917.7471   v.1   135242
  Kin

         King.
         King's handbook of New York
            City 1893.

      Learning Resources Center
   Nazareth College of Rochester, N. Y.

King's Handbook of New York City 1893

King's Handbook of

First Planned, Edited & Published
by Moses King, Boston, 1893

New York City 1893

Second, Enlarged Edition,
with 1029 illustrations,
1020 Pages and
a New Introduction
by A. E. Santaniello

Volume 1

Reissued 1972, New York City
by Benjamin Blom Inc., Publishers

LEARNING RESOURCES CENTER
NAZARETH COLLEGE
WITHDRAWN

Second Edition, Revised and Enlarged
First published in one volume, Boston, 1893
Reissued in two volumes, 1972, by
Benjamin Blom, Inc., New York, N.Y. 10025
New Introduction by A. E. Santaniello

©Copyright 1972 by Benjamin Blom, Inc.

Library of Congress Catalog Card Number 72-87651

Printed in the United States of America

917 747
917 Kin

IN 1973

Benjamin Blom Inc. plans to publish

FEELINGS: My Companions to King's New York

Among the topics this full-length illustrated book will deal with are:

- the attitudes of the shakers and movers of our cities in King's time—the slum dwellers, architects, robber barons—and their counterparts today
- the "gloom and doom" central-city syndrome of Mumford and others
- the ideological thrust of Riis's turn-of-the-century slum photographs, their impact on various classes then, and the continuation of the Riis *weltanschauung* today
- a then-and-now view of Frederick Law Olmsted and Central Park
- the effects of a methodology—in education and elsewhere—based exclusively on secondary to fifthdary sources, bypassing the feelings of those allegedly saved or assisted by solutions thus reached
- some architects and cityplanners today, Frank Lloyd Wright, Philip Johnson, the proponents of the Plan of New York City.

The book's coverage and viewpoint has areas of identity with A. E. Santaniello's introduction to *King's Handbook,* and differences. The author of FEELINGS is the undersigned publisher,

BENJAMIN BLOM

KING'S NEW YORK:

The Dimensions of Fantasy

A. E. SANTANIELLO

WHEN NEW YORK meets whatever fate has been allotted it—Atlantis, Ur, Sodom, Erie, Pa.?—the historian will perhaps have an easier task of reconstruction than the archaeologist. A vast horde of books, graphic art of every imaginable kind await the former; zealously kept mementos preserved on the spot in special libraries, the archives of historical societies, the records of local genealogical associations. The men with pick and shovel, pottery fixatives, and topographical hypotheses will not, however, fare as well. The records of New York's most prized monuments are preserved; the monuments themselves are most often serving as landfill under some suburban patio or protruding, disconsolate and accusing, from a Jersey marshland. Unlike the antiquities of Athens or Jericho, New York's past is likely to be almost entirely a thing of the written word, the silent picture book.

Fragments of ancient cycles of the city's life—Dutch New York, English New York, early Federal, American "Victorian" —may still be found, a few *disjecta membra* preserved anonymously amid alien surroundings, without sense in a casually chaotic cityscape. The respect one feels toward such acts of piety is too often charged with the disquieting suspicion that the building in question has been not so much "preserved" as accidentally overlooked in the latest updating. Inevitably, prolonged exposure to New York begins to erode the very concept of preservation. The headlong, flaming pace of the city, its passion for the new and impatience with anything less, all quickly convince that tomorrow, not yesterday, is being commemorated here. If a surly cynicism ever became the vogue in official mottoes, New York would have best claim to the notorious Ford's "history is bunk," perhaps because it makes its own history so difficult to imagine.

Except for one aspect of that history: the expendability of the past and all its works. This New York characteristic is no reflection of the anxious twentieth century: visitors to the eighteenth-century port felt something of the same pulse and commented on it. The first "pictorial directories" of the city, dating from the 1830s and 1840s, seem to show as many replacements as new buildings on previously undeveloped lots. Granting, of course, the deadly effectiveness of fire in ridding the city of its old (and often new) buildings, one must still conclude that as commercial activity in the city increased, as new industry demanded a new and larger work force close at hand, and as profits urged more lavish display on those who reaped them, New York was ready to sacrifice what it had for what it was confident of having tomorrow. And tomorrow was as limitless as the long island stretching up from the narrow tip where the first Dutch settlers established their village in the seventeenth century. In succession "up-town" became mid, then down, then out of the main circulation of business, financial dealings, fashionable life. Throughout the eighteenth and nineteenth centuries, entrepreneurs courted ridicule by building on the then-accepted, rural, often squalid and untidy edge of the "old" city; some suffered bankruptcy for anticipating the inevitable, many lived to see themselves engulfed by the city whose outer limit they once defined.

Thus it is an experience rooted in New York history that one has today when he leaves the island with its skyline firmly in mind, only to return and be convinced his memory has played tricks on him. Where is . . .? Wasn't there . . .? When did . . .? Such questions insist on the fact of change; others as insistent rise—Why? To whose good? To these questions there are also words by the millions and almost as many theories because the why and the wherefore of New York, the speculation that acts as consolation for a dismantled past, epitomizes the thoughts one is forced to entertain about the nature of cities and their chances of survival today. New York's three-hundred-odd years of history, time which, in another place, has often been marked by a continuity so even as to seem almost without mark, here invites such speculation as might be reserved for the course of an empire.

IN ALMOST ANY DECADE of New York's past there were chroniclers, eager collectors of data and manufacturers of hyperbole. The handbooks, pictorial guides, real estate brochures, and more official compilations occupy hundreds of library shelves. If the city some of the early writers celebrated seems pitifully small, the claims advanced mere presumptiveness, the tone of self-assuredness often convinces. New York was, and always is, on the threshold of immortality, an eternal city no less worthy of the title than any ancient capital. This city was America's claim to greatness, perhaps not as irrefutable a claim throughout the eighteenth and nineteenth centuries as the vastness of its physical size and the limitless physical resources at its command. Certainly such "natural" gifts struck the foreigner with awe and the native with conviction that God had designed it all especially for his use. A new nation so naturally favored had a right to call attention to obvious signs of divine approval and sanctions: "manifest destiny" was consecrated as a religious sentiment before it was honed into a political-military campaign slogan. It was somewhat more difficult to cloak the expansion of a city—devil's plaything—in such religiosity. The myth of man's rural past was vital in his thinking through the eighteenth century; it was a particularly vital myth in America's thinking about itself. Seen in such a light, the artless boasting of New York's historians takes on another quality: it was courageous to claim that a mere city held wonders to match the mountains and canyons, wilderness and woods of this vast continent.

By the last decades of the nineteenth century, however, the endless tracks of America had been claimed if not completely tamed, the physical wonders were captured in all the arts and made familiar through cheap illustration techniques in newspaper and magazine, travel journal, and exhibition. A host of adventurers were numbering the numberless, fencing in the endless, and killing off the countless. Mountains and prairies and wild animals not only could be subdued; they could, even if at times accidentally, be eliminated altogether. But the city obeyed a law different from nature's and seemed to live on and flourish no matter how much it suffered the death of its vital center. To see New York endlessly renew itself, leap up over what had been thought its natural limits, spread and engulf and still search for more—that was to experience a new frontier not likely to be closed or exhausted. And thus the act of writing about New York had in it elements of defiance, a hubris that challenged the archetypal dread of holding man's work up for comparison with God's.

An act of defiance, then, but also an act of defining: New York was quickly recognized as the precursor of an environment toward which modern, technological society was headed. Here commerce and industry create and determine the shape of the community; for proof there was the history of entire areas waxing and waning as "business" dictated. The city grew in response to those considerations and not to the needs of families or individuals, the simpler human imperatives that were the traditional determinants of towns and cities. What would be the cost in the quality of man's life could not be predicted, if the question was even posed in such terms in those heady decades of the late nineteenth century when *progress* was the talisman. Those who felt most acutely the hard reality of a life in bondage to economic necessity—those casually counted millions whose labor kept the machine going so smoothly—were too submerged in the struggle to speculate on its historical implications. They served in much the same manner as the man who hauled his end of the rope to add another granite block to a monument he would not see completed in his lifetime.

But for New York, typical and yet unique, there were in this same end-of-century period many who saw the shape of the future and tried to alter its direction. The great work of Jacob Riis recorded and warned that this new industrial slag heap was made of men and women and children cast off by the machine. Riis saw, and convinced others, that the price was too high and even unnecessary; but it cannot be said that he or those of like mind stopped the forces that were making New York the image of the new technological nightmare. No one would offer these early crusaders for human dignity the affront of saying that they *merely* relieved misery: there were too many who did not try, who ignored the problems, or who thought the victims of poverty and ignorance were the criminal perpetrators of these vices. The tides of immigrants who washed up in New York in the last decades of the nineteenth century and on into the twentieth were often looked upon as a plague, the sins of the old world visited on the new. Reaction against these millions was often chilling in its bluntness, its outspoken discrimination: ". . . the most incorrigible slummers, paupers, and vagrants are the Italians and the Jews. . . . The American-born of this foreign parentage is the most vicious criminal of them all. . . . To the cry of Mr. Riis, 'Abolish the tenements!' there may be suggested an alternative. Why not abolish the tenants?" John C. Van Dyke, who wrote these lines in his *The New New York* in 1909 was no doubt an honorable man, concerned with the fate of his city. His prejudices are distasteful, but equally distressing is the limited vision revealed in his book: he saw that New York had hidden its impoverished workers away in deadly tenements, in all-but-abandoned ghettoes where the necessary public services that make life in a metropolis bearable are totally missing; but he forgot that New York had consistently failed to plan for the masses who built and maintained its greatness. Decent living conditions, a high-minded ideal, perhaps, but a practical necessity, gave way before land speculation, corrupt building codes, venal and indifferent municipal officials. The same can be said of the working conditions of hundreds of thousands, of sanitary conditions, recreation facilities.

Seen from one angle, New York of the late nineteenth century appears an unmitigated disaster, and there were Jeremiahs enough, with pen and, increasingly in the 1880s and 1890s, camera equipment, to record each crack in the civic walls. But not expectedly, a good deal of the literature about the city as it entered the new century is optimistic about the future, proud of the present. A recognizable American trait, perhaps, to assume that anything that big must be "OK," as if the need for discrimination and judgment ended when a certain dimension was reached. Two kinds of literature, then, each with some measure of truth: one chronicled the restless growth of commerce, the increasingly lavish displays of wealth; the other concentrated on the rotting underpinning of the city, its wretchedly housed poor, corrupt government, wasteful lack of urban planning, total disregard for the past, chaotic architectural habits. And together the two kinds of literature are almost an echo of the physical layout of the city: the massive, island-long grid that was to determine, from as far back as 1811, the order of streets, promising stability, logic, free movement; giving more often ironbound conformity, sterility, chaos all the more evident because so logically contrived, like the precise, ritualistic ravings of a psychotic.

THE SOMEWHAT GARGANTUAN CLAIMS that decorated the end papers of *King's Handbook of New York City* and are repeated in the preface suggest that Moses King, indefatigable chronicler of the city, had built a book commensurate with his subject. Such an illustrated history and description of the city, on such a scale, had never been attempted before —and in fact King's *Handbook* does dwarf all previous guides and histories. This single volume, the second edition within ten months of the first, "contains exactly 1,008 pages, more than 1,000 illustrations, thirty chapters, and an index of twenty-four pages with 72 columns, containing over 5,000 items and about 20,000 references." Not just a grab bag of indiscriminate facts, however; a phalanx of city experts and historians defend its authenticity. "The manuscript underwent a thorough revision at the hands of several thousand people, each an authority on the submitted portion. . . ." To all this add the enviable commercial success of the venture: the first edition sold out its 10,000 copies in ten months; the second edition consisted of 20,000 copies, many already spoken for.

Such size, such success evokes the expansiveness of the age, the same spirit that created the World's Columbian Exposition in 1893 and introduced a new world power to the international community. If New York had not always invited commentary and exaggeration, one might conclude that only the Exposition itself, and the expectation of thousands who would tour New York after the rigors of a trip to far Chicago, urged the enterprising King to fill all those columns, consult all those experts. It was, of course, no drawback to the book's chances of success to have such a waiting audience, and King's none-too-modest claims were perfect drawing cards. Whatever the occasion, almost inevitably the book would have taken the shape it has—that was, simply, the way to write about New York. The sheer bulk of material was the main evidence that the city was without parallel, even if Chicago had copped the world's fair. The visitor from Paris, London, Rome, the pedant with fantasies of Troy and Babylon, all had to be convinced that New York was the equal of these, or would be before the second expanded edition of the *Handbook* was exhausted. But the superiority of New York was more than could be proved by brute facts, an individual triumph or two—a Central Park larger than anything in London, newer chateaux than Paris, as many Italians as Rome. Amassing these facts, describing the city's buildings as one by one they began to break through the seven-story ceiling that held down the skyline for so many years, unraveling the strands of the complex financial dealings that radiated from the city—all these were the sum of the mechanical parts, paraded past the reader with proud assertiveness. Such is the identifiable temperament of the book, its link with the intangible American spirit of those fat decades of a gaudy era.

With what relish King and his thousand authorities set about their task can be surmised from a glance at any of the book's thirty chapters. Is the reader for the historical-narrative? He is obliged with an account that encompasses all from the first Indian settlement to the last statistic on the number of factories (25,399) and the receipts for the previous season of grand opera ($200,000, with a deficit of $100,000, just to remind us that while much changes, much abides). Waterways and transport, including the opening of that perhaps naïvely imagined boon to urban living, the elevated rapid transit system, are as important in the book as they are in the development of the city. Today's commuter might well sigh nostalgically as he reads page after page of description of that mighty rail system that serviced the New York region with "first-class equipment" and an "efficient and vigilant management." Where are the pullmans of yesteryear, the "capital system of railways" that was once the Long Island, the twenty separate lines that one could choose from for a Connecticut visit? King ignores the often scandalous financial manipulations that gave the railroads their land and maintained their profits; beyond a bare account of an occasional bankruptcy through "faulty management," we hear little of the matter. A fault, perhaps, but to be expected in a volume designed to attract rather than arouse the reader. Much the same acceptance of existing realities—whether in correctional institutions, insurance companies, trust and investing companies, or in the distribution of charity and relief, the provisions for working class housing, sanitary facilities—in all these areas where corruption kept pace with whatever improvements came about, King hesitated to probe more deeply. In other spheres of urban life, planning, architecture, the total environment, King's values seem restricted. Any building that appears is noteworthy, almost, it would seem, for having been built at the time. And, almost inevitably, for having been built bigger than what it replaced. As for a building's architectural value, relation to other buildings or to the block in which it stands—these were of as little concern to King as to most commentators on the American city.

There was, fortunately, a long tradition of critical observation on New York's peculiar kind of urban squalor, from the writings of William Cullen Bryant and Frederick Law Olmsted, to Henry James and William Grant White. They all protested the airless gridiron that locked out nature and forbade (as it developed in New York) a green, breathing place; they decried the indigestible mess of disparate architectural styles that made up the average street front, and they lamented the increasing defacement by such modern "improvements" as telegraph and telephone and the black tangle of wires they hung about the city. Some of this kind of critical spirit does appear on occasion in King's *Handbook,* as for example in his account of the evolution of Olmsted and Vaux's Central Park. In this long section we learn of the dreary shantytown that held the site before it was re-created and of the difficulties experienced in maintaining the park in the unspoiled and un-"improved" manner in which it was conceived. More of such passages would perhaps have given the book greater significance for us today; but the reader would have been deprived of a greater pleasure—the opportunity to place a contemporary account into a new perspective. In reading King we are aware of so much that is familiar and so much that is remote: the limits of commercial activity may have stood at 42nd Street then, having once held firm at 23rd, at 14th. The data are no longer applicable, but the process is continuing, the center is still moving, occasionally dipping back to a revived section, spreading at times to areas once consecrated to fashionable living, to other things entirely. King's decade of the 1890s was one of particular vigor and growth; but so seem almost all of New York's hundreds. And if the city he describes seems more often than not to have the outlines of a swollen boy rather than a mature and developed adult, could anything different be said about the city's features today? King is writing just as New York is about to evolve a distinctive architectural "face," the noble lineaments that McKim, Mead and White, especially, were to mold for it over the next decades. Whatever criticism can be made of those architects' classical mode, it provided, both in the city and throughout many other American cities, an organizing principle where there had been disarray, buildings in anonymous styles, in no relation to each other or to their environment. The hundreds of buildings, public and private, that King illustrates seem to be in as many styles, few of them completely successful examples of any. Had he compiled a third edition of the *Handbook* a decade later, the image of the city would have been different, more rational if perhaps tamer, lighter in texture and color, even if at times fussy and derivative. It is among New York's misfortunes that exact comparisons cannot often be made; many of King's buildings are long-since gone. On the other hand, many of the next generation's buildings, with which the comparisons might be made, have joined them on the rubbish pile. As usual, one has the book, the illustration, the statistic; the dump has the real thing.

The result is nostalgia, and for many the reason for examining the *Handbook* is to feel that nostalgia, to see broad thoroughfares, crosstown thoroughfares, with traffic actually moving, to learn of store clerks especially trained to serve with utmost courtesy (is it the "training" or the "courtesy" that strikes one). But among the other things King offers us is a study of attitudes, some mercifully abandoned or changed, some lost to our present discomfort, some persisting to our harm. King and his authorities seem convinced that the city is infinitely expandable, its parts always expendable. They revere commerce almost above all other values, almost to the point of insisting that New York exists only for business. They equate the "prosperity and culture of the community" with the private expenditure of money by the wealthy and middle-class. They wax rhapsodic about the latest mansion on Fifth Avenue while holding their noses before the "plague spots" where the newest immigrants fester. They are content to enumerate the free kitchens and charity wards without noticing the root problem of distribution of income, exploitation of cheap labor, greed of speculators of all sorts. They give us an ideal city, and no one can believe in that as a possibility today. New York, where once everything seemed expansible, suffers the fate of hundreds of American cities as it rushes just ahead of financial mayhem, civic disorder, physical decay. It now seems expendable, easily replaced by suburban centers that mimic the city in everything except the one indispensable quality of a city—that they be centers of life, life on every level of meaningful activity. So in reading King's *Handbook* the past of New York, and the causes of its present condition, become clear, a manifest warning.

But the note of warning is not the last heard. Throughout the book a clearer sound is that of the city's endless vitality and life, confused, disordered, senseless. All these things without doubt, but alive nonetheless. None of its imitators, none of the fragmented communities that substitute for it, can lay claim to such life. This is the spirit King's

Handbook captures: the world may be mad, but New York is its capital for all that.

A Note on Moses King

Moses King, editor and chronicler of New York City, was born in England in 1853 and died in Boston in 1909. As a publisher he was widely known for his handbooks and guides to American cities and to the United•States as a whole. Among his massive volumes are the two editions, 1891 and 1893, of the *Handbook of New York City, King's Views of New York City,* 1903, the voluminous *King's Handbook of the United States,* 1891, and *King's Notable New Yorkers.*

1893. — SECOND EDITION. — 1893.

KING'S
·HANDBOOK·OF·
NEW YORK
·CITY·

AN·OUTLINE·HISTORY·
·AND·DESCRIPTION·OF·
·THE·AMERICAN·METROPOLIS·

·WITH·OVER·ONE·THOUSAND·
ILLUSTRATIONS·FROM·PHO-
·TOGRAPHS·MADE·EXPRESS-
·LY·FOR·THIS·WORK·

·PLANNED·EDITED·AND·
·PUBLISHED·
·BY· MOSES·KING, BOSTON, MASS.

THE MATTHEWS-NORTHRUP CO., COMPLETE ART-PRINTING WORKS, BUFFALO, N. Y.

PREFACE TO SECOND EDITION.

NEVER before has any one put forth an illustrated history and description of New-York City in a single volume at all comparable with "King's Handbook." This volume contains exactly 1,008 pages, more than 1,000 illustrations, thirty chapters, and an index of twenty-four pages with 72 columns, containing over 5,000 items and about 20,000 references. The text furnishes an elaborate but condensed history and description of the city itself, and also of every notable public institution and especially interesting feature. The illustrations give many reminders of the past, and furnish an extensive series of pictures of the present city, to an extent many times beyond that of any volume yet published. Every plate was made expressly for this book, and so were nearly all of the original photographs. The whole has been carefully printed on an exceptionally fine quality of paper. It is conceded to be the handsomest, the most thorough, the largest, the most costly and the most profusely illustrated book of its class ever issued for any city in the world.

The original text was prepared with the utmost care, and was the result of the painstaking work of many individuals, principally of Moses Foster Sweetser, Henri Péne du Bois, William Henry Burbank, Lyman Horace Weeks, Henry Edward Wallace, John Collins Welch, Louis Berg and Charles Putnam Tower. The manuscript underwent a thorough revision at the hands of several thousand people, each an authority on the submitted portion, and thus the book became an authentic volume. The text was amplified, rectified, and verified by Mr. Sweetser, the foremost American in this special field of literature. Valuable general assistance was also given by Mr. Tower.

Although the first edition appeared only ten months ago the present volume is not another edition in the ordinary use of the term. It is in fact a new book. Nearly every text page has been reset, and changes of every character have been made throughout the book. About 300 new engravings are inserted, some to replace former ones, but a large part appear for the first time from new originals. The book is now larger and better, with more text and more illustrations. It is indeed a picture of New York in 1893. Its success has exceeded all expectations. The first edition comprised 10,000 copies, and was exhausted in a few weeks. The present edition is 20,000 copies, more than one-half of which are needed to fill orders on hand before publication.

In the second edition the revisions and additions were made by Mr. Sweetser and the undersigned, with the coöperation of more than 3,000 people, who have kindly made revisions or substitutes for the parts in which they had direct interest. Historical works, newspapers, special reports and hundreds of other sources of information, too numerous to permit of specific acknowledgment, have been utilized.

The illustrations are almost wholly from specially-made photographs, upwards of 1,500 negatives having been made by Arthur Chiar, who has shown remarkable skill in photographing exceedingly difficult subjects. Some photographs were made by Frank E. Parshley, John S. Johnston, C. C. Langill and others. The designs for the cover linings and the series of bird's-eye views were made by the New-York Photogravure Company, the President of which is Ernest Edwards.

The entire mechanical work from cover to cover, with slight exceptions, was done by The Matthews-Northrup Company, the famous Art-Printers of Buffalo, whose establishment is one of the most complete in the world, and whose President, George E. Matthews, and Art-manager, Charles E. Sickels, are entitled to much of the credit for the artistic effect of this volume.

If it were usual to dedicate a volume of this character, this one would be dedicated to Charles F. Clark, the President of The Bradstreet Company, to whom I am indebted for substantial aid, valuable suggestions, and hearty encouragement.

And now this second edition is submitted to the public, with the hope that it will be found to be :

> "Good enough for any body,
> Cheap enough for everybody,"

and that the appreciation of the public will necessitate many editions.

MOSES KING, *Editor and Publisher*.

Boston, July 1, 1893.

☞ Corrections and suggestions for future editions are invited.

Historical.

Peter Minuit

Her Dutch Hudson

City Hall 1679.

Diedrich Knickerbocker

Ye earliest chronicler of Nieuw Amsterdam

New York of the Past, from the Earliest Times to the Present.

THE HISTORY of the city of New York, in its Dutch, British, and American periods, abounds in episodes of deep interest, illustrating the development of a petty fur-trading post into the great cosmopolitan metropolis of the Western Hemisphere. Many ponderous volumes have been devoted to this worthy theme, with a wealth of illustration and much grace of literary style; and yet but a part of the wonderful story has been told. In this brief chapter an attempt is made to exhibit a few vignettes from the nearly three centuries of annals pertaining to the Empire City, and to give a few intimations of her lines of advance and of successful endeavor.

Manhattan was the original place-name. *Munnoh* was an Indian word for "island"; in Abenaqui, *Menatan;* in Delaware, *Menatey*; in Chippewa, *Minis*. Thus *Grand Menan*, in the Bay of Fundy; and *Manati*, the ancient Indian name of Long Island; and *Manisees*, the old name of Block Island. *Menatan* was any small island; *Menates* or *Manisees, the* small island. The island on which New York stands was sometimes spoken of as "*the* island," *Manate*, or *Manhatte;* sometimes as "*a* small island," *Manathan, Menatan*, or *Manhatan;* and sometimes as "*the* small island," *Manhaates, Manattes*, and *Manados*. The same root appears in *Manhanset, Montauk (Manati-auke)*, and other Indian place-names. Campanius speaks of "*Manataanung*, or *Manaates*, a place settled by the Dutch, who built there a clever little town, which went on increasing every day."

The first recorded visitor to this jocund region was Verrazano, a Florentine navigator and traveller, who was serving at that time as a French corsair. He sailed from Brittany in the *Dauphine*, in 1524, and cruised up the American coast

Copyright 1892 and 1893 by Moses King.

DUTCH MAP OF NEW YORK, 1656.

from Cape Fear to New-York Bay, where his ship lay at anchor for a few days, sending boats up the river and meeting a kindly reception from the natives. There is a tradition that ships of the Dutch Greenland Company entered the North River in 1598, and wintered there, the crews dwelling in a fort which they had constructed on the shore.

But the first practical and undoubted discovery of our harbor and river was due to Henry Hudson, an English mariner, at that time in the employ of a Holland trading corporation. In 1609 the Dutch East India Company sent Hudson out on a voyage of discovery; and after making landfalls at Newfoundland, Penobscot Bay, Cape Cod and Delaware Bay, he entered the harbor of New York. In his little ship, the *Halve-Maen* ("Half-Moon"), with the orange, white and blue flag of Holland floating from the mast, the bold explorer ascended the Hudson River, through the mountains, nearly to the site of Albany, trading with the native tribes

DUTCH COTTAGE AT NEW YORK, 1679.

on the way. He had hoped and fancied that the grand stream might be the long-sought northwest passage to the East Indies; and when the shoaling water above Albany indicated that it was but an ordinary river, he turned about and dropped down the stream and spread his sails for Europe. He carried back the report that the new-found country contained many fur-bearing animals; and the dwellers under the cold northern skies of Holland needed and prized furs for winter clothing. The very next year some Dutch merchants sent out a ship to trade here, and in its crew were several of the sailors of the *Half-Moon*. In 1611 Adriaen Block visited Manhattan, and carried thence to Europe two sons of an Indian chief, the first New-Yorkers to visit the Old World. The next year Block and Christiaensen were sent across in the *Tiger* and the *Fortune*, by several enterprising Amsterdam merchants, to open trade at Manhattan. Christiaensen built Fort Nassau, near the site of Albany, and started a flourishing trade with the Mohawks; and erected a group of log huts near the southern point of Manhattan (45 Broadway); and Block built here a vessel, the *Onrust* (or "Restless"), in which he explored the coast eastward to Block Island.   This brave little vessel was the pioneer of the vast commerce of New York, which has since that day borne its flags over all seas, and to the remotest ports of both hemispheres.

In 1614 the States-General chartered the United New-Netherland Company, of Amsterdam merchants, to traffic here for three years ; and under the orders of this corporation traders penetrated far inland, and the treaty of Tawasentha was concluded with the Indians.   In 1621 the Dutch Government chartered the West India

"THE DUKE'S PLAN," MADE FOR JAMES, DUKE OF YORK, ABOUT 1664.

Company, with the powers of making treaties, maintaining courts, and employing soldiers ; and three years later their ship *New Netherland* entered the North River, bearing a colony of 110 Walloons, or people of French origin from southern Holland. Some of these stayed at Manhattan, and others scattered throughout the country.

Nearly all who had come to Manhattan hitherto were transient fur-traders and servants of the company. The Walloon immigration marks the first real and permanent colonization of the new land, as a place of homes. The new-comers

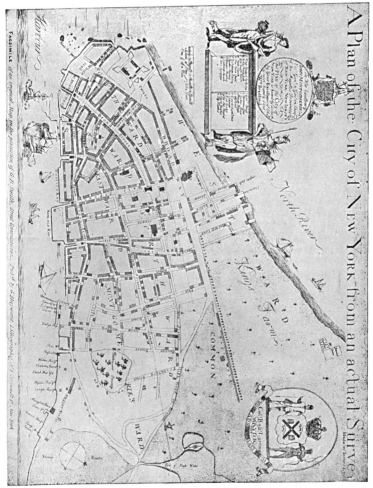

BRADFORD'S MAP OF NEW YORK, 1728.

brought their families, and also horses and cattle, sheep and swine, and farming implements and seed.

In 1625 came the first specimen of the New-York girl, now the delight of two hemispheres, in the diminutive person of Sarah Rapaelje, "the first-born Christian daughter" in the colony. The first white male child born on Manhattan Island was Jean Vigne, who appeared in 1614. His mother owned a farm at the corner of Wall and Pearl streets, and on the hill back of it stood a great windmill. Vigne was a farmer and brewer, and three times schepen of the town. He left no children.

The first director sent out by the West India Company to govern its North-River trading-post was Captain Mey; who was succeeded, in 1625, by William Verhulst. A year later four ships arrived, bringing fresh relays of colonists and 103 head of cattle.

In 1626 the *Sea-Mew* arrived in the harbor, bringing Peter Minuit, the new Director-General, and the first of the four notable rulers of the colony. His earliest official act was the purchase of Manhattan Island from the savages, the payment

being in beads, buttons and other trinkets to the value of 60 guilders (or $24). This policy of purchasing land from the Indians was followed by all the Dutch rulers and colonists.

Manhattan was then a forest-bordered island, swampy along the shores, and rising

RHINELANDER'S SUGAR-HOUSE AND RESIDENCE, BETWEEN WILLIAM AND ROSE STREETS.

inland to low hills crowned with oaks and hickories. On the line of Canal Street tidal marshes and ponds stretched from river to river, and were covered with sea-water at high tide. Wolves and panthers prowled among the rugged ledges and dense thickets beyond, whence an occasional bear sallied forth to dine at ease on the Netherland sheep; and hungry deer ran swiftly southward to trample down the settlers' crops, and enjoy the taste of their corn and wheat. Near the Battery stood a group of the mean precursors of the vast cosmopolitan civilization which was destined to rise on this site; and farther up the island, a few groups of wigwams and communal houses stood in the open valleys, near the corn and tobacco fields of the aborigines. The houses of the Dutch trading-post were of one story, including two rooms, with chimneys of wood, roofs of straw, furniture hewn out of rough planks, and wooden platters and spoons. In 1626 the village had 200 inhabitants, which were augmented to 270 by 1628. About this time it assumed the name of *Fort Amsterdam*, in memory of the metropolis of the Dutch Republic.

The United Netherlands which thus bore Manhattan as a favored child was then conspicuous in Europe in commerce and the mechanic arts. Her dauntless battalions had just shattered forever the power of Spain, and her fleets defied the mariners of England by cruising up and down the English Channel with brooms at their mast-heads. Her cultivation in literature was exemplified in Grotius and DeWitt,

NEW YORK IN 1728, LYNE'S MAP.

THE IRREGULAR PORTION OF THE CITY, AS ORIGINALLY LAID OUT.

Barneveld and William the Silent, and by the great University of Leyden, famous
throughout Christendom.   In art, her Rembrandt and Rubens, Van Dyck and
Teniers, were painting those pictures which are still the admiration of Europe.
The most adventurous spirits of this wonderful nation sought new fields beyond
the sea, and made a deep and enduring impress on the nascent city and common-
wealth.

Most of Minuit's colonists were merely servants of the West India Company,
without the rights of owning land, manufacturing, or trading with the Indians.

NEW YORK IN 1776.   MAJOR HOLLAND'S MAP.

They came to Manhattan only to work for the company, and of this they had enough, building cabins, stone warehouses and mills. Near the Bowling Green (on the site of No. 4 Bowling Green) they also erected Fort Amsterdam, a bastioned earthwork with three sides, and walls crested with red cedar palisades. Minuit sent his secretary, De Rasières, in the barque *Nassau* to Manomet, in Massachusetts, whence

NEW YORK IN 1789. ENGRAVED BY P. R. MAVERICK.

he journeyed to Plymouth, and opened friendly communications and trade relations with the Pilgrim colony. Boston had not yet been founded. About the same time Huyck and Krol came hither as "consolers of the sick;" and began Christian observances in the colony by reading the Scriptures and Creeds in the upper room of the horse-mill. Manhattan in 1629 and 1630 sent to Amsterdam 130,000 guilders' worth of goods, being a large balance in favor of the colony. In 1631 the Manhattan ship-yard built the great ship *New Netherland*, of 800 tons and 30 guns, one of the largest vessels then afloat.

In 1633 Director-General Wouter Van Twiller reached Manhattan in the frigate *Zoutberg*, bringing in a prize Spanish caravel, and having in his company the first accredited clergyman on these shores, Dominie Everardus Bogardus, and the first professional schoolmaster, Adam Roelandsen. While New England depended on her fisheries, and Virginia on the tobacco trade, New Netherland shipped grain to Boston and over-seas, and rich peltries to Holland.

Van Twiller brought with him 104 Dutch troops, the first soldiers to enter Manhattan; and for their proper accommodation he erected barracks, and enlarged and strengthened Fort Amsterdam. His colonists were never so happy as when draining their

"YE EXECUTION OF GOFF, YE NEGER OF MR. MOTHIUS, ON YE COMMONS."

huge pewter tankards; and to provide means for these joyous revels, he erected a profitable brewery. The most conspicuous objects on the island were the tall windmills which he built, and whose slowly revolving arms recalled to the burghers the similar works towering over the far-away meadows of Holland. But Van Twiller, fat and moon-faced, low of stature and dull of wit, was a shrewd trader and self-provider, and secured as his own private property Nutten (Governor's) Island and Blackwell's Island and other valuable properties. He also granted to Roelof Jans 62 acres of land along the North River, between Fulton and Christopher Streets, and reaching Broadway near Fulton Street. In 1671 the heirs sold this domain to Governor Lovelace, and it became incorporated with the King's Farm. This united estate was presented by Queen Anne to Trinity Church in 1703. Van Twiller's successor, William Kieft, little, fussy, fiery and avaricious, ruled from 1638 to 1647; and built a stone tavern near Coenties Slip, the stone church of St. Nicholas, in the fort, and a distillery. In his time hundreds of New-Englanders, flying from religious intolerance, settled in the province, and the Indian tribes of the lower Hudson swept the Dutch settlements with torch and tomahawk, and even shot guards on the walls of Fort Amsterdam. Angered at Kieft's imposition of taxes, and at his unwise Indian policy, the burghers united against him, and inaugurated popular government here. Scores of unarmed and friendly Indians were massacred in their camp at the foot of Grand Street by Dutch soldiers, who also slaughtered 80 more at Pavonia, without resistance, and even larger numbers at Canarsie and Greenwich.   At the end of the Indian war in 1645 there were but 100 persons left at Manhattan, and 1,500 in the province.   The poor little colony, the plaything of a foreign commercial corporation, drooped rapidly, especially after the West India Company began to lose money here, and so its officers planned to absorb the best lands in the new domain and to assume feudal

NEW YORK IN 1778.   THOMAS KITCHIN, SENIOR'S, MAP.   FROM THE LONDON MAGAZINE.

prerogatives, under the title of "Patroons." The States-General, therefore, curtailed the company's privileges greatly, and colonists began to pour in from all parts, so that in 1643 eighteen different nationalities were represented in New Amsterdam alone.

The cosmopolitan growth of the future city was prophesied early in the 17th century by the Amsterdam Chamber, which declared that when its population and navigation "should become permanently established, when the ships of New Netherland ride on every part of the ocean, then numbers, now looking to that coast with eager eyes, will be allured to embark for your island." The accuracy of this prediction has been verified to an extent quite more than desirable, especially during the last half century.

The irregular lines of the lower New-York streets are due to the fact that the colony grew for thirty years before streets were laid out, and the settlers built their cabins wherever they liked. There were but two public roads, the Boston (or Old Post) road, from the Battery along Broadway and the Bowery; and the ferry road, from the fort along the lines of Stone Street and

NEW YORK AND EAST RIVER, FROM BROOKLYN HEIGHTS.

Hanover Square to the Brooklyn ferry at Peck Slip. De Perel Straat (Pearl Street) was on the water side; Water, Front and South Streets all having been reclaimed from the river. Pearl Street is the oldest in New York, and was built upon in 1633, being followed closely by Bridge Street. The most ancient conveyance of property now on record in New York shows that Van Steenwyck sold to Van Fees a lot of 3,300 square feet on Bridge Street for $9.60. The first lot of land granted on Broadway (then called De Heere Straat) was in 1643, to Martin Krigier, who erected here the celebrated Krigier's Tavern, on whose site rose the King's Arms Tavern, afterwards the Atlantic Gardens (9 Broadway).

The next (and last) Director-General was Petrus Stuyvesant, a veteran of the West-Indian wars, wearing a wooden leg banded with silver. He was an autocratic, decided and vigorous ruler; and sturdily fought the colonists, patroons, and Home Government in the interests of the West India Company. Lutherans, Baptists, Quakers and other dissenters from the Reformed religion were persecuted, and

NEW YORK IN 1775. FORT GEORGE, FROM THE HARBOR.

Stuyvesant forbade the mustering of the burgher guard, and ousted the municipal council of the Nine from their honorary pew in the church. Fearful of attack from England and New England, the gallant old soldier fortified the town in 1653 with a breastwork, ditch and sharpened palisades, running from the East River nearly to the North River, and garnished with block-houses. This defensive wall was 2,340 feet long. From Lombard Street it followed the crest of the bluff along the North River as far as the fort. Fort Amsterdam, on the site of the brick block southeast of Bowling Green, was built of small Holland brick, and contained the governor's house, the church, and quarters for 300 soldiers. It stood from 1635 until 1790-91.

The quaint little Dutch seaport was governed from its picturesque stone Stadt Huys, in front of which stood a high gallows. Here often gathered the entire body of the people, from the black-gowned schepens and the richly-clad patroons and merchants down to the common populace, whose men were clad in jackets and wide baggy breeches, and their women in bodices and short skirts. The site of the Stadt Huys is now occupied by No. 73 Pearl Street. Pearl Street was then known

2

as "the Road to the Ferry" (to Brooklyn); and passed through the wall at the Water Gate, which was strengthened by a block-house and a two-gun battery. Before the end of the century these defenses were augmented by the Slip Battery of ten guns, near Coenties Slip ; the Stadt-Huys Battery of five guns ; the Whitehall Battery of fifteen guns ; a wall with bastions and postern gates along the North River ; and stone bastions near Broadway and Nassau Street. An arched gate-way spanned Broadway where that avenue crossed the walls ; and other gates and posterns occurred at convenient points. During the second Dutch dominion it was the duty of the Schout (or Mayor) to walk around the city every morning with a guard, and unlock the gates, after which he gave the keys to the com-mander of the fort. At evening he locked the gates and posted sentries and pickets at exposed points.

Outside the town wall a footpath led to the ponds near by, and because this way had been made by the Dutch lasses going to the ponds to wash clothes, it was called *T'Maagde Paatje*, or the Maidens' Path, and later Maiden Lane. Inside the wall, Broad Street stretched its lines of little gabled brick and stone houses, and a narrow canal ran down its center. Farther down came Whitehall, the fashionable quarter,

VIEW OF NEW YORK IN 1746--MIDDLE DUTCH AND FRENCH CHURCHES.

with prim, bright gardens of dahlias and tulips, and orchards surrounding its quaint step-gabled houses of small black and yellow brick, and Stuyvesant's town house of Whitehall. Bowling Green was at an early day set apart for a parade-ground and village-green, and for public festivities and solemnities, May-poles and the games of the children ; and here also great Indian councils were held. It was for many decades known as "The Plain"; and here, in 1658, was established the first market-house in the city. Every morning the village herdsman passed through the streets, blowing his horn, at which the settlers turned their cattle out from their yards, and they were formed into a common herd, and driven along Pearl Street to the present City-Hall Park, which was then known as *De Vlackte* ("The Flat"). At night the herdsman drove back the cattle, leaving at each citizen's door his own good milch cow. Sometimes, perchance, he lingered in the great cherry orchard, near Franklin Square, from which the modern Cherry Street derives its name ; or loitered along the edge of Beekman's Swamp, now given over to leather-dealers ; or rested under the shadow of the barn-like church, near Whitehall ; or watched the whirling arms of the windmill on State Street. Stuyvesant also founded (in 1658) the village of Niew Harlaem, on the northern part of Manhattan, and began a good highway thitherward. It was during Stuyvesant's time, in 1653, that the West India Company incorporated Niew Amsterdam as a city, with a government modelled on that of Amsterdam, and composed of a schout, two burgomasters and five schepens. The city thus created had 1,000 inhabitants and 120 houses. Moreover, in 1650, Dirck Van Schelluyne, the first lawyer here, had opened his practice.

Between 1656 and 1660 most of the seventeen streets were paved with cobblestones, and provided with gutters in the middle. The first to be paved were De Hoogh Straat (Stone Street) and De Brugh Street (Bridge Street). In 1658 the

NEW YORK IN 1746--LOWER MARKET AND LANDING.

first fire-company came into existence, under the name of "The Rattle Watch." It numbered eight men, who were to stay on watch and duty from nine in the evening until morning drum-beat. At the same time the equipment of the fire-department was prepared, in the importation from Holland of a supply of hooks and ladders and 250 fire-buckets. The gabled ends of the houses faced the streets, and were (even in the cases of wooden edifices) decorated with a checker-work of small black and yellow bricks, all of which were imported from Holland until Stuyvesant's time. Iron figures showing the dates of their erection were fastened in the gables between their zig-zag sides. The main doors of the houses had heavy and well-polished brass knockers ; and over each cresting gable a quaint weather-cock whirled with the breeze. Sitting on the stoops or under the low eaves, or leaning over their half-doors, the burghers discussed the problems of their day amid clouds of tobacco smoke. Every house had its garden, with places for horse and cow, pigs and chickens, and a patch of cabbage and a bed of tulips. The parlor, carpeted only with fine white sand, contained the great camlet-valanced bed, with homespun linen and grotesque patch-work quilts, the iron-bound oaken chest of linen, the corner cupboard, with the small but precious store of plate and porcelain ; the tea-table, stiff Russia-leather chairs, flowered chintz curtains, quaint old pictures, and the fire-place, surrounded with storied Dutch tiles.   The kitchen was the home-room, with the large square dining-table, the vrouw's spinning-wheel, the burgher's capacious chair and pipe, and the immense fire-place, with its hooks and iron pots, and chimney-corner seats sacred to children and stories.   A fair city lot could still be obtained for $50, and the rent of a very good house did not exceed $20 a year.   For there were many troubles still surrounding the good burghers, betwixt the aggressive Yankees on the east, the Swedes on the south, and the aboriginal citizens of the neighboring hills and valleys.   As late as the year 1655 the Indians attacked the town with 1,900 warriors, in 64 canoes, and within three days killed 100 Dutch settlers and captured 150 more, mainly in the suburbs.

Under the lead of Peter Minuit, formerly Director-General of New Netherland, and with the aid of Queen Christina, Swedish colonies had been established on the Delaware River, in 1638, and subsequently enlarged and increased by many expeditions from Sweden.   The Dutch West India Company claimed all this region by right of prior settlement ; and finally, in 1655, Stuyvesant assembled 600 soldiers and seven vessels in the harbor of Niew Amsterdam, and sailed around to the Scandinavian forts, which he captured in succession.   Thus fell New Sweden.   But the heavy cost of these hostilities and of the Indian wars drained the treasury of the West India Company, and paved the way for the approaching fall of New Netherland.

Great Britain had always claimed that the Hudson-River country belonged to her, by virtue of Cabot's discoveries in 1497, and had made several formal protests against the Dutch occupation.   The claim was perhaps not well grounded ; but Britain feared the fast-increasing naval and commercial power of Holland, and determined to reduce it wherever possible.   Gov. Bradford of Plymouth had asserted Great Britain's ownership of Manhattan, in a letter to Minuit ; and Captain Argal had planned to drive away the colonists, with a naval force from Virginia, as early as the year 1613.   The West India Company also applied to King Charles I. for permission to trade to the ports of England and her colonies — a proceeding which did not tend to clear the Dutch title.   Calvert, Lord Baltimore's secretary, informed the Dutch envoy that Maryland extended to the frontiers of New England.   "And the New-Englanders claim that their domain doth reach to Maryland," answered the envoy ; "where then remains New Netherland?"   To which Calvert coldly replied : "Truly, I do not know."   The Connecticut Legislature in 1663 informed Stuyvesant's commissioners that it "knew of no New Netherland province."   The New-England towns on Long Island, in 1663, petitioned Connecticut to annex and protect them, and after several appeals from them, and from Stuyvesant to the English and Dutch governments, the Duke of York, Lord High Admiral of Great Britain, sent out a fleet, which in 1664 appeared before the town, and seized it, subject to negotiations between the home governments.   Stuyvesant cried out, that in preference to surrender, "I would much rather be carried out dead ;" but his clergy and people refused to permit a battle, and the Dutch garrison was allowed "to march out with their arms, drums beating and colors flying."   Since the governments of Great Britain and Holland were in profound peace at this time, the successful naval expedition was in reality a cold-blooded and treacherous buccaneering attack ; but the Duke of York was the brother of the British King, who had granted to him all the territory between the Connecticut and Delaware Rivers.   Moreover, he had more men and heavier guns at the point of dispute.   Captain-General Stuyvesant retired to his Bowerie farm, where for eighteen years, until his death, he dwelt in

OLD CITY OR FEDERAL HALL, TRINITY CHURCH AND WALL STREET IN 1789.
ON THE BALCONY OF THIS FEDERAL HALL WASHINGTON WAS MADE PRESIDENT.

quiet dignity, enjoying a placid rural life. On this lovely and tranquil estate, and on the present site of St. Mark's Church, he erected a chapel wherein he was in due time buried.

Thus closed the Dutch *régime* in New York. Its ruling impulse, the aggrandizement of a commercial company, differed widely from the movements of religious enthusiasm or national pride which inspired the foundations of the English and French colonies in America. From the start, it was a business community, and all its development has been near the original lines of effort. In the present era of mercantile and industrial supremacy, when the sagacity developed by business, and the wealth created thereby, establish religious missions, equip armies, create nations and fill the homes of the people with comfort, New York, London and Paris are the three capitals of the world. The Dutch founders, practical, sagacious and earnest,

JUMEL MANSION, NEAR WASHINGTON HEIGHTS, ONCE WASHINGTON'S HEADQUARTERS.

were influenced by the refined and vivacious French Huguenots, who settled among them, and by their sturdy and enterprising fellow-colonists from New England; while the varied traits of the German Palatines, the Swedish emigrants and many other nationalities tended still further to build up here a cosmopolitan and tolerant community, broad in views, fearless in thought, energetic in action, and free from the limiting provincialisms of Puritan or Cavalier, or of New France or New Spain.

As soon as the town with its 1,500 inhabitants had passed under British rule, it was officially named NEW YORK, in honor of the Duke of York, its new lord. Thus the name of the quiet old provincial town on the English River Ouse, the Eburacum of the Romans, where Constantine the Great was proclaimed emperor, became attached to the future metropolis of the Western World. According to the monkish tradition the name was derived from that of King Ebraucus, who ruled in Yorkshire at about the same period that David reigned in Israel. This ancient sovereign was said to have had twenty wives, twenty sons and thirty daughters; and yet, in spite of these circumstances, he ruled over his people for three-score years. Through the same change of name, "by a strange caprice in history, the greatest State in the Union bears the name of the last and the most tyrannical of the Stuarts."

Holland entered the following year into a two-years' war with Great Britain, whose fleets she well-nigh swept from the seas. By the treaty of Breda, however, she yielded New York to the British, receiving in exchange Surinam and other valuable possessions, which still remain under her flag.

The first British governor was Colonel Richard Nicolls, a wise, tactful and handsome officer, who knew the Dutch and French languages as well as he did his own.

This honest gentleman ruled from 1664 until 1668, and happily conciliated the varied elements in his little principality. Colonel Francis Lovelace, the despotic governor between 1668 and 1672, ordered May races at Hempstead, bought Staten Island from the Indians, and established the first mail between New York and Boston, to be of monthly operation. He also founded the first merchants' exchange on Manhattan. It started its barterings in 1670, when the easy-going Dutch and English shopkeepers began the cus-

tom of meeting every Friday noon at the bridge over the Broad-Street canal. The hour of meeting was marked by the ringing of the Stadt-Huys bell; and the mayor was required to be at the assembly to prevent disturbance. In 1673 a Dutch fleet of twenty-three vessels and 1,600 men entered the harbor and exchanged broadsides with the fort, by which serious losses were occasioned. Then 600 stout Dutch troops were landed, at the foot of Vesey Street, and joined by 400 burghers. The army marched down Broadway to attack the fort, but this stronghold prudently surrendered, and the banner of the Dutch Republic once more floated in supremacy over the city and harbor, and up the Hudson, and over New Jersey and Long Island. The name *New York* was repudiated, and in its place the Lowland com-modores ordained that *New*

FRAUNCES' TAVERN, CORNER OF BROAD AND PEARL STREETS.

Orange should be the title of the city. The new government lasted but little more than a year, and then the province was restored by the States-General to Great Britain; and Edmund Andros, a major in Prince Rupert's cavalry, came over as governor of the territories of the Duke of York in America. In Andros's time, the canal on Broad Street was filled; the tanners were driven out of the city and re-established their tan-pits in the remote district now between Broadway, Ann Street and Maiden Lane; the slaughter-houses were also driven into the country and settled at Smit's Vley, now the intersection of Pearl Street and Maiden Lane; all Indian slaves were set free; and the burghers secured the exclusive right of bolting and exporting flour from the province. The latter monopoly, during its sixteen years of operation, trebled the wealth of the city and ten-folded the value of its real estate, 600 houses having been built and the local fleet augmented to 60 ships.

In 1673, the aggregate value of all the estates in the province was $750,000 ; and a planter with $1,500, or a merchant worth $3,000, was accounted a rich man. A considerable export trade in furs and provisions, lumber and tar was carried on with European ports.   The slaves on Manhattan were rated in value at about $150 each, and had been brought from Guinea and the West Indies.   In 1712, when there were about 4,000 negroes in the city, a hot outbreak of race hatred occurred, and nine whites were slain by negro conspirators in Maiden Lane.   The wildest excitement followed, and fears of a general insurrection ; but the garrison and militia quelled the outbreak with unsparing hands.   Six Africans committed suicide, and 21 were executed, most of them by hanging or by burning at the stake.   One was broken on the wheel, and one hung in chains until he starved.   A similar panic

FEDERAL HALL AND PART OF BROAD STREET, 1796.

broke out in 1741, when conflagrations at Fort George, on the Battery, and elsewhere, were attributed to the slaves acting in collusion with the hostile power of Spain.   In this wild popular frenzy 14 negroes were burned at the stake, 18 hanged, and 71 transported.

In 1683 the governorship was devolved upon Thomas Dongan, an Irish Catholic soldier, then recently lieutenant-governor of Tangier, in Africa, and subsequently Earl of Limerick.   This able and prudent statesman convened in the old fort on the Battery a council and elective assembly which enacted "The Charter of Liberties," providing for religious freedom and liberty of choice in elections, and forbidding taxation without the consent of the people.   The city was now divided into six wards, although its entire assessed value of property lay under £80,000.   After five years of happy rule, Governor Dongan was removed, and New York, New Jersey and the Eastern Colonies were united in the Dominion of New England, with Sir Edmund Andros as Governor-in-Chief, and Francis Nicholson in charge of New York. After the Bostonians had deposed and imprisoned Andros, Jacob Leisler, a German captain of the train-bands, seized the government of New York, and held it for over a year, during which there was one bloody fight between the local train-bands in the fort and British infantry in the town. After Governor Sloughter had arrived, Leisler was tried for treason, and convicted; and suffered the penalty of death by hanging, on the edge of Beekman's Swamp, where the *Sun* building now stands.

During the period between 1690 and 1700, New York carried on a large trade with British East-Indian pirates, sending out liquors, ammunition and other commodities, and at the pirates' haunts exchanging these for Oriental fabrics and carpets, jewels and gold, perfumes and spices. Some of these freebooters were New-Yorkers, and several successful pirate chiefs visited the city. Captain Robert Kidd, "so wickedly he did," recruited at this port most of the buccaneers who sailed with him on his last three-years' voyage to the Red Sea.

Governor Benjamin Fletcher, a luxurious soldier of fortune, and courtier, ruled New York from 1692 until 1698; and received large gifts from the pirates. His successor was the Earl of Bellomont, a pure and honorable governor, who restored the Leislerian (or people's) party to power, and hung all the pirates he could catch. Next came Lord Cornbury, the nephew of Queen Anne, and a silly, venal and bigoted debauchee, who ruled here from 1702 until 1708.

The Dutch Reformed people had long been content to wor-

BANK OF NEW YORK.   MC EVER'S MANSION.   CITY BANK.
WALL STREET, BELOW WILLIAM, IN 1800.

ship in the stone church in the fort; but in 1691–93 they erected on Exchange Street (now Garden Street) the finest church in the province, a quaint and high-steepled brick structure. Next came the Church-of-England people, dissatisfied with services in the fort chapel; and to this society Gov. Fletcher in 1696 gave the revenue of the King's Farm for seven years, which encouraged them to build a new chapel on the site of the present Trinity. The First Presbyterian Church, now on Fifth Avenue, near 11th Street, is descended from the church of the same faith erected on Wall Street in 1719. The quaint towers of the French Huguenot and Middle Dutch Churches rose high above the gables of the houses near Broad Street.

From 1710 to 1719, the little royal court at New York was dominated by Gov. Robert Hunter, formerly a Scottish general under Marlborough, and a friend of Addison and Swift. He founded the court of chancery; fought for religious liberty; and predicted American independence ("The colonies are infants at their mother's breast, but such as will wean themselves when they become of age.")

In 1692 the municipality cut up the Clover Pastures, and laid out Pine and Cedar Streets, and others; and further increased its dignity a year later by appointing a town-crier, dressed in proper livery, and by building a bridge across Spuyten-Duyvil Creek. Four more years passed, and then the night-watch came into existence, to patrol the streets of lonely evenings. The watchmen moved about on duty from nine o'clock until the break of day, traversing their beats every hour, with bells, proclaiming the condition of the weather and the hour of the night. The dark high-ways were lighted by lanterns put out on poles from every seventh house. In front of the City Hall stood the cage, pillory, and whipping-post, as terrors to thieves and slanderers, vagrants and truants; and the ducking-stool, to cool the ardor of scolds and evil-speaking persons. Now also began the era of street-cleaning, when each householder was ordered to keep clean his section of street, and the street sur-veyor received directions to root up weeds. In 1696 the city made its first appro-priation (of £20) for cleaning the streets. At the same time, "the street that runs by the pie-woman's leading to the city commons" was laid out, and became Nassau Street.

Hunter's successor was another gentleman of Scottish origin, William Burnet, the son of the famous Bishop of Salisbury; and after a rule of eight years, he in

MR. EDITOR,

THE accompanying Sketch of the City of New York was taken from the Anchoring Ground near Governor's Island; a Pilot Boat is introduced in the Fore Ground, and a Ship in the distance, sailing towards the Passage of Hell Gates, formed by York and Long Islands.   Your humble Servant,

August 27, 1805.   G. T.

NEW YORK IN 1805.

turn gave place to Col. John Montgomery, another Scot, and an old soldier and member of Parliament. During this period, Greenwich and Washington Streets were made, by filling in along the North River.

With the dawn of the year 1730 a fortnightly winter stage to Philadelphia was established. A year thereafter the municipal authorities imported from London two Newnham fire engines, able to throw water seventy feet high; and organized a fire-department of twenty-four strong and discreet men.

From 1743 to 1753 the city and province were governed by Admiral George Clinton, the son of an earl, who ruled with the rough temper of a sailor, and retired from his administration, enriched by plunder, after many a hot contest with the people. During this period, in 1752, the Royal Exchange was opened, at the foot of Broad Street, with its spacious assembly-hall for merchants, and a famous coffee-room. The Chamber of Commerce received its incorporation in 1770, by Royal Charter.

In 1751 the Assembly appointed trustees to take charge of funds raised for a college; and the next year Trinity Church offered to give the site for the proposed institution. In 1753 the entering class of ten members began its studies in the vestry-room of Trinity; and in another year King's College received its charter. The building was erected in 1756-60, on the site long held by the college, between Barclay, Church and Murray Streets and College Place.

The tremendous power of New-York journalism and publishing, which is now felt all over the continent, began in the humblest way far back in 1693, when the Council invited William Bradford to settle in the city as official printer, for "£40 a year and half the benefit of his printing, besides what served the public." He issued the first bound book in New York, the *Laws of the Colony*, in 1694; and in 1725 began the publication of *The New-York Gazette*, a semi-official organ of Gov. Burnet's administration, printed weekly, on foolscap paper. Nine years later *The Weekly Journal* came into being, to resist the Government, and Zenger, its editor,

The new Trinity Church New York & part y Wall Street.

THE NEW TRINITY. CHURCH AND PART OF WALL STREET.

was sent to prison, and various numbers of the paper were burned by order. The *Gazette* was the organ of the aristocracy, and the *Journal* stood as the champion of the people. After Editor Zenger had languished in prison for nine months, he was tried, and received a triumphant acquittal, to the immense delight of the people, who bitterly resented this first attempt to muzzle the press.

The Brooklyn ferry was started in the earliest days of the colony, and consisted of a flatboat worked by sweeps, the ferryman being summoned by blasts of a horn. It was not until 1755 that a packet began running semi-weekly to Staten Island; and the Paulus-Hook (Jersey-City) ferry began its trips in 1763, followed in 1774 by a ferry to Hoboken.

In the year 1765 the Stamp Act was passed, and the disruption of America and England began. The New-Yorkers forgot their old-time local controversies, and took sides in the new contest. Rivington's *Gazetteer* stigmatized the patriots as rebels, traitors, banditti, fermenters of sedition, sons of licentiousness, and the like; and Gaine's *Mercury* and Holt's *Journal* proclaimed the Royalists to be ministerial hirelings, dependent placemen and informers.

A congress of delegates from nine colonies met at the New-York City Hall and passed a Declaration of Rights and an address to the King. When the stamped paper arrived from England, under naval escort, the Sons of Liberty refused to allow its use, and the Common Council compelled the surrender of the paper to the corporation. The city and province were then under the rule of the venerable Lieutenant-Governor Cadwallader Colden, a Scottish Jacobite and scholar, who lived in New York from 1708 until his death in 1776. He endeavored to repress the popular tumults, but prevented the fort from firing on the rioters. The military commander was Gen. Thomas Gage, who afterwards received from the New-Englanders the brevet title of "Lord Lexington, Baron of Bunker Hill." Major James of the Royal Artillery had his beautiful estate of Ranelagh near the present West Broadway; Sir Peter Parker's estate of Vauxhall was at the foot of Warren Street; and Murray Hill, the seat of Robert Murray, the Quaker merchant, occupied the domain between Fourth and Fifth Avenues, and 36th and 40th Streets.

The Commons, now the City-Hall Park, were often crowded by assemblies of citizens, to whom the tribunes of the people, Sears and Scott, McDougall and Wil-

BROADWAY.   ALMS-HOUSE.   CITY HALL.
BUILDINGS IN CITY-HALL PARK IN 1809.

lett, Livingston and Hamilton, made fiery addresses, although strong detachments of the 16th and 24th British Regiments lay in adjacent barracks. Thence the populace marched to the fort, at evening, bearing 500 lights, and beat against its gates, defied its grape-shot, insulted the officers, spiked the guns of the Battery, and burned Governor Colden's coach, and an effigy of the ruler. The Liberty Pole was set up on the Commons, amid hilarious festivities, attended with a barbecue, and the drinking of twenty-five barrels of beer and a hogshead of punch. Thrice the red-coats of the 24th Regiment cut down this emblem of popular sovereignty, but when they laid it low for the fourth time, the alarm-bells tolled, the shops were closed, and the citizens made a series of attacks on the soldiers. The hottest skirmish occurred on Golden Hill (John Street), where the Sons of Liberty beleaguered and beat a large detachment of the 16th, and themselves received many bayonet-thrusts and other wounds. After this outbreak, the patriots erected on the Commons a lofty iron-bound pole, crowned by a vane bearing the word Liberty. This stood fast until the city fell into the hands of the British army. In 1770 the people erected an equestrian statue of George III. on Bowling Green; and also a marble statue of William

Pitt, at Wall and William Streets. When the British ships laden with taxed tea arrived at New York, the people seized the *London* and emptied all her tea-chests into the river, and compelled the *Nancy* to put about and sail back to England.

On the Sunday after the battle of Lexington, a breathless horseman galloped in over the Boston road, bearing the startling news. The citizens immediately seized the public stores and colony arms; over-rode the local authorities; formed a governing Committee of One Hundred; and enthusiastically welcomed the New-England delegates to the Continental Congress. A few weeks later, the frigate *Asia* fired a broadside through the city, injuring several people, and damaging the houses along Whitehall.

The Provincial Congress, fearing a descent on the city by royalist troops from Ireland, summoned help from New England; and Gen. Wooster marched down

OLD CUSTOM HOUSE AND VICINITY IN 1825.

with 1,800 Connecticut militia, and encamped for several weeks at Harlem, sending out detachments to cover the coast from British marauders. Under this protection the Sons of Liberty seized the Royalist supply-depots at Greenwich Village and at Turtle Bay (at the foot of East 47th Street), and removed thirty cannon from the Battery. The Tories included the landed proprietors, the recent English immigrants, and the Episcopalians; while the patriot party was made up of the Dutch and Huguenots, the New-Englanders and Scots, the Dissenters and the artisans. The influence of the principal families inclined the General Assembly and Provincial Congress strongly toward Royalism; and caused the province to move more slowly in the direction of independence than its neighbors had done. But the great mass of the people were in favor of freedom, and in time crushed out the Tory legislative influences.

During these troublous days, Isaac Sears, one of the leading New-York patriots, rode down from Connecticut, with a band of light horsemen, and destroyed the press and other apparatus of Rivington's *Royal Gazetteer*, and carried off the type to be made into bullets. Early in 1776 Gen. Charles Lee marched into New York with 1,200 Connecticut troops, and encamped on the Commons, whence his detachments

disarmed the Tories, and began to fortify the city. Lee was succeeded by Lord
Stirling, and he by Gen. Putnam; and the Third New-Jersey Regiment and troops
from Dutchess and Westchester Counties and from Pennsylvania entered the city.

Governor Tryon took refuge on the British fleet, and the garrison of the Royal
Irish Regiment was sent away to Boston. As soon as the New-England metropolis
was delivered from the enemy, Washington marched his army to New York; and
here on the 9th of July, 1776, the Continental troops were assembled by brigades to
have the Declaration of Independence read to them. One brigade was drawn up on
the Commons, and in the hollow square Washington sat on horseback while an aide
read the historic document. The same day the citizens pulled down the gilded-lead
equestrian statue of George III. on Bowling Green, and sent it off into Connecticut,

where it was con-
verted into 48,000
bullets; and thus
the   Royalist
troops had "melt-
ed majesty" fired
at them from pat-
riotic muskets.
Three days later
the British frig-
ates *Rose* and
Phœnix sailed up
the Hudson, firing
on the city as they
passed, and tak-
ing post above.
By mid-August

RESERVOIR OF MANHATTAN WATER WORKS ON CHAMBERS STREET, IN 1825.

the hostile fleet in the Bay numbered 437 sail, bearing the armies of Howe, Clinton and Cornwallis, and the King's Guards and De Heister's Hessian division, numbering 31,000 soldiers in all. Again the *Rose* and *Phœnix* sailed past the city,
bound downward, and firing broad-sides through its streets and buildings.

The defences of New York (aside from the Brooklyn lines) consisted of Fort
George, six guns, and the Grand Battery, 18 guns; the Whitehall Battery; and
field-works at Coenties Slip and at Catherine, Madison, Pike, Clinton, Broome, and
Pitt streets, and Grand and Mulberry streets, besides others near Trinity Church,
and heavy barricades in the streets. In due time 21,000 British troops landed at
Gravesend, and shattered Putnam's army of 9,000 men, holding the Brooklyn lines.
Almost a fortnight later five frigates demolished the American defences at Kip's
Bay (foot of East 34th Street), and scattered their garrisons in wild panic, which
was communicated to the troops on Murray Hill, as the English grenadiers advanced.
Putnam retreated from the city by the Bloomingdale Road. The Continentals rallied
on Harlem Heights; defeated the enemy in some hot skirmishes; and then retreated
into Westchester. The military officers had discussed the question of burning the
city, to prevent it being made a winter-quarters for the British army; but Congress
forbade this extreme measure. Nevertheless, on the 21st of September a fire accidentally broke out in a low tavern near Whitehall Slip, and destroyed 493 houses,
obliterating nearly all the North-River side of the city west of Broad Street and
Broadway. The British troops believed that the torch had been applied by the
Americans, and bayonetted or threw into the flames a number of citizens. At mid-

November, Gen. Howe and 9,000 men stormed the outworks of Fort Washington, and compelled the surrender of that strong fortress, the last American post on Manhattan Island. Thenceforward for over seven years New York lay in the hands of the enemy, a prostrate city under martial law, the chief depot for the soldiers and stores of the invading army, and the place of captivity where their prisoners of war were confined. The Dissenters' churches were turned into hospitals and prisons, and the Middle Dutch Church became a riding school for cavalrymen. The municipal government existed no longer, and about the only commerce was that of the sutlers' shops.

In the East River lay the horrible prison ships in whose disease-infested holds so many American soldiers were confined. It is related that in the *Jersey* alone over

BROADWAY, FROM BOWLING GREEN, IN 1828.

10,000 prisoners of war perished. The American officers and dignitaries were consigned to the new jail (now the Hall of Records). Several of the great sugar houses, including Rhinelander's, near William Street, were also used as prisons for captives from the Continental armies. On the 25th of November, 1783, the rear-guard of Sir Guy Carleton's British army embarked at the Battery. The American advance-guard, composed of light infantry, artillery and the 2d Massachusetts Regiment, marched down the Bowery and Chatham, Queen and Wall Streets to the corner of Broadway and Rector Street. After these came Gen. Washington and Gen. Clinton, the City Council, a group of veteran generals, and other functionaries. A few weeks later, Washington bade farewell to his officers, at Fraunces' Tavern, at the corner of Broad and Pearl Streets.

The first American Congress under the Constitution met in 1789, in the handsome old City Hall, at the corner of Wall and Broad Streets. Here, on the gallery overlooking Wall Street, which was packed with vast and silent crowds, Livingston, the chancellor of the State of New York, administered the oath of office to the first President of the United States, April 30, 1789. For a year thereafter New York was the capital of the Republic (as it had been for five years previously); and the President and Cabinet officers, Congressmen and foreign ambassadors and their families made up a brilliant and stately Court circle. The ruins of the great fires, and the squalor of the British garrison's "canvas town," were replaced by new buildings; the streets were cleared from the rubbish which had for years choked them up; and new shops and warehouses showed tempting arrays of wares. Wall Street, the favorite promenade, was brilliant with richly dressed ladies and hardly less showy gentlemen, and the carriages of the Republican aristocracy crowded Broadway down to the Battery. The finest mansion in the city was built in 1790, from the public funds, for the occupancy of Washington and his successors in the

Presidential office.   Before its completion, the seat of government was moved to Philadelphia, and so the splendid house with its Ionic-colonnaded front became the official residence of Governors Clinton and Jay.   It occupied the site of the ancient fort, and was afterwards replaced by the Bowling-Green block.

The holiday of New Year's had been introduced by the first Dutch colonists on Manhattan, and their descendants had kept it up faithfully, and with abundant good cheer.   Washington thus advised a citizen, during one of these receptions :   "The highly favored situation of New York will, in the process of years, attract numerous immigrants, who will gradually change its ancient customs and manners ; but, whatever changes take place, never forget the cordial observance of New Year's Day."

The Tammany Society was formed in 1789, as a patriotic national institution, with a government of a Grand Sachem (chosen from thirteen sachems), a Sagamore, and a Wiskinskie.   Many Indian forms and ceremonials were adopted ; the months

NORTH BATTERY, AT THE FOOT OF HUBERT STREET.

were "moons"; and the seasons were those of snow, of blossoms, of fruit.   With a view of conciliating the hostile tribes on the borders, the society took also the name of Tammany, an Indian chief.   In its early years, some of the most conspicuous and respected of New-Yorkers belonged to this order, which, indeed, did not become a political party institution until the days of the Jefferson administration.

It was impossible for New York to become the permanent capital of the United States, because Congress demanded that the Federal District thus dignified should be ceded to the Nation.   Neither the local nor the State authorities would consent to this alienation of territory and wealth.   Washington made excursions on Long Island and elsewhere, in search of an appropriate location, but without success.   His heart was on the Potomac, where, after a ten years' sojourn at Philadelphia, the National capital was at last established.

The tract known successively as De Vlackte, the Commons, and City-Hall Park, in 1785 contained the Alms House and House of Correction, the public gallows, the Bridewell (on part of the City Hall's site) and the New Jail (now the Hall of Records).   The present City Hall was begun in 1803, Mayor Edward Livingston laying the corner-stone. The front and sides were of Massachusetts marble; but the back, or northern side, was built of red sandstone, because it was thought that the city would never grow to any importance to the northward of the new edifice. As a contemporary writer said, the northern front "would be out of sight to all the world." When this building was finished, in 1812, at a cost of $500,000, it was generally conceded to be the handsomest in the United States.

At the beginning of the century, Broadway had a length of about two miles, paved for little more than half this distance, and lined with comfortable brick houses. Here and there between the houses the view passed down the bay, and out through the Narrows. The homes of the gentry and the rich merchants were along lower Broadway and the Battery, where their occupants could enjoy the beautiful views

BROADWAY.   CITY HALL AND PARK, AND PARK THEATRE.   PARK ROW.

and refreshing air of the bay. At little over a mile from the Battery the paving ceased, and Broadway became a rather straggling road, with houses at intervals, and the indications of streets planned for the future. Broad Street in its width recalled the old canal that once flowed down its centre, but had long since vanished. Wall Street possessed many fine residences, and the handsome Federal Hall. The dry-goods marts occupied much of William Street, which afforded a bright spectacle on days favorable for shopping. Most of the other streets were narrow and winding, and lined with small red-brick houses with tiled roofs. On the west side, where the great fire of 1776 had occurred, the streets had been widened and straightened, and provided with brick sidewalks and gutters. The first sidewalk in the city was on Broadway, between Vesey and Murray Streets, constructed of brick and stone, and hardly a yard wide. The numbering of houses began in 1793. Broadway was built up only as far as Anthony Street; the Bowery Lane, to Broome Street; the East-River shore, to Rutgers Street; and the North-River shore, to Harrison Street. Beyond the steep Anthony-Street hill, Broadway plunged sharply into the Canal

3

Street valley, between the Fresh Water Pond and the Lispenard Meadows. At Astor Place, Broadway ceased, its line being crossed by the wall of the Randall farm.

The favorite duelling ground was a lonely grassy glade in the woods of Wee-hawken, high above the Hudson, and allowing glimpses of New York through the surrounding trees. The combatants were rowed across from the city, and clambered up the rocky steep to the scene of their fight. The most mournful event in Ameri-can duelling annals occurred here, July 11, 1804, when the antagonists were Alexander Hamilton, the first Secretary of the Treasury, and founder of the National financial system, and Aaron Burr, Vice-President of the United States. Hamilton had characterized Burr as a "dangerous man," and helped to defeat his political schemes ; and Burr challenged him to mortal combat. Hamilton did not fire at his antagonist, but Burr, with a carefully aimed shot, mortally wounded him ; and he died the next day, in the presence of his wife and seven children. This dreadful encounter closed the practice of duelling in the civilized States of America ; and at the same time put an end to the public career of Burr.

The development of the higher culture in the Empire City received an impetus in 1784, by the re-chartering of the long-closed King's College, under the more republican title of Columbia College. Twenty years later the New-York Histori-cal Society was organized, followed by the College of Physicians and Surgeons in 1807, and the American Academy of Fine Arts in 1808. The education of the children rested in the hands of parochial, charity and private schools until 1806, when a small public school came into existence, from the contributions of wealthy citizens, and small State and city appropriations. The Free School Society in 1809 erected a large brick building on Chatham Street ; and in 1825, six schools were in operation, not as charities, but open to all comers.

New York may be called the cradle of steam navigation, which has completely revolutionized the world's commerce ; for although other localities had seen at an earlier day vessels propelled by steam, yet here occurred the first profitable and successful ventures in this line on a large scale. In 1807 the *Clermont* was built, from the designs of Robert Fulton, the inventor, and with capital furnished by Chancellor Robert R. Livingston ; and in spite of all the evil prognostications of the conservative, she made a triumphant run from New York to Albany in thirty-two hours. As it took the ordinary packets from four to six days to run between the two cities, the rapid success of steam navigation on the Hudson followed as a neces-sity, especially after 1817, when the time of passage was reduced to eighteen hours.

The navigation of Long-Island Sound by steamboats was soon inaugurated by a line opened in 1818 from New York to New Haven, followed by another to New London, and in 1822 by the New-York & Providence line. The advance from the ugly little *Clermont* and the slow and dirty vessels of her class to the magnificent steamboats of modern days was largely due to a young Staten-Island ferryman, Cornelius Vanderbilt, who came to New York in 1829 and established new and im-proved lines on the Hudson and the Sound.

The first steam vessel to dare the storms of ocean was the *Phœnix*, built by Col. John Stevens of Hoboken, in 1807, and a year later sent around from New-York harbor to Philadelphia, by the sea passage. In 1811 Stevens opened between Hoboken and New York the first steam ferry in the world ; and this was followed the next year by Fulton's lines to Jersey City and Brooklyn. The first steam frigate in the world, the *Fulton*, was built from a Congressional appropriation of $320,000, under Robert Fulton's supervision ; and made its successful trial-trip to Sandy

NEW YORK CITY IN 1851.
A REPRODUCTION FROM A LARGE STEEL ENGRAVING.

Hook in 1814.   Transatlantic steam navigation was inaugurated by the *Savannah*, built at New York in 1819 and sent thence to Savannah, Liverpool, Copenhagen, Stockholm and St. Petersburg.   In 1812 Col. Stevens made the plans for a circular iron-clad war-ship, with screw propellers.

About the year 1810 the city began a rapid development to the northward.   The Brevoort estate, between Broadway and the Bowery road and 11th Street ; Henry Spingler's farm, between 14th and 16th Streets, west of the Bowery ; Nicholas Bayard's West Farm, covering 100 acres between Broadway and McDougall Street, and running north from Prince Street ; the Bayard-Hill estate, between Broadway and the Bowery and Broome Street ; the 260-acre domain established by Sir Peter Warren, in the region of Gansevoort and Christopher Streets ; and many other

estates and farms were invaded by the City Commissioners.   Legions of stalwart laborers levelled the hills and filled the hollows; and new streets were laid out with efficient engineering skill and foresight. Oftentimes the irate landlords assailed the survey-

CORP. THOMPSON'S MADISON COTTAGE, IN 1852.   SITE OF THE FIFTH-AVENUE HOTEL.

ors with dogs, hot water, cabbages and other distressful methods ; but the work went steadily on, especially above Houston Street, whence they laid out the island into parallel numbered cross streets and broad north and south avenues, distinguished by numbers or letters.

When Trinity Church, in 1807, erected St. John's Chapel, in Varick Street, it was regarded as quite beyond civilization, and the parish received much blame for planting their new mission opposite a bulrush swamp, tenanted only by water snakes and frogs.   About the same time, the Lutheran society got into financial straits, and a friend offered to give it four acres of land at the corner of Broadway and Canal Street.   This largess was declined by the church on the ground that the land was not worth the cost of fencing it — which was doubtless true at the time.

The Collect was a broad and placid pond, favored by skaters in winter, and boating parties in summer.   But it lay in the path of the northward advance of the city, and therefore, in 1809, a drainage canal was cut and bordered on either side by shade trees and a pleasant street (afterwards Canal Street).   It was proposed in 1789 to make a public park of this beautiful pond and its shores ; but the scheme came to naught, on the ground that New York would never grow within accessible distance of this lonely region.

The intersection of Leonard and Centre Streets is not far from the centre of the pond, which had a depth of sixty feet.   On the same site now stands the gloomy prison of the Tombs, the abode of so much misery and wickedness.   The Collect was famous as the place where a steamboat with a screw propeller was first tried, in 1796, when John Fitch, its inventor, steamed around the pond several times, in an eighteen-foot propeller.   Among the spectators were Chancellor Livingston and other prominent New-Yorkers. About this time Oliver Evans aroused considerable popular amusement by saying that "The time will come when people will travel in stages moved by steam engines from one city to another, at fifteen or twenty miles an hour."

When Great Britain declared the ports of Continental Europe to be blockaded, and Napoleon retorted by proclaiming all vessels trading with Great Britain liable to seizure, American shipping suffered grave losses; and President Jefferson (in 1807) ordered all our commercial fleets to remain in our ports, and forbade the shipment of cargoes on foreign vessels. He believed that warring Europe, thus deprived of American breadstuffs, would hasten to acknowledge our neutral rights. During this

OLD NEW-YORK POST-OFFICE. SITE OF THE MUTUAL LIFE-INSURANCE BUILDING, ON NASSAU STREET.

year of interdict the shipping of New York's merchant-princes decayed at their anchorages, the warehouses were closed and abandoned, and the clerks were discharged because there was no work for them.

The War of 1812 broke out in the same year that the City Hall received its finishing touches; and within a few weeks the city had fortified her approaches, and sent to sea 26 privateers, manned by 2,239 bold sailors. Such a hornet's nest must needs be closed, and so from 1813 until the end of the war the mouth of the harbor was blockaded by tall British ships-of-the-line. The naval headquarters of the enemy was at Gardiner's Island, east of Long Island, whence their squadrons off Sandy Hook, or blockading New London, could be reinforced or supplied. In expectation of a dash from the enemy, New York was strongly fortified by the voluntary labor of its citizens, and new lines of defence covered the heights of Brooklyn and Harlem, with forts on the islands and at the Narrows and around Hell Gate. The city was held by a garrison of 23,000 men, mostly of the State troops.

The first great trunk line of railway finished from New York to the West was the Erie, which ran its trains as far as Dunkirk, on Lake Erie, in 1851. The line from Albany to Schenectady was opened in 1832, and in 1853 became a part of the newly organized New-York Central, whose rails reached Buffalo a year later. The Hudson-River Railroad, from New-York to Albany, was opened in 1851, and in 1869 became a part of the New-York Central system.

The horse-railroad, of such incalculable importance in street traffic, was inaugurated in 1832, when the Fourth-Avenue line began its trips, running from Prince

Street as far as Murray Hill. The first street-car ever built was made by John Stephenson, with compartments, roof seats, and the driver in the roof.

Another valuable modern convenience, illuminating gas, was introduced in 1825, with pipes traversing Broadway from the Battery to Canal Street.

After the War of 1812, the famous packet lines began their service, the Black-Ball in 1816 and the Red-Star in 1821, running swift and handsome ships nearly weekly between New York and Liverpool, and making the run across eastward in from 15 to 23 days. Depau put four ships on the Havre packet service in 1822; and Grinnell, Minturn & Co. began to send monthly packets to London in 1823. After 1840 Low, Griswold & Aspinwall inaugurated the sailing of clipper-ships to China and California, and their vessels performed the most wonderful feats—as when the *Flying Cloud* ran from New York to San Francisco, making 433¼ statute

FIVE POINTS IN 1859, VIEW FROM THE CORNER OF NORTH AND LITTLE WATER STREETS.

miles in a single day; or the *Sovereign of the Seas* sailed for 10,000 miles without tacking or wearing; or the *Dreadnaught* made the passage from Sandy Hook to Queenstown in nine days and seventeen hours.

The wonderful Erie Canal was built between 1816 and 1825, and became the most prominent factor in the growth of the Empire City, bringing to her docks the illimitable products of the Great West (then without railways), and carrying back much of her vast imports. The telegraph was not then known; and the news of the opening of the canal was carried in 81 minutes 550 miles from Buffalo to Sandy Hook by the successive reports of a line of cannon, ten miles apart. A group of canal boats containing Gov. Clinton and other magnates descended the canal to Albany, and were thence towed down the Hudson to New York, and out to sea, escorted by many flag-bedecked vessels and barges. At Sandy Hook, Governor

Clinton emptied into the ocean a keg of Lake-Erie water, and other unique ceremonials were solemnly and decorously performed.

John Jacob Astor, a native of Waldorf, near Heidelberg, came to the New World in 1784, in his twenty-first year, and entered the fur-trade in the Empire City, keeping also a stock of London piano-fortes. He had himself incorporated as the American Fur Company; bought out the Mackinaw Company and all its forts; established a line of trading-posts across Oregon; and developed a rich China trade. This typical merchant lived on the site of the present Astor House, and frequently entertained Irving, Halleck, and other literary men and scholars.

In 1834 occurred the Anti-Abolition riots, in which for the first time the National Guard was called out to restore order; and a few months later the same potent peace-makers came into service to quell the stone-cutters' riots, and lay under arms on Washington Square for several days. In December, 1835, a fire in the lower part

VIEW FROM THE SCHOOL-HOUSE IN 42D STREET, BETWEEN SECOND AND THIRD AVENUES, IN 1868.

of the city burned over 13 acres, with 700 buildings and $20,000,000 worth of property, and was stopped only at the wide gaps made by blowing up houses with gunpowder. This portentous calamity showed the need of more water for the growing city; and the Croton Aqueduct, begun in 1835, delivered water on Manhattan Island in 1842, and was completed in 1845, at a cost of $9,000,000. The old Manhattan Water Works, whose reservoir stood on Chambers Street, were thus rendered valueless.

The University of the City of New York dates from 1831; the *Sun* from 1833; the *Herald* from 1835; the *Tribune* from 1841; the *Times* from 1851; and the *World* from 1860. Other notable achievements of this period were the opening of the Croton Aqueduct in 1842; the founding of the Astor Library in 1848; and the opening of the World's Fair in the Crystal Palace in 1853.

In 1825 the region north of Astor Place was still devoted to farms and orchards, with a gray old barn on the site of Grace Church, and a powder-house on Union Square. The fashionable summer evening resort was the Vauxhall Garden, stretching from Broadway to the Bowery, near the present Astor Library, and famous for its trees and flowers, band-music and fire-works, and cakes and ale. In the triangle where Third Avenue and Fourth Avenue come together, stood the grocery store of

Peter Cooper, where the uptown lads exchanged berries picked in the Bleecker-Street pastures, for taffy and cakes.

Greenwich village occupied the region about the present Greenwich Avenue ; and to the northward, near West 23d Street, the roofs of Chelsea Village peered over the trees. In 1797 the State Prison of Newgate was opened at Greenwich, and served as a terror to evil-doers during full a quarter of a century.

For a number of years after 1825 the vicinity of St. John's Park was the Court end of the city, with the mansions of the Lydigs, Pauldings and other prominent families. In this vicinity, at the foot of Hubert Street, stood the frowning old North Battery, with its empty embrasures.

The old Potter's Field, now known as Washington Square, became fashionable about ten years later ; and here dwelt the Rhinelanders and Johnstons, Griswolds and Boormans, and other well-known families.

The convergence of several streets where Fourth Avenue met the old Bowery road made it necessary to leave there a broad common, which was at times used as the Potter's Field, much of its area being also covered with rude shanties. Not until 1845 was this rugged and filthy field improved into the present Union Square, which was soon surrounded by fine mansions, and up nearly to the time of the War for the Union remained the Belgravia of Manhattan. Only a few houses were to be seen above Union Square in 1845. Gramercy Park was laid out by Samuel B. Rug-gles, and presented to the owners of the sixty neighboring lots, to induce the erection of attractive houses here. Where the old Boston Road met the Bloomingdale Road lay another broad area of waste land, in olden times a burial-place for the poor, and from 1806 to 1823 the site of a United-States arsenal. Here the first House of Refuge was founded, in 1825, with six boys and three girls ; and remained until it burned down in 1839. During the mayoralty of James Harper (one of the famous publishers), between 1844 and 1847, this dreary region was cleared and beautified, and became the famous Madison Square. The chief house here in 1852 was the little story-and-a-half cottage of Corp. Thompson, on the site now occupied by the Fifth-Avenue Hotel.

One of the most wonderful of modern inventions, the electric telegraph, was inaugurated by the experiments of Prof. S. F. B. Morse, in the University of the City of New York. A line of telegraph was completed from New York to Phila-delphia in 1845 ; to Boston in 1846 ; and to Albany in 1847.

In 1849, Macready, the celebrated English actor, played Macbeth in the Astor-Place Opera House. The populace supposed that Edwin Forrest's ill reception in England, a few years before, had been due to Macready's hostile influence ; and they attacked the Opera House, 20,000 strong, during the play, scattering the police, and breaking the windows with paving stones. The Seventh Regiment cleared the vicinity, after a pitched battle, in which 150 soldiers were severely injured and 70 of the mob.

The commercial and therefore conservative spirit of modern New York naturally held back from the dread hostilities foreshadowed in 1860 ; and by monster petitions and peace societies endeavored to arrest the storm. Mayor Fernando Wood even outlined a plan to make it a free city, like those of mediæval Germany, inviting the trade of the world by nominal duties. But after the first guns were fired, in South Carolina, the spirit of temporizing vanished like a dream, and patriotism and loyalty possessed all classes with full inspiration. Within ten days 8,000 volunteer troops left the city for the South, including the 7th, 6th, 12th and 11th Regiments of militia. In this metropolitan centre also were organized the famous and efficient

THE BLIZZARD OF MARCH 11TH, 12TH, AND 13TH, 1888.
PHOTOGRAPHS TAKEN JUST AFTER THE STORM, BY LANGILL.

societies, the United-States Sanitary Commission and the United-States Christian Commission, and the Union Defense Committee, whose efforts placed 40,000 soldiers under the National colors. New-York City alone sent 116,382 patriotic troops into the field, besides raising scores of millions of dollars for the needs of the Republic.

The terrible Draft Riot of 1863 was caused by popular discontent with the impressment of citizens into the army, a feeling which was intensified by the incendiary editorials of certain Democratic journals, and was not sufficiently discouraged by Gov. Seymour. On July 13th, a mob plundered and burned the provost-marshal's office, at Third Avenue and 46th Street, and then scattered through the city, bent on deeds of rapine and murder. The *Tribune* office was sacked ; the colored Orphan Asylum on Fifth Avenue went up in flames ; the grain-elevators at the Atlantic Docks were burned; and negroes and soldiers were slain or grievously maltreated wherever found. The closed shops, the streets clear of their customary traffic, and even of omnibuses and horse-cars, and many of the houses prepared like fortresses for defence, gave the city a singular and ominous appearance, which was increased by the mad roars of the mob, the clattering of cavalry along the pavement, the roll of volley-firing, and the heavy booming of artillery, sweeping the riotous vermin from the streets. The police behaved with extraordinary valor, but were unable to completely control this vast uprising of foreign-born anarchists, until the arrival of strong military forces, aided by the personal efforts and appeals of the Governor, the Mayor, and Archbishop Hughes. More than 1,000 men were killed and wounded and $2,000,000 of property was destroyed.

The long-continued supremacy of the degraded classes in municipal politics reached its crown of infamy after the close of the War for the Union, when William M. Tweed, a low ward-politician, was elevated to one of the chief offices of the city. In conjunction with other and similar conspirators, he elaborated a shrewd scheme, by which, within a few months, the city was robbed of $20,000,000. The new County Court House alone furnished $7,000,000 of this amount. In 1871, through reason of a disagreement among the municipal officials, the damning documents in the case of "The Ring" passed into the possession of the *New-York Times*, which immediately printed the entire history of this gigantic robbery, and itemized the amounts stolen. The other leading newspapers also came out against the detected thieves, the citizens organized a committee of seventy, and most of the culprits fled to Europe or Canada. Tweed was imprisoned, but escaped to Spain, whence he was returned to the outraged metropolis, and finally died in jail.

The events of later days in New York are familiar to all readers of the newspapers—that is to say, to all Americans. The development of education, of public charities, of artistic and literary culture, of vast works of public utility, have gone forward mightily, and to the great glory of the community. Occasionally, a great financial flurry, like the Black Friday of 1869, or the panic of 1873, threatens to unsettle values and bring ruin to thousands. Now and then a riot occurs, like that of 1871, when 29 policemen and soldiers were killed and wounded, and 104 of their assailants, in the attack of the Irish Catholics on the parading Orangemen. Other years see the rejoicings upon the completion of great public works, like the Park-Avenue improvements, costing $6,000,000, in 1875 ; the blowing-up of Hell Gate, in 1876 ; and the dedication of the East-River Bridge, in 1883.

The year 1886 saw the unveiling of Bartholdi's wonderful statue of "Liberty Enlightening the World," with its attendant civic and National ceremonials. Then also came the trial of the aldermen bribed by persons seeking the franchise of the Broadway Surface Railroad. The same year saw the local Anarchists sent to prison,

WASHINGTON CENTENNIAL EXERCISES IN 1889, AT THE UNITED-STATES SUB-TREASURY.

PHOTOGRAPHED BY JOHNSTON, WHILE THE REV. DR. R. S. STORRS WAS OFFERING PRAYER.

the great street-car strikes, and the twentieth annual encampment of the Grand Army of the Republic.

The most notable event of 1888 was the great blizzard of March 11 – 13, with its stoppage of transportation, food panic, the forming of an ice-bridge across the East River, and other unseasonable phenomena.

In 1889 the hundredth anniversary of the inauguration of George Washington as President of the United States was celebrated here by a three-days' festival, with a naval review by President Harrison, a march-past of 50,000 soldiers from 21 States, a civic parade of 75,000 persons, and other imposing ceremonies.

In 1890 the Holland Society began to identify interesting historic localities connected with the ancient Dutch settlement of New Amsterdam, and to place near them dur-

able bronze tab-
lets, with explicit
inscriptions.   In
the same year oc-
curred the be-
ginning of the
Washington Me-
morial Arch,
erected in Wash-
ington Square, to
replace a tem-
porary triumphal
arch constructed
for the preced-
ing year's Wash-
ington anniver-
sary. At this time,
also, the statue of

THE LOEW BRIDGE, BROADWAY AND FULTON STREET.

Horace Greeley was unveiled.   The year was further distinguished by the great conventions here of the mining engineers, and of the manufacturers of iron and steel.

1891 opened luridly with the burning of the Fifth-Avenue Theatre.   On the 5th of May occurred the dedication of the grand new Music Hall, founded by Andrew Carnegie.   In October the Court of Appeals decided the Tilden Will case in favor of the natural heirs, to the severe loss of the city.   The year was further notable as that in which the Metropolitan Museum of Art was first opened to the public on Sundays.   In 1891, also, came the visit of Prince George of Greece; and then also occurred the attack of a dynamiter on Russell Sage.

The year 1892 was marked by the deaths of several prominent New-Yorkers : John Jay Knox, on February 9th ; Thomas Sterry Hunt, February 12th ; Gen. G. W. Cullum, February 28th ; Edwards Pierrepont, March 6th ; Roswell Smith, April 19th ; William Astor, April 25th ; Sidney Dillon, June 10th ; Cyrus W. Field, July 12th ; and George William Curtis, August 31st.

On the 7th of February 17 persons were burned alive in the Hotel Royal.

In 1892 the wonderfully successful Actors' Fund Fair was held in Madison-Square Garden, where also occurred, at a later date, the world's convention of the Society of Christian Endeavor.   Now also came about the redistricting of the city into thirty Assembly districts, in conformity with the greatly increased population shown by the censuses of 1890.   It may be added, that in 1892 occurred the publi-

ON THIS SITE
WILLIAM BRADFORD
APPOINTED PUBLIC PRINTER APRIL 10TH. A. D. 1693
ISSUED NOVEMBER 8, A. D., 1725
THE NEW YORK GAZETTE
THE FIRST NEWSPAPER PRINTED IN NEW YORK

ERECTED BY THE
NEW YORK HISTORICAL SOCIETY
APRIL 10TH. A. D. 1893
IN COMMEMORATION OF THE 200TH ANNIVERSARY OF THE
INTRODUCTION OF PRINTING IN NEW YORK.

Tablet on the Cotton Exchange.

HERE STOOD
THE MIDDLE DUTCH CHURCH
DEDICATED A. D. 1729
MADE A BRITISH MILITARY PRISON 1776
RESTORED 1790
OCCUPIED AS THE UNITED STATES POST OFFICE
1845-1875
TAKEN DOWN 1882.

THIS TABLET IS PLACED HERE BY
THE MUTUAL LIFE INSURANCE COMPANY
OF NEW YORK.

*Tablet on the Mutual Life Building, corner of
Cedar and Nassau Streets.*

THE SITE OF
LIEUT. GOVERNOR DELANCEY'S HOUSE
LATER OF THE "CITY HOTEL".
IT WAS HERE THAT THE "NON-IMPORTATION AGREEMENT"
IN OPPOSITION TO THE "STAMP ACT" WAS SIGNED OCTOBER 31ST, 1765.
THE TAVERN HAD MANY PROPRIETORS BY WHOSE
NAMES IT WAS SUCCESSIVELY CALLED. IT WAS ALSO KNOWN
AS THE "PROVINCE ARMS," THE "CITY ARMS" AND "BURNS'
COFFEE HOUSE" OR "TAVERN".

THIS TABLET IS PLACED HERE BY THE
HOLLAND SOCIETY OF NEW YORK, SEPTEMBER
1890.

Tablet on the Boreel Building, 115 Broadway.

THIS TABLET MARKS THE SITE OF THE
FIRST HABITATIONS OF WHITE MEN
ON THE ISLAND OF MANHATTAN
ADRIAN BLOCK
COMMANDER OF THE "TIGER"
ERECTED HERE FOUR HOUSES OR HUTS
AFTER HIS VESSEL WAS BURNED
NOVEMBER 1613
HE BUILT THE "RESTLESS" THE FIRST VESSEL
MADE BY EUROPEANS IN THIS COUNTRY
THE "RESTLESS" WAS LAUNCHED
IN THE SPRING OF 1614

THIS TABLET IS PLACED HERE BY
THE HOLLAND SOCIETY OF NEW YORK
SEPTEMBER 1890

Tablet at 45 Broadway.

ON THIS CORNER GREW
PETRUS STUYVESANT'S PEAR TREE
RECALLED TO HOLLAND IN 1664
ON HIS RETURN
HE BROUGHT THE PEAR TREE
AND PLANTED IT
AS HIS MEMORIAL
"BY WHICH" SAID HE "MY NAME
MAY BE REMEMBERED"
THE PEAR TREE FLOURISHED
AND BORE FRUIT FOR OVER
TWO HUNDRED YEARS
THIS TABLET IS PLACED HERE BY
THE HOLLAND SOCIETY
OF NEW YORK
SEPTEMBER, 1890

Tablet at Third Avenue and 12th Street.

THE SITE OF FORT AMSTERDAM
BUILT IN 1626
WITHIN THE FORTIFICATIONS
WAS ERECTED THE FIRST
SUBSTANTIAL CHURCH EDIFICE
ON THE ISLAND OF MANHATTAN.
IN 1787 THE FORT
WAS DEMOLISHED
AND THE GOVERNMENT HOUSE
BUILT UPON THIS SPOT.

THIS TABLET IS PLACED HERE BY
THE HOLLAND SOCIETY OF NEW YORK
SEPTEMBER, 1890

Tablet at 4 Bowling Green.

TO COMMEMORATE THE GALLANT AND PATRIOTIC
ACT OF MARINUS WILLETT IN HERE SEIZING
JUNE 6, 1775, FROM BRITISH FORCES THE
MUSKETS WITH WHICH HE ARMED HIS
TROOPS THIS TABLET IS ERECTED BY
THE SOCIETY OF THE SONS OF THE
REVOLUTION, NEW YORK. NOV. 1892.

DANIEL BUTTERFIELD, FLOYD CLARKSON,
MORGAN DIX, JOHN AUSTIN STEVENS,
DAVID WOLFE BISHOP -- COMMITTEE.

Tablet on the Morris Building.

HISTORICAL TABLETS
RECENTLY PLACED IN THE VARIOUSLY DESIGNATED LOCALITIES.

THE SITE OF THE
FIRST DUTCH HOUSE OF ENTERTAINMENT
ON THE ISLAND OF MANHATTAN
LATER THE SITE OF THE OLD STADT HUYS
OR CITY HALL.
—
THIS TABLET IS PLACED HERE BY
THE HOLLAND SOCIETY OF NEW YORK
SEPTEMBER, 1890

Tablet at 73 Pearl Street, Facing Coenties Slip.

FRAUNCES TAVERN. TO THIS BUILDING
GENERAL GEORGE WASHINGTON
CAME EVACUATION DAY, NOV. 25, 1783
AND ON THURSDAY, DEC. 4
FOLLOWING HERE TOOK
LEAVE OF THE PRINCIPAL
OFFICERS OF THE ARMY
YET IN SERVICE.

Tablet at corner of Pearl and Broad Sts.

cation and sale of the first edition (of ten thousand copies) of *King's Handbook of New-York City.* The summer of 1892 was memorable by reason of the approach of cholera, from Europe, and the detention of many steamships, with thousands of passengers, by the quarantine authorities. By this efficient vigilance the pestilence was prevented from entering the United States. Nearly all the National Guard belonging in New-York City was sent to Buffalo in 1892 to check the destroying agencies of a strike there ; and other detachments were dispatched to Fire Island, to repress insurrection. This same year, 1892, witnessed the burning of the Metropolitan Opera House, and the magnificent ceremonies at the laying of the corner-stone of the Cathedral of St. John the Divine.

In 1893, when Grover Cleveland, a citizen of New York, was inaugurated President of the United States, the magnificent ceremonies of the day were participated in by thousands of Tammany braves, marching through the streets of Washington. During the same springtime occurred the death of Col. E. F. Shepard, the editor of *The Mail and Express.* In April, 1893, the Duke of Veragna, a lineal descendant of Christopher Columbus, visited New York, as the representative of the Kingdom of Spain to the World's Columbian Exposition. He was welcomed with great society and municipal receptions, and for several days was the most conspicuous personage in the metropolis. He also received the freedom of the city, a distinction conferred not more than half a dozen times in a century. Late in April, in New-York harbor, occurred the most imposing of all the pageants commemorating the discovery of America by Columbus. This was the grand naval review, including the best ships of the American fleet, and squadrons of British, French, Spanish, Russian, Italian, Dutch, Brazilian, and Argentine ships-of-war. This event was virtually the inaugural ceremony of the opening of the World's Columbian Exposition, at Chicago, to which New-Yorkers made most liberal contributions of money, and among the most notable features of which will be the exhibits of the people of New-York City.

Thus pauses, for the time, the record of History. What may be in store for the proud New-World metropolis, who can say? She may be destined to sink beneath the waves that gave her life, like the drowned cities of the Zuyder Zee ; or to be irretrievably shattered by hostile armaments, like Tyre ; or to tranquilly fade away into commercial death, like Venice. Yet such fates can hardly be imagined as awaiting the Empire City of the Western World, now in the full flush of her success and power, and leading in the van of modern life and thought. She has appalling problems to face — the inflowing of half-pauperized foreigners, the menace of the submerged tenth, the evils of municipal misgovernment, the rise of a many-millioned plutocracy, and other serious and perilous questions. But public opinion is awakening on all sides to their consideration, and the grand old city will doubtless meet the strong new troubles with stronger new remedies, just as in the days that are past she has faced and conquered so many other threatening perils.

New York of the Present.

A Comprehensive Outline Description of the Whole City—Area, Population, Wealth, Statistics, Etc.

TO-DAY the City of New York is not only the metropolis of the United States, but in population, in wealth, in influence, in enterprise, in all that best distinguishes modern civilization, it is the rival of the great capitals of the Old World.

The Area actually within the limits of the city includes Manhattan Island, Governor's Island, in New-York Bay; Blackwell's, Ward's, and Randall's Islands, in the East River; and a considerable section of the mainland north of the Harlem River, and west of the Bronx. From the Battery, at the southern extremity of Manhattan Island, to the northern line of the city is a distance of sixteen miles. On the island, which is 13½ miles long, the width of the city varies from a few score rods to 2½ miles; and north of the Harlem its greatest width is 4½ miles. The area of Manhattan Island is nearly 22 square miles, or 14,000 acres; and with the section on the mainland, the city has a total of 41½ square miles, or 26,500 acres. In the process of growth and annexation New York has absorbed many villages, once its outlying suburbs, and whose memories even now exist in popular local designations, despite the fact that they have become parts of the metropolis. Thus down-town are Greenwich and Chelsea; farther uptown, in the vicinity of Central Park, Bloomingdale and Yorkville; above the park, Harlem and Manhattanville; then Carmansville, Washington Heights and Inwood; and on the mainland, that was annexed in 1874, are Port Morris, North New York, Claremont, Fairmount, Morrisania, West Farms, Spuyten Duyvil, Mosholu, Williamsbridge, Fordham, Tremont, Mount St. Vincent, Mott Haven and Melrose, and other villages. The insular part of the city is thickly built up and heavily populated, save in certain territories in Harlem, Bloomingdale, Yorkville, and Washington Heights; but even there building is going forward with rapidity. In the annexed district development has been retarded by the lack of transit facilities, but is now proceeding steadily, and this section promises to become an important residential quarter.

The Population has grown in a phenomenal manner during the last half-century. In 1830, it was 202,000; in 1860, 805,000; in 1880, 1,206,500. In 1890 the United-States Census gave the city 1,513,501 population; the Health-Board statistics, 1,631,232; and the police enumeration, 1,710,715. In February, 1892, there was a State enumeration that showed a population of 1,800,891. The yearly vote of the city is one vote for every 7⅔ inhabitants. New York is thus the first city of the United States in population, and that too within a more contracted area than those rivals that come nearest to her in number of inhabitants — Chicago and Philadelphia. The overflow of the city goes out into the surrounding region; and has built up cities, towns and villages that would scarcely have existence were it not for the activity of Manhattan Island.

PRODUCE EXCHANGE TOWER.   "TRIBUNE."   "TIMES."

NEW-YORK CITY.
LOOKING SOUTHWEST FROM THE "WORLD" DOME.

"TIMES."   ST. PAUL'S.   POST OFFICE.   CITY-HALL PARK.

NEW-YORK CITY.
LOOKING WEST FROM THE "WORLD" DOME.

Greater New York comprises the city, with its suburban environs in the State of New York. It takes in the City of New York ; the counties of Kings and Richmond; the southern portions of the towns of Eastchester and Pelham, in Westchester County ; and Long-Island City, the towns of Newton, Flushing, Jamaica and the westerly portion of the town of Hempstead, in Queens County ; making a total area of 318 square miles, with a population of nearly 3,000,000. A commission to enquire into the expediency of consolidating this territory into one city was appointed under an act of the New-York State Legislature, in 1890, and has reported in favor of the project. Andrew H. Green, the father of the movement, is also the President of the Commission. Greater New York will thus be the second city of the world, leaving Paris behind ; and still provided with a line of great suburban cities pertaining to New Jersey, and hence isolated from its political life, though united with it socially and industrially.

The Nationalities represented in New York make it the most cosmopolitan city in the world. It has more Irish than Dublin, and more Germans than any German city except Berlin. There are sections almost entirely given over to people of foreign birth or descent, each nationality forming a colony by itself. Thus, we have the French, the German, the Italian, the African, the Chinese, the Hebrew, the Spanish and the Arab colonies. The English-speaking foreigners, as the Irish, the English and the Scotch, have assimilated more readily with the native population ; and so have the Germans, to a considerable extent. Other nationalities have kept themselves more nearly intact.

The Surroundings of few cities are more remarkable than those of New York. The urban territory and the surrounding country is historic ground. In the lower streets many old houses still stand, or localities are distinguished that recall Revolutionary and pre-Revolutionary days ; and on the hills of upper Manhattan, and in the Trans-Val region, modern enterprise has not yet destroyed all the ancient landmarks. Along the west flows the noble Hudson, renowned as one of the world's most beautiful rivers ; and on the east, the East River leads into Long-Island Sound. Up and down Long Island are numerous beautiful and historic villages ; and along the south shore of the island extend the great popular summer-resorts, Coney Island, Rockaway Beach, Sheepshead Bay and their rivals. The harbor is one of the largest, safest and most beautiful in the world. A hundred navies could ride at anchor upon its waters. The Lower Bay, almost surrounded by the shores of Long Island, Staten Island and New Jersey, is a magnificent sheet of water. Coming up through the Narrows, between the picturesque shores of Long Island and Staten Island, the view is enchanting ; and the land-locked upper harbor, sheltered by the hills of the two islands and of New Jersey, with the point of Manhattan Island reaching down into it between the two great rivers, the indications of a phenomenal commercial energy exhibited on every hand, the Statue of Liberty, and the towering buildings of the city, present a scene never to be forgotten.

The Municipal Administration is conducted mainly by the Mayor and the heads of departments, several of whom are chosen by popular vote, and the others appointed by the Mayor. Municipal legislation is in the hands of the Board of Aldermen, which consists of 32 members, including 29 from Manhattan Island, 2 from beyond the Harlem, and a president elected at large. Previous to 1892 there were only 25 Aldermen.

The City Finances, according to the last report of the Comptroller, for the year ending January 1, 1893, shows the receipts were : From taxes, $33,232,725 ; from other sources, $5,552,856 ; moneys borrowed, $27,665,053. Total receipts,

$66,450,635. The expenditures were by appropriation, $34,732,289, and on special and trust accounts, $30,586,068. The total funded debt was $155,161,974; or, less the amount in the sinking fund, $98,629,567. This debt is bonded at from 2½ to 7 per cent. interest, a considerable part of it being at 2½ and 3 per cent., a handsome testimonial to the credit of the city.

For the year 1893 the final estimate of appropriations allowed amounted to $34,444,155. Of that sum $3,000,000 is provided for by receipts from miscellaneous sources, leaving nearly $35,000,000 to be raised by taxation. Of this amount $4,948,582 was for interest on the city debt; $1,499,021 for the redemption and installments of the principal of the city debt; $3,554,458 for State taxes and State common schools; $3,014,020 for the Department of Public Works; $1,096,455 for the Department of Public Parks; $2,223,425 for the Department of Public Charities and Correction; $5,309,886 for the Police Department; $2,200,000 for the Department of Street-Cleaning; $2,223,134 for the Fire Department; $4,480,448 for the Board of Education; $1,139,890 for Judiciary Salaries; and $1,305,177 for Charitable Institutions.

The Judiciary is partly elected and partly appointed by the Mayor. The elected officials are the seven judges of the Supreme Court, with a salary of $17,500 each; the six judges of the Superior Court, with a salary of $15,000 each; the six judges of the Court of Common Pleas, with a salary of $15,000 each; in the Courts of General Session, one Recorder and three judges, salary, $12,000 each; the six judges of the City Court, with a salary of $10,000 each; in the Surrogate Court, two Surrogates, $15,000 each; in the District Court, eleven justices, $6,000 each; Sheriff, $12,000 and half the fees; and District Attorney, $12,000. The principal appointed officials are fifteen Police Justices, $8,000 each; six Assistant District Attorneys, at $7,500 each; and one Commissioner of Jurors, at $5,000. Legal advice can be secured from 6,000 lawyers.

Political Divisions separate the city into thirty Assembly, eight Senatorial and ten Congressional districts. At the last election, in 1892, 284,984 votes were cast, or twenty per cent. of the total State vote. Within fifteen miles of the New-York City Hall there is a vote of about 500,000, or forty per cent. of the State.

The Police Department numbers 3,906 men, and has a deservedly high reputation for efficiency. The arrests number about 85,000 yearly.

The Fire Department has 1,400 employees, in twelve battalions; and over 200 pieces of apparatus, including 91 steam fire-engines, four water-towers and three fire-boats. There are 1,200 miles of wire and 1,235 boxes for the fire-alarm telegraph. Fire destroys over $4,000,000 of property in this city every year.

The Number of Buildings includes 90,000 dwelling-houses in the city, and 25,000 business-houses, making a total of more than 115,000. Over 1,100 new buildings, valued at more than $13,000,000, are erected yearly. The real-estate valuation for purposes of taxation is $1,464,247,820, which fixes the actual value at over $4,400,000,000. The assessment value of personal property is $321,609,518, making a total of $1,785,857,338. The tax rate is $1.90 per hundred.

The Deaths in 1890 were 40,103, at a rate of 23.51 in a thousand; in 1891, 43,659, or 24.73 in a thousand; and in 1892, 44,329, or 24.26 in a thousand.

Streets, Sewers, Water, Etc.— There are 575 miles of streets; 444 miles of sewers, constructed at a cost of over $22,000,000; 685½ miles of water-mains, and 8,800 hydrants; and 16 public bathing places, used yearly by 4,000,000 bathers. The streets are lighted at night by 26,524 gas-lights and 1,535 electric lights. The city has 144 piers on the North and East Rivers; and 13 public markets.

135242

MURRAY STREET.   CITY HALL.   WARREN STREET.

NEW-YORK CITY.
LOOKING WEST-NORTHWEST FROM THE "WORLD" DOME.

CITY-HALL PARK.   COUNTY COURT-HOUSE.   COURT OF GENERAL SESSIONS.

NEW-YORK CITY.
LOOKING NORTH FROM THE " WORLD " DOME.

LEARNING RESOURCES CENTER
NAZARETH COLLEGE

The Public Buildings belonging to New York include the City Hall, a fine example of the Italian Renaissance architecture; the County·Court-House, an imposing Corinthian structure of white marble, which nominally cost many millions, and is a memorial of the peculations of the notorious Tweed ring; the Jefferson-Market Court-House, a handsome building of brick and sandstone, in the Italian Gothic style; the Hall of Records, in City-Hall Park; the Tombs, a substantial and grim-appearing edifice, in the purest Egyptian style; the new Court-House, just approaching completion, near the Tombs; the famous Castle Garden, at the Battery, long used as a receiving station for immigrants; and many department buildings. Two other imposing public structures, both works of engineering skill, belong in part or in whole to the city—the East-River Bridge to Brooklyn, and the Washington Bridge, over the Harlem River.

The Water-Supply comes from the Croton water-shed, about 30 miles from the city. Besides natural lakes in that region, there are artificial reservoirs giving a total storage capacity of 17,150,000,000 gallons. Work now in progress in the construction of new dams will more than double this storage capacity. The supply is practically unlimited, and with abundant storage facilities 350,000,000 gallons a day would be assured. Water is brought down to the city by the old aqueduct, which has a carrying capacity of 75,000,000 gallons each day. The new aqueduct which was opened in 1890 has a carrying capacity of 320,000,000 gallons each day. It cost over $25,000,000. In the city proper there are storage and receiving reservoirs that will hold 1,266,000,000 gallons. The daily consumption is 170,000,000 gallons, and the present storage capacity at the watershed would meet all needs for three months.

The Militia constitutes a full brigade of the National Guard of the State. There are seven regiments, two batteries, one cavalry troop, and one signal corps, with 896 officers and 4,268 men. Besides these there is a Naval Battalion.

Local Traffic is effected by the elevated railroads, horse-cars and cable-cars, and the Fifth-Avenue stage-line. There are five lines of elevated roads (33 miles), under one management, four running practically the length of Manhattan Island, from the Battery to the Harlem River; and the fifth extending out into the trans-Harlem district. There are 17 surface street-car railroad companies, running cars over 42 main lines and branches. One line across town in Harlem and up Washington Heights (seven miles) has been operated by cable for several years; and cable-power is about to be substituted for horse-power on Broadway and Third Avenue.

The Ferries (with the exception of the East-River Bridge and the several Harlem-River bridges) afford the only means of communication between Manhattan Island and the surrounding localities. There are 38 ferry lines, including thirteen to Brooklyn, and thirteen to New Jersey.

Steam Railways to the number of 23 serve New York directly. Only four of these enter the city proper—the New-York Central & Hudson-River, the New-York & Harlem, and the New-York, New-Haven & Hartford, which come into the Grand Central Depot, at 42d Street; and the New-York & Northern, which has a depot at 155th Street and Eighth Avenue. The depot of the Long-Island Railroad is at Long-Island City; and on the New-Jersey side of the Hudson River are the depots of the Pennsylvania, the Baltimore & Ohio, the New-Jersey Central, the Delaware, Lackawanna & Western, the Erie, the Lehigh-Valley, the New-Jersey Southern, the Ontario & Western, the West-Shore, and many connecting lines.

Steamboats run from New York to Albany, Troy and other ports on the Hudson River; to Boston, Newport, Providence, Bridgeport, New Haven, Fall River and other New-England ports; to Long Branch, Sandy Hook and elsewhere on the

New-Jersey coast; and to many places on Long Island. There are over thirty such lines, and not fewer than 150 steamboats thus employed, including the palatial boats that are in commission on the Sound routes to Boston, on the Hudson River, and on the summer routes to Sandy Hook and Long Branch. For speed, safety, beauty and elegance of appointments these boats surpass anything in the world.

Coastwise and Ocean Traffic to and from the port of New York reaches enormous proportions. In the trans-Atlantic fleet there are over 120 steamships, belonging to fourteen regular lines to Europe, and lines to Brazil, Central America, the West Indies, Mexico, Venezuela, Trinidad, Newfoundland and other foreign ports, and to the chief Atlantic domestic ports. In the European fleet the great ocean greyhounds are floating palaces that represent the perfection of modern marine architecture. From foreign ports the yearly arrivals of steamships number 3,000, and sailing vessels reach about the same number. From domestic ports there are 1,700 steamships and 14,000 sailing-vessels. The total tonnage of the shipping at this port is 5,000,000 yearly.

Federal Interests of paramount importance are concentrated in New York, which is second only to Washington in this particular. The Custom House, the Assay Office and the Sub-Treasury, all close together on Wall Street, represent the Federal Government financially. Here is the main port of entry for foreign trade for the whole country. The foreign commerce of New York for the last fiscal year amounted to $1,061,000,000, being more than half the total for the United States (which reached $2,010,000,000). The imports at New York reached $576,000,000, including $113,000,000 in coffee, $48,000,000 in sugar and molasses, $37,000,000 in silks, $30,000,000 in woollens, $21,000,000 in cottons, and $19,000,000 each in hides and rubber. The exports of goods reached $462,000,000, mainly in provisions, petroleum, cotton and tobacco.

At the Sub-Treasury the receipts sometimes exceed $1,227,000,000 a year. Enormous quantities of bullion are annually passed through the Assay Office.

The Post Office is the centre for the railway mail service of the Eastern and Middle States, and the distributing point for foreign mail. More than 3,000 men are employed. The United-States Courts hold sessions in the Post-Office building.

Immigration pours a steady tide into the United States through the port of New York. Immigrants were formerly received at Castle Garden, but they are now landed at Ellis Island, where the United-States Government takes charge of them. In the ten years after 1881, the number of immigrants at New York averaged about 380,000 yearly. In 1891 they reached 430,887; and in the year closing June 30, 1892, 446,000.

The Military Department of the East has its headquarters here, and the Major-General and his staff reside on Governor's Island. Detachments of troops are in garrison at Fort Hamilton and Fort Wadsworth, which face each other across the Narrows on the Long-Island and Staten-Island shores respectively; at Fort Schuyler, upon Throgg's Neck, where the East River and Long-Island Sound meet; and at Willett's Point, on the Long-Island shore, opposite Fort Schuyler. These fortifications would, perhaps, be of small avail against the heaviest modern naval armaments, but the Government is improving the defences at these stations, and projecting new works at Sandy Hook and Coney Island, so that the city and harbor shall have adequate protection in case of war.

The United-States Navy-Yard (virtually a part of New York, although across the East River, in Brooklyn) is the most important naval station in the country; and employs over 2,000 men continually. The dry dock cost over

COURT OF GENERAL SESSIONS.　　POLICE COURT.　　CENTRE STREET.　　"STAATS ZEITUNG."

NEW-YORK CITY.
LOOKING NORTHEAST FROM THE "WORLD" DOME.

"STAATS ZEITUNG."   CITY-HALL BRANCH ELEVATED RAILROAD.   WILLIAM STREET.

NEW-YORK CITY.

LOOKING EAST-NORTHEAST FROM THE "WORLD" DOME.

$2,000,000, and is unequalled anywhere in the world.   The Government property covers 144 acres, and has a mile of water-front.   Besides the shops and officers' houses, there are Marine barracks and a naval hospital.

The Wealth concentrated in the hands of residents of New York is almost inconceivable.   Many vast fortunes have been made here ; and many enormously wealthy Americans have come here to live and enjoy the fortunes accumulated elsewhere.   A recent table of the wealth of New-York's millionaires estimates that at least two New-Yorkers are worth more than $100,000,000 each ; six more have above $50,000,000 each; more than thirty are classed as worth between $20,000,000 and $40,000,000 ; and 325 other citizens are rated at from $2,000,000 to $12,000,000 each.

The Commerce and Finance cannot be adequately measured in words or figures.   The aggregate transactions every day reach an amount so stupendous that the figures are beyond comprehension.

The Banks include 47 National banks, with a capital of $50,000,000, and resources of over $500,000,000 ; 47 State banks, with a capital of $18,000,000, and resources of $185,000,000 ; 27 savings-banks, with deposits of $325,000,000, from 800,000 depositors ;   and 19 trust-companies, with capital of $20,000,000, or gross assets of $270,000,000.

The Clearing House does a business amounting to from $35,000,000,000 to $50,000,000,000 yearly, and its daily transactions range from $125,000,000 to $250,000,000.   Since it commenced in 1853 it has transacted business to the enormous amount of over $1,000,000,000,000.

The Stock Exchange has a membership of 1,100 ; and its aggregate transactions amount to many millions of shares a year.   The Produce Exchange has 3,000 members ; and the Maritime Exchange, 1,365.   There are 2,362 members in the Consolidated Exchange, where often in a single day 75,000 shares of stock are dealt in, and where almost incalculable quantities of petroleum are sold yearly. There are also ninety-six Trade-Associations.   In and about Wall Street 289 of the leading railroads of the country have their main or important offices.

The Office Buildings comprise many notable structures.   In the down-town business-districts alone, there are several hundred great office-buildings which are hives of industry.   Many of them have a business population every day more than equal to the population of a large country village.   Such buildings as the Mills, the Equitable, the Havemeyer, the Bennett, the Potter, the Pulitzer, the Times, the Washington, the Columbia, Temple Court, the Western Union, the Postal-Telegraph-Cable, the Mutual Life, the Jersey Central, the Lackawanna, and a score of others, are notable for their grandeur and solidity and elegant appointments.

The Manufactures in 25,399 factories give employment to over 350,000 people, who make every year $765,000,000 worth of goods, of which clothing, books and papers, cigars and pianos, constitute the largest amounts.

The Publishers of the United States are well represented or located in New-York City, where more books are yearly published than in all the rest of the country combined.   There are thirty leading publishing concerns, and others of lesser importance.   In periodical publications there is even more activity.

The Papers and Periodicals comprise 43 daily newspapers.   Of these, six are German, three Italian, two Bohemian, one Spanish and one French.   There are nine semi-weekly papers, 221 weekly, and 48 bi-weekly.   The monthly publications lead off with *Harper's Magazine*, the *Century*, *Scribner's*, the *Cosmopolitan*, the *North American Review*, and the *Forum*, and run up a list of 394.   There are 14 bi-monthlies and

21 quarterlies. All the varied social, religious, literary, political and business interests are served by these periodicals. The most important groups are : Religious, 53 ; commercial, 15 ; sporting, 8 ; art, 5 ; literary, 64 ; mechanical, 5 ; socialist, 2 ; secret societies, 9 ; legal, 3 ; theatrical, 6 ; scientific, 7 ; medical, 22 ; educational, 12 ; agricultural, 3 ; and fashions 7. The serial publications include papers in the following languages : German, 58 ; Spanish, 17 ; Bohemian, 6 ; Italian, 5 ; French, 4 ; Armenian, 3 ; Swedish, 3 ; Portuguese, 2 ; and Polish, Finnish, Russian, Danish, Slavonic, and Hungarian. There are 14 papers for the Hebrew race.

The Churches own and occupy more than 600 church buildings, valued with their land and foundings at upwards of $75,000,000. They represent every phase of religious belief, and together they have a seating capacity of nearly 300,000. The Protestant Episcopal Church leads, with 103 churches ; closely followed by the Roman Catholic, with 85 ; then come the Presbyterian, with 75 ; the Methodist-Episcopal, 69 ; the Baptist, 51 ; the Jewish, 50 ; the Reformed Dutch, 32 ; the Lutheran, 23 ; the Congregationalist, 11 ; the Reformed Presbyterian, 5 ; the African Methodist Episcopal, 6 ; the United Presbyterian, 6 ; the Unitarian, 3 ; the Universalist, 3 ; and all others, including Swedenborgians, Moravians, etc., 60.

Religious Work in conjunction with the churches is served by many societies and associations. Most prominent among these is the American Bible Society, which, since it started in 1816, has published over 56,000,000 copies of the Bible ; has printed the Bible in more than eighty different languages and dialects ; has had receipts of nearly $26,000,000 ; and owns a large building, valued at nearly $500,000. The Young Men's Christian Association is housed in its own building, that cost $500,000, and it occupies a broad field of usefulness in promoting the spiritual, intellectual, social and physical welfare of the community. It supports fourteen branches, of which the most important are the Young Men's Institute, in the Bowery, and the Railroad Branch, which occupies a house on Madison Avenue, built and presented to it by Cornelius Vanderbilt. In local missionary work the New-York City Mission and Tract Society is preëminent, maintaining churches, libraries, missions, gymnasiums, and Sunday-schools. Each of the leading denominations supports one or more missionary societies, publication-houses, and organizations for the propagation of their religious tenets. Three-score missionary societies cover the foreign and home fields.

The Charities (according to a published directory of the charitable and benevolent societies) number more than 700, not including scores of small associations, that never appeal to the public. More than 200 are prominent, and labor unremittingly and effectively in relieving the poor and suffering of every class and nationality. Many of these associations maintain hospitals and homes. Besides all the hospitals, there are a score of homes for the poor, sick and convalescent. Thirty asylums are provided for orphans and destitute children ; fifteen asylums for the blind, the insane, the deaf and the crippled ; twenty homes for the aged ; and numerous temporary refuges for the poor and friendless. Some of these are municipal institutions ; and others receive municipal aid. But, aside from civic appropriations, charitable contributions from private sources yearly amount to many millions of dollars. In addition, much is given in the form of permanent endowments and new buildings. The Children's Aid Society alone maintains twenty-two industrial and nine night schools ; keeps open six lodging houses ; has every year under its charge 37,000 boys and girls ; and spends nearly $400,000 annually. Another notable and unique charity is the Fresh-Air Fund, through which poor children are sent into the country every summer.

NEWSBOY'S LODGING-HOUSE.   APPROACH TO BROOKLYN BRIDGE.

NEW-YORK CITY.
LOOKING EAST-SOUTHEAST FROM THE " WORLD " DOME.

DROOKLYN BRIDGE.   FRANKFORT STREET.   HEALY BUILDING.

NEW-YORK CITY.
LOOKING SOUTHEAST FROM THE " WORLD " DOME.

The Charitable and Correctional Institutions of the city are located chiefly on the islands in the East River. Blackwell's Island, 120 acres in extent, has the penitentiary, almshouse, workhouse, charity hospital, hospital for incurables and other institutions. Over 7,000 persons, including criminals, charity patients, officials and attendants live upon the island, which is maintained chiefly by convict labor. A recent proposition that is being favorably entertained looks to the removal of these institutions to a location on the main land, and the transformation of the island into a beautiful public park. On Randall's Island are the Idiot Asylum, the House of Refuge, Nursery, Children's Hospital, and Infants' Hospital and schools. The usual population of the island is between 2,500 and 3,000. On Ward's Island are the Insane Asylum for Males, the Ward's-Island Hospital, the State Emigrant Hospital, and other noble institutions. On Hart's Island is another insane asylum and a branch of the Work-House; and on North Brother Island is the Riverside hospital for contagious diseases. At Islip, Long Island, is an insane asylum. The city maintains the Bellevue, Emergency, Gouverneur, Harlem, Reception and Fordham hospitals in the city proper. Municipal aid to the amount of nearly $1,250,000 is given for the support of 29 private or State asylums, reformatories and charitable institutions, and altogether the city pays out for these purposes more than $3,300,000 annually.

The Hospitals of New York are not surpassed elsewhere in the world for extent, completeness of appointment, and general excellence of management. The most skilful medical service is at the command of the suffering; and the reputation of the physicians for skill has travelled even to Europe, so that in recent years European physicians have sent patients across the water to New-York hospitals for treatment in special cases. Particularly is this true of surgery, in which New-York practitioners are without superiors. The leading hospitals are Bellevue, established in 1826, and maintained by the city; New York, chartered by King George III. of England in 1771, and opened to the public in 1791; Roosevelt, opened in 1871, and supported by the endowment of James H. Roosevelt; St. Luke's (Protestant Episcopal), incorporated in 1850; St. Vincent's (Roman Catholic), 1857; Lebanon (Hebrew), 1889; Mount Sinai, opened in 1855; New-York Eye and Ear Infirmary, 1820; New-York Ophthalmic, 1852; Presbyterian, 1857; and the Sloane Maternity and Vanderbilt Clinic, endowed by the Vanderbilt family to the amount of $1,000,-000. Other hospitals devoted to special diseases bring the number of these institutions up to nearly seventy. There are dispensaries and infirmaries for the free treatment of the sick in all parts of the city, to the number of over fifty.

The Educational Work of New York is preëminent, and her teaching facilities yearly attract thousands of students from all parts of the country. The public-school system, broad in scope and thorough in instruction, is in charge of a Board of Education composed of 21 commissioners. The number of school buildings is 135, and in these 240,000 children are taught by 4,200 teachers. There are 108 grammar schools, 118 primary schools and departments, 29 evening schools, two colleges, one training school, one nautical school, and 48 corporate schools in reformatories and asylums. The College of the City of New York has a yearly attendance of 1,100 young men; and the Normal College of 2,800 young women. These two institutions complete the system of public schools.

Advancing beyond the public schools we find educational institutions of higher grade, that in number and in character combine to make New York one of the great university-towns of the world. In the front rank stands Columbia College, one of the five oldest and greatest colleges of the country. With its five departments, Arts, Mines, Law, Political Science, and Medicine, and its Barnard College for Women, it is in effect, as well as in name, a university. Scarcely second to Columbia is the University of the City of New York, which has three well-equipped departments. Both these institutions have had brilliant careers, and the names of scores of men like Barnard, Drisler, Chandler, Quackenbos, Dwight, Morse, Mott, Butler and others, great in various branches of professional attainment, are identified with them. There are 3,000 students yearly instructed in these two universities.

The Union Theological Seminary (Presbyterian), and the Episcopal General Theological Seminary are the next most prominent higher educational institutions. Combined they have a yearly register of over 300 students. To these must be added the medical schools, Bellevue, Physicians and Surgeons, University, Homœopathic, and a dozen like institutions, in special fields. There are several prosperous Catholic colleges, like Manhattan, St. John's, and St. Francis Xavier.

The prominent law-schools are those connected with Columbia College and the University of the City of New York, both unsurpassed in facilities and thoroughness of training; and drawing students from all parts of the world.

Private schools of all grades are numerous. The Cooper Union Schools for free instruction in the sciences, mathematics, art, engraving, telegraphy, and other branches, is one of the grandest philanthropic institutions in existence. Over 4,000 students are taught yearly, most of whom are young tradesmen or mechanics who attend the evening classes. The Trade School is another institution on a large scale for practical instruction in common employments.

The Libraries, special and general, are numerous and large. The Aguilar Free Library and the Free Circulating Library have several branches each; and the Apprentices' Library contains nearly 95,000 volumes. The millions left by the will of Samuel J. Tilden provided a great free library; and even now that the will has been set aside, the generosity of one of the heirs will in the near future make up a part of the loss. The Mercantile Library is the largest circulating library in the city. It contains 245,000 volumes. The Astor Library, richly endowed by the Astor family, with a quarter of a million volumes, mostly valuable for reference rather than for popular reading, is much frequented by students and investigators.

The useful Columbia-College Library has over 160,000 volumes. At the Cooper Union there are 34,000 volumes of a miscellaneous character, and several hundred newspapers and magazines are regularly received. The library of the New-York Historical Society is valuable in Americana. The Lenox Library contains more rare editions of Bibles, Shakespeariana and Americana, and ancient manuscripts than other institutions in this country. It has only a few more than 70,000 volumes, but most of these are priceless in value. The libraries at the City Hall; the Bar Association, 38,000 volumes; the American Institute, 14,000; the New-York Society, 90,000; the Bible Society, 4,000 rare volumes; the Law Institute, 42,000; and the Young Men's Christian Association, 40,000, are useful institutions. There are more than a score others of lesser importance, generally serving the needs of some special class. The libraries attached to the Art Museum and the colleges and seminaries, as Union Theological Seminary (70,000), St. Francis Xavier (25,000), and Manhattan College (17,000), are also note-worthy.

In Art and Architecture, New York leads the country. It is the Mecca towards which artists from all other sections turn. The studios of America's greatest painters, sculptors and designers are here, and the native school of art has always displayed its fullest and most admirable powers in this city. To-day the names of

SHOT TOWER.   SPRUCE AND WILLIAM STREETS.

NEW-YORK CITY.
LOOKING SOUTH FROM THE "WORLD" DOME.

WILLIAM STREET.   PRODUCE EXCHANGE TOWER.

NEW-YORK CITY.
LOOKING SOUTH-SOUTHWEST FROM THE "WORLD" DOME.

such painters as Huntington, Inness, Chase, Millet, Weir, Porter, Parton, Beck-with, J. G. Brown, Blum, Crane, Gay, Moran and Shirlaw, and of such sculptors as St. Gaudens, Elwell, Ward, Warner, Hartley, and scores of others not less accomplished, sufficiently uphold the claim of New York to preëminent distinction in this respect.   The general art taste of the community is revealed on every side, especially in the local architecture, which has attained to a remarkable degree of excellence during the last few years.   The Vanderbilt houses, the Stewart mansion, the Union-League-Club buildings, the Madison-Square Garden, the Metropolitan Opera House, the Casino, the Carnegie Music Hall, St. Patrick's Cathedral, the City Hall, the Tribune Building, the Times Building, the World Building, the Academy of Design, Grace Church, the Produce Exchange, the Mutual-Life and the Equitable-Insurance buildings, the Imperial, Astor, Savoy, Holland and New Netherland hotels, the Tiffany house, the new Court House, Trinity Church ; the record might be continued for pages without exhausting the list of buildings that give architectural distinction to the city.   The Huntington mansion, the Metro-politan Club House, the Cathedral of St. John the Divine, the New-York *Herald* and the Manhattan Life buildings, and a score of other residence and business structures are either projected or in process of erection.   Every conceivable style and variation of style is represented by admirable examples, Colonial in the houses of old Greenwich and Chelsea villages, Gothic in Trinity and other churches, Doric in the Sub-Treasury building, Corinthian in the Court House, Ionic in the Custom House, Egyptian in the Tombs, Italian Renaissance in the City Hall and the Produce Exchange, Florentine in the Lenox Library and the W. K. Vanderbilt house, Moorish in the Tiffany house, the Temple Emanu-El and the Casino, Vene-tian in the Academy of Design, Byzantine in the German Catholic Church of the Most Holy Redeemer and St. George's Church, and contemporaneous "Queen Anne" in the Union-League Club House, and many private residences around about Central Park.   Nor in this connection can the public statues and memorials be ignored.   Among them are many admirable examples of art, such as the Farragut statue, by Augustus St. Gaudens ; the equestrian Washington, by H. K. Browne ; the Indian Hunter, the Horace Greeley, and the Washington, by J. Q. A. Ward ; the Union-Square Drinking-Fountain, by Olin Warner ; the Diana, on the Madison-Square-Garden tower, by Augustus St. Gaudens ; the Still Hunt, by Edward Kemys ; the Egyptian Obelisk in Central Park ; the Tigress and Young, by Auguste Cain ; the Washington Memorial Arch, by Stanford White ; the Grant Mausoleum ; and the magnificent colossal Statue of Liberty, on Bedloe's Island, by Bartholdi.

The Metropolitan Museum of Art easily stands at the head of institutions of its character in this country.   It now has treasures valued at over $6,000,000, housed in a building that has already cost nearly $1,000,000, and is not yet completed.   In these galleries are many famous pictures presented to the Museum from the Stewart and other private collections, the Wolfe collection of pictures by modern masters (valued at half a million), the Marquand old masters, the Di Cesnola collection of Cypriote antiquities, the E. C. Moore collection of ceramics, the Brayton-Ives Jap-anese swords, the Marquand, Charvet and Jarves glass, the Stuart and Astor laces, the Drexel and Brown musical instruments, the Baker Egyptian mummy and other cloth, the Ward Assyrian antiquities, a remarkably large collection of casts from the antique, and other valuable and interesting possessions.   The New-York Historical Society has a valuable collection of portraits of distinguished Americans, the Durr collection of old Dutch paintings, the Abbott collection of Egyptian antiquities, the Lenox Nineveh marbles, and other art-treasures second only in extent and value to the possessions of the Metropolitan Museum. In the Lenox Library there is a precious collection of pictures, including works of most of the great masters of modern times. Recent bequests bring this institution into close rivalry with the Metropolitan Museum and the Historical Society.

The private galleries in New York are not equalled by those in any other American city. The finest collections belong to the Vanderbilts, the Astors, the Belmonts, the Havemeyers, the Rockefellers, H. G. Marquand, J. A. Bostwick, Thomas B. Clarke, C. P. Huntington, Henry Hilton, D. O. Mills, Jay Gould, Morris K. Jesup, J. W. Drexel, Robert Hoe, and many other eminent collectors, who constitute a band of picture lovers and buyers such as no other American community can boast of. The portraits in the Governor's room at the City Hall, and in the Chamber of Commerce, and the Academy of Design's collection of works by its members are interesting. All the leading clubs possess good paintings, and they make exhibitions of these and loaned pictures from time to time. Nearly all the fashionable hotels show fine collections of paintings in their saloons, offices and public rooms. Not much attention has yet been given to art in New-York church interiors. In St. Thomas's, the Church of St. Mary the Virgin, the Church of the Transfiguration, the Church of the Heavenly Rest, Grace Church, St. Patrick's Cathedral and Trinity Church, there are mural paintings, mosaic and sculptured reredoses, statuary and painted windows. A score of art-stores show the best productions of American and European painters, and during the season there are numerous exhibitions. The National Academy of Design has autumn and spring exhibitions ; the Society of American Artists, the Salmagundi Club, the Etching Club, the American Water-Color Society, and other art organizations hold annual exhibitions.

The Parks of New York are commensurate with its great development. Bowling Green was the first public park ; and the fashionable folk dwelt about it in the old Dutch and Colonial times. In the main part of the city the principal reservation for the people is Central Park, one of the handsomest public breathing-places in the world. It contains 840 acres, which have been beautified at an expense of over $15,000,000, with landscape-garden features, statuary, play-grounds and promenades. Part of the park is still left in a state of nature. Morningside Park (of 32 acres) and Riverside Park (of 178 acres), the latter overlooking the Hudson River for nearly three miles, are two of the most beautiful public places in the city. Many smaller squares and parks are generally made attractive with shrubbery and flowers. North of the Harlem River are six parks : The Van Cortlandt, of 1,070 acres ; the Bronx, of 653 acres ; the Crotona, of 135 acres; St. Mary's, of 25 acres ; Claremont, of 38 acres; and Pelham-Bay, of 1,740 acres. At present these properties, which cost the city $10,000,000, are unimproved. They are distant from the populated part of the city, but are already much frequented by those who wish a rustic outing in the wild woods and pastures. In time these parks, which are connected by parkways, will form a system that in extent, in natural beauty and in adornment will have no rivals. A new park on the west bank of the Harlem River at Washington Heights is also projected.

Amusements numerous and varied enough to suit all tastes and all purses range in character from the Metropolitan Opera House to the low concert-saloons of the Bowery and Eighth Avenue. The legitimate theatres are thirty-six in number, and at least five others are projected or building. Several of these remain open the year round, comic opera holding the stage throughout the summer months. All of them have a season of at least forty weeks. The Metropolitan Opera-House is the home of German and Italian grand opera, and during the last ten years the productions there have been on a scale of magnificence and musical excellence rivalling the most famous European opera-houses.   The receipts for the opera season have amounted to about $200,000 annually, in recent years, leaving a deficiency of $100,-000 to be made good by assessments upon the stockholders, who are the leaders in wealth and society.   The Madison-Square Garden, a large and architecturally beautiful structure, has an amphitheatre where horse-shows and dog-shows patronized by fashion are held, and where the circus annually exhibits.   In addition, it has a theatre, a restaurant, a roof-garden, a concert-room, and a ball-room.   The old Academy of Music, once devoted to grand opera, but now given over to the spectacular drama ; the luxurious Fifth-Avenue ; Palmer's and the Star, both rich with memories of Lester Wallack ; the handsome Casino, where comic opera reigns the year round ; Amberg's and the Thalia, where performances in German only are given ; Daly's, and the Lyceum, with their admirable stock companies ; the handsome Garden Theatre ; the Madison-Square Theatre, with its permanent farce comedy ; these are the most important.   In all the legitimate theatres combined there is a seating capacity of nearly 60,000.   The dime-museums and other low-priced places will accommodate at least 10,000 more.   Even with this total the supply does not exceed the demand.   It is estimated that every year there is spent in New York for amusements of this character at least $6,000,000.

In Chickering Hall, Music Hall, the Lenox Lyceum, the Berkeley Lyceum, Hardman Hall and the concert-room of the Metropolitan Opera-House most of the high-class musical entertainments are given.   Notable concerts of the year are those by the Philharmonic Society, the Symphony Society, the Oratorio Society, the Boston Symphony Orchestra, the Liederkranz and the Arion Society.

Clubs and Clubmen are legion throughout New-York City.   Every conceivable social, political, religious, professional and business interest is concentrated in this manner.   A list of the leading clubs in the city would include the names of over fifty, such as the Union League, Manhattan, Union, Metropolitan, Lotus, Century, New-York, St.-Nicholas, Colonial, Aldine, Authors', University, German, Knickerbocker, New-York Athletic, New-York Racquet, Players' and Manhattan Athletic.   All these have comfortable homes, and the houses of many are palatial.   The purely sporting clubs and associations, such as the American Jockey Club, the American Kennel Club, the Coney-Island Jockey Club, the yacht clubs, the bicycle clubs, and so on down to those of minor importance will number a hundred or more, and there are at least 150 clubs of a miscellaneous character.   There are fully 300 clubs of good standing in New York, with a membership of upward of 100,000.   Few men of New York do not belong to at least one club, and most of them have membership in several.   The desirable clubs are usually full to their extreme limit.

The Hotels, comprising about a thousand of all kinds, include a full hundred excellent hotels, a large proportion of them strictly first-class, with a world-wide reputation.   The Fifth-Avenue, Windsor, Gilsey, Hoffman, Imperial, Brunswick, Brevoort, Plaza, Murray-Hill, Buckingham and Astor House are notable.   Recent important additions to the list either just completed or building are the Holland House, the Waldorf, the Savoy and the New Netherland.

The Water Ways.

The Harbor and Rivers — Piers and Shipping — Fortifications
and Quarantine — Exports and Imports — Oceanic and
Coastwise Lines — The Ocean Greyhounds.

THE harbor of New York is perhaps the most interesting in the world, for it
has been the portal of a new world and a new life for millions of men and
women. It is as beautiful, furthermore, as it is interesting, from the hill-girt gateway of the Narrows up into the broader spaces between Bayonne and Gowanus,
with the high blue Orange Mountains crowning the view to the northwest, the
rampart-like Palisades frowning down the Hudson, and verdant islands here and
there breaking the vivid blue of the bay. On all sides the assembled cities encircle
the waters with their masses of buildings, the forests of masts by the waterside, the
immense warehouses and factories along the pier-heads, and the spires, domes and
towers of the beautiful residence-quarters beyond. At night, the harbor is girded
about by myriads of yellow and colored lights and white electric stars, and dotted
with the lanterns of vessels in motion or at anchor.

The Lower Bay and its tributary Raritan Bay and Sandy-Hook Bay are
formed by a triangular indentation of the coast, between Monmouth County, N. J.,
Staten Island and Long Island, partly protected from the sea by Sandy Hook and
Coney Island, and the long bar and shoals extending between them. The channel
is devious and at times difficult, and numerous buoys, beacons and light-houses mark
out the path of the inbound ships. At the head of the Lower Bay the maritime
route leads through the Narrows, a magnificent water-gate a mile wide, hemmed in
between the bold hills of Staten Island and Long Island, and bordered by heavy
batteries. Beyond this remarkable portal opens the Upper Bay, or New-York Harbor, an admirable land-locked haven eight miles long and five miles wide, the grand
focal point of North-American Atlantic commerce.

The Water-Front of Manhattan Island available for vessels is about 25 miles
long, 13 miles being on the North River, 9 on the East River, and the rest on the
Harlem River. There are seventy-three piers on the East River, below East 11th
Street ; and seventy on the North River, below 12th Street.

On one side of the harbor is the mouth of the magnificent Hudson River, flowing down for 300 miles, from the Adirondack Mountains, navigable for 148 miles to
Albany and Troy, and the outlet of the Erie Canal, bringing down immense supplies of grain from the West. On the other side is the entrance to Long-Island
Sound, "The Mediterranean of the West," giving an admirable marine route to the
ports of New England and the remote East. The strategic position of the city, for
purposes of commerce, is one of unapproachable strength and excellence, and has
been skillfully availed of by the merchants and public men of this active community ;

and the commerce of the East and the West converges here in immense volume, on the waters of one of the finest American harbors.

The East River is a deep and swift tidal strait twenty miles long, joining New-York harbor, at the Battery, with Long-Island Sound, at Willett's Point. Most of the western shore is formed by New-York City ; and the eastern shore includes Brooklyn, and other communes of Long Island. It is the avenue of a vast commerce, and with its many ferry-boats and immense white steamboats flying to and fro presents a pleasantly animated scene. The narrow channel of Hell Gate, near Astoria, was for two and a half centuries a terror to mariners, with its swift eddies and currents, setting over a reef of sharp rocks. Between 1870 and 1885 these ledges were undermined and blown up with nitro-glycerine, by Gen. Newton and a corps of engineers, at a cost of many millions of dollars ; and since that time navigation here has been much less perilous.

Harlem River is an arm of East River, seven miles long, partly navigable for small vessels, and connecting near its head with the much-winding Spuyten-Duyvil Creek, a shallow tributary of the Hudson River. These two streams separate Manhattan Island from the mainland, and form the proposed route of the ship-canal between them.

The North River, on the western shore of the great city, preserves a name applied for nearly three centuries to that stretch of the Hudson River extending in front of Manhattan. The old Dutch colonists named the Delaware the *South River,* and the Hudson they called the *North River.* It is a noble straight-channeled reach of deep water, a mile wide and a score of miles long, and gave ample soundings for the *Great Eastern,* as it does now for the *Campania,* the *Spree* and the *New York.*

The lower water-side streets are occupied generally by small irregular buildings, sail-lofts, the haunts of riggers and outfitters, ship-owners and ship-chandlers, mysterious junk shops, and a vast variety of drinking-places, sailors' boarding-houses, and shops for small-wares. Street-railways run along the pier-heads ; and a continuous crowded and noisy procession of drays and carts pours up and down the streets, or entangles itself in hopeless blocks, overflowed by tides of objurgations and hearty profanatory expletives.

The Piers and Wharves are for the most part exceedingly irregular and rather unsightly, being of various lengths, and constructed of wood, upon myriads of piles, around and between which the free tides swirl and eddy. Though devoid of the architectural symmetry and structural massiveness of European quays, the waterfront of New York is well-fitted for its uses, and has also a singular picturesqueness and diversity of outline and character. Some years ago a well-considered plan was devised and begun, to replace the crazy-looking wharves with a systematic and imposing line of stone piers and docks ; but this transformation is a very costly process, and has made but little advance. In 1892 the Legislature passed a bill providing " for the recreation and health of the people of New York by setting aside certain piers along the river-front." The plan involves the construction of very large two-story pavilions on the pier-ends, the lower stories being devoted to commercial purposes, and the high-arched upper floors forming fresh-air gardens, with music and flowers and sea-views, for the pleasure of the people. The piers at Barclay and Perry Streets, on the North River, are being fitted up for this fortunate service ; and there are to be four similar roof-gardens on the East-River front.

In going up the North-River side, from the Battery, there is a continual succession of varied and busy scenes, the headquarters of the Coney-Island steamboats; the huge piers of the Pennsylvania Railroad ; the trim vessels of the New-Orleans, Bos-

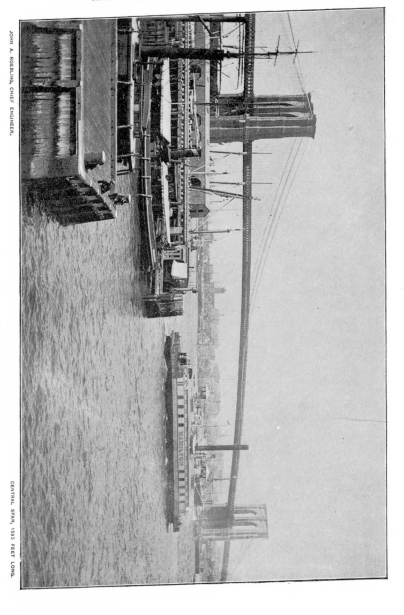

JOHN A. ROEBLING, CHIEF ENGINEER.

THE EAST RIVER, OR NEW YORK AND BROOKLYN, SUSPENSION BRIDGE.

ACROSS THE EAST RIVER FROM CITY HALL PARK, NEW YORK, TO BROOKLYN.

CENTRAL SPAN, 1595 FEET LONG.

THE BOWLING GREEN BUILDING.   BROADWAY.   BOWLING GREEN.   PRODUCE EXCHANGE.

BOWLING GREEN AND THE BOWLING GREEN BUILDING—THE BEGINNING OF BROADWAY.

THE BOWLING GREEN OFFICE BUILDING.

BOWLING GREEN, THE BEGINNING OF BROADWAY.

THE NORTH RIVER, ALSO CALLED THE HUDSON. STEAMSHIP "NEW YORK" STARTING FOR SOUTHAMPTON.

JERSEY CITY AND THE PENNSYLVANIA RAILROAD STATION IN THE DISTANCE, AND BABBITT'S GREAT SOAP WORKS IN THE FOREGROUND.

ton, and Savannah steamships ; the huge white floating palaces of the Sound lines to Fall River and Providence and Norwich ; the docks of the Hudson-River lines ; the Morgan and Old-Dominion boats ; and the resting-places of the unrivalled ocean-greyhounds of the American, Guion, White Star, Cunard and French lines. Along the East River a great space is given up to the large sailing-ships, bringing in cargoes from all parts of the world, and with their lofty masts and long yards interwoven against the sky. Then come the grain-laden canal-boats from the West, hundreds of fruiters from the West Indies, and a line of ferries, above which appear several dry-docks, followed by iron-foundries, lumber-yards, and old steamers laid up in ordinary. Almost every variety of vessel is found in these waters, the brilliant excursion-steamboats, melodious with band-music, and waving with flags and

streamers ; ark-like canal-boats from the Great Lakes, distended with wheat and corn ; the swift Norfolk schooners, redolent of fine tobacco and of early vegetables ; oyster-boats from the Connecticut coast, small and pert in outlines and motion ; huge full-rigged ships from Calcutta, laden with indigo ; sooty steam-barges from the Pennsylvania coal-regions ; Nova-Scotia brigs, laden with fine apples and potatoes ; heavy old whalers, making port after long Arctic voyages ;

UNITED-STATES BARGE OFFICE, BATTERY PLACE.

schooners from the West Indies and Honduras, crammed with tropical fruits ; fishermen from the Grand Banks, heroes of the saltest northern seas ; Mediterranean merchantmen, with rich cargoes from the Levant ; and hundreds of other types, each full of interest and attraction. The loom of the great environing cities, the breadth and life of the confluent waters, the intense and joyous activity of motion, combine to give this cosmopolitan picture an unusual breadth and life.

Space fails to tell of the Barge Office at the Battery, and its customs inspectors and sailors' dispensary ; of the natty flotilla of the Battery boatmen ; of Ellis Island and its great buildings for the reception of immigrants ; of the United-States Navy Yard, at Brooklyn, the chief naval station of the Republic ; of the wonderful docks on the Brooklyn side, the home of a universal commerce ; and of scores of other interesting scenes which surround the gateway of the New World.

The Military Defences of New-York City are formidable, as far as the old style of warfare goes. It remains to be seen how efficient they may be when confronting the untried and uncertain naval monsters of the new era; and acting under the support of chains of torpedoes, dynamite guns, and the battle-ships of the new American navy. New mortar-batteries of great power are about to be constructed on Sandy Hook and near Long Island, to command the remote Lower Bay; and Fort Lafayette and other points will be occupied by immense steel turrets.

Fort Wadsworth, the most powerful of the military defences of New York, is a three-tiered casemate work of granite, on the Staten-Island shore of the Narrows. On the heights above stands the heavily-armed Fort Tompkins; and along the channel-side extends a line of water-batteries. From this place a triple fire, water-line and casemate and plunging, could be converged upon a hostile vessel in the narrow channel.

On the Long-Island shore, at the Narrows, opposite Fort Wadsworth, and only a mile distant, glower the heavy stone casemates of Fort Hamilton, on a military reservation of 96 acres. Just off-shore, on an artificial island, stands Fort Lafayette, built in 1812–22, and celebrated as a prison for political captives and disloyal persons during the civil war. The inflammable parts of the fort were burned in 1868, and the remaining buildings are used now only for storing ordnance supplies.

Fort Wood, on Bedloe's Island, is a star-shaped work, finished in 1841, and mounted then with seventy guns. The wonderful colossal statue of Liberty Enlightening the World rises from a pedestal on the parade-ground.

Willett's Point was fortified in 1862, by the National Government, to close the entrance to the East River from Long-Island Sound. It is the headquarters of the Battalion of Engineers, U. S. A. Across the entrance of the East River looms the ponderous casemated defence of Fort Schuyler, whose construction was begun in 1833.

Governor's Island, within 1,000 feet of the Battery, and six miles inside of the Narrows, is the headquarters of the Military Department of the East, and the usual residence of the commanding general. It is a beautiful island, of 65 acres, with a far-viewing parade-ground, surrounded by fine old trees and the quarters of the officers; an arsenal containing scores of heavy cannon and endless pyramids of cannon-balls; magazines and hospitals; the headquarters of the Military Service Institution, with its library and picture-gallery; and the interesting Military Museum, rich in battle-flags, weapons ancient and modern, and Indian curiosities. The chief defence on Governor's Island is Fort Columbus, a star-shaped stone fort mounting 120 guns, and with enclosed barracks for the artillerists. On the point toward the Battery stands Castle Williams, an old-fashioned and picturesque three-story fortress, circular in shape, built between 1808 and 1812.

The Quarantine Station defends the port of New York (and with it the entire continent) against the entrance of dangerous and pestilential diseases. The danger of epidemics being brought in by foreign vessels was guarded against as early as 1647; and in 1716 the Council ordered that all West-Indian vessels should be detained at Staten Island. In 1758 the Provincial Legislature enacted laws for the protection of the port in this regard, and established a quarantine station at Bedloe's Island. One of the first measures of the State Legislature, in 1784, was a re-enactment of this law. Ten years later, the station was moved to Governor's Island, but the citizens of New York were rather uneasy at having the pest-house so near them. In 1801, therefore, it was again transferred to Tompkinsville, Staten Island, where it remained for more than sixty years. But in the course of time, as Staten Island became thickly settled, its people made serious objections to the continuance of so undesirable a neighbor ; and in 1857 the State Legislature ordered the selection of another site. This was found at Sandy Hook, but the opposition of New Jersey rendered it impossible. The next move appeared in the erection of buildings for the purpose at Seguin's Point, on the south part of Staten Island. The neighboring residents were incensed at the project, and attacked the establishment by night, and set fire to it. This summary process approved itself to the people of Tompkinsville, who also made a night attack upon the existing station, and thoroughly destroyed it. Richmond County was forced to pay for these nocturnal raids, but the result justified the acts, and the State gave up its attempt to establish the quarantine here. In 1859 a commission including Horatio Seymour, John C. Green, and Gov. Patterson adopted the idea of a floating hospital ; and the old steamship *Falcon* entered upon the duty, with an anchorage below the Narrows. In 1866–70 the artificial Swinburne Island was constructed, on the sand-bar of West Bank, and now has rows of hospital wards, a crematory and mortuary, and a dock and break-

BAY AND HARBOR FROM BEDLOE'S ISLAND, ABOUT 1840.

water. Hoffman Island, built in 1868–73, is a quarantine of observation and isolation, for immigrants who have been exposed to dangerous epidemics. The Lower Quarantine is marked by yellow buoys, and has a ship moored for a floating station, where vessels from infected ports are boarded. Their arrival is signalled thence to the main Quarantine Station, six miles above, on Staten Island, from which the proper officials go down to board them. The swift little tug-boat of the station passes the day in rushing from one incoming vessel to another, and the health-officers are kept busy in inspecting their passengers and crews. In a single year 7,600 vessels and 370,000 passengers have been examined here. The New-York quarantine is the most complete, thorough and efficient in the world.

The harbor is guarded from law-breakers, and "wharf-rats," mutineers and rioters, river-thieves and smugglers, as much as possible, by the police of the Thirty-Sixth Precinct, which has jurisdiction over the waters and wharves adjoining the city, along both rivers, and down as far as Robin's Reef. The police headquarters is on the steamboat *Patrol*, and several row-boats are continually moving along the rivers and up into the docks, manned by officers of the law, looking after thieves, fires, lost property, suicides and drowned persons.

The Exports and Imports of America find their foremost clearing-houses in this peerless harbor, with its rich adornments of Nature, and improvements and defences of art. One hundred years ago the total export and import trade of the United States was below $50,000,000 annually. At present (including specie) it is over $2,000,000,000, of which the imports reach $900,000,000. The exports of cotton are over $290,000,000; of grain, breadstuffs and provisions, $480,000,000; and of specie, $80,000,000. The foreign commerce for 1891 and 1892 was the largest in the history of the Nation. Nearly two-fifths of the exports of the Republic go from New York, which sends out $460,000,000 yearly, to $107,000,000 from New Orleans, $74,000,000 from Baltimore, $70,000,000 from Boston, and $37,-000,000 from Philadelphia. Two-thirds of the imports to the United States enter at the port of New York. Less than one-fourth of the trade is under the American flag, which has a tonnage of 1,000,000 in the foreign trade, and 3,700,000 in the coastwise trade, besides 87,000 in the fisheries. New York owns 2,000 sailing vessels, of 409,000 tons; 1,000 steamers, of 375,000 tons; and 900 canal-boats and lighters, of 167,000 tons.

During a single year over 2,000 grain-laden steamships sail from New York, which ships one-third of the American grain and breadstuffs, in spite of its heavy port and storage charges. The hold is filled with grain in bulk; the between-decks with grain in bags. The port has a storage capacity of 26,000,000 bushels, in 22 stationary elevators and 31 floating elevators; and grain-ships can be loaded at the rate of 458,000 bushels an hour.

New York receives every year over 200 tramp steamships, 136 from transatlantic ports, and the rest from other American harbors. Many of them come to this great maritime clearing-house for orders, or enter in ballast, seeking cargoes. These wanderers of the seas have engines of low power, with small consumption of coal, and cross the ocean in from fifteen to twenty days, with cargoes of heavy character, and including all sorts of merchandise. Here also are seen the singular tank-steam-ships, partly owned by the Standard Oil Company, and carrying over seas from 30,000 to 35,000 barrels of oil, pumped into the hold, which is divided into half-a-dozen or more great tanks. One of these singular floating reservoirs can be filled with petroleum in twelve hours. On their return-voyages from Europe the tanks are partly filled with water-ballast. Vessels of somewhat similar construction are employed in transporting molasses from Cuba.

There are several score of fruit steamers plying between the Central-American and West-Indian ports and New York, bringing bananas and cocoanuts, oranges and pineapples, and mostly sailing under the Norwegian flag. Between the outer hull of steel and the inner hull of wood opens a considerable space, which is packed with charcoal, for refrigeration. They have triple-expansion engines, steam steering-gear, and, in many cases, twin-screws, and are built for the trade, with three open decks and separated deck-planks, to ensure free circulation of air, and prevent the fruit from becoming heated. Their seasons are spring and summer, after which most of them go into the grain and general freighting business to and around Europe.

Before the days of steam, the Atlantic Ocean was traversed by several famous packet-lines, like the Black Star ships of Grimshaw & Co., the Black Ball line of C. H. Marshall & Co., the old Black Stars of Williams & Guion, the packets of the Tapscot Line. The largest accommodations were for 30 cabin and 20 second-cabin, and a varying number of steerage passengers in a ship, the rates being higher than in the modern steamships. These ocean racers were built on the finest and most graceful lines, with vast expanses of canvas spread from their towering masts ; and their passages across were of remarkable swiftness. The *Red Jacket* made the transatlantic voyage in 13 days and $1\frac{25}{60}$ hour; and the *Dreadnaught* in 1860 made the run from New York to the Irish coast in 9 days and 17 hours. In 1864 the clipper *Adelaide* left New York at the same time as the Cunard steamship *Sidon*, and entered Liverpool before her, in $12\frac{1}{3}$ days. At the present time many sailing ships ply to and from the port of New York, and among them are enormous four-masted steel vessels, with a capacity of 6,000 tons of freight.

The science of steam navigation, which has revolutioned modern commerce, changed the aspect of naval warfare, made travel by sea speedy and pleasant, and united the remote places of the earth, had its beginning in the noble harbor of New York. Various Spanish and German, British and American inventors claimed to

NEW-YORK HARBOR, FROM EAST-RIVER BRIDGE, IN 1893.

have discovered the principles of marine engines, at periods running from the Middle Ages down to the close of the eighteenth century ; but it was reserved for Robert Fulton to practically apply this idea, and to perfect and develop it, so that his fleet of vessels had an immediate economic value for transporting passengers and freight.

This successful demonstration of a great new principle resulted in a rapid spread of the discovered power all over the maritime world. Fulton's *Clermont* was launched at Jersey City, in 1807, and ascended the Hudson River to Albany. Almost at the same time, John Stevens, of Hoboken, built the *Phœnix*, and sent her around to Philadelphia, the pioneer of all ocean-going steamers. Following New York's example, the St.-Lawrence River received a steamboat, in 1809 ; the Ohio and Mississippi, in 1811 ; and the Scottish Clyde, in 1812. The first steamship to cross the ocean was the *Savannah*, built at New York, and equipped with folding paddle-wheels, which were taken out and laid on the deck when not in use. In

1819 this little 380-ton vessel steamed from Savannah to Liverpool, Cronstadt, and Copenhagen. In 1838 Brunel's steamship *Great Western*, of 1,340 tons, steamed from Bristol, England, to New York, in fifteen days; and the *Sirius* ran across from London and Cork to New York.

In 1850 the Collins Line began its operations, and built up a fleet of five magnificent American steamships — the *Pacific*, *Arctic*, *Adriatic*, *Baltic*, and *Atlantic*, built at a cost of $4,000,000, and operated under a large subsidy from the United-States Government. The first two were lost at sea ; the cost of the voyages far exceeded the receipts ; the subsidy was withdrawn ; and in 1858 the Collins Line ceased to run.

There are now thirty great transatlantic steamship lines between New York and Europe, some of them with several sailings each week. They have eighty-five passenger steamships, bringing to New York yearly nearly 100,000 cabin passengers, four-fifths of whom are returning Americans. Their eastern ports are Liverpool, Southampton, London, Newcastle, Hull, Moville (Londonderry), Queenstown, and Glasgow, in the British Islands ; Havre, Bordeaux, and Boulogne, in France ; Antwerp, Rotterdam, and Amsterdam, in the Low Countries; Copenhagen, in Denmark; Hamburg, Stettin, and Bremen, in Germany ; Christiania and Christiansand, in Scandinavia ; and several Mediterranean ports. The capital embarked in these lines is $500,000,000. The offices of most of the steamship lines are on lower Broadway, or at "Steamship Row," on Bowling Green, where they occupy a block of ancient brick houses once dwelt in by the merchant-princes of New York.

The American Line is the successor of the old Inman Line, which began operations in 1850, under the title of the Liverpool, New-York & Philadelphia Steamship Company. The Inman Line was purchased in 1886 by the International Navigation Company, of Philadelphia ; but it was not until early in 1893 that the company was able to naturalize the two steamships *New York* and *Paris*, and start them running under the flag of the country in which they were actually owned. The ceremonies of transferring the ships to the American flag on the *New York* were appropriately performed on Washington's Birthday by President Harrison, in the presence of the members of his cabinet, and a large gathering of distinguished and representative United-States citizens, invited by the International Navigation Company to witness this most interesting ceremony. The placing of this most magnificent fleet under the Stars and Stripes has attracted an immense patronage from American travellers. Not content with merely changing the flag and name of the line, the management, recognizing the enormous advantages of Southampton as a terminal point in Great Britain over any other available port, started their newly-named service to a new terminus in England. The American Line ships *Paris*, *New York*, *Berlin* and *Chester* now sail every Saturday to Southampton. It will be noticed that, in addition to other changes, the words *City of* in the names of the ships have been dropped. These steamships are so well known to transatlantic travellers that it seems hardly necessary to describe them minutely. The *Paris* has made the fastest westbound transatlantic voyage on record, her time being 5 days, 14 hours and 24 minutes, while her sister-ship, the *New York*, has the honor of holding the record of some of the fastest voyages made to the eastward. These two American steamships are provided with double bottoms, so that the inner skin would keep out the water if the outer one were broken. They have twenty water-tight compartments, separated by solid bulkheads, and fronted by an immensely thick collision-bulkhead, near the bow ; and twin screws, each driven by an independent triple-expansion engine, so that if one becomes disabled, the ship can be brought

AMERICAN LINE;—THE "NEW YORK" AND "PARIS," TWIN-SCREW STEAMSHIPS.
INTERNATIONAL NAVIGATION COMPANY. NEW PIERS 14 AND 15, N. R. OFFICES, 6 BOWLING GREEN.

into port with the other engine. The number of cabin passengers carried by these steamships is limited to the number they can seat at table at one sitting. All possibility of overcrowding is thereby avoided. These steamers are each 580 feet long and 59 feet deep, and the extreme breadth is 63¼ feet. They have a displacement of 10,500 tons each, and 20,000 horse-power. Each ship carries many of its first-cabin passengers on the promenade and saloon decks, some in suites of sitting-room, bed-room, bath-room and toilet-room, and others in rooms arranged with berths folding up like those in a Pullman car, so that by day the place becomes a pleasant sitting-room. The other first-class cabins, on the main and upper decks, are of greater size than usual, and elegantly and comfortably furnished. The dining saloons are spacious rooms of singular beauty and convenience, with high arched ceilings and choice architectural and artistic decorations. Every device calculated to increase the comfort of passengers has been combined in these splendid ships, which are at once swift, secure and sumptuous, as strong as battle-ships and as luxurious as Belgravia drawing-rooms. The kitchens are isolated, and ventilated into the funnels.

HELL GATE, FROM GREAT BARN ISLAND, ABOUT 1825.

Hydraulic power is used instead of steam for the daily work of steering, hoisting out supplies, and many other duties ; and its operation is very nearly noiseless.

The rates of first-cabin passage are from $60 to $650, depending on the ship, the season, the number in a state-room, and the location. All these steamers have spacious state-rooms, ventilated by electric-driven fans and other devices, and containing scientific plumbing and other modern improvements.

The International Navigation Company has contracted with The William Cramp & Sons Ship and Engine-Building Company, of Philadelphia, for the construction of several new steamers of the highest order known to naval architecture, and when this magnificent fleet of modern steamships is afloat, the company will maintain a weekly service to Southampton and a weekly service to Antwerp, calling at Southampton and Boulogne. It is readily appreciated that these two ships, with their promised sisters, among the largest, finest and fastest vessels in the world, are a valuable acquisition to the United-States Navy.

The American Line and the Red Star Line (both of which are owned by the International Navigation Company) land their passengers directly on the company's piers, and thus save them the inconvenience, discomfort and exposure of being transferred by small tenders. American Line and Red Star Line cabin tickets are interchangeable; the return portion is available by either line, as the passenger may

AMERICAN LINE, NEW PIERS 14 AND 15, NORTH RIVER.

choose. The International Navigation Company has recently acquired the largest and finest pier property in New-York harbor, near the Cortlandt-Street ferry of the Pennsylvania Railroad, and known as New Pier 14, or Washington Pier. They also own New Pier 15. They are rapidly fitting up these piers with a second story, and in the most improved manner; and New Pier 14 will be in many respects the most commodious pier in the world, with admirable provision for passengers and freight.

The offices of the company are at 6 Bowling Green, New York; 307 Walnut Street, Philadelphia; 32 South Clark Street, Chicago; 3 Cockspur Street, London; Canute Road, Southampton; and 22 Kammenstrasse, Antwerp.

The White Star Line (or Oceanic Steam Navigation Company), founded in 1870, sent out in 1875 the *Britannic* and *Germanic*, steamships of a new type, of great length and equipped with powerful compound engines. Fourteen years later, in 1889, the magnificent *Teutonic* and *Majestic* were launched, each of them 582 feet long, and of nearly 10,000 tons displacement. In March, 1891, the *Majestic* crossed from Queenstown to New York in 5 days, 18 hours, and 8 minutes, and the *Teutonic* made the same voyage in 5 days and 16½ hours, the average being 20⅓ knots an hour, and the swiftest day's run reaching 517 knots. Each of these giants of the sea can carry 1,200 passengers and 2,500 tons of freight; and each of them cost above $2,000,000. They are built of Siemens-Martin steel, and each is propelled by two independent sets of triple-expansion engines, with manganese bronze propellers. They are minutely divided by athwart-ship and longitudinal bulk-heads, ensuring rigidity, strength and security. There are family and single-berth state-rooms, ivory-and-gold Renaissance saloons, smoking-rooms decorated with embossed leather and fine marine paintings, a library-room with well-filled book-cases and luxurious furniture, and many other very comfortable departments.   The first-cabin rates are from $80 to $600, depending on the steamship, the season, and the location of the state-room.   Among the other vessels of the line are the *Oceanic*, its first boat; the *Belgic*, *Gaelic* and *Adriatic;* and the *Coptic*, *Doric* and *Ionic*.   All these were built at Belfast, Ireland.   The company's dock is at the foot of West 10th Street.   The twin-screw steamships *Bovic*, *Tauric*, and *Nomadic*, and the *Runic* and *Cufic*, are used for freight exclusively, and cross in ten days.   In a single voyage, the *Nomadic* has carried 9,591 tons of freight; and the *Cufic* has brought to New York at one time 77,000 boxes of tin-plate.

The Cunard Line was established by Samuel Cunard, of Halifax, David McIver, of Liverpool, and George Burns, of Glasgow; and began its voyages in the year 1840.   Its official title was the British & North-American Royal Mail Steam Packet Company.   The first Cunarders were paddle-wheel vessels, of wood, and bore the names — *Britannia*, *Acadia*, *Columbia*, and *Caledonia*.   Those four steam-

PECK SLIP, EAST RIVER.

ships carried the mails between Liverpool, Halifax and Boston, for which the company received $400,000 yearly.   The mail service has ever since been an important perquisite of the Cunard Company.   The fleet was increased by the *Hibernia*, in 1843; the *Cambria*, in 1845; the *America*, *Niagara*, *Europa* and *Columbia*, in 1850; the *Asia* and *Africa;* the *Persia*, in 1855; and the *Scotia*, in 1862.   The *China*, launched in 1862, was the first iron screw steamship in the Cunard fleet.   In 1874, the *Bothnia* and *Scythia* were launched; and in 1881, the *Servia*.   In 1884-85, appeared the *Etruria* and *Umbria*, each of over 8,000 tons, and in their day the sovereigns of the seas.   The *Campania* and *Lucania* began to run in 1893, and are each of nearly 13,000 tons and 25,000 horse-power, with a length of 625 feet.   The Cunard New-York fleet includes the *Campania*, *Lucania*, *Etruria*, *Umbria*, *Aurania*, *Gallia*, *Servia* and *Bothnia*, sailing on Wednesdays and Saturdays for Queenstown and Liverpool.   The first-cabin fare from New York to Liverpool is from $60 to $125.   The Cunard dock is at Pier 40, N. R., at the foot of Clarkson Street.

ELLIS-ISLAND IMMIGRANT STATION, IN NEW-YORK HARBOR.
THE LANDING-PLACE FOR IMMIGRANTS.

The Guion Line dates from 1864, when its great new steamships succeeded its line of wooden sailing-packets, established in 1842. The construction of the *Arizona*, in 1879, inaugurated the wonderful rivalry which has since stimulated the ocean lines to increase the size, speed and comfort of their ships. The *Arizona* was of 5,164 tons, and crossed in 7 days and 3½ hours ; and her sister-ship, the *Alaska*, built in 1881, of 6,932 tons, and 11,000 horse-power, made a still better record. These two enormous ships have accommodations for about 1,200 passengers and 2,000 tons of freight each. The other vessels — the *Nevada, Wisconsin,* and *Wyoming* were built at Jarrow, England, between 1868 and 1870, and are smaller. All the Guion boats are of iron, with water-tight compartments. The cabin passage rates vary from $50 to $100, and upward, according to the ship or the location of the berth. The Guion dock is at the foot of Grand Street, Jersey City.

The Anchor Line, founded in 1852, by Thomas Henderson, has on its service between New York and Glasgow, six fine steamships, with weekly sailings. The

SOUTH STREET AND HARBOR, AND JEANNETTEE PARK.

Ethiopia, Devonia, Circassia and *Anchoria* are each of between 4,000 and 5,000 tons. The *Furnessia,* of 6,500 tons, is a fine vessel, with electric lights, water-tight compartments, and a rich furnishing. The *City of Rome,* built in 1881, at Barrow, has a gross tonnage of 8,415, with four masts, three funnels, and a magnificent equipment for passenger accommodation. The Anchor cabin fares from New York to Glasgow are from $50 to $100. The Anchor dock is at Pier 54, N. R., foot of West 24th Street. The route is across to the bold north coast of Ireland ; up Lough Foyie to Moville, where passengers for Londonderry get on a tender ; across the North Channel and the Firth of Clyde ; and up the wonderfully interesting River Clyde for 25 miles to Glasgow. This company also has Mediterranean and Indian services.

The National Line, founded in 1863, runs from New York to Liverpool and London, and has twelve large steamships, once favorite passenger-boats, but now entirely devoted to freighting. In a single trip one of these vessels has carried over 1,000 head of cattle.

The Atlantic Transport Line, running every ten days between New York and London, is also devoted to freight.

The Bristol City Line, at the foot of West 26th Street, and the **Manhanset Line,** for Avonmouth, whose pier is at Jersey City, have a large freight business with Bristol and South Wales, served by weekly steamships on each route. The English coast is also reached by the Hamburg-American and North German Lloyd steamships, calling at Southampton, from or for New York every day or two.

The Allan-State Line, between New York, Londonderry, and Glasgow, was founded in 1872 by a Glasgow company, under the name of the State Line. The New-York fleet includes the Clyde-built steamships *State of California, State of Nebraska,* and *State of Nevada,* strong and comfortable vessels of iron or steel, with saloons amidships, and electric-lighted parlors and sitting-rooms and state-rooms on the main deck. The *California* was built on the Clyde, in 1891, and is 400 feet long, with a tonnage of 4,500, eight water-tight compartments, triple-expansion engines, steel boilers, and accommodations for 1,000 passengers. This line carries large quantities of freight, and is thus able to make very low rates for passengers who are not in a hurry to get across. Its first-cabin rates are $40, or $75 for the trip over and back. The steamships leave the foot of West 21st Street Thursdays. The Allan Line also sends out freight steamships, which bring back passengers.

The Wilson Line owns thirty vessels, with a tonnage of 114,000, mainly devoted to freighting. There are four services from New York, running to Hull, London, Newcastle and Antwerp. The Hull steamships sail from Hoboken (cabin fare, $45), and carry no steerage passengers. The London steamships include several 4,500-ton vessels. They are largely devoted to carrying cattle, and make long and leisurely passages.

The Compagnie Generale Transatlantique, usually known as the "French Line," serves the route between New York and Havre with six fine express mail steamships, *La Touraine, La Bourgogne, La Normandie, La Champagne, La Bretagne* and *La Gascogne.* Each of these vessels can accommodate 1,300 passengers, and carries 2,500 tons of freight. Several of them were built at St. Nazaire, France, by the company; and so also was *La Touraine,* with a tonnage of 10,000, and

NEW-YORK CENTRAL & HUDSON-RIVER RAILROAD COMPANY'S ELEVATOR.

12,000 horse-power, and costing $2,000,000.   She has made the run from Havre to
New York in six days and 8½ hours.   The French Line ships are of steel, with
water-tight compartments and cellular bottoms.   In the latter part of the voyage
the vessels command pleasant views of the Channel Islands and the great naval city
of Cherbourg, and then swing around the French coast to Havre and the mouth of
the Seine.   The pier is No. 42, N. R., at the foot of Morton Street.   The office is
at 3 Bowling Green, Augustin Forget being the general agent for the United States.

   The Bordeaux Line, originating in 1880, runs three British-built steamships,
the *Chateau Lafite, Panama* and *Tancarville*, making the voyage in nine days.

   The Netherlands-American Line calls at Boulogne-sur-Mer.

   The North German Lloyd (Norddeutscher Lloyd) is one of the greatest
steamship companies the world has ever seen, and its flag floats proudly on every
sea.   It was formed in 1856, by Herr H. H. Meier, who amalgamated the shipping
interests of Bremen, and its five maritime companies, into one powerful union.
The steamships *Bremen, New York, Hudson* (afterwards burnt), and *Weser* (afterwards sold) were built at Greenock, and began running in 1858; the *Hansa* came on
in 1861; the *America*, in 1862; the *Hermann*, in 1865, and other steamers in the
fifteen following years, until a great sea fleet was created.   In 1881, the splendid
express steamer *Elbe* began running; in 1882, the *Werra* and *Fulda*; in 1883, the

HOBOKEN FERRY PIER, NORTH RIVER, FOOT OF CHRISTOPHER STREET.

Eider and *Ems;* in 1885, the *Aller;* in 1886, the *Trave* and *Saale;* and in 1888,
the *Lahn*.   All these vessels were built at Glasgow.   The later additions to the
fleet, the *Kaiser Wilhelm II., Spree* and *Havel* were built at Stettin, Germany.
The twelve Lloyd express steamers are of about from 4,500 to 7,000 tons each,
and carry 1,150 passengers and 2,000 tons of freight.   They leave New York
(Hoboken) semi-weekly, crossing in about seven days to Southampton, within two
hours' ride of London; and thence running along the English Channel and the
North Sea to Bremerhaven, which is 1½ hours by railway from Bremen.

   The comforts of the Lloyd ships are unexcelled.   The promenade-deck is 200
feet long, and the whole width of the ship, sheltered by awnings, lit by electricity,
and made melodious by the orchestra daily.   A broad stairway leads to the saloon,
of great size, and superbly furnished, with rare carvings, paintings, mirrors, book-
cases, and plush curtains, and perfectly lighted and ventilated.   The saloon is
amidships, and occupies the entire width of the vessel, the sides being taken up by

NORTH GERMAN LLOYD STEAMSHIP COMPANY.
PIERS AT HOBOKEN.   OFFICES AT 2 BOWLING GREEN, NEW YORK

cozy alcoves, with lounges and small tables.   The ladies' cabin, in the gallery above, on the upper deck, is richly adorned with paintings, and has many divans and easy chairs.   The state-rooms are on the saloon-deck, nearly all outside, of large dimensions, white, airy and comfortable.

The North German Lloyd has 59 ocean steamships, including lines from Bremen to Baltimore, weekly; to Antwerp, Lisbon and Brazil, monthly; to Buenos Ayres and Montevideo, every ten days; to India and China, monthly; to the Australian ports, monthly; and branch lines from Hong Kong to Japan; and from Singapore to Java and Sumatra and the German colony of New Guinea.   No other steamship company has so great a tonnage.   The general agents are Oelrichs & Co., 2 Bowling Green, New York,— a firm that has existed for almost a century.

The Hamburg-American Packet Company is the oldest German transatlantic line, having been founded as early as the year 1847.   Nine years later it sent out its first steam vessel, the predecessor of a magnificent fleet of 54 steamships now owned by the company, and running on sixteen lines, reaching Boston, Baltimore, and Philadelphia, as well as New York, and also plying to the West Indies and the Spanish Main.   Safety, speed and comfort are the three prime objects of the line, and it has already forwarded over two million passengers, between the Old World and the New.   The Express Service, from New York to Southampton and Hamburg, is served by four of the noblest and most magnificent of the great ocean steamships, the *Fürst Bismarck, Augusta Victoria, Normannia,* and *Columbia.* The two first-named were built at the Vulcan Works, at Stettin, and the others at Govan (Scotland) and Birkenhead.   These greyhounds of the sea are constructed of steel and teakwood, with double bottoms and numerous water-tight compartments. They are from 10,000 to 12,000 tons each, with a horse-power of from 13,000 to 16,000, and a speed of from 19 to 20¾ knots an hour.   The *Fürst Bismarck* has made the run between New York and Southampton in 6 days and 11¾ hours, the fastest time between those ports, and the transit between New York and London is made regularly in less than a week by this route.   After leaving Southampton, the Express steamships in 24 hours run across the North Sea to Cuxhaven, at the mouth of the River Elbe, whence the passengers are transported to Hamburg by railway. These majestic vessels are among the swiftest plying between America and the Continent of Europe, and their passengers are landed almost in the heart of the Old World.   Their safety is increased by powerful turtle-backs at stem and stern, and also by complete twin-screw systems, so that if one engine, boiler, shaft, or screw should be disabled, the ship could be propelled by the other set.

The furnishing of the Hamburg steamships is sumptuous, the saloons having been decorated by eminent European artists.   The white and gold furniture of the music-room, the rich damask hangings of the ladies' saloon, the carved dark-wood panels of the main saloon, the great glass cupola, all give the impression of the state apartments in some Old-World palace.   The state-rooms are unusually large and airy, some of them arranged in suites, for families.

Besides the Express Service, there is the Regular Service of the Hamburg-American Company, from New York to Hamburg direct, touching at Havre on the return. Its first-cabin fares are from $45 upward.   It employs the iron and steel steamships *Bohemia, Dania, Gellert, Gothia, Moravia, Rhætia, Rugia, Russia, Scandia, Slavonia, Suevia, Venetia, Virginia, Wieland,* etc.   These great ships are divided into water-tight compartments, and heated by steam, lighted by electricity, and have their state-rooms on the main deck, with abundant light and air.   This is a route by which the traveller gets many comforts for comparatively little money.

MAIN SALOON FIRST CABIN.

LADIES RECEPTION ROOM.

FÜRST BISMARCK.

MUSIC ROOM.

SMOKING ROOM.

HAMBURG-AMERICAN PACKET COMPANY.
PIERS AT HOBOKEN.   OFFICES AT 37 BROADWAY, NEW YORK.

The general office of the Hamburg-American Line is at 37 Broadway, New York, and the docks of the steamships are at Hoboken, with good accommodations for their varied traffic.

The Union Line is operated by the Hamburg-American Packet Company, and maintains the steamships *Sorrento, Marsala, Amalfi,* and *Taormina* on the direct route between New York and Hamburg, taking steerage passengers only.

The Red Star-Line is one of the most prominent of the Atlantic steamship lines, running weekly from New York to Antwerp and from Philadelphia to Antwerp, and is owned by the International Navigation Company, the proprietors of the American Line. Although the steamers of this line do not enjoy the reputation of being "ocean greyhounds," they make the voyage between ports in nine or ten days, and compare favorably in this respect with other Continental lines. The steamships *Friesland, Westernland, Noordland, Waesland, Pennland, Rhynland, Belgenland, Switzerland,* etc., are magnificent specimens of naval architecture, and especially constructed for the Atlantic trade. They are not excelled in comfort and safety by any steamers afloat. Their construction is in excess of the rigid requirements of the British Lloyds and Bureau Veritas, under whose inspection they were built. They are very comfortably arranged, with family rooms, dining-rooms on saloon-deck, electric lights, isolated kitchens, saloons artistically decorated with rare woodwork and paintings, perfect ventilating apparatus, and smoking-rooms with tiled floors and mahogany walls. The voyage eastward leads past the Scilly Islands and the Lizard, whence the course is laid up the English Channel, in sight

RED STAR LINE STEAMSHIP "FRIESLAND." OFFICES, 6 BOWLING GREEN.

of Eddystone Rock, the Bill of Portland, the Isle of Wight, Hastings and Dover, with the French coast on the starboard side. Then the steamship heads across the North Sea, passing Dunkirk and Ostend, entering the Scheldt River at Flushing, 47 miles from Antwerp. This port was chosen as the Continental terminal on account of its central geographical position, within a few hours' railway ride of

Paris, Strasburg or Frankfort, and in the very heart of the quaint and fascinating Low Countries, and because it avoided the extremely disagreeable "Channel crossing" which is so dreaded by many experienced travellers. The rates by this line vary from about $50 to $135, according to the season, steamer and location of

RED STAR LINE STEAMSHIP "WESTERNLAND," OFFICES, 6 BOWLING GREEN.

room. The offices of the company are at 6 Bowling Green, New York; 307 Walnut Street, Philadelphia; and 32 South Clark Street, Chicago; the General European Agents are von der Becke & Marsily, 22 Kammenstrasse, Antwerp.

The White Cross Line runs between New York and Antwerp, with the steamships *Hermann* and *De Ruyter.*

The Insular Navigation Company (Empreza Insulana Navegaçao) runs every three weeks from New York to the Azore Islands in nine days (fare, $60), to Madeira (by transfer) in eleven days ($75), and to Lisbon in fifteen days ($90). It is a Portuguese line. The *Vega* and *Peninsular* are finely equipped 4,000-ton steamships.

The Mediterranean Trade is accommodated by several lines, and by many "ocean tramps," bringing to New York yearly 1,500,000 boxes of Sicily oranges and lemons, 600,000 barrels of Spanish grapes, and vast quantities of nuts and dried fruits. Many passengers for Southern Europe and the Levant avail themselves of these routes, which lie far south of the storms and ice of the North Atlantic. There are lines of steamships running monthly from New York by the Mediterranean Sea and Suez Canal to the ports of India, China and Japan. They are usually laden with heavy freights, and bring back valuable cargoes of tea.

The Mediterranean traffic has of late years assumed important proportions, and employs extensive fleets. The recent enterprise of the North German Lloyd and Hamburg-American lines in placing some of their finest vessels on the route from New York to Genoa has been rewarded by large passenger-lists, and this method of entering upon European travel is destined to be increasingly popular. Thus the tourist's land journey begins in the innermost centres of ancient art and civilization.

The **Netherlands-American Steam-Navigation Company** was founded in 1872, and runs semi-weekly steamers from New York (Hoboken) to Rotterdam or Amsterdam, touching at Boulogne-sur-Mer to land passengers for Paris, four hours' distant by railway.   The fleet includes the steamships *Spaarndam, Maasdam, Veendam, Werkendam, Amsterdam, Obdam, Rotterdam, Didam, Dubbeldam, Edam, Schiedam,* and *P. Caland,* the first seven having been built at Belfast, and the next two at Rotterdam (in 1891).   The Netherlands steamers are four-masters, with four decks and eight water-tight compartments, and very commodious equipments.   They are lighted by electricity and heated by steam, and have commodious and comfortable state-rooms, saloons, smoking-rooms, and other advantages, together with unusually low rates of fare, making this the cheapest of all the Continental lines. The first-cabin rates are from $55 to $70.   The route traverses the Atlantic Ocean

NETHERLANDS-AMERICAN LINE STEAMSHIP "SPAARNDAM," OFFICE 89 BROADWAY, PIER IN HOBOKEN.

and the English Channel, with pleasant views of the coasts of England and France and the port of Boulogne, and ascends the River Maas, an arm of the Rhine, fourteen miles, by Vlaardingen and Delfthaven, to Rotterdam.   The steamships sailing on Wednesday do not call at this port, but go on to Amsterdam, traversing the costly North-Sea Canal from Ymuiden, about fifteen miles.   Either of these great ports has favorable railway communication with Paris, Vienna, Berlin and all other cities of Continental Europe.   The magnificent Rhine steamboats start directly from Rotterdam, running to Düsseldorf, Cologne, Bonn, Coblenz, Mayence and Mannheim, which is close to beautiful Heidelberg and the grand old cathedral-cities of Worms and Spires, and within six hours of Switzerland.   The Netherlands-American piers are at the foot of 5th Street, in Hoboken; and the offices are at 39 Broadway, in the vicinity of Bowling Green, New York.

The Netherlands-American Line is preferred by many travellers who wish to avoid the discomforts of the Channel passage, and to be landed directly on the Continent, where a comfortable journey by railway will lead them to the great metropolitan cities of Germany, France and Italy, or to the mountain-glories of Switzerland. Although the Netherlands steamships are large and well-equipped, the rates of passage are relatively very moderate, and purchase a high value in good and comfortable accommodations. This is therefore one of the most popular of the prominent Continental lines, and is fully patronized during the seasons of travel by many well-known American and European families.

The **Thingvalla Line** in 1879 began its voyages from New York to Norway and Sweden, with Scandinavian officers and crews and flag, and bearing the mails. The run takes from eleven to twelve days; and the first-cabin fares are $50 and $60. The *Hekla*, *Thingvalla*, *Norge* and *Island*, make fortnightly sailings from Hoboken to Christiania and Christiansand, in Norway, and Copenhagen, in Denmark.

The **North German Lloyd Mediterranean Service**, inaugurated in 1891, runs about weekly the fast express steamships *Fulda*, *Werra*, *Ems* and *Kaiser Wilhelm II*. They reach Gibraltar in eight days, and thence in less than three days arrive at Genoa, in some cases proceeding to Naples, where connections are made by Lloyd steamers running to Palermo, and also, during the winter season, with special North German Lloyd steamers between Genoa and Alexandria, Egypt. Travellers desiring to reach Italy, Switzerland, the Riviera, Southern France, Sicily, Egypt and the Nile can do so in the shortest possible time, and in the most convenient manner, by these Mediterranean lines of the North German Lloyd Steamship Co. The route from New York to the Mediterranean is on southern latitudes, ensuring comparatively smooth trips and pleasant passages during the winter months, and a corresponding degree of comfort for travellers.

The **Hamburg-American Packet Company's Mediterranean Express Line** runs a fine winter-service of twin-screw express steamers from New York. They cross the Atlantic in less than seven days, and make their first call at Algiers, thus offering a direct means of communication between New York and that celebrated winter-resort. From there they go to the superb bay of Naples, where connection is made for Sicily, Rome and the East. Leaving this port, the Hamburg-American steamship the next day reaches Genoa, convenient to the Riviera, the Italian Lakes, and Switzerland. The Hamburg-American Packet Company also once a year, generally at the beginning of February, sends one of its magnificent twin-screw express steamers from New York on a cruise to the Mediterranean and the Orient, touching at Gibraltar, Genoa, Ajaccio, Alexandria (for Cairo and the Pyramids), Jaffa (for Jerusalem), Smyrna, Constantinople, Athens, Malta, Syracuse, Palermo, Naples and Algiers. The excursion lasts about ten weeks, and embraces the principal places of a region whose every inch of soil abounds with stirring reminiscences of ancient lore and history, in the regions rich with countless treasures of art which surround "the Storied Sea."

The **Anchor Line** also sends steamships every ten days from New York to Gibraltar, Naples, Genoa, Leghorn, Messina and Palermo.

The **Florio Italian Line** sails fortnightly from New York for Gibraltar, Marseilles, Genoa, Naples, Messina and Palermo, connecting with steamships for Egypt, the Black Sea and the West Indies. They take a far southerly course, below the range of ice, fogs and gales.

The **Fabre Line** sends the *Neustria*, *Massilia*, and other steamships from Brooklyn to Naples and Marseilles every two or three weeks.

Peabody's Australasian Line is owned and operated by Henry W. Peabody & Co., of 58 New Street, New York, one of the most important of the large mercantile houses engaged in the foreign commerce of the port of New York. The business of this firm extends to nearly all parts of the globe, but is more especially with Great Britain, Australasia, India, the Philippine Islands, and Yucatan, in all of which countries they have either their own branch houses or regularly established agents. They are also well known, and have extensive dealings in Mexico, Central and South America, the West Indies, and South Africa. It is, however, in connection with the Australian shipping and commission business, which has for a long

time been one of the most important mercantile interests of the port of New York, that the firm of Henry W. Peabody & Co. is perhaps best known. In this business, which comprises the purchasing and shipping to the British colonies of Australia and New Zealand of the products of the United States and Canada of every description, Henry W. Peabody & Co. have taken a foremost place since 1859. They established between the United States and Australia the regular line of sailing vessels known as Peabody's Australasian Line, of which the present firm are still the proprietors. In this service Henry W. Peabody & Co. have constantly under charter or loading, in New York, first-class ships, in which they take all freight offering for the various Australian ports.

The Western Seas, to their uttermost ends, are traversed by steamships and sailing vessels, loaded by or for the Empire City.

To the Southern and Gulf coasts, the West Indies, and the Central-American and South-American ports, there are several first-class sea-routes, served by fine vessels, and much used for winter excursions, as well as for freighting. An inexpensive voyage of two or three days conducts the traveller from the snow-bound northern coasts to lands of perennial summer, the lovely semi-tropical Bermudas, the ever-popular Bahamas, the Lesser Antilles, the summer-lands of Cuba, Hayti and Jamaica, and the coasts of Mexico and the Spanish Main.

HENRY W. PEABODY & CO.'S OFFICES, 58 NEW ST.

The Red-Cross Steamships *Miranda* and *Portia* visit Halifax, Nova Scotia, and St. John's, Newfoundland (fare, $34; or $60 for the round trip of twelve days). The route lies through Long-Island Sound, and requires fifty hours from New York to Halifax, and an equal time thence to St. John's.

The Mallory Line's Maine and Maritime Provinces Service is maintained by a steamer sailing from Pier 21, E. R., every Saturday afternoon and reaching Bar Harbor Monday morning, Eastport Monday afternoon, and St. John, New Brunswick, Monday evening. C. H. Mallory & Co., at Pier 20, are the agents.

The Maine Steamship Company sends out its swift new 2,000-ton steamships *Manhattan* and *Cottage City* thrice weekly, at 5 P. M., from Pier 38, E. R. (foot of Market Street). During the same night they traverse Long-Island Sound, and the next morning they stop at Cottage City, Martha's Vineyard. Sailing thence eastward through Vineyard Sound, and past lone Nantucket, and up along sandy Cape Cod, the boat reaches Portland at nightfall, 27 hours from New York.

The Metropolitan Line sends its large and powerful freight-steamships thrice weekly, from Pier 11, N. R., to Boston, by the outside passage around Cape Cod.

The Clyde Steamship Company has lines of steamers running between Boston, New York, Philadelphia, Baltimore, Washington, Norfolk, New Berne, Richmond, Troy, Albany, Wilmington, N. C.; Georgetown, S. C.; Charleston, S. C., and Jacksonville, Fla.; and on the St.-John's River between Jacksonville, Palatka and Sanford and intermediate landings; also between New

VESSEL OF HENRY W. PEABODY & CO.'S AUSTRALASIAN LINE.

York and Turks Island, Haiti and Santo Domingo, and other West-India ports. Their line between New York, Charleston, and Jacksonville, comprises the steamers : *Iroquois, Cherokee, Algonquin, Seminole, Yemessee* and *Delaware*, which sail from the company's wharf, Pier 29, E. R., on Mondays, Wednesdays and Fridays.

The Clyde steamships for the far South pass down the beautiful harbor of New York in the glory of the late afternoon, traversing the Narrows, and rounding the lonely Sandy Hook. In about fifty hours they reach the historic city of Charleston, the pride of South Carolina, passing into the harbor by the famous Fort Sumter and Fort Moultrie. Here the vessel sojourns for about eight hours, giving ample opportunity for an inspection of the city, rising undaunted from the ruins of bombardments and earthquakes. From Charleston a short and pleasant voyage outside of the Sea Islands of Carolina leads down to the low semi-tropical coast of Florida, the land of flowers and oranges. The great steamship enters the St.-John's River, and runs up its broad course for 25 miles, to the city of Jacksonville, from which railway or river routes reach all parts of the State. Clyde's St.-John's River Line runs thence southward up this famous river for 193 miles, by Green Cove Springs, Palatka, Astor, Blue Springs, and many other landings, to Sanford, the terminal point of seven railways, and the main distributing point for South Florida. The general office of the Clyde Line is at 5 Bowling Green ; and its dock is at Pier 29, E. R., at the foot of Roosevelt Street, under the great Brooklyn Bridge. The steamers of the West-India Line leave from Pier 15, E. R., as advertised.

The Clydes have been active in the building and management of steamships for more than half a century.   Thomas Clyde, the founder of the house, was a co-laborer with John Ericsson, as early as 1837, in introducing the screw-propeller.   He built the steamship *John S. McKim,* the first screw-steamer ever constructed in the United States for commercial purposes, and was one of the originators and owners of the first line of propellers — the Ericsson Line, which to-day has a service between

CLYDE'S STEAMSHIP PIER, AT FOOT OF ROOSEVELT STREET, NEW YORK.

Philadelphia and Baltimore.   The *John S. McKim,* by the way, was a twin-screw ship.   This steamer conveyed Col. Jefferson Davis and his regiment of Mississippi troops from New Orleans to one of the Mexican ports during the Mexican War. Strange to say, it was a Clyde steamship, the *Rebecca Clyde,* which brought President Jefferson Davis, of the Confederacy, a prisoner from Savannah to Fort Monroe, in 1865.   In 1871 the Clydes built for their ship *George W. Clyde,* the first compound engine ever set up in this country, and in 1886 built the first large triple-expansion engines in America.   They were placed in their ship *Cherokee.*   In 1888 the Clydes also built the steamer *Iroquois,* the first steel steamship ever built for commercial purposes in this country.

The Old Dominion Steamship Company has a fleet of eight large steamships, the *Seneca,* 3,000 tons, *Guyandotte* and *Roanoke,* 2,354 tons each, the *Old Dominion, Wyanoke, Richmond,* and *City of Columbia.*   Their sailings are from the foot of Beach Street, Pier 26, N. R., New York, at 3 P. M., four times a week to Norfolk, Old Point Comfort and Newport News, Va., in 24 hours (fare, $8, including meals and state-room berth); three times a week to Richmond in 36 hours (fare, $9) ; and thrice a week to West Point, Va.   At Norfolk connection is made with the company's auxiliary steamboat, *New Berne,* running through the sounds.

The Ocean Steamship Company is a favorite route between New York and Georgia, Florida and the Gulf States. Its splendid steamships, *Kansas City, Nacoochee, City of Augusta, City of Birmingham, Chattahoochee* and *Tallahassee* leave New York every Tuesday, Thursday and Saturday, at mid-afternoon, reaching Savannah in from 44 to 55 hours, and connecting there with the Waycross Short Line, the Central Railroad of Georgia, and other routes to the chief points of the Southeastern States. The voyage is full of interest and refreshment, and gives a delightful rest to a tired man or woman, and a marvellous change of climate, from the blue winter ice of the North to the orange-groves and perennial gentleness of the South, or, in summer, from the blazing heats of the Gulf States to the bracing breezes of Yankeeland. The first few hours of the voyage are made charming by the vast and impressive panorama of New-York Bay and the Navesink Highlands, and the last two hours by the ascent of the Savannah River, with its historic fortresses, tropical jungles and ancient rice and cotton plantations. Between these two landward episodes are forty hours on the open sea, with all its mystery, its rest-

OCEAN STEAMSHIP CO. OF SAVANNAH (SAVANNAH LINE), PIERS 34 AND 35, NORTH RIVER, FOOT OF SPRING AND CANAL STREETS.

fulness, and its invigoration. The Ocean Steamship Line also runs steamships between Boston and Philadelphia and Savannah. It has one of the finest covered piers in New York, at the foot of Canal and Spring Streets, with a handsome and capacious building containing its general offices. The steamships were built on the Delaware River, under the inspection of the highest boards of survey, and are of iron and steel, with triple-expansion engines, and divided into water-tight compartments. Among the fleet are the fastest merchant vessels on the American coasts. The state-rooms are larger than those on the transatlantic steamships, and each has two roomy berths, and is lighted by electric lights. The saloons are finished in polished satinwood and white mahogany, with rich upholstery, curtains and carpets to match. There are well-appointed smoking-rooms for the men, on the hurricane-deck.   The promenade-deck is spacious and secure, and affords a capital place for health-giving walks. R. L. Walker is the New-York agent of the Ocean Steamship Company, at New Pier 35, N. R. The business of the Savannah Line is so immense that it is necessary to utilize the adjoining pier.

The St.-Augustine Steamship Company sends the *City of St. Augustine*, a freight-steamer, every three weeks from the foot of Clinton Street to St. Augustine, Florida.

The Cromwell Steamship Company dispatches a steamer every Wednesday and Saturday from Pier 9, N. R., New York, to New Orleans direct. The fleet includes the largest and finest vessels in this coastwise trade, built of iron, exclusively for this route, and first-class in every respect.   The cabin fare is $35 ; and return tickets good for six months cost $60.   This is a six days' voyage, the round trip, with four days at New Orleans, taking sixteen days.

The Morgan Steamship Line of the Southern Pacific Company, dispatches every Tuesday, Thursday and Saturday from New Pier 25, N. R., one of its steamships *El Norte, El Monte, El Sol, El Rio, El Mar, El Sud, El Paso, Excelsior* and *El Dorado*, bound for New Orleans.   They are devoted entirely to freighting, and carry out vast cargoes destined to the Mississippi and Red-River points and to

SOUTHERN PACIFIC CO.'S STEAMSHIP "EL SUD."

Louisiana, Mississippi, Texas, New and Old Mexico, Arizona and the Pacific Coast. The Morgan Line steamers also run regularly from New Orleans weekly to Port Tampa, Punta Gorda, Key West and Havana (for passengers and freight) ; and also to Bluefields, Nicaragua (passengers and freight) ; with frequent freight-boats to Brazos de Santiago, Texas.   The Southern Pacific is also interested in the Occidental and Oriental Steamship Company, running the steamers *Oceanic, Gaelic,* and *Belgic* from San Francisco to Honolulu (7 days), Yokohama (17 days ; fare, $200), and Hong Kong (25 days; fare, $225). At Yokohama they connect with the Nippon Yusen Kaisha steamers for Hiogo, Nagasaki, and Chinese, Corean and Siberian ports; and at Hong Kong with lines for Chinese ports, Formosa, the Philippines, Java, Australia, Calcutta and Bombay. The New-York offices are at 343 Broadway and 1 Battery Place (Washington Building).

The Mallory Steamship Lines (New-York & Texas Steamship Co.) with their own steamships and connections carry freight and passengers to all points in

MALLORY S. S. LINES. NEW-YORK & TEXAS S. S. CO., PIERS 20 AND 21 EAST RIVER.

Texas, Colorado, Arizona, Utah, New Mexico, California, Mexico, Georgia, Florida, Alabama, etc., and the South and Southwest; and also to Eastport and Bar Harbor, Maine, St. John, N. B., and all points in New Brunswick, Nova Scotia, etc. These lines were established in 1866, and are the only lines of freight and passenger-steamships running "from Maine to Texas." There are three distinct routes — the Texas Route, the Georgia-Florida Route, and the Maine and Maritime Provinces Route. The fleet comprises eleven iron steamships, aggregating 30,772 tons. The most modern of these ships are lighted by electricity, steered by steam-power, and equipped with the most approved appliances for safety and comfort. The saloons are on the hurricane deck, and are lighted from large domes above, as well as from wide windows in the sides. The promenade decks are protected by awnings, and afford a pleasant exercising ground. The state-rooms are large and airy, and eligibly situated on the main and hurricane decks. There are also comfortable and attractive smoking-rooms, and many other conveniences for the sea traveller.

The Texas Service is maintained by semi-weekly sailings every Wednesday and Saturday at 3 P. M., from Pier 20, E. R., to Galveston, Texas, which is reached in six or seven days. During the cotton season in Texas the service is tri-weekly

7

Tuesdays, Thursdays and Saturdays. The Saturday boats stop at Key West, Florida, making connection there with the Plant Steamship Line for Havana, which is only ninety miles distant. From Galveston, the chief sea-port of Texas, all parts of the Lone Star State may be visited by railway. There is also a large passenger-travel by the Mallory Line from New York to Galveston, and thence into Colorado and on to the Pacific Coast, or down into Old Mexico.

The Georgia-Florida service is maintained by weekly sailings at 3 P. M. every Friday from Pier 21, E. R., New York, reaching Brunswick, Georgia, in about 62 hours. Brunswick is a fast-growing and very charming city, half buried in live-oak and palmetto groves and Spanish moss, and the coast terminus of the Brunswick & Western Railroad and the East-Tennessee, Virginia & Georgia system. Thence the steamers continue on to Fernandina, on a land-locked harbor inside of Amelia Island, and giving access to all parts of Florida by the Florida Central & Peninsular Railroad. The Mallory steamships lie at Piers 20 and 21, E. R., close to the Fulton Ferry, where also are the offices of C. H. Mallory & Co., the general agents.

The New-York & Cuba Mail Steamship Company (Ward Line) owns the *Niagara*, *Saratoga*, and *City of Washington*, etc., running from Piers 16 and 17, E. R. (foot of Wall Street), New York, every Wednesday. They reach Havana in from four to five days, connecting with steamers for all parts of the West Indies, and for Mexico and the Spanish Main, England, France and Spain. Ward's Wednesday steamers from New York go to Havana and Matanzas.

Ward's Mexican Line, including the *Yumuri, Yucatan, Orizaba, City of Alexandria,* etc., leaves New York every Saturday, and goes on from Havana to Progreso (the port for Merida, in Yucatan), Vera Cruz (263 miles by rail from Mexico), Tuxpam and Tampico, returning by Campeche, Progreso and Havana. The company's steamer *Manteo* runs between Campeche, Laguna and Frontera. The Wards also send fortnightly the steamships *Cienfuegos* and *Santiago* to Nassau, arriving in three days, and thence running through the Bahama Islands, and around to beautiful old Santiago de Cuba, and 325 miles further to bright modern Cienfuegos. This is a favorite excursion-route in winter, and affords various interesting combination and round tours. The single cabin fares are : From New York to Havana, $35 ; to Nassau, $40 ; to Progreso or Vera Cruz, $55 ; to Santiago, Cienfuegos, Tuxpam or Tampico, $60 ; to Campeche, $70 ; to Frontera or Laguna, $75 ; with steerage at about half these rates. The Ward fleet includes several very handsome and commodious vessels, efficiently managed.

The Compania Trasatlantica is a Spanish mail line, sending steamships every ten days from Pier 10, E. R., New York, to Havana, the voyage taking four days. The steamer sailing on the 20th of each month also goes on to Progreso and Vera Cruz, in Mexico ; and the steamer on the 30th goes from Havana to Santiago de Cuba ; La Guayra and Puerto Cabello, in Venezuela ; Sabanilla, Cartagena, and Colon, in Colombia ; and Puerto Limon. At Havana, close connections are made for Spanish ports. The passage-rates (from which 25 per cent. is discounted for excursion-tickets) are : From New York to Havana, first-cabin, $37, second-cabin, $25, steerage, $17 ; to Progreso, $55, $35 and $20 ; Vera Cruz, $60, $40 and $25 ; to Santiago de Cuba, $65, $45 and $30 ; to La Guayra, $80, $60 and $45 ; to Cartagena, $93, $72 and $54 ; to Cadiz, Spain, $190, $145 and $50.

The Quebec Steamship Company has weekly sailings from January to June, and fortnightly the rest of the year, between New York and Bermuda, the fine 2,500-ton iron steamship *Trinidad*, making the voyage in about 50 hours. The fares are $30 for the first cabin, and $20 for the second cabin. The dock is at

FORT WADSWORTH, THE SCHOOL SHIP AND WAR-VESSELS.
VIEWS TAKEN IN NORTH RIVER AND NEW-YORK HARBOR.   PHOTOS BY JOHNSTON.

New Pier 47, N. R., at the foot of West 10th Street. The Quebec Line also sends steamers every ten days from New York to St. Croix, St. Kitts, Antigua, Montserrat, Guadaloupe, Dominica, Martinique, St. Lucia and Barbadoes, at fares varying at from $50 to $60. These vessels connect in the Windward Islands with steamships for the other West Indies, and for England and France. The Bermuda Line is much patronized in spring and fall by persons in search of health or respite from bad weather, who find delight in the serene climate of these beautiful coral islands, abounding in flowers and fruits, and one of the impregnable and strongly garrisoned naval stations of the British Empire.

The Atlas Steamship Company owns a favorite line of steamers sailing to the West Indies from Pier 55, N. R., carrying the United-States mails, and offering great inducements to passengers visiting the many interesting ports in the West Indies. Chief among the health-resorts is the British island of Jamaica, renowned for its luxuriant foliage and unequalled facilities for the tourist in the shape of magnificent roads, with good hotels and liveries in every town. The company also has a coastal service sailing regularly around the island, and a trip in one of these steamers, visiting all the ports, cannot be equalled as a yachting voyage in these summer seas. For invalids desiring a winter-resort where they can

ATLAS MAIL LINE TO THE WEST INDIES, PIER 55, NORTH RIVER.

obtain abundant sunlight and an equable temperature, Jamaica offers what cannot be obtained in any other island near the United States. The many mineral springs are wonderful in their cures of neuralgia, gout, rheumatism, etc., and buildings have been erected for the use of invalids visiting the springs. The coffee, tobacco, sugar and banana plantations are well worth a visit, and the fact that many are conducted by American capital renders them doubly attractive. Making Jamaica his headquarters, the tourist can at regular dates embark on the Atlas steamers, and visit Hayti, Costa Rica, and the Spanish Main, whose old towns (bearing the marks and carrying the reminiscences of their Spanish rulers and privateering captains) are full of interest. The spacious and luxurious passenger accommodations offered on these steamers are worthy of note. The saloons and state-rooms are above the main deck, which insures the minimum of motion, perfect ventilation, and freedom from unpleasant smells from holds or engines. The state-rooms are large, well lighted and comfortably furnished ; each room having two berths and a sofa, and electric lights. The company since its formation, twenty years ago, has never lost a life by shipwreck — and being its own insurer offers the best guarantee that every precaution is taken for safe navigation. The company's fleet includes the steam-ships *Adirondack, Alene, Athos, Alvo, Ailsa, Andes, Alps, Alvena, Claribel, Adula* and *Arden.* These steamers, of from 2,200 to 2,500 tons each, were built on the Clyde and at Belfast, and fill the necessary requirements of the British and American Passenger Acts. The agents of the Atlas Line are Pim, Forwood & Co., at 24 State Street, New York.

The **New-York & Porto-Rico Line** sails from the Atlantic Dock, Brooklyn, every fortnight, for the famous Spanish island of sugar, coffee, and cotton.

The **Trinidad Line** has its pier at the Union Stores, Brooklyn, and brings from the far-away British island, under the Venezuelan Andes, large cargoes of tropical products. Its steamboats sail every ten days, carrying cabin passengers.

The **Central-American Company** sends its steamships *Jason* and *Argonaut* from Atlantic Dock, Brooklyn, fortnightly, to Kingston (Jamaica), Greytown (Nicaragua), Belize, Livingston, Truxillo, and other tropical ports.

The **Pacific Mail Steamships** sail from the foot of Canal Street, Pier 34, N. R., every ten days, for Colon, connecting there with the Panama Railway for the Pacific Coast. The distance by this route from New York to San Francisco is 5,220 miles ; and the fare is $90, or $40 for forward-cabin passengers. The time is about 25 days. The steamships are the *Columbia, City of Para, Newport* and *Colon.*

The **Red "D" Line**, at Harbeck Stores, sends out the large American-built iron steamships *Venezuela, Caracas*, and *Philadelphia* every ten days to the chief ports of Venezuela. The fare is $80 ; or $50 for second-class. The steamships are of 2,500 tons burden or more ; and have water-tight compartments, electric lights and bells, large smoking-rooms and social halls, and other comforts. The route leads from New York through the Mona Passage, between San Domingo and Porto Rico ; and at six days out reaches the quaint Dutch island-colony of Curaçoa, 1,763 miles from Sandy Hook. Thence a night's run of 111 miles leads to Puerto Cabello, a busy coffee-port, thirty miles by railway from beautiful Valencia. Another night voyage of seventy miles takes one to La Guayra, celebrated in Kingsley's *Westward Ho*, and twenty-seven miles by an Andes-climbing railway from Caracas, the mountain-girt capital of Venezuela. The smaller Red " D " steamer *Merida* runs regularly over the 214 miles from Curaçoa to Maracaibo, a city of 35,000 Venezuelans, exporting hides, coffee and cocoa, and standing near a great inland sea.

The Red "D" steamers are very comfortable, and well-appointed for travellers ; and they run through seas of remarkable historic interest and picturesque beauty. The legends and traditions of the Spanish Main are of wonderful charm, and when they are studied in connection with the rich tropical scenery of these regions, they acquire a new value.

The general managers of the Red "D" Line are Boulton, Bliss & Dallett, at 135 Front Street, New York, where passages may be obtained, and state-rooms selected.

The **Clyde West-India Line** sends steamships to Turks Island, Hayti, Puerto Plata, Samana, Sanchez and San-Domingo City.

The **Royal Dutch West-Indian Mail Line** (Koninklijke West-Indische Maildienst) has the *Prins Willem I.* and five other steamships, leaving New York every three weeks, and running to Port au Prince, $60; Aux Cayes, Jacmel, and Curaçoa, $75; Puerto Cabello, La Guayra, Cumaná, and Carúpano, $80; Trinidad and Demerara, $90; and Paramaribo, $100. From the last port the ships cross the Atlantic to Havre, France, and Amsterdam, Holland.

The **Sloman Line** runs freight-boats between New York and the Brazilian ports.

Norton's Freighting Vessels sail to the ports of the River Plate.

Busk & Jevons send occasional vessels down the South-American coast.

The **Booth Line** sends a monthly steamship to Para and Manaos (on the Amazon River), and another to Para, Maranham and Ceara, with passenger accommodation at from $75 to $125.

The **Bays, Rivers and Sounds** for more than a hundred miles about New York are traversed by great fleets of passenger-steamers, varying in size from the tiny craft which visit the nearer islands to the immense and magnificent vessels which traverse Long-Island Sound and the Hudson River. No other port in the world has such noble boats as these last mentioned, which, with their superb halls, grand staircases, and spacious dining-rooms, resemble floating hotels of the first-class. In summer an immense passenger and excursion business is done by the suburban steamboats, especially by those running to Coney Island and Rockaway Beach, to Sandy Hook and the coast toward Long Branch, and to the Fishing Banks outside.

The **Fall-River Line** has its headquarters at the foot of Murray Street, whence in the pleasant season it dispatches at late afternoon two of the vessels of its fleet, the *Puritan, Pilgrim, Plymouth,* or *Providence.* They arrive early the next morning at the Massachusetts port and cotton-manufacturing city of Fall River, whence connecting trains run to Boston in eighty minutes. These are undoubtedly the largest, most magnificent, and most perfectly-equipped vessels in the world, used for interior navigation. They are lighted by electricity, steered by steam, enlivened by orchestral music, and provided with meals *a la carte.* In spring, autumn and winter the Fall-River line sends out but one boat daily.

The **Providence Line** steamboats leave from Pier 29, N. R., at late afternoon daily (except Sunday), from May to November, and traverse the entire length of the East River, Long-Island Sound, and Narragansett Bay, arriving at six o'clock the next morning at Providence, Rhode Island. Parlor-car trains connecting run to Boston, 42 miles, in 75 minutes; and to Worcester. The *Connecticut* and *Massachusetts* are beautiful vessels, decorated in white and gold, with dining-rooms on the main decks, and fine orchestras.

The **Norwich Line** steamships *City of Worcester* and *City of Boston* leave Pier 40, N. R., New York, at 5 o'clock, P. M., and run eastward up the Sound to New London, where passengers take the trains at early morning for Boston, Worcester and other New-England cities. This is a very commodious route, served by large and handsome first-class steamboats, and giving easy access to Yankee-land.

The **Stonington Line** sends a fine steamboat at 5.30 o'clock every afternoon from New Pier 36, N. R., up Long-Island Sound to the quaint little Connecticut port of Stonington, where it connects with swift trains to Boston and other New-England cities. This route is served by the new steel steamers *Maine* and *New Hampshire* and other fine boats; and is especially desirable in winter, or when rough sea-winds make the longer Sound routes uncomfortable.

Other Eastern Lines are those to Saybrook and Hartford, daily, ascending the picturesque Connecticut River; to Bridgeport, the busy manufacturing city on the Connecticut shore; to New Haven, the seat of Yale University; to Stamford, South Norwalk, New Rochelle and Port Chester; and to the towns on the north shore of Long Island, like Sea Cliff and Sands Point, Roslyn and Glen Cove, Sag Harbor and Shelter Island, Southold and Whitestone.

The Hudson-River Day-Line Steamers traverse the most beautiful and interesting river-scenery in the world. Not the Rhine, the Danube, or the Rhone can

claim superiority to this glorious stream of the New World, with its cliffs and mountain-guards, its legends of centuries, and its thronging poetic, literary and artistic enrichment, made

HUDSON-RIVER STEAMER "NEW YORK."

still more famous in the Columbian year of 1893 by having peacefully floated the greatest aggregated naval power ever brought together at any one

HUDSON RIVER STEAMER "ALBANY."
HUDSON-RIVER DAY LINE STEAMERS, "NEW YORK" AND "ALBANY," DESBROSSES-STREET PIER, N. R.

point in the history of the world. During the pleasant season the great iron steamboats *Albany* and *New York* leave Desbrosses-Street Pier and 22d Street Pier, N. R., every day (except Sunday) at early morning, and reach Albany at about 6 P. M. They are of about 1,500 tons each, built at Wilmington, Delaware, with over 3,000 horse-power, and a speed of nearly 25 miles an hour. Since these boats are for tourists only, they carry no freight, and are therefore far more comfortable, with broad open spaces, dining-rooms on the main decks, private parlors with bay-windows, and immense grand saloons on the promenade-deck, with almost continuous windows. They are finished in hard-wood, furnished with mahogany, carpeted with Axminster, and decorated with choice paintings by Cropsey, Satterlee, Bierstadt and other masters. These are in every respect the finest vessels of their class afloat. The boat touches first at the attractive suburban city of Yonkers. About noon it reaches West Point, amid the magnificent Highlands of the Hudson, where Grant and Sherman, Sheridan and Lee, learned the art of war, and where Scott, Custer and Kilpatrick are buried. A little later, and Newburgh is reached, with its great Washington triumphal arch towering on the hill. Next comes Poughkeepsie, with its famous bridge far overhead. The Catskill Mountains loom grandly in the west, as the steamer goes on, passing innumerable other vessels, of all degrees, and viewing along the shore scores of quaint old villages and historic country-seats. It is a voyage in Paradise ; and the huge iron steamer itself, being used only as a pleasure-boat, has the lightness, grace and beauty of a royal yacht. A trip on these Hudson-River Day-Line steamers, on a pleasant day, is a joy never to be forgotten afterwards. The general offices are at the Desbrosses-Street Pier, in New-York City.

The Homer Ramsdell Transportation Company's magnificent iron steamers, running between New York and Newburgh, leave New York on week

RAMSDELL LINE TO NEWBURGH : HOMER RAMSDELL TRANSPORTATION CO., FOOT OF FRANKLIN ST., NORTH RIVER.

days at 5 P. M. and on Sundays at 9 A. M., and leave Newburgh every evening in the week at 7 P. M. They stop both ways at Fishkill, Cornwall, Cold Spring, West Point and Cranston's, and on the down trip also at 129th Street. The trip covers the grandest part of the Hudson River. The fare is fifty cents. Besides furnishing the usual accommodations for passengers and freight, special accommodations are provided for horses and perishable freight.

This company is the successor of the firm of J. & T. Powell, who established a line of sloops in 1802. The freighting business was continued by means of sailing vessels until about 1830, when steamboats were first employed. In 1835 Thomas Powell built the steamer *Highlander*, and she was run on the route until 1848, when the barge *Newburgh*, built by Powell, Ramsdell & Co., replaced her ; ·in 1851 the barge *Susquehanna* was built, and ran in connection with the *Newburgh;* and in 1870 the barge *Charles Spear* was purchased, and with the *Susquehanna* and *Minisink* formed a daily line, each of the boats making two trips a week.

Powell, Ramsdell & Co. were succeeded by Homer Ramsdell & Co. in 1865, and the business was carried on under that name until 1880, when Mr. Ramsdell and his sons (the grandsons of Thomas Powell) formed the present company. In 1886-7 a return was made to the use of steam in the forwarding business, and the barges were replaced by the handsome steel propellers *Newburgh* and *Homer Ramsdell*, which afford to the public express freight accommodations unsurpassed by any other water or railroad line in the country.

The distance between New York and Newburgh is sixty miles, and the wonderful expanse of the Hudson River between the two cities include some of the finest scenery in the world, the tremendous rocky walls of the Palisades, the broad expanses of the Tappan Zee, the legend-crowned villages of Tarrytown and . Peekskill, the busy scenes around Haverstraw and Nyack, the palaces of the millionaires about Yonkers and Dobbs Ferry, the magnificent gateway of the Highlands, the State National Guard's camp-ground at Peekskill, the gray old United-States Military Academy at West Point, the far-viewing summer-hotels of Cornwall, and then the venerable and beautiful city of Newburgh, the home-port of the Ramsdell boats. Nearly two centuries ago a band of Lutheran exiles from the devastated Palatinate of the Rhine settled here, under the patronage of Queen Anne ; and since that far-past day the present great, flourishing and enterprising city has grown up on these pleasant hills. The New-York pier of the Homer Ramsdell Transportation Co. is at the foot of Franklin Street, North River.

Other Hudson-River Lines lead to Yonkers, Tivoli, Nyack, Peekskill, Fishkill, Fort Lee, Sing Sing, Tarrytown, etc.

New-Jersey Ports are reached by a fleet of white steamers ploughing the

CENTRAL PARK.   THE NEW NETHERLAND.   THE SAVOY.   THE PLAZA.   THE DALHOUSIE.
58TH STREET, LOOKING EAST FROM SIXTH AVENUE.

waves daily to Elizabethport and Keyport, New Brunswick and Bergen Point, Sandy Hook and Red Bank, South Amboy, Perth Amboy, Atlantic Highlands, etc.

The Ferry Boat, as now in use around New York, was designed by Fulton and Stevens, and is remarkably well adapted to its uses, especially with regard to the terminal floating bridges and the spring piles along the slips. The first ferry was established in 1642, by Cornelius Dircksen, from near Peck Slip to Fulton Street, Brooklyn; and for nearly two centuries the transits were made in barges, row-boats or pirogues. From 1814 to 1824 horse-boats were used, being propelled by horses working a wheel by means of a treadmill between twin-boats; and these in turn were succeeded by steam ferry-boats. Scores of these vessels now traverse the waters around the city, carrying the suburbans to and from their work, and are well crowded morning and evening. They are swift, staunch and powerful craft, much more serviceable than they appear; and they make quick and frequent passages, when the fogs and floating ice of winter do not hinder. There are dozens of these routes to Brooklyn and Long-Island City, Jersey City and Hoboken and many other localities, the fare being from one cent upward. On account of their light draft, good speed and great strength, armed New-York ferry-boats were found useful as gun-boats on the Southern rivers, during the civil war; and Capt. Zalinski thinks that they would be valuable adjuncts in the naval defence of the Empire City when armed with pneumatic dynamite guns. Staten Island is reached by large ferryboats running in twenty-five minutes from the Battery to St. George.

FULTON FERRY, FOOT OF FULTON STREET, EAST RIVER.

The waters about New York are traversed by about 400 tow-boats or tugs, equipped with very powerful engines, and competent to pull the heaviest ships, or strings of laden canal-boats. Most of them are below 100 tons each; but the Pennsylvania Railroad twin-screw tugs *Amboy* and *Raritan*, the ocean-tug *Luckenback*, and the mighty drawers of canal-boats — the *Vanderbilt* and the *Oswego* — reach above 250 tons each. Some of these tow-boats have engines of 900 horse-power.

Yachts and Yachting, with an endless number of yachting and boat-clubs, are conspicuous features hereabouts. Nowhere else in the world are there such fleets of white-winged racing boats, flying like huge birds over the harbor and rivers, and swooping away in great bevies up the Sound eastward to Newport. The regattas and cruises of the many local yacht-clubs are events of the liveliest interest, and eager tens of thousands follow them far out to sea, beyond the Scotland Lightship. The patriarch of all these noble maritime amusements is the New-York Yacht Club, the oldest in the United State (founded in 1844), which has in its fleet 200 boats. Many steam-yachts also cruise about Manhattan, varying in magnitude from the puffy little naphtha-launch up to the superb sea-going private steamships of the Vanderbilts, Bennetts, and other rich families.

EAST RIVER --- THE BROOKLYN BRIDGE --- SOUTH STREET.

JEANETTE PARK, COENTIES SLIP, EAST RIVER, LOOKING TOWARD BROOKLYN, SHOWING THE CANAL-BOAT FLEET.

BIRD'S-EYE VIEW FROM WASHINGTON BUILDING, LOOKING SOUTHWEST.

BIRD'S-EYE VIEW FROM WASHINGTON BUILDING LOOKING SOUTHEAST.

Transportation and Transit.

Railroads—Steam, Elevated, Cable, Horse and Electric—
Stages, Subterranean Transit, Etc.

THE need of opening communication between New York and the West was recognized as early as the days of Queen Anne, when the first attempt was made in this direction. The Colony appropriated £500 to certain men to open a route from the Hudson River westward, the first section being from Nyack to Sterling Iron-works, over which a road was ordered wide enough for two carriages, with the overhanging boughs of the trees cut away. In 1673 Col. Francis Lovelace, the second British Governor of New York, established a mail-route between New York and Boston. This primitive establishment consisted of a single messenger, who, for the "more speedy intelligence and dispatch of affairs," was ordered to make one round trip each month, with letters and packages. The Puritan town to the eastward having thus been accommodated, in 1729 certain enterprising spirits established a fortnightly line of stages to Philadelphia, the Quaker town to the southward. In the same year (so sure was the march of progress), proposals were issued for a foot post to Albany. In 1793 the running time of the "small, genteel, and easy stage carriages" between New York and Boston was between three and four days, and three trips were made weekly each way. The fare was four-pence a mile.

The subject of intercommunication between the little fringe of settlements along the Atlantic Coast and the great Mississippi-Ohio Valley was one of the most cherished projects of George Washington. As a Provincial military officer, or member of the Virginian House of Delegates, or commander-in-chief of the American armies, or President of the United States, he always kept this theme in view, and in person crossed the Virginian mountains, and examined the valleys of the Potomac and the Mohawk, to find the best route for a canal. He regarded the West ("the flank and rear of the Union," as he called it) as likely to be lured away from the Republic by Great Britain, on the north, or by Spain, on the south. As he remarked : "The Western States hang upon a pivot. The touch of a feather would turn them any way." The crops of the West could not be moved to market, so great was the expense of transportation. To carry a ton of wheat from Buffalo to New York cost $100, where it now costs $1.50. Great arks floated down the Delaware, Susquehanna and Ohio Rivers, laden with produce ; but the voyage was very long, and the returns were uncertain. The first attempt to relieve this blockade was made by building canals, beginning with the one opened in 1802 from the lower Mohawk to Oneida Lake and Lake Ontario. The completion of the Erie Canal, in 1825, revolutionized the commerce of America, and gave New-York City the place of commercial metropolis of the continent. Pennsylvania, Maryland and Virginia attempted to win the West by similar constructions, but their canals reached only to the foot of the Alleghany Mountains. Ohio, Indiana and Illinois built canals connecting the Ohio and Mississippi Rivers with the Great Lakes, at Cleveland, Toledo and Chicago; and by the year 1840, 8,500 miles of canal were in operation.

But a new unifying and civilizing agency was about to enter the world's service. In 1826 the Stockton & Darlington Railway, in England, showed the feasibility of moving trains by steam-power. In 1827 a tramway of three miles was built near Quincy, in Massachusetts, to transport granite from the quarries to tide-water. New York had cut off the Western trade of the other Atlantic ports, by its Erie Canal; and Baltimore hastened to avail itself of the newly discovered mechanism of the rail-

NEW-YORK CENTRAL & HUDSON-RIVER RAILROAD TRACKS ABOVE 98TH STREET.

way, to offset the canal. Accordingly, the Baltimore & Ohio Railroad was chartered in 1827, and began grading in 1828. The first locomotive used in America was the *Stourbridge Lion*, imported from England, and started on the Carbondale & Honesdale Railroad, in 1829. It was too heavy for the unsubstantial rails then in use, and had to be given up. The second locomotive to run in America was called *The Best Friend of Charleston*, and was built at the West-Point Foundry Works, on the Hudson, in 1830. It belonged to the South-Carolina Railroad, which for some years was the longest continuous line in the world. Another locomotive from the same works was placed on the Mohawk & Hudson Railroad, in 1831. In the meantime, the Baltimore & Ohio line had been using horses to draw the trains between Baltimore and Frederick; and had made elaborate experiments to see if the cars could not be propelled by sails.

With all the Atlantic States reaching inland by lines of iron rails, New York also advanced in the same direction, and the result appears in a remarkable system of railways, excelled by none in the world outside.

The New-York Central & Hudson-River Railroad is the only route which runs from New-York harbor to the Great Lakes over the territory of a single State. Its main line, from New York to Buffalo, 441¾ miles, is one of the most perfectly appointed and equipped railways in the world, and for the greater part of its course

GRAND CENTRAL RAILROAD STATION, 42D STREET AND VANDERBILT AVENUE.

NEW-YORK CENTRAL & HUDSON-RIVER RAILROAD: NEW-YORK & HARLEM RAILROAD: NEW-YORK, NEW-HAVEN & HARTFORD RAILROAD.

RIVERDALE STATION, N. Y. C. & H. R. R. R.

has four parallel tracks, of which two are reserved for passenger trains exclusively. The company controls nearly 5,000 miles of steel-rail track, and has 1,169 locomotives, 1,300 passenger cars, 40,500 freight and other cars, and 136 steamboats and other craft. The sum of $17,000,000 is paid yearly to the 27,000 employees of the company, being more than half of the working expenses of the road. The cost of the road and equipment has exceeded $165,000,000, which is mainly represented by capital stock of $100,000,000, and a funded debt of $65,000,000. In a single year the New-York Central company has carried more than 20,000,000 tons of freight, equalling the movement of nearly 4,000,000,000 tons for one mile; and 22,000,000 passengers. The Grand Central Station on 42d Street, enormous, well-placed and commodious, covers 257,312 square feet, and contains 19 tracks, and the general offices of several railways. Daily 50,000 persons arrive at or depart from this

MOTT-HAVEN STATION, 138TH STREET, NEW-YORK CENTRAL & HUDSON-RIVER RAILROAD.

station, on 245 trains, of 800 cars. The stations at Mott Haven, at Riverdale, and elsewhere are very commodious and highly available. The Central trains (and also those of the routes to New England) traverse Manhattan Island, from the Grand Central Station to the Harlem River, by a series of sunken tracks and viaducts whose construction cost many millions of dollars. Then they follow for over 100 miles the eastern shore of the Hudson River, "the Rhine of America," crossing the inflowing streams on massive bridges, and passing the mountain-promontories by rock tunnels

or broad artificial terraces. Scores of famous villages and cities and historic localities are passed ; and along the route the magnificent panorama of the Hudson River
and its enwalling mountains and fruitful plains is unrolled before the delighted vision.
Here is the dark·line of the Palisades, frowning across the placid Tappan Zee ; the
classic region where the names of Major André, Benedict Arnold, Mad Anthony
Wayne, Hendrick Hudson, Captain Kidd and George Washington are oddly combined with those of the Livingstons and Philipses, with the valorous trumpeter
Anthony Van Corlaer and Jan Peek, and Rambout Van Dam ; the noble Highlands
of the Hudson, the Dunderberg and Anthony's Nose, Storm King and Cro' Nest ;
the historic batteries of West Point, where the art of war was studied for years by
Grant and Sherman, Sheridan and McClellan, Lee and Longstreet ; Newburgh, with
its triumphal arch and Washington's headquarters ; Poughkeepsie, the seat of Vassar
College ; and noble views of the Catskill Mountains, the home of Rip Van Winkle.
At Albany the New-York Central line turns up the great natural highway which
the Mohawk River cut through the Alleghany Mountains ; and for nearly 300 miles

"EMPIRE-STATE EXPRESS," NEW-YORK CENTRAL & HUDSON-RIVER RAILROAD.
FASTEST LONG-DISTANCE TRAIN IN THE WORLD.   PHOTO. BY A. P. YATES, OF SYRACUSE, N. Y.

traverses the grandest railway route in the world, with its continuous four tracks,
side by side. On this rosary-chain are strung numerous important cities, like Schenectady and Amsterdam, Utica and Rome, Syracuse and Rochester, closing at thronged
and busy Buffalo, "The Queen City of the Lakes." On the great highway of nature
between New York and Buffalo, some of the most remarkable of railway runs have
been made, crowning the world's record for long-distance rapid transit. September
14, 1891, a train traversed the stretch of 436 miles between New York and East Buffalo
in 425¾ minutes, making on some sections a speed of 78 miles an hour. As a result
of this experimental trip, the New-York Central established its Empire-State
Express, which daily makes the run between New York and Buffalo in 8 hours and
40 minutes, an average of over 52 miles an hour. This is the fastest long-distance
train in the world.

8

At Buffalo the through trains of the New-York Central pass on to the rails of the lines for the farther West, the Lake-Shore, or the Michigan Central. Some of the finest trains in the world serve this magnificent route to the West, with Wagner drawing-room cars, buffet, smoking, dining, café and library cars, and standard,

MORRISANIA STATION, NEW-YORK CENTRAL & HUDSON-RIVER RAILROAD.

buffet and private-compartment sleeping-cars. The New-York and Chicago Limited, the Southwestern Limited, the North-Shore Limited, and the Chicago, St. Louis and Cincinnati Express-trains are marvels of comfort and luxury.

The old terminal station of the Hudson-River Railroad, at 30th Street and Tenth Avenue, New York, is mainly used as a freight depot, although passenger trains for all stations on the western side of Manhattan Island, up to Spuyten Duyvil, are still despatched thence.

The northern connections of the Central lines are made mainly at Albany, Troy, Herkimer and Utica, and reach Saratoga and the Adirondacks, both shores of Lake Champlain, Montreal and Ottawa, the Green Mountains of Vermont, and the Thousand Islands of the St. Lawrence. Myriads of metropolitans every year seek these scenes of vernal beauty for their season of summer rest.

The history of the New-York Central Railroad dates back to the earliest days of the railroad in America. Its first link was the Mohawk & Hudson, chartered in 1826, and completed in 1831, and afterward re-named the Albany & Schenectady. This was the first railroad in New-York State, and for a long time stationary engines were used on parts of its line. Another route westward from the Hudson, the Schenectady & Troy, received its charter in 1836, and began operations in 1842. Meanwhile, the Utica & Schenectady had been opened in 1836, and the Syracuse & Utica in 1839; the Auburn & Syracuse in 1838, and the Auburn & Rochester in 1841 ; the Lockport & Niagara-Falls in 1838, and the Attica & Batavia and Tonawanda lines (afterward united as the Buffalo & Rochester) in 1842. All these and other roads were consolidated under the special law of 1853 into the New-York Central Railroad Company, giving a through route between Albany and Buffalo.

Several other connecting lines were subsequently leased, and then merged into the New-York Central system. The Hudson-River Railroad was chartered in 1846, and opened from New York to East Albany in 1851. In 1869 occurred the consolidation which made up the New-York Central & Hudson-River Railroad.

The New-York & Harlem Railway, operated by the New-York Central, was chartered in 1831. It reached 14th Street in 1832; 32d Street in 1833; Yorkville in 1834; Harlem in 1837; Williamsbridge in 1842; White Plains in 1844; Dover Plains in 1848; and Chatham Four Corners in 1852. The line cost $23,-500,000 to build and equip, and is 127 miles long, from New York to Chatham, where it connects with the Boston & Albany Railroad. It was leased in 1873 for 401 years to the New-York Central Company, which pays eight per cent. on the capital stock, and interest on the funded debt. This picturesque route to the north follows the Bronx, Neperhan and Croton Valleys for many miles, through the pleasant farming lands of Westchester, Putnam and Dutchess Counties, and near the

SWITCH TOWER CONTROLLING ALL TRAINS ENTERING THE GRAND CENTRAL DEPOT.

Taconic Mountains. Among the charming summer-resorts near the line are Lake Mahopac and the Berkshire Hills, and farther connections lead to the finest scenery of the Green Mountains.

The West-Shore Railroad was organized in 1880, and the following year became possessed of the Jersey-City & Albany line, from Weehawken to Fort Montgomery. The first through-train between Weehawken and Buffalo was run in 1884, but the road passed into the hands of a receiver during the same year, and in 1885 was sold to a new company, which leased it to the New-York Central & Hudson-River Railroad for 475 years. The West-Shore route thus became an important and interesting division of the Central system. It follows the western bank of the Hudson River nearly to Albany, and thence crosses the rich midland counties to Buffalo on a route nearly parallel with that of the New-York Central line. The West-Shore trains may be reached at the Pennsylvania depot in Jersey City, or at Weehawken (by ferry from Jay Street or West 42d Street).

The Rome, Watertown & Ogdensburg Railroad Co. was organized in 1860 by the amalgamation of the Watertown & Rome Railroad Co. and the Potsdam & Watertown Railroad Co., and has since acquired by consolidation numerous small lines in the northern part of the State, and also, on April 14, 1886, the Utica & Black-River Railroad, which, up to that time, was its chief competitor. The Rome, Watertown & Ogdensburg Railroad and its leased lines were leased in perpetuity to the New-York Central & Hudson-River Company March 14, 1891. The New-York Central, appreciating the value of this new acquisition, and its capabilities of becoming the largest and most important tourist traffic route in America, proceeded at once, with its usual enterprise, to raise to Trunk-Line standard that portion of the newly acquired property patronized by summer-travel. This has been accomplished by hard work and the outlay of a very large sum of money,— nearly $1,000,-000,— in permanent improvements, and relaying the road with heavy steel rails, renewing and reballasting the road-bed, replacing wooden bridges with strong new ones of stone and iron, etc., all of which enables the company to inaugurate a new era in Northern New-York passenger service. The improvement of the equipment and service has kept pace with the road-bed. Standard locomotives, capable of hauling the heaviest passenger trains at high speed, have been added to the motive power. In carrying out the policy of developing summer-travel, by offering every facility, the New-York Central & Hudson-River Railroad has placed in service new fast trains, through from New York and from Buffalo to points on the Rome, Watertown & Ogdensburg Railroad, equipped with new coaches, new Wagner sleeping and drawing-room cars, and buffet smoking and library cars.

The Dunkirk, Allegheny-Valley & Pittsburgh Railroad, from Dunkirk to Titusville, was recently leased by the New-York Central & Hudson-River Railroad.

The Pennsylvania Railroad was incorporated in 1846, and chartered in 1847, to build a line from the Harrisburg and Lancaster route to Pittsburgh or Erie. The State system of transportation, built between 1828 and 1834, at a cost exceeding $14,000,000, consisted of a railway from Philadelphia to Columbia, 82 miles; a canal thence to Hollidaysburg, 172 miles; the Portage Railway, across the Alleghany Mountains to Johnstown, 36 miles; and the railway thence to Pittsburgh, 104 miles. This route resulted in great benefit to the sections through which it passed, but it was a slow, costly and complicated system, and proved unremunerative to the State. For years the route between Philadelphia and Columbia was served only by horse-cars, making the transit in nine hours, with relays every twelve miles. The superior facilities offered by New York and Baltimore threatened to leave Pennsylvania out of the race, as a competitor for Western trade, and therefore local patriotism was highly stimulated to construct a new and first-class route across the State. The project was advocated by the press and in public meetings; and committees went from house to house asking subscriptions to stock. With the funds thus raised, and under the wise direction of Chief Engineer J. Edgar Thompson, the Pennsylvania

PENNSYLVANIA RAILROAD, JERSEY-CITY STATION.
FERRIES TO DESBROSSES STREET AND TO CORTLANDT STREET, NEW YORK.

Railroad began its construction works in 1847, between Harrisburg and Lewistown ; and in 1854 the entire route, from Philadelphia to Pittsburgh, went into operation. In 1861, after a contest of six years, the company bought the State lines, for $13,570,000. Mr. Thompson held the presidency of the company from 1852 until his death, in 1874, when he was succeeded by Col. Thomas A. Scott, who had been for twenty-four years connected with the company, and had been vice-president since 1860. After constructing its magnificent trunk line across the Keystone State, the company prolonged its routes farther westward by securing control of several lines to the great trade-centres of the West ; gained an admirable entrance to New York by acquiring the United New-Jersey lines ; found an outlet at Baltimore by getting control of the Northern Central Railroad ; completed and opened the Baltimore & Potomac line, to Washington ; and came into possession of numerous minor routes.

The New-Jersey part of the Pennsylvania system includes the plant of the United New-Jersey Railroad and Canal Companies, leased in 1871, for 999 years,

PENNSYLVANIA RAILROAD DEPOT, JERSEY CITY, INTERIOR OF TRAIN-HOUSE.

at a deservedly high rental. This confederacy was formed in 1831, by the practical unification of two companies chartered a year before — the Delaware & Raritan Canal and the Camden & Amboy Railroad, both of which were finished in 1834. Two years later the United Companies got control of the Philadelphia & Trenton line (opened in 1834), and in 1867 they consolidated interests with the line of the New-Jersey Railroad & Transportation Company from New Brunswick to Jersey City. The section from Jersey City to Newark was opened in 1834, and for some years was used only by horse-cars. In 1836 it reached Rahway ; and in 1839 its trains arrived at Philadelphia.

The new passenger station at Jersey City is larger than the Grand Central Depot in New York, and has a length of 653½ feet, with a width of 256 feet, and a height of 112 feet. It is reached from New York by the steam ferry-boats of the com-

PENNSYLVANIA RAILROAD : FREIGHT DEPOT, WEST STREET.

pany, running from Cortlandt Street and Desbrosses Street. The Pennsylvania Railroad has already bridged West Street at their Cortlandt-Street ferry, and is rapidly putting into service a fleet of double-deck ferry-boats, so that eventually passengers will be able to pass from Cortlandt or Desbrosses Streets to the upper decks of the ferry-boats, above the confusion of West Street, and thence on the same level to their trains in the Jersey-City station.

The Southern Pacific Company, one of the greatest transportation systems in the world, has spacious offices in New-York City, whence sails its important

MOTT-HAVEN CANAL.

Morgan Line of steamships for New Orleans. This efficient link by sea unites New York with the eastern end of the Southern Pacific Railway system, at New Orleans, for purposes of freighting goods. Passengers from New York may go to New Orleans by the New-York Central or Erie, the Pennsylvania or Baltimore & Ohio, the Piedmont Air Line or Chesapeake & Ohio, or the Atlantic Coast Line ; or by the Cromwell steamships every Saturday from New York to New Orleans. At New Orleans, the quaint old French capital of the Gulf States, begins the renowned Sunset Route, through the lowlands of Louisiana, across the richest and most populous sections of imperial Texas, up the weird Rio-Grande valley, across the New-Mexican Sierra Madre, and over the mysterious tropical plateaus of Arizona

SOUTHERN PACIFIC COMPANY -- " MORGAN LINE," -- PIER 25, NORTH RIVER.

and Southern California. Northward, along the coast, the line runs by San Francisco, past the wonderful scenery of the Mount-Shasta Alps, to Portland, on the mighty Columbia River ; and its rails run eastward across the Sierra Nevada to Ogden, on the Great Salt Lake of Utah. At San Francisco the line connects with the sea-route, which penetrate still deeper into the sunset, the Occidental and Oriental and the Oceanic lines for Hawaii and Japan, New Zealand and Australia, China and India. Many travellers also visit Mexico by the Sunset Route, crossing the Rio Grande at Eagle Pass, or at Laredo or El Paso.

The Southern Pacific Line enjoys peculiar advantages from its connection with such amazingly rich States as Texas and California, and its close relations with Mexico and Louisiana. It is an important and impressive trans-continental route, first-class in equipment and service, traversing many great cities, and scenery oftentimes unspeakably grand, and for many years a favorite line with veteran travellers and experts in journeying. The New-York offices are at 343 Broadway, and at 1 Battery Place, in the Washington Building.

The Reading Railroad System—Lehigh Valley Division—is one of the great lines of travel of America, and well entitled to the appellation, "The Scenic Route." For more than four hundred miles the tracks of its main line, extending from New York to Buffalo, traverse a region rich in natural beauty and in human interest, while the remaining portions of the thousand miles of track, which constitute this single division, penetrate the great mountain ranges and lovely valleys of Pennsylvania, with their wealth of agricultural and mineral resources, and their picturesque scenery. The eastern termini of the Scenic Lehigh Valley Route are at New York and at Philadelphia. In New York the passenger-station is at the foot of Liberty Street, North River, occupied jointly by the Central Railroad of New Jersey and the Reading System. In the new depot in Jersey City, a structure remarkable for its spaciousness and for the convenience and tastefulness of its interior, the tourist may pause to admire the train which is to bear him westward. A feature which strikes him most favorably, and which he will observe wherever he may journey upon the lines of the Reading System, is the complete absence of the smoke, soot and cinders which are attendant upon the use of soft coal, all locomotives being fueled exclusively with clean, hard Pennsylvania anthracite. The coaches are handsome and comfortable, being furnished with the most approved devices for heating, ventilation and lighting. Luxurious drawing-room, dining and sleeping cars complete the equipment of rolling stock. The road is double-tracked, of the most substantial construction, and the track and trains are protected by an improved block system and automatic signals.

Westward from New York the line traverses the most attractive portion of New Jersey, entering the Keystone State and the gateway of the world-famed Lehigh Valley at the city of Easton, picturesquely perched on a group of hills at the confluence of the Lehigh and Delaware Rivers. At the historic town of Bethlehem, 89 miles from New York, the line from the latter city forms a junction with a branch from Philadelphia, which is 56 miles to the southward. The Reading's

READING RAILROAD SYSTEM -- LEHIGH VALLEY DIVISION. DEPOT IN JERSEY CITY.

main passenger-station in Philadelphia is at Market and 12th Streets, in the very centre of the city, almost adjoining the City Hall, and in close proximity to all the chief hotels and places of interest.   It is a magnificent new structure, impressively beautiful in its architectural aspect, and of great size and convenience of arrangement.   The road is elevated through the central portion of the city, and its course hence to Bethlehem lies through a diversified and interesting region of suburban villages and fertile farms.   Beyond Bethlehem there is a chain of thriving industrial towns to interest the man of business, while the æsthetic taste is gratified by a swiftly changing panorama of beautiful scenery.   At Allentown connection is made with another division of the Reading System, reaching Reading, Harrisburg, Gettysburg and other points in the Schuylkill, Lebanon and Cumberland valleys.   As the track follows the graceful curves of the Lehigh River, there flashes into view many a beautiful vista of mountain and valley and stream.   Mauch Chunk, with its encircling peaks, the famous "Switchback" and Glen Onoko require no extended mention.   Glen Summit is a noted summer-resort on the crown of Nescopec Mountain, overlooking the romantic vale of Wyoming.   The cities of Wilkes-Barre, Scranton and Pittston are centres of the coal-producing industry reached by this line.   At Waverly it crosses the line dividing Pennsylvania and New York, and runs through the picturesque lake region, reaching Ithaca, Sheldrake, Cayuga, Geneva and other favorite resorts on Seneca and Cayuga Lakes, and also Clifton Springs.   Rochester is reached by a short branch road diverging from the main line.   At Batavia the trains are divided, some of the cars going to Buffalo and others to Niagara Falls.   Through coaches, parlor, dining and sleeping cars are run to Chicago from New York and from Philadelphia, by way of Buffalo, and also by way of Niagara Falls.   To the latter Mecca of the tourist the "Scenic Lehigh Valley" is a very attractive route, by reason of its picturesque scenery; and to all classes of travellers the line commends itself by its directness, its promptness, and its general excellence of service.   The principal New-York City ticket office is at 235 Broadway.

WEST STREET, FOOT OF LIBERTY STREET.

The Central Railroad of New Jersey provides transit to many charming residential places in New Jersey.

The commodious depot at Communipaw is reached by ferry from the foot of Liberty Street, North River. In conjunction with the Philadelphia & Reading Railroad this line forms a part of the famous Royal Blue Line from New York to Philadelphia, Baltimore, Washington, and the South and West. It traverses the entire length of the garden-like little State, bringing to the New-York market the products of New Jersey and Pennsylvania. Running westward, it passes through Elizabeth and Easton, Allentown and Mauch Chunk, and the marvellous anthracite coal region between Tamaqua and Scranton, including the whole length of the Valley of Wyoming and the Lehigh Valley. Its suburban service every evening conducts a vast peaceful army of business men from the rush and roar of the metropolis to the flourishing towns and villages of Central New Jersey,— to many towns such as Greenville, Bayonne City, Newark, Elizabethport, Elizabeth, Roselle, Cranford, Westfield, Fanwood, Netherwood, Plainfield, Dunellen, Bound Brook and Somerville.

The three steamers of the Sandy-Hook Route, owned and operated by the Central Railroad Company, include the *Monmouth, Sandy Hook* and *St. Johns*, leaving Pier 8, North River, foot of Rector Street, daily and Sunday during the summer season, at frequent intervals, for Atlantic Highlands, connecting there for Highland Beach, Navesink Beach, Normandie, Rumson Beach, Seabright, Low Moor, Galilee, Monmouth Beach, Long Branch, Elberon, Deal Beach, Asbury Park, Ocean Grove, Avon, Bel Mar, Como, Spring Lake, Sea Girt, Manasquan, Brielle and Point Pleasant. This route is one of the most popular in America during the

TRAIN-HOUSE OF THE GRAND CENTRAL STATION, ON 42D STREET.

summer season, when every one tries to escape from the arid streets of the great metropolis, and find the cool breezes which enliven the ocean-shore.

There is also an all-rail route from the foot of Liberty Street, New York, to the above-named coast-resorts, and also to Red Bank, Lakewood, Atlantic City, Tom's River, Bay Side, Barnegat Park, Forked River, Waretown and Barnegat Bay.

• The entire coast-line, from Sandy Hook to Barnegat Inlet, is an almost continuous summer-resort, with enormous hotels, colonies of handsome cottages, camp-meeting grounds, and all the other accessories of modern watering-place life. The memories of Grant and Garfield still haunt the bluff of Long Branch ; the State troops of New Jersey encamp along the plains of Sea Girt ; the light-houses flash across the sea from the Navesink Highlands and Barnegat ; the Methodists assemble their devout classes at Asbury Park and Ocean Grove ; and the perfume of the pines

CENTRAL BUILDING : CENTRAL RAILROAD OF NEW JERSEY, LIBERTY AND WEST STREETS, NEW YORK.

overflows the sands of Key East. In a way, this strip of wave-beaten coast, in winter "The Graveyard of the Sea," in summer becomes the most popular and delightful suburb of the great city, abounding in piquant varieties of scenery and of humanity.

The Delaware, Lackawanna & Western Railroad had its inception in the little Ligett's-Gap Railroad, down in Pennsylvania, which was incorporated in 1832, and 19 years later became the Lackawanna & Western, running from Scranton northwest to Great Bend. Two years later, upon consolidating with the Delaware & Cobb's-Gap Railroad, it took its present title, although the line did not reach the Delaware River until 1856. A year later, the company leased the Warren Railroad, then just opened from the Delaware River to New Hampton Junction, N. J. Meantime, the Morris & Essex Railroad, chartered in 1835, had been built from Hoboken across the hill-country of northern New Jersey to Phillipsburg, which it reached in 1866; and two years later it was favorably leased to the Delaware, Lackawanna & Western, which thus secured a terminal on New-York harbor. While thus triumphantly planning its route to the seaboard, the company also turned its attention northward and westward, securing the line to Owego and Ithaca in 1855; that to Syracuse and Oswego, in 1869; that to Utica and Richfield Springs in 1870; and that from Binghamton to Buffalo, in 1882. These and other annexed routes and new sections constructed, gave the company its present splendid system, reaching from opposite New York to Lake Ontario and Lake Erie and down through the coal-regions of Pennsylvania to Wilkes-Barre, Scranton and Northumberland. These routes are served by 550 locomotives and 36,000 cars of all kinds. The eastern terminal of the Lackawanna system, at Hoboken, is reached

DELAWARE, LACKAWANNA & WESTERN RAILROAD : DEPOT IN HOBOKEN.

by ferries from Barclay Street and Christopher Street, New York. The through main line from New York to Scranton, Elmira and Buffalo, 409 miles long, is traversed daily by several express-trains, connecting at Buffalo with the routes for the farther West. This Lackawanna route leads to some of the most charming summer-resorts in northern New Jersey, like Lake Hopatcong, Budd's Lake, and Schooley Mountain, and the noble scenery of the Delaware Water Gap and Pocono

Mountains. The Morris & Essex Division gives access to the most beautiful of all the suburbs of New York, the villages around the Orange Mountains, the Oranges, Montclair, Summit, Short Hills, Madison and Morristown, whose pure highland air and pleasant scenery are widely celebrated. The suburban traffic on this division has assumed great proportions, and is yearly increasing, on account of the desire of New-York business men to keep their families and to spend their own leisure days

ELEVATED RAILROAD NEAR COENTIES SLIP, EAST RIVER.

in the beautiful region of New Jersey, where the climate is of such sovereign salubrity that people are sent hither, even by physicians in Europe, as to a sanitarium. The suburban train-service is kept up to the highest point of efficiency, and affords the best of facilities, whether one goes northward on the route by Passaic and Mountain View, or westward by Newark and Orange, Summit and Madison. Largely on this account, the region of the Orange Mountains, so richly endowed with landscape-beauty and pastoral charm, has become perhaps the favorite residence-district in the outer suburbs of New York, and presents the aspect of a great park, adorned with hundreds of pleasant country-seats and dozens of dainty hamlets.

The Delaware, Lackawanna & Western Railroad Building, at William Street and Exchange Place, completed and opened in 1892, is one of the notable structures of the financial district. It measures 85 feet on William Street, and 60 on Exchange Place, is ten stories in height, and is in the Italian Renaissance style of architecture. The materials of construction are granite for the foundation and basement, and Indiana limestone above. The imposing entrance-arch on Exchange Place is supported on piers of polished granite. A pleasing effect has been gained by facing the masonry of the lower two stories, and leaving that of the upper stories rough, as the blocks of stone came from the quarry. The building is first-class in all respects.

The Baltimore & Ohio Railroad has a large interest in the Staten-Island Rapid Transit Railroad and its warehouse and shipping piers on the Bay of New

DELAWARE, LACKAWANNA & WESTERN RAILROAD COMPANY.
GENERAL OFFICES : EXCHANGE PLACE AND WILLIAM STREET.

York, and turns its freight traffic to this terminal, reaching the Arthur-Kill Bridge to Staten Island by its New-York Division, from Cranford, N. J. From the bridge the cars run over the Staten-Island Rapid Transit Railroad to St. George, whence they are conveyed on floats to the pier at New York. Passengers for the Baltimore & Ohio routes to the South and West cross the ferry from Liberty Street to the station of the Central Railroad of New Jersey, at Communipaw, and take the vestibuled Pullman trains of the Royal Blue Line for Philadelphia and Baltimore, Pittsburgh and Cincinnati, Chicago and St. Louis.

The New-York, Ontario & Western Railway was organized in 1866, under the name of the New-York & Oswego Midland Railroad, and opened its entire line in 1873, but passed into the hands of receivers the same year, and was afterwards sold and reorganized. The Ontario & Western owns and leases 500 miles of track, and runs from New York to Oswego, having branches to Scranton, Ellenville, Edmeston, Delhi, Rome and Utica, and a trackage right over the West-Shore road from Cornwall to Weehawken. Ferries run from Jay Street and West 42d Street to the terminal station at Weehawken, whence for over fifty miles the line follows the Hudson River, with many beautiful episodes of scenery. From Cornwall it turns westward through the rugged spurs of the Highlands, and beyond Middletown it crosses the Shawangunk Mountains. After passing Summitville, the line ascends the Delaware Mountains, which are surmounted at Young's Gap, 1,800 feet above the sea. The Middle Division of the route is celebrated for its picturesque scenery and for its many trout-streams, and great forests abounding in game. Next come

ELEVATED RAILROAD, AT COENTIES SLIP.   PRODUCE EXCHANGE TOWER.

the picturesque counties of Sullivan and Delaware, in the outer ranges of the Catskill Mountains, and abounding in bright lakes. After a long run across the hilly farm-lands of Chenango and Madison, the road bends around the broad Oneida Lake for more than a score of miles, and descends the valley to Oswego, one of the chief ports of Lake Ontario. Connections thence to the northward and westward are offered by the Rome, Watertown & Ogdensburg line, reaching from the St.-Lawrence Valley to Niagara Falls.

The New-York, Lake-Erie & Western Railroad forms one of the grand routes between the Empire City and the West, and, in spite of its many financial vicissitudes, has an enormous business, and controls dozens of tributary lines. The Legislature in 1825 ordered the surveying of a State road through the southern tier of counties, from the Hudson River to Lake Erie ; but the project was soon abandoned as impracticable. In 1832 the New-York & Erie Railroad Company received incorporation, and Col. De Witt Clinton, Jr., reconnoitred its projected route. The company was organized in 1833, and the route was surveyed the next year, by Benjamin Wright, at the cost of the State. New surveys occurred in 1836, and parts of the line were begun. The credit of the State was granted to the amount of several million dollars ; and in 1841 a section of track between Goshen and Piermont went into operation. Nevertheless, a year later the road passed into the hands of a receiver ; and it required subscriptions of $3,000,000 to the stock, by the merchants of New York, to energize the work. At last, on May 14, 1851, the great task was completed, and two trains ran over the entire line, from the Hudson River to Lake Erie, bearing the President of the United States and Daniel Webster, and a great company of notables. It was intended that the Erie line should end at Piermont, on the Hudson, but the directors soon saw that their terminal should be at New York, and therefore they arranged with the Union, Ramapo & Paterson, and Paterson & Jersey-City Railroads, to run trains over their lines from Suffern to Jersey City. The Erie Company owns or leases 800 locomotives, 450 passenger cars, and 42,000 freight and other cars and controls 3,000 miles of track. The Erie station at Pavonia Avenue, Jersey City, is reached by ferries from the foot of Chambers Street and West 23d Street. The line runs out across northern New Jersey to the Delaware Valley, which it follows for nearly 100 miles through a country of great landscape beauty. Then it crosses the mountains to the Susquehanna Valley, and so reaches the cities of the southern tier, and passes on to Dunkirk or Buffalo. There it connects with the main routes to the West and Southwest, the Chicago Express and the St.-Louis Express running through with wonderful speed and security. The Erie also has vestibuled trains to the Pennsylvania coal regions.

CORTLANDT-STREET FERRY, NORTH RIVER.

9

The **Delaware & Hudson Canal Company** is a corporation chartered by the State of New York in 1823, mainly to transport coal from the Pennsylvania coal-fields to New York. The canal was begun in 1825 and finished in 1828, and was twice enlarged, first in 1844 and again in 1862, to admit vessels of 150 tons capacity. It extends from Rondout, on the Hudson, to Port Jervis, on the Delaware, 59 miles ; thence 24 miles up the Delaware Valley, to Lackawaxen ; and thence 26 miles to the coal-region at Honesdale. This was one of the most important works of the great era of canal-building, which just preceded the rise of the railways. The capacity of the canal, with its equipments, is about 2,500,000 tons per annum.

The celebrated Gravity Road from Carbondale to Honesdale, over which millions of tons of coal are carried, was begun in 1827 and finished in 1829.

Between 1827 and 1829 the Canal Company built a railway from Honesdale to the coal-mines, and placed thereon the first locomotive that ever ran upon a railroad in the Western hemisphere. This pioneer engine, the *Stourbridge Lion*, was brought across from Liverpool on the packet-ship *John Jay*, in 1829, and passed to Honesdale, by river to Rondout, and thence by canal. In 1860 the company owned 108 miles of canal and 23 miles of railroad ; in 1870 it leased in perpetuity the Albany & Susquehanna line ; and in 1871 it leased the Rensselaer & Saratoga line and its branches. Subsequently it built a new line along the west side of Lake Champlain, from Whitehall nearly to Montreal, giving a straight route from Albany to the metropolis of Canada and traversing a country of rare beauty and diversity of scenery. Trains run from New-York City to Montreal, 384 miles, without change, in less than 12 hours, reaching Albany over the New-York Central & Hudson-River Railroad. The world-renowned Ausable Chasm is reached from Port Kent, on the Champlain Division.

Apart from its enormous freighting business, in coal and other commodities, the Delaware & Hudson Railroad system has a very large and lucrative tourist and summer-travel business. It affords the best route between New York and other southern points, and Montreal, Ottawa or Quebec, the historic old Canadian capitals ; and also to Lake George and Lake Champlain, with their exquisite scenery of land and water, mountain, island and beach, and the famous Hotel Champlain, at the station of the same name, three miles south of Plattsburg ; to the heart of the Adirondacks, with stages running from its stations to Blue Mountain-Lake, Long Lake, Schroon Lake, and Keene Valley, and by connecting line to Saranac Lake to the remote interior of the Adirondack wilderness, by the Chateaugay Railroad from Plattsburg ; to Ticonderoga, Crown Point, and Plattsburg ; to Saratoga, the queen of summer-resorts ; and to Rutland and other interesting points in southern Vermont. The Delaware & Hudson lines southwestward from Albany reach the famous resorts of Howe's Cave, Sharon Springs, and Cooperstown, on Otsego Lake ; and pass downward to Binghamton, and southward into the valley of Wyoming.

The Delaware & Hudson Canal Company's building is an immense and imposing fire-proof structure, generally known as the Coal and Iron Exchange. It is on Cortlandt Street, at the southeast corner of Church Street. It is not an "Exchange" building, excepting in name ; but it is the property of the Delaware & Hudson Canal Company, for whom it was built in 1874–76, and whose main offices are located therein. Here centres the executive administration of the line, and here is the focal point of its enormous and lucrative coal-trade. The great building was designed by Richard M. Hunt, and to-day is one of the finest office-buildings in the city, having all the modern appliances and conveniences, and being occupied by an interesting group of administrative and executive headquarters.

DELAWARE & HUDSON CANAL COMPANY.
COMPANY'S BUILDING, CALLED "THE COAL AND IRON EXCHANGE," CORTLANDT AND CHURCH STREETS.

DESBROSSES-STREET FERRY AND PASSENGER-STATION, WEST STREET, NORTH RIVER.

The New-York, New-Haven & Hartford Railroad was formed in 1872 by a consolidation of the New-York & New-Haven and the Hartford & New-Haven Companies. The line begins at Woodlawn, N. Y., and runs to Springfield, Mass., 122½ miles, its total trackage, owned and leased, exceeding 900 miles. The com-

A NORTH-RIVER FERRY BOAT.

pany runs its trains from Woodlawn to New York over the Harlem Railroad, by virtue of an agreement made in 1848, the tolls paid to the Harlem being about $1,000 a day. The company owns 200 locomotives and 5,000 cars, and has a first-class road-bed and equipment. The entrance to the great gate-way of land-travel from New-York to New England and the remoter East is the Grand Central Depot, and the only route leads over the rails of the New-York, New-Haven & Hartford line.

All the railway trains between New York and Boston pass over this route, at least as far as New Haven, beyond which they may follow the Springfield Route, the Air Line or the Shore Line. This company also controls the New-Haven &

Northampton line; the Hartford & Connecticut-Valley Railroad; the Naugatuck Railroad, from Stratford Junction to Winsted, Conn. ; the Shore Line, from New Haven to New London, Conn. ; and several other minor lines.

The New-York & New-England Railroad runs from Boston to Fishkill-on-Hudson, N. Y., with branches to Providence, Worcester, Springfield, Norwich, Woonsocket, Pascoag, Rockville, and other Eastern cities. Its trains enter the Grand Central Depot in New-York City by passing over the New-York, New-Haven & Hartford line from Willimantic, or Hartford, Conn. Every day the famous "White Train" leaves New York and Boston at 3 P. M., always making the run between the two cities in exactly $5\frac{3}{4}$ hours, with only four stops in the 213 miles. They run between Willimantic and Boston, 86 miles, without a stop. This route is shorter by twenty miles than any other between Boston and New York ; and is served by parlor-cars, dining-cars, royal buffet smoking-cars, and other fine coaches, whose colors of white and gold are very unusual and attractive. The White Train runs by way of Willimantic and the Air Line ; and there is also a train leaving New York and Boston at noon, and running by way of Hartford. The New-York and New-

NEW-YORK & NEW ENGLAND RAILROAD : "THE WHITE TRAIN," BETWEEN NEW-YORK AND BOSTON.

England Company also owns the famous Norwich Line of steamboats, between New York and New London, Conn., where it connects with trains for Boston. The route of these lines is so favorable, that it receives a great amount of travel, and will always be a favorite avenue to the eastward. The Washington Night Express runs between Boston and Philadelphia, Baltimore and Washington, by way of the Poughkeepsie Bridge, the Reading system and the Baltimore & Ohio Railroad, giving very good and comfortable facilities for transit between the metropolis of New England and the capital of the Republic.

The New-York & New-England Railroad gives convenient access to many of the most famous cities and towns of Connecticut and the adjacent States, like Danbury, famous for its hats; Waterbury, whose watches are not unknown ; Willimantic, where 1,500 operatives make the famous six-cord sewing cotton ; Putnam, with its score of busy mills ; Norwich, on the pleasant hills at the head of the Thames ; New London, always charming as a summer-resort; and busy groups of manufacturing communities in Rhode Island and Massachusetts. The first-class equipment of the railway and its efficient and vigilant management give it great value as one of the foremost avenues leading eastward from New York, and ensure its increasing success and popularity in the future.

The New-York & Northern Railway has its station at 155th Street and Eighth Avenue, on the upper part of Manhattan Island, and runs thence northward 54 miles, between the main line and Harlem route of the New-York Central Railroad, to Brewster, on the Harlem line. It follows the valley of the Harlem River as far as Kingsbridge, and thence strikes across Van Cortlandt Park and into Yonkers, to which it runs many rapid-transit trains daily for the convenience of suburban residents. Beyond this point it reaches Tarrytown, Sleepy Hollow and Pocantico Hills, in the region made classic by the genius of Washington Irving. Farther north, the line passes near Croton Lake, the great reservoir of the New-York water-supply ; and Lake Mahopac, a favorite summer-resort among the wooded hills of Carmel. At Brewster the route meets the tracks of the Harlem Railroad and the New-York & New-England Railroad, crossing the latter on its way from Boston to the Hudson River. The stretch of 51 miles from High Bridge to Brewster, operated by the Northern Line, belongs to the New-York, Westchester & Putnam Railway, the successor of the New-York & Boston Railroad. It was opened in 1880, and is under a fifty years' lease to the Northern line. Various plans have been suggested to run through trains from Boston to New York by way of Brewster and the New-York & Northern, and thus to secure for the New-York & New-England Company an independent entrance to the metropolis. The terminal station of the Northern line is easily reached from lower New York by the Elevated Railroad, on Sixth Avenue or Ninth Avenue.

The Long Island Railroad for a long time had its eastern terminus at Hicksville, but in 1844 it reached Greenport ; and the mails between New York and

SOUTH-FERRY STATION--ELEVATED RAILROAD.

Boston were then carried by this route, being transferred by steamboats from Greenport to the Connecticut shore. The company was chartered in 1834. By successive consolidations and leases the company now controls more than 500 miles of track on Long Island, including two nearly parallel lines, each about 100 miles long, from Brooklyn and Long-Island City to Sag Harbor and Greenport. Branches lead to Long Beach, Rockaway and Manhattan Beach, on the ocean front ; and to Flushing, Whitestone, Great Neck, Oyster Bay, Northport and Port Jefferson, on Long-Island Sound. This capital system of railways brings to the metropolis the abounding farm-products of the island, and gives access to the scores of suburban villages and famous seaside resorts. The Hunter's-Point station of the Long-Island Railroad is reached from New York by the ferries from James Slip and East 34th Street.

The New-York and Sea-Beach Railroad connects at Bay Ridge with the boats of the Staten-Island Rapid Transit Company, from the foot of Whitehall Street, the terminus of the elevated roads and the Broadway and Belt-Line surface roads.

ELEVATED RAILROAD AT 110TH STREET AND NINTH AVENUE.

From Bay Ridge it runs down to West Brighton, Coney Island. In 15 minutes, Brooklyn passengers connect with it by the Brooklyn City Elevated Railroad. It is a double-track standard-gauge line, six miles long, opened in 1879.

The Brooklyn, Bath & West-End Railroad, reached by ferry from Whitehall to 39th Street, Brooklyn, leads in 6⅜ miles to Coney Island. It was built in 1864; and in 1892 began running to the tide-water ferry-house, by the South-Brooklyn Railroad & Terminal Company's costly new roadway.

The Brooklyn & Brighton-Beach Railroad is a double-track line, 7½ miles long, running from Atlantic Avenue, Brooklyn, to Brighton Beach, across Flatbush.

The Staten-Island Rapid-Transit Railroad is reached by ferry from the foot of Whitehall Street; and gives access to all the important villages on "the American Isle of Wight." The Rapid-Transit Company was chartered in 1880, and in 1886 opened its line from Arrochar to Bowman's Point, opposite Elizabethport. In 1884 it effected a ninety-nine years' lease of the Staten-Island Railroad, chartered in 1851, and seven years later completed from Clifton to Tottenville. The lines of this company have a considerable value as leading from the metropolis to the rising suburban villages on the island. Their chief service, however, is in handling the enormous freight brought by the Baltimore & Ohio Railroad hither, across the Arthur-Kill Bridge, and down to tide-water at St. George and other points.

Local Transit.—The immense population of the metropolis of the New World and the necessity of moving myriads of men daily to and from their place of business, have given rise to many successive problems as to transportation, whose solutions have been of an interesting and ingenious character. The great length of the island, and its separation from the shores on either side by broad and deep tidal estuaries have given the necessary travel thereon a unique character, compelling successive developments of the modes of locomotion.

Stage Coaches were the first means employed for local transits. Departing at stated and infrequent intervals, and with much fanfare of horns, they ran from the taverns on the lower part of the island, over the Old Boston Post Road and the

FIFTH-AVENUE STAGE AT THE CATHEDRAL.

Bloomingdale Road, to the little embowered hamlets on the north. These vehicles went through many evolutions, and increased amazingly in numbers, until lower Broadway at times was almost blockaded with their huge and swaying forms. This main artery of the city retained its omnibuses for many years after they had disappeared from the other avenues, and only relinquished them when the vastly more comfortable street-car system came into use. The modern development of the old-fashioned stage-coach is now seen on Fifth Avenue, which is traversed every few minutes by low-hung stages, beginning their courses at Bleecker Street and running north along the elegant patrician thoroughfare to 86th Street, at the Metropolitan Museum of Art, the last mile or more being alongside Central Park. Some of these conveyances used in pleasant weather have seats on their roofs, and it is a favorite diversion to ride up the Avenue thereupon, especially in the late afternoon, observing the splendid panorama of architecture and metropolitan life.

Street-Cars.—In the course of time the rattling omnibuses of the provincial era were found ill-adapted to the transportation of the ever-increasing thousands of urban travellers, and ingenious inventors set to work to discover some new method of transit, at once more competent and more comfortable. This was found in the horse-car, whose idea is a gift from the city of New York to the civilized world, and has been of inestimable benefit to mankind. Nearly thirty years after their adoption here they were first introduced in Europe by George Francis Train, a citizen of New York, and now they are in constant use in hundreds of cities of Europe, Asia and Oceania, besides American cities and villages from Seattle to Key West.

The New-York & Harlem, the first street-railway in the world, was chartered in 1831, and in 1832 opened its entire line from Prince Street to Harlem Bridge. The cars were like stage-coaches, balanced on leather springs, and each having three compartments, with side-doors; while overhead sat the driver, moving the brake with his feet. From this germ has grown up the present immense and efficient street-car system of the Empire City, which is used by millions of passengers and reaches almost every part of

ORIGINAL TRAM CAR

DESIGNED and BUILT by JOHN STEPHENSON in 1831.

the island, with its lines along both water-fronts and up nearly all the north and south avenues and across town at a score of points. It was for a time thought that the introduction of the elevated railways would ruin the business of the street-cars, but this result has not followed, and the surface lines are still as fully employed as ever.

The **First & Second Avenue Line** runs from Fulton Ferry to the Harlem River, with branches to Worth Street and Broadway and to Astor Place and Broadway, and to the Astoria Ferry.

The **Third-Avenue Railroad** is one of the ancient street-car lines, its charter dating from 1853. The company has 28 miles of track, from the City Hall to Harlem (130th Street), with branches from Manhattan Street to 125th Street, E. R., and on Tenth Avenue from 125th Street, near Manhattanville, to 186th Street.

The **Fourth-Avenue Line** runs from the Post Office to the Grand Central Depot, with a branch to the Hunter's-Point Ferry. The Madison-Avenue line runs from the Post Office to Mott Haven.

The **Sixth-Avenue Railroad** was chartered away back in 1851, and runs from the Astor House (Vesey Street and Broadway) to Central Park. The line properly begins at Canal and Varick Streets, but the track thence to Vesey Street and the branch along Canal Street are owned in common with the Eighth-Avenue Company. The company owns 120 cars and 1,100 horses.

The **Seventh-Avenue Line** runs from Whitehall to Central Park, and beyond to Washington Heights. It owns 420 cars and 1,200 horses. The cost of construction was $4,500,000.

The **Eighth-Avenue Railroad** controls 20 miles of track, from Broadway and Vesey Street to the upper part of the island. It was chartered in 1855.

The **Ninth-Avenue Line** has 16 miles of track, extending from Broadway and Fulton Street to Manhattanville (125th Street). It was chartered in 1859.

The **Cross-Town Lines** include those on Charlton, Prince and Stanton Streets; from the Hoboken Ferry by Christopher, 8th and 10th Streets to the Greenpoint Ferry; from the 23d-Street Ferry by Grand and Vestry Streets, to the Desbrosses-Street Ferry (to Jersey City); from the Grand-Street Ferry to the Cortlandt-Street Ferry; along 23d Street, from the Erie Ferry to the Greenpoint Ferry; and many others.

The **Northern Wards** also have numerous street-car lines, reaching Morrisania, Tremont, Fordham, West Farms, Port Morris and other villages north of the Harlem River.

The **Broadway Line** is one of the latest-built of the street-car routes. It traverses Broadway, from the South Ferry to Central Park, giving admirable facilities for reaching all parts of this grandest thoroughfare of the world. The construction of the line met with a most determined opposition from a great number of citizens, who feared that their favorite commercial avenue would be ruined by the introduction of the rails; and a charter was obtained only after protracted controversies, and resulted in grave municipal complications. But the anticipated annoyances have not been realized, and the line is now one of the most important and useful in the city; and happy was the day for New-Yorkers when the old-fashioned, slow, cumbersome and noisy omnibuses gave way to the swift, quiet and neat horse-cars.

Cable-Cars, so successfully used in many American cities, are about to be introduced in New York on several of the main lines of tramway, and notably on Broadway and Third Avenue, whose routes have been constructed with this modern system of propulsion, so that passengers may be, and are, carried by them for marvelously low fares. The trolley system of electric railways will probably get an entrance into New York in time, although it has been unable to overcome a certain singular prejudice felt here against it, in spite of the success of the trolleys in so many other cities.

The Elevated Railroad is the crowning achievement in solving the problems of rapid transit. By its aid the New-Yorkers fly through the air from end to end of their teeming island at railway speed and in comfortable and well-appointed cars. The simplicity of their structure and the free gift to the companies of the right of way enable these routes to be built at a fraction of the cost of the urban rapid-transit lines in other great cities. Instead of being whirled through the darkness and monotony and poisonous air of almost continuous tunnels (as in London), the New-Yorkers are borne along, swiftly and comfortably, high up above the streets, in view of the wonderful changing panorama of the Empire City, and in a fresh and wholesome atmosphere. A ride on the London Metropolitan Railway is a depressing necessity; but a flight along the New-York elevated rails is a refreshment.

The movement for elevated railways grew very strong in 1866, and during the following year more than forty plans were submitted to the Legislature. The system of Charles C. Harvey was accepted, and the inventor was allowed to build an experimental track along Greenwich Street from the Battery to 29th Street. If it succeeded Harvey was to have permission to extend the line to the Harlem River,

PASSENGER ELEVATOR AND STATION, ELEVATED RAILROAD,
EIGHTH AVENUE AND 116TH STREET.

but if it failed it must be taken down. The system was commenced in 1867, but the means of locomotion then used was a wire rope drawn by a stationary engine. This method was unsuccessful, and the matter lay in abeyance for several years. The company failed in 1870, and was succeeded by the New-York Elevated Railroad Company, which began the use of small locomotives on the tracks. The Manhattan Railway Company was formed in 1875, and in 1879 it leased, for a term of 999 years, the New-York Elevated Railroad and the Metropolitan Elevated Railway, both of which were chartered in 1872 and opened in 1878. The lease was modified in 1884. The New-York line cost $20,500,000 for construction and equipment, and the Metropolitan cost $23,300,000. The Manhattan Company has about 300 locomotives and 1,000 cars, and carries 215,000,000 passengers yearly.

In 1891 the Manhattan Company secured control of the Suburban Rapid-Transit Railroad, running from 129th Street and Third Avenue, in Harlem, and through Mott Haven and Melrose to Central Morrisania (171st Street and Third Avenue).

This system is in process of extension to West Farms, Bronx Park, Fordham and other localities.

The main elevated railway lines are along the East Side, on Second and Third Avenues, two parallel routes from the lower part of Manhattan Island to Harlem ; the Sixth-Avenue line, along the middle of the island ; and the Ninth-Avenue line, nearer the Hudson River, from South Ferry to Central Park and the Harlem River, at West 155th Street. The railways are carried on girders resting upon wrought-iron lattice columns, usually along the line of the curb-stones, and from 37 to 44 feet apart. In some cases each side of the avenue has its elevated track, one for the up-trains, the other for the down-trains. Elsewhere the girders run clear across the narrower streets, and the two tracks are brought close together over the middle

CABLE-CARS ON THE EAST-RIVER BRIDGE, NEW-YORK END.

of the street. On some of the wider and less crowded avenues, the columns and tracks are placed in the middle. The stations are about one-third of a mile apart ; and in the busy hours of the day trains pass them about every minute, drawn by powerful locomotive engines. The crowded junction points of the lines, the stations in mid-air, the swallow-flight of the light trains, the perfect system and discipline of the arrangements, command admiring wonder, and make an especially vivid impression upon foreign visitors. The lofty curving trestles of iron near 110th Street were justly characterized by De Lesseps as one of the most audacious of engineering feats.

Projected Subterranean Transit.—However rapidly the facilities are increased, the needs of the city seem to increase even more rapidly, and the capacity of the elevated lines is already overstrained, especially at certain hours of the day. Consequently, new methods are in process of being worked out, and all possible routes between the Battery and Harlem are being studied by competent engineers.

In the belief that the existing surface and elevated railways occupy as much of the land and air of the city as can properly be used, attention has been directed to subterranean routes, to be bored under Broadway for its entire length.   The Rapid-Transit System proposed in 1891 by William E. Worthen, the chief engineer of the commission, provided for a tunnel under Broadway and the Boulevard, from the Battery to Spuyten Duyvil, containing four railway tracks, the outside ones for local trains and the inside ones for express trains, running at forty miles an hour. From 14th Street the East-Side branch diverges up Fourth and Madison Avenues to the Grand Central Depot.   The trains were to be run by electric power, and the stations and tunnels ventilated by powerful fans and brightly lighted by electricity. The lines and plan of construction were approved by the Mayor and Common Council.   Yet this system failed to be realized, and many new schemes for other routes and methods have since been brought before the Rapid-Transit Commissioners.   The tendency seems to be towards more extensive elevated railway services, especially between the Battery and Fort George.

America is the Temple of Liberty, and New York is its Beautiful Gate.   Other portals there are : Boston and Baltimore, New Orleans and San Francisco, and many more, but their aggregate of travel and traffic falls below that of this imperial city.   In the days of the Cæsars all roads led to Rome ; but in this happier century all routes, by sea or land, converge upon this wonderful harbor.   Millions of European immigrants have first touched the land of peace and freedom here ; and armies of travellers in search of pleasure or variety, or along the lines of trade and commerce.   Here centre the routes of travel between the rich and prosperous North and the happy and beautiful South, and between earnest New England and her daughter States of the West.   Hundreds of thousands of people from all parts of the Republic visit the great city every year for its own sake, because nowhere else are there such abundant facilities for pleasure, for enlightenment, for business. Here, therefore, is the supreme clearing-house for travellers of all kinds, and on all errands.

Along these close converging tracks of steel, each more noble than the Appian Way, hundreds of trains arrive and depart daily, with every variety of traveller, from the Westchester suburban to the New-Zealand globe-trotter.   The White Train and other famous convoys fly thence to New England and the remoter East ; the Empire-State Limited and the Erie Flyer to the North and West ; the Royal Blue and the powerful Pennsylvania trains to the West and South ; and scores of other routes have their almost continuous processions of cars, bound for innumerable destinations.   Nowhere else in the world is there such a focal point of travel as this.

Another interesting feature in the relation of New-York City to the railway systems of America appears in its overmastering financial control of many of their chief lines.   It is hardly possible to construct and equip a new route anywhere without securing some part of the needed capital from this treasure city ; and if the enterprise is promising and feasible there is always plenty of money at hand for the purpose.   The little rock-bound cañon of Wall Street has furnished the means to construct thousands of miles of track in all the country between Tampa Bay and Eastport, and between Sonora and Seattle.   The great trust-companies of New York are the guardians of incalculable amounts in mortgage-bonds and other obligations, and at their offices many railway companies, both near and far, pay their dividends.   The Vanderbilt, Gould, Corbin and other far-reaching systems have their headquarters here, and from this impregnable financial fortress control the destinies of unnumbered myriads of American people.

Thoroughfares and Adornments.

Streets, Avenues, Boulevards, Alleys, Ways, Parks, Squares, Drives, Monuments, Statues, Fountains, Etc.

I
N NEW YORK all roads lead not to Rome, but to the Battery. There the city had its beginning; and to-day, after three centuries of municipal existence and of steady expansion northward, the stupendous commercial and financial interests of the metropolis are still in that vicinity. The trains of the elevated railroads all run to the Battery, and all the principal street-car lines trend in that direction. Naturally a topographic tour of the city begins at that point.

The Battery was once the court end of the town. Fortifications were erected here by the first Dutch settlers. Castle Garden was once a fort on a ledge in the

BATTERY PLACE--WASHINGTON BUILDING.   PRODUCE EXCHANGE

bay, connected by a causeway with the main land. As time wore on, the Castle became a peaceful summer-garden and a concert-hall. The Lafayette ball was given there in 1824, and there Jenny Lind, the Swedish Nightingale, made her American *debut*. From 1855 to 1891 Castle Garden was the immigrant-depot, and many millions of persons from Europe have passed through its portals on their way to make homes for themselves in the New World. Now the Garden has changed character again. It will soon be devoted to a public aquarium, where many varieties of dwellers in the water may be seen. The United-States Revenue Barge-Office is situated there, on the water-front. Battery Park contains about 21 acres. It is well kept, with green lawns, flowers and shade-trees, and is a delightfully cool place in summer time. In colonial days the homes of New-York's wealth and aristocracy looked down upon this lovely spot. Several of the old houses still remain, but for the most part they have made way for huge warehouses and gigantic office buildings.

Bowling Green, a small triangular plot on the northern confines of Battery Park, is rich with traditions. Here stood the equestrian statue of King George III. Lord Cornwallis, Lord Howe, Sir Henry Clinton, George Washington, General Gates, Benedict Arnold, Talleyrand and other famous folk lived in this vicinity. Just south of the Green is the site of Fort Amsterdam, built by the Dutch in 1626. The Produce Exchange, the Welles Building, the Standard Oil Company Building, the Washington Building, the Columbia Building and other notable architectural structures now distinguish the locality.

Broadway, which starts from Bowling Green, is one of the longest and grandest business thoroughfares of the world. It is not always imposing, but it is always

WHITEHALL STREET, LOOKING TOWARDS BROADWAY. ARMY BUILDING.

interesting; and in general appearance, variety of scenes and impressive air of business and social activities it has, all in all, no rival on either continent. It is the main business artery of the city. On and about it, down-town, are hundreds of great buildings, bee-hives of industry, some of which have a business population equal to that of a country-town. The street is packed from sunrise to sunset with processions of merchandise, trucks, vehicles and cars, and the sidewalks are crowded with hurrying thousands, all on business intent. There are few loiterers and few pleasure-seekers in this part of the town. Financial institutions, shipping interests, the wholesale dry-goods and other branches of business monopolize lower Broadway and the adjacent streets.

At its inception Broadway is dignified with the great buildings that have already been referred to as surrounding Bowling Green; and the offices of the foreign consuls and the steamship companies and immigrant boarding-houses jostle them.

At every step northward appear tall buildings, the Columbia, Aldrich Court, the Tower, the Consolidated Exchange, the Manhattan Life-Insurance Company, the

PRODUCE EXCHANGE.   STEAMSHIP ROW, BOWLING GREEN.   STATE STREET

Union Trust Company, the United Bank, and others. Opposite Wall Street is Trinity Church and graveyard, breaking the monotony of the busy scene. Once Broadway ended at this point, and meandered beyond as a green country-lane. The

LOWER BROADWAY, LOOKING NORTH, FROM MORRIS STREET TO TRINITY CHURCH.

imposing Equitable Building, extending from Pine to Cedar Streets, stands where in 1646 good old Jan Jansen Damen lived, and shot the bears that prowled about his orchards. More great buildings : the Boreel, the Williamsburg City Fire, the

Mutual Life, the *Evening Post,* the Western Union, the *Mail and Express,* the *Herald,* — and then Broadway reaches Park Row and City-Hall Park. There is St.-Paul's Chapel, its back turned to the great thoroughfare. Opposite is the National Park Bank, and beyond is the famous Astor House, and the Post Office. A little farther on, not on Broadway, but within sight, across City-Hall Park, are

BROADWAY AND FIFTH AVENUE, SOUTH FROM MADISON SQUARE.

the Potter Building, and the newspaper buildings — the *Times, Sun, Tribune, World,* and *Staats-Zeitung.* In the park itself are the City Hall and the Court-House, and just beyond is the Stewart Building. The East-River Bridge terminates at City-Hall Park, in the midst of these noble architectural piles. The Postal-Telegraph-Cable Building, at the corner of Murray Street, and its neighbor, the Home Life-Insurance Building, will be imposing 13 and 14-story structures. The quadrangle formed around the southern end of the City-Hall Park by the newspaper

BROADWAY AND SIXTH AVENUE, NORTH FROM 34TH STREET.

buildings, the City Hall, and the Post Office is, without doubt, the grandest square on the American continent.

From the City Hall northward as far as Grace Church, at 10th Street, wholesale business-houses practically monopolize Broadway. At Duane Street rises the elegant twelve-story building of the Mutual Reserve-Fund Life Association, a splendid fire-proof stone structure. At Leonard Street the New-York Life-Insurance Building attracts attention, and near Lispenard Street is the fine edifice of the Ninth National Bank. Just beyond is Canal Street, in its name a reminder of the time when a canal ran across the island. Farther north are the Metropolitan Hotel

BROADWAY, FROM PARK PLACE TO CHAMBERS STREET.
OPPOSITE CITY-HALL PARK.

and Niblo's Theatre, the conspicuous Rouss Building, the Manhattan Savings Institution, the newly remodelled Broadway Central Hotel, the old New-York Hotel, then the Stewart dry-goods emporium, occupying an entire block between Broadway and Fourth Avenue, 9th Street and 10th Street, and then the beautiful Grace Church. At 11th Street is the first-class dry-goods establishment of James McCreery & Co. In this vicinity a literary centre has grown up. The publishing house of D. Appleton & Co. is a few blocks below in Bond Street ; Charles Scribner's Sons, in Broadway, opposite Astor Place ; the Aldine Club and the Astor Library, in Lafayette Place ; the University of the City of New York, in Washington Square ; the Cooper Union and the Mercantile Library, in Astor Place ; the American Book Co., a monopoly of the school-book business; Wm. Wood & Co., in 10th Street ; the

FOURTEENTH STREET, BETWEEN FIFTH AND SIXTH AVENUES.

United-States Book Co., in 16th Street ; Dodd, Mead & Co., in 19th Street ; and other publishing houses and new and second-hand book-stores are near at hand in all directions.

At 13th Street, leaving the Star Theatre, where for a generation shone the genius of Lester Wallack, Broadway at 14th Street debouches into Union Square, and, deflecting slightly to the west, pursues the rest of its course up-town diagonally across the avenues, instead of parallel to them.

Here is the retail shopping district, from 10th Street to above 23d Street. In Broadway, 14th Street and 23d Street principally, the prominent retail establishments are the wonder and the admiration of all who see them, and in extent and in

MRS. WILLIAM H. VANDERBILT.   WILLIAM D. SLOANE.   MRS. ELLIOTT F. SHEPARD.   WILLIAM K. VANDERBILT.   ST. THOMAS CHURCH.   DR. HALL'S CHURCH.

FIFTH AVENUE, LOOKING NORTH FROM 51ST STREET,

SHOWING THE VANDERBILT RESIDENCES, AND ST. THOMAS EPISCOPAL AND THE FIFTH-AVENUE PRESBYTERIAN CHURCHES.

variety of goods they are not surpassed elsewhere in the world. It has been estimated that the trade in this district annually amounts to over $500,000,000. A few
play-houses are still found as far south as 14th Street, but the main theatre-region
is in Broadway, or within about a block's distance, between 23d and 42d Streets.
Within that distance — about a mile — are Proctor's 23d-Street Theatre, the Madison-Square Garden, the Garden Theatre, the Madison-Square Theatre, Koster &
Bial's, the Lyceum, the Fifth-Avenue, Herrmann's, Daly's, the Bijou, Palmer's,
the Standard, Harrigan's, the Park, the Casino, the Metropolitan Opera House, the
Manhattan Opera House, the Broadway, and the new Empire Theatre. Broadway is
also an avenue of great hotels. Up-town it has the St. Denis, at 11th Street ; the St.
George, at 12th Street ; the Morton, at 14th Street ; the Continental, at 20th Street ;
the Aberdeen and Bancroft, at 21st Street ; the Fifth-Avenue and the Bartholdi, at
23d Street ; the Albemarle, at 24th Street ; the Hoffman, at 25th Street ; the St.
James, at 26th Street ; the Victoria and the Coleman, at 27th Street ; the Gilsey
and the Sturtevant, at 29th Street ; the Grand, at 31st Street ; the Imperial, at 32d
Street ; the Marlborough, at 36th Street ; the Normandie, at 38th Street ; the Oriental, at 39th Street ; the Gedney, at 40th Street ; the Vendome, at 41st Street ; the
St. Cloud and the Metropole, at 42d Street ; the Barrett, at 43d Street ; and the
Gladstone, at 59th Street.

Above 42d Street Broadway yet maintains something of the residential character
that long ago disappeared from it below. Many large apartment-houses face it as
it nears Central Park, at 59th Street. There with another turn westward it broadens
out into a wide asphalt-paved thoroughfare, with a shaded parkway in the center,
and is henceforth known as the Boulevard. It is a long but exceedingly interesting
walk up Broadway from Bowling Green to Central Park — about five miles.

The Boulevard, virtually a continuation of Broadway, beginning at the Park,
goes on for nine miles farther, through the pleasant upper part of the city that is
being rapidly covered with handsome houses, apartment-buildings and churches. It
passes over the hillside between Riverside Park and Morningside Park, where
Columbia College, the Protestant-Episcopal Cathedral and the Grant Monument are
soon to rise, and down into the ravine at Harlem, and then up again upon historic
Washington Heights, still a region of beautiful country-homes of old New-York
families, and on to the end of the island at Spuyten-Duyvil Creek, by the old Kingsbridge road. The Boulevard includes two capital roadways, separated by a central
strip of lawns, trees, and flowers. When finished, it will be one of the most beautiful driveways in the world, traversing, as it does, the remarkably picturesque
region between Central Park and the Hudson River, much of the way over high
ground, commanding beautiful views.

Fifth Avenue is celebrated the world over as the grand residence street of the
aristocratic and wealthy families of the metropolis. In recent years business has
encroached upon its boundaries, but despite all it still maintains its prestige and its
brilliant character. There was a time when some people regarded residence in Fifth
Avenue as an indispensable requisite to pre-eminent social recognition. In recent
years this notion has been decidedly relaxed, and grand residences of prominent
people arise on many of the cross streets immediately out of the avenue, and in Madison Avenue, Park Avenue, around the various squares and parks, in the newly-laid-
out streets, and in other favored localities ; but nevertheless a luxurious residence in
Fifth Avenue is a sort of stamp, or patent of rank. From Washington Square for
a distance of nearly four miles northward, Fifth Avenue is lined with handsome
residences, club-houses, churches and hotels that give abundant evidence of wealth

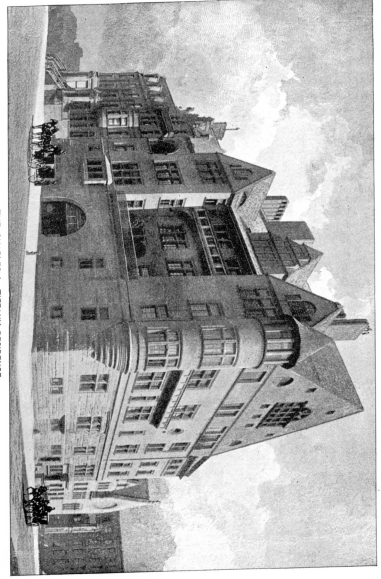

THE CHARLES L. TIFFANY RESIDENCE.
MADISON AVENUE, NORTHWEST CORNER OF SEVENTY-SECOND STREET.

12 3 0 STREET.
JOHN DWIGHT.
MOUNT MORRIS AVENUE.

MOUNT MORRIS PARK.

and luxurious tastes. In the lower part of the avenue many of the old New-York families still hold their mansions, despite the proximity of trade. Between 14th and 23d Streets, business has almost entirely pushed out residences, and only a few years will elapse before it will be in full possession of the usurped territory. The Manhattan Club has gone up-town to 34th Street ; the Lotos is preparing to move ; and the Union must soon follow. The *Judge*, the Methodist Book Concern, and the Mohawk buildings, three large, handsome structures, have been erected recently, and are prophetic of the transformation now taking place in this part of the avenue.

PARK AVENUE, LOOKING NORTH FROM 55TH STREET.

ST. BARTHOLOMEW'S CHURCH. MANHATTAN ATHLETIC CLUB. HOLY TRINITY CHURCH.

MADISON AVENUE, LOOKING NORTH FROM 42D STREET.

PRESBYTERIAN HOSPITAL. CHARLES F. CLARK. JOHN KING.

MADISON AVENUE, EAST SIDE, BETWEEN 69TH AND 70TH STREETS.

At 23d Street, Fifth Avenue crosses Broadway and makes the western border of Madison Square. From this point northward to 42d Street business is in the ascendant. Many of the private houses that once lined the avenue are gone, and many of those that remain are not used for residences. Art-galleries, book-stores, *bric-à-brac* shops, fashionable millinery and dressmaking establishments, publication offices, clubs and hotels are rapidly making this an aristocratic business street.

Above 42d Street are the palaces of some of New York's millionaires. The Vanderbilt houses are regarded as the finest examples of domestic architecture in the United States. They do not stand entirely alone, however, in respect to beauty. The Stevens house, now owned and occupied by ex-Secretary-of-the-Navy William C. Whitney; the C. P. Huntington mansion, nearly completed; the houses of Robert Goelet, R. F. Cutting, and others add distinction to the mile of avenue between 42d Street and Central Park; and in the same district live, less pretentiously but none the less elegantly, such well-known New York aristocrats as Governor Roswell P. Flower, Darius O. Mills, Henry M. Flagler, Ogden Goelet, Washington E. Conner, Russell Sage, Chauncey M. Depew, and William Rockefeller. Above 59th Street, facing the Park, are other splendid mansions, among them the home of Henry O. Havemeyer, and the Robert L. Stuart house.

Fifth Avenue is the great hotel thoroughfare of the city. In that respect it surpasses even Broadway, its closest rival. It has the Brevoort, at Clinton Place; the Berkeley, at 9th Street; the Lenox, at 12th Street; the Logerot, at 20th Street; the Glenham, at 22d Street; the Fifth-Avenue, at 23d Street; the Brunswick, at 25th Street: the Victoria, at 27th Street; the Holland, at 30th Street; the Cambridge and the Waldorf, at 33d Street; the St. Marc, at 39th Street; the Hamilton

HARLEM VIEW, LOOKING EAST FROM 137TH STREET.

and the Bristol, at 42d Street; the Sherwood, at 44th Street; the Windsor, at 46th Street; the Buckingham, at 50th Street; the Langham, at 52d Street; and the Plaza, Savoy and New Netherland, at 59th Street.

Fifth Avenue is also a street of churches. On it stand Ascension (Episcopal), at 10th Street; the First Presbyterian, at 12th Street; the Collegiate Reformed, at 29th Street; the Brick Presbyterian, at 37th Street; the Jewish Temple Emanu-El, at 43d Street; the Divine Paternity (Universalist), at 45th Street; the Heavenly Rest (Episcopal), near 45th Street; the Collegiate Reformed, at 48th Street; St. Patrick's Cathedral (Roman Catholic), at 50th Street; St. Thomas (Episcopal), at 53d Street; and the Fifth-Avenue Presbyterian, at 55th Street.

Fifth Avenue, moreover, is the main resort of the clubs, nearly all of which have taken possession of old-time residences. Among them are the following: the Union, at 21st Street; Sorosis, near 25th Street; the Reform, at 27th Street; the

JEANNETTE PARK, COENTIES SLIP.

Calumet, at 29th Street; the Knickerbocker, at 32d Street; the Manhattan, at 34th Street; the New-York, at 35th Street; the St.-Nicholas, at 36th Street; the Union League and the Delta Kappa Epsilon, at 39th Street; the Republican, at 40th Street; the Lotos, near 45th Street; the Democratic, near 49th Street; the Seventh-Regiment-Veteran, above 57th Street; the Metropolitan, at 60th Street: and the Progress, at 63d Street.

Among the public and semi-public institutions on Fifth Avenue are: Chickering Hall, Delmonico's, St. Luke's Hospital, the Roman Catholic Orphan Asylum, and the Lenox Library. With its handsome residences, numerous hotels, churches, clubs and other institutions, and with Washington Square at its southern terminus, Madison-Square and the Reservoir in Bryant Park breaking its course, and the 59th-Street Plaza and Central Park illuminating its northern extension, Fifth Avenue is certainly one of the most magnificent thoroughfares of the world.

SOUTH STREET, NORTH FROM THE BATTERY.

Madison Avenue, which, only a block away, runs parallel with Fifth Avenue, contains the Villard Florentine palace, part of which is now the home of Whitelaw Reid, the editor of the *Tribune,* and ex-United-States Minister to France. The Tiffany house, at Madison Avenue and West 72d Street, is one of the most unique and attractive dwelling-houses in America. It was built for and is owned by Charles L. Tiffany, the founder and senior member of the world-famous jewelry house of Tiffany & Co. It was designed by Stanford White, of McKim, Mead & White, and Louis C. Tiffany. The interior was designed by Louis C. Tiffany, son of the owner, who, with other members of the same family, occupies the house. The architecture contains many quaint and delightful features of the old Dutch style; and the lofty and ornate façades and picturesque roof are prominent features of up-town New York. On the same avenue stand other mansions scarcely less notable. Madison Avenue, too, might well be termed "the Avenue to the Gods," for imposing shrines of worship, in a greater number than on any other thoroughfare in the city,

EDISON BUILDING.　　　STOCK EXCHANGE.　　　MILLS BUILDING.

BROAD STREET, NORTH TO WALL STREET.

of many denominations and many creeds, rise up at every few corners throughout its whole length. At its beginning has just been completed the magnificent white marble edifice of the Metropolitan Life Insurance Company.

Sixth Avenue rivals Broadway, 14th Street and 23d Street in its retail stores. Several of the large dry-goods establishments are there, and hundreds of smaller shops. It contains the Jefferson-Market Court-House at 10th Street; the Greenwich Savings Bank, at 16th Street; the Masonic Hall, at 23d Street; and the Union Dime Savings Institution, at 32d Street; besides which there is little of noteworthy architectural character in the avenue. It has a large resident population, in apartments over stores, and is the main thoroughfare of the Tenderloin District.

Seventh Avenue, extending from Greenwich Avenue to Central Park, is a residence-street for people of moderate means, and has many retail stores. The State Arsenal is at 35th Street; the Osborne Flats, at 52d Street; Tattersall's, at 55th Street; Hotel Grenoble, at 56th Street; Music Hall, at 57th Street; and the Central-Park Apartment-houses, at 59th Street.

West Street and South Street are the water-front thoroughfares, leading from the Battery along the North River and East River respectively. Along the former are the piers of most of the great ocean-steamship lines and of the Hudson-River and Long-Island-Sound boats. Much of the South-American shipping comes

DREXEL BUILDING.   MILLS BUILDING.   PRODUCE EXCHANGE.   STOCK EXCHANGE.   WILKS BUILDING.

BROAD STREET, SOUTH FROM WALL STREET.

to the East-River front, and sailing vessels predominate there. Near the mouth of the East River, at the Battery, large fleets of canal-boats tie up. The piers on all the river-fronts, with one exception, are wooden or iron structures.

Eighth Avenue is the West-Side cheap thoroughfare. The upper part of the avenue toward 59th Street is respectable, and contains several notable public buildings.

Central Park West is that part of Eighth Avenue that faces Central Park from 59th Street to 110th Street. It is a beautiful street, and is being built up with artistic and expensive private houses and handsome apartment-hotels. The Dakota, the San Remo, the San Carlo, and the La Grange, are among the finest houses of their kind in the city. The American Museum of Natural History, in Manhattan Square, and the Cancer Hospital look upon Central Park West.

Wall Street is a short and narrow thoroughfare, but it is second only to Lombard Street, London, in the magnitude, importance and far-reaching influence of its financial operations. Both its sides are lined for about half their length with some of the costliest office and bank buildings in this country; here, too, are the Sub-Treasury, the Assay Office, and the Custom House. Once the outer wall of the city, surmounted by a stockade, ran where the street now is. Hence comes the name of the street. Times have changed since that day when watchful sentinels paced this wall, guarding the little village of New Amsterdam from the Indians and the wild beasts. Even as late as 1697, when a grant of land was made to Trinity Church, it was described as "in or near to a street without the North Gate of the city, commonly called Broadway." The Sub-Treasury stands on the site of the first City Hall, afterward called the Federal Hall.

Nassau, Broad and New Streets take a great deal of the overflow of Wall Street. In Broad Street is the main front of the handsome white-marble building of the Stock Exchange, and several elegant office-buildings — the Mills, the Edison, and the Morris. In Nassau Street is the Clearing House, and many banks and banking houses. The majestic Mutual Life-Insurance Building stands on the site of the Middle Dutch Church, which was used for a riding-school by the British soldiers during the Revolution, and was afterwards the New-York Post-Office. In 1728 the Dutch society bought this land for £575; in 1861 the United-States Government paid the church $200,000 for it; and in 1881 the insurance company bought it for $650,000. It is probably worth now fully $750,000.

Printing-House Square is at the north end of Nassau Street. The appellation is popular rather than official. It is an open space, or plaza, at the intersection of Park Row and Nassau and Spruce Streets, abreast of the City-Hall Park; and

WALKER STREET. -- HARRY HOWARD SQUARE. -- CANAL STREET.

is bordered by the offices of the great newspapers. The statues of Benjamin Franklin and Horace Greeley are appropriately placed as the presiding geniuses of the locality.

Franklin Square is only known and only important because the firm of Harper & Brothers still keep their publishing-house there. A century and less ago this was one of the fashionable quarters of the town. The old mansions have disappeared, and a tenement-house population and small manufacturing establishments now occupy the land. The square is pretty well covered over by the network of tracks and depots of the Elevated Railroad.

BROADWAY, FROM THE BROADWAY CENTRAL HOTEL TO GRACE CHURCH.
BOND STREET TO TENTH STREET.

The Bowery is historic ground.   In the good old pre-colonial days it was a pleasant country lane, running between the "Boweries" or farms of the worthy Dutch burghers.   Its rural character departed years and years ago, and for a long time its name was synonymous with all the worst phases of vice in the slums of the great city.   The swaggering "Bowery Boy" tough then ruled the precinct, which was redolent with depravity. ⁀ In recent years the Bowery has risen from its low ·estate, and possesses many enterprising business establishments, successful banks,

" CHINATOWN "--MOTT STREET, WEST OF PARK ROW.

and public institutions.   A flavor of cheapness from the surrounding tenement region still clings to it, but the decent German and Hebrew elements now chiefly dominate the neighborhood.

The Five Points, once so infamous, was renovated some years ago.   Crime and poverty no longer control it..   In their place have come mission schools, chapels and manufactories, and industrious working people.   New streets and open squares have been laid out by the municipal authorities, and the district is generally improved sanitarily and socially.

Mott, Pell and Doyers Streets and vicinity are now given over to the Chinese. There is a large population in the district just west of the Bowery and Chatham Square.   The district is a veritable "Chinatown," with all the filth, immorality and picturesque foreignness which that name implies.

Second Avenue in its southern limits is the great German⁀thoroughfare.   A large German population exists to the east of it ; and its cafés, gardens and other places of public resort are for people of that nationality.   About 10th Street was the farm of Peter Stuyvesant, the last Dutch Governor of New Amsterdam.

Baxter Street is still monopolized by the cheap clothing-dealers, who have made the name of the street famous.

Thompson Street is the centre of one of the largest negro colonies in the city, and has given rise to a very readable book, "The Proceedings of the Thompson-Street Poker Club."

Hanover Square, at the junction of Hanover, Pearl and William Streets, is the centre of the cotton trade, and here, too, is the stately Cotton Exchange. In this locality, in days gone by, lived many of New York's wealthy merchants, and after the French Revolution many notable French *emigrés*. Here is an important station of the Elevated Railroad, greatly utilized by the men connected with the Stock, Cotton and Produce Exchanges.

Lafayette Place, a short street between Astor Place and Great Jones Street, is distinguished as the location of the Mission of the Immaculate Virgin, the Astor Library, the Protestant Episcopal Diocesan House, the DeVinne Press (printers of *The Century Magazine*), and the offices of several publishing concerns and religious societies. In the row of houses opposite the Astor Library, and known as "the Colonnade Row," lived John Jacob Astor and other rich merchants, two generations ago. The north end of the Row is owned and occupied by *The Churchman.*

Astor Place, just north of Lafayette Place, has the Mercantile-Library Building, the Eighth-Street (Jewish) Theatre, and the statue of Samuel S. Cox. In front of the Opera House, which then occupied the present site of Clinton Hall (the Library Building), occurred the "Forrest-Macready riot," in 1849. Astor Place was once a fashionable residence-quarter.

Parks and Squares are generously provided for New-York people. Large public parks and small open squares are scattered about in all districts, especially

MULBERRY BEND, THE ITALIAN QUARTER.

where they can be readily availed of for the children of the poor. Few if any cities of the world now have as great an acreage of parks, and the spirit of the people is steadily favorable to even more such open places, that conduce to the general health

CENTRAL PARK AND FIFTH AVENUE, NORTH FROM 59TH STREET.

and happiness of the community, and this too notwithstanding the high value of every square foot of land in the city.

Central Park is one of the most beautiful and one of the most famous urban parks in the world. It covers the territory between Fifth and Eighth Avenues and 59th and 110th Streets, a tract over 2½ miles long by half a mile wide, including an area of 840 acres. There are about 400 acres of wooded ground, part of which is still in the natural state, while the rest has been improved by the planting of trees, shrubs and vines. There are nine miles of carriage-ways, six miles of bridle-paths, and thirty miles of foot-paths. The Park has been beautified with handsome architecture, landscape gardening, statues and other works of sculpture. There are nineteen entrances, over which it was once proposed to erect imposing arches, a plan that may yet be carried out. Transverse roads from east to west, in open cuts below the level of the Park, accommodate business traffic, which is not allowed within the Park limits. Park-carriages are run for the convenience of visitors. The Park was begun in 1857, during the mayoralty of Fernando Wood ; and has cost over $16,500,000, inclusive of maintenance, which has been over $300,000 a year. Frederick Law Olmsted and Calvert Vaux directed the landscape design, and Calvert Vaux and J. W. Mould superintended the architectural features. Washington Irving and George Bancroft Davis were consulting members of the first Park Board, and General Egbert L. Viele was the first engineer. Central Park is twice the size of Regent's Park or Hyde Park, in London ; and in the world is exceeded in size only by the Great Park at Windsor, the grounds at Richmond, Phœnix Park in Dublin, the gardens at Versailles, the Bois de Boulogne at Paris, and the Prater in Vienna. None of these equals it in beauty.

Starting from 59th Street, one comes first upon the Ball Ground, a ten-acre plot in the south-west corner, where the boys are privileged to play base-ball and cricket. Near this is the Dairy ; and just to the north-east is the Carrousel, with swings for children. Adjoining is the Common, or Green, of sixteen acres, where the sheep

THE OBELISK, IN CENTRAL PARK.

are pastured. On the east side, at Fifth Avenue and 64th Street, is the Menagerie, partly housed in the Arsenal, and partly in pens and wooden houses. There is a large and varied collection of wild animals, elephants, lions, hippopotami, tigers, bears, camels, seals, monkeys and birds. Just to the east of the Green is the Mall, a grand promenade, over 200 feet wide and a third of a mile long, overshadowed by rows of noble elms. Here are many statues; at the southern end, the beautiful Marble Arch, over an underground pathway; and near the middle the Music Pavilion, where concerts are given on Saturday and Sunday afternoons. The goat carriages for the children are kept here; and on the cliff to the left is the arbor, covered with gigantic wisteria vines, that in springtime make a wonderful show of purple blossoms. Close at hand is the Casino, a restaurant for this section. To the north the Mall terminates in the Terrace, the chief architectural feature of the Park.

TERRACE, FOUNTAIN AND LAKE, IN CENTRAL PARK.

There is an Esplanade on the shore of the lake, and the Bethesda Fountain stands there. A central stairway leads down to the Esplanade under the road, beneath which is a tiled hall with arched roof. On either hand outside are other flights of steps. The Terrace is built of a light-brown freestone, with beautiful decorative details, and very intricate carvings of birds and animals.

The Lake covers twenty acres, and is given over to pleasure-boats in the summer and skating in the winter. Beyond the Lake is the Ramble, a spot beautiful with sylvan paths, waterfalls, natural groves, thickets of underbrush and exquisite bits of scenery. Next is the Receiving Reservoir for the city water, and on its margin rises the lofty terrace of the Belvedere, with a picturesque tower fifty feet high, affording a magnificent view of Manhattan Island and all the surrounding country. To the east of the Reservoir are the Obelisk and the Metropolitan Museum of Art; and to the north again, the new Croton Reservoir, which fills nearly the entire width of the Park. At the extreme northern section there is less adornment, but none the less beauty; and, withal, much of historical interest. From Great Hill, with its Carriage Circle, there is a view of Harlem and Washington Heights. Harlem Mere

11

is at the foot of the hill upon which stands the old Block-House; and McGown's-Pass Tavern is near McGown's Pass, the scene of skirmishes between the British and the Continental troops in 1776. The North Meadow, a fine grassy lawn of nineteen acres, is largely set apart for tennis-players and picnic-parties.

Other lakes than these already mentioned are the Conservatory Water, where the boys sail little boats; the Lily Pond, which has a valuable collection of water-lilies, Egyptian lotus and other beautiful flowers; and the Pond, where swans and

BOAT-HOUSE AND LAKE IN CENTRAL PARK.

other aquatic birds disport themselves. The water area of the Park is: lakes, 43¼ acres; reservoirs, 143 acres. The place is much frequented in all seasons of the year. It is not unusual for 150,000 people to visit it on a single pleasant day in summer; and 15,000,000 visit it every year.

Riverside Park, next in importance to Central Park, is on the east bank of the Hudson River, extending from 72d Street north to 130th Street, a distance of three miles, with an irregular width, averaging about 500 feet, and an area of 178 acres. That part of it farthest from the river, and known as the Riverside Drive, has been laid out in lawns, driveways and walks, the uneven contour of the land being carefully preserved. Throughout the length of this charming thoroughfare, which is on the crest of a hill, there is a wide-sweeping view of the Hudson River and the Jersey shore as far north as the Palisades. On the east line of the Park is Riverside Drive, upon which are built elegant private residences, facing the west; and this section is becoming one of the favorite places of residence of New-York millionaires, whom the encroachment of trade is driving out of the other districts. To the west a substantial granite wall borders the Drive, and below this, sloping to the river's edge, is an uneven tract of land as yet unimproved, and abounding in fine old trees. A plan will probably be carried out to fill in the river to the outside pier line for the entire length of the Riverside Park, and raise an embankment above the present level of the New-York Central & Hudson-River Railroad, bridges across the tracks

SCENES AND ORNAMENTAL STRUCTURES.
IN CENTRAL PARK.

STATUES, BUSTS AND ORNAMENTS.
IN CENTRAL PARK.

STATUES AND ORNAMENTAL WORK,
IN CENTRAL PARK.

connecting the embankment with the hillside. This arrangement would give the city a water-front park unequalled for beauty elsewhere in the world. At the northern end of Riverside Park is the tomb of General U. S. Grant.

Morningside Park is a strip of land about 600 feet wide and more than half a mile long, with an area of 32 acres, extending north and south upon the eastern slope of Bloomingdale Heights, north of 110th Street and west of Eighth Avenue. It overlooks Central Park and Harlem, and commands a view of Washington Heights and the country to the north and east. The land at the foot of the hill has been laid out in a handsome landscape design, and against the face of the cliff has been constructed a heavy granite wall with projecting bastions and broad stairways leading up to the parapetted promenade on the top.

Madison Square, bounded by Fifth Avenue, Broadway, Madison Avenue, 23d Street and 26th Street, is the chief popular resort of the central districts. It covers nearly seven acres, and in summer is charming with shade-trees and beds of flowers. The Seward and the Farragut statues are inside the park, and the Worth Monument is at the northern corner. Here are ornamental and drinking fountains, and

MENAGERIE IN CENTRAL PARK.

in the season beds of beautiful water-lilies. The Square is much frequented by prettily dressed children with their nurses, and withal is thoroughly delightful.

Union Square, at Broadway, 14th Street, 17th Street, and Fourth Avenue is 3½ acres in extent. Here are the Lafayette, the equestrian Washington and the Lincoln statues, a pretty fountain in the centre, a large drinking fountain surmounted by the figures of a woman and two children, a small and artistic drinking fountain designed by Olin T. Warner, a paved plaza on the north bordered by a row of colored gas-lamps, an ornamental structure and a cottage with a reviewing balcony. The plaza is a favored place for large outdoor mass-meetings.

Washington Square has a character peculiar to itself. It is at the lower end of Fifth Avenue, an open space of about nine acres, once the Potter's Field. New-York society, driven successively out of Bowling Green, Bond Street, Bleecker Street and elsewhere down-town, has made a sturdy stand for two generations in Washington Square. The north side is lined by old-fashioned red-brick houses, with white-marble trimmings, in which dwell the Coopers, the Rhinelanders, and other aristocratic families. On the east side is the imposing white-stone castellated structure of the University of the City of New York, hallowed by many associations. The dormitory of this building has for a generation at least been the bachelor home of artists and men of letters, and many a recluse has buried himself from the world in its quiet

BOW BRIDGE, IN CENTRAL PARK.

precincts. In the next block is the Asbury Methodist Episcopal Church, and the modern Benedict Chambers, principally occupied by artists. On the south side of the Square small shops catering to the neighboring tenement population, have crept in to a considerable extent. Some of the old historic houses remain, and several apartment-buildings. The feature of that side of the Square, however, is the Judson Memorial Baptist Church. On the west side are fine private residences and apartment-hotels. The principal ornament of the Square is the white-marble Washington Memorial Arch, where Fifth Avenue begins. There is a fountain, a statue of Garibaldi, a bust of Alexander L. Holley, beds of flowers, shade-trees, and hundreds of seats that are generally occupied by poor people from neighboring tenements.

STATUES AND BUSTS.

IN CENTRAL PARK.

THE CAVE, LAKE, OLD FORT, AND ORNAMENTAL STRUCTURES.
IN CENTRAL PARK.

City-Hall Park has been shorn of much of its original dimensions. A century and more ago it was "The Open Field" outside the city limits, and great mass-meetings were held there.   Once it was the only park in the city, and the land now

occupied by the Post-Office Building was within its limits twenty-five years ago. The City Hall, the County Court-House, the ancient Hall of Records, and a fire engine-house take up much of the open space of the Park, which has about eight acres. There are two fountains, plenty of shade, and many flower-beds. The asphalt-paved plaza in front of the City Hall is the favorite resort of the fun-loving boot-blacks and newsboys of the neighborhood.

Bryant Park consists of five acres, between Fifth and Sixth Avenues, and 40th and 42d Streets, on the site once occupied by the famous Crystal Palace, which was burned in 1858. On the Fifth-Avenue side is the old Reservoir, from which until 1884 it was

GARIBALDI STATUE, IN WASHINGTON SQUARE.

called Reservoir Park. It preserves the memory of William Cullen Bryant merely in the name, its only statue being a bust of Washington Irving.

East-River Park is on the bluff overlooking the East River, at the foot of 86th Street. Although of limited area, it is very airy, and commands a fine view of the river far up toward Long-Island Sound. It has been fitted up particularly for the comfort of the babies and young children and their mothers, from the adjacent tenements.

High-Bridge Park is the name given to the 23 acres that surround the Reservoir and buildings of the city water-works at the Harlem River and 170th Street.

Manhattan Square, covering about 15 acres, at Central Park West and 77th and 81st Streets, is an annex to Central Park. It is the site of the Museum of Natural History, but the grounds have not been fully laid out nor cared for.

Mount-Morris Park, along Fifth Avenue, from 120th to 124th Street, in Harlem, is over a score of acres in extent. It contains a rocky and well-wooded hill, surrounded with pretty stretches of level land. There is a plaza on top of the hill from which an extensive view is obtained ; and shaded paths, and other natural and artificial adornments make this one of the handsomest of the city's smaller breathing places.

Gramercy Park is a private enclosure of 1½ acres, between 20th and 21st Streets and Third and Fourth Avenues. It is a part of the old Gramercy farm. Looking out upon it are the homes of David Dudley Field, the late Cyrus W. Field, John Bigelow, Hamilton Fish, ex-Mayor Abram S. Hewitt, and other well-known wealthy New-Yorkers. There, too, was the home of the late Samuel J. Tilden ; and next to it is the Players' Club, that Edwin Booth established. In the Gramercy-Park Hotel reside several eminent theatrical and musical artists.

Stuyvesant Square, four acres in extent, on Second Avenue, between 15th and 17th Streets, is a part of the old Stuyvesant farm. Private residences surround it ;

and on the west side rise St. George's Episcopal Church and the Friends' Meeting-House and Seminary. On the east side is the New-York Infirmary for Women and Children. It is an aristocratic neighborhood, but the Square is mostly used by the East-Side tenement dwellers.

Mulberry-Bend Park is a projected new small park between the Bowery, Park Row, Canal, Pearl and Elm Streets. The commission to acquire the property was appointed in 1888, and in 1892 completed its work. The cost of acquiring the property has been about $2,000,000.

The New Park System above the Harlem River has been planned upon magnificent proportions. The lands were selected by a commission, in 1884 ; and were acquired by the city at a cost of about $9,000,000. There is a fraction over 3,945 acres in the territory, which includes six parks and three parkways. Up to the present time these breathing-places have been left in an absolute state of nature and it is not proposed ever to "improve" them artificially. They are somewhat removed from the popular sections of the city, and mostly frequented by picnic and excursion parties in summer, and skating parties in winter.

Pelham-Bay Park is in Westchester County, outside the city limits. It contains 1,756 acres on the shore of Long-Island Sound, Hunter's Island and Twin Island being included within its limits. The land belonged to the Pell family two centuries ago, and the old manor-house is still standing. Here Ann Hutchinson, fleeing from Puritan persecutions in New England, settled, and was murdered by the Indians. In the Revolution much fighting occurred over all this ground. The Park has a very picturesque shore-line, nearly ten miles long.

Van-Cortlandt Park contains 1,132 acres, and is part of the property once owned by the Van-Cortlandt family. The old family mansion is still preserved, a quaint Dutch building of stone, with terraced lawns commanding views of the Palisades and the Hudson River. There Washington had his headquarters while carrying on operations for the expulsion of the British from New-York City. "Vault Hill" on this property was the burial-place of the Van-Cortlandt family ; and "Indian Field" was an aboriginal place of interment, as many graves indicate. There is a large lake, covering sixty acres ; and a parade-ground for the city regiments of the National Guard has been laid out, on a level meadow of 120 acres.

ALEXANDER L. HOLLEY BUST, IN WASHINGTON SQUARE.

Bronx Park contains 661 acres, lying on both sides of the Bronx River, a shallow and narrow stream whose picturesqueness has made it a favorite with New-York artists. It is proposed to establish here a botanical garden, like that at Kew.

Crotona Park, 135 acres, lies between Tremont and West Farms, and contains the Bathgate Woods. It commands views of the Palisades and the Brooklyn Bridge.

St.-Mary's Park occupies 25 acres, part of the old Gouverneur-Morris estate, near Morrisania. It is a pleasant undulating region, with views of river and Sound.

Claremont Park, of 38 acres, is between Inwood and Tremont, beyond the Harlem River. It is a triangular valley, rich in vegetation.

The Parkways which connect these parks will be handsome roads 600 feet wide. Between Pelham Park and Bronx Park is the Bronx and Pelham Parkway; between Crotona Park and Bronx Park, the Crotona Parkway; and between Bronx Park and Van-Cortlandt Park, the Mosholu Parkway.

WASHINGTON IRVING BUST, IN BRYANT PARK.

Other Parks are simply small open places with walks, flowers, shrubbery and seats, and generally less than half an acre in extent. These are the principal places of the kind : Abingdon, Beach-Street, Boulevard (2), Canal - Street, Christopher - Street, Cooper-Institute, Duane-Street, Five-Points (called Paradise Park), Grand-Street, Jackson, Sixth-Avenue, Cedar, Jeannette, Boston-Road (2), Fulton-Avenue (2), and Tompkins (with 10½ acres).

A new park is to be laid out on the eastern slope of Washington Heights, overlooking the Harlem River, from 155th Street to the bluff at Fort George, a distance of over two miles.

Statues, Busts and Sculpture adorn the parks and public places. There are in the city about fifty portrait-statues and busts and ideal works of sculpture, almost half of which are in Central Park. Several are very admirable works of art, and on the whole the collection will compare favorably with that in any other American city.

The Washington Memorial Arch had its inception in the celebration in 1889 of the Centennial anniversary of the inauguration of Washington as first President of the United States. The temporary arch which was part of the street decoration of the occasion spanned Fifth Avenue on the north side of Waverly Place. The structure, which was designed by Stanford White, the architect, was so generally admired that arrangements were perfected to perpetuate it in white marble. Now it stands in Washington Square, facing the lower end of Fifth Avenue, fifty feet south of Waverly Place, and spanning the main drive of the Square. The Arch is the finest structure of its class in this country. Each of the square piers is 64 feet around, and they are 30 feet apart; from the ground to the centre of the arch space is 47 feet. With the frieze, the attic and the coping the structure is 77 feet high. The frieze is carved with a design showing 13 large stars, 42 small stars, and the initial "W" regularly repeated. American eagles are carved on the two keystones; in the panels of the piers are bas-relief emblems of war and peace; and in the spandrils of the arch figures of Victory. The roof of the arch is ornamented with carved

WASHINGTON MEMORIAL ARCH.

WASHINGTON SQUARE, BEGINNING OF FIFTH AVENUE.   JUDSON MEMORIAL CHURCH SHOWS THROUGH THE ARCH.

rosettes in panels. At the base of the piers are two simple pedestals, on which will be placed symbolical groups of figures. On the north panel of the attic is this inscription, from Washington's inaugural address: "Let us Raise a Standard to which the Wise and the Honest can repair. The Event is in the Hands of God." On the opposite panel is this dedication: "To Commemorate the one-hundredth anniversary of the inauguration of George Washington as the First President of the United States." Below the frieze and above the centre of the arch are carved the words: "Erected by the People of the City of New York." The cost of the structure was $128,000, and the amount was raised by popular subscription. The corner-stone of the arch was laid May 30, 1889; and the main work was completed in April, 1892.

Garibaldi, in bronze, by G. Turini, is in Washington Square. It was presented to the city by Italians of the United States, and erected in 1888.

Alexander L. Holley is commemorated by a heroic bronze bust, placed upon a simple square column, upon which an inscription states that the memorial was

BRYANT PARK -- SIXTH AVENUE, 41ST TO 42D STREETS.

erected by mechanical engineers of two continents. The bust is the work of J. Q. A. Ward, and is in Washington Square, where it was unveiled in 1890.

Washington Statues in the city are three in number. An important one is the colossal bronze statue by J. Q. A. Ward, at the entrance of the Sub-Treasury building in Wall Street, which is on the site of Federal Hall, where Washington took the oath of office as first President of the United States, April 30, 1789. On the pedestal is the stone upon which Washington stood when he took the oath. The statue was unveiled November 26, 1883.

Another statue of Washington in the city is a copy of the Houdon statue in the Capitol at Richmond, Virginia, reduced in size. It stands in Riverside Park, near 88th Street; and was a gift to the city from the children of the public schools.

The Equestrian Washington, the most satisfactory of the Washington statues, is in Union Square. It is the work of Henry K. Browne. It is of heroic size, and an excellent piece of sculpture.

Liberty Enlightening the World is probably the best-known statue in the United States. It stands in New-York Bay, on Bedloe's Island, formerly the place of execution of pirates; and is one of the most conspicuous objects in view, either from the surrounding shores or from the decks of ocean vessels bound through the Narrows. It is admired for its magnificent proportions, and by general consent it is admitted to be one of the world's greatest colossi and the largest made in modern times. The draped female figure, of *repoussé* copper, 151 feet high, is crowned with a diadem, and holds lifted high in the right hand a torch that is lighted by electricity at night. The left hand clasps close to the body a tablet bearing the inscription "July 4, 1776." Some of the dimensions of the figure are interesting; the nose is nearly four feet long, the right fore-finger eight feet long and five feet in circumference; and the head fourteen feet high. The statue weighs 25 tons; and the cost (over $200,000) was defrayed by popular subscription in France. The sculptor Bartholdi, who made the Lafayette statue in Union Square, conceived the idea, and modelled the figure (it is said) from his mother. The pedestal upon which the statue stands is 155 feet high, a square structure of concrete and granite. It

MOUNT MORRIS PARK, FIFTH AVENUE, 120TH TO 124TH STREETS.

was designed by Richard M. Hunt, the architect, and erected under the supervision of General Charles P. Stone, engineer. It cost $250,000, and was paid for by a popular subscription in the United States, the greater part of which was raised by the efforts of *The World*. Surrounding the island is a sea-wall, and the statue stands on an elevation in the centre of an enclosed space made by the double walls of old Fort Wood. The statue was unveiled in October, 1886.

Benjamin Franklin, of heroic size, in bronze, keeps watch over the newspapers from his pedestal in Printing-House Square. The statue was designed by E. Plassman, and was given to the city by Captain Benjamin De Groot, an old New-Yorker. It was unveiled in 1872.

Horace Greeley, in heroic bronze, faces Franklin, seated on an arm-chair on a pedestal at one of the doorways of the Tribune Building, corner of Nassau and Spruce Streets. The statue was dedicated in 1890, and was paid for principally by the *Tribune* owners. It is one of the best statues in the city, and is the work of John Q. A. Ward.

WASHINGTON STATUE, ON WALL STREET.

Samuel S. Cox, when a Congressman, befriended the letter-carriers in National legislation, and they remembered him in a statue that stands in Astor Place, and was dedicated in 1891. It is the work of Miss Louisa Lawson.

William E. Dodge, a bronze by J. Q. A. Ward, was paid for by merchant friends, and erected in 1885 at the junction of Broadway, Sixth Avenue and 35th Street.

Washington Irving's bust, presented to the city in 1866 by Joseph Weiner, is on a pedestal in Bryant Park.

Lafayette, an animated figure, done in bronze, by Bartholdi, stands in Union Square. It was erected in 1876 by French residents of New York, and bears two inscriptions upon its pedestal : "To The City of New York, France, in remembrance of sympathy in time of trial, 1870-71 ;" and "As soon as I heard of American Independence my heart was enlisted, 1776."

Lincoln is commemorated in a bronze statue which stands as a complement to the equestrian Washington, in Union Square. This fine work of Henry K. Browne was paid for by a popular subscription, and erected in 1868. The martyr President stands in the attitude of addressing an audience, and the angularity and ungracefulness of his figure are expressed with painful exactitude. A low curb of granite surrounds the pedestal, and on this are inscribed Lincoln's famous Gettysburg words, "With Malice Toward None, With Charity For All."

The William H. Seward Statue in Madison Square is from a design by Randolph Rogers. The Secretary of State is represented seated in a chair, beneath which are piles of books, and upon the pedestal is the inscription : "Governor, U.-S. Senator, Secretary of State, U. S." The statue was unveiled in 1876.

The Admiral Farragut Statue in Madison Square is by general consent one of the finest examples of contemporaneous American art in sculpture. It is the work of Augustus St. Gaudens, and a present to the city from the Farragut Memo-

rial Association. The brave admiral is represented as standing on the deck of his vessel, with field glasses in hand, and coat blowing in the breeze. The curving pedestal is decorated with bas-relief female figures, ocean waves, and appropriate bits of marine design.

General Worth is commemorated by a granite obelisk, in the triangle formed by Broadway, Fifth Avenue and 26th Street (Madison Square). On the south face of the plinth is a bronze bas-relief of General Worth on horseback. The east face has the motto, "Ducit Amor Patriæ;" the west face the motto, "Honor to the Brave;" and on the north side is the name and the dates and places of his birth and death. Raised bands are placed at regular

FRANKLIN STATUE, IN PRINTING-HOUSE SQUARE.

LIBERTY ENLIGHTENING THE WORLD.
STATUE, BY BARTHOLDI, ON BEDLOE'S ISLAND, NEW-YORK HARBOR.

GREELEY STATUE, IN PRINTING-HOUSE SQUARE.

intervals about the shaft, and upon these are carved the names of battles with which General Worth's fame was identified. The plot of land on which the monument stands is surrounded by an iron fence ornamented by appropriate military designs, and the shaft also has upon it a bronze coat-of-arms of New-York State and a group of military insignia. The monument was erected by the city in 1857.

Commodore Cornelius Vanderbilt, in bas-relief, is on the façade of the Hudson-Street freight-depot of the New-York Central & Hudson-River Railroad.

Governor Peter Stuyvesant, with his wooden leg most conspicuous, is a wooden statue in front of the Stuyvesant Insurance Company's office, 165 Broadway.

Gutenberg, the father of modern printing, and **Franklin,** America's eminent printer, both modelled by Plassman, adorn the façade of the *Staats-Zeitung* Building, looking out upon Printing-House Square.

Beethoven, in Central Park, is commemorated by a colossal bronze bust on a granite pedestal near the Music Pavilion of the Mall. It is the work of the German sculptor Baerer, and was erected in 1884 by the Männerchor German singing society.

Robert Burns is also on the Mall, in Central Park, a bronze seated figure on a rock, modelled by John Steele, of Edinburgh, and presented to the city in 1880 by Scottish citizens.

Sir Walter Scott, in Central Park, also of bronze, of heroic size, the work of Steele, and a present from resident Scotchmen, is seated opposite the Burns statue, on an Aberdeen-granite pedestal. It was unveiled in 1872.

Fitz-Greene Halleck, in Central Park, of bronze, the work of Wilson MacDonald, is on the Mall. It shows the poet seated in a chair, with note-book and pen in hand. It was erected in 1877.

The Shakespeare Statue, by J. Q. A. Ward, is a standing figure in

COX STATUE, IN ASTOR PLACE.

bronze, at the southern entrance to the Mall, in Central Park. It was unveiled, May 23, 1872, on the 300th anniversary of the great dramatist's birth.

The **Indian Hunter**, by J. Q. A. Ward, a life-size ideal figure of an Indian, bow and arrow in hand, bending eagerly forward and holding his dog in leash, is just west of the Mall, in Central Park, and is a very spirited and admirable group.

The **Eagles and Goat** in Central Park is an interesting bronze by the French sculptor Fratin, presented to the city in 1863 by a wealthy resident, Gurdon W. Burnham.

The **Bethesda Fountain,** the most ambitious work of sculpture in Central Park, stands

DODGE STATUE, AT BROADWAY AND SIXTH AVENUE.

on the Esplanade at the foot of the Terrace, on the shore of the Lake. The design, by Miss Emma Stebbins, the New-York sculptor, represents the angel blessing

JAMES FOUNTAIN, IN UNION SQUARE.

the waters of the Pool of Bethesda. The figure of the winged angel is poised easily upon a mass of rocks from which the water gushes, falling over the edge of the upper basin, which is supported by four figures symbolizing Temperance, Purity, Health and Peace. In her left hand the angel holds a bunch of lilies, flowers of purity, and over her bosom are the cross-bands of the messenger. The basin of the fountain contains lotus, papyrus, Indian water-lilies, and other rare water-plants.

General Simon Bolivar, the Liberator of South America, is represented by an equestrian statue that stands on the west side of Central Park, near 81st Street. It is a replica of the Bolivar statue by R. De La Cora, in Caracas, Venezuela; and was a present from the South-American Republic to the City of New York in 1884.

WASHINGTON EQUESTRIAN MONUMENT, IN UNION SQUARE.

Daniel Webster is an heroic bronze statue on the West Drive in Central Park, made by Thomas Ball, at a cost of $65,000. Gurdon W. Burnham presented it.

Mazzini, a bronze bust, is on the West Drive of Central Park. It is of heroic size, upon a high pedestal. Turini, the Italian sculptor, made it, and Italian residents of New York, admirers of the great Italian agitator, presented it to the city in 1878.

The Seventh-Regiment Monument is on the West Drive of Central Park, not far from the Webster statue. It represents a citizen soldier at parade rest, leaning on his musket. It was modelled by J. Q. A. Ward, and was erected in 1874, to commemorate the patriotism of those members of the Seventh New-York Regiment who fell in battle during the civil war.

The Falconer, an ideal bronze figure, modelled by George Simonds, stands on a bluff in Central Park. George Kemp presented it to the city in 1872.

Commerce, an allegorical female figure in bronze, of heroic size, is the work of the French sculptor Bosquet. It is in Central Park, near the entrance at Eighth Avenue and 59th Street, and was erected in 1866, a gift from Stephen B. Guion.

Alexander Hamilton, a granite statue in Central Park, stands near the Museum of Art. Ch. Conradts, the sculptor, designed it for the son of Hamilton, John C. Hamilton, who presented it to the city in 1880.

Prof. S. F. B. Morse is honored with a bronze statue, of life-size, modelled by Byron M. Pickett, and erected in 1871 by the Telegraph Operators' Association. It is in Central Park, near the 72d-Street entrance, on Fifth Avenue. Prof. Morse was present at the dedication.

The Pilgrim, an heroic bronze statue on the Grand Drive, in Central Park, was a gift from the New-England Society of New York, in 1885. It is a picturesque and noble statue, by J. Q. A. Ward, to commemorate the landing of the Pilgrims on Plymouth Rock. It represents a strong-faced, alert, and resolute hero, in the quaint English costume of 1620.

The Alexander Von Humboldt bronze bust in Central Park was a gift from the German residents of the city, in 1869. It was designed by Prof. Gustave Blaeser, of Berlin; and stands near Fifth Avenue and 59th Street.

The Thomas Moore bust near the southeastern corner of Central Park, was modelled by Dennis B. Sheehan, and put in place by the Moore memorial committee, in 1880.

LAFAYETTE STATUE, IN UNION SQUARE.

Schiller, the German poet, is remembered in a bronze bust by C. L. Richter, that is set up on a sandstone pedestal in the Ramble, in Central Park. It was the first piece of sculpture to be erected in the Park; and was presented by German residents, in 1859, less than three years after the Park was begun.

The Still Hunt, in Central Park, by Edward Kemeys, represents a crouching American panther preparing to leap upon its prey. It is on a high ledge near the Obelisk.

The Tigress and Young, a fine bronze group, came from the hand of the French sculptor, Auguste Cain. It stands west of the Terrace in Central Park, and was a gift in 1867 of twelve New-Yorkers.

The Egyptian Obelisk, in Central Park, is one of the most interesting historical relics in the metropolis. It was presented to the city, through the Department of State, in 1877, by the Khedive of Egypt, Ismail Pasha. It was transported to this country under the direction of

LINCOLN STATUE, IN UNION SQUARE.

Lieut.-Com. H. H. Gorringe, U. S. N., at the expense of William H. Vanderbilt. The monolith is of granite, 69 feet high, and weighs 220 tons. It is the sixth in size of the famous obelisks of Egypt, and was erected in the Temple of the Sun, at Heliopolis, 3,500 years ago, by King Thothmes III. The hieroglyphic inscriptions upon it relate the titles of Thothmes, and his illustrious descendant, King Rameses II., who lived 200 years after Thothmes. Until the reign of Tiberius it stood in

SEWARD STATUE, IN MADISON SQUARE.

the Temple of the Sun, and then it was removed to Alexandria, where it remained until it crossed the water to the New World. The obelisk was old in the days of the Roman Empire; antedates the Christian Era by fifteen centuries; looked down upon the land of Egypt before the siege of Troy; and was familiar to Moses and the Israelites in bondage. It now stands on a knoll near the Museum of Art, an impressive reminder of a far-away past. The severities of the American climate may cause the gradual obliteration of the venerable inscriptions on the obelisk, and great care has been taken to protect these annals of the past by covering them with paraffine and other protective materials. Another obelisk, of similar size, stood with this before the Temple of the Sun, and now adorns the Queen-Victoria Embankment, along the Thames, in London. Both were of the rose-red granite of Nubia.

COLUMBUS STATUE, 59TH STREET, BROADWAY AND EIGHTH AVENUE.

The James Fountain, in Union Square, was designed by Adolf Donndorf, of Stuttgart, and dedicated in 1881. It was a gift to the city from D. Willis James. The ornate base, of Swedish granite, supports a beautiful group of a benignant mother and two children, cast in bronze, at Brunswick, Germany.

The Christopher Columbus Monument stands on the Circle, where Eighth Avenue, Broadway, the Boulevard and West 59th Street meet, at the southwestern corner of Central Park. It is a tall column, ornamented with bronze reliefs, anchors, and ships' prows, and crowned with a statue of the great discoverer. One inscription attributes its erection: "By the initiative of *Il Progresso Italo-Americano*, the first Italian daily newspaper in the United States, Cav. Carlo Barsotti, editor and proprietor." . . . . Another inscription reads thus : "To Christopher Columbus, the Italians resident in America.

Scoffed at before, during the voyage menaced, after it chained, as generous as oppressed, to the world he gave a world. Joy and glory never uttered a more thrilling call than that which resounded from the conquered ocean, at sight of the first American island. 'Land ! Land !' On the 12th of October, 1892, the fourth centenary of the discovery of America, in imperishable remembrance."

FARRAGUT STATUE, IN MADISON SQUARE.

The John Ericsson Statue, commemorating the illustrious Swedish-American, whose discoveries in naval science were of vast importance, was unveiled April 26, 1893, in the presence of the international fleet and of many Swedish gymnastic, singing and social societies, and military companies. It was designed by J. S. Hartley, and cast in bronze by the Gorham Manufacturing Company ; and stands on a pedestal of polished Quincy granite, bearing four historical panels in relief. The statue is on the Battery, near the Barge Office, and facing toward Jersey City. It was erected by an appropriation from the City of New York. On the base is this inscription : "John Ericsson. The City of New York erects this monument to the memory of a citizen whose genius has contributed to the greatness of the Republic and to the progress of the world."

ERICSSON STATUE, NEAR BARGE OFFICE, IN BATTERY PARK.

Judge John Watts, Recorder of the city during the British occupation, and one of the most sagacious and influential citizens of the older New York, is commemorated by a noble bronze statue in Trinity Churchyard. It was modelled by George W. Bissell, and erected by Gen. John Watts de Peyster. The unveiling took place in 1892. The calm statue looks down on the wild whirl of Broadway.

WORTH MONUMENT, IN MADISON SQUARE.

Archbishop Hughes stands in bronze, of heroic size, in the grounds in front of St. John's College, Fordham. The prelate is represented clad in a silken robe, addressing an audience. The statue, which is the work of W. R. O'Donovan, is placed on a granite pedestal. It was unveiled in 1891. Hughes was a poor Irish immigrant gardener, who bravely fought his way through college, and was made priest in 1825, bishop in 1838, and archbishop of New York in 1850. He was a patriot during the Secession War; and in 1841 founded the now flourishing St. John's College.

ARCHBISHOP JOHN HUGHES STATUE, ST. JOHN'S
COLLEGE, FORDHAM.

Regina Sodalium is a statue of the Virgin Mary, at St. John's College, Fordham, erected in 1887, by the students.

Other statues that are contemplated are the equestrian General W. T. Sherman, by Augustus St. Gaudens, to be placed at the Boulevard and West 72d Street; the Nathan Hale, by MacMonnies, to be erected in the City-Hall Park, by the Sons of the Revolution; the Horace Greeley, a gift from the printers of the United States, to be set up at Broadway, Sixth Avenue and 32d Street; the Columbus-Pinzon monument, with gigantic statues, to be erected in Central Park by Spanish residents of the city; J. Q. A. Ward's statue of Roscoe Conkling; and many others, commemorating distinguished citizens, and others.

New York has made a good beginning in adorning her public places with these memorials of the great men of the world. There are many more to be thus honored, among her own sons, as William Cullen Bryant the poet; Robert Fulton, the father of steam navigation; Valentine Mott, the foremost physician of his time; John Jay, the illustrious jurist, and scores of others. Thanks to Ward and St. Gaudens, the statuary work in New York is more worthy and artistic than that of any other American city, and includes some of the choicest memorial work of the present century. The cosmopolitan character of the city is thus illustrated, for the statues include New-Englanders, Virginians and Westerners, Scots, Englishmen and Irishmen, Frenchmen and Italians, Germans and Swedes, Spaniards and Dutchmen, West-Indians and South-Americans, Syrians and Egyptians.

New York is too great in spirit and in appreciation to be confined by provincial preferences. It honors valor, genius, honor, wherever found. Imperial Rome was hospitable to the gods of the world; joyous Paris has welcomed the fine arts to her studios and boulevards; and imperial and joyous New York craves and honors noble men and their memories and achievements.

REGINA SODALIUM STATUE, ST. JOHN'S
COLLEGE, FORDHAM.

SUB-TREASURY.   ASSAY OFFICE.   CUSTOM HOUSE.

THE WASHINGTON STATUE IN FRONT OF UNITED STATES SUB-TREASURY.

WALL ST., NORTHEAST CORNER OF NASSAU ST. ON THIS SPOT GEORGE WASHINGTON WAS INAUGURATED PRESIDENT.

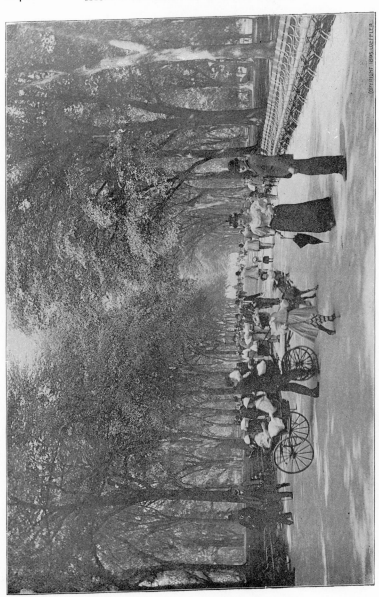

COPYRIGHT 1895, LOEFFLER.

CENTRAL PARK: THE GOAT WAGONS ON THE MALL.

VIEW TAKEN BY LOEFFLER IN 1895.

CENTRAL PARK: THE BOAT HOUSE AND LAKE.

COPYRIGHT 1895 LOEFFLER.

GENERAL U. S. GRANT'S MONUMENT.

RIVERSIDE PARK, MORNINGSIDE HEIGHTS.   VIEW TAKEN IN JANUARY, 1897.

Overhead and Underfoot

Bridges, Tunnels, Sewers, Water, Aqueducts, Reservoirs, Lighting by Gas and Electricity, Telegraphs,
Telephones, Etc.

THE exigencies of life in modern municipalities compel the utilization of space overhead and underground; so closely are the people crowded and restricted for room. In New York, the East River and the Harlem River are bridged to allow of quick egress to the surrounding country; and projects are in hand for more bridges and several tunnels across and under the East and North Rivers, and beneath the Narrows from Staten Island to Long Island. Electric-light, telephone and telegraph wires are still suspended from buildings and poles, although many miles of them have already gone into the subways, where it is proposed that all shall follow in due course of time. Beneath the principal streets there is a network of pipes of all descriptions; sewers, water-mains, pneumatic tubes, gas-mains, steam-heating pipes, subways for wires, and, in Broadway, Third Avenue, Tenth Avenue and 125th Street conduits for street-car cables. Beneath sidewalks the abutting property-owners build vaults and sub-cellars, thereby adding valuable room to the establishments above ground. Were it not for all these conveniences overhead and underground, the normal activity of the metropolis would find itself hampered to a serious extent.

The Bridges, aside from the ornamental structures in the parks, comprise fourteen which belong in whole or in part to New York. One is across the East River; and others span the Harlem, connecting Manhattan Island with the mainland.

The East-River Bridge, more popularly known as the Brooklyn Bridge, was erected to meet the pressing necessity for a better means of communication between New York and Brooklyn than was offered by the ferry-boats. In this generation Brooklyn has become essentially a part of the great metropolis in the intimacy of its business and social relations. To a remarkable degree the population of the Long-Island city is made up of those who are employed or who do business on Manhattan Island, and are thus compelled to make the trip twice a day across the East River. It was inconceivable that these two communities would be willing always to remain dependent upon ferriage, which is at times slow and inadequate. As far back as 1819 a civil engineer named Pope published a scientific paper in which he advocated a suspension-bridge across the East River. The same idea was taken up in 1829, when a private corporation was organized, and elaborated plans for a bridge from Brooklyn Heights to Maiden Lane, at an estimated cost of $600,000. In 1849 public agitation of the matter was revived, and the daily newspapers urged that the work be undertaken. John A. Roebling, the successful engineer, had long entertained the idea; and in 1860 at the suggestion of W. C. Kingsley, a wealthy contractor, he publicly outlined his plan. It was not, however, until after the civil war, which had accustomed the public to big undertakings and lavish expenditures, that the scheme was definitely developed.   There were several rival projects ; but Roebling, who had just finished the Cincinnati Suspension-Bridge across the Ohio River, was taken into consultation with Kingsley, Henry C. Murphy and others, and his plans were adopted.   A private company was chartered in which were Roebling, Kingsley, Murphy, John T. Hoffman, S. B. Chittenden, John Roach, Henry E. Pierrepont and others.   This concern was known as the New-York Bridge Company, and work was at once entered upon.   Roebling was chosen Chief Engineer in 1867, and his son, Washington A. Roebling, Assistant Engineer.   The elder Roebling drew the original plans and specifications; but he died suddenly in 1869, while engaged in the preliminary surveys, before the actual work of construction had begun.

BROOKLYN BRIDGE PROMENADE -- LOOKING TOWARD NEW-YORK.

The son took his father's place ; and, beginning in January, 1870, carried the enterprise through to a successful conclusion, after thirteen years of difficult work. Through exposure and overwork he broke down in health and became an invalid. For ten years, confined to his house on Columbia Heights, Brooklyn, he, with the assistance of his wife, directed the work to the end.   From the window of his sick room he watched the progress of construction through a telescope, day by day, hour by hour, supervising as thoroughly and as efficiently as though he had been on the spot.   It was a wonderful display of indomitable will power and of mechanical genius.   But it was rough sailing sometimes.   In 1874 the Legislature took the enterprise out of the hands of the private corporation that had initiated it, and empowered the twin cities to go ahead with the project, Brooklyn to pay two-thirds and New York one-third of the cost, the control of the bridge during its construc-

EAST RIVER, OR NEW-YORK AND BROOKLYN, BRIDGE.
ACROSS THE EAST RIVER FROM NEW YORK TO BROOKLYN.

tion and afterwards to remain in the same relative proportions in the hands of the authorities of the sister municipalities. Many unforeseen delays arose, of political as well as of mechanical character. New problems in engineering had to be met ; experiments made ; and new devices and working machinery invented. For a time there was much public distrust of the management, which on the New-York side was in the hands of the notorious Tweed ring, and once the work was entirely stopped. But the municipal plunderers were overthrown before they had succeeded in getting their fingers into the bridge treasury ; the seemingly well-nigh insuperable mechanical difficulties were overcome; and the bridge was finally completed and opened to general traffic, in May, 1884. There was a grand military procession, President Arthur and his Cabinet, and Governor Cleveland and his staff, being present. There were speeches by William C. Kingsley, Hon. Abram S. Hewitt, and Rev. Dr. Richard S. Storrs ; the bridge was illuminated, and fireworks were displayed ; and the creator of the work, Col. Roebling, watched the proceedings through the faithful telescope at his house, where later in the day the distinguished people who had participated in the celebration went to congratulate him. The estimate for the construction of the bridge was $8,000,000 ; but owing principally to the amplifica- tion of the original plans it cost when completed about $15,000,000.

Statistics of the bridge will be interesting even to the unprofessional reader, for the structure is one of the highest achievements of modern engineering, and ranks as one of the great wonders of the world. There is a central span across the river 1,595 feet long and 135 feet above high-water mark. At each end this span springs from a tower, resting upon a caisson. These foundations are of solid con- crete, resting upon rock, 78 feet below the water-level on the New-York side and 45 feet on the Brooklyn side of the river. The Brooklyn caisson is 168 x 102 feet, and the New-York caisson 172 x 102 feet ; and each caisson contains over 5,000 cubic yards of timber and iron, and over 5,000 cubic feet of concrete, the weight of the caisson being about 7,000 tons, and of the concrete filling 8,000 tons. At the water-line the towers are 140 x 50 feet, and of solid masonry in the lower part, being hollow the rest of the way up to the bases of the great arches. The arches, of which there are two in each tower, are 117 feet high, and the capstones are 271 feet above the water. Travel passes through these arches, the floor of the bridge being across the towers at the bases of the arches. At their summits the towers are narrowed to 120 x 40 feet. In the New-York tower are 46,395 cubic yards of masonry, and in the Brooklyn, 38,214 cubic yards. Behind each tower are the anchorages, 930 feet distant. They are massive granite structures, each 129 x 119 feet at base, 117 x 104 feet at top, 89 feet high in front and 85 feet in rear. On each anchorage is an arrangement of iron bars to which the cables are fastened, and an anchor-plate weighing 23 tons. The four cables upon which the bridge is suspended are bound to the anchor-chains, then pass through 25 feet of masonry, and come out of the walls of the anchorages on the water side, about 80 feet above high-water mark. They are then carried over the tops of the towers and in the middle of the river-span they drop to the level of the roadway, 135 feet above the water. From these cables hang at regular intervals smaller steel cables that are braced and tied together and that hold the floor beams upon which the bridge proper is laid. The four large cables are each made of 5,434 galvanized steel oil-coated wires, which are not twisted, but which, lying parallel, are pressed compactly together and then bound tightly with other wires, the whole making a solid cable 15¾ inches in diameter. Each cable thus finished is 3,578½ feet long, and has a supporting power of 12,200 tons in the middle of its sag. The cables were made where they are, and this part

THE WASHINGTON BRIDGE, ACROSS THE HARLEM RIVER.
FROM 181ST STREET AND TENTH AVENUE TO AQUEDUCT AVENUE.

of the work was not begun until June, 1877. Steel wire ropes were stretched between the tops of the towers, and from these were suspended movable platforms for
the workmen. The steel wires were drawn across in place and then bound into a
cable as they hung in mid-air. Between the towers and the anchorages the spans
are also suspended from these cables at a height of from 68 to 119 feet above the
street levels. The New-York approach from the terminus to the anchorage is 1,562

APPROACH TO THE WASHINGTON BRIDGE.

feet in length; and the Brooklyn approach, 971 feet. Heavy arches of masonry
support these approaches, and the streets are crossed by steel truss-bridges. The
space under these archways is utilized for storage and other business purposes.

The total length of the bridge is 1¼ miles; the width is 85 feet. In New York
the terminus is in Park Row, facing the City-Hall Park, and in Brooklyn at Fulton
and Sands Streets, the terminus of nearly all the elevated and surface railway-lines
in that city. There is an elevated promenade in the middle of the bridge, and seats
are placed at the towers for those who wish to rest and enjoy the view. The fare
for pedestrians was formerly one cent, but the promenade has now been made free,
and consequently the bridge is thronged, especially in hot summer nights and holidays, by those who wish to enjoy the view of the river and harbor and the two
cities, and the refreshing river breezes. On each side of the promenade is a drive
for vehicles, and a railway track, upon which trains are run at intervals of a minute
or less during the entire day. The cars are run by cable from a power-house on the
Brooklyn side. The car-fare is three cents, or ten tickets for 25 cents, and the trip
over is made in about six minutes. During the construction of the bridge twenty
persons were killed by accidents, and many others were injured. Since it was opened
to traffic several notoriety-seekers have jumped from it into the river below. One
of these divers, Stephen Brodie, survived the ordeal. The others were killed. The
bridge has a capacity of 45,000 pedestrians and 1,440 vehicles each hour. It is the
longest suspension-bridge in the world. Bridges not suspension that exceed it in
length are the Maintenon aqueduct of stone, 13,367 feet; the Firth of Forth bridge,
10,321 feet; and the Victoria (over the St.-Lawrence), the Parkersburg (West Va.),
and the St.-Charles (Mo.) iron bridges. The yearly receipts from the bridge
exceed $1,250,000, and the expenses are less than $1,000,000. Over 43,000,000
passengers are carried across every year, and fully 12,000,000 people walk over. As
many as 160,000 passengers have been carried in a single day, but the daily average
is about 120,000.

HIGH BRIDGE (OR "CROTON AQUEDUCT BRIDGE") ACROSS THE HARLEM RIVER.

The Washington Bridge across the Harlem River, from 181st Street and Tenth Avenue on Manhattan Island to Aqueduct Avenue on a part of the old Ogden estate on the mainland, is another notable structure. It connects Washington Heights and the so-called Annexed District, two sections of the city that will in a few years be ranked among its handsomest and most popular residence-quarters. The bridge was completed in 1889, and cost nearly $2,700,000. It is a massive structure of granite approaches and piers and iron and steel spans ; and it is much admired for the beauty of its proportions and lines, as well as for its grandeur and substantial character. Its total length, including the span of the bridge proper across the river and the New-York Central Railroad and New-York & Northern tracks on the east bank, the masonry approaches and the arched granite passages, is 2,384 feet. The east abutment is 342 feet long, with four arched passage-ways of masonry. The abutment on the west shore is 277 feet long, with three arches. The two central spans are of steel, and describe beautiful parabolic curves. They are each 510 feet long, and in the center 135 feet above high-water mark. Their construction was notable in that it successfully tested a new device in engineering. The arches were made and placed in position by sections. One section was firmly anchored in the abutment, and then the next section was sent out on travellers, to be fastened to the extremity of the first, and so on, until the entire space was spanned, when the arches were keyed in the center as stone arches are. The superstructure is very handsome. With a roadway fifty feet wide, and two pathways each fifteen feet wide, there is abundant accommodation for travel. There are heavy granite parapets, pierced with loop-holes, polished buttresses, artistic bronze lamp-posts, and many semi-circular niches in the parapet, with low granite steps or seats. The bridge is one of the most popular places of public resort in the city. The view from it is superb, taking in the Harlem River to the north and south, the city farther in the distance, the wide sweep of the beautiful Annexed District, even as far as Long-Island Sound to the east, and Fort George, Spuyten Duyvil and Kingsbridge, and the surrounding country to the west and north.

High Bridge spans the Harlem River at 175th Street and Tenth Avenue, a third of a mile below Washington Bridge. It was built to carry the old Croton Aqueduct across the river and valley at that point, and is 1,460 feet long, from bluff to bluff. Arches resting upon thirteen solid granite piers support the structure. The crown of the highest arch is 116 feet above high-water mark. Large cast-iron pipes enclosed in brick masonry convey the water across the bridge. The structure is not provided with a carriage-way, but there is a wide walk for foot-passengers, who are numerous in summer-time, attracted by the beautiful view, and the enjoyment of the park and picnic grounds at each terminus, and the open country at the eastern end. On Manhattan Island the water-pipes terminate in the pretty High-Bridge Park, where there is a reservoir, a lofty stand-pipe, a gate-house, and other appurtenances of an important water-station.

The McComb's-Dam Bridge (or Central Bridge), an old wooden draw-bridge, has long existed across the Harlem at the northern terminus of Seventh Avenue. It has had much local celebrity, for Seventh Avenue, south of the river, and Jerome Avenue, its continuation north of the river, have for a generation constituted the favorite drive for New-Yorkers outside of Central Park. North of the river the avenue extends to the Jerome-Park racing-track, and thence on to Yonkers; and it is lined with many well-known road-houses. A new bridge with approaches is now building to take the place of the old one, and this will be, when completed, one of the greatest works of the kind in the world. It will consist of a viaduct, a bridge, and steel approaches. The viaduct on the west side of the Harlem has been completed. It is in effect an extension of 155th Street from the ridge of Washington Heights on a gentle decline to the river; an ornate steel structure 60 feet wide and 1,602 feet long, with a driveway and two sidewalks. At the Washington-Heights abutment it is 65 feet above the ground, and it crosses above the elevated railroad at Eighth Avenue, with which connection is made by stairways. The bridge will be 731 feet long, and 32 feet above high-water. It consists of an immense swing span, or draw, 400 feet long, resting upon a cylindrical pivot-pier in mid-river; and four fixed spans at the ends. The terminal piers are of masonry, and there are ornamental copings and watch-towers. Two approaches, 50 feet wide, have been arranged at the east end of the bridge. They will consist of steel lattice spans resting upon masonry piers, carrying roadway and sidewalks 50 feet wide, one approach being 350 feet, and the other 1,740 feet long. The total cost of this pontifical improvement will be over $2,000,000. The Department of Public Works has built the viaduct, and the Department of Parks has charge of the construction of the bridge and its approaches.

The New-York Central & Hudson-River Railroad Bridge crosses the Harlem at Park Avenue and 134th Street, a great draw-bridge over which come all trains from New England and Northern New York that enter the Grand Central Station. Work has begun upon a new bridge at this point. It will be a draw-bridge of iron and steel, elevated 24 feet above high-water mark, and it will cost about $500,000. In connection with the bridge, elevated approaches will be constructed, to supersede the present Park-Avenue viaduct for about a mile south of the river, to 106th Street. The approaches will cost about $500,000.

Other Harlem Bridges present no particular points of interest. They include the following-named: At Second Avenue is an iron railway draw-bridge, with a foot-way, intended mainly for the trains of the Suburban Transit and the Harlem-River branch of the New-York, New-Haven & Hartford Railroad. At Third Avenue there is an iron draw-bridge for public travel, resting on stone abutments and iron piers in

THIRD-AVENUE, OR HARLEM, BRIDGE.

the water. It is usually known as Harlem Bridge. At Madison Avenue is an iron draw-bridge for general traffic. At Eighth Avenue is the iron railroad bridge of the New-York & Northern Railroad, by which connection is made with the elevated railroad system of the city proper. At Dyckman Street is an old wooden foot-bridge, that from time out of mind has connected Washington Heights with Fordham. At 224th Street, on the plain above Fort George, is the Farmer's Bridge, an antique structure, the name of which sufficiently indicates its purpose. At the junction of the Harlem River and Spuyten-Duyvil Creek, where Kingsbridge Road crosses

13

the water, there is another old bridge. The United-States Government is deepening the creek into a ship-canal, and the old bridge is soon to be torn down and a new structure that will not interfere with navigation will take its place. Where Spuyten-Duyvil Creek empties into the Hudson there is a draw-bridge for the New-York Central & Hudson-River Railroad.

Contemplated Bridges and Tunnels, and those in process of construction, respond to the demand for additional and improved facilities for reaching New Jersey, Long Island and the northern parts and suburbs of the metropolis, a demand created and constantly made more urgent by the overcrowding of Manhattan Island, both in its business and in its residence quarters.

The North-River Bridge is the most important of these undertakings. It will be built by the New-York & New-Jersey Bridge Company, and ground has already been broken for the foundations on both sides. The bridge will be a combined cantilever and suspension structure, with a single river-span of 3,200 feet, two side-spans of 1,000 feet each, and a short span of 300 feet on the New-York side, making a greater length than the present East-River Bridge. The distance above high-water mark will be 150 feet, and at the middle of the structure 193 feet. There will be two main towers, 500 feet high, with bases 120 x 250 feet, extending

HARLEM RIVER AND HARLEM BRIDGE, AT 130TH STREET AND THIRD AVENUE.

about 250 feet below the water to hard rock. On the New-Jersey side the terminus will be at Niles Avenue, Weehawken, and the New-York end will be between 70th and 71st Streets. From the latter point a viaduct 100 feet wide, with four main railroad tracks and three lines of sidings, will run through private property to a point between Eleventh and Twelfth Avenues, and thence down-town to 44th Street. This viaduct, running all the way through the blocks between streets and avenues, will be built of steel and stone. A Grand Union station, modelled after the St. Pancras Station in London, will cover the blocks between Eighth Avenue, Broadway, and 42d and 44th Streets, 400 feet on Broadway and 1,300 feet back to the avenue. Seventh Avenue and 43d Street will be arched over, the grade of the depot being above the street level. The railroad offices will be there, and also a great transferring mail station. The depot will be laid with twenty tracks, and on the bridge there will be six tracks, with room to add four more. The bridge, which it is estimated will cost $40,000,000, is intended for railroad trains exclusively, and not for general traffic. It will give the great railroads which are now compelled to bring passengers and freight by ferry into New-York City a route direct to the heart of the metropolis.

The Citizens' Bridges between New York and Brooklyn will be two in number. Legislation has been granted, and the preliminary work entered upon. Both will be suspension bridges, controlled by one company; and they will cost about $25,-000,000. Both will have a common terminus on the New-York side, between Delancy and Rivington Streets, and from that point connection will be made by elevated structures with the present elevated railroad system. One bridge will extend to Broadway, in Williamsburg, and the other with a long approach to Fulton Street, between Bridge and Little Streets. They are designed to connect the Eastern District of Brooklyn with the central business section of New York. They will be open to general traffic, and the cars that cross them will be run in connection with the Union Elevated Railroad of Brooklyn.

The Corbin Bridge has been planned to cross the East River from Long-Island City to a point on the New-York side between 37th and 42d Streets. This will be for cars only, so as to give the Long-Island Railroad entrance into New-York City. A tunnel across the city to the North - River - Bridge Depot, connecting with the Grand Central Station at 42d Street and Fourth Avenue, is also part of this plan. The bridge will

SUBURBAN ELEVATED RAILWAY BRIDGE, AT SECOND AVENUE AND 129TH STREET.

be built of iron and steel, at a cost of $12,000,000. Besides the terminal piers, there will be a mid-river pier, built on Man-of-War Rock. The structure will be 135 feet above high-water mark.

The Blackwell's-Island Bridge will extend from 64th Street, New York, to Long-Island City. A company was chartered to construct this bridge in 1867. The project has been recently revived, and work may be begun soon. There will be central piers on Blackwell's Island, abutments in Long-Island City and in New York near 64th Street, and two short river-spans. On the Long-Island side there will be elevated approaches extending nearly two miles inland, and a branch running into Brooklyn. On the New-York side there will be two approaches, one extending to the Grand Central Station at 42d Street, and the other farther north. The bridge will be 150 feet above high-water, and will be for general traffic and for railroad trains. Ground was broken for this great work in 1893.

The Astoria Suspension Bridge across the East River, from 90th Street to Astoria, Long Island, has been talked of, and will probably be built in the course of time.

A Tunnel under the Narrows between Staten Island and Brooklyn has been projected. The design is to divert railroad traffic from New Jersey south of Jersey City across Staten Island to Long Island, and eventually thus to make a short route from the coal fields and the West across Long Island and the Sound to New England.

The Hudson-River Tunnel has not yet been a fortunate enterprise. It was planned to connect Jersey City with New York for the accommodation of the railroads. Begun in 1874, work was soon suspended, not to be resumed until 1879.

The shafts on the New-York side were begun in 1882, but again for lack of funds all work was stopped in the same year. In 1887 the work was resumed, only to be suspended in 1892. At the present time, 1,550 feet have been opened from the New-Jersey shore, and about 550 from the New-York side. The entire width of the river at that point is 5,600 feet. The plans provide for a tunnel of elliptical shape, 23½ feet high and 21½ feet wide on the outside, and 18½ feet high and 16½ feet wide inside, to be lined with brick and steel plates, and to rest in blue clay and rock 25 to 50 feet below the river-bed. In Jersey City the tunnel starts from the foot of 15th Street, and in New York from the foot of Morton Street. When completed, the New-York terminus will be in the vicinity of Washington Square.

The Park-Avenue Tunnel extends from 49th Street to 106th Street, and through it run all the railway trains that come into the Grand Central Depot. From 42d Street to the south end of the tunnel the tracks are in the yards of the railroad company, or in open cuts; and these are bridged at the intersecting streets. The tunnel is brick-arched; is in three parts, separated by walls; and has four tracks and sidings. The middle of the avenue immediately over the tunnel is laid out in little parkways with green grass, trees and shrubbery, between the streets. Iron fences enclose these spots, and in them there are openings in the roof of the tunnel by which means ventilation is secured. The tunnel is owned and operated by the Harlem Railroad Company; and at 106th Street it terminates in a viaduct, which in turn is succeeded by an open cut to the Harlem River. What is practically an extension of this tunnel goes under Park Avenue from 40th Street to 34th Street. It is used for horse-cars only, and has several approaches from the street.

The Water-Supply of New York is of the utmost interest. A little more than fifty years ago the people got their water from private wells, and were very

HARLEM RIVER AND SECOND AVENUE BRIDGE, AT 129TH STREET.

well supplied, for Manhattan Island abounded in springs that gushed out of the living rock, pure and wholesome. In time, however, this source of supply began to be inadequate, and in 1774 a reservoir was built between Prince and White Streets, east of Broadway. Into this water was pumped from the wells, and distributed through the city in wooden pipes. In 1778 a committee of citizens recommended that Rye Pond in Westchester County should be made into a reservoir by building a dam, and that the water should be brought down to a city reservoir through iron pipes, crossing the Harlem River on a bridge. To this end the Manhattan Water-works were chartered, but the company got no further than to build a reservoir in Chambers

Street, between Broadway and Centre Streets, and to try to support the city with well-water by the plan before attempted. The scheme failed for the second time. Many events served to call attention to the inconvenience and danger resulting from a continuance of this condition of things, and several plans for a better water-supply were brought out from time to time. The great fire of 1834 was a conclusive argument against the folly of longer delay; and in that year, the Legislature having given the needed authority, a survey of the Croton streams was made, and in 1835 the work of constructing reservoirs and an aqueduct was definitely undertaken. The Croton water-shed is about thirty miles north of New-York City, on high land, in a remarkably healthful region. The water is exceptionally good, and is little exposed to contamination, while the flow through thirty miles of conduit to the city has a tendency still further to purify it. Croton Lake is fed by Croton River and other smaller streams, and this was formed into a reservoir, five miles long, by erecting a dam which raised the water forty feet. Then a conduit of brick, stone and cement was built in the shape of a horse-shoe, 8½ feet perpendicular diameter and 7½ feet

PARK AVENUE, NORTH FROM 98TH STREET. N. Y. C. & H. R. R. R. TRACKS.

horizontal. This conduit begins at Croton Lake, and runs to the Central-Park Reservoir. It crosses 25 streams below grade; has 16 tunnels from 160 to 1,263 feet long; and it was designed to carry about 60,000,000 gallons each day. It drew from Croton Lake and other natural and artificial reservoirs, which were then utilized, with a storage capacity of 9,500,000,000 gallons, or about three months' supply for the city. The aqueduct crosses the Harlem River upon the High Bridge, at the city end of which there was built a high-service reservoir, holding 11,000,000 gallons, a tower, and pumping machinery. Thence it goes to the Central-Park reservoirs. On Fifth Avenue, between 40th and 42d Streets, a distributing reservoir with a capacity of 20,000,000 gallons was constructed. The work of providing for this system was completed in 1842. The water was turned on upon July 4th of that year, amid the greatest enthusiasm of the people. There was a military and civic procession, eight miles long, and other forms of celebration in September of the same year. In less than forty years the city had outgrown this means of supply. The aqueduct was forced to the point of carrying nearly 100,000,000 gallons a day, but even that was not sufficient for the needs of the population. The upper stories of high buildings and even of residences on high land could get no water at all, and the storage capacity of the reservoirs was so limited that a short dry spell always made a water famine imminent. Public agitation for an increased supply began before the year

1880. Commissioners were appointed to consider various plans for relief, and they approved of Croton as an ample and pure supply. An extension of the reservoirs and the construction of a new and improved aqueduct was recommended. This work was at once entered upon, under the provisions of a special act of the Legislature, passed in 1883, and the metropolis is being provided with a water system that will be unsurpassed in any other city of the world. The construction of the aqueduct taxed engineering skill and financial management to the utmost. Unforeseen difficulties were encountered that retarded progress, and the frauds of contractors, who lined parts of the tunnel with thin shells of brick instead of with thick rubble walls, made it necessary to have a great deal of that part of the work done over again.

GATE HOUSE, CROTON AQUEDUCT.
MANHATTAN AVENUE AND 135TH STREET.

But as finally completed the aqueduct is a solid, and will be an enduring achievement.

The total length of the masonry conduit, from Croton Dam to the 135th-Street gate-house, where the tunnel ends, is $30\frac{3}{4}$ miles; from the latter point to the new reservoir in Central Park there are $2\frac{1}{3}$ miles of pipe line, making the total length of 33 miles. There are 38 shafts, from 28 feet to 350 feet deep, several of them left open to the surface so as to give access to the aqueduct for repairs when needed. The average depth of the tunnel beneath the ground is 170 feet, but at South Yonkers it was built in an open trench for the distance of a half-mile, and also at the Pocantico River and Ardsley it comes to the surface. At each of these three places there are blow-outs and waste weirs, by which the flow of water can be turned off at any time for the purpose of making repairs and cleansing the aqueduct. The tunnel begins at Croton Dam, and at its head is a handsome granite gate-house, set in a recess that was blasted for it out of the solid rock, 30 feet below the top of the old dam. The water flows from the lake through this house into the tunnel, and makes its way to the city by the force of gravity, no pumping being required, as the grade, though light, is continuous to the Harlem River. The flow is about two miles an hour. From the Croton Dam to a point a mile above Jerome Park the aqueduct is of horse-shoe form, 13.53 feet high and 13.60 feet wide; then it becomes circular, 12.3 feet in diameter. At the Harlem River there is a fine piece of engineering in the inverted siphon by which the water is carried under the river to the High-Bridge station. A circular tube of brick, $10\frac{1}{2}$ feet in diameter, goes down into the river for 1,300 feet; passes under the river-bed, and comes up on the west bank as a shaft 400 feet high. Through this the water flows and climbs the hill on its way to the gate-house at 135th Street. At this point the single tunnel ceases, and the water is distributed by pipe lines, eight iron pipes 48 inches in diameter, laid a few feet below the surface and diverging in different directions carrying it. Four of these pipes go direct to the Central-Park Reservoir, and the others supply the demands of the

Harlem District. No other tunnel in the world is equal to this in size or in the difficulty of the task that its construction imposed. The Hoosac Tunnel and the Mt.-Cenis Tunnel are each 5 miles long, and the St.-Gothard Tunnel 9½ miles, as against the 33 miles of this aqueduct, which consumed five years in building. Of brick-work alone there were 312,258 cubic yards, equal to thirty large 14-story office-buildings. Material was excavated to the amount of 3,250,000 cubic yards. The aqueduct was completed and the water turned on in the summer of 1890. The cost of the construction, exclusive of lands, engineering, superintendence, etc., was $19,612,000, as against the engineers' estimate of $18,957,000.

The new aqueduct has a flowing capacity of 300,000,000 gallons a day. A reservoir will soon be built on the site of the present Jerome Park, in order to provide for the needs of the growing annexed district. The aqueduct will keep this reservoir full, and after leaving there will be able to carry 250,000,000 gallons a day down to the Central-Park reservoir, thus allowing 50,000,000 gallons a day for the annexed district, nearly two-thirds as much as the entire city had under the old service. Then the old aqueduct can still be depended upon for at least 75,000,000 gallons a day, and the pipe lines from the Bronx River can bring down 20,000,000 a day. So it is possible to have a daily supply of at least 350,000,000 gallons. The present demand is for a little more than 175,000,000 gallons daily. It has been shown that even in dry weather the Croton-River watershed can be depended upon for fully 250,000,000 gallons a day.

Now that the aqueduct has been completed, the question of storage is engaging the attention of the municipal authorities. The present storage capacity of the Croton watershed, natural and artificial, is 17,150,-000,000 gallons ; at Croton Lake, 500,000,000 ; Boyd's Corner reservoir, 2,700,000,000 gallons ; Middle Branch, 4,000,000,000 ; East Branch, 4,500,000,000; Bog Brook, 4,050,000,000 ; Kirk Lake, 500,-000,000 ; Lake Mahopac, 500,000,-000 ; Lake Gilead, 300,000,000 ; and Barrett Pond, 150,000,000 ; total, 17,150,000,000. Tributary to the above and included in the estimate are the smaller lakes, Gillead, Gleneida and Waccabuc, and White Pond. The East Branch, which has a depth of 67 feet of water, and the Bog Brook, with a depth of 60 feet, were finished in the summer of 1892. In addition, three reservoirs are in process of construction, and will be completed

HIGH SERVICE STATION, 98TH STREET, NEAR COLUMBUS AVENUE.

in 1894. These are Reservoir D on the Western Branch, near Carmel, capacity 10,000,000,000 ; Titicus River, 7,000,000,000 ; and Amawalk Reservoir, on the Muscoot Branch, 7,000,000,000. Thus the storage capacity will be increased to 40,100,-000,000 gallons. Still another dam is under way, which is known as the New Croton

Dam, on the Cornell site. The Aqueduct Commissioners have let the contract for this structure, which was begun in the fall of 1892. The dam will be located five miles south of Croton Lake. It will be a wall of solid masonry, 264 feet high and 1,500 feet long, and will cost over $6,000,000. By its construction a reservoir 16 miles long will be erected, with a storage capacity of over 30,000,000,000 gallons. The water thus held will set back and submerge the present Croton Dam 35 feet. Hundreds of farms and houses now in the valley will have to be abandoned, and in 1893 the city authorities began their destruction.

At High Bridge there is a reservoir with a capacity of 10,000,000 gallons, and with two pumping-engines of an aggregate capacity of 10,000,000 gallons a day.

RESERVOIR, FIFTH AVENUE, 40TH AND 42D STREETS.

There can be distributed to high points on the island 20,000,000 gallons a day. In 98th Street, near Columbus Avenue, there is another water-tower and three Worthington high-service engines, with a pumping capacity of 25,000,000 gallons a day. The new retaining reservoir that occupies nearly the entire width of the northern part of Central Park will hold 1,000,000,000 gallons, and the receiving reservoir below it 150,000,000 gallons more. The reservoir at Williamsbridge holds 140,000,000 gallons ; and the distributing reservoir at Fifth Avenue and 42d Street 20,000,000. The new reservoir at Jerome Park will have a capacity of 1,300,000,000 gallons. The total storage capacity at the source of supply and within the city limits by reservoirs completed, building, and arranged for amounts to 84,600,000,000 gallons, sufficient to supply the city at its present rate of demand for two years. It is calculated when all this work is completed the municipal needs will be provided for, for the next fifty or seventy-five years. Water is distributed throughout the city by iron water-mains beneath the street surface. Of these there were on January 1, 1892, 685.48 miles, with 7,129 stop-cocks and 8,752 fire hydrants, and this branch of the water service is being constantly extended. The average daily consumption of water is nearly 100 gallons per capita. Consumers pay for the water, the annual charges ranging from $4 to $18 for each house, with extra rates for special service, and for houses more than fifty feet wide. In hotels, breweries, large office-buildings, manufacturing establishments, stables and other places where water is used in large quantities, meters are put in, and the water is measured and charged for at the rate of one dollar for each thousand cubic feet. A fixed rate is charged to some business establishments. There are 24,264 meters, and they register an annual consumption of over 30,000,000 gallons. The total water revenue from all sources amounted for the year 1891 to $3,375,140. The annual receipts go to pay the interest on the debt, and to the sinking fund, which is intended in time to extinguish the debt.

Lighting the Public Streets in the olden time was a duty imposed upon individual citizens. The first street-lighting was ordained by decree of the corporation in 1697, when it was ordered that every seven householders should unite to pay the expense of burning a candle in a lantern, suspended on a pole from the window of every seventh house on nights when there was no moon. But even this provision was so inadequate that the worthy burghers who were out late at night — that is until 9 or 10 o'clock — continued to carry their own lanterns to dispel the gloom. In 1762 public lamp-posts, with lamps burning oil, were first maintained at city expense, and this method continued down to 1825. Experiments with gas were made as early as 1812, but it was not until 1823 that practical steps were taken to introduce this new illuminating medium. In that year the New-York Gas-Light Company was incorporated, with a capital of $100,000, and given the right to the city south of Canal Street; and in 1825 pipes were first laid down. In 1830 the privilege of supplying gas to the northern part of the island was given to the Manhattan Gas-Light Company, which was incorporated with a capital of $50,000. The people did not take kindly to this innovation. They protested against the use of gas in the streets, for fear of explosions; and many of the old residents would not allow it to be introduced into their houses, holding to what they considered the safer use of oil-lamps and wax-candles. To-day the city is served by seven gas-companies, the Consolidated, Equitable, Standard, New-York Mutual, Central, Northern and Yonkers. The Consolidated is the oldest company, and has 810 miles of gas-mains in the streets. It is the successor of the two original gas companies, combined with several others of later existence. It has a capital stock of $35,430,-000, and seven stations, with an aggregate capacity of 30,000,000 cubic feet a day. Both coal-gas and water-gas is manufactured. The Equitable has 136 miles of mains below 74th Street, and manufactures 6,000,000 cubic feet of water-gas daily. The New-York Mutual, with 123 miles of mains, also manufactures water-gas, supplying the lower half of the city with 4,000,000 cubic feet a day. The Standard principally serves the up-town East-Side with water-gas through 140 miles of mains, at the rate of 4,000,000 cubic feet a day. The Central and the Northern supply the trans-Harlem district with coal-gas, the former with 800,000 cubic feet a day, through 64 miles of mains; and the latter with 250,000 cubic feet a day, through 38 miles of mains. The Yonkers, a suburban company, has 18 miles of mains. In many cases more than one of these companies have mains in the same street. The total miles of gas mains is 1,325, and the total capacity of all the companies is over 45,000,000 cubic feet daily. The Equitable pays an annual franchise fee to the city of over $140,000. There are 540 miles of streets and 69¼ acres of parks and public squares lighted, at a cost varying from $12 to $28 a year for each lamp, according as there is competition or not in the territory lighted, or as the company's charter may have fixed the price.

Electric Lighting of streets costs the city from 40 to 50 cents a night for each lamp. There are six companies, the Brush Electric Illuminating Company, the United-States Illuminating Company, the Thomson-Houston Electric-Light Company, the Mount-Morris Electric-Light Company, the Harlem Lighting Company and the North-River Electric-Light and Power Company. On the first of January, 1893, the city had 26,524 gas lamps, 1,535 electric lights, and at Woodlawn Heights 152 naphtha lamps, at a yearly cost of nearly $800,000.

EDISON ELECTRIC ILLUMINATING CO., 26TH STREET, BETWEEN BROADWAY
AND SIXTH AVENUE.

The Edison Electric Illuminating Company of New York, the general offices of which are at Pearl and Elm Streets, was organized in 1880. It was the first company to supply electricity for incandescent lighting on a commercial basis, and is the largest concern of its class in existence in the world. Its business is the generation and sale of electric currents for all purposes, but especially for incandescent and arc lighting, heat and power. Its principal generating station and general offices are located in the company's building at Pearl and Elm Streets. This new station is planned to be the largest and most efficiently equipped establishment of its kind. When completed, it will have an equipment for generating current equivalent to over 20,000 horse-power. The dynamos are of the multi-polar Edison type of the latest design. The engines are of the marine multi-expansion style, with inverted cylinders, and are connected direct to the dynamos. The boilers are of the extra heavy, water tube safety type, intended for 200 pounds steam pressure, and the whole steam plant is fitted with all the recent economizing devices to be found in marine and stationary engineering practice. The general offices of the Company occupy an upper floor of the building, and are to be very extensive.

The company also operate stations at 255 and 257 Pearl Street, 47 to 51 West 26th Street, and 117 to 119 West 39th Street, and also an annex station in the basement of the Produce-Exchange Building. It is also erecting another station on the premises 118 to 122 West 53d Street. The up-town buildings occupy lots measuring 50 by 100 feet. That at Pearl and Elm Streets, when completed, will cover an area 75 by 200 feet. All the newer buildings are owned by the company, and have been erected for its own use. The company's oldest station, at 255 and 257 Pearl Street, was built under the direct supervision of Thomas A. Edison, in 1882–83, and its successful operation was the real inauguration of incandescent electric lighting as a commercial enterprise. In the

few years of the company's existence its business has grown rapidly. The entire plant now supplies current for an equivalent of about 200,000 incandescent lamps. Its operations cover all that portion of the city extending from the Battery to Central Park, included between Third and Eighth Avenues. Current is distributed over this territory by means of over 500 miles of conductors, which occupy 160 miles of underground three-wire conduit. It is led away from the stations to the net-work of "main" conductors by a system of "feeders." From the "main" conductors service wires lead to the premises of the consumers. The station buildings are all constructed on one general plan, and are absolutely fire-proof. A peculiar feature of their design is the placing of the boiler-rooms in the upper stories of the building, in-

EDISON ELECTRIC ILLUMINATING CO., PEARL AND ELM STREETS.

stead of on the ground-floor, while above the boilers are placed large coal-bunkers of 1,000 tons' capacity in the up-town stations and 3,000 tons' capacity in the new Elm-Street station.

The up-town stations are each capable of generating electric current equivalent to 6,000 horse-power, exclusive of the 53d-Street station, which may ultimately have a capacity of possibly 8,000 horse-power. The new Elm-Street station, with its capacity exceeding 20,000 horse-power, will be able to supply current for an equivalent of over 200,000 incandescent lamps, all connected at one time. Permits to view the stations should be applied for at the general offices.

The Sewer System is on a scale commensurate with the importance of this branch of municipal economy. As early as 1676 sewers were built on Manhattan Island. These were simply box-drains of wood or stone, and at first were intended only to relieve low areas of storm water. Very soon, however, they were built of brick, and connections were made with buildings, so that they could carry off the usual sewage matter. It was not until 1849 that the character and the method of construction of the sewers were definitely laid down by the municipal authorities. The supervision of the work was then placed in the hands of a city department. At that time about seventy miles of sewers of a miscellaneous character existed. They were built four feet in diameter. Many of these old sewers exist to the present day. In 1860 the egg-shaped sewer was introduced, with the dimensions of 4 x 3 feet or 4 x 2.8 feet. In 1865 a Legislative act authorized a general sewerage system. There were then in use 200 miles of sewers, partly of vitrified pipe, which was first laid in 1864. In 1870 the Department of Public Works was created, and put in charge of the sewers of Manhattan Island. To the Department of Public Parks were assigned the sewers of the trans-Harlem territory. Under these arrangements the system has been improved and brought to its present state of efficiency.

The sewage is disposed of by discharging it into tidal water, where it is rendered innocuous by dilution, and by the natural flow of water it is carried away from the city. Thus the sewers empty into the Harlem, North and East rivers along fifty miles of river-front. There are about 140 outlets, most of which are at the ends of piers, where swiftly running water takes the sewage immediately and carries it seaward. The entire city below the Harlem is sewered in the most approved manner, and the work above the Harlem keeps pace with the growth of population there. The city is divided into 26 drainage areas or districts, each of which is practically independent, with its own pipes and mains and outlets.

The sewers are laid in all the principal thoroughfares. They have all the latest improvements for ventilation and flushing, and some of the pipes are imbedded in concrete. They are on the system for carrying off sewage and rain-water combined. The average demand made upon them is nearly 100 gallons for each head of population each day, but their capacity is largely in excess of that. The smallest pipe is 12 inches in diameter. The largest sewers are in Canal Street, between Washington Street and the North River, 8x16 feet ; in Canal Street between Washington Street and Broadway, 7x10 feet ; and in 110th Street, between Fifth Avenue and the East River, 8x12 feet. All the main sewers are entered and traversed by workmen for the purpose of cleaning or repairing them. In 1892, there were 444 miles of sewers and 5,314 receiving-basins. The total extent of construction in 1891 was over six miles, three-quarters of which was of brick mains. The maintenance of sewers costs the city yearly $130,000, and the new work completed in 1891 cost over $500,000.

Electric Wires are maintained by the various telegraph, telephone and electric-light companies, and the Police and Fire Departments, strung on poles and attached to roofs. Formerly there was a vast and intricate net-work of wires over all the city, especially in the business sections ; and the avenues and streets showed a forest of tall poles, many of them carrying several hundred wires. Even now, despite the development of the subway system, hundreds of poles and thousands of miles of wire are still in mid-air, and over 2,000 miles are attached to the elevated-railroad

BAXTER STREET.
ONE PHASE OF LIFE IN THE METROPOLIS.

structure. But Broadway, Wall Street, and other main thoroughfares are now void of the erstwhile objectionable poles.

Electrical Subways have been constructed in nearly all the principal streets south of Central Park, and to a lesser extent elsewhere. They are designed to accommodate all the wires that are now hanging overhead. This municipal undertaking is in charge of the Board of Electrical Control. It had its inception in 1884, when, after nine years of opposition by interested parties, a bill for the purpose of compelling corporations operating electrical conductors to place them underground was passed by the Legislature. Legal delays hindered the inception of the work; and, although subways were built, it was not until 1889 that the provisions of the law began to be seriously enforced. In that year the municipal authorities took upon themselves the task of compelling the companies to use the subways, and to that end they proceeded to cut the wires and chop down the poles in the leading thoroughfares where subways had been built. Within a year nearly 5,000 poles and 6,000 miles of wire were thus removed, and there were over 12,000 miles of wire placed underground. Since that time the work of constructing subways and putting the wires into them has progressed without serious interruption. At present, there are over 200 miles of trench, containing several thousand miles of duct, and this construction will accommodate over 100,000 miles of wires.

The Postal Telegraph-Cable Company was organized in 1881, mainly by persons interested in the manufacture of compound steel and copper wire, and of an automatic system of telegraphic transmission. The theories which led to the construction of its original lines were found to be mistaken. The property was capitalized upon a basis supposed to be justified by the great earning capacity which the superior construction and the proposed machine transmission were believed to render practicable. The company was re-organized in 1885 upon the moderate capital of $5,000,000, and, being largely controlled by John W. Mackay, also principal owner of the Commercial cables, was operated in close connection therewith. The property now comprises not only the excellent plant of the original Postal Company, but all that was saved from the wreck of the Bankers' & Merchants', and several other smaller telegraph properties, which have been rebuilt and re-equipped, together with new lines of much greater extent than all the original plants above mentioned, covering the South to Savannah, Ga., the Southwest to New Orleans, and the West to Denver, covering the principal points in Kansas and Colorado, and the Northwest, to principal points in Iowa, Nebraska, Wisconsin and Minnesota. By its connection with the large telegraph system of the Canadian Pacific Railway Company, it reaches the Maritime Provinces — the Dominion of Canada, Manitoba, and British Columbia; and thence, in connection with the Canadian Pacific Railway, owns an extensive system of new lines, covering the Pacific Coast as far south as San Diego. The whole comprises by far the most extensive, best organized, and most thoroughly equipped system of telegraph that has ever been in competition with the Western Union Telegraph Company and the Anglo-American cables, and the best evidence of its permanence is found in the fact that excellence of service and constant, persistent competition in honorable and not destructive methods, has been its policy from the beginning. The directors and executive officers of the company are as follows: John W. Mackay, George S. Coe, W. C. Van Horne, J. W. Mackay, Jr., Albert B. Chandler, Charles R. Hosmer, James W. Ellsworth, William H. Baker, Edward C. Platt, John O. Stevens, George G. Ward; Albert B. Chandler, President and General Manager; Vice-Presidents, George S. Coe and William H. Baker.

BROADWAY AND DEY STREET.
SHOWING MERCANTILE NATIONAL BANK, WESTERN UNION TELEGRAPH BUILDING, AND "THE MAIL AND EXPRESS."

Its executive officers have for more than four years past been in the Washington Building, No. 1 Broadway, comprising about twenty rooms on the upper floor of that commodious building. The necessity for combining these offices with the main operating rooms, and other departments of the company now occupying widely separated quarters, led to the construction of a building for the company, which is now in process of erection, on Broadway, corner of Murray Street, New York, directly opposite the City Hall, which will be one of the largest and handsomest office-buildings in the country. It will be 14 stories in height, exclusive of basement and cellar, and will rise about 175 feet above the street, with a Broadway front of over 70 feet, a Murray-Street front of 156 feet, and a wing 30 by 50 feet. The first four stories will be built of Indiana limestone, and the upper portion of the building will be of light gray brick, with terra-cotta trimmings. George Edward Harding & Gooch are the architects. The Postal Telegraph and Commercial Cable companies will occupy the eleventh, twelfth, and thirteenth floors, the corner-office of the first floor level with the street, and a portion of the basement and cellar. The rest of the building will be rented.

The Commercial Cable Company was organized in 1884 by John W. Mackay of California, and James Gordon Bennett, proprietor of *The New-York Herald*, for the purpose of establishing permanent competition, and affording an accelerated and reliable service at a moderate tariff, between the Old and New Worlds. Cables were laid during the same year, and business was begun in December, 1884. The company signalized its advent by reducing the cable rates twenty per cent. Its competitors instituted a rate-war by reducing their rates to twelve cents a word, and the Commercial met this by coming down to 25 cents a word, and appealing to the public for support in its fight against monopoly and the excessive rates that had

previously existed. From May, 1886, to September, 1888, this rate-war was continued, but was finally compromised by all the companies agreeing to hold to the charge of 25 cents a word. Thus the Commercial Company deserves the credit of bringing about a reduction in rates, fifty per cent. of what they

SECTION OF ATLANTIC CABLE CARRIED IN PROCESSION.

had been, to the lowest figure at which it has been shown that the service can be profitably done. The company has two complete routes to Europe, and the duplex system that is used practically doubles the capacity of the cables. The cables are submarine and underground from the office in New York to Paris and to within 100 miles of London, only that short distance being by overhead wire. The landing-places are at New York, Rockport (Massachusetts), Canso (Nova Scotia), Water-

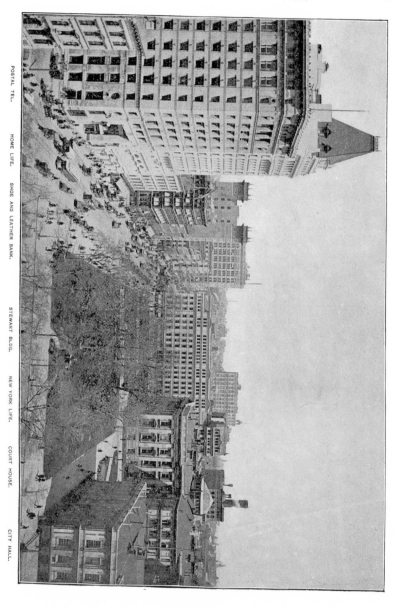

BROADWAY, AT THE NORTHWEST CORNER OF THE CITY HALL PARK.
VIEW FROM THE MURRAY STREET PATH, LOOKING NORTHWARD.

POSTAL TEL.   HOME LIFE.   SHOE AND LEATHER BANK.   STEWART BLDG.   NEW YORK LIFE.   COURT HOUSE.   CITY HALL.

GEO. EDW. HARDING & GOOCH, ARCHTS.

POSTAL TELEGRAPH BUILDING—POSTAL TELEGRAPH-CABLE CO.

BROADWAY, NORTHWEST CORNER OF MURRAY STREET, WEST SIDE OF CITY HALL PARK.

EXCHANGE PLACE.   GEO. EDW. HARDING & GOOCH, ARCHTS.   STOCK EXCHANGE.

COMMERCIAL CABLE BUILDING—21 STORIES HIGH—COMMERCIAL CABLE BUILDING CO.

BROAD STREET, WEST SIDE, BETWEEN WALL STREET AND EXCHANGE PLACE.

WESTERN UNION TEL.   "MAIL AND EXPRESS."   ST. PAUL'S.   ASTOR HOUSE.   POSTAL TEL.

BROADWAY, LOOKING NORTH FROM DEY STREET.

VIEW SHOWING WEST SIDE OF BROADWAY FROM DEY TO CHAMBERS STREET.

POSTAL-TELEGRAPH-CABLE COMPANY'S BUILDING.
BROADWAY AND MURRAY STREET, FACING CITY HALL PARK.

ville (Ireland), Bristol, and Havre. Nearly 7,000 nautical miles of cable are in operation. To this company must also be credited the reduction of time in the transmission of messages beneath the Atlantic; and by the adoption of automatic working, and the introduction of typewriters for taking the messages, a point of excellence in accuracy, speed and reliability never before attained has been reached. It is an interesting bit of history that during the great blizzard of March, 1888, the only means of communication between New-York City and the rest of the world was by the Commercial Cable. Messages were sent to London, whence they were cabled back to Boston. The Commercial Cable and the Postal Telegraph Companies are allies, the latter being the land system. The Directors are: John W. Mackay (President), James Gordon Bennett, George G. Ward (Vice-President and General Manager), George S. Coe, John W. Mackay, Jr., Albert B. Chandler, Sir Donald A. Smith, Wm. C. Van Horne, Charles R. Hosmer, E. C. Platt (Treasurer), Gardiner G. Howland, Richard Irvin, Jr., and Thomas Skinner.

The **Western Union Telegraph Company** occupies a handsome and well-appointed building in Broadway, corner of Dey Street, and has 137 branch-offices in different parts of the city. The main building is at present the finest equipped telegraph office in the world. The company has the largest telegraph system ever established. It has 21,000 offices and 750,000 miles of wire. The company leases the two cables of the American Telegraph & Cable Company from Nova Scotia to Penzance, England, which are extended to New-York City direct by the company's own cables; it also connects with the four cables of the Anglo-American Telegraph Company, Limited, from Valentia, Ireland, to Heart's Content, Newfoundland, and from Brest, France, to St. Pierre, Miquelon; and with the cable of the Direct United-States Cable Company from Ballinskelligs, Ireland, to Rye Beach, N. H. It has thus the service of seven Atlantic cables, as well as direct connection with the South-American cable at Galveston, Texas; and messages may be sent from any of its offices to all parts of the world.

Pneumatic tubes extend under Broadway from 23d Street to Dey Street. They belong to the Western Union Telegraph Company, and through them messages are sent a distance of about $2\frac{1}{2}$ miles. Similar tubes extend from Dey to Broad Streets.

The **American District-Telegraph Company** is an adjunct of the Western Union, and does a messenger-service business exclusively.

The **Mutual District Messenger Company**, with its main offices at Broadway and Grand Street, is the only serious rival of the A. D. T. Company.

The **Metropolitan Telephone and Telegraph Company** conducts the telephonic communication of New York, and its system comprises eight central offices, upwards of 30,000 miles of underground wire, and about 9,000 subscribers' stations. The system is in direct communication with those of Brooklyn and the principal towns in New Jersey, and also with that of the Long Distance Telephone Company, whose wires extend through the Eastern States in all directions, so that a New-York subscriber can reach any one of *eighty thousand* other subscribers scattered through New York, the New-England States, Pennsylvania and Ohio. Of the eight exchanges in New-York City the four more important, viz.: those at Broad Street, Cortlandt Street, Spring Street and 38th Street, are placed in fire-proof buildings of a special type. There are two reasons why a telephone exchange building should be impregnably fire-proof. One is the enormous cost of the apparatus, which is equally susceptible to damage by water as by fire, so that a slight fire is as much to be feared as a serious one. Another is that the crippling of an important exchange would result in heavy loss to the many patrons. It is not generally known

METROPOLITAN TELEPHONE AND TELEGRAPH COMPANY.
TELEPHONE BUILDING, CORTLANDT STREET, BETWEEN BROADWAY AND CHURCH STREET.

how great the use of the telephone is in large cities.   There are many subscribers in
New York who call for from between 60 and 70 connections a day, while some run
up to as high as 130 a day.   In order, then, to sufficiently protect both its own interests and those of its subscribers, the company has been obliged to design special
telephone buildings, which are at once thoroughly fire-proof and properly adapted,

TELEPHONE OPERATING OR SWITCH-ROOM, ON CORTLANDT ST., METROPOLITAN TELEPHONE AND TELEGRAPH CO.

from roof to basement, to the requirements of a modern telephone central office.
The largest of these new telephonic centres is at 18 Cortlandt Street.   It is a handsome eight-story building, and the only sign of its special vocation is the familiar
blue bell hanging over the entrance.   The cloud of overhead wires formerly insepara-
ble from a telephone exchange is entirely absent, as the wires are all underground.
In the basement of the building is a large department where some 15,000 or 16,000
wires enter from the subways.   These are all encased in heavy lead-covered cables,
from the terminals of which other wires extend up through the building to the eighth
story, the whole of which is occupied by the operating department, or exchange
proper.   Here a huge switchboard extends around three sides of the building in an
unbroken curve about 250 feet long.   This switchboard is the largest of its kind in
the world.   It contains all the most improved devices for metallic circuit working,
and was completed a few years ago at a cost of about $400,000.   It can accommodate
6,000 subscribers' lines, and about 150 operators are required to answer the calls and
facilitate the conversations that are constantly passing through it.   A telephonic
switchboard is the most complicated electro-mechanical device known to science.
This particular one contains more than 260,000 separate electrical instruments, none
of which has less than three wires soldered to it.   Hundreds of miles of fine insu-
lated wire pass through the board and connect the different parts together.   All of
this has to be kept in perfect order, as a single defect may throw more than one
line temporarily out of service.
   The other exchanges referred to are of the same general type as that just
described, differing only in minor details and in switchboard capacity, each district

exchange having accommodation for from 1,200 to 3,600 subscribers' lines. A most interesting feature of the New-York telephone service, is that, practically, the entire system of conductors is under ground. During the past four or five years the Metropolitan Company has expended several million dollars in removing its pole lines and replacing them by costly underground cables. It has put down over 400 separate cables, containing an aggregate of more than 30,000 miles of wire. Underground cables radiate from every central office to points from which groups of subscribers can conveniently be reached. All the exchanges are connected together by several hundred underground wires, and some 500 wires, laid underground the entire distance except across the Bridge, join the various New-York exchanges with the principal exchange in Brooklyn. The wires are made into cables containing generally fifty-one pairs of conductors ; these cables are covered with a lead armoring, and are drawn into iron pipes laid under the streets. The adoption of underground cables has been accompanied by so many electrical and mechanical difficulties as to necessitate a complete remodeling of the company's plant. This work has been carried out during the past four years, and is typified by the construction of the model telephone build-

ings already described. The Metropolitan Telephone Company employs a staff of about 800 persons ; and its pay-roll amounts to over $600,000 a year. The operators, who number about 400, are nearly all girls ; they pick up the work very quickly, and give good satisfaction, alike to the company and to the subscribers. At each exchange a suite of rooms, consisting of dining-room, reading and work room, wardrobe and lavatory, are provided for the use of the operators. This department is in charge of a matron, who serves light refreshments and attends to the comfort of the girls generally when they are off duty. An important part of the organization is composed of the technical depart-

METROPOLITAN TELEPHONE AND TELEGRAPH CO., 38TH-STREET BUILDING.

ments that have to do with the construction and equipment of the offices, lines and subscribers' stations, the maintenance of the vast and complicated plant, and the inspection of the many thousands of lines and telephone sets. Each part of the work is done by a special staff, working under a responsible chief, the reins of

METROPOLITAN TELEPHONE AND TELEGRAPH CO., BROAD AND PEARL STREETS.

authority gradually centralizing through the general manager, executive committee, president and board of directors. Accurate record is kept of the work of every individual throughout the entire organization, so that the history of any of the tens of thousands of wires and instruments belonging to the company, and of every transaction connected therewith, is always available. The volume of business done by the company is almost incredible. The average number of telephone connections each day in New York City is about 120,000. Of these, 99 per cent. occur between the hours of 8 A. M. and 6 P. M. A permanent service is kept up at all the offices, but the use of the telephone at night is comparatively slight. The busiest hours of the day are from 11 A. M. to noon, and from 2 to 3 P. M. During those two hours probably nearly one-half of the entire day's business is conducted, and both plant and staff are working at high pressure. An eminent professor of political economy has said that the question of telephone rates was the most difficult problem that had ever been submitted to him, so complicated are the conditions involved. This opinion will be appreciated when it is considered that in a city like New York the entire plant and organization of the telephone system must be designed and arranged to stand the strain of performing almost one-half of the day's work within the short period of two hours. This is a condition of affairs not met with in any other industry.

The American Telephone & Telegraph Company maintains long-distance telephone lines for direct communication with Boston, Philadelphia, Washington, Pittsburgh, Harrisburg and intermediate points, the list altogether embracing 150 important cities and towns. The company has an extensive local service.

Cable Conduits for street-cars are laid underground in Broadway and Seventh Avenue for one line, in 125th Street and Tenth Avenue for another, and in Third Avenue. The conduits are of brick and cement, with iron frames supporting the cable pulleys. On the Broadway route, from the Battery to Central Park, the two conduits with their spurs are nearly twelve miles in length. In Third Avenue there are over sixteen miles of conduit, and in 125th Street and Tenth Avenue ten miles.

The New-York Steam Company supplies steam-power and heat to consumers through pipes laid underground. The company has been in business since 1882, and has fifteen miles of pipe in use in its down-town district, south of Duane Street. Six hundred business consumers and 300 residences are supplied.

Life in the Metropolis.

Hotels, Inns, Cafés, Restaurants, Apartment Houses, Flats, Homes, Tenements, Etc.

WHEN travellers came to the New Netherland settlement in its early days they were entertained at the expense of the Directors of the West India Company. This custom became in time such a burden that in 1642 Director-General Kieft built at the Company's expense a tavern, a quaint stone building near the present Pearl Street and Coenties Slip. This was the first tavern on Manhattan Island, and in later years it became the Stadt Huys. The following year Martin Krigier built and opened Krigier's Tavern, at Bowling Green, and this soon became the fashionable resort for the townspeople as well as for visitors from abroad. This house subsequently became the King's-Arms Tavern, and in Revolutionary days it was the headquarters of General Gage. To the generation of a quarter of a century ago it was the Atlantic Gardens, a popular pleasure-resort.

Many little taverns began to spring up about this time, and Director-General Stuyvesant compelled them to be licensed. In 1676 six wine and four beer taverns were licensed, with permission to sell strong liquors. The rates of charges were regulated as follows : lodging, three and four pence a night ; meals, eight pence and one shilling ; brandy six pence a gill ; French wines, fifteen pence a quart ; rum, three pence a gill ; cider, four pence a quart ; beer, three pence a quart ; mum, six pence a quart. There were other restrictions, especially in regard to serving liquor to the Indians. If an Indian was found drunk on the street, the tavern-keeper who sold him the liquor was fined ; and when it could not be discovered which tavern-keeper was guilty, all the residents of the street were mulcted to make up the amount of the fine.

In Revolutionary days there were many public houses, the memory of several of which still remains bright. Fraunce's Tavern was probably the most famous in its day, and is best remembered now. It was originally the homestead of a member of the distinguished De-Lancey family, and was a handsome brick building, erected in 1730, on the corner of Pearl and Broad Streets. It was sold in 1762 to Samuel Fraunce, who opened it as the *Queen Catharine*. It was well patronized, and many receptions, balls and other social gatherings were held in its assembly-hall. There several societies met for their Saturday-night convivialities, and there the Chamber of Commerce had its headquarters for a long time. Washington made his headquarters there ; and in the assembly-room delivered his farewell address to the officers of the Continental Army, in 1783. Burns Coffee-House was also a De-Lancey homestead, standing on Broadway just north of Trinity churchyard, where the Borcel Building now is. It had many different names and many changes of proprietors. The Sons of Liberty made it their rendezvous, and during the British occupation it was much favored by the military officers. In 1793 it was torn down, and the City Hotel put up in its place.

About the same time and later there was the Bull's Head, in Bowery Lane, with cattle-pens and the public slaughter-house near it. The old Bowery Theatre, now the Thalia, occupies its site. The Merchants' Coffee-House was on the corner of Water and Wall Streets; and there were other coffee-houses. Tea-gardens were numerous, and opposite the present City-Hall Park was the famous La-Montagne garden and tavern. In the country, on the banks of the East River, were several houses, where turtle feasts, which were important social events, occurred once or twice a week. On the North River in Greenwich Village were two very popular gardens; and there was the Vauxhall, near Broome Street, in Broadway, once owned by John Jacob Astor. Nor was the old Dutch Vauxhall, at the corner of Warren and Greenwich Streets, forgotten.

Since the nineteenth century came in, the hotel history of New York has been mainly a record of steady development toward the perfection of luxurious living that prevails at the present time. Many of the old hotels remain, although a large number have gone the way of all things material. French's Hotel until a few years ago occupied the site of the Pulitzer Building, and was a popular house of its day, but it is now well nigh forgotten. The Golden Eagle Inn was another famous place. The building stood until 1893, back of the Broadway Central Hotel. It was redolent with memories of old-time theatrical folk and politicians.

Now New York has over one hundred thoroughly good hotels, with a score standing pre-eminently at the head of the list. There are 250 more of the second and third class; and of all grades there are fully 1,000. Over $150,000,000 in capital is invested in them. Of the best of these nearly three-quarters are conducted on the European plan, but among those on the American plan are several of the most famous. Prices in the better American-plan hotels range from $3 to $6 a day for a single room with board, and almost any figure beyond that for extra accommodations. At the European-plan houses single rooms are charged at from $1 to $3 a day; and again in this case, there are better accommodations for those who want to pay more. At all these hotels, of either class, there is every convenience for comfortable living; and at the best there is nothing to be desired in the way of luxurious furnishings, charming surroundings, perfect service and exceptional cuisine. In these respects several of the leading New-York hotels cannot be surpassed.

Not alone by the travelling public are these establishments patronized. Many New-York families make their homes in them the year around, to avoid the annoyances attendant upon housekeeping, and to secure much more of comfort, luxury and freedom. It is this assurance of permanent patronage that has done much to promote the excellence of New-York hotels during the present generation, and particularly during the last decade. Several of the best American-plan hotels are sustained chiefly in this way, and the tendency among many well-to-do people is more and more toward that style of living.

The great hotel district is between 23d and 59th Streets, and Fourth and Seventh Avenues. There are admirable hotels outside those limits, as in Union Square; in Broadway, below 14th Street; and in Fifth Avenue, between 23d Street and Washington Square, and elsewhere; but they are few in number and are overshadowed by their modern rivals up-town. In that territory, which is a little less than two miles long by a half mile wide, are half of the leading hotels of the metropolis, and a census of the district would show half of the hotel population living in them.

HOTEL WALDORF.
FIFTH AVENUE, NORTHWEST CORNER OF 33D STREET.

The Hotel Waldorf (American and European plans), built by William Waldorf Astor, and opened in 1893, is said to have cost $5,000,000. It has a frontage of 100 feet on Fifth Avenue, and 250 feet on 33d Street; and is twelve stories, or 180 feet high. It is a diversified and picturesque German Renaissance structure, designed by H. J. Hardenbergh, and abounding in loggias, balconies, gables, groups of chimneys, and tiled roofs. One of the chief features is the interior garden court, with fountains and flowers, walls of white terra cotta, frescoes and stained glass. The Empire dining-hall is modelled after the grand *salon* in King Ludwig's palace at Munich, with frescoes, satin hangings, upholstery and marble pillars, all of pale green, and Crowninshield's beautiful frescoes. Among the other rooms are the Marie Antoinette parlor, superbly frescoed by Will H. Low, N. A.; the Turkish smoking-room, with its low divans and ancient Moorish armor; the ball-room, in white and gold, with Louis XIV. decorations; and the café, abounding in carved English oak and leather hangings.

The Hotel New Netherland (European plan) is one of New York's newest hotel palaces. It stands as the highest achievement attainable in these times in hotel construction. In situation it is unrivalled, and in furnishings and general equipment it is almost unequalled. In the announcement of the hotel the proprietor claims it is "the most elegant, the safest, the strongest and the most complete hotel palace in the world. Every scientific appliance for ventilating, heating, plumbing and electric lighting. The privacy of a home. The furnishings of a palace. The table of an epicure. Absolutely fire-proof." No one can dispute these claims. It is situated on Fifth Avenue and 59th Street, immediately at the main portal of Central Park. It extends for 100 feet on Fifth Avenue and 125 feet on 59th Street, and rises to the majestic height of 234 feet, the tallest hotel structure in the world, and looms up loftily by the side of the neighboring Plaza and Savoy hotels. It overlooks not only Central Park and the magnificent Fifth Avenue, but all of the main part of New-York City. Built as securely against fire as can be done, its rooms on any floor provide every luxury and convenience that can be furnished by any hotel. Its main floor, with its onyx, mosaic and marble finish, is probably the grandest hotel rotunda on either continent, and from the three floors beneath the street level to the topmost of the seventeen stories above the street the New Netherland is uniformly a complete and perfect structure. It is conducted on the European plan, with restaurants, cafés, and private dining and banquet rooms that are practicably unsurpassable. Its proprietor is Gen. Ferdinand P. Earle, who is one of the most noted of the hotel landlords of modern times.

The Fifth-Avenue Hotel (American plan) has borne a conspicuous part in the public life of the metropolis, and has been identified with the most notable local events of the generation, since its opening, in 1859. Both location and management have contributed to this prosperity. The house fronts upon Madison Square, the most charming of the smaller parks of the city, at the junction of Broadway and Fifth Avenue, the two great thoroughfares. It is unequalled in the number and spaciousness of its corridors, halls and public rooms, and the commodious character of its guest-rooms. The proprietors are Hitchcock, Darling & Co.

The Windsor Hotel (American plan), seven stories high, substantial, dignified, and inviting in outward appearance, occupies the entire block on Fifth Avenue between 46th and 47th Streets, extending toward Madison Avenue nearly two hundred feet, and overlooking a broad open space in the rear which affords the hotel magnificent light and ventilation. The proprietors are Hawk & Wetherbee.

HOTEL NEW NETHERLAND.
FIFTH AVENUE, NORTHEAST CORNER OF 59TH STREET, AT MAIN ENTRANCE TO CENTRAL PARK.

The Hotel Savoy (American and European plans) is one of the most notable structures in this country. It is a palace of the highest order of art, and in every detail are seen the results of the most perfect workmanship. It is one of the most elegant and comfortable and safest hotels in the world, and occupies a site of remarkable beauty and interest. Even so long ago as 1870 William M. Tweed selected this as the choicest site for a hotel on Manhattan Island; and here he began the construction of the Knickerbocker Hotel. Before the shattering of the Tweed Ring, $250,000 had been spent here on the Titanic foundations of the never-to-be-realized Knickerbocker. The locality, so desirable even in that far-past day, is now simply marvellous in its combination of advantages, with the improvement of rapid transit, the development of Central Park, and the concentration in this immediate vicinity of the wealth, fashion and aristocracy of the Western Hemisphere. To occupy this fine strategic position, looking down on Fifth Avenue and the Plaza, and the main entrance to Central Park, the Hotel Savoy was built, and opened in 1892. It is twelve stories high, and the façades are in the rich efflorescence of Italian Renaissance architecture. This vast structure, with its long fronts on Fifth Avenue and 59th Street, is absolutely fire-proof, being of the steel-framed construction, with every beam and column of steel. The partitions and the arches between the floor-beams are of hard burnt terra-cotta. The walls are of Indiana limestone. The public apartments of the Savoy are of extraordinary interest and beauty. The table-d'hote dining-room, in Greek and Renaissance architecture, is one of the richest in the world, encased with Siena marble and rouge jasper, green and white Killarney marbles, satinwood and white holly, sculptures and frescoes. The breakfast-room is English in style; the billiard-room is Pompeian; and the drawing-rooms reproduce the decorative effects of the epochs of Louis XIV., XV. and XVI., and the First Empire. The lobby, main corridor and foyer are finished in Numidian marble, with wonderful sculptured ceilings. There are 135 bath-rooms, with mosaic floors and enamelled tiled walls. The electric plant has a capacity of 6,400 candle-lights, and the fixtures are unsurpassed. The Savoy also has a fine livery, a theatre-ticket office, a celebrated restaurant, and a huge safe, with separate safe-deposit boxes for the free use of guests. Many of the rooms are arranged in suites, with private halls and bath-rooms. The bridal or state suite, on the second floor, looking out over the Plaza, and through the main entrance over Central Park, is one of the most sumptuous and enchanting apartments on either continent. It is a reproduction of the boudoir of Marie Antoinette, in the Trianon Palace, at Versailles. It was occupied in 1893 by the Infanta Eulalia of Spain.

The architect of this vast and imperishable combination of ingenious devices for security and luxury of living was Ralph S. Townsend. The capitalists who built it were Judge P. Henry Dugro and F. Wagner. The men who manage this marvellous caravansary and its army of employees are veterans in the art of hotel-keeping.

Only one block distant is the Elevated Railway, by which in a few minutes the guest can reach the farthest parts of "Down-town;" and past the Savoy's doors rumble the stages of the Fifth-Avenue line, giving quick access to the swell residence, theatre and shopping districts. And around the great balconies and porticoes of the Savoy sweep the bird-songs and flower-perfumes and fresh airs of the world-renowned Central Park, which has nowhere a rival in beauty. It hardly needs be said that the Savoy cuisine is unsurpassed, in America or Europe; or that its wines, selected by a *connoisseur* and specially imported, and kept in lonely cellars two stories below the street, are of the very choicest. The house is kept on both the American and European plans, and is now being enlarged.

HOTEL SAVOY.
FIFTH AVENUE, SOUTHEAST CORNER 59TH STREET, OPPOSITE MAIN ENTRANCE TO CENTRAL PARK.

The Plaza Hotel (American and European plans) is one of the most attractive public houses in the wide world, and represents the highest possibilities attained in the art of constructing and keeping great modern caravansaries. Its situation is peculiarly advantageous, in the most delightful and aristocratic residence-quarter in America, almost surrounded by the homes of distinguished families, the architectural splendors of the "swellest" club-houses and the most fashionable churches. At its opposite corners are the gorgeous New Netherland and the palatial Savoy hotels. Its front is on the matchless Fifth Avenue, with its unceasing processions of beauty and elegance, on the sidewalks and in the line of carriages, and just at one side opens the main entrance to Central Park, the goal for all fashionable drives. One entire side of the hotel looks down close by on the Park, with its rocky hills, deep thickets, and little ponds, as wild in appearance as a scene deep in the New-Hampshire mountains. In the heart of the great city, and within a few minutes of its finest churches, theatres and art-galleries, you are still on the very verge of the loveliest pleasure-ground in America, with its drives and rambles, its lawns and forests, its statuary and fountains.

The Plaza Hotel to an unusual degree combines beauty and convenience. Rising majestically from the broad asphalt-covered Plaza to the height of eight full stories, in brick and brownstone, diversified but not overladen with terra cotta and polished marble, balconies and cornices, it shows rich and tasteful effects on all sides, and the simple beauty of Italian Renaissance architecture. There is nothing of the narrow-tower effect about this broad-based and dignified structure, but its 500 feet of frontage on three streets suggests comfort, rest and security. This effect is increased by its absolutely fire-proof construction. The ventilating arrangements of the rooms and halls are very ingenious and effective; and the equipment for lighting the house includes one of the finest electrical plants in the country. A large part of the main floor is finished with choice marble mosaic pavements, silvered ceilings, enfoliated bronze columns, counters of Mexican onyx, woodwork of mahogany, and fine paintings. Here are the reception-rooms, with their Gobelins tapestries; and the great lounging-room, where ladies and gentlemen meet, amid Persian rugs, dainty tables, rich easy-chairs, costly paintings, and other attractive features. The pink parlor and the blue parlor, facing Fifth Avenue, on the second floor, are furnished in white and gold, with onyx tables, delicately frescoed ceilings, and walls finished *en panel*, in embossed silk drapery in delicate colors. The great dining-room, 80 by 40 feet, has a graceful arched roof, 30 feet high, rich in frescoes and fretted gold; and is finished in dead white and gold, with stained-glass windows and polished oak furniture. The walls are adorned with paintings of the Five Senses, executed in Paris. The Restaurant and Café are beautiful and attractive rooms, of great size, on the 59th-Street side; and the bar-room is equipped with onyx counters and *prima-vera* furniture. The public apartments are adorned with many paintings of the first order, including Pope's life-like pictures of horses, lions and dogs, and Cowles's "Shoshone Falls." There are 400 guest-rooms, most of them *en suite*, and all of them large and airy, with broad corridors laid with heavy red velvet carpets. As it stands, the Plaza Hotel cost more than $3,000,000, and was opened to the public in 1890. The proprietor is F. A. Hammond, for many years a prominent figure among the Bonifaces of America.

On the block below, on Fifth Avenue, at the corner of 57th Street, is the Cornelius Vanderbilt mansion, which in 1893 was so enlarged and remodelled as to make it the rival of any residence on the continent. At the opposite corner of 57th Street is the palatial residence of C. P. Huntington, now approaching completion.

THE PLAZA HOTEL.

FIFTH AVENUE, WEST SIDE, FROM 58TH STREET TO 59TH STREET, AT FIFTH-AVENUE ENTRANCE TO CENTRAL PARK.

Holland House (European plan), at Fifth Avenue and 30th Street, is in some respects the leading hotel of America ; and ranks as the equal of any hotel in the world. Its excellence of construction, its perfection in the furnishings, and its admirable management made the Holland House a marked success from the day of its opening. It has a frontage of 250 feet, on the most noble and aristocratic thoroughfare of the New World, and rises far above the surrounding buildings with impressive and monumental effect. Although so immense and preëminent, the exceeding delicacy of its architectural details, and the fineness of its design, make this one of the most attractive and beautiful secular structures on this avenue of palaces. The architects and designers were George Edward Harding and Gooch; the style is a modification of the Italian Renaissance ; and the material of the walls is a fine gray Indiana limestone. The portico, one of the richest in America, is decorated with admirable stone carvings. The main staircase and corridors are wonderful works of art, in carved Siena marble and bronze. A London magazine recently characterized this as the handsomest staircase of its kind in America. The hotel office, in Italian Renaissance, and encased in Siena marble, contains among its many conveniences an enormous safe, in which are a number of steel safe-deposit boxes for the use of the guests. On the main floor is the Restaurant, with a seating capacity of 300 persons ; the equal in all its details of any room devoted to this purpose in this country. On the same floor is the Café, with its furnishings in the manner of the famous English palace of Holland House ; its exquisite screens of glass, marble and bronze ; and its delicate tones of gray and pale yellow. The Buffet, in a soft yellow and golden brown, has high wainscots of panelled wood. The Foyer, on the parlor floor, is lighted by four immense *torchères*, bearing electric lights, and is furnished in the most attractive style. The Ladies' Reading-room, with pale satin and plush hangings, contains files of newspapers and dainty writing-desks. The drawing-room is in the style of Louis XVI., with its walls covered with salmon-tinted satin damask, embroidered portières, furniture in the Adams and Chippendale styles, and fawn-colored Axminster carpet. The Gilt Room is a reproduction of the famous Gilt Room in the historic Holland House at London, in Elizabethan architecture, with carved wainscotting, quaint heraldic devices, gold-crown ornaments, interesting antique furniture in natural cherry and gold, olden-style fire-places, English parquet floors, Flemish chandeliers, and magnificent plush curtains embroidered with fleur-de-lys. One of the bridal suites is in Louis XV. style, with satin *brochè* hangings and furniture, and curtains of Brussels point lace ; and the other is in the style of the First Empire, with upholstering of French tapestry, and curtains of point lace. Each of the 350 rooms is furnished and decorated in a distinctive style. A special feature of each is an electric indicator by which a guest, without waiting for a bell-boy, may signal direct to the office for any of 140 various articles. This indicator, known as the Herzog Teleseme, is in fact one of the great conveniences of Holland House ; it is the most perfect of all signalling systems. It comprises a dial sunk into the wall, and connected by electricity with the office ; upon this dial is printed 140 articles at times needed by travellers, and the guest has only to move the pointer until it points at the desired object, and then press an electric button, whereupon the clerk in the office, thus apprised, will send up, without further instructions or delay, the desired newspaper, or bottle, or food, or servant, or any other needed thing. The rooms have brass bedsteads, red-birch woodwork, Wilton carpets, and the best modern furniture. Holland House is entirely fire-proof, and contains the most perfect sanitary plumbing. Its walls and floor-arches are of porous terra cotta, which is a non-conductor of heat, cold or noise ; and even the heating pipes are encased in asbestos,

HOLLAND HOUSE.
FIFTH AVENUE, SOUTHWEST CORNER OF THIRTIETH STREET.

The floors and stairways are entirely of marble mosaic and cement. All impaired air is sucked out of the building by enormous exhaust air-shafts and a hollow roof-chamber. The house has five noiseless hydraulic elevators, marvels of elegance. The table-ware was made to order, from special designs, and bears the Holland arms. The silverware is of special designs by the Gorham Manufacturing Co. ; the china is Royal Worcester porcelain ; the glass is special English crystal ; and the table-linen was woven to order in Scotland. Holland House is under the proprietor-ship of H. M. Kinsley and Gustav Baumann, famous among American hotel-keepers. They are also proprietors of "Kinsley's," Chicago, a restaurant and catering estab-lishment, known all over the world for its excellent cuisine.

The Hotel Imperial (European plan) cost about $2,300,000. Architecturally, it is as admirable as it is conspicuous, being built of light-colored brick, and richly ornamented. The main corridor is in African marble ; the grand staircase is in marble and Mexican onyx ; the ceiling of the corridor is a reproduction from the Vatican, in pale blue and gold ; the dining-room reproduces the boudoir of Marie Antoinette, in gold and white ; the café is in white mahogany, with blue, white and gold ceiling ; the bar-room is in the style of an apartment of a French chateau.

The Hoffman House (European plan) is famous the world over for its mag-nificent banquet-hall and its art-gallery, no less than for its cuisine and its general excellence as a hotel. It is on Broadway, between 24th and 25th Streets, and its front takes up nearly the whole block. It has a sightly and beautiful location. The Broadway front of the house dates from 1864 ; and the eight-story fire-proof annex on 25th Street was erected in 1882–85, in Italian Renaissance architecture. The great Banquet Hall of the Hoffman is 60 feet square, with beautiful allegorical paintings. The bar-room contains Bouguereau's painting, "Nymphs and Satyr," Correggio's "Narcissus," Chelmonski's "Russian Mail Carrier," and other price-less paintings and sculptures.

The Buckingham (European plan), at Fifth Avenue and 50th Street, opposite St. Patrick's Cathedral, was opened in 1876. It is richly finished within, princi-pally in mahogany and oak. Many families make their homes there, especially those who come from a distance to spend the winter in town. It has the quiet elegance of a refined home. The neighborhood is the most elegant in America.

The Gilsey House (European plan) has been a successful establishment for nearly twenty years. The building is a handsome structure of white marble and iron, on the corner of Broadway and 29th Street, in the busy portion of the up-town district. Its guest-chambers are finely appointed, and it attracts the patronage of travellers who are very wealthy and extremely particular, especially army and navy officers, congressmen, coal operators and mine owners, and railroad magnates. The restaurant is famous for its excellence, and has been approved by many lovers of good living. The proprietors of the Gilsey are James H. Breslin & Brother.

The Hotel Bristol (American plan) is very favorably situated, at the corner of Fifth Avenue and 42d Street, overlooking the ancient reservoir and Bryant Park, and convenient to the Grand Central Station. It is an aristocratic and elegant house.

The Hotel Normandie (European plan), at Broadway and 38th Street, has 200 rooms and an excellent restaurant. All its floors are of iron beams and brick arched work, so that the house is absolutely fire-proof. It is first-class in its appointments. Its architect was W. H. Hume. Gen. Ferdinand P. Earle is the proprietor.

The St. James (European plan), at Broadway and 26th Street, under its suc-cessive owners, has been the resort of the better class of sporting men, especially those interested in the turf. Many theatrical stars have been patrons of the house.

The Hotel Grenoble (American and European plans) ranks among the most charming of the public houses of the great metropolis. The situation is very advantageous, either for permanent residents, among those happy families who escape the exasperations of modern housekeeping, or for transient visitors to the city, who find here at once a luxurious and aristocratic home and a locality peculiarly convenient for excursions down-town. The hotel is very favorably placed, and covers the entire block fronting on Seventh Avenue, from 56th Street to 57th Street, its grand façade being 394 feet long and seven stories high, and in attractive architecture. The section reaching to 57th Street is of red brick and Scotch sandstone, and contains exclusively suites of rooms, furnished or unfurnished. The more ornate part of the building, reaching to 56th Street, constructed of Pompeian and buff brick and red and white terra cotta, has a handsome portico. The whole struc-

HOTEL GRENOBLE, SEVENTH AVENUE, FROM 56TH STREET TO 57TH STREET.

ture is adequately equipped as a first-class modern hotel. All visitors are delighted with the beautiful white-and-gold dining-rooms, the spacious and elegant office, the exquisitely equipped café, the white mahogany furniture of the ladies' parlors and reading-room, the wonderful mosaic floorings, the ingenious fire and burglar alarms in every room, the six rapid-running Otis elevators, and the liberal endowment of electric lights. The Grenoble occupies very high land, which helps with the perfect drainage and sanitary conditions to make it an exceptionally healthy house. Only two blocks distant are the unrivalled landscape beauties of Central Park, with its lakes, lawns, woods, crags, and charming drives and rambles. People who want to go down-town will find the Elevated Railway only a block away from the Grenoble; while the Boulevard cars are an equal distance, and the Belt Line two blocks away. The Broadway cable-cars pass the very doors of this hotel. The proprietor of the Grenoble is William Noble, who has large hotel interests elsewhere, especially at Lake George, where he owns the Fort William Henry Hotel.

The Hotel Cambridge (American and European plans) is at the southwestern corner of Fifth Avenue and 33d Street, with its main entrance immediately facing the main entrance of the Waldorf, which is directly across the street.   It has a

modest exterior, in harmony with the exclusiveness and the quiet elegance of the interior.   But it has all of its several floors arranged into the choicest and most desirable apartments for families and travelling parties. It was planned and is conducted as an elegant home for families — many from the North and East making it their winter home ; and many ,from the South and West occupying a large part of it in the

HOTEL CAMBRIDGE, FIFTH AVENUE AND 33D STREET.

summer.   Besides its permanent guests, the Cambridge enjoys a very choice patronage of well-to-do people, who come here for a day, a week, or longer, and prefer this hotel by reason of its quiet elegance, its handsomely furnished apartments, and its exquisite cuisine and service.   The hotel is conducted by Henry Walter, who became the proprietor in 1893, after having been the successful proprietor and genial host of the Albemarle Hotel of New York for fifteen years.   The Cambridge is most advantageously situated on a high point in America's famous social thoroughfare — the unapproachable Fifth Avenue.   In its immediate vicinity are the great theatres, famous clubs, noted churches, and grand public institutions.   It is of easy access to surface cars and elevated trains, and past its doors go the Fifth-Avenue stage coaches.   The Cambridge is provided with modern improvements, gas and electric lights, elevators, perfect sanitary plumbing, and elegant appointments.   Its service is commendable.   Its rates range from $5 a day upward, on the American plan ; and from $2 a day upwards on the European plan.   During the short period of its present management the Cambridge has become a favorite resort of foreign diplomats, a number of whom may usually be found here.   A notable feature of the Cambridge is its quietude, and another is its convenient situation.   It is far enough away from Broadway to avoid all its commotions, and yet close enough to enjoy its conveniences.   Only one block away is the 33d-Street Elevated Railroad station, which provides rapid transit up-town and down-town, and yet the hotel is entirely apart from it.   A short distance away is the Fourth-Avenue tunnel, through which one can reach the Grand Central Station in six minutes, yet no trains can be seen or heard.

The **Park-Avenue Hotel** (American and European plans), on Park (Fourth) Avenue, from 32d to 33d Streets, is one of the greatest of the New-York hotels. It was built by the late A. T. Stewart, with the definite purpose of securing at any cost a house of accommodation that should be fire-proof, comfortable in every way, and in its public rooms magnificent. With his colossal fortune behind it, this project was nobly achieved. Within a year or two the entire building has been improved, refreshed and thoroughly modernized, adding $150,000 to the original cost of $3,000,000. The Park-Avenue is the most obviously and manifestly fire-proof hotel in America. The broad arches overhead in the chambers tell of uninflammable floors everywhere. It gives one a very restful sense of security to feel thus guaranteed against one of the worst of perils. The chambers are high and airy, well lighted and heated, and supplied with hot and cold water. There are 500 rooms, all newly furnished and decorated. The Park-Avenue is a vast and imposing quadrangular palace, surrounding a spacious courtyard which is beautified with evergreen trees, flowers and fountains, and where the famous Lanzer Orchestra plays exquisite music. All the inside rooms open upon this scene of fairyland, which is especially brilliant under the colored electric lights of evening. The situation is admirable, fronting on the Fourth-Avenue street-car line, not far from

PARK-AVENUE HOTEL, PARK AVENUE, FROM 32d STREET TO 33d STREET.

the Grand Central Station, and only a few minutes' walk from Madison Square or Bryant Park, and two or three squares from the Third and Sixth Avenue Railways, leading everywhere. All the public rooms are floored with mosaic, with bronze and gold reliefs on walls and ceilings, the richest of furniture, and many choice works of art, in paintings and statuary. The Park-Avenue Hotel is under the proprietorship of Wm. H. Earle & Sons, of the well-known Earle family, who are famous in the annals of American hotel development for more than a third of a century.

The Murray Hill (American and European plans), on Park Avenue, 40th and 41st Streets, is a great and handsome building of seven stories and ornamental towers, with accommodations for over 500 guests. It is elegantly appointed, and is an establishment of the highest class. Many New-England people sojourn at this very quiet and attractive hostelry, on high ground, near the Grand Central Station, but quite secluded from its noise and uproar.

The Victoria (American and European plans), at Fifth Avenue, 27th Street and Broadway, is a high and roomy structure, inclined to exclusiveness in its patronage. The hotel jumped into sudden fame a few years ago, when Grover Cleveland, on his election to the Presidency, made it his headquarters when in New York.

The Hotel Brunswick (European plan), eligibly located on Madison Square, at Fifth Avenue and 26th Street, is much favored by English tourists, and is patronized also by the wealthy young men about town. The house has a high reputation for its admirable service and for its restaurant, than which it is claimed by many there is none better in the city. The parades of the Coaching Club start here.

The Gerlach (European plan), on West 27th Street, near Sixth Avenue, was built in 1890, by Charles A. Gerlach, its present manager. It is an imposing eleven-story fire-proof house, with elevators, electric lights, sumptuous dining-rooms, and many fine suites. The Gerlach is chiefly for permanent residents, but receives numbers of well-to-do transients, as well, and finds a particularly large and profitable patronage in the winter season.

The Hotel de Logerot (European plan), at Fifth Avenue and 18th Street, occupies the grand old Fifth-Avenue mansion of Gurdon W. Burnham, with two others adjoining, refitted and elegantly refurnished for the present use. It is very fashionable and very aristocratic, and the landlord is a genuine nobleman, Richard de Logerot, Marquis de Croisic, who has a good standing in New York's "400."

The Clarendon (American and European plans), on Fourth Avenue and 18th Street, is favored by many English people and families, who come to make an extended stay in the city.

The Everett House (European plan), in Union Square, at the corner of Fourth Avenue and 17th Street, attracts many professional people, lecturers, authors and actors. Henry M. Stanley has been a frequent guest there. The locality is very convenient for people who wish to be near to the life of the great city, and its manifold amusements and diversion.

The Brevoort House (European plan), in Fifth Avenue, near Washington Square, is a quiet and aristocratic hotel that has long been in favor with English tourists. The cuisine of the Brevoort has always been considered one of its attractions. Sam Ward, that prince of epicures and most genial of entertainers, lived there at one time; and his nephew, F. Marion Crawford, the novelist, describes the house and his uncle's favorite corner in his novel of *Doctor Claudius.*

The Albemarle (European plan), on Madison Square, at the junction of Broadway and Fifth Avenue and 24th Street, is a quiet and exclusive place, numbering among its guests many permanent residents and foreigners of distinction.

The Grand Union Hotel (European plan) is located at Fourth Avenue and 42d Street, just across the street from the Grand Central Station. It is architecturally unassuming, but it is very large, its dimensions being 200 by 135 feet. It contains over 500 sleeping-rooms, and does the largest business of any hotel in New York, in respect to the number of guests entertained. The features which first strike the visitor to the hotel are its cleanliness and quaintness, and an air of home comfort which is lacking in many hotels. The walls of the public rooms are covered with paintings, mostly by American artists, of a high order of excellence. There are also a number of examples of foreign schools, purchased by the proprietors at the Paris *Salon.* One of the cafés is devoted to curious old colored prints, and another to prints relating to the early history of New York. Several large rooms on the ground floor are set apart for reading and writing, and are abundantly supplied with stationery, books, papers and illustrated periodicals. This is a popular feature with the travelling public, who appreciate having a comfortable place in which to lounge, read and write. The hotel has the reputation of being one of the most profitable in the country. Simeon Ford, the senior proprietor, having been asked to account for the continued and growing success of the Grand Union, in spite of the building of many new and elegant hotels, said : "In the first place, we have a location which, for transient business, is unique. We are just across the street from the Grand Central Station, and travellers, instead of having to struggle with hackmen and expressmen, can step across to our house, and we deliver their baggage in their rooms in a few minutes, without charge. Then, again, we have a moderate-priced house. We give a nice room for a dollar a day, but, if people want to pay more, we have handsome suites which cost four or five dollars a day. Our food is of the best quality obtainable, and well cooked ; and we don't ask

GRAND UNION HOTEL, FOURTH AVENUE, FROM 41ST STREET TO 42D STREET, OPPOSITE GRAND CENTRAL DEPOT.

enough for it to bankrupt a man. We are cranks on the subject of cleanliness. We are eternally scrubbing and mopping. Then again we are within easy distance of all the best shops and theatres. But, above all, we attribute our success to the fact that we try to take good care of our guests and make them feel at home, and we try our best to impress upon our employees that we get our living out of the travelling public, and that they are entitled to some consideration, and when our employees do not agree with us on this point we ask them to "seek fresh fields and pastures new."

The St. Denis Hotel (European plan), at Broadway and 11th Street, opposite Grace Church, has for many years been one of the well-known landmarks of the metropolis, and has been celebrated in Howells' works and other choice modern literature. In 1875 the hotel property was leased by William Taylor, who had served a long apprenticeship with his elder brother, in the famous Taylor's saloon, at Broadway and Franklin Street. This was, perhaps, the most magnificent restaurant ever seen in America. When Mr. Taylor assumed the charge of the St. Denis, his first work was to reconstruct it ; and this skilful renovation so greatly increased its good fame and patronage that it was found necessary to construct a very large addition. There are

ST. DENIS HOTEL, BROADWAY AND 11TH STREET.

many points of attractiveness about the hotel, the conveniences and compactness of the office, the quiet and spacious reading-room, the dainty parlors, and the famous Colonial dining-room, a triumph of refined architecture. The whole establishment is pervaded by such an air of home comfort, and is, withal, so convenient to everywhere, that people who once visit it as guests afterwards make it their domicile while in New York. The equipments of the house, as to steam heating, electric lighting, ventilating, and hydraulic elevators, are supplemented by a perfect corps of polite and well-disciplined attendants.

The situation of the St. Denis is exceptionally good, being midway between the up-town residence quarter, and the down-town business quarter, and facing on Broadway, the brightest and most fascinating street in the world. Looking across from the hotel parlors and public rooms, the stranger might fancy himself in some venerable cathedral town of England, for the wide spaces fronting the St. Denis are occupied by the beautiful Gothic edifice of Grace Church and its rectory and connecting buildings, set amid rich velvety lawns. It is a scene full of peaceful and restful suggestions. On the opposite corners are the great retail dry-goods houses of James McCreery & Co., and Hilton, Hughes & Co., the successors of A. T. Stewart & Co. A few minutes' walk above the St. Denis is the brilliant Union Square, and the shopping district extends on all sides. The restaurant of the St. Denis is widely and pleasantly known, as a place where delicious cooking, elegant surroundings and attentive service are combined with very reasonable rates. These recognized facts make the restaurant a favorite resort for shopping parties and many other people of fashion, as well as for the guests of the hotel.

The Broadway cable-cars pass the doors almost every minute, and give quick access to the City Hall or the Battery, and to the up-town squares or Central Park. Within easy walking distance, also, are the 9th-Street and 14th-Street stations of the Third-Avenue and Sixth-Avenue Elevated Railways.

The St. Denis has many points of attraction which may not be found in the great up-town hotels; and prominent among these is the absolute coziness of its public rooms, which, indeed, do not seem in the least like parts of a hotel, but rather like pleasant nooks in a refined home. Yet there are so many of these charming rooms, for divers uses, that they are never crowded or uncomfortable; and from their windows one can watch the vast and perpetual human tides flow up and down Broadway, with the cathedralesque gray spires of Grace Church looking calmly down on the busy and brilliant scene.

The Astor House (European plan), on Broadway, Barclay and Vesey Streets, is the leading hotel down-town, and one of the famous houses of the city. For two generations it has been noted, and its solid granite front, nearly opposite the Post Office, makes a conspicuous feature of that part of Broadway. It is an old-fashioned and conservative establishment, substantially furnished, and kept in good style. On the ground floor along the street fronts are stores, but back of the stores opens the great rotunda, which is a much-frequented eating-place for noon-day meals.

The Metropolitan (European plan), at Broadway and Prince Street, is still a favorite with merchants from the South and West. It is near the centre of the wholesale dry-goods district, and is a commodious six-story structure. The dining-room is one of the largest in the city. Niblo's Theatre has an entrance here.

The Morton House (European plan), on 14th Street, has been favored by theatrical folk, who until within a few years made their rendezvous in Union Square.

The Union-Square Hotel (European plan), at Fourth Avenue and 15th Street, has accommodations for 400 guests. It is strictly fire-proof.

The **Westminster Hotel** (American plan), in a quiet location at Irving Place and 16th Street, is exceedingly convenient to the shopping district and the places of amusement, being but a few steps from Union Square and the rush of Broadway, and a few minutes' walk from Madison Square and Gramercy Park. It enjoys the distinction of being a first-class family and transient hotel, having an apartment-house connected with it. The Westminster is the home of many families of means, who find here quiet elegance and refined conservatism. The hotel was named in honor of the Duke of Westminster, whose coat-of arms appears on its stained windows, stationery and menus. It was a favorite home of Charles Dickens, Christine Nilsson, and Profs. Tyndall, Huxley and Proctor; and has always been much in vogue with English travellers. The dainty drawing-rooms, recently refurnished in the French style; the cream-and-white Colonial dining-room, with its rich-hued curtains, hard-wood floors and rugs; the many commodious guest-rooms, newly carpeted and furnished; and many other attractions, give a quiet distinction to this house. Here also come many native and foreign members of the diplomatic force, drawn thither, perhaps, by the proximity of the house to Gramercy Park, now or formerly the home of statesmen and men of affairs like Hamilton Fish, Samuel J. Tilden, John Bigelow, Cyrus W. Field, David Dudley Field and Abram S. Hewitt.

The Westminster is a remarkable example of an ancient hostelry which has

WESTMINSTER HOTEL, IRVING PLACE AND 16TH STREET, NEAR UNION SQUARE.

never lost its hold upon the public favor, and which is fresher, cleaner, brighter and more modern than scores of hotels erected in New York within five years. Although nestled away in its quiet nook on Irving Place, the Westminster is within two blocks of a station of the Third-Avenue Elevated Railway, whereby the explorer may reach all parts of Manhattan in a trice. The house is practically fire-proof, withal.

The Broadway Central Hotel (American and European plans), at 665 to 675 Broadway, opposite Bond Street, is probably the largest public house in New York, and has accommodated as many as 1,200 guests at one time. On this memorable site La Farge, a sagacious French investor, built the La Farge House, which was opened in 1856. Back of the hotel stood the Tripler Hall, the scene of Jenny Lind's triumphs. The hall was remodelled into Burton's New London Theatre, then the largest in New York ; and subsequently into the Winter Garden, where Edwin Booth played *Hamlet* for 100 consecutive nights. In 1869, after La Farge's death and the burning of the Winter Garden, the entire property was acquired by the late E. S. Higgins, the carpet manufacturer, who erected here the most palatial hotel in New York, at first known as the Southern Hotel, and

BROADWAY CENTRAL HOTEL, BROADWAY, OPPOSITE BOND STREET.

afterward as the Grand Central Hotel. The grand dining-hall occupies the locality made famous by Jenny Lind and Edwin Booth, where Adelina Patti made her first public appearance, and where Rachel met her first American audience. After making fortunes for several proprietors, the house in 1892 passed into the proprietorship of the Hon. Tilly Haynes, a well-known and public-spirited Massachusetts man, who has made a notable success of the United-States Hotel, at Boston. The original cost of the Broadway Central was $2,000,000, and nearly a quarter of a million more was spent by Mr. Haynes in thoroughly renovating, refitting, refurnishing and modernizing it up to the times in every regard. It is a solid and spacious structure, with seven stories above the main floor, and very spacious and comfortable public rooms. It is admirably protected against fires. Its cuisine is noted for its excellence. It is in a singularly interesting part of the city, close to Bleecker Street, the Latin Quarter of New York ; Washington Square, the site of the triumphal arch ; Lafayette and Astor Places, with their libraries, and the centre of the publishers' quarter ; the Bowery, with its picturesque humanity ; and the Cooper Institute. Only a few blocks north is the group of buildings pertaining to Grace Church, one of the handsomest sights in the metropolis. In front of the hotel flow the vast and impressive human tides of Broadway. From this central locality one may ride up or down-town by elevated railway or by the cable cars on Broadway, reaching the Battery in 15 minutes, and Madison Square in much less time. Guests can get rooms here, on the European plan, for from $1 a day upward ; or full board, on the American plan, for from $2.50 a day upward.

The Hotel Marlborough (American and European plans), on Broadway, from 36th Street to 37th Street, is a solidly built and modern red-brick structure of 400 rooms, perfectly fire-proof, and with a general luxuriousness in all details, broad lobbies, ample billiard-rooms, well-trained servants, and a famous table.

The Hotel Métropole (European plan), is eligibly placed, at the corner of Broadway and 7th Avenue and 41st Street, and has large and comfortable accommodations. The building is completely fire-proof.

The Hotel Vendome (American plan), at Broadway and 41st Street, is largely availed of as a home for families, having many fine suites and a pleasant dining-room.

The San Remo (European plan) is an immense and imposing edifice, finely situated on the high ground of West 75th Street, and facing on the lawns, woods and waters of Central Park. The rooms in the San Remo are all in suites.

The Hotel Beresford (European plan) is a very large new hostelry, fronting on Central Park, at 1 West 81st Street. It is in a charming section of the city, not far from the American Museum of Natural History.

Other Noted Hotels might be mentioned, but out of the thousand hotels there are too many worthy of notice to be described in one brief chapter. The following is merely a partial list of the better class : Grand, Earle's, Gedney, Oriental, Barrett, Madison-Avenue, Wellington, America, Sinclair and Cosmopolitan.

Nationality in Hotels is represented by several establishments. The best-known is the Hotel Martin, in University Place, a French house that is also well patronized by Americans, and is of the better class. Another French hotel is the Hotel Monico, in 18th Street ; and still another, the Hotel Français, in University Place, that, oddly enough, is kept on the American plan. The Hotel Griffon, in 9th Street, is a French hotel, favored by French and Spanish artists, and musical and literary folk. Spaniards put up at the Hotel Español, in 14th Street ; and Italians at the Hotel Del Recreo, in Irving Place ; and there are several Spanish and Italian boarding-houses that are practically hotels on a small scale. On the East Side,

German hotels are numerous, but generally they are no more than lodging-houses above lager-beer saloons and restaurants ; and somewhat similar in character, without the saloon appendage, is a hotel exclusively for colored persons.

Cheap Hotels thrive mainly down town in the business district, or among the tenements. The best of them are respectable, and quite up to the requirements of the class of patronage to which they cater. On the lower West Side there are several large houses of this description, where rooms can be had for 75 cents and sometimes as low as 50 cents a night. They are considerably patronized by marketmen from Long Island and New Jersey, and clerks and porters in the markets and wholesale stores thereabouts, whose business requires them to be on duty for the early marketing before sunrise in the morning. At and around the Battery are houses of about the same class and price as the marketmen's hotels, but designed especially for the accommodation of immigrants, who were a good source of profit when Castle Garden was the immigrant receiving station. In the vicinity of City-Hall Park, where the all-night work of the newspaper offices and the Post Office naturally calls together a large night population, there are other hotels of this description, and several, like the Cosmopolitan and Earle's, that are of a higher grade. These places have but little else than their cheapness to commend them. Most of them are restricted to the accommodation of men only, and are well patronized by poor respectable persons.

Another step, literal as well as metaphorical, brings us to the very cheap hotels that flourish in the Bowery and vicinity, on the East Side, and on West Broadway, South Fifth Avenue, and adjacent streets on the West Side. These establishments are exclusively for men, and in them you will find the apotheosis of misery and vice. Petty thieves, hopeless drunkards, toughs and reprobates of all kinds, loafers and unfortunates whom fate has served unkindly in the struggle for existence congregate there night after night. Only the pencil of a Hogarth or the pen of a Dickens could do justice to this phase of metropolitan life. The general public knows very little about these houses of despair, save as occasionally it may read in the daily newspaper of the death there of some man who was once respected and influential among his fellow citizens, until drink dragged him down to the level of these Bowery dives. The hotel of this class generally has a high-sounding name and much glare of gas-light outside. Within, it is one or two floors or lofts in what was once a business building. Sometimes plain wooden partitions divide the room into many little closets, each with a cot bed ; more frequently the sleeping apartment is a huge dormitory, with a score or more of cots, foul mattresses on the floor, or wooden bunks, with a single old army blanket for the bed-clothing. A single room in the most aristocratic of these places is 25 cents a night, and beds are put down at 10 and 15 cents, and in the very worst of the class at 7 cents. Some of the signs advertise that a hot or cold bath is free to all guests, and at others the price of a night's lodging includes a glass of whiskey. The patronage of these establishments is large, and the proprietors grow rich. In 1892 there were 116 such houses, with accommodations for 14,172 persons.

Restaurants and Cafes are abundant, of all grades, from Delmonico's famous establishment, where it will cost you from $3 upward for a good dinner, to the cheap down-town eating-houses. There are several thousand establishments of this kind, and New York has come to be very much like Paris in respect to patronizing them. For the most part men live so far from their places of business that it is necessary for them to take their luncheons, and often their dinners, away from home, and for much the same reason it is the custom with many people to dine out when they attend the theatres and other places of amusement. More than that, however, thousands of families of all grades in financial means find it more economical and convenient to go to restaurants for their meals than it is to maintain home establishments. They have all the comforts of home except the kitchen and dining-room-attachment with the consequent care, expense of rent and annoyance of servants. Add to these the army of other folk who live in furnished rooms and take their meals at restaurants, and the thousands of citizens of foreign birth who have brought with them from across the water the ingrained national habit of patronizing cafés, and you have the abundance of restaurants and cafés accounted for. Nearly all the large hotels have great public restaurants for the accommodation of others than their regular guests. Every nationality that helps to make up the cosmopolitan character of New York has its own eating and drinking places.

Delmonico's restaurants are known all over the world. The name has been a familiar word among the epicures of two continents for nearly three-quarters of

DELMONICO'S : FIFTH AVENUE, BROADWAY AND 26TH STREET.

a century. There are two establishments in New York managed by the Delmonicos. That with which the public of this generation is most familiar occupies the entire building at Broadway, 26th Street and Fifth Avenue. The gentlemen's Café is on the Broadway side, and the public dining-room looks across Fifth Avenue into Madison Square. On the floors above are private parlors and dining-rooms, and the elegant banquet and ball room, which is famous as the scene of the Patriarchs' balls, of innumerable brilliant social events, and of nearly all the grand banquets that have been given for a generation. Many of the belles of the "Four Hundred" have made their *débuts* at Delmonico's. The place is the social centre of the wealthy and exclusive portion of New York.

The down-town establishment is at Beaver and William Streets, in a handsome eight-story building, erected in 1890. It stands on the site of the old Beaver-Street

DELMONICO'S.
BEAVER AND WILLIAM STREETS, OPPOSITE THE COTTON EXCHANGE.

House, which was erected in 1836 by Peter and John Delmonico, who were as famous in their day as their successors are now, and established in 1827, not far from this site, the business which has been so successful ever since. John died in 1843, and Lorenzo Delmonico was admitted to partnership. In 1848 Peter retired. Lorenzo died in 1881, and his nephew Charles succeeded to the business. Charles died in January, 1884, and two months later the firm which is now in existence was organized. The members are Rosa, Lorenzo Crist, Charles Crist and Josephine Crist Delmonico. The famous Delmonico restaurant at 22 Broad Street was closed in 1893.

The Café Savarin, in the Equitable Building, is one of the most celebrated of dining-rooms. Its ladies' restaurant is a beautiful room, on the main floor.

Roof Restaurants are becoming important features of down-town daily life. The upper parts of the Mills, Central, Equitable and other buildings have them.

Fleischmann's Vienna Model Bakery, Café and Restaurant, at Broadway and 10th Street, attracts many by its specialties in Vienna coffee, bread and ices. There is a plaza in front of the building, provided with a canvas roof and growing vines, where guests may dine in garden-like surroundings during the heated term.

The Dairy Kitchen in 14th Street is a curiosity. It is an enormous establishment where several thousand people are fed every day. There is orchestral music day and evening, and much glitter and show. The prices are moderate, and the food and service correspond.

The Columbia, in 14th Street, with very showy and attractive appointments, and clean and stylish in its service, is a good example of the popular second-class restaurants on a large scale.

Dry-Goods-Store Restaurants.— Several of the large bazaar stores, like Macy's and Hearn's, have restaurants. These do a large business, and are much to the convenience of shoppers from out of town, who chiefly patronize them. They are not first-class in cooking or in service. A peculiar custom distinguishes them from all other restaurants. Elsewhere prices are wholly in multiples of five cents. Here, however, prices are in parts of a five-cent standard. You get a cup of coffee for six cents, and other dishes for seven, nine, thirteen, nineteen and twenty-one cents, and so on. It is the bargain counter extended to the lunch table, and you always feel that it is bargain-day comestibles that you are getting.

Table d'Hote Dinners are served at several hundred places, from the Murray Hill and Hotel Brunswick down through many grades to the very cheap Bohemian resorts, where a dinner with wine costs 35 cents. Several restaurants up-town, like the Hotel Hungaria, Martinelli's, Moretti's, and Riccadonna's have more than a local reputation for good cooking. In the French quarter in the vicinity of Bleecker Street, and elsewhere down town, are several unique and low-priced establishments of this character.

Novelty in Restaurants is in abundant variety. In the Chinese district are several Chinese restaurants, dirty, foul-smelling and cheaply furnished. National viands of a mysterious character and national drinks are served at reasonable prices. Those who go slumming take in these restaurants, but they are not often disposed to pay a second visit. Hebrew restaurants are numerous on the East Side, and even in the wholesale business district. They make a specialty of serving "strictly Kosher" meat, and many of them are of a very good character. There is a cheap Japanese restaurant on the East Side, and meals in Japanese style are excellently served at the private Japanese Club. In East Broadway and vicinity are several Russian restaurants. Spanish cooking prevails at several places off Park Row. In

Mulberry Street are Italian restaurants of low order, and in Division Street are Polish eating-places. Of a much higher grade are the restaurants, cafés and summer-gardens in Second Avenue, below 14th Street. They are in effect public club-rooms, where Austrians, Swiss, Hungarians and sometimes Germans spend their evenings. All are liberally supplied with foreign and American periodicals, and they serve odd foreign eatables, and beer, wine and coffee of exceptional quality.

Cheap Restaurants keep company with the cheap hotels in location and in general character. They are feeding-places of the vilest character, where the staple article of food is hash or beans, with bread and butter, and tea or coffee, for 10 cents. Other dishes are at corresponding prices. Sidewalk stands will serve in their respective seasons an oyster, a little fish, an ear of corn or some other simple eatable for a cent; and all the year-round at the St.-Andrew's Coffee-Stands the poor can get a bowl of hot tea or coffee for a cent, and plain food quite as cheap. A tour of these parts of the city will reveal much gastronomic atrocity.

Drinking Saloons exist by the thousand all over the city. Of course, all the hotels have their bar-rooms, and most of the restaurants supply beer, wine or liquors, either with or without food. There are German lager-beer saloons everywhere, wine shops in the Italian and French quarters, "vodka" shops among the Russians, "nomadeo" bars among the Chinese, and liquor saloons on every other corner. The drinking-places are licensed by the Board of Excise Commissioners, and pay fees according to the character of their business. They are under certain restrictions regarding location near a church or school-house, the number permitted in a single block, hours of closing, etc., and they are not permitted to keep open on Sunday. It is almost needless to say that these conditions are continually ignored by the saloon-keepers. There are 9,000 licensed places in the city, and many more that exist in violation of the law. The licensed places pay to the city every year $1,500,000, which goes to the Police Pension Fund, etc. Hundreds of these places are very elegant, with heavy plate and cut glass, rich carved wood, fine frescoes and other decorations, and valuable pictures. Kirk's, at Broadway and 27th Street, and Stewart's, in Warren Street, near Broadway, are particularly famous for their collections of rare oil paintings, the most famous of all being the saloon of the Hoffman House, in 24th Street.

The Private Home Life of the wealthy and middle classes of New-Yorkers is a measure of the prosperity and culture of the community. Evidences of good living multiply on every hand in the handsome buildings and sumptuous interiors.

If old Peter Minuit, the first Governor-General of the Dutch colony in New Netherland, could drop in here to-day he would open his eyes in wonder, and would probably think himself bewitched. He bought all this Manhattan Island from the Indians for $24, which was about ninety cents for one thousand acres. Some of the land is now worth several times $24 per square foot, and the present market value of that original $24 worth of real estate is over $2,500,000,000. Changes in methods of living, in the details of food and shelter, have kept pace with this wonderful development in values of real estate. The men and women of to-day find it difficult in their luxurious, or at least comfortable, houses to realize how their ancestors lived here two centuries and more ago. The first houses were of wood, generally of one story, with two rooms and a high peaked roof, thatched with straw. The chimneys were also of wood, and there was much danger of fire. Furniture was of the rudest description, generally made of rough planks. Wooden platters and pewter spoons prevailed, but there were a few pieces of porcelain in the village, family heirlooms from Holland. Between that way of existence and living in the Vanderbilt mansion

16

or the Plaza Hotel there is a great gulf.   After a time the colonists began to build
their houses of brick, and they bore the date of the building in iron letters.   The
roofs were tiled or shingled, and there was always a weathercock.   Furnishings
were meagre ; sanded instead of carpeted floors, a little solid silver, but more
wooden or pewter ware, stiff-backed chairs and settees and tiled mantles.   Home life
was simple.   Around every house was a garden and pasturage for live stock.   The
mynheer smoked his pipe at the fire-place or under the projecting eaves of his house,
and the good vrouw found her only dissipation in running around the neighborhood
to gossip.   But even as far off as that, a custom was established that has been maintained down to the present time.   All tenants intending to move were compelled by
law to vacate by noon of May 1st.   There is the origin of New York's May moving.
Rents were then $25 to $100 a year.   Think of that in contrast now, with $7,000
for a flat.   Houses were then worth from $200 to $1,000.   Few traces are left of
that old time,˙ but when you come down to the Colonial days, and the early part of
the present century, it is different.   Down-town, where business is in the ascendant,
over on the East Side among the foreign population, in the historic Ninth Ward, in
Greenwich and Chelsea villages, in Washington Square, you find these houses, generally shabby enough, but with an air of gentility even in decay, with their fine old
wrought-iron railings, diamond window-panes, arched doorways, fan-lights and
carved mantels and balustrades; and in the upper part of the island a few old historic
country mansions exist, redolent with memories of the past.   But the domestic life
of New York is no longer in that environment.   Now you cannot buy even an old
house in a decent neighborhood, in the city proper, for less than $10,000, and a
single ordinary lot is worth more than that, even without a house on it.   The
majority of the single private residences are worth from $25,000 to $50,000 each.
Below $25,000 there is not much to be found of a desirable character, and in good
neighborhoods.   Above $50,000 in value come the houses of the millionaires,
occupying several city lots, splendid examples of architecture, and decorated and
furnished at lavish expense.   A list of these homes of the wealthy would number
several hundred that might reasonably be called palaces.   Rents are high, even for
ordinary houses.   It is possible to rent as low as $600 or $800, but either the house
will be old and without modern improvements, or the locality objectionable.   For a
tolerably decent house in the heart of the city from $1,000 to $2,000 must be paid;
and the figure must be increased to $3,000 and upwards if something desirable is
sought.   The West Side above 59th Street has within a few years developed into
the most agreeable residence-quarter.   Rents there are a trifle lower than farther
down-town, while the houses are in every way more attractive architecturally, and
more modern and convenient in arrangement.   In all respects this section of the
metropolis might justly be taken as an example of the perfection of attainment in
the contemporaneous home-life of a great city.   In the country annexed district
across the Harlem, values and rentals are at a lower figure, because municipal
improvements have not yet wholly reached there.

   Apartment Houses, it has been said, hold more than half of the middle-class
population of Manhattan Island.   Real estate is so valuable and consequently rents
so high that to occupy a house is quite beyond the reach of a family of ordinary
means, and the suburbs on account of their inaccessibility are out of the question.
Consequently apartments and flats have become a necessity, and a system of living,
originally adopted for that reason, has now become very much of a virtue.   Apart-
ment-life is popular and to a certain extent fashionable.   Even society countenances
it, and a brownstone front is no longer indispensable to at least moderate social

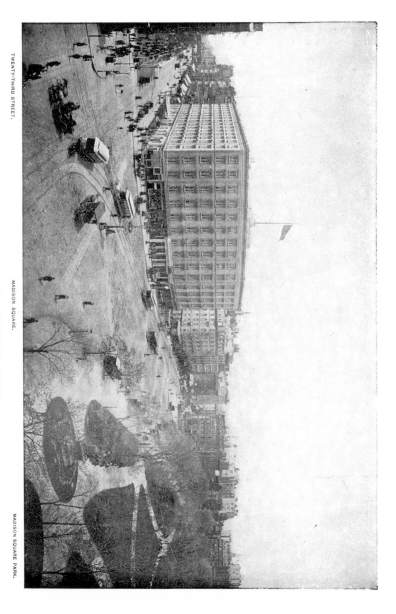

TWENTY-THIRD STREET.

MADISON SQUARE.

FIFTH AVENUE HOTEL AND MADISON SQUARE.

MADISON SQUARE, JUNCTION OF FIFTH AVENUE AND BROADWAY AND 23D AND 24TH STREETS.

MADISON SQUARE PARK.

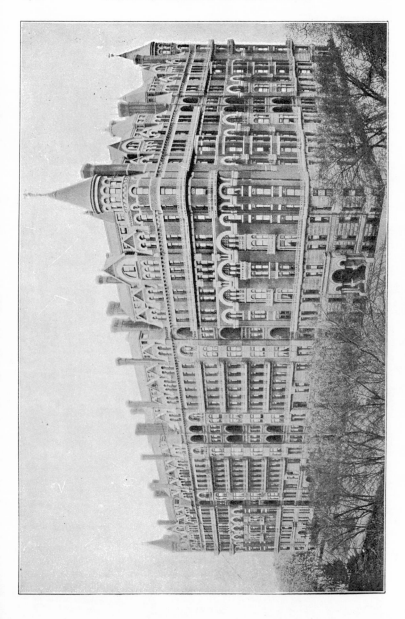

THE CENTRAL PARK APARTMENT BUILDINGS.

59TH STREET, 58TH STREET AND SEVENTH AVENUE, FRONTING CENTRAL PARK.

THE HOFFMAN HOUSE, MADISON SQUARE.

BROADWAY, WEST SIDE, FROM 24TH TO 25TH STREETS. VIEW SHOWING THE REMODELED AND REBUILT HOTEL OF 1896.

THE HOTELS WALDORF AND SCHERMERHORN.

FIFTH AVENUE, FROM THIRTY-THIRD TO THIRTY-FOURTH STREETS.   IN PROCESS OF COMPLETION IN 1897.

standing. And as for wealthy folk who are not in society, they are taking more and more to apartments. There is a great difference in apartments. You can get one as low as $300 a year, or you can pay as high as $7,000 or even more annually; in the former case you will be the occupant of a flat, but below that rental figure the flats degenerate rapidly into tenements. But even the low-priced flats have much to commend. They have generally five or six small rooms with private hall, bathroom, kitchen-range, freight-elevator for groceries, etc., janitor's service, gas chandeliers, very fair woodwork and wall-paper and often steam-heat. Between $25 and $50 a month rental the difference is chiefly in location, in number of rooms and minor details of finish. A small family with refined tastes and no social ambitions can have an agreeable home of this kind for $50, or possibly $40 a month, the latter figure in Harlem. There are in such flats many comforts that are lacking in houses in the suburbs, and the drawbacks are only contracted quarters, impossibility of privacy, and the chance of annoyance from other tenants. Above $50 a month the apartment may be of seven, eight or nine rooms, handsomely finished, and with much luxurious show in the way of tiled floors, marble wainscot in the public halls, carved over-mantels, stained glass and other fine appointments. In houses where the apartments rent for from $50 upward there are uniformed hallboys at the public entrance, and when you reach the $1,000 a year figure there will be a passenger elevator and other conveniences. On the West Side are the majority of the medium-priced apartments, renting from $30 to $75 a month, and also several of the highest class houses of the kind. In Harlem the variety and the number is greater, with almost none of the first rank. On the East Side there are more of the low-priced flats, and on Fifth Avenue, Madison Avenue and adjacent streets a few of the best quality.

Most of the handsomest apartment-houses in the city are in the vicinity of Central Park. One of the largest and best, is the Dakota, at Central Park West and 72d Street. It is a many-gabled building in the style of a French chateau, and is elegant in all its appointments. In 59th Street near Seventh Avenue are the Central-Park, or Navarro Flats, which include several independent houses constructed as a single building. Architecturally they are notable with Moorish arches, numerous balconies, grand entrances and highly ornamental façades in the Spanish style. In interior appointments the houses are not surpassed in the world. The structure cost $7,000,000. The different houses in the group are known as the Madrid, Granada, Lisbon, Cordova, Barcelona, Valencia, Salamanca and Tolosa.

Other superior apartment-houses on the West Side in the neighborhood of the Park are the Osborne, Grenoble, Wyoming and Van Corlaer, in Seventh Avenue; the Strathmore, Windsor, Rutland, Albany and Pocantico, in Broadway; the Beresford, San Remo, La Grange, Endicott and Rutledge, in Central Park West; and the Nevada, on the Boulevard. In Madison Avenue are several elegant modern houses of the highest class, with rents up to $2,000 to $4,000 a year, like the Earlscourt, St. Catherine, St. Honore, Hoffman Arms, and Santa Marguerita. In Columbus Avenue are the Brockholst and Greylock; and in Fifth Avenue are the Hamilton and the Knickerbocker. In the central part of the city are the Gramercy-Park, Anglesea, Chelsea, Florence, Westmoreland, Douglas, Beechwood and many others. The Croisic, Benedict, and Alpine are exclusively bachelor apartments.

Lodging and Boarding-Houses afford accommodations for living to a considerable per cent. of the community. High rents have much to do with this, as well as the desire to escape housekeeping cares and the necessities of the thousands of young unmarried people who find employment here away from their family homes.

Most persons of moderate means who hire a house find themselves obliged to rent rooms or to take boarders to help pay expenses, and hundreds go into the business of thus catering to the needs of the homeless, purely as a money-making enterprise. These houses are as widely diverse in character as the people whom they serve. A mechanic or laborer can hire a room for $2 a week, and get board for from $3 to $5 a week ; the wealthy bachelor may pay $25 or more a week for his suite of rooms and as much more for his board. Every individual caprice and purse can find something to suit. Broadly stated, it is not possible to get board and room in a respectable house in a fairly good locality for less than $7 or $8 a week. For that there will be wholesome food, but the room will be a small side-room, or a cramped attic-room, under the roof. For comfortable sleeping quarters with good board, $10 a week is about the lowest figure. Of that amount $4 or $5 a week is reckoned for the board, and the balance for the room-rent. The majority of clerks and others on small salaries bring their expenditure below the $10 limit by sacrificing comforts. These figures can be carried to any extreme that individual taste and means shall dictate.

The Tenements display the lowly side and often the dark side of New-York life. It is not possible to locate the tenement-house population within any closely defined limits. In general, it may be said to hold parts of nearly all the streets below 14th, except a part of the old Ninth Ward, which is distinctively the Native-American section of the city, and in and about Washington Square and lower Fifth Avenue, clinging to the river-front on either side, monopolizing almost entirely the East Side nearly over to Broadway. Above 14th Street on the East Side it is supreme east of Third Avenue as far as the Harlem River, with the exception of a part of lower Second Avenue and a few side-streets here and there. On the West Side it comes from the river-front as far east as Sixth Avenue, with oases of better homes here and there, and this as far north as about 59th Street. The territory above 59th Street to 125th Street has very little of this population. Tenement-houses are as a rule great towering buildings, many of them squalid and in bad repair, and devoid of any but the rudest arrangements for existence. They are packed with human beings. In a single block between Avenue B and Avenue C and 2d and 3d Streets there are over 3,500 residents, and a smaller block on Houston Street contains 3,000 people, which is at the rate of 1,000,000 to the square mile. That section is altogether populated at the rate of 500,000 to the square mile, which is as if the entire population of the city should be crowded into a space less than two miles square.

The picture of life in these quarters repeats what has been so often written of the misery of the poor in great cities. Frequently half a dozen people eat, sleep, and somehow exist in a single room, and tenants who have two or three rooms generally keep boarders besides their own large families. Monthly rents range from $1 a room upward, and $10 a month will sometimes secure a small stuffy apartment of three or four rooms. The landlords of these rookeries become very rich out of the needs of the poor tenants. Most of these old tenement-houses are occupied by immigrants just from Europe. When they have been here a short time they are inclined to seek better quarters in new and improved, although still cheap enough, buildings that are being put up in recent years. But the condition of living is not materially changed ; it is only different in degree of squalor and unhealthfulness.

Of all grades, good, bad and indifferent there were in 1891, according to the report of the Board of Health, 34,967 front and 2,391 rear tenement-houses, containing 1,064,703 persons above five years of age and 106,708 below that age ; about two-thirds of the entire population. In this estimate 150 first-class apartment-houses are not included, but the medium-priced flats and apartments.

THE **City and County of New York** are identical in their boundaries, and were consolidated in their governments by act of the Legislature, April 30, 1874. The Mayor, Aldermen and Commonalty of the City of New York is the name of the corporation representing the city and county. It is a public corporation, and as such its charter is always subject to amendments or alterations by the State Legislature. All local administration of both city and county affairs is in the hands of this corporation. The city has had a corporate existence since the charter for the town of New Amsterdam was granted, in 1657, by Peter Stuyvesant, representing the West India Company and the States-General of Holland. Other charters were granted from time to time afterward, superseding existing ones, and important amendments were made to them. These amendments and all other legislation pertaining to the city were codified in the New-York City Consolidation Act, passed by the Legislature in July, 1882. This act, with later additions, makes a volume of 1,100 pages. Since 1882 the Legislature has passed many laws relating to New-York City, some of which, while not in definite terms amending any of the sections of the Consolidation Act, do so in effect.

General Provisions Pertaining to Departments and Officers provide that a majority of a Board in any department constitutes a quorum to perform and discharge business. No expense can be incurred by any of the boards or officers unless an appropriation for it has previously been made by the Board of Estimate and Apportionment ; and in any year for any purpose the expenditures must not exceed the appropriation. The heads of departments, except in specified cases, appoint and remove chiefs of bureaus (except the Chamberlain) and clerks and employees, without reference to the tenure of office; but the men must be informed of the cause of the proposed removal, and be allowed an opportunity of explanation. In case of removal, a statement showing the cause is filed in the department. The numbers and duties of clerks and other employees, except as is otherwise provided, with the respective salaries, are fixed by the heads of departments, subject to the revision of the Board of Estimate and Apportionment. The heads of departments and the commissions appointed by the Mayor report to him once in three months, and at such other times as he may direct, the reports being published in *The City Record*. They must furnish him at any time such information as he may demand. The heads of departments and of bureaus (except the Police Department) are required to furnish to any tax-payer desiring them true and certified copies of books and accounts upon payment in advance at the rate of five cents for every hundred words. Books, accounts and papers in all departments and bureaus, except the Police Department, are open at all times to any tax-payer, subject to reasonable rules. In every department or board there is kept a record of its transactions accessible to the public. Once a week a brief abstract is made of all transactions, and of all contracts awarded and entered into for work and materials of every description, along with notices of appointments and removals from office and changes in salaries ; and these are all printed in *The City Record*, a publication issued daily at the city's expense, and containing many details as to the municipal life.

The Legislative Department is vested in a Board of Aldermen, including a President and Vice-President. Formerly there was a Board of Aldermen, another of Assistant Aldermen, and another of Councilmen ; and collectively they were known as the Common Council. This name still survives, and is applied, semi-officially, to the Board of Aldermen.

The Board of Aldermen chosen in November, 1892, for a term of two years, instead of one year, as hitherto, consists of 31 members. Of these 28 were elected in that part of the city below the Harlem River ; one in the 23d Ward, and one in the 24th Ward (on mainland, north of 170th Street). The President of the Board, elected at large, is the thirty-first member. The salary of members is $2,000 a year ; and that of the President is $3,000. The Aldermen take office in January succeeding their election in November. A majority constitutes a quorum. The Comptroller, the Commissioner of Public Works, the Corporation Counsel, and the President of the Board of Commissioners of each department are entitled to seats in the Board, and to participate in its discussions, but are not members of the Board nor entitled to vote. Every legislative act is by resolution or ordinance. No resolution or ordinance is passed except by a vote of a majority of all members elected to the Board. In case any resolution or ordinance involves the expenditure of money, or the laying of an assessment, or the lease of real estate or franchise, the votes of three-fourths of the members are necessary to its passage. No money can be expended for a celebration, procession, formal ceremony, reception or entertainment of any kind, unless by the votes of four-fifths of all the members. Every resolution or ordinance is presented to the Mayor for his approval. He should return it approved or disapproved within ten days after receiving it, or at the next meeting of the Board after the expiration of ten days. It takes effect as if he had approved it, unless he returns it, with his disapproval in writing, within the specified time. If disapproved, and again passed by the votes of at least two-thirds of the members elected, but in no case by a less vote than is required by its character, it also takes effect.

The Board of Aldermen has power to make, continue, modify and repeal such ordinances, regulations and resolutions as may be necessary to carry into effect all the powers vested in the corporation and for the fuller organization and carrying out of the powers and duties of any department. It has the power to enforce such ordinances by ordaining penalties in sums not to exceed $100 for every violation. It is part of its duty to regulate the use of the streets, sidewalks and other public places, especially in regard to traffic, obstructions, openings for gas and water mains and sewers, paving, grading and cleaning, naming, numbering of houses and other needs. It regulates the disposition of ashes and garbage, the public cries and noises, the use of fire-arms, the conduct of places of public amusement, the management of the markets, the licensing of cartmen, cabmen, junk-dealers, pedlers, intelligence-offices, etc., and the sale of meats, fruits and vegetables. Its duties and powers are multifarious. In general it can exercise authority over everything that pertains to the domestic economy of the community. The municipal ordinances of the Board have all the force of statute law, and are enforced by the police authorities and the courts.

The Board can so far invade the province of legislation that it can establish measures for the suppression of vice and immorality, for restraining and prohibiting certain kinds of business and for preventing the obstruction of the North and East rivers by ships mooring or anchoring in the channels ; and the Board can require the public officials to carry into effect its decrees. But there are some things that the Board is especially prohibited from doing. The municipality cannot deprive

PARK PLACE, FROM BROADWAY TO CHURCH STREET.

itself of its legislative power over the streets and their use. Any attempt to do so by contract, either expressed or implied, would not only be revocable at pleasure, but would be null and void. The city has no authority to grant to anyone the right to construct and maintain in the streets a railway for private gain. The Board has no power to appropriate any portion of a street to private use, to the exclusion of the public.

The Executive Department is vested in the Mayor and the heads of the departments. The Mayor is elected at the November general election, for a term of two years, commencing January 1st after his election. His salary is $10,000 per year. It is the duty of the Mayor to communicate to the Board of Aldermen, at least once a year, a general statement of the finances, government and improvements of the city ; to recommend to the Board of Aldermen all such measures as he shall deem expedient ; to keep himself informed of the doings of the several departments ; and generally to perform all such duties as may be required of him by the city ordinances and the laws of the State. The Mayor is a magistrate. He appoints clerks and subordinates to aid him in the discharge of his official duties, and renders every three months to the Board of Aldermen a statement of the expenses and receipts of his office. The aggregate yearly expenditure must not exceed $20,000. He regulates and controls by appointment or license, auctioneers, public exhibitions, immigrant-passenger-agents, solicitors of hotels, etc. He is by virtue of his office one of the Commissioners of Immigration. The Mayor can be removed from office for cause by the Governor of the State.   Formerly the Mayor's appointments were reviewed by the Board of Aldermen.   Now, however, he holds (with a few exceptions) the appointing power entirely independent of that body.

The Finance Department is in charge of the Comptroller, who is elected for three years, and has a salary of $10,000.   The department, which is in many respects the most important and most influential branch of the municipal organization, has control of the fiscal concerns of the corporation, and there all accounts of other departments are subject to inspection and revision.   The Comptroller furnishes to each head of department, weekly, a statement of the unexpended balance of the appropriation available for his department.   There are five bureaus in this department. 1st : For the collection of revenue from rents and interest on bonds and mortgages, and revenue arising from the sale or use of property belonging to or managed by the city, and for the management of the markets.   The chief officer of this bureau is called the Collector of the City Revenue and Superintendent of Markets.   2d : For the collection of taxes ; the chief officer of which is called the Receiver of Taxes. 3d : For the collection of assessments and arrears of taxes and assessments, and of water-rents.   The chief officer is called the Collector of Assessments and Clerk of Arrears.   4th : For auditing, revising and settling all the city's accounts, the auditing bureau, under the supervision of the Comptroller.   The chief officers are two Auditors of Accounts, appointed or removed at the pleasure of the Comptroller. 5th : For receiving all moneys paid into the treasury of the city, and for the paying of money on warrants drawn by the Comptroller and countersigned by the Mayor. The chief officer is called the Chamberlain.   The Comptroller publishes in *The City Record,* two months before the election of charter officers, a full and detailed

CITY-HALL PLACE :   CENTRE, PARK, CHAMBERS AND READE STREETS.

statement of the receipts and expenditures and the cash balances or surplus of the corporation during the year ending the first day of the month in which such publication is made.

The City Chamberlain is appointed by the Mayor for a term of four years.   He gives a bond for $500,000, and has a salary of $25,000 per year, out of which he pays his assistants and clerks.

The Board of Commissioners of the Sinking-Fund is composed of the Mayor, Recorder, Chamberlain, Comptroller, and Chairman of the Finance Committee of the Board of Aldermen. It has power to sell or lease at public auction, or by sealed bids, any city property except wharves or piers.

The Board of Estimate and Apportionment is composed of the Mayor, the Comptroller, the President of the Board of Aldermen, and the President of the Board of Taxes and Assessments. It has meetings at intervals throughout the year, when called by the Mayor. In October and November it makes a provisional estimate of the amounts required to pay the expenses of conducting the public business of the city and county in each department and branch thereof, and of the Board of Education, for the next financial year, and to meet the interest and debt account and taxes due the State. These estimates are scrutinized by the Board of Aldermen, and subsequently revised by the Board of Estimate and Apportionment. They are finally determined late in December, sometimes on the last day, and then they become the appropriations for the ensuing year. The Comptroller prepares and submits to the Board of Aldermen before its yearly meeting a statement setting forth the amounts authorized by law to be raised by tax in that year for city purposes, and also an estimate of the probable amount of receipts of the treasury of the city during the current year from all sources of revenue of the general fund. A summary of the finances of the city is as follows : The entire amount of taxes received by ordinance of the Board of Aldermen for the year 1892 was $33,232,725. The rate of taxation is about $1.85 per $100, upon a valuation of real and personal estate of over $1,700,000,000, and the rate upon the assessed valuation of the personal estate of such companies as are subject to local taxation thereon, amounting to nearly $80,-000,000, is $1.68 per $100.

The total funded debt of the city and county :

December 31, 1892, was $155,161,974
Deducting the amount held by the Commissioners of the Sinking
Fund as investments, and cash, ... 56,532,407

Left the net funded debt, ... $ 98,629,567

The general tax rate for 1892 was $1.85 on each $100 of assessed valuation, which is the lowest in thirty years, and lower than the rate in any other large city in the United States. The amount to be raised by taxation in 1892 was $33,725,556, besides which the city has and expends an income of about $3,000,000 a year, from fees, licenses, and other sources. The total assessed valuation of the city, real and personal, is $1,828,264,275, an increase of over $42,000,000 since 1891. Of this amount, $71,306,402 is corporation property, exempt from State taxes, and paying a rate to the city of $1.71 on each $100.

The Department of Public Parks is under the care of the Board of Park Commissioners, four in number, who are appointed by the Mayor, for terms of five years. The President of the Board draws a salary of $5,000 a year. The other members serve without pay. The Board has the care and maintenance of all the parks in the city, and also of certain streets in the vicinity of Central Park, such as Fifth Avenue, Morningside Avenue, and 72d, 110th and 122d Streets. It is assisted by a superintendent, an engineer of construction, and a superintending gardener.

The Police Department is under the charge of the Board of Police. It consists of four persons, known as Police Commissioners of the City of New York. They receive their appointments from the Mayor, and hold their offices (unless sooner removed) for six years, at a salary of $5,000 each. The Board is authorized and empowered to make, adopt and enforce rules and regulations for the government, discipline, administration and disposition of the police department and police force and its members. The police force consists of one superintendent, at a salary of $6,000 ; four inspectors ; captains, not exceeding one to each fifty patrolmen ; sergeants, not exceeding four to each fifty patrolmen ; detective sergeants, not ex-

BROADWAY, LOOKING NORTH FROM BARCLAY STREET. THE POST OFFICE.

ceeding forty ; surgeons not exceeding fifteen in number ; and patrolmen, etc., making 3,639. The Board of Police appoints all the members, and selects and appoints to perform detective duty as many patrolmen, not exceeding forty, as it deems necessary.

The **Department of Public Works** is under the charge of the Commissioner of Public Works, who is appointed by the Mayor, and holds his office for four years, at a salary of $8,000. The chief duties of the department pertain to the water-supply ; the altering, opening, paving and lighting of the streets ; and the care of sewers and drainage. These duties are divided among eight bureaus.

The **Department of Docks** is managed by a board of three commissioners, appointed by the Mayor, each of whom is paid $5,000 a year. The board has control of all the dock property of the city — which is a considerable portion of the entire river-front at the lower end of the city — and makes repairs, improvements, etc.

The **Department of Street-Cleaning,** the name of which fully describes its mission, is under the control of a single commissioner, whose salary is $6,000 a year. He is appointed by the Mayor. He is assisted by a deputy of his own selection, whose salary is $4,000 a year ; and employs nearly 1,500 sweepers and 500 carts.

The Department of Health is under the charge of the Board of Health, which consists of the President of the Board of Police, the Health-Officer of the Port, and two officers to be called Commissioners of Health, one of whom must be a practising physician. The commissioner who is not a physician is president of the Board. They are appointed by the Mayor, independently of the Board of Aldermen, and, unless sooner removed, hold their offices for six years. The salary of the president is $5,000 a year ; of the other commissioner, $4,000. The authority of the Board extends over the waters of the bay, up to and within the quarantine limits established by law, but not to interfere with the powers and duties of the Commissioners of Quarantine or of the Health-Officer of the Port. The total number of deaths in the city during 1892 was 44,329, or 24.26 to each thousand inhabitants. The number of births registered was 49,447 ; the number of marriages, 16,001. The amount of. money expended by the Board yearly exceeds $400,000. The summer corps of physicians inspected in July and August 40,193 tenement-houses ; visited 348,318 families ; and treated 23,834 sick persons. It is the duty of the Board to make quarterly and yearly reports to the Mayor of all its operations. The Mayor can at any time call for a fuller report. The Mayor and one Commissioner from the Department of Health, the Commissioner of Public Works, one delegate from the Bureau of Inspection of Public Buildings, and the Commissioner of the Department of Street-Cleaning are required by law to meet yearly between November 15th and December 30th to consider the subject of tenement and lodging-houses, and to make

POST OFFICE.   WORLD, TIMES AND POTTER BUILDINGS.   PARK ROW.   ANN STREET.

such recommendation in the laws affecting them as they deem best ; and to cause such recommendation to be sent to the Governor of the State, and the Senate and Assembly, yearly, on or before January 15th. They are also to consider the execution of the laws, and recommend to the Board of Health such changes as they deem best. There are two bureaus in the department. The chief officer of one is called the Sanitary Superintendent. He must have been for ten years a practising physician.

He is the chief executive officer of the department. The chief officer of the second bureau is called the Register of Records. In this bureau are recorded, without fees, every birth, marriage and death, and all inquisitions of coroners, which are taken within the city. The Board takes cognizance of the condition of any building, excavation, or premises; of any business pursuit, and of any phase of city life, which may

HALL OF RECORDS, OR REGISTER'S HALL, NEAR PARK ROW, IN CITY-HALL PARK.

affect public health, or the healthfulness of the city, and has powers which are virtually absolute to compel changes. The powers of the Board include the supervision of the repairs of buildings, in so far as sanitary condition is concerned; the regulation and control of public markets, in matters affecting cleanliness, ventilation and drainage; and the prevention of the sale of improper articles; the removal of matter on the public streets which may lead to results dangerous to life or health; the prevention of accidents by which life or health may be endangered; and generally the abating of all nuisances. It is the duty of the owner or person interested in every building or premises, to keep it in such manner that it is not dangerous or prejudicial to life or health. Every person violating or refusing to comply with the provisions of the law in these respects, or with the regulations of the Board, is guilty of a misdemeanor. The Board may remove or cause to be removed, to a place designated by it, any person sick with a contagious, pestilential, or infectious disease; and it has power to provide and pay for the use of such proper places. It may enclose streets and passages, to forbid and prevent all communication with houses or families infected with disease. It may issue a proclamation, declaring every place where there is reason to believe a pestilential, contagious or infectious disease actually exists, to be an infected place within the meaning of the health laws of the State. After such proclamation is issued, all vessels arriving in the port of New York from such infected places, together with their officers and crews, passengers and cargoes, are subject to quarantine for such period as is necessary, and it may regulate or prohibit internal intercourse by land or water with such infected places. It is the duty of the Board to aid in the enforcement of all laws of the State applicable in the city to the preservation of life and the care of health, including the laws relative to cleanliness and the sale of deleterious drugs and foods. It is authorized to require reports from hospitals, prisons, schools, places of amusement, etc. It is to omit no reasonable means for ascertaining the existence and cause of disease, sending such information to health authorities elsewhere, with such suggestions as it may see fit. The Board, the Health-Officer and Quarantine Commissioners are to co-operate to prevent the spread of disease and to ensure the preservation of health. The Board is authorized from time to time to alter, annul or amend the sanitary code. It keeps a general complaint book, in which may be entered by any person in good faith, any complaint of a sanitary nature, giving the names of persons complained of and date of the entry, with suggestion of remedy; and such complaints are to be investigated. It is the duty of all boards and officers having charge of any property controlled by public authority, to report upon and give knowledge of anything affecting sanitary conditions to the Health Board. False reports on these matters from any one required to make reports are misdemeanors. Prompt action in such cases is required of prosecuting officers, and police justices. The Sanitary Code, consisting of 219 sections, is made up of the sanitary ordinances adopted by the Department of Health ; and is of profound value in fighting epidemics and other menaces.

The Board of Excise, with rooms at 54 Bond Street, corner of the Bowery, acts under a law of the State, the same that applies in most respects to cities of over 30,000 inhabitants. It is composed of three members, who are appointed by the Mayor, for a term the same as his own, and receive salaries of $5,000 each. The Board issues licenses for the sale of spirituous liquors, wines, ale and beer, to saloons, hotels, restaurants, drug and grocery stores, and collects the license fees therefor. The receipts of the Board for 1892 were $1,523,780. Aside from paying the expenses of the Board, this sum was used as follows : New York Fire-Relief Department, $75,000 ; police pensions, $307,000 ; charitable institutions for the support of children committed by magistrates, $667,000 ; general fund of the city, $350,000.

The Law Department has at its head the Counsel to the Corporation, who receives his appointment from the Mayor, for a term of four years, and draws an annual salary of $12,000. The department has charge of the law business of the corporation and its departments, the management of legal proceedings relating to the laying out of streets, and the preparation of all deeds, leases, contracts and other legal papers connected with any department, and is at all times the legal adviser of the city officials. There are two bureaus in the department, in charge respectively of the Corporation Attorney and the Public Administrator. Certain actions in behalf of the city, such as for the recovery of penalties, etc., are conducted by the Corporation Attorney. The Public Administrator collects and takes charge of the property of persons dying intestate, and is, in effect, a public executor. The District Attorney is the prosecuting officer of the city and county. He is elected by the people for a

JEFFERSON-MARKET POLICE-COURT, SIXTH AND GREENWICH AVENUES.

term of three years, receiving a salary of $12,000 a year. His six assistants, whom he appoints, receive salaries of $7,500 a year each. The Recorder is elected for fourteen years. He receives a salary of $12,000. The City Judge and the Judges of General Sessions are elected for fourteen years, at yearly salaries of $12,000. The Police Justices, fifteen in number, are appointed by the Mayor, at $8,000 a year. The Courts of Special Sessions are held by them, at the Tombs ; and there are six police-courts, in various parts of the city.

The Harlem Municipal Building, at the corner of Sylvan Place and 121st Street, is a large building erected in 1891–92, and containing the rooms of the Harlem courts, and the local branches of various municipal departments. In its imposing architecture and modern equipments it is worthy of this dignity.

The Criminal Court Building, erected in 1891–93, occupies a site alongside the Tombs, with which they are connected by a bridge across the street, connecting the cells and the court-rooms. The building is in the German-Romanesque style, and the architects were Thom, Wilson & Schaarschmidt. The wings are crowned by pediments, and adorned with statuary. The building is of great size, and its internal arrangements are admirably adapted for the serious and solemn purposes for which this temple of justice was erected. With its brilliant coloring and lofty façades, the court-house forms a striking contrast to the low, dark and massive Tombs. In it will be held the courts of Oyer and Terminer, General Sessions of the Peace, Special Sessions of the Peace, and one or more police courts; and it provides proper office-accommodations for the judges and clerks of these courts, for juries and grand juries, and for the district attorney and other officers. It occupies the square bounded by White, Franklin, Centre and Elm Streets.

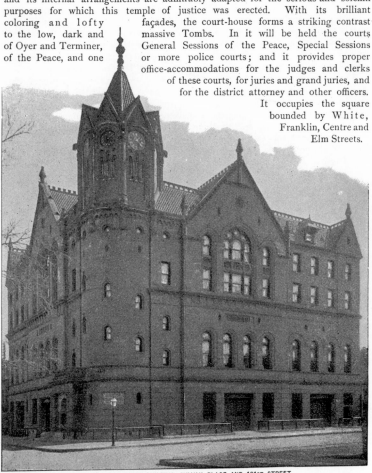

HARLEM MUNICIPAL BUILDING, SYLVAN PLACE AND 121ST STREET.

THE CRIMINAL LAW COURTS (UNFINISHED) AND THE TOMBS.
CENTRE STREET, WEST SIDE, FROM FRANKLIN TO LEONARD STREETS.

NINETEENTH-WARD POLICE-COURT, 191 EAST 57TH STREET.

The Department of Public Charities and Correction is under the charge of the Board of Charities and Correction, which consists of three persons known as Commissioners. They are appointed by the Mayor, at a salary of $5,000 each. The department possesses and exercises full and exclusive powers for the government, management, maintenance and direction of the several institutions, buildings, premises and properties belonging to the city, and situated upon Blackwell's, Ward's, Randall's and Hart's Islands ; of all places provided for the detention of prisoners (except Ludlow-Street Jail, which is under the Sheriff) ; and of all hospitals belonging to the city, except such as are conducted by the Department of Health, and especially of the Alms-house and Workhouse ; of the nurseries for poor and destitute children on Randall's Island ; and of the county lunatic asylum and the lunatic asylum upon Ward's Island ; and of the Potter's Field, and especially, also, of the penitentiary and city prison. There is in the department a Bureau of Charities and a Bureau of Correction. The former has charge of matters relating to persons not criminal ; the latter of matters relating to criminals. The Board of Public Charities and Correction also maintains on Ward's Island an asylum for inebriates.

The Fire Department is under the exclusive charge of the Board of Fire-Commissioners, consisting of three persons known as Fire-Commissioners. They are appointed by the Mayor and Board of Aldermen, and hold their offices for six years, unless sooner removed. Their salaries are $5,000 each. There are in the department three bureaus. One is charged with the duty of preventing and extinguishing fires, and of protecting property from water used at fires. The principal officer is called the Chief of the Fire-Department. Another bureau is charged with the execution of all laws relating to the storage, sale and use of combustible materials. The principal officer is called the Inspector of Combustibles. Another bureau investigates the origin and cause of fires, under the Fire Marshal.

The Department of Street-Improvements, Twenty-Third and Twenty-Fourth Wards, is in charge of a single commissioner, elected by the people of those wards. Its jurisdiction is north of the Harlem River, and corresponds to that of the Department of Public Works in the rest of the city.

The Department of Taxes and Assessments assesses taxable property, real, personal and corporation, upon which is levied a tax sufficient to meet the expenses of conducting the business of the city and county government in each department, court, etc., including the interest on the City debt, the principal of any stock or bonds that may become due, and the proportion of the State tax for the next fiscal year. It is governed by a Board of three commissioners, appointed by the Mayor for six years each. The salary of the President is $5,000 a year, that of the other members $4,000. The Commissioners are assisted by a Secretary, a Chief Deputy, and 16 Deputy Tax Commissioners ; a Board of four Assessors ; and a clerical force. The President is by law one of the members of the Board of Estimate and Apportionment, controlling the financial affairs of the city ; and of the Armory Board, charged with the purchase of land and the erection and equipping of armories for the militia. The Board of Assessors apportion the cost of local improvements, and levy it upon the property benefited.

The Department of Buildings has charge of all matters relating to buildings. The Department has full power in passing upon questions of the mode of construction or material to be used in the erection or alteration of any building ; also plumbing and drainage of all buildings ; and light and ventilation of tenements ; and stairways, fire-escapes and other exits in theatres and other public buildings ; with power to make all details of construction conform to the intent and meaning of the law. Its office is at Fourth Avenue and 18th Street.

The Board of Education includes 21 Commissioners appointed by the Mayor, and supervises the free public schools. The office is at 146 Grand Street.

Other Civic Duties are fulfilled by the Commissioners of Accounts, the Aqueduct Commissioners, the Board of Armory Commissioners, the Commissioners of the Harlem-River Bridge, and the Civil-Service Supervisory and Examining Board.

The City Hall has been in its time the finest piece of architecture in the country, but it is surpassed now by many buildings of more imposing structure, if not so classical in their architectural style. It was built between the years 1803 and 1812, at a cost of over $500,000. Its front and east and west sides are of marble, but sandstone was regarded as good enough for the rear, the city being at that time mostly on its front. In 1890 the rear was painted, making all sides uniform in appearance. The city has so outgrown it that many other buildings have to be used for the public offices. An enormous new City Hall, of white marble, is to be built in 1893-95, at a cost exceeding $4,000,000. Richard M. Hunt, Napoleon Le Brun and Wm. R. Ware form the advisory committee of architects. The City-Hall Park, in the very midst of the swarming denizens of the metropolis of the Western Continent, and with its broad sweep of ground, fountain, trees, and plots of grass, forms a redeeming feature to the brick and mortar, granite, marble and asphalt, that rule nearly everywhere else for many square miles on the lower end of Manhattan Island. The park and the City Hall together have been for this century the chief centre and historic place in the city. The Brooklyn Bridge, terminating in such close proximity, has added to the importance of the location. Celebrations of note have made them memorable. October 23, 1812, "The City Hall was like a Sea of Fire" in consequence of Perry's victory on Lake Erie. Here the citizens became wild with enthusiasm on the

LUDLOW-STREET JAIL.　　　　　　　　ESSEX-MARKET COURT.
ESSEX-MARKET POLICE-COURT, ESSEX ST. AND ESSEX-MARKET PLACE.

17

opening of the Erie Canal, in 1825, and a correct forecast was made of the future supremacy of the city above all other cities of the Republic. It witnessed the return of Lafayette to this country half a century after its independence was declared, the Republic meantime having taken rank as one of the chief nations of the globe. One of the greatest of modern events, the laying of the Atlantic Cable, was here celebrated, with a keen appreciation of what it implied to mankind. The sorrows of the Nation have been here expressed, when Lincoln and Grant, the accepted leaders and heroes of the century now nearing its close, were viewed in their inanimate clay by mourning thousands, before going to their final resting places. The interior of the building is made memorable by its relics of the past, and works of art commemorating great events and distinguished statesmen. The Governor's Room contains furniture that was used by the first Congress of the United States, held in Federal Hall, in Wall Street. There are two desks used by Washington, one while he was President. There are portraits of Washington, Jefferson, Hamilton, Jay, and Lafayette, and busts of Washington and Franklin, by the most distinguished artists of their times. The portraits of many later statesmen adorn the walls.

The Mayors of the City have been elected since the charter was amended in 1830. Previous to that time they were appointed by the Common Council. John Cruger, first president of the Chamber of Commerce, with a distinguished record during the Revolutionary War, was mayor of the city from 1739 to 1744, and again from 1757 to 1766. De Witt Clinton, before becoming governor of the State, and under whose administration the Erie Canal was opened, was mayor for several terms, none succeeding each other. Fernando Wood came into unenviable prominence during his second administration, by pursuing a conciliatory policy toward the criminal and corrupt elements of the city. It was during the administration of A. Oakey Hall that the Tweed ring was in full possession of the reins of government, and defiant of public opinion. Its power was broken at the general election in November, 1871. Wm. F. Havemeyer then came a second time to the chair. Tweed soon died in a felon's cell, while some of his companions were sent to prison and others became exiles in foreign lands. Following is a list of mayors with their terms of service since the town has been known by its present name : Thomas Willet, 1665–1667; Thomas Delavall, 1666, 1671, 1678; Cornelis Steenwyck, 1668, 1670, 1682, 1683; Matthias Nicolls, 1672; John Lawrence, 1673, 1691; William Dervall, 1695; Nicholas De Meyer, 1676; Stephanus Van Cortlandt, 1677, 1686, 1687; Francis Rombouts, 1679; William Dyer, 1680–1681; Gabriel Minvielle, 1684; Nicholas Bayard, 1685; Peter de la Noy, 1689–1690; Abraham de Peyster, 1692–1695; William Merritt, 1695–1698; Johannes de Peyster, 1698–1699; David Provoost, 1699–1700; Isaac de Riemer, 1700–1701; Thomas Noell, 1701–1702; Philip French, 1702–1703; William Peartree, 1703–1707; Ebenezer Wilson, 1707–1710; Jacobus Van Cortlandt, 1710–1711–1719–1720; Caleb Heathcote, 1711–1714; John Johnson, 1714–1719; Robert Walters, 1720–1725; Johannes Jansen, 1725–1726; Robert Lurting, 1726–1735; Paul Richards, 1735–1739; John Cruger, 1739–1744; Stephen Bayard, 1744–1747; Edward Holland, 1747; 1757; John Cruger, 1757–1766; Whitehead Hicks, 1766–1776; David Matthews (Tory), 1776–1784; James Duane, 1784–1789; Richard Varick, 1789–1801; Edward Livingston, 1801–1803; DeWitt Clinton, 1803–1807; Marinus Willett, 1807–1808; DeWitt Clinton, 1808–1810; Jacob Radcliff, 1810–1811; DeWitt Clinton, 1811–1815; John Ferguson, 1815; Jacob Radcliff, 1815–1818; Cadwallader D. Colden, 1818–1821; Stephen Allen, 1821–1824; William Paulding, 1825–1826; Philip Hone, 1826–1827; William Paulding, 1827–1829; Walter Bowne, 1829–1833; Gideon Lee,

THE CITY HALL.

IN CITY-HALL PARK, OPPOSITE MURRAY STREET, BETWEEN BROADWAY AND PARK ROW.

1833-1834; Cornelius W. Lawrence, 1834-1837 ; Aaron Clark, 1837-1839 ; Isaac L. Varian, 1839-1841 ; Robert H. Morris, 1841-1844 ; James Harper, 1844-1847 ; William V. Brady, 1847-1848 ; William F. Havemeyer, 1848-49 ; Caleb S. Woodhull, 1849-1851 ; Ambrose C. Kingsland, 1851-1853 ; Jacob A. Westervelt, 1853-1855; Fernando Wood, 1855-1858; Daniel N. Tiemann, 1858-1860 ; Fernando Wood, 1860-1862 ; George Opdyke, 1862-1864 ; C. Godfrey Gunther, 1864-1866 ; John T. Hoffman, 1866-1868 ; Thomas Coman (acting mayor), 1868 ; A. Oakey Hall, 1869-1870 ; William F. Havemeyer, 1871-1874 ; William H. Wickham, 1875-1876 ; Smith Ely, 1877-1878 ; Edward Cooper, 1879-1880 ; William R. Grace, 1881-1882 ; Franklin Edson, 1883-1884 ; William R. Grace, 1885-1886 ; Abram S. Hewitt, 1887-1888 ; Hugh J. Grant, 1889-1892 ; and Thomas F. Gilroy, 1893-1894.

The Seal of the City had its origin in colonial and Dutch times.   The commercial activity at first was in the purchase of furs from the Indians, and nothing was so potent in bringing about a trade as gunpowder, whiskey or flour.   The contracting parties were sailors and Indians.   Hence we have on the seal a sailor and an Indian, representing the traders, and two beavers and two barrels, representing the articles traded in ; and the windmills of Holland, celebrated in the 17th as well as in the 19th centuries, are represented, and the four arms serve for the quarterings.   An eagle surmounts the shield, and in this we have a more modern intimation. The first seal, for New Amsterdam, was granted in 1654, the town having been incorporated the preceding year.   For this the seal of the Duke of York was substituted under Governor Nicolls, in 1669, and was continued in use until 1686.

The Courts and Judicial Powers and Proceedings.—The term "City Hall of the City of New York," when used in any law of the State, includes, for all legal purposes, all buildings designated by the Board of Aldermen for the use of the courts or public offices within that part of the city bounded by Chambers Street, Broadway, Park Row, Centre Street, Mail Street and Tryon Row ; but rooms used by any of the courts of the city and county of New York are deemed a part of the City Hall for the purpose of holding a court.   The First Judicial District of the State consists of the city of New York.   The library of the Law Institute is in the Post-Office Building, under the care and management of the Justices of the Supreme Court of the First Judicial District, who are its trustees.   It is open to the public. The Justices of the Supreme and Superior Courts and the Judges of the Court of Common Pleas have power to commit to the Inebriate Asylum, under the control of the Commissioners of Charities and Correction, for a term not to exceed two years, actual inhabitants of the city who are unfit for conducting their own affairs on account of habitual drunkenness.   The Circuit and District Courts of the United States are held in the Post-Office Building.   The original jurisdiction of the former is in suits arising under the revenue, copyright and patent laws; and in civil law and equity suits between citizens of different States ; its appellate jurisdiction is from the United-States District Court.   The latter has jurisdiction in admiralty and maritime cases, in cases where an alien sues on tort in violation of a treaty or the laws of nations, and in suits instituted in the United States by and against foreign consuls.   The State courts, — the Supreme Court and the Court of Oyer and Terminer, are held in the County Court-House.   The former is the general law and equity court of the State, and the latter is the criminal branch of the same.   The appellate branch of the Supreme Court, known as the General Term, passes on appeals from the trial justices of the court, the final appeal being from the General Term to the Court of Appeals, which sits at Albany.   The salaries paid the Justices of the First Judicial District are $17,500 each a year, this being $11,500 a year more than is paid to the justices of the other districts of the State, the city and county of New York paying the additional amount. Of the city courts the Court of Common Pleas for the City and County and the Superior Court of the County are courts of record, and each of them has six judges, who are magistrates. The courts have concurrent jurisdiction with the Supreme Court of the State within the city limits. They both hold general terms, final appeals being made to the Court of Appeals. They sit in the County Court-House. The jurisdiction of these courts is about the same; the former has appellate jurisdiction in cases from the city and district courts, its decisions being final. The salaries paid the judges are $15,000. The City Court, formerly called the Marine Court, sits in the City Hall. It has six Judges, who hold office for six years, with salaries of $10,000 a year each. It is the lowest of the courts of record. It tries actions to the amount of $2,000. It has a limited maritime jurisdiction, and also a general term. The District Courts are inferior civil courts. There

are eleven of them, held as follows: First, Chambers Street, corner Centre Street; 2d, corner of Pearl and Centre Streets; 3d, 125 Sixth Avenue; 4th, 30 1st Street; 5th, 154 Clinton Street; 6th, 61 Union Place; 7th, 151 East 57th Street; 8th, 200 West 22d Street; 9th, 150 East 125th Street; 10th, 158th Street, corner of Third Avenue; 11th, 919 Eighth Avenue. The Surrogate's Court is held at the County Court-House. It adjudicates in matters pertaining to wills, and administrates matters pertaining to deceased persons. The Court of General Sessions of the Peace is held at 32 Chambers

COURT OF GENERAL SESSIONS, 32 CHAMBERS STREET.

Street by the Recorder, the City Judge and two Judges of the Court of General Sessions, each of whom holds office for fourteen years, at $12,000 a year. Its jurisdiction is similar to that of the Oyer and Terminer. Appeals are to the General Term of the Supreme Court, and finally to the Court of Appeals, except when the judgment is of death, when the appeal is to the Court of Appeals direct.

The Police Courts are inferior criminal courts, having original jurisdiction over minor offenses. Before them are brought, every morning, prisoners arrested and held over night in the police stations and city prisons. Drunkenness, assault and battery, and thieving, are the complaints most frequently dealt with. Nearly all cases in which punishment is inflicted are disposed of by fines or short terms of imprisonment in the city institutions on Blackwell's Island. The police justices have power to examine and hold for trial persons accused of serious crimes. They have great latitude in the exercise of their powers, and much of their work is to adjust minor neighborhood differences, and dispose of petty offenders, without resorting to actual legal proceedings. They are fifteen in number, and are appointed by the Mayor for terms of ten years, at salaries of $8,000 a year. Three police justices, without a jury, constitute the Court of Special Sessions of the Peace. This court has jurisdiction over all misdemeanors, and is held at the Tombs. The locations of the six police courts are as follows : 1st District, the Tombs ; 2d, Jefferson Market ; 3d, 69 Essex Street ; 4th, 57th Street, near Lexington Avenue ; 5th, 121st Street and Sylvan Place (in the Harlem Municipal Building) ; 6th, East 158 Street and Third Avenue, Morrisania.

The County Court-House, adjacent to the City Hall, is in Corinthian architecture, of Massachusetts white marble, and occupies a space of 250 by 150 feet. Kellum was the architect, and was succeeded by Leopold Eidlitz. The original design was noble, but suffered disfigurement by large additions ordered by the city government. It was begun in 1861, but the dome is not yet finished. The Court-House is an inadequate showing for the $10,000,000 it cost the city. Its construction was a basis for a considerable part of the peculations of Tweed and his associates. The new City Hall will enclose this structure on three sides, and probably at no distant date it will be taken down.

The Hall of Records, or Register's Office, is used for courts as well as records. It is the only public building that dates back to the times of the Revolution. Many loyal citizens were imprisoned in it while the British held the city, and it was afterward used as a debtors' prison. It is near Park Row, in City-Hall Park. This historic (but very unattractive) edifice is to be demolished to make room for the new palace of the city government, which will reach within 50 feet of Broadway, Centre Street, and Chambers Street. The Hall was built in 1757, as a suburban prison, on the Boston Road. The patriots confined here in the Revolution suffered inexpressible horrors, and died by thousands.

Jurors.—The Commissioner of Jurors is the judge of the qualifications of petit or trial jurors. He hears and determines claims for exemption. The persons to serve as grand jurors are taken from the lists of petit jurors by a board consisting of the Mayor and certain designated judges of the court. The board meets yearly, on the first Monday in September, and elects one of its number as chairman. Four members comprise a quorum. Not less than 600, nor more than 1,000, are chosen from the lists of persons qualified to serve as petit jurors, to serve as grand jurors of the Courts of Oyer and Terminer and General Sessions, until the next list is prepared. The names on these lists are deposited in a box, and the names of persons to serve as grand and trial jurors are drawn by chance. A grand jury is drawn for every term of the Court of General Sessions, and may be drawn for the Court of Oyer and Terminer. A trial juror is to be not more than seventy years of age, and he is to be the owner, or the husband of a woman who is the owner, of personal property of the value of $250; and he is to be able to read and write the English language understandingly. Certain persons are exempt, as clergymen, physicians, lawyers, teachers, editors, reporters, members of the National Guard, and others. A person trying to escape jury duty by bribery, false statement or illegal means, or one who assists another to do the same, is guilty of a misdemeanor.

The Court of Arbitration.—The Governor nominates and with the consent of the Senate, appoints an arbitrator, to be known as the Arbitrator of the Chamber of Commerce. His salary is fixed and paid by it. In a controversy brought before the arbitrator, the parties to it may each appoint an additional arbitrator if he desires. Upon application of parties interested, contracts, written or oral, are to be interpreted and construed. The parties to any controversy or dispute, arising or

THE COUNTY COURT-HOUSE.
BROADWAY AND CHAMBERS STREET, IN CITY-HALL PARK.

being within the port of New York, or relating thereto in various respects, may voluntarily submit it to the Court of Arbitration. An award being made, an order must, at the instance of either party, be filed at the office of the County Clerk. An award for the payment of money or the delivery of property requires, on request being made, a judgment to be entered. Such judgment has the same force as a judgment of the Superior Court.

The County Officers are elected for three years. The Sheriff of the county is paid a salary of $12,000, and half of the fees paid into the office. There is an under-sheriff, and deputies not to exceed twelve in number. The salary of the County Clerk is $15,000 in full for all services. The salary of the Register is $12,000 a year. There are four coroners, each receiving a salary of $5,000. When a person dies from criminal violence or casualty, or suddenly, when in apparent health, or unattended by a physician, or in prison, or in any unusual or suspicious manner, it is the duty of the coroner to subpœna a coroner's physician, who views the body of the deceased person, or makes an autopsy, as may be required. The testimony of such physician, and of other witnesses, constitutes an inquest. The coroner may call a jury, if he deems it necessary, or if a citizen should so demand. It is the duty of a citizen who may have become aware of the death of a person as here stated, to report such death to a coroner or any police officer, and a person who wilfully neglects this is upon conviction guilty of a misdemeanor. Any person who wilfully disturbs the body or clothing of a person so dying is guilty of a misdemeanor. A coroner is the only officer who has the power to arrest the Sheriff.

The Port Wardens of the Port of New York are nine in number, three of whom are nautical men, appointed by the Governor, with the consent of the Senate. They elect one of their number as president, and one as vice-president. The appointments are for three years. It is the duty of the Board, or some of them, on being notified, to go aboard of any vessel to examine the condition and stowage of the cargo, and if there are any goods damaged to seek the cause, and to enter the same upon the books of the office. The members of the Board are exclusive surveyors of any vessel that has been wrecked, or is deemed unfit to proceed to sea. They are to specify what damage has occurred, and record in the books of the office full and particular accounts of surveys made on vessels; and they are judges of repairs necessary to make vessels seaworthy again. They have exclusive powers over the survey of vessels and their cargoes arriving in the port of New York in distress.

Quarantine for the protection of the public health is provided for by the laws of the State for the port of New York. The Quarantine establishment consists of warehouses, anchorage for vessels, hospitals, a boarding station, crematory, and residences for officers and men. The Health-Officer is appointed by the Governor and Senate for four years. He receives a salary of $12,500 a year. He appoints and dismisses at pleasure two Assistant Health Officers. There are three Commissioners of Quarantine, at a yearly salary of $2,500 each, who, with the Mayors of New York and Brooklyn, constitute a board that erects hospitals, docks, etc., and has care of the Quarantine property. On Swinburne and Hoffman Islands, in the Lower Bay, fifteen miles from the city, and between Staten Island and Sandy Hook, are the chief hospitals. Persons from infected ships are taken there. Vessels from non-infected ports are boarded from Clifton by the Health-Officer and his assistants.

Pilots and Pilotage.— The Board of Commissioners of Pilots consists of five persons, each holding his office for two years. Three are elected by the Chamber of Commerce, and two by the presidents and vice-presidents of the marine-insurance companies of the city, composing the Board of Underwriters. The commissioners license for such time as they think proper as many Sandy-Hook pilots as they deem necessary, for the port of New York. Candidates are subject to examination pertaining to the duties to be performed by them, and are required to give bonds in two sureties, not exceeding $500 each, for the faithful performance of their duties. Pilots for the safe pilotage of vessels through the channel of the East River, known as Hell-Gate pilots, are appointed by the Governor with the consent of the Senate, on recommendation of the Board of Port-Wardens of New York. This board makes the rules and regulations under which they act.

The Post Office is the chief architectural representative of the Federal Government in the city. It occupies a specially favored site — the lower end of what was once the triangular City-Hall Park. More people daily come in view of it than of any other building in the city. In its rear it has the City Hall and park, and the

THE UNITED-STATES POST OFFICE, BROADWAY, PARK ROW AND MAIL STREET.

western terminus of the East-River Bridge ; and close to it are the two great thoroughfares, Broadway and Park Row. A dozen streets converge towards it ; the great newspaper offices with their newer architecture tower over it ; and the elevated cars and the street-cars carry hundred of thousands of people daily past it, or pour them out near by. At night the spaces around it are illuminated with almost the brilliancy of day. Here the heart-throb of the city is more than anywhere else evident. The building was no doubt designed to reflect the power and dignity of the Federal Government. Its cost was $10,000,000, including the furniture. The architecture is Doric and Renaissance. It extends 340 feet on Broadway, 340 feet on Park Row, and 290 feet on Mail Street, facing the park. It is made of a light-colored granite. Its height is five stories. The United-States Circuit and District Courts here hold their sessions. In handling the mail of New-York City, 1,561 clerks and 1,175 letter-carriers are employed. The Post-Office receipts for the fiscal year ending June 30, 1892, were $6,783,202. The expenditures reached $2,568,-700, leaving a net revenue of $4,214,502. There are 18 branch post-office stations, 20 sub-stations, 100 agencies for the sale of postage stamps, and 1,770 street letter-boxes, attached to lamp-posts, and located in hotels, clubs, and large business buildings.

The Postmaster of New York is Charles Willoughby Dayton, appointed by President Cleveland in 1893, to succeed Cornelius Van Cott, appointed by President Harrison in 1889. His predecessor was Henry G. Pearson, appointed by President Garfield, in 1881. Thomas L. James was postmaster during President Hayes's administration, and went into President Garfield's cabinet as Postmaster-General, in 1881.

The Bureau of Animal Industry, at 18 Broadway, is under the Department of Agriculture of the United-States Government. The duties are the inspection of all live animals intended for export to Europe. The exportation of cattle exceeds that of all other animals. The special object of the office is to detect cases of pleuro-pneumonia and other contagious diseases in animals. The veterinary inspector of the port has a corps of assistants at the stock-yards. The inspection of the cattle-carrying steamers comes within the jurisdiction of the office. All cattle exported are tagged, showing the sources of shipment. There are offices in Brooklyn, Jersey City and many other points, for detecting the contagious diseases of animals.

The New-York State Fish-Commission, consisting of five members, is appointed by the Governor. It has its chief office at 83 Fulton Street. Its object is to disseminate the fry of food-fish in public waters throughout the State. There are five hatcheries for the propagation of the fry from the eggs of the female fish. They are as follows : The Adirondack, Saranac P. O. ; Franklin County ; Cold Springs P. O., Long Island ; Fulton Chain, Old Forge P. O. ; Sacandaga, Newton Corners ; Chautauqua, Caledonia P. O. There is a shell-fish department, for the surveying and granting of franchises to the holders of oyster grounds.

The United-States Immigrant Bureau, on Ellis Island, New-York Harbor, is under the charge of the Commissioner of Immigration and a staff of officers. The principal function of this bureau is to inspect and examine arriving immigrants ; and to see that the provisions of the laws forbidding the landing of certain prohibited classes, namely : convicts, lunatics, idiots, paupers, persons likely to become public charges, or suffering with contagious or loathsome diseases, contract laborers, and polygamists, are carried out. All immigrants are landed at Ellis Island, which covers an area of 6 acres. For the twelvemonth ending June 30, 1892, the immigration was 445,987, including 81,592 from Germany, 60,233 from Austria-Hungary, 59,205 from Russia, 58,687 from Italy, and 47,635 from Sweden and Norway.

·The General Culture·

THE ancient history and traditions of New York, its immense increase and con-
servation of wealth, and the gathering here of the brightest men and women in
the Republic, combine with many other causes to make of the Empire City one of
the foremost educational centres of the Western World. This leadership is not
dependent upon any single institution, or any special line of study, or any individual
group of influences. Besides its two universities, which stand among the foremost
exponents of the German system, it has schools of medicine, theology, law, art, and
music second to none in efficiency and value of results. Students in New York work
and play with equal and intense zest, as the merchants of the city do, for the electric
air of Manhattan allows no place or time for bucolic stagnation. In the great libraries and art-galleries, museums and hospitals, the scholar finds numberless object-
lessons, and extends the bounds of his observation far beyond his text-books.

The first schoolmaster in New Amsterdam was Adam Roelandsen, who enjoyed
a monopoly of teaching the round-faced little Dutch children. After a time this
pioneer of pedagogues fell into ill repute, so that his pupils all departed, and he was
forced to earn a scanty living by taking in washing. Not even as a launderer was
he permitted to dwell in the New World, for in 1646 he was publicly flogged and
banished from the country. A year before this exile began, Adrien Jansen Van
Olfendam opened a school, and met with good success, his price for a year's tuition
being two beaver-skins. This lucrative business stimulated Jan Stevenson to open
another school in 1648.

Four years later, in response to the earnest appeals of Captain-General Stuyvesant, the first public school was founded, to teach reading and writing and the
knowledge and fear of God. The teachers were, successively, Dr. La Montagne,
William Verstius, Harmen Van Hoboken and Evert Pietersen, who received $14.50
a month, besides $50 a year for board. In 1658 the burghers erected a new school-
house, and the West India Company sent over the learned Dr. Curtius, who founded
here a flourishing Latin school, using his spare time in practising as a physician.
After his return to Holland the academy was conducted by Dominie Ægidius Luyck,
the private tutor of the Director's children.

The Free Public Schools of New York are remarkably efficient, and have received many commendations from competent authorities. They number more than
300, including about 100 each of primary and grammar schools, 48 corporate schools,
and 29 evening schools. The enrolment of pupils is in the vicinity of 240,000, and
the average daily attendance exceeds 160,000. There are 4,200 teachers; and the

expense of the schools to the city is $5,000,000 a year. The children learn their letters in the lower primary schools, and thence advance, after rigid and careful examinations, through the various grades of the grammar schools, studying the English branches, drawing, vocal music, and (if desired) French and German. All such as may desire a higher education, and have passed the examinations, are provided

GRAMMAR SCHOOL NO. 94, AMSTERDAM AVENUE AND 68TH STREET.

with collegiate instruction, free of cost; the boys in the College of the City of New York, and the girls in the Normal College. In the evening schools, education is given to 22,000 young people who are obliged to support themselves by working during the day. The discipline in all the public schools is stringent and rigid, and teaches the desirability of system and subordination. There are 40 manual training schools, with 430 teachers and 20,000 pupils, doing an admirable and efficient practical work.

Children between eight and fourteen years of age are compelled by law to attend school; and a group of twelve agents of truancy continually look up the delinquents, and enforce the statute. The more vicious and incorrigible truants are sent to reformatories. Since this efficient organization has been at work, many thousands of loitering and unemployed children have been placed in school; and the number of children arrested by the police for crimes or under suspicion has dwindled from 1,200 to 500 yearly. The public property used for school purposes exceeds $15,000,000 in value. A department of public instruction for teachers is attached to the American Museum of Natural History, with series of lectures on subjects illustrated by the vast collections of that institution.

The College of the City of New York was established in 1848, under the name of the Free Academy, and in 1866 received its present name, and the powers and privileges of a college. Instruction and the use of text-books and apparatus are free to young men of New-York City. There are three courses of study, classical, scientific and mechanical, each of five years' duration; and a two years' post-graduate course in civil engineering. The rather picturesque buildings of the college are at Lexington Avenue and 23d Street, and contain valuable collections and apparatus, a large work-shop, and a library of 28,000 selected volumes. There are about 40 professors and tutors, and 1,100 students. The college costs the city $160,000 a year, and stands in the place of the usual city high school, although its range of studies is much higher than that followed in high schools.

The Normal College For Women occupies a great building, which with its grounds takes up the block bounded by Park and Lexington Avenues, and East 68th and 69th Streets. The building was erected at a cost of nearly $500,000, and contains a spacious hall, three lecture-rooms and thirty recitation rooms. About 2,800 students are at work in the college and the adjacent kindergarten and primary training departments. More than 5,000 graduates have gone out from this institution, and eighty per cent. of them have become teachers in the public schools. The Normal College costs the city $100,000 a year, and is widely renowned for the perfect discipline maintained among its students.

The Board of Education, at 146 Grand Street, is the supervising legislative body, and is made up of 21 Commissioners appointed by the Mayor, who also appoints three inspectors in each school district, while the Board names five trustees in each ward.

The Universities.—The beginnings of the movement for liberal education in New York appeared in 1703, and funds were raised for the purpose soon afterward by legislative authority. The two great institutions for higher education in New-York City, Columbia College and the University of the City of New York, pursue mainly the continental European methods. They have relatively little under-graduate work, their strong efforts being in the direction of higher academic study and special professional work. Of their 3,000 students fewer than one-fifth are under-graduates, but more than one-fourth are graduates of other colleges. Like other first-class metro-

COLLEGE OF THE CITY OF NEW YORK, LEXINGTON AVENUE AND EAST 23D STREET.

politan universities, they are constrained to maintain their graduate departments at the highest rate of efficiency; while their magnificent professional schools could almost carry the entire organizations if needed. In these regards, they differ from nearly all other American universities, which mainly seek to house and train many young under-graduates, and whose professional schools fail to meet their cost. They have no dormitories, and from this cause college associations and intimacies, as generally understood, are little known. There has been considerable discussion, but very little probability, of uniting Columbia and the University of New York under the same roof, each to retain somewhat of its own corporate existence, traditions and special work, and both to co-operate in a unified higher education. Some form of federation may in time be adopted.

Columbia College is the lineal successor to King's College, which was chartered in 1754, with the Archbishop of Canterbury and a number of prominent gentle-

NORMAL COLLEGE, TRAINING DEPARTMENT.

men of England and New York as governors. The first president was the Rev. Dr. Samuel Johnson, of Connecticut, who convened the earliest college class, numbering eight young men, in the vestry-room of Trinity Church. Trinity was the most efficient friend of the new institution, and granted to it lands now of enormous value. A handsome stone building, one side of a projected quadrangle overlooking the Hudson River, was opened in 1760. After a time Dr. Johnson sought rest, feeling the weight of years ; and the Archbishop of Canterbury sent over the Rev. Myles Cooper, a fellow of Queen's College, Oxford, to succeed him, in 1763. Dr. Cooper was an ardent loyalist, and wrote strongly against the growing sentiment of American independence, until finally a mob attacked his lodgings in the college, and he escaped with difficulty to England, in 1775. During the Revolution the library and apparatus were scattered, and the college building served as a military hospital. Among the young men who had been educated here were Alexander Hamilton, John Jay, Gouverneur Morris, Robert R. Livingston, and other leading patriots of New York.

When the war ceased, and the city restored her waste places, this institution was revived, under the more appropriate name of Columbia College. Among its students were De Witt Clinton and John Randolph of Roanoke. From 1784 to 1787 Columbia was officially styled a university, with projected faculties of Arts, Divinity, Medicine and Law, although it had but 40 students. The president from 1787 to 1800 was William Samuel Johnson, a son of the first president, and withal a friend of the famous Dr. Samuel Johnson, of England, and a United-States Senator from Connecticut. From him the administration passed nominally to Benjamin Moore, Bishop of New York. The presidencies of William Harris (1811–29), William Alexander Duer (1829-42), and Nathaniel F. Moore (1842–49) followed thereafter. The presidency of Charles King extended from 1849 to 1864, and witnessed the removal of the college from College Place to its present location, the founding of the Law School and the planning of the School of Mines, and the nominal addition of the Medical Department. The presidency of Dr. F. A. P. Barnard lasted from 1864 to 1889, during which period the college prospered greatly. In 1890 the Hon. Seth Low, a graduate of the college, and a well-known political reformer and business

NORMAL COLLEGE.
PARK AND LEXINGTON AVENUES, EAST 68TH AND EAST 69TH STREETS.

man, and ex-mayor of Brooklyn, was elected president. The college chairs have been occupied by such men as Anthon and Drisler, in the classics ; Adrain, Anderson and Van Amringe, in mathematics; Chandler, in chemistry ; McVickar, in political economy ; Boyesen, in the Germanic languages ; and many other illustrious scholars in various departments.

In 1801 Dr. David Hosack, of the Medical School, bought for a botanical garden the domain called Elgin, which the State purchased from him and gave to the college in 1814, to replace a township of land granted long before, and lost when Vermont (in which it lay) became a State. Elgin covered nearly the domain included between Fifth and Sixth Avenues and 47th and 51st Streets, then nearly four miles from the city, but now in its very heart. When the delightful green and the venerable sycamores of the original site on College Place had become only a little oasis in a great roaring world of commercial activity, the college resolved to move to its uptown estate, and plans for a noble group of buildings were prepared by Upjohn, the famous Gothic architect. Pending their erection, Columbia bought and occupied the old Deaf and Dumb Asylum and grounds ; and there it still remains, for the civil war of 1861–65 put an end to its ambitious scheme of building. The Elgin estate is of enormous value, and yields large revenues to the college.

The college buildings form almost a double quadrangle, covering the block between Madison and Fourth Avenues and 49th and 50th Streets, with handsome and commodious brick buildings, in collegiate Gothic architecture. The library is a noble hall, with a triple-arched roof on iron trusses ; 160,000 volumes, arranged by subjects ; long lines of tables for readers ; and an admirable system of service. Seven hundred serial publications are kept on file in the reading-room. In one of the stack-houses is the precious Torrey Herbarium, with its 60,000 volumes ; and the astronomical observatory occupies the tower.

Columbia has developed into a great and powerful university, with 226 professors and officers and 1,630 students. Its college under-graduate department is relatively small, the main strength being given to the professional and advanced schools. There are no dormitories, or other institutions for residence. Plans are being actively developed to augment the already large endowments, and to move the university to a new site, covering $17\frac{1}{2}$ acres, at Bloomingdale, near the inchoate Protestant-Episcopal Cathedral. The land has already been purchased; and Charles F. McKim, Charles C. Haight and Richard M. Hunt, the eminent architects, are serving as a commission to lay out the new site.

The University faculties of Law, Medicine, Mines, Political Science, Philosophy, and Pure Science, taken together, constitute the University, offering advanced study and investigation in private

COLUMBIA COLLEGE, SCHOOL OF ARTS,
MADISON AVENUE AND EAST 50TH STREET.

or municipal law; medicine and surgery; mathematics and pure and applied science; history, economics and public law; and philosophy, philology and letters. Columbia has an extensive system of co-operation, by which it confers benefits upon others and obtains for its own students increased opportunities. This system embraces Barnard College, the Teachers College, the Union Theological Seminary, Cooper Union, the Metropolitan Museum of Art, and the American Museum of Natural History.

The School of Arts occupies the range of buildings along Madison Avenue, and has nearly 50 professors and instructors and 300 students.

The School of Mines was founded in 1864, and ten years later occupied the costly new building erected for its use. Among the earlier professors were Gen. F. L. Vinton, Thomas Egleston, Charles F. Chandler (now Dean of the school), and John S. Newber-

ry, the latter of whom brought hither his unrivalled geological and palæontological collections. The seven courses are: Mining engineering, civil engineering, electrical engineering, metallurgy, geology and palæontology, analytical and applied chemistry, and architecture; and the students are given practical instruction in geodesy, mining, metal-

COLUMBIA COLLEGE : LIBRARY AND OPEN QUADRANGLE,
MADISON AVENUE AND 49TH STREET.

working and other departments. There are also three graduate courses, of two years each, in electrical engineering, sanitary engineering, and special courses. The department of architecture, under the charge of Prof. William R. Ware, is the foremost architectural school in America, and has a large number of enthusiastic students, under competent and careful instruction.

The School of Law, of which Professor William A. Keener is Dean, was organized in 1858 under the direction of Professor Theodore W. Dwight, and is recognized as one of the leading law-schools of the country. It has a three years' course of study in private and public law, leading to the degree of LL. B. It has a staff of ten instructors, with 315 students. The famous commentaries of Chancellor Kent are an outgrowth of lectures delivered by him at Columbia.

The School of Political Science, an outgrowth of the School of Law, was founded in 1880, under Prof. John W. Burgess, "to prepare young men for the duties of public life." It has already won a high measure of success, in teaching constitutional history and law, history of political theories, political economy and social science, Roman law and comparative jurisprudence, administrative law, international law and history.

The School of Philosophy was founded in 1890, for advanced courses in philosophy, philology and letters.

The School of Pure Science, an outgrowth of the School of Mines, began in 1892, for advanced courses in pure (as distinguished from applied) science.

The College of Physicians and Surgeons, the medical department of Columbia College, was chartered in 1807; and six years later, the School of Medicine of the college, which dated from 1767, united with it. In 1860 this college became nominally a department of Columbia, and in 1891 became an integral part of it. In 1884 William H. Vanderbilt presented $500,000 to the college, which with this gift

purchased land and erected a building at 59th Street, near 10th Avenue. A few months later Mr. Vanderbilt's daughter, Mrs. William D. Sloane, and her husband gave $250,000 for the erection of the Sloane Maternity Hospital, under the control of the college; and still later Mr. Vanderbilt's four sons gave $250,000 for the

COLLEGE OF PHYSICIANS AND SURGEONS, 437 WEST 59TH STREET.

construction of the Vanderbilt Clinic and Dispensary. The college has 50 instructors and 570 students. It is equipped with electric lights, Worthington pumps, etc.

Barnard College, at 343 Madison Avenue, has professors appointed by the President of Columbia. It is practically a section of Columbia, with the same entrance examinations, the use of the same extensive library, and the receipt of the same degrees. Here women may secure an education identical in quality and official recognition with that given to men. Founded in 1889, it was named for the late President of Columbia College. It has its own botanical and chemical laboratories. Its 85 students are mainly New-York girls, whose parents prefer that their daughters should live at home during their college education.

NEW-YORK TRADE-SCHOOL, FIRST AVENUE, 67TH AND 68TH STREETS.

The University of the City of New York was planned in 1829 and 1830, in several meetings of public-spirited merchants and professional men, and incorporated in 1831. The idea was to offset Episcopalian and conservative Columbia with an undenominational modern university. Until 1883 a part of the Council was elected by the City Legislature, and it was forbidden that any religious denomination should have a majority in the Council. John Taylor Johnston and Charles Butler, recent Presidents of the Council, have served in it respectively forty-six years and fifty-six

UNIVERSITY OF THE CITY OF NEW YORK, WASHINGTON SQUARE, EAST, AND WAVERLY PLACE.

years. The property of the University, all of which has come from gifts and bequests, amounts to about $2,000,000. The University building, on Washington Square, erected in 1832–35, is a conspicuous structure of light-colored limestone, in Gothic architecture, and contains the Council-room, with its many portraits of distinguished members of the Council, and the class-rooms and laboratories, museum and observatory of the Department of Arts and Science. In ancient days many famous authors, artists and scholars dwelt in this noble building, where Prof. S. F. B. Morse discovered the recording telegraph, Dr. John William Draper made the first photographs from the human face, and Theodore Winthrop wrote *Cecil Dreme*. The University has about 100 professors and instructors and 1,330 students. The Chancellors have been Drs. James Matthews, Theodore Frelinghuysen, Gardiner Spring, Isaac Ferris, Howard Crosby, John Hall and Henry M. MacCracken.

In 1891–92 the University took an important step, in purchasing for $300,000, a new site, intended in particular for the College of Arts and Philosophy, the technological schools, and the Graduate Seminary. The School of Law, the School of Pedagogy, and part of the Graduate Seminary work will remain upon Washington Square, where a new building will be erected, of which probably seven or eight stories will be rented for business purposes, while two or three stories will be reserved for the schools named, and for University offices, and popular lectures. The Medical School will continue as at present. The new site is an elevated plateau of twenty acres, accessible by railway in less than twenty minutes from 42d Street. It is to be known as "University Heights," and is admirably adapted to University purposes.

The Department of Arts and Science dates from 1832, and for over half a

LOOMIS LABORATORY, UNIVERSITY MEDICAL COLLEGE, 414 EAST 26TH STREET.

century consisted of a college on the approved American plan, with from 100 to 150 students. University College now has twenty-six professors and lecturers, and its classical and scientific courses lead respectively to the degrees of Bachelor of Art and Bachelor of Science. Among its professors have been the Drapers, Vethake, McIlvaine and Robinson; John Torrey, the botanist; Tayler Lewis, the philologist; George Bush, the commentator; Nordheimer, the Hebraist; Henry P. Tappan, the philosopher; Davies and Loomis, the mathematicians, and S. F. B. Morse, the inventor.

The School of Civil Engineering and **the School of Chemistry**, two well conducted institutions for technical training, are controlled by the Faculty of Arts and Science, which also conducts

The School of Pedagogy, founded in 1890, to give higher training to teachers, in psychology and ethics, the theory and practice of pedagogy, and the history, classics and systems of education. There are 260 students in the school.

The Graduate Seminary, founded in 1886, receives candidates for the degrees of Master of Arts or Science, and Doctor of Philosophy. Over 100 graduate students are in attendance, and thirty special courses are provided.

The Department of Law, with its under-graduate and graduate schools, has its lecture-room and library in the fine old University building. The foundation of this faculty was carefully planned in the year 1835, by the Hon. B. F. Butler, then Attorney-General of the United States. The council of the University adopted his plans, and Mr. Butler accepted the office of Senior Professor. The Law school was soon suspended, and again opened in 1858; but it is only during the past few years that it has advanced to a prominent rank. As Prof. Stoddard remarks, in that period "it has changed its character from a school of law forms to a school of jurisprudence;" and develops at once the systematic study of statute law and the observation of professional methods of research and practice. The Dean and Senior Professor is Austin Abbott, LL. D.; and there are three other professors and six lecturers. The

MCKIM, MEAD & WHITE, ARCHTS.

COLUMBIA COLLEGE LIBRARY AND SURROUNDING COLUMBIA COLLEGE BUILDINGS.

MORNINGSIDE HEIGHTS: MORNINGSIDE AND AMSTERDAM AVENUES, BETWEEN 116TH AND 120TH STREETS.

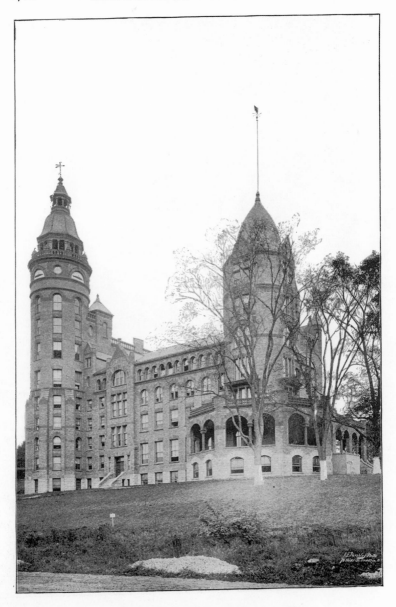

WEBB'S ACADEMY AND HOME FOR SHIP BUILDERS.

SEDGWICK AVENUE AND ACADEMY STREET, HARLEM.

MISS ANNIE BROWN'S SCHOOL FOR GIRLS. NOS. 711, 713, 715 AND 717 FIFTH AVENUE, WEST SIDE, BETWEEN 55TH AND 56TH STREETS.

THE TEACHERS' COLLEGE.

MORNINGSIDE HEIGHTS: WEST 120TH STREET, NEAR AMSTERDAM AVENUE.

course is of two years, with several advanced courses in the graduate year. There are 240 students (nearly half of them college graduates), including also ten women. The Graduate Law School was opened in 1891, with 40 pupils, and requires the completion of five subjects for the degree of Master of Laws. The University also gives popular courses of lectures on law, in particular to business women, every winter. This lectureship is endowed by the Women's Legal Education Society.

Theology is not taught by the University; but in 1890 an alliance was formed with the Union Theological Seminary, by which students of either institution are admitted under easy conditions to the libraries and lecture-courses of the other. Also, the graduates of Union Seminary may receive the degree of Bachelor of Divinity.

The Faculty of Medicine (University Medical College), founded in 1841, numbered among its earlier members Drs. Valentine Mott, Bedford, Post, Draper, and Paine. Its buildings are on 26th Street, near the East River, fronting Bellevue Hospital, and near the ferry-entrance to the great city charities. They consist of the central edifice, which includes the offices, with the lecture-room and amphitheatre, either of which seats 500 students; the west wing, in which are the Dispensary, and eight "section rooms"; and the east wing, to which the anonymous giver of $100,000 for its erection attached the name of the Loomis Laboratory, after the senior professor. Its five floors contain the five laboratories of Materia Medica, Physics, Chemistry, Physiology, Biology and Pathology. There are 23 professors, and 35 lecturers. Three winter courses, each comprising eight months' study, are required for the degree of M. D. The University Medical College has 640 students, of whom 30 came from Canada, 30 from Russia, and many others from Central and South America, and other countries. Among its 6,000 graduates have been many illustrious physicians and scientists.

UNIVERSITY MEDICAL COLLEGE, 410 EAST 26TH STREET.

The Medical Schools bring wide renown to the great metropolis for their magnitude and their very unusual opportunities for imparting a practical education. Many of the foremost of American physicians live in New York, and here also are brought thousands of patients requiring the care of the most skillful specialists. The notable museums, libraries and scientific societies also afford rich stimulus to the student, and tend to elevate more and more the spirit of the profession. Here occur the meetings of the laryngological, dermatological, clinical, microscopical, medico-historical, medico-legal, neurological, obstetrical, medico-chirurgical, surgical, pathological, ophthalmological, therapeutical and other cognate societies. Here also are held the fortnightly meetings of the

POST-GRADUATE MEDICAL SCHOOL AND HOSPITAL, 226 EAST 20TH STREET.

New-York Academy of Medicine, which dates from 1847, and has for nearly half a century studied how best to promote the public health, to raise the standard of medical education, to advance the honor of the profession, and to cultivate the science of medicine. The Academy maintains a library of more than 50,000 volumes, which is open to the people all day long; and it also subscribes for and keeps on file all the current medical periodicals and monographs, showing the latest results of professional research in all countries. Students are able to live in New York at an expense not exceeding that attending life at other educational centres, and also find more frequent opportunities for partial self-support. They are broadened by the myriad influences of the metropolitan city, and may become in a sense citizens of the world, while preparing for the arduous professional life before them. If their opportunities and advantages are fully availed of, they will enter upon the practice of the healing art with a better equipment of special and general knowledge than can usually be acquired by students in the quiet cloisters of secluded rural colleges.

The noted medical schools of Columbia College and the University have been hereinbefore described.

Bellevue-Hospital Medical College owes its inception to the construction of an amphitheatre for clinical lectures at Bellevue Hospital, in 1849, followed eight years later by the erection of a pathological building. The college began its work in 1861, with lectures on military surgery, a theme of vital interest at that time ; and has since developed into one of the leading medical schools of America, under the lead of men like Mott, Flint, Hammond and Doremus. The institution occupies a part of the grounds of Bellevue Hospital, at the foot of East 26th Street, and close to the East River. The contiguity of the great public hospital, with the numberless opportunities there afforded for obtaining a practical knowledge of both the duties and the resources of the medical profession, places it in the power of the Bellevue students to enter upon their life-duties competent to meet intelligently every emergency. Almost every physical ill which they may encounter in future practice comes under their observation here, and also the most modern scientific and skilful means of relief, as given by sagacious physicians. The hospital clinics afford object-lessons in every variety of disease requiring indoor treatment ; and the Bureau of Medical and Surgical Relief for the Outdoor Poor at its clinics illustrates the best treatments in minor surgery, and of commoner and less grave diseases, especially in disorders of children. The bureau was organized and elaborated by the Faculty of the college, and has been of immense service to the poor, whose profound respect for the skill of the attendants is justly deserved. Over 40,000 patients are treated here every year. The college has graduated upwards of 4,000 doctors. It has 35 instructors and 550 students (60 of whom are foreigners, mainly from Canada and the West Indies). A recent addition to the college buildings is the Carnegie Laboratory, a five-story building containing three general laboratories and a large auditorium. The President of the college is William T. Lusk, M. D.

The New-York Post-Graduate Hospital and Medical School has a plain and substantial brick building at 226 20th Street, near Second Avenue. This institution dates from 1882, and is intended to give practising physicians opportunities to see and study the newest discoveries in medical and surgical science. Its clinics diffuse the freshest knowledge.

The New-York Homœopathic Medical College and Hospital received its charter in 1861, and has been very successful. Its building, at 63d Street and Avenue A, is well equipped for the curriculum of lectures, clinics, and demonstrations, which extend over a period of three years. The Dean is Timothy Field Allen, M. D., LL. D., with whom serves a body of 28 instructors. The pupils number 130.

The New-York College of Dentistry, chartered in 1865 and opened in 1866, is at 23d Street and Third Avenue, and has 40 instructors and 250 students. The dean is Dr. Frank Abbott. It educates students in the scientific and chirurgical requirements of the science, with series of lectures on operative and mechanical dentistry, and daily practice and demonstration at operations in the chair, and careful laboratory practice.

The College of Pharmacy of the City of New York was founded in 1829, and gives instruction in chemistry, materia medica, botany, pharmacognosy, pharmacy, physiology, and physics, by afternoon lectures, quizzes, and laboratory work. The buildings, on West 68th Street, near Ninth Avenue, contain valuable museums and apparatus, spacious laboratories and lecture-room, and the largest pharmaceutical library in America. The course includes thirty hours a week, for two years; and converts druggists' apprentices into thoroughly equipped and scientific pharmacists, fitted to understand and compound all manner of medicines. There are 400 students, including about a dozen foreigners. The president is Samuel W. Fairchild.

The Women's Medical College of the New-York Infirmary for Women and Children was chartered in 1865, as an outgrowth of a dispensary which was founded in 1854, and the hospital which was added thereto in 1857. The sessions of the college are held in a handsome and commodious new building on Stuyvesant Square, near the Infirmary. There are 30 professors and instructors, and about 90 students (including 16 foreigners), the course covering three years. Dr. Emily Blackwell is the Dean.

N.-Y. COLLEGE OF DENTISTRY, 205 EAST 23D STREET NEAR THIRD AVENUE.

The **New-York Medical College and Hospital for Women** dates from 1863, and has about 40 students in homœopathic medicine, at 213 West 54th Street.

The **Eclectic Medical College** of the City of New York, founded in 1865, is composed of 21 instructors and 80 students. It is at 239 East 14th Street.

The **School of Ophthalmology and Otology** is connected with the New-York Ophthalmic Hospital (201 East 23d Street), and gives a complete course of study in diseases of the eye, ear and throat.

COLLEGE OF PHARMACY, 209 EAST 23D STREET.
(OCCUPIED UNTIL 1893.)

Nurses' Training-Schools.—Large hospitals find their best development in large cities ; and among their most valuable agencies are their corps of trained nurses. Conversely, the training-schools for nurses must be intimately associated with hospitals, where the students may daily observe the practical workings of their profession. There are over 300 pupils in the nurses' training-schools connected with the Charity, the Bellevue, the New-York and St. Luke's Hospitals. One of the largest of these is the one connected with the New-York Hospital, where 60 pupils are enrolled.

The **D. O. Mills Training-School for Male Nurses** occupies a substantial brick building erected in 1888 in the Bellevue-Hospital grounds, at the foot of East 26th Street. It is arranged and fitted up as a home for the nurses during their two-years' course of study, which is on the same lines as that of the Training-School for Female Nurses, nearly opposite. Two classes have been graduated from the school, and there are now 54 inmates, all of whom serve in the male wards of the hospital. It is a generous educational charity, founded by Darius O. Mills.

The **Columbia College of Midwifery,** 242 West 33d Street, is another manifestation of the healing art. It was incorporated in 1883. Connected with it is the Dispensary for Diseases of Women.

The **College of Midwifery** of the City of New York was organized in 1883, and in 1884 became connected with the Nurses' Training-School of the Woman's Infirmary and Maternity Home, 247 West 49th Street.

The **New-York College of Massage,** also at 247 West 49th Street, was organized in 1884.

The **New-York College of Fine Forces,** at 4 West 14th Street, was chartered in 1887. It teaches chromopathy, mind cure, patho-mechanism, magnetic massage, and solar magnetics. E. D. Babbitt, M. D., is dean.

Veterinary Colleges and Hospitals have arisen from the vast investments in American live-stock, the annual losses of millions of dollars by contagious diseases, the need of scientific inspection of meat and milk, and the ruin caused by quack horse-doctors. With its organized Veterinary Society of graduates, its two veterinary colleges and its two hospitals, New York is one of the foremost educational centres as to the arts of healing domestic animals. The students are taught the theory and practice of veterinary medicine, anatomy (with dissections) and surgery, pathology and obstetrics, therapeutics and microscopy, ophthalmology, and bacteriology; with scientific care, and abundant illustrations and experiments.

The New-York College of Veterinary Surgeons and School of Comparative Medicine, chartered in 1857, is at 332 East 27th Street. It has ten professors and four lecturers; and over 100 students, attending lectures on equine anatomy, bovine pathology, horse-shoeing, and many connected subjects. Many of its graduates are appointed veterinary surgeons for the United-States Army. The hospital of the college affords opportunities of observing the diseases of domestic animals, and their treatment, and also of witnessing surgical operations. The President is Dr. William T. White.

The American Veterinary College dates from 1875; and has its home at 141 West 54th Street, where the American Veterinary Hospital receives and treats disabled horses and dogs, admitting patients at all hours. The President is Dr. A. Liautard; and there are 16 instructors and 130 students.

Religious Instruction.—The Empire City has long been recognized as an admirable drill-ground for students in the fields of religion and philanthropy. Here are thousands of the most formidable heathen in the world, whose condition demands amelioration; and other thousands of earnest and devoted Christians, always studying and practicing methods of beneficence. Many of the foremost clergymen in the Republic occupy pulpits here; and the headquarters and conventions of various denominations seek this great metropolitan focus. Large opportunities are also afforded for students to support themselves in mission-work, teaching and parochial assistance.

D. O. MILLS TRAINING SCHOOL FOR MALE NURSES, 431 EAST 26TH STREET.

The General Theological Seminary of The Protestant Episcopal Church was established by the General Convention in 1817; it began instructions in 1819; and was incorporated in 1822. Since that date, it has graduated 1,200 men, of whom 34 have become bishops. It is governed by a Board of Trustees, composed of the Bishops of the Church, the Dean, 25 appointees of the House of Deputies of the General Convention, and 25 men elected by former contributing dioceses. There are twelve professors and instructors, and 131 students in holy orders. Ninety of these are college-graduates, including seven from colleges in Sweden, and others from colleges in Canada, Persia and Turkey. Tuition is free, to properly accredited candidates. There are rooms for 117 students in the seminary; and each of these pays $225 a year for the room and its care, coal and gas, and board.   The buildings are on Chelsea Square, between 20th and 21st Streets and Ninth and Tenth Avenues.   In 1880 the square was occupied only by two grim old stone edifices ; but since that date there has been erected a series of handsome brick and stone buildings, in collegiate Gothic architecture.   The Memorial Chapel of the Good Shepherd has a melodious chime ; a reredos of exquisitely carved

UNION THEOLOGICAL SEMINARY, PARK AVENUE, FROM 69TH TO 70TH STREETS.

alabaster, adorned with the Good Shepherd and eight Evangelists and Apostles, in statuary marble; and ten storied windows of English stained glass.   The beautiful Hobart Hall contains the library of 23,000 volumes, with an open timber roof, and many interesting portraits.   The velvety green lawns and the groups of shrubbery between the buildings and the extent and massive construction, and the quiet dignity of the seminary buildings make a charming oasis of verdure and peace in the vast whirl of the city's secular life.

The Union Theological Seminary occupies a range of handsome buildings on Lenox Hill, along Park Avenue, between 69th and 70th Streets.   This location was occupied in 1884 ; and the buildings form a quadrangle, and include offices and lecture-rooms, library, chapel and gymnasium, museum and reading-room, and many furnished chambers for the students.   The library, containing 70,000 volumes and 50,000 pamphlets, was built up on the basis of the library of Leander Van Ess. The seminary was founded in 1836.   Since 1857 the Directors have made a yearly report to the General Assembly, though now the institution is not under ecclesiastical control.   Its officers give their assent to the standards of the Presbyterian Church; but the seminary is open to students from any Christian denomination. There are 13 members of the Faculty, and 150 students.   Among the professors are

GENERAL THEOLOGICAL SEMINARY OF THE PROTESTANT EPISCOPAL CHURCH.
CHELSEA SQUARE, NINTH AND TENTH AVENUES, 20TH AND 21ST STREETS.

Thomas S. Hastings (President), George L. Prentiss, Philip Schaff, Marvin R. Vincent, Charles A. Briggs and Francis Brown.   The seminary has endowed instructorships in vocal culture, elocution and sacred music ; and lectureships in the evidences of Christianity, the relations of the Bible to science, and hygienic instruction.   The course of study covers three years.   The recent trial of Dr. Briggs on doctrinal points profoundly affected Union Seminary.

The **Jewish Theological Seminary,** founded in 1886, in 1892 occupied the handsome residence at 736 Lexington Avenue ; and has three preceptors and fifteen students.   The course lasts nine years, and educates young Hebrews to be rabbis or teachers.   The seminary is maintained chiefly by the New-York, Philadelphia and Baltimore synagogues. The president of the Faculty is Dr. Sabato Morais.

MANHATTAN COLLEGE, BOULEVARD AND WEST 131ST STREET.

The **New-York Missionary Training College** aims to prepare persons devoid of an elaborate liberal education, for city and foreign missionaries and evangelists, by spiritual and scriptural studies of the Bible and theology, and a practical and experimental training.   The college, a fire-proof five-story building at 690 Eighth Avenue, is occupied by the men-students.   Berachah Home, at 250 West 44th Street, and the annex at 453 West 47th Street, are for the women. The course is three years in length.   There are about a dozen instructors and 200 students, of whom 90 are women.   A score come from Canada, and there are others from Scotland, England, Germany, Switzerland, Russia, India, Japan and Hayti.

The **New-York Deaconess Home and Training-School of the Methodist Episcopal Church,** at 241 West 14th Street, has about a score of inmates, studying the Bible, elementary medicine, hygiene, nursing and other requisites for the sisterhood of service among the poor and the sick.   Graduates of the school become probationers, and these become uniform deaconesses, devoted entirely to Christian labor with the wandering and sorrowing, the poor and the orphan, the sick and the dying.

The **International Medical Missionary Training Institute** is at 118 East 45th Street, with a ladies' branch at 121 East 45th Street.

St. John's College was founded in 1841 by Archbishop John Hughes, on the famous old Rose-Hill estate at Fordham, and its first President was John McCloskey, who became the first American Cardinal.   In 1846 the college passed into the hands of the Jesuits, who have ever since controlled its destinies with singular ability and devotion, preparing many young men for high achievements.   St. John's has several massive and imposing stone buildings, looking out on a broad lawn, which is adorned with a bronze statue of Archbishop Hughes.   The college conducts three courses of study, collegiate, academic and scientific, and about 350 students are engaged therein.   The surrounding country and the St. John's estate are very picturesque and attractive, and the avenues of ancient elms add beauty to the grounds.

The College of St. Francis Xavier is a Jesuit institution, opened in 1847 and chartered in 1861, and now having twenty instructors and over 300 collegiate students. Its handsome and imposing buildings are at 39 to 59 West 15th Street and 30 to 50 West 16th Street, near Sixth Avenue. The library contains 25,000 volumes, and the museum and herbarium have large and valuable collections.

ST. FRANCIS XAVIER CHURCH AND COLLEGE, ROMAN CATHOLIC. 36 WEST 16TH STREET, BETWEEN FIFTH AND SIXTH AVENUES.

Manhattan College is another great Catholic institution. Its stately build-ings overlook Manhattanville and many leagues of the Hudson River and the Pali-sades. It was founded by the Brothers of the Christian Schools in 1853, and received a charter in 1863. It has twenty-two instructors and 300 students, one-third of whom are collegiate. It possesses a fine library and museum.

The Academy of the Sacred Heart is at Manhattanville (130th Street and St.-Nicholas Avenue), where it occupies a group of stone buildings in a pleasant

CONVENT OF THE SACRED HEART, ST. NICHOLAS AVENUE AND 130TH STREET.

park of lawns and groves. It has about 250 students, mostly boarders, cared for by the Ladies of the Sacred Heart, who also conduct a large day-school at 49 West 17th Street, and a boarding and day academy at 533 Madison Avenue.

The Academy of Mount St. Vincent, under the care of the Sisters of Charity, is just above Riverdale, on the banks of the Hudson River. Near the academy stands the stone castle of Font Hill, built by Edwin Forrest for his home, and now a part of the religious institution, whose domain covers sixty-three acres. The 200 girls studying here wear blue uniform dresses, and French is the language spoken. The property of this academy is valued at nearly $1,000,000.

St.-Louis College, at 224 West 58th Street, has 75 pupils. It was founded in 1869, by Rev. Père Ronay, for Catholic boys of refined families.

The La-Salle Academy, at 44 and 46 2d Street, has 130 pupils, under the care of the Christian Brothers.

The Holy-Cross Academy, is at 343 West 42d Street. It has 250 girl-students.

St. Catharine's Convent is at Madison Avenue and East 81st Street.

St. Vincent Ferrers Convent, at Lexington Avenue and East 65th Street, has fine buildings, and a capable body of teachers.

Catholic Parochial Schools, with large and costly buildings and appliances, are numerous.

The Catholic Private Schools, of which there are a dozen of a high order, are for Catholic children. Among them are the Ursuline and Villa Maria Acade-mies, the Holy Rosary, St. Augustine's and St. Cecilia's.

Trinity-Church Schools include a group of interesting Episcopal institutions, such as the parochial school for boys, on Trinity Place ; the girls' school of St.

Paul's on Church Street; and the night schools for men and women. The industrial schools of the parish teach sewing to more than 2,000 women; and the Sisters of St. Mary conduct a training-school for girls to learn household service.

The St. John Baptist and St. Mary's Schools are private institutions for girls, at 231 East 17th Street and 8 East 46th Street. St. Mary's (founded in 1867) has 160 girls, under the Sisters of St. Mary. It is an expensive and efficient school.

The Riverside School, at 152 West 103d Street, is an Episcopal private school, with 100 pupils.

The Friends' Seminary, at 226 East 16th Street, has 125 students.

St. Matthew's Academy, at 156 Elizabeth Street, is attended chiefly by children of the Evangelical Lutherans.

The Society for Ethical Culture was founded in 1888 for the study and practical teaching of the science of ethics, based on purely humanitarian grounds as distinguished from the theological basis of Christian ethics. Prof. Felix Adler has long been prominently identified with the society, of which he was one of the founders. Religious services are held every Sunday at Chickering Hall, corner of Fifth Avenue and West 18th Street, and the society is actively engaged in benevolent work. It is about to erect a half-million-dollar building up town.

Art Education.—New York is the foremost of American cities in regard to art, and its public galleries, private collections, and sales-galleries are of more than continental reputation, and include many noble works, both of the old masters and of the best modern schools. It is therefore natural that several well-attended art-schools have grown up amid such surroundings. Even the public schools teach drawing to all their pupils; and several famous artists admit to their studios promising students. The American Academy of Fine Arts was founded in 1802, mainly by merchants, and opened its collections to art-students in 1825. But the policy was narrow and churlish; and in the same year the students withdrew and, under S. F. B. Morse and A. B. Durand, formed the New-York Drawing Association.

ACADEMY OF THE SACRED HEART, 49 WEST 17TH ST., NEAR SIXTH AVE.

The National Academy of Design, whose art-schools occupy a part of the Venetian palace at Fourth Avenue and 23d Street, grew out of the New-York Drawing Association. The schools are open both to men and women, in morning, afternoon and evening sessions. There are classes in sketching, and drawing from antique statuary and living figures, with lectures on perspective, anatomy, and composition. The pupils average 250.

The **Metropolitan Museum of Art** has art-schools which give careful technical instruction in free-hand and mechanical drawing, designing, painting, modelling,
architecture, and other branches.   A travelling scholarship has lately been endowed,
to enable competent male students in painting to have the benefit of European
instruction also.

The **Art-Students' League of New York,** founded in 1875, is in its elegant
new building at 215 West 57th Street; and has day and evening classes of men and

MOUNT ST. VINCENT ACADEMY, RIVERDALE, BEYOND THE HARLEM RIVER.

women studying portraiture, composition, sketching, modelling, and drawing and
modelling from sculptures or from live models.   Among the students here have been
Church, Remington, De Thulstrup, Howard Pyle, and other well-known men.   Among
the instructors are Beckwith, Mowbray, Weir, Chase, St. Gaudens and Kenyon Cox.

The **Gotham Art Students** are at 17 Bond Street.

The **Harlem Art Association,** at 149 East 125th Street, affords art instruction for the residents of upper New York.

The **Society of Decorative Art,** at 28 East 21st Street, has classes in fine
needle-work, china-painting, fan-painting, water-colors, and other branches of art;
and aims to thoroughly train women, each in one kind of decorative work.

The **School of Industrial Art and Technical Design for Women,**
founded in 1881 by Mrs. Florence E. Cory, is at 134 Fifth Avenue, and successfully
teaches designing for carpets, wall-paper, cretonne, calico, silk, linen, portières,
carved and inlaid work, stained glass, lace, decorated cards, china, and all industrial
art manufactures.

The **American Art School** (A. L. Blanchard's), at 326 Fifth Avenue, near
33d Street, was established in 1879, and teaches drawing and all branches of
painting, and especially tapestry painting.

The **New-York Institute for Artist-Artisans,** at 140 West 23d Street, is a
school founded in 1888 by eminent firms, citizens and artists to develop distinctive
American art and artisanship combined, and to popularize art and make it vital, domestic and national.   A *N.-Y. Times* editorial says, " It is by all odds the best, most democratic, most thorough and promising art-school in the country.   It is leading the van in
industrial art-education."   There are departments in Illustration, Painting, Sculpture,

Architecture, Textiles, Wall-paper, Ceramics, Wood-carving, Metal and Jewelry work. The terms are $50 a year, with a few prize-scholarships. John Ward Stimson, previously so successful at the Metropolitan Museum, is the educational director.

The Woman's Art-School in the Cooper Union maintains classes in painting, oil-color, drawing from the antique and from life, photo-color, photo-crayon, painting porcelain photographs, pen and ink drawing, retouching negatives, designing for silks and windows, and preparation for teaching art. It is intended to supply to women of taste and capacity, from anywhere, a free education in some one professional branch of art, in morning and afternoon classes. The night school of art has over 1,000 pupils in cast-drawing, form-drawing, decorative designing, ornamental drawing, rudimental drawing, modelling in clay, perspective drawing, mechanical drawing and architectural drawing. The students are instructed by able artists, like Gifford and Weir, and are provided with lectures on various branches of art. Over 400 persons study in the Woman's Art-School, and a still larger number in the night school, and there are always many more applicants than can be received. These Cooper-Union schools are among the very foremost enlightening influences in America, and have disseminated practical æsthetic ideas for many years.

Music Instruction is well provided in New-York City, for here is the musical centre of the Union, and all musicians depend mainly upon the New-York verdict. Here the German, English and Italian operas are presented as nowhere else in America, and the great musical societies render the best oratorio and orchestral compositions. Music is taught in the public schools; and by hundreds of private teachers throughout the city.

ST. CATHERINE'S CONVENT, MADISON AVENUE AND EAST 81ST STREET.

The Metropolitan College of Music was founded in 1886, as a vocal school, and in 1891 received incorporation as a college. It occupies many rooms, at Nos. 19 and 21 East 14th Street; and has 20 professors, among whom are Dudley Buck, Harry Rowe Shelley, R. H. Woodman and other well-known musicians.

19

The New-York College of Music was founded in 1878, and has more than a score of instructors and 700 pupils. The handsome building at 128-130 East 58th Street was erected for the college, and has a commodious concert-hall. Among the instructors are Alex. Lambert, Mme Fursch-Madi and Walter Damrosch.

The New-York Conservatory of Music is at 5 East 14th Street.

The German Conservatory of Music is at 7 West 42d Street.

The Liederkranz Schools are free for instruction in vocal music for young men and women, in the Liederkranz building, on East 58th Street.

Industrial and Scientific Training is accomplished through numerous important institutions, like the Hebrew Technical School, with its 140 students; the manual-training department of the College of the City of New York; and the Workingman's School, of the United Relief Works of the Society for Ethical Culture, at 109 West 54th Street, in which Felix Adler is interested.

MOUNT SINAI HOSPITAL.   CHURCH OF THE DOMINICAN FATHERS.   ST. VINCENT FERRERS CONVENT.   65TH STREET.

ST. VINCENT FERRERS CONVENT, LEXINGTON AVENUE AND EAST 65TH STREET.

The Cooper Union, one of the greatest popular educators in America, occupies a seven-story brown-stone building, covering the block at the intersection of Seventh Street and the Bowery, and Third and Fourth Avenues. One of its chief features is the Free Night School of Science, giving a thorough instruction in mathematics, and mechanics, in a five-years' course. The night schools of science and art have over 3,000 students, most of whom work at their trades during the day. The pupils must be fifteen years old, and acquainted with the rudiments of education. The Union costs $50,000 a year, which is derived from the rentals of stores in the building and from the income of the endowment. Among its interesting features are the library of 32,000 volumes; the reading-room, with 500 magazines and newspapers on file, and visited by 600,000 persons yearly; the evening Elocution Class, with 150 attendants; the Literary Class, with 200 debaters and declaimers; the free Saturday-evening lectures, by celebrated scholars and scientists; the free class in

Stenography and Type-writing, numbering 40 women ; the Free School of Telegraphy for women, with 40 women ; and the Woman's Art-School.

Peter Cooper was born when New York contained 27,000 inhabitants, and reached only to Chambers Street ; when there was not a free school in the city ; and in the first presidency of George Washington. He died in 1883. He was a plain and practical man, and a successful inventor and manufacturer ; and a million dollars of his wealth was devoted to the construction and endowment of the Cooper Union, " dedicated to Science, to make life intelligent, and to Art, to make life beautiful."

Columbia Grammar School, on 51st Street, near Madison Avenue, was founded in 1764, as a Preparatory Department of Columbia College, and was transferred by the trustees to the entire control of the late Dr. Charles Anthon. It is a first-class private school, with 20 instructors, and fine school-rooms and gymnasium.

COOPER UNION, IN JUNE, 1893, JUNCTION OF THE BOWERY, THIRD AND FOURTH AVENUE AND 7TH STREET.

The New-York Trade-School, at First Avenue, 67th and 68th Streets, was founded by Col. Richard T. Auchmuty, in 1881, to enable young men to learn certain trades, and to give young men already in those trades an opportunity to improve themselves. This school covers nearly an acre of ground, and is attended yearly by 600 young men, from all parts of the United States and Canada. Connected with the school is a lodging house, accommodating 100 young men, where well-furnished rooms are rented at a moderate cost. The average age of the young men in the day classes is 19 ; those in the evening classes are younger. Until the present year the New-York Trade-School has been supported as well as managed by Col. Auchmuty, but recently it has received an endowment of $500,000 from J. Pierpont Morgan. The workshops at the school are always open to visitors. The pupils are taught by skilful mechanics the right ways of working, and also why work should be done in a certain way, by thorough, direct and friendly methods. The classes in Bricklaying have erected several great buildings. The evening classes work three evenings in each week. The classes in Plumbing, under the careful supervision of the Master Plumbers' Association, have a shop 37 by 115 feet in area, perfectly

equipped. The classes in Carpentry have built some of the Trade-School edifices, in admirable style. The classes in House, Sign and Fresco Painting are supervised by the Master Painters' and Decorators' Association, and have a wide reputation. The classes in Stone-cutting, Blacksmith's Work, Printing and Plastering, are all of great efficiency and service.

The Nautical School is a very interesting department of education, intended to prepare boys for service in the American merchant-marine. It numbers about 80 lads, between 16 and 20 years old, who are under the care of United-States naval officers, the entire institution being governed by the city Board of Education. The school occupies the old war-ship *St. Mary's,* sometimes at the foot of East 28th Street, or anchored in the harbor, and every year mak-

BARON HIRSCH FUND TRADE-SCHOOLS, 225 EAST NINTH STREET.

ing long practice cruises to Europe or the islands of the Atlantic. Besides the usual English branches, the lads are taught orally and practically in making knots and splices ; the names and uses of rigging and sails, bending and loosing, reefing and furling ; the management and steering of boats, by rowing, sculling or sailing ; the compass, boxing and steering, and taking bearings; heaving the lead and marking log and lead lines ; swimming and floating ; and many other details needful for sea-life. There is a post-graduate course, fitting students for the position of mates. All instruction is free, as the *St. Mary's* is practically one of the New-York public schools. It is in no sense a reformatory, and only willing and well-accredited boys are admitted.

Webb's Academy and Home for Shipbuilders was planned and built by William H. Webb, an eminent New-York shipbuilder, and incorporated in 1889. It was opened in 1893, to serve a double purpose : As a home for infirm and unfortunate shipbuilders, and their wives, and as a school for young Americans who desire to learn how to build ships and marine engines, and have no money to pay for skilled instruction. The tuition includes all the details of shipbuilding and marine engineering, theoretical and practical ; and the students are boarded and taught free of cost. The stately tall-towered building is in handsome Renaissance architecture, and stands in a park of thirteen acres, on Fordham Heights, overlooking the Harlem River. Besides its dormitories and parlors, library and hospital, it has spacious draughting-rooms and an immense laying-out room.

The **Teachers College,** the first established in America, offers courses in pedagogy, and gives opportunity for studying children from the kindergarten to the end of the high school, and also for observation and practice in teaching. It has students from eighteen States, including many experienced teachers and college graduates. Its aim is to bring modern life and the modern school more into touch with each other, and to train teachers able to accomplish this result by teaching in accordance with the principles of the new education. In 1892 the college received a gift of a valuable building site on Morningside Heights, adjoining the future site of Columbia College, and entered upon the work of raising a building fund of $700,000. In 1893 a permanent charter was granted, the name being changed from New-York College for the Training of Teachers, by which it had been known since

HOLY CROSS PAROCHIAL SCHOOL, 240 WEST 43D STREET.

its foundation in 1889, to Teachers College; and an alliance was formed with Columbia College by which its students, whether men or women, may become candidates for the degrees of A. B., A. M., and Ph. D., given by Columbia College, and the students of Columbia College may pursue courses in the Teachers College leading to such degrees. An especial feature of the work in its new quarters will be the Mechanics-Arts Building, than which no more commodious edifice for a similar purpose exists. There are 34 officers and several hundred students. The college occupies the old Union Seminary, at 9 University Place, pending the completion of the new structures on Morningside Heights.

Commercial Colleges have attained a high rank as educational institutions. It is natural that this great metropolitan centre of commercial activities, the chief port of entry and clearing-house of the continent, should have thousands of students of business forms and principles. For many years the commercial colleges of New York have been fitting great numbers of young people for practical service in the counting-rooms and offices of the city, and preparing them to become expert accountants and book-keepers in positions of trust and responsibility. The standard of commercial honor is higher in New York than in London or Paris, and among most of its business men their word is as good as their bond. In the normal condition of affairs here, apart from the infrequent panic of a financial crisis or the fever of speculation, the rectitude of the commercial spirit follows the lines of absolute truth. Much of this nobility in the life of trade came from the grand old merchants of the early days of New York, who held honor as high and stainless as the members of any learned or military profession have ever done. Much of it also is derived from the teachings of the business colleges of the city, where the sentiments of exactness and precision are taught step by step with those of vigilance and enterprise.

Packard's Business College and School of Stenography is one of the institutions of New York. It was located in the then new building of the Cooper Institute in 1858, where it remained five years, then removing to more spacious

PACKARD'S BUSINESS COLLEGE, NORTHEAST CORNER 23D STREET AND FOURTH AVENUE.

quarters in the Mortimer Building, corner of 22d Street and Broadway, where it stayed seven years, when, in 1870, it occupied the entire fourth story of the Methodist Building — now McCreery's — at the corner of Broadway and 11th Street. In 1887 it took possession of its present admirable quarters, at the corner of 23d Street and Fourth Avenue, occupying the entire upper part of the building formerly held by the College of Physicians and Surgeons. The notable fact of this institution is its hold upon its students, which comes from its individualizing system of instruction and government. The Packard boys and girls are never reckoned *en masse*, but have unusual opportunities to impress their individuality upon their teachers, as they afterwards have upon the world. While being thoroughly educated for business — that is, for clerkships of all kinds — they are also educated for citizenship. While bookkeeping, arithmetic, penmanship and phonography are the principal technical studies of the school, especial care is given to the study of English, commercial law, civil

PARISH SCHOOL, CHURCH OF OUR LADY OF MT. CARMEL. 445 EAST 115TH STREET.

government, and questions of public interest. One of the constant exercises of the school is public speaking, which receives intelligent and discriminating attention, and constitutes a charming feature of the course of training. During the past thirty-five years many thousands of graduates have been sent out of this school, and are holding important places in the foremost enterprises of the city. Among its constituents are merchants, bankers, legislators, lawyers, ministers, and physicians, and among its friends and patrons many of the most eminent men of the country. Its proprietor and president, S. S. Packard, is a recognized leader in his line of work, having given more time and achieved a fuller measure of success in it than any other man. He is, in fact, the pioneer business-college man, and the man whose impress is most firmly fixed upon that specialty of education represented by the business college. Through Mr. Packard's efforts, mainly, has been carried

WORKINGMEN'S SCHOOL, SOCIETY FOR ETHICAL CULTURE, 109 WEST 54TH STREET.

forward the Business Education Exhibit at the World's Fair, which will undoubtedly form a remarkable spectacular effect, and in impressiveness will lead the educational exhibits of the great Exposition. In short, the Packard College, while being a marked feature of the great metropolis, is a recognized American institution.

Physical Culture is given much consideration. Among the great gymnasiums of the city are those of the New-York Athletic Club, at 55th Street and Sixth Avenue ; the Racquet and Tennis Club, at 27 West 43d Street ; the Young Men's Christian Association, at 23d Street and Fourth Avenue, and at Mott Haven ; and the Berkeley Ladies' Athletic Association, on 44th Street, near Fifth Avenue. The Turnverein conducts a school for 1,000 children, between the ages of six and fifteen,

DICKEL'S RIDING ACADEMY, 124 TO 136 WEST 56TH STREET.

in which, besides the usual studies, the young people are taught in calisthenics and other branches of gymnastics.

Dickel's Riding Academy, at 124 to 136 West 56th Street, is the most famous of the excellent schools of equestrianism which abound in the vicinity of Central Park ; and is also the oldest institution of this kind in the city. From the very first Dickel's has enjoyed the patronage of the best families of New York, and therefore it has long since acquired a social *prestige* of great value. The riding takes place in a spacious, airy and well-ventilated hall, floored with tan-bark, and bordered at either end with large galleries. Every evening there is a considerable assemblage of patrician equestrians, who ride to music, while their friends enter-tain themselves in the galleries, and watch the brilliant sight. Instruction is given under the personal supervision of Charles W. Dickel, and begins with the teaching of persons entirely unacquainted with riding, imparting to them confidence, gracefulness and strength in the saddle. Even the most timid and fearful girls, who at first have to be held onto the saddles, in a short time acquire a notable mastery over their steeds, and are able to enjoy the long gallops in Central Park. The academy also teaches the most difficult achievements in rough field riding, including proficiency in leaping and other delights of experienced horsemen. At certain hours the ring is set apart for the use of Troop A, N. G., S. N. Y., which is so celebrated for its splendid equestrianism. It is natural that this exercise-ground of the best families should be guarded against unworthy intruders, and no one can be admitted to the classes without satisfactory introduction or references. The hall of the ring is of attractive and appropriate architecture, with a fine Louvre roof, for copious air and light, and ingenious truss-supports. On one side are a great number of lockers and dressing-rooms, from which the equestrian issues fully equipped, from spurs to

INTERIOR OF DICKEL'S RIDING ACADEMY, 124 TO 136 WEST 56TH STREET.

riding-hat and gloves. The academy is under the proprietorship of Dickel & Kroehle, both well-known in the world of horse-lovers.

Other Riding Schools are mostly near Central Park, whose roads and bridle-paths afford fine opportunities for equestrian practice and exercise. Durland's, near the Eighth-Avenue entrance to the Park, at the Grand Circle, is one of the largest equestrian schools in the world. Other riding academies are the Boulevard, at 60th Street; the Central Park, at 58th Street and Seventh Avenue; the Belmont, on 124th Street; the West End, at 139 West 125th Street; and Antony's, at 90th Street and Fifth Avenue. These institutions have well-equipped riding-rings and saddle-horses, with competent teachers, and some of the evening classes are inspired by pleasant music.

Dancing Schools are numerous and varied, where this graceful art is taught to thousands of young people. Among the foremost terpsichorean academies is Dodsworth's, whose patrons come from the select circles of the city, and are instructed in all the most modern forms of dancing.

Rutgers Female College, at 56 West 55th Street, was founded by Chancellor Ferris, in 1838, and for many years held a very high rank. After it lost its fine buildings on Fifth Avenue, the institution declined; but of late many influential friends have risen to sustain it. Rutgers now has sixteen instructors. The president is George W. Samson, D. D., and the lady principal is Mrs. James T. Hoyt.

Fencing Classes are taught by Prof. H. Armand Jacoby, at the New-York Athletic Club, and at 75 West 44th Street (Prof. Jacoby is also the instructor of Troop A); M. Gouspy, at the Racquet and Tennis Club; Frederick and Heins, at the Turnverein; M. Regis Senac; and several other masters of swordsmanship.

The **New-York Institution for the Instruction of the Deaf and Dumb,** on Washington Heights, opened in 1818, as a free school for residents of the State, has 16 instructors and over 300 pupils, including many in articulation and auricular perception; trade-schools, with instructors for the several branches; and a department for technical and applied art.

NEW-YORK INSTITUTION FOR THE INSTRUCTION OF THE DEAF AND DUMB, ELEVENTH AVENUE, NEAR 162D STREET.

The Institution for the Improved Instruction of Deaf Mutes, on Lexington Avenue, between 67th and 68th Streets, has 20 instructors and 200 pupils. It was founded in 1867, and teaches the oral method, by articulation and lip-reading, not using the deaf and dumb alphabet. The building is an attractive one; and near it stands the four-story fire-proof structure of the Technical Training Department and Art-Studio, metal-working, wood-working, natural philosophy and art-studios, each having one full floor. The children are also taught sewing, cooking, dress-making and other useful avocations; and a kindergarten is provided.

St. Joseph's Institute for the Improved Instruction of Deaf Mutes, at Fordham, has commodious modern buildings, and an industrial department.

The New-York Institution for the Blind, at 34th Street and Ninth Avenue, is another beneficence of far-reaching value, founded in 1831, and now occupied by 30 instructors and 240 pupils. Here the unfortunate who have lost or never seen the light of day are educated in literature and in the essentials of a sound musical education, and also in piano-tuning and other useful avocations, with a view to becoming happy and self-supporting members of society. The library contains over 3,000 volumes, many of them in raised letters. Since its origin, upwards of 1,500 persons have been instructed here, a number of whom have attained success and distinction in the business and professional walks of life.

INSTITUTION FOR THE IMPROVED INSTRUCTION OF DEAF MUTES, LEXINGTON AVENUE, EAST 67TH AND EAST 68TH STREETS.

The school has been the source of many original improvements in the methods and appliances used in educating the blind, the latest and most important of which is the New-York Point System of Tangible Writing and Printing, for literature, music and mathematics.

Private Schools, Seminaries and Academies in great numbers are found scattered throughout New-York City, giving every variety of education, and largely patronized by the well-to-do families of the city.

The American Academy of the Dramatic Arts, 19 and 21 West 44th Street, is the principal training school for the professional theatrical stage in this country. The faculty numbers twenty prominent professionals. This academy was founded in 1884 under the name of The Lyceum Theatre School of Acting. It was the first and only institution of its kind in this country. Since 1884 nearly 300 students have graduated from the American Academy of the Dra-

NEW-YORK INSTITUTION FOR THE BLIND, NINTH AVENUE AND 34TH STREET.

matic Arts, and most of them are playing in various theatrical companies. Its president is Franklin H. Sargent. In 1892 it moved to the Berkeley Lyceum, on West 44th Street, where it utilizes the beautiful theatre, besides class and rehearsal-rooms.

The Berkeley School has a magnificent new fire-proof building, at 18 to 24 West 44th Street, with a front of Indiana limestone and Roman brick, in Ionic architecture. On the ground floor is the armory and gymnasium, occupying 85 by 100 feet. The first floor contains a library, large dining-room, offices and reception-rooms. The library and hall are embellished with four superb memorial windows. On the second and third floors are the school and class-rooms ; and the upper floors

contain a studio and a laboratory, with dormitories for twenty students. The main halls and toilet-rooms are wainscoted in marble and floored with mosaic. The building is heated by hot water, with inlets for fresh air upon every floor and in every room. An original system of ventilation is employed, by which the vitiated air is drawn from every room through a smoothly-masoned flue, to a chamber on the fifth floor, opening from which to the outside air is a Blackman propeller-fan run by an electric motor, which can change the air in the entire building in four minutes. The athletic grounds of the school, known as the Berkeley Oval, comprise ten acres, with thirty tennis courts, a quarter-mile running track, and a straight-away 220 yards running track, together with a boat-house and thirty boats upon the Harlem River. The Oval is 130 feet above the

BERKELEY SCHOOL, 20 WEST 44TH STREET, NEAR FIFTH AVENUE.

level of the Harlem River, and affords a superb view of the Harlem and Hudson valleys. The Berkeley School has made an enviable reputation as a preparatory school, and has sent nearly 200 boys to the leading colleges within twelve years, 90 per cent. of them going to Harvard, Yale, Columbia and Princeton, where their scholarship has attested the thoroughness of their preparation. The systematic physical instruction afforded, together with the discipline and proficiency acquired by the students in the military drill, have been no small factors in the success which the school has obtained. The school was founded by the present head master, John S. White, LL. D., a graduate of the Boston public schools and of Harvard University, Class of 1870, where he took the first classical honors. The Berkeley School has 30 instructors and 300 students.

Collegiate School, a private school for boys, at 241 and 243 West 77th Street, has a continuous history running back to the early settlement of the Island of Manhattan by the Dutch. The first school-master was an official of the Dutch West India Company, with Wouter Van Twiller, in 1633. This is, therefore, the oldest school now in existence in America. The new building, occupied in the fall of 1892, adjoins the new Collegiate Church on West-End Avenue. The school has classical, scientific and commercial studies, and military drill. There are twelve teachers in the Primary, Intermediate and Senior departments. Many boys are prepared here for college. The head master is Lemuel C. Mygatt, A. M.

Weingart Institute, at 22 and 24 East 91st Street, between Madison Avenue and Fifth Avenue, is a select day and boarding school, with kindergarten, under the direction of S. Weingart. It occupies two handsome and commodious four-story buildings on the highest and healthiest ground in the city, and within half a block of Central Park. One building is devoted to school purposes entirely, and the other is the residence of the principal and the boarding pupils. The ground-floor is occupied by a spacious gymnasium, equipped with the most approved modern appliances. Both buildings are well adapted to their educational uses, and are fitted up in a thorough and efficient manner. The grades of the school are kindergarten, primary, intermediate, junior and senior, the latter department preparing for the leading colleges and scientific schools. All the English branches are taught by competent American teachers. As a large portion of the pupils are of Germanic origin, the German language forms a regular part of the course. The Weingart Institute was founded in 1882, on 55th Street; and the thorough intellectual, physical and moral training it gives its pupils has caused its continual growth and prosperity.

The Lenox Institute, founded in 1888, at 334 and 336 Lenox Avenue, is practically a German gymnasium, or college preparatory school, with business, primary and kindergarten classes also. It has men teachers, and boy and girl pupils.

The Hebrew Free School Association, founded in 1864, has four large schools and 3,200 students, with daily sessions from 4 to 6 P. M. (except Fridays and Saturdays). The pupils also attend the public schools.

The Baron Hirsch Fund, established by a wealthy Berlin banker, and with headquarters at 45 Broadway, conducts a series of day and night schools for children and adults of the Russian and Roumanian Hebrew race, to teach them to become good citizens, giving instruction in trades, and in American elementary studies. It also furnishes tools to mechanics; loans small sums to deserving persons; and endeavors to prevent the Hebrews from congregating in the cities.

Other well-known institutions include the following: The Columbia Grammar School, at 34 and 36 East 51st Street, near Columbia College, a preparatory school for all colleges and scientific schools; Dr. Sachs's Collegiate Institute, at 38 and 116 West 59th Street, fronting on Central Park; William Freeland's admirable and efficient Harvard School, 578 Fifth Avenue, corner of 47th Street, fits many lads for the leading colleges. Still others are the Barnard School for boys, at 119 West 125th Street, with 120 pupils; Callisen's School for boys, 131 West 43d Street; Morse's English and Classical School for boys, 423 Madison Avenue; Dr. Chapin's Collegiate School for boys, 721 Madison Avenue; Cutler's Private School for boys, 20 West 43d Street; the Dwight School for boys, 1479 Broadway; the Irving School for boys, 20 West 59th Street; Halsey's Collegiate School for boys, 34 West 40th Street; Lyon's Classical School for boys, 6 East 47th Street; McMullen's Private School for boys, 521 West 161st Street; Richard's School for boys, 1475 Broadway; the University Grammar-School for boys, 1473 Broadway; the West-End

Avenue School for boys, 208 West-End Avenue ; the Woodbridge School for boys, 32 East 45th Street ; Madame Ruel's Boarding and Day School for girls, 26 East 56th Street ; the Brearley School for girls, 6 East 45th Street ; the Classical School for girls, 1961 Madison Avenue ; the Misses Ely's School for girls, Riverside Drive, near 85th Street ; the Comstock School for girls, 32 West 40th Street ; the English and French Schools for girls, 148 Madison Avenue and 55 West 47th Street ; Miss Perrin's Girl's School, 244 Lenox Avenue ; the Van Norman Institute for girls, 2 West 71st Street ; Mrs. Weil's School for girls, 711 Madison Avenue ; Misses Peebles and Thompson's School for Young Ladies, 32 East 57th Street ; Rev. C. K. Gardner's School for Young Ladies, 601 Fifth Avenue ; the Misses Grahams' School for Young Ladies, 63 Fifth Avenue ; Miss Anna C. Brackett's School, 9 West 39th Street ; Miss Emily A. Ward's Riverside School, 50 West 104th Street ; and the Heidenfeld Institute, for both sexes, 824 Lexington Avenue.

A commanding advantage which New York has over other American cities, for purposes of education, is its massed treasures of art, literature and humanity. The Astor, Lenox and Mercantile Libraries, and other great collections of books ; the Metropolitan Museum and several other very rich collections in art ; the American Museum of Natural History ; the moving life of the parks and avenues, architecture in every form, philanthropy organized to benefit millions, oratory and dramatic art, consecration and self-sacrifice — almost every form of civic and social life may be observed and entered into, in the proud metropolis of the New World. The contemplation of these manifold phases makes versatile men and women.

Cooking Schools, wherein is taught the art of preparing and cooking food to the best advantage, comprise several well-equipped institutions, ranging from the simple cooking-classes of the charity schools to the scientific academies.

The New-York Cooking School, in the United Charities Building, elevates the poor by free lessons in plain cooking, marketing, nurses' cooking, etc., and has nearly 1,000 pupils yearly. A large dining-room is attached.

Maillard's New-York Chocolate School is at 114 West 25th Street, where free lessons are given on Monday, Wednesday and Friday afternoons, from October to June, in the art of making a cup of chocolate or cocoa.

Kindergartens and other peculiar schools show the imperial beneficence of New York. Here have been instituted great numbers of schools for the dependent and defective classes. The New-York Kindergarten Association has opened numerous schools for the very young children in the tenement-house districts.

The Children's Aid Society conducts 22 admirable day and night industrial schools, and 14 kindergartens. The 15,000 poor Italians in New York are aided by three industrial schools in Leonard, Sullivan and Crosby Streets, where more than 1,200 children and adults are taught in ordinary studies and in carpentry, cooking, sewing, etc. Similar schools are maintained in the Five-Points Mission House, with cooking classes and other practical features. The House of Industry, at 155 Worth Street, teaches type-setting, carpentry, and other industries, to about 300 children ; and has a well appointed kindergarten. St. Joseph's Home, on Great Jones Street, is an enormous Catholic mission, with industrial and other schools attached. The Catholic Protectory has large trade-schools for boys, and sewing-schools for girls.

Besides these, are the great reform schools, like the New-York Juvenile Asylum, founded in 1851, with 70 instructors and 1,100 pupils ; the House of Refuge, on Randall's Island, founded in 1825, with 50 instructors and 1,000 pupils ; and the New-York Catholic Protectory, with 50 instructors and 1,500 pupils. These enormous schools are liberally conducted, and accomplish inestimable good.

The Higher Culture

Art Museums and Galleries, Scientific, Literary, Musical and Kindred Institutions, Societies and Organizations.

I N THE interest of the United States the New-Yorkers never rest. They are at work unceasingly, in order that they may give to the Americans all the types of beauty and of elegance. Even the least lavish among them — those who do not buy miniatures, vignettes of the eighteenth century, art-objects of Japan — pay cheerfully for perfection, the price of which is fabulous. In their estimate of value, it is not the actual worth, but the art truer than truth, that counts.

Elsewhere there are skies, fields, plains, forests, brooks under dark leaves, delicious corners of shade ; but in New York, there are flowers that are living jewels made of light. In New York, myriads of periwinkles, forget-me-nots, rose-bushes and geraniums, uniformly embroidered on miles of lawn, are as if cut out of an endless cloth, regularly woven and inexhaustible.

Elsewhere there are Queens, Princesses, great ladies, and peasants ; but in New York there are women prodigiously dressed, young and beautiful — not only because they are, but because they wish to be young and beautiful — and representing plastically the ideal of thoughts human.

Elsewhere intelligent men read journals, books, scientific pamphlets, everything ; and in comparison with New-Yorkers, most of whom are too busy to read, are little informed and provincial, because ideas are in New York in the air that one breathes. In London and Paris, the only cities in the world that New York might not surpass in higher culture if it ceased to labor, art-galleries, literary, scientific and artistic societies, museums, are in the charge of the government.

The Metropolitan Museum of Art, in Central Park, near Fifth Avenue and 82d Street, in a stone and brick building on the site formerly called Deer Park, was formed as the result of a meeting instigated chiefly by the art-committee of the Union League, in October, 1869, wholly in reliance upon the public spirit of New-Yorkers. It was incorporated in 1870, and soon thereafter purchased a collection of pictures, which it exhibited, together with loaned objects of art, in a leased building at 681 Fifth Avenue. In 1873, before its lease had expired, it rented the Douglas mansion, 126 West 14th Street ; having in 1872 purchased from General L. P. di Cesnola the antiquities unearthed by him in Cyprus. Gifts were received, in money and objects of art, with members' subscriptions, and an offer from the Park Commissioners to furnish a building in the Park if the museum should be transferred thither. In 1871 the Legislature had passed an act authorizing the Department of Public Parks to erect a building for the purposes of a museum, and to enter into an agreement for its occupancy by the Metropolitan Museum of Art. The first portion of the proposed building was finished and inaugurated in 1880. By the agreement just mentioned the museum was opened to the public without charge four days in the week. The second, or south, wing of the building was completed and occupied in 1889 ; the third is now in progress. In 1890 petitions were circulated in the city requesting that the museum be opened to the public on Sundays without charge. The Trustees complied, at the cost of large pecuniary sacrifices, and submitting to an inevitable deficit. Out of 751,856 visitors in 1892, 246,988 came on Sundays. This

loss has been in part made up by increased appropriations from the city.

The Cyprus collection has no parallel anywhere for extent and value. It comprises stone sculptures, sarcophagi, inscriptions, alabastra, ivories, lamps, pottery, terra-cotta statuettes, bronzes, glass, gems, jewelry and other objects in gold and silver ; Assyrian, Egyptian, Phœnician, Greek and Roman in character, and of dates from the earliest times to later than the Christian era; many of its objects and classes of objects are unique. The museum's collection of glass was increased by a purchase from Charvet by Henry G. Marquand, and by him presented to the Museum ; also a later collection presented by J. J. Jarves ; making the

INTERIOR OF THE METROPOLITAN MUSEUM OF ART.

entire collection of glass the most valuable known. There are magnificent collections of Babylonian, Assyrian, and other ancient cylinders, seals and inscribed clay tablets ; Egyptian, Greek, Roman, Indian and American antiquities, the last in gold and silver, as well as pottery and stone; modern sculptures and bronzes; the Huntington collection of memorials of Washington, Franklin and Lafayette ; the E. C. Moore collection of ancient terra-cotta statuettes, ancient and modern glass, Oriental enamelled and other pottery, and objects of art in metal, ivory, etc.; the Coles collection of tapestries and vases; the Lazarus collection of miniatures, enamels, jewelry and fans; the Drexel collection of objects of art in gold and silver ; the C. W. King collection of ancient gems, purchased and presented to the museum by John Taylor Johnston ; the collection of Oriental porcelain purchased from S. P. Avery ; the Japanese swords from the Ives collection ; the unique collection of musical instruments of all nations, presented by Mrs. John Crosby Brown, with a smaller collection presented by J. W. Drexel ; the Baker and other collections of ancient textile fabrics from the Fayoum, in Egypt ; the pictures, gold medals and other objects commemorative of the laying of the Atlantic Cable, presented by the late Cyrus W. Field ; the models of inventions by the late Captain John Ericsson, presented by George H. Robinson ; the reproductions of ivory carvings, exhibiting the mediæval continuance of the art ; the collec-

METROPOLITAN MUSEUM OF ART.
CENTRAL PARK, NEAR FIFTH AVENUE AND 82D STREET.

20

tion of Renaissance iron work, the Della Robbia altar-piece, the metallic reproductions of gold and silver objects in the imperial Russian museums, all presented by Henry G. Marquand; the McCullum, Stuart and Astor laces; the collection of architectural casts, made from a fund bequeathed by the late Levi H. Willard, amounting to $100,000; the sculptural casts, presented by H. G. Marquand; and the beginning of a series of casts, purchased by subscription, intended to illustrate progressive art from the earliest examples to the later Christian; drawings by the old masters, collected by Count Maggiori of Bologna, Signor Marietta, Professor Angelini and Dr. Guastala, purchased and presented by Cornelius Vanderbilt; with another smaller but equally fine collection presented by Mrs. Cephas G. Thompson; a large collection of paintings by old Dutch and Flemish masters; another exceedingly important and valuable collection of paintings by old masters and painters of the English school, presented by Henry G. Marquand; the noble galleries of modern paintings bequeathed by the late Catharine Lorillard Wolfe; other galleries of masterpieces by modern artists, including the most famous works of Rosa Bonheur (presented by Cornelius Vanderbilt) and Meissonier (presented by Henry Hilton). The Metropolitan Museum of Art would be a museum of the first class even if it were limited to any one of the collections that it includes; but its symmetry and extent are as remarkable as its rapid growth, especially when we reflect that its creation and increase are due wholly to private enterprise. Besides the advantages furnished to artists, artisans and art-students in copying and designing from its collections, the museum has also, during the greater period of its existence, maintained an institution called the Art-Schools, in which the fine arts and decorative arts, in their chief branches, are taught, and lectures on art are given. In coöperation with Columbia College an arrangement has been made, under which the College provides for the delivery of lectures on art during each winter season, at the Museum, and the Museum supplies the illustrative material for the lectures. These plans will have much effect in developing art-taste in New York.

The American Museum of Natural History, in Central Park (77th Street and Eighth Avenue), was incorporated in 1869, for the purpose of establishing and maintaining in New-York City a museum and library of natural history. The first president was John David Wolfe, who was succeeded by Robert L. Stuart, now both deceased. The present officers are: Morris K. Jesup, President; James M. Constable and D. Jackson Steward, Vice-Presidents; Charles Lanier, Treasurer; John H. Winser, Secretary and Assistant Treasurer; and William Wallace, Superintendent of Buildings.

The museum held its first exhibition in the old arsenal, where the Verreaux collection of natural-history specimens, the Elliot collection of North-American birds, and the entire museum of Prince Maximilian of Neuwied were displayed. It was not until June, 1874, that the corner-stone of the first building in Manhattan Square was laid. A new portion has recently been added which greatly strengthens the effect of the architectural design — a not very pronounced tendency to the Romanesque. The building proper is of brick, with a front of red granite from New Brunswick and Canada. The imposing and ornamental entrance is of Massachusetts granite. The seven arches resting on short polished pillars of stone make a commanding and dignified front. The structure is so designed that it can be extended to occupy the whole of Manhattan Square, which has been set aside for that purpose; wings will be added as the collections require them, and the liberality of the city allows. The plans are now ready for the addition of another wing, to provide the much needed additional space for the exhibit of material now stored in the

AMERICAN MUSEUM OF NATURAL HISTORY.
CENTRAL PARK WEST, BETWEEN WEST 77TH AND WEST 81ST STREETS.

building. The expenses are paid by the city, by the board of trustees, and by sub-scriptions. In birds, mammals, insects, fossils, minerals, shells, and implements of the aborigines of our own and foreign lands, the collections are extremely rich and note-worthy ; the library on many subjects is unequaled by any other in the country. The collections of woods and building stones of the United States, presented by Morris K. Jesup, are far the most extensive and valuable in America and, possibly, in the world. Most conspicuous in the other departments are : The American gems and gem minerals, exhibited at the Paris Exposition by Tiffany & Co. (these brilliant and precious stones were purchased for and presented to the museum by J. Pierpont Morgan, one of the trustees); the collection of Prof. James Hall, the State Geologist ; the Spang collection of minerals; the Jay collection of shells, pre-sented to the museum by Catherine L. Wolfe; the D. J. Steward collection of shells ; and a series of specimens on Mammalian Palaeontology, the result of original research and investigation under the direction of Prof. H. F. Osborn. Prominent in the department of Ethnology and Archæology are the collections of Lieut. Emmons, H. R. Bishop, Jones, Terry, and Sturgis ; the celebrated collection of jade objects made by George F. Kunz; the Harry Edwards collection of entomo-logical specimens ; and the private collection of Andrew E. Douglass.

The different departments of the institution are designated as :

Public Instruction — Prof. Albert S. Bickmore, Curator.

Geology, Mineralogy, Conchology, and Marine Invertebrate Zoology — Prof. R. P. Whitfield, Curator.

Mammalogy, Ornithology, Herpitology, Ichthyology — Prof. J. A. Allen, Curator.

Mammalian Palaeontology — Prof. Henry Fairfield Osborn, Curator.

Archaeology and Ethnology — James Terry, Curator.

Taxidermy — Jenness Richardson, Taxidermist.

Entomology — William Beutenmuller, Curator.

Library — Anthony Woodward, Ph. D., Librarian.

Every object, however small, is labeled with its scientific and common appella-tion, its description, and its history. The catalogues record the investigations, the researches and the studies of ages. The trustees encourage the use of the halls and study-rooms for the holding of receptions, exhibitions and business meetings of the different scientific societies of the city and country. The aim of the institution is to establish a post-graduate university of natural science, that shall be as complete in all its appointments as any similar institution in London or Paris.

The National Academy of Design, at the northwest corner of 23d Street and Fourth Avenue, was formed in 1826, of the New-York Drawing Association, and is the American Ecole des Beaux-arts, the American equivalent of the Royal Academy and of the Salon. In its act of incorporation, passed April 5, 1828, are the names of Samuel F. B. Morse, Henry Inman, Thomas S. Cummings, John L. Morton, Asher B. Durand, Charles Ingham, Frederick S. Agate and Thomas Cole. It has in its list of students names of the most eminent artists. The schools directed by the Academicians, instructed by the ablest professors, are opened the first Monday in October and closed in the middle of May. The instruction is free. There are composition classes, costume classes, sketching classes from casts, from the living model, draped and undraped, painting classes, lectures, prizes to deserv-ing students, and exhibitions of works by artists. The students have access to the books of an art library, the value of which is inestimable. The spring and autumn exhibitions of the National Academy of Design introduce the work of American artists to the critics and to the public.

The Academy building, designed by P. B. Wight, is of white and dark marble, in the beautiful Venetian Gothic architecture. It has a double stairway to the main entrance, with massive balustrades. The building was paid for by public subscriptions. There are about 100 Academicians and 50 Associates.

The American Water-Color Society, at 52 East 23d Street, founded in 1866, makes a very popular yearly exhibition at the National Academy of Design of the works of painters in water-colors, members of the society and others, and awards the William T. Evans prize of $500 to the painter of the picture adjudged by a vote of the society to be the most meritorious of the exhibition. The society has 100 members.

The Kit-Kat Club, at 20 West 59th Street, founded in 1881, and incorporated in 1884, is a working club of artists. There are classes three times a week, at

NATIONAL ACADEMY OF DESIGN, FOURTH AVENUE AND 23D STREET.   LYCEUM THEATRE.

night, without professors. The members criticise the work of each other. There are informal receptions called smoking parties, and annual exhibitions of *tableaux vivants.*

The New-York Etching Club is at 49 West 22d Street. Its catalogues contain an etching and a portrait of every member of the club, and short essays on the art of the etcher. There are about 50 members.

The Society of American Artists, at 215 West 57th Street, was founded in 1877, by artists dissatisfied with the National Academy of Design. Several Academicians are members, and one, W. M. Chase, is President of the society. Its purposes are the same as those of the National Academy of Design. It has brilliant May exhibitions, well-contested prizes, a large membership, and Parisian artistic ideals. Among the members are Abbey, Beckwith, Blashfield, Bridgman, Appleton Brown, Chase, Church, Duveneck, Cox, Gay, Gifford, LaFarge, Millet, Pearce, Picknell, St. Gaudens, Vedder, Vinton, and Weir.

The Art-Students' League, at 215 West 57th Street, was organized in 1875, and incorporated in 1878. There, every day, are life, portrait, sketch, modelling, composition and costume classes. There are frequent lectures, art-receptions and exhibitions. There are a dozen class-rooms in the Fine-Arts Building.

The Architectural League of New York, at 215 West 57th Street, was organized in 1881. It has monthly meetings, lectures and dinners, an annual exhibition and banquet (in December) and prizes. Its president is Russell Sturgis ; and the membership is large and influential, including St. Gaudens, Ward, McKim, Tiffany, Ware, Upjohn, Renwick, Rich, Port, Bruce Price, Le Brun, Hunt, Gibson, Robertson and other well-known men.

The American Fine-Arts Society was formed in 1889, by a combination of the Society of American Artists, the Architectural League of New York, and the

Art-Students' League of New York, for the purpose of erecting a building for their home, and for a headquarters of the graphic arts in New York. They jointly own and occupy the exquisite building erected by them, at a cost of $400,000, at 215 West 57th Street, between Broadway and Seventh Avenue. The architect was Henry J. Hardenbergh ; and the façade reproduces that of the house of Francis I. in Paris. The materials are pink granite and Indiana limestone. The building was finished in 1892. The large Vanderbilt gallery valued at $100,000 was presented to the

AMERICAN FINE-ARTS BUILDING, 215 WEST 57TH STREET.

society by George W. Vanderbilt ; and together with the South Gallery, forms an admirable place in which to display pictures to the best effect.

The Associated Artists, at 115 East 23d Street, is a corporation founded by Mrs. Candace Wheeler, its President, to paint ceilings and decorative panels, and for the manufacture of artistic patterns in silk, and artistic prints in cotton. It has done a great work in the elevation of textile industry, and its goods have been largely copied, even by European manufacturers. The embroideries and needle-woven tapestries which have come from this society, having been worked under Mrs. Wheeler's supervision, are widely celebrated for their beauty. The business is managed and run by women.

Other Art Organizations include the Society of Painters in Pastels, with its yearly exhibitions ; the New-York Water-Color Society, which was organized in 1890 ; the Art Guild, the Salmagundi, the Artists' Fund Society and others.

The New-York Institute for Artist-Artisans, at 140 West 23d Street, founded in 1881, and directed by John Ward Stimson, former director of the Metropolitan Museum of Art Schools, is a training school for all the arts, kept constantly in touch with the various trade guilds and associations. The arts are taught in their application to various branches of trade. The school is under the patronage of influential men and women of the city,

ASSOCIATED ARTISTS, 115 EAST 23D STREET.

and interests every person who cares for the progress of American industrial art.

The Cooper-Union Free Night Schools of Science and Art, at the Cooper Institute, are open to all applicants at least fifteen years of age, whether they are or are not residents of the city. In the scientific department are taught mathematics, chemistry, astronomy, electrical measurements, mechanics, mechanical drawings. In the art department are taught mechanical, architectural, perspective, cast, form, ornamental, figure and rudimental drawing, decorative designing and modelling in clay. There are lectures, exhibitions, prizes and diplomas.

The Cooper-Union Woman's Art-School, at the Cooper Institute, is open to all applicants at least sixteen and not over thirty-five years of age. There are classes in oil-painting, life and cast drawing, designing and normal drawing, pen and ink illustration, crayon photograph, lectures on art and on anatomy, exhibitions, diplomas. There are supplementary afternoon classes for women who study art as an accomplishment, or have the means to pay for tuition.

The Society of Decorative Art, at 28 East 21st Street, incorporated in 1878, exhibits and sells art-work of women, pottery, china, tiles, plaques, embroideries, hangings, curtains, book-cases, cabinets, table and other house linen, articles for wardrobes of infants, panels for cabinet work, painting on silk for screens, panels and fans, decorated bills of fare, and works of like description. A subscriber of $100 may nominate a pupil for one year in any of the free classes taught by the society. A subscriber of $10 may place one pupil unable to pay for tuition in the china, water-color or fan-painting classes, for five free lessons. A subscriber of $5 may nominate one pupil for six free lessons in art needlework, the pupil's ability to be determined by the first two lessons. The society charges 10 per cent. commission on its sales, and it sells nothing that its committees have not approved.

The Exchange for Women's Work, at 329 Fifth Avenue, is devoted to the sale of artistic articles, mainly made by poor gentlewomen, and often of great beauty and originality of design.

The Municipal Art Society was organized in 1893, for the development of a higher art taste in the city, and a purer sentiment in its monuments, parks and public buildings, and for the appropriate decoration of public places with works of sculpture, painting, mosaic or stained glass. Foremost artists are enrolled in this most commendable organization, which has a semi-official relation to the municipal government. The President is Richard M. Hunt. The Executive Committee includes three architects : E. H. Kendall, W. B. Bigelow, and Henry J. Hardenbergh ; three artists : E. H. Blashfield, Will H. Low, and George W. Maynard ; three sculptors : Augustus St. Gaudens, J. Q. A. Ward, and Olin L. Warner ; and three laymen : August Belmont, J. Armstrong Chanler, and W. T. Evans.

The Art Stores of the American Art Association, 6 East 23d Street ; of Moore, in West 17th Street ; of Thomas B. Clarke, 4 East 34th Street ; of S. P. Avery, Jr., W. C. Baumgarten & Co., Boussod, Valadon & Co., Cottier & Co., L. Christ Delmonico, Durand Ruel Brothers, H. J. Duveen & Co., Knoedler & Co., Reichard & Co., Herman Schaus and A. W. Conover (successors of Wm. Schaus), and Sypher & Co., in Fifth Avenue ; of H. B. Herts & Co., Frank Hegger, Tiffany & Co., and Wunderlich, on Broadway ; of Frederick Keppel, Wernicke and many others, have in their books records of private collections only a little less interesting than their wares, to the public of New York. But these records are sealed. It is not by them that one may know what treasures are hidden behind many severe, ordinary, uninviting brownstone fronts of New-York houses. However, they may be known, for many of these treasures appear at loan exhibitions frequently. When known, they are not difficult of access.

Everybody in New York is interested in the industrial phase of the arts, if one may judge by the attraction which the shop-windows have for the crowds, the increasing taste for beauty being displayed everywhere, the popularity of exhibitions of handicraft, and the interest displayed to learn the value, the history, and the names of buyers of works of art.

The Private Art Collections of New York include those of Mrs. Astor, Samuel P. Avery, Heber R. Bishop, James B. Colgate, R. L. Cutting, Charles A. Dana, W. B. Dinsmore, Henry Hilton, C. P. Huntington, G. G. Haven, Henry G. Marquand, J. Pierpont Morgan, Levi P. Morton, Darius O. Mills, Oswald Ottendorfer, J. W. Pinchot, Charles Stewart Smith, Mrs. Paran Stevens, Mrs. W. H. Vanderbilt, Cornelius Vanderbilt, W. K. Vanderdilt and C. F. Woerishoffer. The most valuable collection is the one formed by William H. Vanderbilt. Not one is limited to paintings. Samuel P. Avery has paintings, bronzes of Barye, and the greatest private collection of etchings extant ; Heber R. Bishop has an unsurpassable collection of jades ; Charles A. Dana, of vases of china ; and Henry G. Marquand has classified in appropriately designed rooms, Persian, Japanese, Arabic and Hispano-Moresque, the most valuable antique tapestry, porcelain arms and art-objects. The value of the private art-collections in New York is calculated at $8,000,000. In 1885 the paintings collected by George I. Seney, 285 in number, brought $650,000. Meissonier's "1807," presented by Henry Hilton to the Metropolitan Museum of Art, cost the late Alexander T. Stewart $67,000. The portrait

BIRD'S-EYE VIEW OF FIFTH AVENUE.

NORTH OF 51ST STREET.

by Rembrandt, which Henry G. Marquand bought from the Marquis of Lansdowne and presented to the Metropolitan Museum of Art, cost $25,000 and expenses. The paintings shown at one of the annual receptions of the Union League were insured for $400,000. In 1883 a loan collection of paintings and various objects of art at the National Academy of Design was insured for more than $1,000,000. The sales at one exhibition of the National Academy of Design aggregated $40,000. Mr. Drewry, secretary of the Kit-Kat Club, and art-editor of the American Press Association, estimates at 4,000 the number of professional artists in New York. Among these are the foremost painters and sculptors of America, enriching the Empire City with the art of Paris, the statuary of Athens, the architecture of Italy.

The Fifth-Avenue Art-Galleries are famous all over the continent, wherever there are *connoisseurs* and lovers of the best works of art. They occupy a building

admirably designed for the purpose, at 366 and 368 Fifth Avenue, between the houses of the Manhattan Club and the New-York Club. This perfectly planned structure was erected expressly for the purpose, by the Caswell estate, after plans wrought out by the late Henry O. Avery, the well-known architect. The upper floor, only one flight from the street, is occupied by the commodious and well-lighted galleries in which Samuel P. Avery, Jr., displays constantly the choicest works of European and American art. Mr. Avery has devoted himself to this business for over twenty years, and makes annual visits to Europe to give commissions to celebrated artists, and to purchase the choicest paintings at the great art-centres. In these unrivalled

FIFTH-AVENUE ART GALLERIES, 366 AND 368 FIFTH AVENUE.

galleries may be seen examples of almost all the best-known painters of Europe and America, exquisite French landscapes, *genre* pictures, brilliant marines, and all the wide range of modern art. The patrician mansions of New York secure their choicest pictures here, and many a hamlet among the New-England hills or on the limitless Western prairies has been enriched by paintings from this magnetic centre of art. The works exhibited and sold here have been selected with the finest and most highly-trained æsthetic taste, and are the crown-jewels of each year's studios and *salons*. The Avery galleries are lighted from above, with broad sky-lights; and what may be called the domestic effect of pictures is shown also in the contiguous private rooms, where the paintings are exhibited in the side-lights from windows.

Ortgies & Co., the best-known and longest-established art-auctioneers in New York, occupy the great galleries on the ground-floor of the Fifth-Avenue Art-Galleries building, extending around to 35th Street. These galleries have 5,000 square feet of hanging space, and 5,300 square feet of floor area, with perfect overhead lighting. They were specially designed for the exhibition and sale by auction of paintings, sculptures, books, *bric-à-brac,* engravings, etc. During the past twenty years this firm has conducted nearly thirty picture-sales, each of which brought over $30,000, at least seven bringing over $100,000 each. Among these were the collections of John Taylor Johnston, $328,286; Albert Spencer, $284,025; and J. F. Kensett, $137,944. At times of these great sales, or when unique collections of porcelains and other artistic property are offered, the galleries are crowded with the very flower of metropolitan society. The firm is made up of John Ortgies and Robert Somerville, with Samuel P. Avery, Jr., as special partner.

Frank Hegger's Photographic Depot, at 152 Broadway, is the best-known and most popular establishment of its kind in America. The spacious store is a

HEGGER'S ART ESTABLISHMENT, 152 BROADWAY, NEAR LIBERTY STREET.

magazine packed with everything that is choice in water-colors, etchings, engravings, photographs of every possible description, and unmounted views from all parts of the globe. "If you can't get them at Hegger's, you can't get them in this country," is a well-deserved compliment and literally true. Hegger's is always abreast with the time, and the selections which continually replenish his stock are made with the taste and judgment of a man of travel and a knowledge of the best one sees as a traveller. It is a case of a man fitted by every natural inclination and gift to his vocation, and who has become conspicuous among us by the natural development and vast public utility of his business. The absence of the Hegger establishment from New York would leave an aching void to the eyes of thousands to whom his show-windows and port-folios are a perpetual source of intellectual refreshment and æsthetical delight. The Broadway sidewalk is often blockaded by the throng attracted by his ever freshly renewed and ever novel and interesting displays, and brokers and business men, hot with the fever of mid-day business, break suddenly away from their drive for gain to "run in and see what Hegger has new," and jostle grave divines and college professors in their investigations of the huge sample books.

The Tiffany Glass and Decorating Company of New York.— It is without doubt evident to every careful observer that a strong artistic taste is rapidly developing among us, and that the American people are ultimately destined to become deeply imbued with an unprecedented love for all forms of material beauty,

architectural, pictorial and decorative. The phenomenal growth and expansion of the Tiffany Glass and Decorating Company, of 333-341 Fourth Avenue, are sufficient evidence of this fact, as such an organization could not exist without a large clientage of art-loving people. Take the subject alone of colored glass windows, and it is in the memory of all that only a

TIFFANY GLASS AND DECORATING COMPANY, FOURTH AVENUE AND 25TH STREET.

few years ago most Americans were contented with imported windows, or with poor imitations made here. In both cases the windows were but copies of mediæval work, seldom equalling the originals, and never showing an advance, either in artistic qualities or improvement of method, or even mechanical skill, over the windows of the Middle Ages. All this is now a thing of the past. To-day America leads the world in the making of colored glass windows; a result brought about mainly through the investigations and experiments of Louis C. Tiffany, an artist of rare ability, having a most exquisite appreciation of color values and their relations, one to another. He intuitively took up the subject where the mediævalist left off, viz.: The study and the unfolding of the inherent properties of the glass to their fullest extent, both in color and in texture, in order to obtain in the glass itself light and shade, through depth and irregularity of color, in union with inequality of surface, in that way hoping to avoid the dullness, opacity and thinness which invariably accompany the use of paint, and are marked characteristics of European glass-work.

Moreover, he endeavored to obtain effects in this obstinate material which were hitherto deemed impossible. Among other things he introduced the use of opales-

BEETHOVEN MÆNNERCHOR, 210 FIFTH STREET.

cent glass. He softened the hard lead lines by plating glass over glass, and he developed the mosaic system of work, substituting it for glass-painting.

In a word, he originated a system of work which requires the strictest attention of the artist, a method founded on the most perfect practice of the mosaic system, an artistic method *par excellence.* The result is that a Tiffany window made by the company that bears his name is indeed a thing of beauty, and for which the demand is growing from day to day, and so fast, that the company is compelled to carry constantly in stock over a hundred tons of glass in the raw state, and employ a large corps of artists exclusively for this branch of its business. Just as the Glass Department has grown, in the same way every other one has developed, until in the studios of the company all forms of artistic handicraft are found. Churches, houses, hotels and theatres are decorated and furnished throughout. In fact, both domestic and ecclesiastical work of every description is undertaken by the company. The demand for its work has been so great that an increase of capital became a necessity, and the company now has a paid-up cash capital of $400,000. The artistic department is under the immediate direction of Louis C. Tiffany; the general management is under the care of Pringle Mitchell; while the Board of Direction is composed of a number of well-known men, viz.: John C. Platt, John DuFais, Henry W. de Forest, George Holmes, Von Beck Canfield and J. A. Holzer.

Music in New York has shown a remarkable and vigorous development. This city knew all Wagner before Paris accepted *Lohengrin.* It has capital orchestras, choral societies, music clubs, conservatories, professors, lectures by musical experts, and exquisite private performances.

The Philharmonic Society, organized in 1842 by Uriah C. Hill, a violinist,

NEW-YORK MÆNNERCHOR, 203 EAST 56TH STREET.

native of New York, who had studied with Spohr at Cassel, is composed of professional orchestra players and a non-professional president. It gave at the first concert, December 7, 1842, the Symphony in C Minor of Beethoven, which seemed far above the faculty of appreciation of a public so little educated musically as the public of New York was then; but it had a high aim and never faltered. It led the public taste. In 1867 the membership was increased to 100 players. At that time Carl Bergman was its conductor, and remained in office until 1876. Dr. Leopold Damrosch was conductor, 1876-77; Theodore Thomas, 1877-1878; Adolph Neuendorff, 1878-79; Theodore Thomas, 1878-91; and Anton Seidl.

The Symphony Society was organized in 1880 by Dr. Leopold Damrosch. Its Symphony Orchestra, the only permanent one in New York, is directed by Walter Damrosch. Its concerts are brilliant social events.

The Oratorio Society, organized in 1873, is under the skilful direction of Walter Damrosch. Its predecessors in the place that it occupies were the Church

LIEDERKRANZ, 58TH STREET, BETWEEN LEXINGTON AND FOURTH AVENUES.

Music Association, the Mendelssohn Union and the Harmonic Society. Like the Harmonic Society, it gives every year during Christmas week a performance of the *Messiah.* It has given and continues to give, with perfect art, works like Bach's *Passion Music,* Berlioz's *Messe des Morts,* Handel's *Judas Maccabeus,* Haydn's *Creation* and *Seasons,* Schumann's *Paradise and the Peri,* Liszt's *Christus,* Grell's *Missa Solemnis,* and the cantatas of Dr. Damrosch.

The Mendelssohn Glee Club was organized in 1866 by Joseph Mosenthal, a violinist, a pupil of Spohr, and a native of Cassel, who became an influential organist of the Episcopal Church in New York, and resigned from Calvary Church not to yield to a fashionable craze for boy choirs. The club gives concerts invariably excellent.

The Manuscript Society, organized in 1889 for the performance in public of unpublished works of American composers, has for president Gerritt Smith.

The Musurgia, devoted exclusively to part songs for men's voices, is under the direction of William R. Chapman, who also directs the Rubenstein (part songs for women) and Metropolitan Musical Societies, for the study of music.

Orpheons, of Swiss and French, are represented by several organizations.

Church Choral Societies, which Trinity Church encouraged so effectively when New York had no other music than the music of churches, have been organized in various sections.

The New-York Maennerchor, founded in 1870, in 1887 erected its spacious and handsome building on 56th Street.

Maennerchors and Saengerbunde, mainly Germans, are numerous.

The Deutscher Liederkranz, at the north side of East 58th Street, between Park and Lexington Avenues, gave to New York the fervor of German lyrism. It was organized in 1847, and incorporated in 1860, and it has steadily given, in concerts, in cantatas, in courses of instruction that have powerful influence, the best works of the German composers. It has admirably produced works like Mozart's *Requiem,* Liszt's *Prometheus,* and Mendelssohn's *Walpurgisnacht.* Its membership is composed of active members who are

ARION SOCIETY, PARK AVENUE AND EAST 59TH STREET.

musicians or students in the perfect school of vocal music provided by the club, and others to whom the seductive social features only of the club have appealed. Its membership includes 1,200 Germans and German-Americans, 200 Hebrew-Americans, and 100 Americans of British origin. There are female choruses. The conductor is Heinrich Zöllner, of Cologne, whom the club called to New York in 1890. The festivals of the Liederkranz, especially the annual Carnival, are thoroughly artistic. The club-house of the Liederkranz is a large brownstone building in the style of the German Renaissance. The president is William Steinway.

The Arion Society, with its home at the corner of Park Avenue and 59th Street, was organized by fourteen seceding members of the Liederkranz in 1854. They gave their first concert in the Apollo Rooms, at Broadway and Canal Street ; produced an operetta *Mordgrunbruck,* in 1855 ; another, *Der Gang Zum Eisenhammer,* in 1856 ; furnished the choruses in the first Wagner opera performed in America, *Tannhäuser,* August 27, 1859 ; performed *Der Freischutz* in 1869 ; and gave brilliant Carnival meetings and masquerade balls that are still maintained. In 1871, the Arion brought Dr. Leopold Damrosch from Breslau. In 1870, it occupied 19 and 21 St. Mark's Place, and in 1887 it entered its present beautiful palace. It is, unlike the Liederkranz, almost exclusively German. It has no chorus of mixed voices. It gives concerts, balls, and operettas in the large hall on the third floor of its graceful building. The lower story is of Berea sandstone, the rest of buff brick and terra cotta. The style is early Italian Renaissance. The groups of heroic size at the roof are Arion on a huge shell borne by dolphins accompanied by Tritons on the Park-Avenue side, and Prince Carnival with Terpsichore and the Genius of Music on the 59th-Street side.

The **Music Hall,** founded by Andrew Carnegie, at the corner of 57th Street and Seventh Avenue, has a main hall or auditorium for concerts, smaller rooms for chamber music, studios, rehearsals, fairs, and a gymnasium. The building, opened in May, 1891, is of mottled brick and terra cotta, in the style of the Venetian Renaissance. The house decoration is of pale salmon color, produced by a stenciling of white on a background of old rose. Music Hall is the home of the Oratorio Society. The Symphony and other societies play there.

The **Lenox Lyceum,** on Madison Avenue, near 59th Street, on the site of the Old Panorama, has the most beautiful but not the best in acoustics of the New-York music halls. The stage is under a shell-shaped building. The façade is of colored marbles. The style is early Italian Renaissance. The building was opened in January, 1890, and is fitted for concerts, fairs, banquets, balls and other festivals.

Semi-Artistic Societies and Scientific Organizations find in New York their great headquarters on the Western Hemisphere, and their collections and proceedings win the attention of the world.

The **New-York Historical Society,** at 170 Second Avenue, southeast corner of 11th Street, founded in 1804, incorporated in 1809, has a library of 100,000 volumes of reference, in large collections of scarce pamphlets, maps, newspapers, manuscripts, paintings and engravings, records of every phase in the progress of New York. Egbert Benson, DeWitt Clinton, William Linn, Samuel Miller, John N. Abeel, John M. Mason, David Hosack, Anthony Bleecker, Samuel Bayard, Peter G. Stuyvesant and John Pintard were its founders; and it never lacked the liberality, the public spirit, the influence and the labor of men like these. John Pintard gave paintings, books and manuscripts; James Lenox, marbles of Nineveh; Luman Reed, Thomas J. Bryan, Louis Durr, the New-York Gallery of Fine Arts and the American Art Union, paintings, books and statuary. The home of the society was in the City Hall from 1804 to 1809, in the Government House from 1809 to 1816, in the New-York Institution from 1816 to 1832, in Remsen's Building in Broadway from 1832 to 1837, in the Stuyvesant Institute from 1837 to 1841, in the

New-York University from 1841 to 1857. It could not be predicted in 1857, when the society took possession of its present edifice, that in less than half a century the rooms would be over-crowded. They are a solid mass of books and paintings and statuary and antiquities. In the Department of Antiquities, the larger collections consist of the celebrated Abbott Collection of Egyptian Antiquities, purchased for the institution in 1859; the Nineveh Sculptures; and a considerable collection of relics of the American aborigines. The Gallery of Art includes 835 paintings and 63 pieces of sculpture. Here, in addition to the society's early collection of paintings and sculpture, is the largest and most important gal-

AMERICAN INSTITUTE HALL, 1079 THIRD AVENUE, BETWEEN 63D AND 64TH STREETS.

lery of historical portraits in the country, together with the original water-colors, 474 in number, prepared by Audubon for his work on Natural History ; the famous Bryan Gallery of Old Masters, presented to the society by the late Thomas J. Bryan in 1867 ; and the extensive Durr Collection, presented in 1881. The society is to erect a new building on a site which it has purchased, facing Central Park and the Museum of Natural History, on Central Park West, between 76th and 77th Streets. It will have a fire-proof building for its invaluable library, gallery and museum, and a large hall for meetings and lectures.

The American Institute, for the promotion of domestic industry, at 111 to 115 West 38th Street, gives every year in the fall, for two months, in the large building on Third Avenue, between 63d and 64th Streets, an exhibition of the latest inventions for advancing commerce, agriculture, manufactures and the arts. It awards premiums and certificates of merit, and publishes reports of its proceedings. Its library, of 15,000 volumes, interesting to scientific men, is freely opened to all the members and friends of the Institute. The American Institute was founded in 1828, and now has 2,000 members. The Polytechnic Association, Farmers' Club, and Photographic Section of the Institute hold frequent public meetings, lectures, and discussions.

AMERICAN GEOGRAPHICAL SOCIETY, 11 WEST 29TH STREET.

The American Geographical Society, at 11 West 29th Street, founded in 1852 and chartered in 1854, had for its first President the historian George Bancroft. It has a library of 25,000 volumes, an extensive collection of 8,000 maps, a treasury of valuable information not easily accessible elsewhere, and here well classified. It gives lectures by famous travellers and geographers, and issues a quarterly bulletin. Its privileges and advantages are for its 1,500 members, whose annual dues are $10.

The New-York Academy of Sciences was founded in 1817, under the name of the Lyceum of Natural History, which was changed in 1876. It began in 1824 the publication of *Annals*, and in 1881 of *Transactions*, wherein its labors are recorded. It has a valuable library of 8,000 volumes ; and meetings Monday evenings in Hamilton Hall of Columbia College. It has 300 members. Prof. John S. Newberry is President.

The American Society of Civil Engineers, founded in 1852, has an active membership of about 1,600, composed of engineers of good standing, and at least ten years' experience. Its house, at 127 East 23d Street, contains a large lecture hall, a library of 17,000 volumes — the finest and most comprehensive library on civil engineering in the country — and various other apartments. There are meetings of the society twice a month at its house, and an annual convention, which is held in the larger cities in rotation. The *Transactions* of the society are published monthly, and make two large volumes a year. The President is William Metcalf ; the Secretary, Francis Collingwood ; and the Treasurer, John Bogart.

21

The American Society of Mechanical Engineers, organized in 1880, with 40 members, now has on its membership roll the names of 1,600 mechanical engineers of good standing. Among the honorary members are Prof. Francis Reuleux of Berlin, and Sir Henry Bessemer of

England. There are two stated meetings of the organization a year — the annual meeting in November, which is held in a large hall in the society's house at 12 West 31st Street, and an annual convention in the spring, which may meet in any city. The society has a free public library, purely technical, of about 4,000 volumes. The *Transactions* of the society are published yearly, in a volume of about 1,000 pages. The President is Eckley B. Coxe, of Drifton, Pa.; the Secretary, Prof. Frederick R. Hutton of Columbia College ; and the Treasurer, William H. Wiley.

The American Institute of Mining Engineers, founded in 1871, numbers 2,000 members, including also metallurgists and chemists, many of them foreigners. It usually has three meetings a year, in different cities, and

AMERICAN SOCIETY OF MECHANICAL ENGINEERS.
12 WEST 31ST STREET.

the proceedings are published. The secretary is R. W. Raymond, 13 Burling Slip.

The American Numismatic and Archæological Society of New York has frequent meetings in its rooms at the Academy of Medicine Building, 17 West 43d Street. It was founded in 1858, and has 225 members. The cabinets contain 8,000 coins and medals ; and the library is the finest collection of numismatic books in America.

The American Ethnological Society was organized in 1842, by Albert Gallatin, John R. Bartlett, George Folsom, A. I. Cotheal, Francis L. Hawks, Theodore Dwight, Jr., Edward Robinson, Charles Welford, W. W. Turner, Henry R. Schoolcraft, A. W. Bradford, John L. Stephens, and Frederic Catherwood. Its first president was the Hon. Albert Gallatin, followed by the Rev. Dr. Edward Robinson, the Hon. George Folsom, and Dr. John Torrey. Its objects are the prosecution of inquiries into the origin, progress, and characteristics of the various races of men, especially into the origin and history of the aboriginal American nations, and the phenomena connected therewith ; the diversity of languages, the remains of ancient art, and traces of ancient civilization in Mexico, Central America, and Peru ; the arts, sciences and mythology of the American nations; and the earthworks and other monuments of the United States. Besides its resident membership, the society has numerous corresponding members in different countries. It has published three volumes of ethnological contributions, and gathered a considerable library and many ancient relics, which are deposited in the American Museum of Natural History, where its regular meetings are held. The officers are : President, Alex. I. Cotheal ; Corresponding Secretary, A. S. Bickmore; Recording Secretary, Rev. Dr. Browne ; Librarian, Anthony Woodward.

The **New-York Genealogical and Biographical Society,** incorporated in 1869, designs to procure and perpetuate whatever may relate to genealogy and biography, particularly of families and persons associated with the State of New York. Its library and hall, at the Berkeley Lyceum, 23 West 44th Street, are open to members and to others introduced by them. Gen. James Grant Wilson is the president. Meetings are held on the second and fourth Fridays of each month, excepting in July, August and September. *The New-York Genealogical and Biographical Record,* now in its 24th volume, is published under its supervision. The society has also published, as its first volume of collections, "Marriages from 1639 to 1801 in the Reformed Dutch Church, New York." Other volumes will follow, the intention being to print correctly the Record of the Reformed Dutch Church in New Amsterdam and New York.

The **American Chemical Society,** organized in 1876, has meetings in December and August, in various cities, and includes nearly all the leading American and many foreign chemists. It has published many valuable papers and journals. The New-York Section meets monthly at the University, on Washington Square.

The **New-York Mathematical Society** is of a national character. Among its 250 members are the prominent mathematicians in America. The meetings are held at Columbia College, on the first Saturday of each month. The society's *Bulletin* is the only journal in the English language devoted to historical and critical mathematical work. The officers are: President, Dr. Emory McClintock; Vice-President, Prof. Henry B. Fine; Secretary, Dr. Thomas S. Fiske; Treasurer, Harold Jacoby; Librarian, Prof. D. A. Murray; other members of the Council, Prof. Thomas Craig, Prof. W. Woolsey Johnson, Prof. J. E. Oliver, Prof. J. K. Rees, and Prof. J. H. Van Amringe.

The **American Microscopical Society** devotes itself to a study of microscopy, histology, optics, and kindred works. It was founded in 1865, and five years later was incorporated. It holds fortnightly meetings at 12 East 22d Street.

Other learned bodies are: Academy of Anthropology, in the Cooper Union; American Metrological Society on 49th Street, near Madison Avenue; New-York Horticultural Society, 26 West 28th Street; New-York Public Health Association, 12 West 31st Street; Electric Club, 17 East 21st Street; Sorosis, a society of women; and the Archæological Institute.

Debating and other Societies; clubs of authors, artists, newspaper men; informal meetings in modest rooms of lovers of poetry, worshippers of the beautiful, searchers of light and truth, merchants who are art-lovers; artists who are not Bohemians; exalted dilettantism, are contributors to the greatness of New York as active, as indefatigable as its famous men of business. The rapid growth of a high civic pride in New York is largely attributed to these agencies of enlightenment, stimulating among the people a municipal self-respect almost equal to that of Athens, or Florence, or Chicago.

The **Fowler & Wells Company** is a scientific institution that has a worldwide reputation. For nearly sixty years its founders and owners have maintained an office in the city of New York, and have been the recognized leaders in the phrenological, physiological and hygienic sciences, and for half a century they have been the main educators in these branches of useful study. They are classed in a business way as phrenologists and publishers, but they might well be called a scientific and educational institution. They occupy the building at 27 East 21st Street, near

Broadway, where is carried on the work inaugurated by Orson S. Fowler and Lorenzo N. Fowler in 1835. These men were the first in America to give the science of phrenology a practical value by making special delineations of character. They began work in a small way, but steadily increased its scope. In 1843 they were joined by Samuel R. Wells, who subsequently married Charlotte Fowler, the sister of his partners. In course of time both the Fowlers withdrew from the house. Orson, who was one of the most famous phrenologists of the world, died in 1887. Lorenzo still practices his profession in London. Mr. Wells conducted the business of the original house until his death, in 1875, and his widow, Charlotte F. Wells, assumed the management until 1884. Then the Fowler & Wells Company was incorporated, with Charlotte Fowler Wells, President; Nelson Sizer, Vice-President and phrenological examiner; Dr. H. S. Drayton, Secretary and general editor of the company's publications; and Albert Turner, Treasurer and business manager.

FOWLER & WELLS CO. AND AMERICAN INSTITUTE OF PHRENOLOGY,
27 EAST 21st STREET, NEAR BROADWAY.

The company publishes *The Phrenological Journal*, of which the ninety-fifth volume has just been completed, a number of serial publications, and a large list of standard works on phrenology, physiognomy, ethnology, physiology, psychology and hygiene. It has handsome business offices and spacious editorial rooms, lecture-rooms and phrenological parlors, where examinations are made and charts given daily, indicating choice of pursuits, means of culture, etc. An outgrowth of the business of the concern is the American Institute of Phrenology, which was incorporated as an educational institution in 1866. Among the original incorporators were Horace Greeley, Rev. Dr. Samuel Osgood, Judge Amos Dean, Henry Dexter, Samuel R. Wells, Lester A. Roberts, Edward P. Fowler, M. D., and Nelson Sizer. Each year, beginning on the first Tuesday in September, a course of instruction in practical phrenology is given by a corps of experts, under the direction of Prof. Sizer, the President of the Institute. An interesting feature in the lecture-room of the Fowler & Wells Company's building is a large collection of casts of the heads of people who have been prominent in various ways in past years; also, skulls from many nations and tribes, as well as animal crania, illustrative of phrenology, and constituting a free public museum, and material for instruction in the institute.

The Literary Culture.

Libraries and Reading Rooms. Public, Club, Society and Private.

THE libraries of New York are nearly perfect. They have not only quantity and quality; they have availability. In this respect they are easily in advance of those of the great cities of Europe. There books accumulate, while librarians, literary men whom the government has rewarded with sinecures, study special works, or write on special subjects. The American business education has admirably mingled book-lore, literary tact and commercial order in the formation and management of libraries. Here books are classified, catalogued, inventoried, better than was ever imagined. If the treasures be not as rich as in countries that have lived ages, the service of such treasures as there is is quicker, surer and more gratifying. At the Bibliothèque Nationale one may obtain any books, but the process is slow, and at the end of it one is in a doubt that may not be solved, for there is no way of telling if the books obtained were not less valuable than others obtainable. The libraries of New York are without secrets.

The Astor Library, on the east side of Lafayette Place, is an ideal public library of works of reference. As it has no artificial light, the building must be closed at sunset. As it has a perfect system of classification, book catalogues, card catalogues, and the quickest and ablest of librarians and assistants, its hours count double. There are not all the treasures of the British Museum and the Bibliothèque Nationale, but the fact is not easily discovered. "He gives twice who gives quickly," says the ancient proverb. The Astor Library gives quickly. Suggested by Washington Irving and Dr. J. C. Cogswell to John Jacob Astor, the library was founded by virtue of a codicil of Mr. Astor's will, which bequeathed for the purpose $400,000. It was incorporated January 1, 1849. The trustees were Washington Irving, William B. Astor, Dr. Cogswell, and others. Then there were 20,000 volumes, the cost of which had been $27,000. In 1854 the library was opened to the public. In 1859 William B. Astor, son of the founder, built a second hall in Lafayette Place, and gave, in all, $550,000. In 1864 Dr. Cogswell made a printed catalogue of the library, which then numbered 100,000 volumes. In 1881 John Jacob Astor, grandson of the founder, erected the third hall of the library, his gifts exceeding $800,000.

The building, of brownstone, has 200 feet of front and 100 feet of depth. The exterior is graceful, the interior is as bright as a house of glass. The entrance is through a Pompeian vestibule, bordered with pedestals of colored marble, on which are busts in white marble, sculptured by a Florentine artist, of the great and wise men of ancient Greece and Rome. There is a wide stairway to the Middle Hall, where are the librarians and the catalogues, tables for women, a department for students of patents, alcoves for special students, and in glass-covered cases curious autographs, specimens of missals, books of hours, early typography and marvels of the art of book binding. The south building is the hall of science and art ; the north building is that of history and philosophy. There are 90 alcoves ; each alcove has 20 presses ; each press has 7 shelves, with a capacity for 175 volumes.

ASTOR LiBRARY, LAFAYETTE PLACE, BETWEEN ASTOR PLACE AND GREAT JONES STREET.

The ground floor, yet unused for books, may hold 250,000 volumes. There, in the south room, used by the trustees for their meetings, is a collection of paintings, presented to the library by William Waldorf Astor, comprising works of Saintin, Madrazo, Toulmouche, Knaus, Gifford, Leroux, Muller, Meissonier, Schreyer, Berne-Bellecour and Lefebvre. There are marble busts of John Jacob Astor, Dr. Cogswell and Washington Irving ; a portrait of William B. Astor, by Eastman Johnson ; of Alexander Hamilton, by Huntington ; of Daniel Lord, by Hicks ; and of Fitz-Greene Halleck, by Prof. S. F. B. Morse. This collection is open to the public every Wednesday. Frederick Saunders is the chief librarian.

The Astor Library contains 250,000 books and 15,000 pamphlets. Each year the library has more than 50,000 readers, reading nearly 200,000 books, besides 8,000 visitors to the alcoves. The trustees are the Mayor, *ex-officio*, Hamilton Fish, Dr. T. M. Markoe (president), Prof. Henry Drisler (secretary), J. L. Cadwalader, Rt. Rev. H. C. Potter, S. V. R. Cruger, Robbins Little (superintendent), Stephen H. Olin, Edward King (treasurer) and Charles H. Russell. This is the foremost American library in mathematics, Egyptology, South American and Mexican history, and Orientalia. It is a free reference library, open all day, and affording a delightful retreat for scholars.

The Lenox Library, on Fifth Avenue, between 70th and 71st Streets, is a curiosity of the world. It is the library of a bibliophilist, made public. The gift of James Lenox, a retired merchant of New York, who loved books immeasurably, it was incorporated January 20, 1870. It was the private collection of Mr. Lenox, a mysterious, fabulously beautiful and valuable collection, guarded in a house which was a fortress ; it became a public collection, as free as the trees in the Central Park. Mr. Lenox would not show his books to his friends ; braved public opinion by refusing to let Prescott consult his Mexican manuscripts ; barred the great book-binder, Matthews, between two doors of a vestibule, that he might neither quit nor catch a glimpse of the sacred library room ; and at one stroke, in the gravest deliber-ation, gave his treasures to the world. He named nine trustees, including himself; gave the land, the books, and funds for a building ; and in 1875 the Lenox Library was a dream realized. The building is of white stone,, a solid and graceful struc-ture, with two projecting wings. The entrance is by two massive gateways, a court, wide stairs, and a vestibule laid in tiles of white marble, between walls skirted with a dove-colored marble base. The stairs to the upper stories are of stone, and have balustrades in iron scroll-work. The rooms have vaulted ceilings, the walls priceless paintings, the cases for books inestimable works. There are missals, Bibles, incun-abula, Americana, master-pieces of ancient and modern literature in original editions, curiosities of printing that most book-lovers have heard of and never seen elsewhere. There are autographs, ceramics, glassware. There are paintings by Landseer, Gains-borough, Bierstadt, Turner, Ruysdael, Peale, Delaroche, Stuart, Reynolds, Munkacsy. There are marble busts of great sculptors. There are the marvelous Drexel musical

LENOX LIBRARY, FIFTH AVENUE, 70TH AND 71ST STREETS.

library, and the Robert Lenox Kennedy collection. There are the admirable books of the R. L. Stuart legacy, and those of Evert A. Duyckinck. The number of vol-umes exceeds 70,000. The library is open, free, from 10 to 5, except in July, August and September. The architect of the building was Richard M. Hunt.

The **Mercantile Library** is at the junction of 8th Street, Astor Place and Lafayette Place, on the sixth and seventh floors of a substantial building of buff brick and red sandstone, erected by the trustees of the library and the Clinton-Hall Association.   It is a reference library and a circulating library for members, whose

annual dues are $5. Works of art and other costly publications must remain in the library rooms as books of reference, but standard, instructive, popular, historical and scientific books are kept in circulation. The library was founded November 9, 1820, by clerks of merchants.   In 1821, in one room at 49 Fulton Street, it had 150 members and 700 volumes.   In 1826, in the building of Harper & Brothers, in Cliff Street, it had 6,000 volumes.   In 1828 the merchants, made enthusiastic by the achievement of the clerks, organ-

MERCANTILE LIBRARY, ASTOR PLACE, 8TH STREET AND LAFAYETTE PLACE.

ized the Clinton-Hall Association for the purpose of giving a building to the library. This association, in 1830, erected the first Clinton Hall, on the corner of Nassau and Beekman Streets, where Temple Court now stands,   In 1854 the association and its books were removed to the Astor-Place Opera-House, which had been re-modelled for the purpose.   In 1891 the historic opera-house was taken down, and in its place was built the present Clinton Hall.   The library rooms have shelf space for 475,000 volumes.   There are 50,000 volumes in the department of works of reference, and 245,000 in the entire library.   The librarian is W. T. Peoples.

The **New-York Society Library** is the oldest in the city.   It was at first the Public Library, founded in 1700 during the administration of the Earl of Bellomont ; augmented in 1729 with the library presented to the Society for the Propagation of the Gospel in Foreign Parts, by Dr. Millington, Rector of Newington, England ; and until 1754 in the inefficient charge of the corporation of the city.   Then several citizens united with it their private libraries, and placed the entire collection, which they called the City Library, in the charge of trustees.   In 1772 George III. granted a charter to the trustees, in the name of the "New-York Society Library." The establishment is still the property of a corporation, the shares in which have a market value, but any person may, with the approbation of the Board of Trustees, become a member of the corporation and be entitled to one right in the library for every sum of $25 paid to the treasurer. There are yearly dues on all shares, except the free shares. The amount has been increased at various times since 1819, when it was $4. Now the maximum is $10. These annual dues may be commuted by the payment of $125 for the annual payment of $10, $75 for the annual payment of $6, and $50 for the annual payment of $4, on the respective rights subject to these payments. Until 1795 the library was in the City Hall, and it was in reality the first Library of Congress. Then a building, large and remarkable for its time, was erected especially for the library in Nassau Street, opposite the Middle Dutch Church. In 1836 this building was sold. The books were removed to the rooms of the Mechanics' Society, in Chambers Street, and remained there until 1840, when a new building of the library, at the corner of Broadway and Leonard Street, was finished. In 1853 this edifice was sold, and the books were kept in the Bible House until 1856, when the present library building, at 67 University Place, was finished. In 1793 there were 5,000 volumes; in 1813, 13,000; in 1825, 16,000; in 1838, 25,000 volumes. There are at present 90,000 volumes. Many valuable gifts have been made to the library. The most notable one was made by Mrs. Sarah H. Green, a gift of $50,000 from the estate of her husband, John C. Green. The income is used for the purchase of books, one half of which circulate among the members. The other half are costly illustrated works and are placed in a department called the "John C. Green Alcove." The librarian is Wentworth S. Butler. He

was appointed in 1856, and is the sixth incumbent since 1793. A list of persons holding rights in the Society Library includes nearly all of the most ancient and wealthy families of the city.

The Free Library of the General Society of Mechanics and Tradesmen (formerly the Apprentices' Library), at 18 East 16th Street, circulates its books, without charge, among persons approved by the General Society of Mechanics and Tradesmen. This society, founded in 1785 for the relief of widows and orphans, gave free instruction to apprentices, when there were no free schools. When its exclusive benevolence in that respect was a little impaired by the establishing of

NEW-YORK SOCIETY LIBRARY, 67 UNIVERSITY PLACE.

public schools, the society began to circulate freely the books of its library. The library was formed in 1820, in rooms of the Free-School Building. In 1821 it was in the society's building in Chambers Street; in 1832, in a building in Crosby Street, extending to 472 Broadway. The present building was adapted to library purposes in 1878. In the cases on the walls are interesting relics, old books, deeds, flags, the

APPRENTICES' LIBRARY, 18 EAST 16TH STREET.

skull (yellow as ivory) of a famous pirate, an iron key of the Bastile, old newspapers and playbills. There are 95,000 volumes, having a yearly circulation of 250,000, absolutely free, with the exceptions of books of the De Milt bequest, the charge for which is trivial. William Wood, who originated the idea of forming the Apprentices' Library of New York, established the one in Boston. He also signed the first call for a meeting which resulted in the establishment of the Mercantile Library. J. Schwartz is the librarian.

The New-York Historical Society maintains, at 170 Second Avenue, an establishment that is at once a library, an art-gallery and a museum. It has been in existence since 1804. There are in the library 100,000 books, 2,700 bound volumes of newspapers and large collections of pamphlets and manuscripts. On American history and genealogy a vast quantity of information is available. The art-gallery contains many works of the earliest American artists, such as Benjamin West, the Peales, Stuart, Trumbull and Durand, and also a large number of paintings by old Italian masters. The Abbott collection of Egyptian antiquities, the Lenox collection of Assyrian sculptures, rare and curious medals and coins and specimens of Mexican and Indian antiquities constitute the museum. The establishment is open daily excepting Sundays and the month of August. Admission may be had by means of an introduction by a member of the society.

The Young Men's Christian Association Library occupies a rectangle in the magnificent building of the Association, at the southwest corner of 23d Street and Fourth Avenue. There are three tiers of books, on three sides. The books in the upper tiers are reached by winding stairways and balconies. William Niblo bequeathed $150,000 to the Association for the purchase of books and the support of the library. In 1870 there were 3,500 volumes; there are at present 42,000. The northern end of the room is occupied by the librarian, Reuben B. Poole, and his assistants. He has classified the library in accordance with the Dewey decimal system and Cutter's dictionary catalogue. The library is varied and valuable. It has 43 early-printed Bibles which antedate 1700, including the Koburger Bible of 1477, Luther's Bible of 1541, the Bishop's Bible of 1568, and one in French of the eighteenth century, bound in marvellous covers of mosaic leather. A relic of great interest is a musical manuscript of the thirteenth century, containing the Ambrosian ritual for the entire year. The manuscript is decorated with brilliant miniatures and initial letters. It has an autotype of the Codex-Alexandrinus, a printed fac-simile of the Frederico-Augustanus Codex, and a photographic fac-simile of the Codex-Vaticanus (1889–90). It has many works on art useful to architects and decorators, and representative works in different languages. The collected portraits number about 17,000, including one unique collection of 8,000, in 35 volumes, formed mainly by John Percival, Earl of Egmont, A. D. 1 to 1736. This library is almost the only one that is open evenings and holidays. The hours are from 8.30 A. M. to 10 P. M.

Membership in the Association includes the privileges of the library; and all reputable persons, male or female, are admitted to its use, whether members or not.

The Cooper-Union Library, in the Cooper Institute, is one result of the work of the six intelligent, benevolent and public-spirited trustees, to whom Peter Cooper deeded in fee simple, on April 29, 1859, an extensive property, with the injunction that it, "together with the appurtenances and the rents, issues, income and profits thereof, shall be forever devoted to the instruction and improvement of the inhabitants of the United States, in practical science and art." There are 34,000 bound volumes, besides 471 newspapers and periodicals on file, and a complete set of the Patent-Office reports. All are accessible to the public every day, including a part of Sunday. There were last year 1,650 readers daily.

The Maimonides Library, 203 East 57th Street, corner of Third Avenue, was founded by District Grand Lodge No. 1 of the Order of B'nai B'rith, in accordance with its law that commands intellectual advancement. It contains about 40,000 volumes. The library is general in character and contents. Its departments of political and social science and education are very full. Special interest is devoted also to Jewish literature. There are books written by Jews and other writers on Judaic topics, in all languages, besides books in every branch of knowl-

HISTORICAL SOCIETY.   BAPTIST TABERNACLE.
NEW-YORK HISTORICAL SOCIETY, SECOND AVENUE AND EAST 11TH STREET.

edge. The library is easily accessible to the public every day except Saturdays and Jewish holidays. The librarian is Max Cohen.

The Free Circulating Library has four library buildings, situated at 49 Bond Street, 135 Second Avenue, 226 West 42d Street and 251 West 13th Street, and a distributing station at 1943 Madison Avenue, near 125th Street. The library was incorporated March 15, 1880, and re-incorporated under special charter April 18, 1884. Its object is clearly defined in its title. In March, 1880, it occupied two rented rooms at 36 Bond Street, and circulated 1,004 volumes. In May,

NEW-YORK FREE CIRCULATING LIBRARY,
251 WEST 13TH STREET.

1883, it had a new library building at 49 Bond Street, and then gave circulation to 6,983 volumes. It has a special Woman's Fund, founded in 1882, for the employment of women and the purchase of books. In 1884 Oswald Ottendorfer founded the Second-Avenue Branch, in the centre of the German district. It is called the Ottendorfer Library, and is maintained with the aid of a special fund of $10,000 and of frequent contributions of the founder. In 1887 Miss Catherine Wolfe Bruce founded the 42d-Street Branch, and gave $30,000 for its maintenance. The building was opened in 1888. It is called the George Bruce Memorial Library. The 13th-Street Branch, founded by George W. Vanderbilt, was opened July 6, 1888. The ten founders who contributed $5,000 or more each, were John Jacob Astor, Miss Catherine Wolfe Bruce, Andrew Carnegie, Mrs. Benjamin H. Field, Julius Hallgarten, Henry G. Marquand, Oswald Ottendorfer, Jacob H. Schiff, George W. Vanderbilt and Mrs. C. F. Woerishoffer.

There were also 22 patrons, each of whom gave $1,000 ; 80 life-members, each contributing $200 ; 62 associate members, paying $25 a year; and 154 annual members, at $10 a year each. The city government grants to the library from $10,000 to $15,000 a year, in accordance with the State Legislative Act of 1886, to encourage the growth of free public libraries. The library has 65,000 volumes, and a yearly circulation of 500,000. The cost of distribution per volume is smaller than in the great libraries of Boston, Chicago or Baltimore.

The Columbia-College Library, at 41 East 49th Street, has 160,000 volumes, beside the libraries of the Huguenot Society, the New-York Academy of Science, and Townsend's Civil-War Record. The Avery Architectural Library has 9,000 volumes, richly illustrated, on architecture, decoration and the allied arts. Over 900 different serials are currently received. The library includes all the standard works of reference indispensable to students, the costly classics, the masterpieces of literature, the scientific works and books of law. The library is open day and evening, to students and scholars. George H. Baker is librarian.

The Law Libraries include the noble collection of the Law Institute, in the Post-Office Building ; the 41,000 volumes of the Bar Association's Library, at 7 West 29th Street, between Broadway and Fifth Avenue ; and the admirable and extensive collections of the law-schools of Columbia College and the University. The Harlem Law Library, on West 125th Street, near Lenox Avenue, is for reference. The Law Library of the Equitable Life-Assurance Society, at 120 Broadway, is intended for the use of the officers of the society, the tenants of the building, and members of the Lawyers' Club. It has 14,000 volumes.

Theological Libraries of great value are found at Union Theological Seminary (70,000 volumes) and the General Theological Seminary (23,000 volumes), including several special collections of historical interest. There is also one in the Methodist Book-Concern building.

Medical Libraries.—The Mott Memorial Library, at 64 Madison Avenue, has 3,000 medical and surgical books, mainly collected by Dr. Valentine Mott, and free to medical students and physicians. The library of the New-York Academy of Medicine (50,000 volumes) is at 17 West 43d Street ; that of the New-York Hospital (25,000 volumes), 6 West 16th Street, founded in 1796, and open free daily. The great medical schools have very extensive and valuable libraries.

Special Libraries include those of the American Numismatic and Archæological Society (6,000 books and pamphlets), at 17 West 43d Street ; the American Geographical Society (25,000 volumes and 8,000 maps), at 11 West 29th Street ; the Gaelic Society (1,200 volumes), at 17 West 28th Street ; the New York Genea-

logical and Biographical Society (2,500 volumes), at 19 West 44th Street ; the American Institute Library (14,000 volumes), at 113 West 38th Street ; the Museum of Natural History Library (27,000 volumes), in Central Park West ; the American Society of Civil Engineers (17,000 volumes), at 127 East 23d Street ; and the American Society of Mechanical Engineers (5,000 volumes), at 12 West 31st Street. There is a Free Circulating Library for the Blind at 296 Ninth Avenue.

The Produce Exchange and the Maritime Exchange have good libraries for their members.

The Masonic Library is at Sixth Avenue and 23d Street ; and the Odd Fellows' Library is at 2374 Park Avenue.

The Young Women's Christian Association, at 7 East 15th Street, has a library of 13,000 volumes ; and there are other libraries for women at 19 Clinton Street, and 16 Clinton Place.

Seamen's Libraries are provided by benevolent persons, to be carried away on ships for the diver-

MOTT MEMORIAL FREE MEDICAL LIBRARY, 64 MADISON AVENUE, NEAR EAST 27TH STREET.

sion and solace of the mariners. The headquarters of this work of the Seamen's Loan Libraries is at 76 Wall Street, under the care of the American Seamen's Friend Society. The Protestant Episcopal Mission Society Library for seamen is at 21 Coenties Slip ; the Seamen's Library, at 34 Pike Street ; the New-York Port Society Library, at 46 Catherine Street.

Miscellaneous Libraries include the First-Ward, at 135 Greenwich Street ; the Broome-Street ; the Five-Points Mission at 63 Park Street ; the Benjamin-Townsend, at the foot of East 26th Street ; the Children's, at 590 Seventh Avenue ;

the Harlem, at 2,238 Third Avenue; St. Mark's Memorial, at 228 East 10th Street; Washington-Heights, at Amsterdam Avenue and 156th Street; St. Barnabas, at 38 Bleecker Street; the Lorraine, at 41 West 31st Street.

The Aguilar Free Library was established in 1886, and has departments at 197 East Broadway, 721 Lexington Avenue, and 624 East 5th Street.

The libraries of clubs like the University, Century, Lotos and Press Clubs have invaluable standard and reference books. The Grolier Club has an inimitable collection of books about books; the Players' Club, a valuable collection of books about the drama; the Aldine Club is forming a collection of books about book-making.

The Private Libraries of Robert Hoe, missals, manuscripts and general literature; of William Loring Andrews, typographical curiosities, New-York City relics and books bound by Roger Payne; of Samuel P. Avery, master-pieces of book-binding; of George Beach de Forest, Elzevirs, books with vignettes of the eighteenth century, books with original illustrations; of C. Jolly-Bavoillot, Romanticists of France; of Marshall Lefferts, Americana; of C. B. Foote, works by modern English and American authors; of Rush C. Hawkins, first books printed everywhere, Incunabula; of Beverly Chew, works of the Elizabethan era; are easily accessible to serious students.

Three hundred members of the Grolier Club are men who have formed libraries. Every literary, artistic or simply social circle has its library. In New York where men have the distinctive business air of the ancient Venetian merchants, the fate of a man in search of a fortune may not be enviable, but the fate of a man in search of knowledge is the fate of a favorite of the gods.

FIFTH AVENUE, LOOKING NORTH FROM 42D STREET.

Shrines of Worship·

Cathedrals, Churches, Synagogues and Other Places of Religious Worship and Work.

NEARLY all religious creeds are represented in New York. The ecclesiastical annals of the city form a most interesting chapter in its history, and the churches have played an important part all through its development. Earnest men have filled its pulpits. Many of its charitable, educational and reformatory institutions owe their origin to the labors of the clergy, nobly seconded by zealous laymen.

The multiplication of churches has kept a fairly even pace with the increase in population. From 1638 to 1697 the Reformed Dutch Church was the only place of worship. The coming of the British in 1664 gave the Church of England a foothold on the island, and in 1697 its first house of worship was erected, on the site of the modern Trinity. From 1697 to 1770 the number of churches increased but slowly, and in the latter year fifteen ecclesiastical edifices sufficed for the ten different denominations. The outbreak of the Revolution temporarily suspended all thoughts of church extension, and it was not until the coming of more peaceful times that the churches began to multiply. In 1845 there were 245 houses of worship in the city. Now there are 600, with nearly an equal number of Sunday-schools. The average attendance is 150,000. These 600 churches, representing nearly all religious faiths, and many styles of architecture, provide sittings for nearly half a million worshippers, and, with the land on which they stand, have a valuation of $75,000,000. Their yearly disbursements, including salaries, amount to $5,000,000. The combined membership of all the religious societies of the city, including Protestant, Catholic and Hebrew organizations, is not far from 700,000, not quite one-half the total population. This includes, however, the large claims made by the Catholic Church, whose method of including baptized infants, as well as adults, in estimating church-membership, differs wholly from that of the Protestant Church.

The religious history of New York is remarkably free from the bitter persecutions that characterized the early history of many of the other colonies. The early Dutch settlers were a kindly and tolerant folk, in the main, and the English had not been long in possession of the Province when the outbreak and successful issue of the War of Independence gave liberty of conscience and faith to all religious opinions. The early law, forbidding the holding of public worship other than that allowed by the authorities, never very strictly enforced, and easily evaded ; the brief imprisonment of a few Quaker refugees from Massachusetts ; the hanging of a Roman Catholic for alleged complicity in the Negro Riot of 1741, with the added accusation of being a Catholic priest ; a Baptist and a Presbyterian clergyman imprisoned for brief periods, and a Lutheran minister forbidden to preach in the Province — these form the scanty annals of religious persecution.

The churches have shared in the northward migration of the citizens. The early edifices were in the extreme southern portion of the island ; but when the city began its journey to the north, they began to desert the old historic sites, and seek new ones in the up-town districts, leaving scarcely a score in their old locations. To-day the finest of the city's churches stand where forty years ago were green fields and the pleasant country-seats of the magnates of the city.

The Collegiate Reformed Protestant Dutch Church was the first ecclesiastical organization in New York. In 1628 the Rev. Jonas Michaelius reached the "Island of Manhattas," and immediately organized a church, with the worthy Director Minuit as one of the elders. The meetings were held in the loft of a horse-mill until 1633, when a small wooden church was built in Broad Street. In the same year the Rev. Everardus Bogardus came over from Holland, with Adam

COLLEGIATE CHURCH, 5TH AVENUE AND WEST 48TH STREET.

Roelandsen, a schoolmaster, who opened the first church-school in America, the latter still in existence as the Collegiate Grammar School. In 1642 a small stone church was erected within the walls of Fort Amsterdam, and called St. Nicholas, in honor of the patron saint of Manhattan, and here for half a century the early Dutch settlers met for worship. The first Dutch church outside the walls of the fort was built in 1693 in Garden Street (now Exchange Place). The Old Middle Church was built in 1729, in Nassau Street, and the North Church in 1769, in William Street. For nearly a century and a half these three churches, forming but one parish, then and now called the Collegiate Reformed Protestant Dutch Church (although the name does not appear upon the records, and has no legal authority), were the only Reformed Dutch churches in the city.

The Collegiate Church received a royal charter from King William III. in 1696 ; and now has four churches and as many mission chapels, all under the control of a central body called the Consistory, composed of the ministers of the four congregations, with twelve elders and twelve deacons, chosen from the congregations. During the 264 years of its existence the church has had twelve different houses of worship

and thirty-one ministers, many of the latter widely known for eloquence and commanding influence, including John Henry Livingston, William Linn (who was chaplain of the first Congress of the United States), Jacob Brodhead,

Philip Milledoler, John Knox, Thomas De Witt, Joseph T. Duryea, William Ormiston, and Thomas E. Vermilye.

The consistory of the parish meets monthly, in the consistory-room of the church at 48th Street; and the congregations, besides holding their own communion services, join in the reception of the Lord's Supper once yearly, in the church at 29th Street. The parish has 2,146 communicants. The Reformed Dutch churches in the city number 22, besides several missions and chapels. Of these, the four churches mentioned as under the control of the consistory of the Collegiate Church constitute, technically, a single parish, as is the case in the Episcopal Church with Trinity and its chapels. These four are at Second Avenue and 7th Street; at Fifth Avenue and 29th Street; at Fifth Avenue and 48th Street, and at West-End Avenue and 77th Street. The senior minister of the Collegiate Church is the Rev. Talbot W. Chambers, S. T. D., LL. D., and as such he has a general oversight of the whole parish.

MIDDLE COLLEGIATE CHURCH, SECOND AVENUE AND 7TH STREET.

The Middle Collegiate Church built its first shrine in 1729, on Nassau Street, on the site now occupied by the Mutual Life-Insurance Company. Its second church, from 1839 to 1887, was in Lafayette Place. In 1891–92 a third edifice was erected, at Second Avenue and 7th Street, to hold a site for religious worship well down-town. It is a handsome structure in the Gothic style of architecture, built of limestone, with a graceful spire. The pulpit is an object famous among old New-Yorkers, having originally been in the church in Lafayette Place. It is of pure statuary marble. The windows are of stained glass, made by the Tiffany Glass and Decorating Co.; and present a unique and very brilliant feature by reason of receiving their illumination, day and night, from electric lights behind the glass. The subjects of the windows are from the life of Christ, after designs by Heinrich Hoffmann of Dresden. The minister in charge of the Middle Church is the Rev. John Hutchins. In connection with this church is a hand-

COLLEGIATE CHURCH, FIFTH AVENUE AND WEST 29TH STREET.

22

some Church House, facing on 7th Street, and thoroughly equipped with reading-rooms, gymnasium, and all the appliances for aggressive modern church work.

The **Marble Collegiate Church**, at Fifth Avenue and 29th Street (popularly known as "the Marble Church"), is a massive marble building, erected in 1851 – 1854, in a simple type of Gothic architecture. The large auditorium is attractively decorated, and contains a triple organ, with electric wires connecting the different parts. The old bell which hung in the belfry of one of the Collegiate churches stands at the left of the entrance, bearing an inscription stating that it was cast in Amsterdam in 1768. A special feature of the church is its work among the apartment-houses and large hotels in the vicinity, and its courtesy to strangers is famous. The Rev. Dr. David James Burrell is the minister in charge, with two assistants.

The **Fifth-Avenue Collegiate Church**, at Fifth Avenue and 48th Street, is a strikingly beautiful edifice, of Newark sandstone, in the decorated Gothic architec-

COLLEGIATE REFORMED CHURCH, AT WEST-END AVENUE AND 77TH STREET.

ture of the fourteenth century, with a lofty spire, flying buttresses, numerous gables, and a colonnaded entrance-porch on the avenue. A flying buttress on the northern corner supports a small spire, which adds to the symmetry of the front. The interior has a lofty groined roof, resting upon exquisitely carved stone and marble pillars. The organ-gallery is picturesque, and the walls are delicately tinted. The church was dedicated in 1872. The minister in charge, Dr. Edward B. Coe, is one of the most esteemed preachers in the city.

The **West-End Avenue Collegiate Church**, at West-End Avenue and 77th Street, was built in 1891 – 92, after designs by R. W. Gibson; and is a large and imposing structure in quaint Flemish architecture, with decorated crow-step gables and many pinnacles, and ornate dormer-windows in the roof. The interior is decorated in old ivory effects and harmonious tints of orange. Dark cross-beams under the roof carry out the Flemish idea. Pillars of Tennessee marble support the arches. The pulpit and choir-stalls are elaborately carved ; and the communion-table is copied from that in Leonardo de Vinci's picture of "The Last Supper." The minister in charge is the Rev. Henry Evertson Cobb.

The Fulton-Street Prayer-Meeting is the outcome of a missionary enterprise of the Collegiate Reformed Church, and the meetings have been held in the Consistory building, at 113 Fulton Street, since they were begun, in 1857, with no deviation from the original plan, which was "to give merchants, mechanics, clerks, strangers and business men generally, an opportunity to stop and call upon God amid the daily perplexities incident to their respective avocations." The meetings are held daily, at noon, and continue for one hour, but the visitor is at liberty to leave at any time. When the desire is expressed, prayer is offered for individual needs and perplexities, and the meetings have been a source of comfort and encouragement to thousands.

The First Collegiate Reformed Church of Harlem began with the election of John LaMontagne as deacon, in the year 1660, when Harlem was a venturesome journey from the little burgh of New Amsterdam. For the long period of 105 years the good burghers of Harlem were compelled to depend upon their "Vorleser," or reader, and the help of neighboring clergy-

men, for their Sunday instruction in the Scriptures. Good old Dominie Selyns occasionally used to ride over to the little settlement on the Harlem from his Brooklyn charge, in the days of Peter Stuyvesant ; and later, Dominies Drisius and Niewenhuysen came now and then from the lower end of the island for a Sunday service ; but it was not until just before the outbreak of the Revolution that a minister was settled over the church, Rev. Martinius Schoonmaker, who has had eight successors. The present church, a plain building with pillared front, on 121st Street, near Third Avenue, was dedicated in 1835. Its minister is Rev. Dr. Joachim Elmendorf.

The Second Collegiate Reformed Church of Harlem has its beautiful Gothic house of worship at 267 Lenox Avenue, at the corner of 123d Street. Rev. W. J. Harsha is the pastor.

SECOND COLLEGIATE REFORMED CHURCH OF HAR-LEM, LENOX AVENUE AND WEST 123D STREET.

The South Reformed Dutch Church, at Madison Avenue and East 38th Street, is one of the oldest ecclesiastical organizations in the city. Its earlier history, previous to the year 1812, is connected with that of the Collegiate Church, of which it formed a part. The first South Church, erected in Garden Street, in 1693, was a solid and substantial building, with an imposing belfry and round-arched windows. The old church was torn down in 1807, to make room for a larger building, destroyed by fire in 1835. Previous to this, in 1812, the South Church had become independent of the North and Middle Collegiate Churches, and assumed the title of "The Ministers, Elders and Deacons of the Reformed Protestant Dutch Church in Garden Street in the City of New

York," which is still the legal title of the society. Differences of opinion regarding the advisability of rebuilding on the old site led to the formation of a new society, which built the church now owned by the Asbury Methodists, in Washington Square, while the old society erected a church in Murray Street, followed in 1849 by a larger and more imposing building on Fifth Avenue. This was sold in 1890, and the present Gothic stone church, formerly Zion Episcopal Church, was purchased and re-decorated. The large memorial window in the west end, representing the Nativity, Baptism and Resurrection of Our Lord, is the work of the Tiffany Company. The first minister of the South Church after its separation from the Collegiate Church was Dr. James M. Matthews, who became Chancellor of the University of the City of New York in 1834. The Rev. Roderick Terry, D. D., is now in charge, and the parish is prospering.

SOUTH REFORMED DUTCH CHURCH, MADISON AVENUE AND 38TH STREET.

The Madison-Avenue Reformed Church, at the corner of 57th Street, an imposing Gothic brownstone building, was erected in 1870. The society, formerly known as the Northwest Reformed Church, was organized in 1808, and worshipped in a church on Franklin Street until 1854, when it moved to a more eligible location on East 23d Street. The Madison-Avenue Church has a seating capacity of 1,000, and with its galleries, groined roof and picturesque arrangement of round arches, the interior is extremely attractive and commodious. The minister is Rev. Dr. Abbott E. Kittredge.

The Thirty-Fourth Street Reformed Dutch Church, at 307 West 34th Street, was organized in 1823, and its first church was a modest brick structure at Broome and Greene Streets. Under the ministerial care of Dr. Jacob Brodhead and Dr. Samuel A. Van Vranken it attracted large and fashionable congregations. Dr. Brodhead was one of the most eloquent preachers of his day, and Dr. Van Vranken possessed pulpit talents of a high order. Later, the ministerial charge was assumed by the Rev. Dr. George H. Fisher and the Rev. Henry V. Voorhees, both noted preachers. In 1860 the present large Gothic church was built. It is of brick, with yellow stone front and double towers, and the interior is plain and comfortable, with free pews and a very sweet-toned organ. Previous to the building of the new church, the members of the Livingston Reformed Church, then worshipping in a hall on 33d Street, united with the 34th-Street parish, adding materially to its strength and influence. The minister is the Rev. Dr. Peter Stryker, a writer, lecturer, and active worker in the temperance cause.

The Bloomingdale Reformed Church is at 68th Street, where it crosses the Boulevard. It is one of the most impressive and stately of all the churches in this region, and has a noble Gothic spire. The Rev. Madison C. Peters is the pastor.

Trinity Church is the chief edifice of the Protestant Episcopal Church, which maintains the prestige that it secured as the State Church two centuries ago, and in wealth and influence easily distances all rivals. Bishop Henry C. Potter is at the head of the diocese, and the Church is ministered to by men of wide fame. It has churches for Englishmen, Frenchmen, Italians, Germans, Africans, Chinese, and Spaniards; and for soldiers, seamen, deaf-mutes, and prisoners.

Trinity Church is the second oldest religious organization in the city proper. It was organized under the provisions of an Act passed by the Colonial Assembly of 1693, but the royal charter establishing the Parish of Trinity Church was not granted until 1697. The services of the Church of England had been introduced immediately after the arrival of the British fleet in 1664, and were held in old St. Nicholas Church, within the Fort, until March, 1697, when a small

MADISON-AVENUE REFORMED CHURCH, MADISON AVENUE AND EAST 57TH STREET.

wooden building was opened on the site of the present Trinity Church. This stood unchanged for nearly forty years, when it was virtually rebuilt. The close of the Revolution left the Episcopalians, many of whom had remained loyal to King and Parliament, in small favor with the patriots; but with the restoration of order came wiser counsels. The ritual was revised by omitting the obnoxious prayer for the King, and with the consecration of the first American bishops in 1784, and the General Convention in 1785, which organized the Protestant Episcopal Church in the States of America, officially declared to be loyal to the new government, came the beginning of a growth that has made that church the most powerful Protestant denomination in New York. St. George's and

BLOOMINGDALE REFORMED CHURCH, BOULEVARD AND WEST 68TH STREET.

St. Mark's remained the only other Episcopal churches in the city until 1794, when the increasing population necessitated a second parish, and Christ Church was organized. As the population has increased, other parishes have been formed, and new churches erected ; and there are now 84 Episcopal churches and chapels in the city, with 35,000 communicants, and a vast network of parochial charities. Trinity still remains the wealthiest single church corporation in the United States. Most of its annual income of half a million dollars comes ·from what remains, after many generous gifts, of the royal grant of the Queen's Farm, made in 1705, and comprising a large tract of land along the North River, between Christopher and Vesey Streets, now in the heart of the business part of the city. This property is valued at $9,000,000. At the outbreak of the Revolution Trinity was closed for a time, owing to the persistent refusal of the clergy to omit the prayer for the King. It was re-opened after the British occupation, only to be destroyed a few days later in the great fire of 1776. The second church was built in 1788, on the same site on Broadway, opposite the head of Wall Street. The third, that is to say, the present Trinity Church, was finished in 1846, from the designs of Richard Upjohn. It is a stately Gothic edifice, with an exquisite sharply pointed ornate spire, rising to a height of 284 feet, and carrying a melodious chime of bells. On either side is a quiet graveyard, with many interesting memorials of men and women of the past. The interior is lofty and spacious, with a groined roof borne aloft by sandstone columns. The pews are of carved oak. The chancel is enriched by a fine altar and reredos of white Caen stone, with mosaics and cameos, a memorial to William B. Astor from his sons. Of the many benefactions of Trinity, from its early gift of a communion-service and an altar-cloth to a church at Rye, down to the present time, none has been of greater service to the city than the numerous chapels which she has erected and still maintains. The first was St. George's, now an independent parish, opened in 1753, and endowed by Trinity with a generous gift of over a quarter of a million dollars ; then came St. Paul's, in 1766 ; St. John's, in 1807 ; Trinity Chapel, in 1856 ; St. Chrysostom's, in 1869 ; St. Augustine's, in 1877 ; and St. Agnes' and St. Luke's, in 1892. Trinity has over 6,000 communicants. The music in this church is famous for its beauty, a full cathedral service being sung every Sunday morning, with a full choral vesper service later in the day.

Of the large income enjoyed by Trinity not a cent is hoarded. The expenses of keeping up the estate ; the support of the chapels ; the large yearly grants to twenty-four parishes ; the payment of taxes and assessments ; and the maintenance of the several parochial schools and other parish charities exhaust the yearly income. Of the former rectors of Trinity three have been made bishops of the Church, and one was banished from the State for his royalist proclivities, and became bishop of Nova Scotia. The Rev. Dr. Morgan Dix is the rector of the parish.

St. Paul's Chapel is the oldest church edifice now remaining in the city, and the oldest of the chapels of Trinity Parish. It stands in its ancient location at the corner of Broadway and Vesey Street, Vesey being the name of the first rector of the mother church. It was built in 1764-66, before the troublous times of the War of Independence, and with its simple but impressive architecture of the style of a century and a half ago ; its exquisite spire, recalling one of Sir Christopher Wren's, standing where seemingly it ought not, on what is now the rear end of the building ; and its quiet God's Acre surrounding it, it is one of the picturesque features of lower Broadway. The spacious interior is interesting, not so much for its architectural or decorative beauties (of which indeed it makes but scanty show), as for its oldfashioned look, and the hints it gives of the simple taste and moderate ideas of

TRINITY CHURCH -- PROTESTANT EPISCOPAL.
BROADWAY, BETWEEN RECTOR AND THAMES STREETS, AT THE HEAD OF WALL STREET.

splendor which belonged to the men of the past. Many interesting events have taken place within St. Paul's, but none surpass in impressiveness the solemn service of thanksgiving there, which Washington and the civic authorities attended in simple state, after the inauguration ceremonies in 1789 of the first President of the United States, in the old City Hall, hard by. The centennial anniversary thereof was celebrated within these walls in 1889. A tablet in the rear wall of the chapel, facing Broadway, commemorates the bravery of General Richard Montgomery, the hero of Quebec; and in the churchyard are monuments to Emmet, the Irish patriot; George Frederick Cooke, and others. The Rev. Dr. James Mulchahey is in charge. The music is rendered by a double quartette and a chorus choir of 27 voices.

St. John's Chapel, on Varick Street, was built by Trinity Parish, between 1803 and 1807, in a region then just beginning to be fashionable for homes. It is a quaint and venerable edifice, surrounded by factories and tenements, and the only church within a great area. The front presents a high Corinthian porch, supported by four massive columns of sandstone. The church-yard, in effect like a diminutive park, with trees and shrubbery, lies on either side. The position which St. John's occupies makes it a conspicuous as well as a picturesque object, as seen from the Sixth-Avenue Elevated Railroad, just below Canal Street. Its quaint hewn-oak spire, with a tower clock, rises above the surrounding buildings, 214½ feet high. The Rev. Philip A. H. Brown is in charge. The music is famous.

Trinity Chapel, on 25th Street, near Broadway, was erected in 1851-56 by Old Trinity, for the accommodation of the up-town communicants of the parish. It is a pleasing brownstone Gothic edifice, of the most substantial construction; and is probably the only one of the chapels of Trinity which could support itself if the aid of the mother-church were withdrawn. The plans of the building were designed by Richard Upjohn, and the interior is peculiar in being simply a lofty nave, with arcades along the sides to indicate the position of the aisles, if they had not been omitted. This causes the building to seem very long and narrow; but the great height of the walls and

ST. JOHN'S CHAPEL, PROTESTANT EPISCOPAL, VARICK STREET.

the open roof make an impressive and satisfactory interior. The spacious chancel ends in an apse of seven bays, and paintings fill the tympanums of the sanctuary. The interior is chastely decorated, the corbel pillars in the nave being ornamented with gold leaf. The reredos is of Caen stone and alabaster. Adjacent to the church are the vestry-room and the parish-school building. The Rev. Dr. Swope was a long time in charge of Trinity Chapel, which is now ministered to by the Rev. Dr. William H. Vibbert. The music at the chapel is under the direction of Dr. Walter B. Gilbert, organist and choir-master, and is largely of modern forms.

ST. PAUL'S CHAPEL--PROTESTANT EPISCOPAL.
BROADWAY AND CHURCH STREET, FROM FULTON STREET TO VESEY STREET.

St. Chrysostom's Chapel, at the corner of Seventh Avenue and West 39th Street, is a commodious Gothic edifice, of brownstone, equipped with auxiliary schools and mission and guild rooms. It dates from 1869, and is a power for good in a crowded poor district. Rev. T. H. Sill is the clergyman.

St. Augustine's Chapel is one of the striking architectural features of the city.

TRINITY CHAPEL, PROTESTANT EPISCOPAL, WEST 25TH STREET, BETWEEN BROADWAY AND SIXTH AVENUE.

One of the chapels of Old Trinity, erected in 1876-77 in East Houston Street, between the Bowery and Second Avenue, it stands in the most densely populated part of New York, and, according to the *London Times*, of the whole world. The church cure is a region where all grades of poverty, and almost all forms of vice abound. The buildings consist of the chapel proper and the Mission House. The former, entered through a broad archway with tiled walls and floor, and timbered ceiling, is cruciform, with an open Gothic roof and richly decorated in warm colors. It is handsomely and completely furnished, and seats nearly a thousand. The font is a Caen monolith, and the black iron lectern and oaken altar, placed in Trinity Church at its consecration, are fine specimens of the ecclesiastical art of that period. In the west transept Roger's statue of 'Isaac' is seen. There are four services on Sunday,

ST. CHRYSOSTOM'S CHAPEL, PROTESTANT EPISCOPAL, SEVENTH AVENUE AND WEST 39TH STREET.

the spire cross being illuminated at all night services. The bell is one of the oldest in the country, having been made in 1700, and given in 1704 by the Bishop of London to the first English parish-church in New York. The Mission House contains a large hall, rooms for the day and night-schools, guild-rooms, a music-room, and various offices. Besides the Sunday-school, that occupies twenty different rooms, ten of which are in the basement of the chapel proper, there are a day-school for boys, a night-school for young men and women, a sewing-school with dressmaking and millinery classes, a house-school for teaching girls all kinds of housework, the parish cooking-school, and a number of guilds and societies. The Rev. Dr. Arthur C. Kimber is in charge, with three assistants.

St. Cornelius' Chapel, on Governor's Island, is maintained by Trinity Church, under an arrangement with the War Department, for army officers and soldiers who may desire to attend divine services; and for baptisms, burials, weddings and other ceremonials in the garrison.

St. Agnes' Chapel, near the Boulevard, on West 92d Street, is the newest and most magnificent of Trinity's chapels. Its cost was about $800,000, and it was opened for public services in 1892. St. Agnes' is a cruciform Romanesque building, of striking design and treatment. The main front is of brownstone, flanked and crowned by plain granite walls. The lower stage is occupied by a portal of three deep and heavily-moulded arches. The upper stage is pierced by a large arched window, and the intervening frieze is decorated with emblems of the four Evangelists. The tower is a straight

ST. AUGUSTINE'S CHAPEL, PROTESTANT EPISCOPAL,
107 EAST HOUSTON STREET.

shaft of granite, with belts of brownstone; and the belfry stage is ornamented with arches and spandrils of the same material. A large square lantern rises above the roof-line, at the intersection of the nave and transepts, and forms the dominating feature of the exterior. The interior treatment is elaborate and costly, the richest effects centering in the aspidal chancel, which has a massive rail of white marble, filled with rich inlaid work in green marble. The same material is used in the construction of the pulpit, lectern and altar. The ceiling has a background of gold, upon which are painted in rich colors heroic figures of the Apostles, each bearing an emblem. In the centre is a large representation of Christ, the Triumphant

King, seated upon a throne. The walls of the chancel are broken by window openings, arches communicating with the vestries, and recesses backed with glass mosaics, having ornamental work in relief. The beautiful Morning Chapel is on the west side, opening into the transept and nave by two large archways. In the rear of the church are the parish-house and the rectory. The chapel seats about 1,200 people. All the interior decorative work, including the windows, was done by the Tiffany Glass and Decorating Company. The architect was William A. Potter. The minister in charge is the Rev. Dr. Edward A. Bradley. The grounds surrounding St. Agnes' are effectively adorned with lawns, trees and shrubs.

Grace Church, on Broadway, near 10th Street, is, with the exception of Trinity, the wealthiest Episcopal corporation in New York. The parish was organized in 1808, and the first church stood at the corner of Broadway and Rector Street, then a fine residential quarter. The present location was selected in

ST. AGNES' CHAPEL, PROTESTANT EPISCOPAL, NEAR THE BOULE-
VARD, ON WEST 91ST AND WEST 92D STREETS.

1844, and was thought to be very far up-town. The graceful white limestone church, in the Decorated Gothic style, is one of the architectural features of Broadway, and its spire, once of wood, but now of marble, is one of the most exquisite in the city. The group of buildings belonging to Grace Church comprises the rectory, on the north, connected with the church by Grace House, erected in 1880 by Mrs Catherine L. Wolfe, and containing the vestry and clergy-rooms, library and reading-room ; the Chantry, adjoining the church on the south, also the gift of Miss Wolfe ; and Grace Memorial House, in the rear, on Fourth Avenue, erected by the Hon. Levi P. Morton in 1880 in memory of his wife, and used as a day-nursery for small children. Grace Chapel, at 132 East 14th Street, was erected by the parish in 1876 to replace the former chapel, built in 1852, and destroyed by fire in 1872. Grace-House-by-the-Sea, at Far Rockaway, Long Island, was opened in 1883 as a

GRACE CHURCH — PROTESTANT EPISCOPAL.
BROADWAY, NEAR 10TH STREET, AT THE HEAD OF LOWER BROADWAY

summer home for poor women from tenement houses.   Liberal support is given to
this and the many other parochial charities, and generous contributions are made to
aid benevolent work outside the parish limits.   The architect of Grace Church was
James Renwick.

Few if any of the churches surpass Grace in beauty of interior design and decoration.   It is impressive and magnificent.   In the eastern end a large chancel
window, the gift of Miss Wolfe (as are also the altar and the lofty reredos), is filled
with English stained glass.   The groined roof of the nave is supported by graceful
columns ; and the clere-story and side windows contain some of the finest examples
of the glass-worker's art.   A beautiful memorial porch forms the entrance ; and the
chime of bells in the belfry rivals that of Trinity in sweetness.   Grace has long been

GRACE MEMORIAL HOUSE, FOURTH AVENUE, NEAR 10TH
STREET, IN REAR OF GRACE CHURCH.

noted for fashionable weddings.   The
Bishop of New York, the Rt. Rev.
Henry C. Potter, was long rector of the
parish.   He was succeeded in 1883 by
the Rev. Dr. William R. Huntington.

Christ Church was the second parish of the Episcopal Church organized
in New York, dating back to 1794, when
a church was built on Ann Street.   Here
a goodly congregation soon gathered,
under the Rev. John Pillmore, one of the
first Wesleyan itinerants sent over from
England, who labored for a time with
the brethren of the John-Street Church,
but later joined the Episcopalians.   The
parish grew rapidly, and in 1823 its
former accommodations became too
straitened for its needs, and a larger
church was built on Worth Street, where
the parish remained in peace and prosperity until it migrated up-town in 1854,
building and occupying the present St.
Ann's Church on West 18th Street.   In
1859 a church at Fifth Avenue and 35th
Street was purchased from the Baptists,
and here again the parish rested and
throve for more than thirty years.   In

1890 Christ Church removed to its present site, at the corner of 71st Street and the
Boulevard.   The architect was C. C. Haight.   Among the prominent rectors of
the parish have been Dr. F. C. Ewer, the founder of the ritualistic church of St.
Ignatius ; the Rev. Hugh Miller Thompson, a preacher of nervous and picturesque
force ; and Dr. William McVickar.   Dr. J. S. Shipman has been the rector for
sixteen years.

St. George's Church began its independent existence in 1812.   The first
church, a chapel of Trinity, was built in 1752, at Beekman and Cliff Streets.   The
more modern building, erected in 1845, is a graceful brownstone structure, in the
Gothic style, and a prominent landmark on the East Side, in Stuyvesant Square.
Formerly it had two noble spires, but they became weakened, as the result of a
fire.   They were taken down, and have never been replaced.   For many years the

Rev. Dr. Stephen H. Tyng, the elder, was rector, and his sturdy preaching brought the church well to the front in the Episcopal body. The Rev. Dr. William S. Rainsford became rector in 1881, and since then many changes and improvements have been made in the working methods of the parish, which is one of the most active in the city, and the largest in the country, having 2,600 communicants. One of the most important of its parochial agencies is St. George's Memorial House, adjoining the church. It was erected in 1888, the gift of J. Pierpont Morgan, in memory of Mr. and Mrs. Charles Tracy. It is built of red sandstone, and contains school-rooms, club-rooms, clergy-rooms, gymnasium, library and reading-room, and is the centre of much philanthropic work among the poorer classes in the neighborhood.

St. Mark's Church was organized in 1791. The present church at Second Avenue and 10th Street was consecrated in 1829, and is one of the few survivors of old colonial style of ecclesiastical architecture, with lofty pillared porch and a sharply tapering steeple. The interior preserves its olden quaintness, and is pleasingly decorated. Many memorial tablets adorn the walls; and on the east side of the outer wall, an ancient stone bears

ST. MARK'S CHURCH, PROTESTANT EPISCOPAL, STUYVESANT STREET AND SECOND AVENUE.

ST. GEORGE'S CHURCH, PROTESTANT EPISCOPAL, STUYVESANT SQUARE AND EAST 16TH STREET.

witness to the fact that Governor Petrus Stuyvesant lies buried in the vault below. When the doughty Dutch Captain-General retired from office, after the surrender of the province to the English, he withdrew to his "Bouwerie," or farm, in the vicinity of the present Stuyvesant Square, then two miles from the centre of the city. He built a small chapel adjoining his manor-house, and here the Rev. Henry Soleyns was wont

CHURCH OF THE HEAVENLY REST, PROTESTANT EPISCOPAL, FIFTH AVENUE, ABOVE 45TH STREET.

to preach on Sunday afternoons. In a vault underneath the chapel the Governor was laid to rest, after his death in 1682, to be followed, in 1691, by Henry Sloughter, the English royal governor, and still later, by Daniel Tompkins, an early governor of the State.   At one time the Methodists held meetings in the chapel, commonly called the "Two-Mile-Stone Meeting House," from its distance from the centre of the city.   It was taken down in 1793, and the offer of Petrus Stuyvesant, a descendant of the Governor, to present the ground and 800 pounds in money to Trinity for a church, was accepted.   The church was built in the years 1795-99, and long bore the name of "St. Mark's in the Bowery."   It is still the spiritual home of many descendants of the old families.   The Rev. Dr. J. H. Rylance is the rector.

The Church of the Heavenly Rest, at 551 Fifth Avenue, was built through the efforts of Dr. Robert S. Howland, then rector of the Church of the Holy Apostles.   The parish originated in services held in the hall of Rutgers Female College, in 1865.   The narrow front of the church, ornamental in design and surmounted by angelic

figures, gives little promise of the spaciousness of the interior, which is cruciform in shape, and contains some of the finest wood-carving and stained-glass windows in the country.   Polished marble pillars support the roof ; the walls are richly frescoed and adorned with beautiful paintings ; and Ary Scheffer's *Christus Consolator* forms the altar-piece.   The entire effect of the interior is one of extreme and satisfying richness, refinement, beauty and peace.   The Church of the Heavenly Rest is one of the fashionable shrines of the city, and the wealth of its members is shown in their liberal support of public and parochial charities.   The rector is the Rev. Dr. D. Parker Morgan.

St. Thomas's Church, at Fifth Avenue and 53d Street, was organized in 1823 ; and its first church stood at Broadway and Houston Street, then a rural suburb.   The parish attained to a high degree of prosperity under

ST. GEORGE'S MEMORIAL HOUSE, 207 EAST 16TH STREET, IN REAR OF ST. GEORGE'S CHURCH.

the rectorship of Dr. Francis L. Hawks, but as early as 1843 the need of a location farther up-town began to be felt, and in 1870 the present magnificent edifice was opened for worship.   The church is one of the most imposing architectural features of the city, and was regarded by the architect, Upjohn, as the masterpiece of his long career as a church architect.   The church and the adjoining rectory are built of brownstone, in the Gothic style ; and, with the grounds and furnishings, represent a value of nearly one million dollars.   The interior is one of the finest in the city, with monolithic columns supporting the nave, a central dome at the intersection of the nave and transept, an apsidal chancel adorned with a series of cartoons by LaFarge, and a reredos in old gold by St. Gaudens, representing the Adoration of the Cross by cherubs and angels.   The chancel is flanked by shallower recesses, in which is built

St Luke's 483 Hudson St

St Michaels Amsterdam Ave and 99th St

FIVE PROTESTANT EPISCOPAL CHURCHES

St THOMAS' CHURCH 5TH AVE

Zion & St Timothy 332 West 57th St

St Mary the Virgin 228 West 45th St

PROTESTANT EPISCOPAL CHURCH EDIFICES.

23   ST. LUKE'S.   ST. MICHAEL'S.   ST. THOMAS'.   ZION AND ST. TIMOTHY.   ST. MARY THE VIRGIN.

the great organ, in two parts, for a double choir, whose rendering of church music is famous throughout the country. The entire decoration of the chancel, including the costly works of LaFarge and St. Gaudens, is a memorial from Charles H. Housman to his mother; and to his generosity the church also owes the angelic figures with musical instruments, after Fra Angelico, by LaFarge, which form the decorations above the organ. Other memorials are the chime of bells in the tower, rivalling those of Trinity in sweetness, the cross surmounting it, and many stained-glass windows and other fittings of the interior. While St. Thomas's is a church for the wealthy, it is by no means neglectful of the claims of the poorer classes. In addition to its numerous benevolent societies, it maintains St. Thomas's Chapel, on 60th Street; a German mission; and St. Thomas's House, in the rear of the chapel, erected in 1872 by Hon. and Mrs. Roswell P. Flower as a memorial to their son, Henry Keep Flower. The rectors of St. Thomas have been : Rev. Cornelius R. Duffie ; Rev. Dr. George Upfold, later bishop of Indiana ; Rev. Henry J. White-house, some time bishop of Illinois ; Rev. Dr. Edmund Neville ; Rev. Dr. William F. Morgan ; and the present incumbent, Rev. Dr. John W. Brown.

St. James's Church grew out of a chapel-at-ease erected in 1810 at 69th Street and Park Avenue, for the convenience of those New-York families whose country-

ST. JAMES'S CHURCH, PROTESTANT EPISCOPAL, MADISON AVENUE AND EAST 71ST STREET.

seats were in the vicinity of Hamilton Square (now Lenox Hill). This was succeeded by an edifice erected in 1869 on the north side of 72d Street, between Lexington and Third Avenues,— the present church having been built in 1884 at the northeast corner of Madison Avenue and 71st Street. It is an imposing Gothic building, designed to have a lofty tower in the Florentine style. It has an apsidal chancel at the side of the tower ; a smaller round tower ; and a loggia, with bold projections, forming with the two gables a very beautiful and picturesque effect. The interior is extremely pleasing. A tower-room, with a notable stairway, opens upon the chancel, which is very deep, with two arches and an apsidal sanctuary. At the east end is a large gallery. The interior finish is oak, and the entire scheme of decoration is chaste and harmonious. There is a vested choir ; and the building contains two choir-rooms, a large parish-room, a library, a guild-room, and a kitchen. In the tower are three large brass tablets, having representations of the two former buildings of the parish, and inscribed with the names of former vestrymen. The rector, the Rev. Dr. Cornelius B. Smith, began his work in 1867.

St. Luke's Church, at Convent Avenue and 141st Street, is an impressive Romanesque brownstone church, designed by R. H. Robertson, and opened in 1892. It cost $275,000. It occupies very high ground, on Washington Heights; and the rectory is the old mansion of Alexander Hamilton, known as "The Grange." Old St. Luke's, at 483 Hudson Street, was built in 1821, in Green-

ST. LUKE'S CHURCH, PROTESTANT EPISCOPAL, AND ALEXANDER HAMILTON'S "THE GRANGE," CONVENT AVENUE AND 141ST STREET.

wich Village, and in 1892 became a chapel of Trinity Parish. It is in a densely settled part of the city, and is supported as a mission. When it was sold to Trinity, the records and traditions of the parish were transferred to the new and magnificent church on Washington Heights. The Rev. Dr. Isaac H. Tuttle, rector of old St. Luke's for 42 years, is now rector emeritus of the migrated parish; and the Rev. Dr. John T. Patey is the active rector.

Calvary Church was built in 1837, on Fourth proved to be too far up- organized in 1835, and its first church was Avenue, near 35th Street. The location town for the prosperity of the parish, and in 1842 the church was moved to the corner of 21st Street. Five years later it was taken down, and the present brownstone building erected, in the old English style of architecture. The interior arrangements and decorations are extremely good. The lofty groined roof is supported by slender columns springing out in graceful pointed arches; the side walls are panelled; and the arched windows are filled with richly colored

CALVARY CHURCH, PROTESTANT EPISCOPAL, FOURTH AVENUE AND EAST 21ST STREET.

glass. Calvary has long been one of the leading Episcopal parishes, and with Calvary Chapel and the Galilee Rescue Mission on East 23d Street, and a goodly number of parochial charities, it is the centre of much beneficent activity. There are 1,600 communicants. The rector is the Rev. Dr. H. Y. Satterlee. The congregational singing at Calvary is very fine, trained singers being scattered throughout the congregation. The new building which is to be occupied by the Church Missions House is slowly rising into view, on Fourth Avenue, just north of Calvary Church.

The Church of the Ascension, at Fifth Avenue and 10th Street, is an attractive brownstone edifice, erected in 1840. Its founder was Dr. Manton Eastburn, afterwards bishop of Massachusetts; who was succeeded by Dr. Gregory T. Bedell, afterwards bishop of Ohio; Dr. John Cotton Smith; and Dr. E. Winchester Donald, who in 1892 succeeded Phillips Brooks as rector of Trinity Church, in Boston. In 1888-89 the church was beautified by a new chancel, furnished by Stanford White, and adorned with angel figures by St. Gaudens, mosaics by Maitland Armstrong, a richly carved memorial pulpit and walls of Siena marble. Above these is the largest ecclesiastical painting in America, representing the Ascension.

ST. ANDREW'S CHURCH, PROTESTANT EPISCOPAL, FIFTH AVENUE AND EAST 127TH STREET.

This magnificent picture was the work of John LaFarge, and took two years to execute, its cost having been $30,-000. It was the gift of the Misses Rhinelander. The parish has been widely known for its generous gifts, including a hall at the Theological School near Alexandria, Va.; a hall and church for Kenyon College, at Gambier, Ohio; and the Church of the Ascension, at Ipswich, Mass.

St. Andrew's Church was organized in 1829, and built its first ecclesiastical home during the following year. The early growth of the parish was feeble, owing to its remote situation, far up-town; and it was not until the year 1873 that the need of large accommodations became sufficiently urgent to cause the erection of a more spacious church, which remained in use until the opening of the present edifice, in 1889, at Fifth Avenue and 127th Street. The exterior is picturesque in appearance, with a stately corner tower carrying a sweet chime of bells, gabled entrances, and a pleasing roof-line. The interior is churchly and impressive in the best sense, with lofty nave, lower side aisles, transepts, baptistery and apsidal chancel. Slender shafts, surmounted by a clere-story pierced with many windows, and spanned by graceful pointed arches, support the lofty arched roof. Two narrow lancet windows light the chancel, and between them is a large painting of *The Call of St. Andrew,* the patron-saint of the church. The chancel and transepts open out into smaller spaces through pointed arches, adding greatly to the perspective effect. The color scheme is in terra cotta, relieved by lighter lines on the faces of the arched ribs of the roof. The first rector of the parish was the Rev. George L. Hinton. Later incumbents have been the Rev. Dr. James R. Bailey, who withdrew to join the Roman Catholic Church, and became Archbishop of Baltimore; the Rev. Dr. Francis Lobdell; and the present rector, the Rev. Dr.

George R. Van De Water, one of the strongest preachers and leading organizers in the city. The communicant list numbers 1,500 ; and St. Andrew's is noted for the variety and liberality of its gifts.

The Church of the Holy Communion, at Sixth Avenue and 20th Street, was erected in 1846 by Mrs. Anna C. Rogers, in obedience to the dying request of her husband, that "a church might be built, to the glory of God, where rich and poor might meet together." Mrs. Rogers's brother, Dr. William A. Muhlenberg, the founder of St. Luke's Hospital, became the first rector. It was a free church from the beginning, and the first in the country to establish early communions, weekly celebrations, daily prayers, and a boy choir, and the first to organize a sisterhood. The group of buildings includes the church and rectory, in brownstone, after designs by Upjohn ; a Sisters' House ; a home for aged women ; and other edifices. The church is cruciform in shape, and the interior is plain but churchly in its decorations. The Rev. Dr. Henry Mottet is rector.

The Church of the Transfiguration, at 5 East 29th Street, is better known as "The Little Church around the Corner," from the fact that its rector once

CHURCH OF THE TRANSFIGURATION (THE LITTLE CHURCH AROUND THE CORNER), PROTESTANT EPISCOPAL, EAST 29TH STREET, BETWEEN FIFTH AND MADISON AVENUES.

read the funeral service of the Church over the body of an actor, after a neighboring clergyman had refused, telling the friends of the deceased to go to "the little church around the corner." This simple incident has made the church an object of affectionate regard to the whole dramatic profession, many of whom have shown their interest in a substantial manner. The parish was organized in 1849 by the present rector, Dr. George H. Houghton, and early in the following year a part of the rambling but picturesque church was erected. The building has grown by degrees, as need arose and funds were forthcoming, and is now a long low structure, with a single transept and many beautiful and costly decorations. The church has 600 communicants, and is recognized as a very earnest body of communicants. Services are conducted three times a day throughout the year. The rectory adjoins the church. There is a Transfiguration Chapel on West 69th Street, between the Boulevard and Columbus Avenue.

St. Ann's Church is engaged in an interesting field of work among the deaf-mutes, in whose behalf the parish was organized by the rector emeritus, the Rev. Dr. Thomas Gallaudet, in 1852. For several years the services were held in the chapel of the University of the City of New York and the lecture-room of the New-York Historical Society. The church, on 18th Street, near Fifth Avenue, was purchased in 1859. The main interest attaching to the parish is its peculiar field of work among the deaf-mutes, of whom there are more than 100 among the communicants. This free church has five services on Sunday, and two on every other day, and is open all day for private prayer and meditation. The Rev. Dr. Edward H. Krans became rector of the parish in 1892, being pastor of the hearing persons, Dr. Gallaudet devoting his energies to the deaf-mutes. The Rev. John Chamberlain is a co-laborer with Dr. Gallaudet in the Church Mission to Deaf-Mutes, incorporated in 1872.

St. Bartholomew's Church, one of the largest and most fashionable in the city, was organized in 1835, the congregation for many years worshipping in a church in Lafayette Place. The imposing building at Madison Avenue and 44th Street was finished in 1876. It is a fine example of the Lombardo-Gothic style, with lofty decorated front and a campanile tower with open belfry. The interior is handsomely treated in polychrome. Polished Scotch granite columns, carrying a triforium gallery and a clere-story, support the lofty nave roof, and all the appointments bespeak the wealth of the congregation. The rector is the Rev. Dr. David H. Greer. Aside from the usual benevolent and missionary activities of a well-organized parish, there is St. Bartholomew's Parish House, on East 42d Street, near Third Avenue, erected in 1891, the gift of Mrs. William H. Vanderbilt and Cornelius Vanderbilt. It is a costly stone and brick building, and is made the centre of an im-

ST. BARTHOLOMEW'S CHURCH, PROTESTANT EPISCOPAL, MADISON AVENUE AND EAST 44TH STREET.

portant religious and humane work among the poor of the East Side.

All Souls' Church, at Madison Avenue and 66th Street, is one of the most attractive Episcopal temples in the city, and is the home of the parish ministered to by the Rev. Dr. R. Heber Newton, the somewhat iconoclastic preacher. The parish was organized in 1859, and early in 1861 its first edifice, on West 48th Street, was consecrated as a memorial to the Rev. Dr. Henry Anthon. In 1890 the parish bought the property of the Church of the Holy Spirit, selling its former place of worship, and taking possession of the beautiful stone church which it now occupies. The building is in the Romanesque style, with a massive tower and an imposing front on Madison Avenue; and the interior is quaint and attractive, with richly tinted walls and a series of fine paintings on the rear wall of the chancel.

The Church of Zion and St. Timothy was formed in 1890 by the union of the two Episcopal parishes of Zion and St. Timothy,

ALL SOULS' CHURCH, PROTESTANT EPISCOPAL, MADISON AVENUE AND EAST 66TH STREET.

the latter having an organization dating back to 1853, while the former was formed in 1810, when the English Lutheran Church Zion conformed to the Episcopal Church.

ST. BARTHOLOMEW'S PARISH HOUSE, 205 EAST 42D STREET.

The new Church of Zion and St. Timothy, at 332 West 57th Street, was erected in 1891. It is early Gothic in design, treated in a simple and massive manner, and with an avoidance of carving and minute detail, in order to bring the design within the rightful use of brick and stone, the latter being employed only when needed to strengthen the walls. A massive tower, with strongly marked pier-braces at the corners, is placed in the north of the main front, the plainness and severity of the latter being relieved by the staircase pinnacle and the deeply recessed doors and windows. On the 57th-Street elevation three sharply pointed gables relieve the monotony and give character to the design. The same simplicity of treatment marks the interior. The level of the sanctuary is several feet above the choir floor, giving greater dignity to altar and reredos, and the use of the customary chancel-arch has been avoided. The roof and side walls are on the same lines as those of the nave, but greatly enriched by extra braces in the open timber-work of the roof. A system of double trusses, supported by clustered stone columns at the four transept angles, divides the nave from the aisles and chancel, giving an appearance of greater length to the interior. The roofs are constructed entirely in open timber-work, in natural hard pine, colored to suit the expression of the interior, the walls of which are finished in red brick, relieved by gray brick in wide bands. Connected with the church there is a large parish-house, of similar construction. The combined parish is in charge of the Rev. Henry Lubeck, with the former rector of Zion Church, Dr. Charles C. Tiffany, as rector emeritus.

The Church of the Holy Trinity, at Madison Avenue and East 42d Street, was erected in 1873. It is near the Grand Central Depot, and its variegated brick and ivy-covered walls and lofty corner tower make it a conspicuous object. The parish was founded in 1864, by the younger Stephen H. Tyng, and the result of his early labors was a remarkable growth in many directions. In 1888 the Rev. E. Walpole Warren, an English "missioner," was called to the rectorship. He has introduced many new agencies for increasing the effectiveness of the parish. Holy Trinity has always been marked by the co-operation of its laymen, the practical character of its preaching, and its adherence to the "evangelical" school of churchmanship. It has a specially commendable boy choir. The parish has 840 communicants, with nearly a score of societies.

The Church of St. Mary the Virgin, at 228 West 45th Street, is the most ritualistic of the Episcopal churches of New York, with a daily celebration, an elaborate ceremonial, and all the usages of the advanced Anglo-Catholic school. The parish was organized in 1868, and the church was opened in 1870. It is a small Gothic building, and the interior is chiefly notable for its white marble altar, tabernacle and altar-screen; the hanging sanctuary lamps, and the sculptured figures of Christ,

CHURCH OF THE HOLY TRINITY, PROTESTANT EPISCOPAL, MADISON AVENUE AND EAST 42D STREET.

the Virgin and St. John; and of St. Paul (as founder of the British Church), on the pulpit. The Sunday and festal services are largely choral, and of the most elaborate and beautiful character. The parish is active in good work among the poor, supporting mission-house, schools, guilds, and other agencies for charitable work. The Rev. Thomas McKee Brown is rector and founder; and the church has 600 communicants, lovers of good deeds as well as æsthetic forms.

The **Church of the Incarnation,** at Madison Avenue and East 35th Street, is a modern Gothic temple, in a pleasant residence-quarter. The Rev. Dr. Arthur Brooks is the rector; and the Rev. Newton Perkins has charge of the Chapel of the Reconciliation, at 246 East 31st Street. The church is a picturesque structure, built of dark sandstone, with many buttresses, a quaint entrance porch on the Madison-Avenue front, and a solid-looking square tower, at the corner nearest the intersection of the street and avenue. The spire was carried in 1892, after remaining thirty years incomplete, to its present height, as seen in the illustration. The front of the church is literally covered with ivy. It grows thickly around the bases of the buttresses at the side of the building, quite concealing the size of the church, which is one of the largest in the city.

All Angels' Church, at the corner of West-End Avenue and West 81st Street, was built in 1890. The society came into existence about the middle of the century, and had its first building in what is now Central Park. It occupies a corner-lot of 100 by 102 feet, and is 140 feet long, the builders having adopted the shrewd device of placing it diagonally. Dr. Charles F. Hoffman is the rector, and Rev. S. DeLancey Townsend, associate-rector.

The Church of Holy Trinity, at Lenox Avenue and 122d Street, Harlem, is one of the recently erected Episcopal shrines. The building was consecrated in 1888, and is Italian Gothic in style, and substantially constructed of rough-faced Indiana limestone, with brownstone trimmings. A massive tower with long, narrow openings surmounts the main entrance on 122d Street, and the long frontage on Lenox Avenue is agreeably diversified by

CHURCH OF THE INCARNATION, PROTESTANT EPISCOPAL, MADISON AVENUE AND EAST 35TH STREET.

two gables and a small spire, breaking the monotony of the roof-line. The main feature of the spacious interior, which has a seating capacity of 1,200, and is cruciform in shape, with lofty arched roof, is the chancel, which is extremely decorative in its treatment. An oaken communion table, surrounded by the chancel rail, occupies the centre, and the Bishop's chair is behind it. The walls are finished in polished variegated marble, above which the effect of small galleries is produced by arched openings. There are two transept galleries, and the walls are decorated in terra cotta and buff. On the first floor of the Lenox-Avenue side are the parish parlors, and above them, the Sunday-school rooms. The parish was organized in 1868, and the Rev. William N. McVickar became the first rector. He was succeeded in 1884 by Dr. Randolph H. McKim, during whose term of office the parish grew rapidly, establishing in 1884 Holy Trinity Chapel and Holy Trinity Mission House and Day Nursery, on East 112th Street. The first church was built in 1870, on Fifth Avenue, at the corner of 125th Street. Under its successive rectors, Holy Trinity has enjoyed a continually increasing measure of prosperity, culminating in the present beautiful edifice, and a communicant list of 1,000. The Rev. Dr. C. D'Witt Bridgman is rector. The architect was William A. Potter.

St. Michael's Church, at Amsterdam Avenue and 99th Street, is one of the five picturesque and impressive ecclesiastical buildings which the Episcopalians have recently erected in the upper part of the city. St. Michael's parish was organized in 1807, the first church having been built the previous year. The second church was erected in 1854, and for many years the parish had but a feeble growth, owing to its situation far up-town. But in recent years the city has stretched out in this direction, and the increase in population has brought increasing prosperity, together with the need of larger accommodations. The pres-

ent stately structure, of Indiana limestone, in the Italian style of the twelfth century, was consecrated in 1891, and it is a noteworthy instance of modern intelligent ecclesiastical architecture, planned by Robert W. Gibson, the sides of the nave, aisles, and outer cloister porch rise one behind the other in three successive groups, all surmounted and dominated by the massive corner tower, rising to a height of 180 feet, and carrying a chime of bells. The windows and arcades are round-arched. The interior, in the shape of a Latin cross, is spacious and impressive. Massive square columns separate nave from aisles, and support the lofty roof, which is panelled in wood. The wide round arches have ornamental faces, and the side walls are treated in terra cotta. The windows are filled with cathedral glass, and there are two

CHURCH OF THE HOLY TRINITY, PROTESTANT EPISCOPAL, LENOX AVENUE AND WEST 122D STREET.

large windows in the transepts. The church has sittings for 1,600 people. The total cost of the building, which is the crowning success of the 48 years' toiling of the rector, the Rev. Dr. T. M. Peters, in the upper part of the city, was nearly $200,000.

The Cathedral of St. John the Divine. — In 1885 the authorities of the Episcopal Church in the Diocese of New York began to agitate the subject of a cathedral, worthy of the increasing growth of the Church, and for a centre of its numerous religious and charitable activities. The result of the preliminary meetings and the public agitation of the subject was the receipt of subscriptions sufficient to warrant the purchase, at $850,000, of an eligible site between 110th and 113th Streets and Morningside and Tenth Avenues, then occupied by the Leake and Watts Orphan Asylum. Designs were then invited from the leading architects of the world; and after careful examination of the plans submitted, four were chosen for a second competition. Those of Heins & LaFarge were finally accepted, as a basis for beginning the work, the details of which will be determined as it proceeds. The

CATHEDRAL OF ST. JOHN THE DIVINE. (PROTESTANT EPISCOPAL.)
MORNINGSIDE PARK.

corner-stone was laid on St. John's Day, December 17, 1892, by Bishop Potter. In the amended drawings the ground-plan has the shape of a cross, the arms of which are formed by the nave and transepts and chancel, with central and side aisles. The general exterior design is that of a group of seven towers; two at the west front; a large central tower or lantern over the crossing of the transepts and nave; and four smaller flanking towers at the angles of the cross. There are to be entrances in each of these flanking towers, as well as in those on the west. The central tower alone is crowned by a spire, which is to dominate the group. Around the chancel will be seven apsidal chapels, each capable of seating 150 persons; and a high arcaded balustrade will crown the cornices of the side-aisles, whose buttresses will

ALL ANGELS' CHURCH, PROTESTANT EPISCOPAL, WEST-END AVENUE AND WEST 81ST STREET.

be surmounted by figures of angels with folded wings. The cathedral will face towards the west, and the chapels will appear to rise abruptly from the retaining wall of Morningside Park.

The principal dimensions of the cathedral, as proposed, are as follows: Total length outside, 520 feet. Width across the front, 192 feet; across the transepts, 290 feet. Width of the front towers, 57 feet, and their height 248 feet. The width of the four flanking towers will be 43 feet, and their height 158 feet. The total exterior diameter of the central tower is to be 116, and its interior diameter 96 feet, with a height of 253 feet for the vaulting, and 445 feet from the floor of the cathedral to the top of the cross. The chancel will have a depth of 120 feet, and the nave will be 60 feet in width, with a length of 180 feet and a height of 105 feet, while the front gable will tower aloft to the height of 164 feet. The building will be constructed in the most substantial manner, and its total cost will probably reach $6,000,000 or more, of which it is proposed to expend $200,000 yearly until the construction is completed. As seen from the streets of Harlem the spire of the cathedral will appear higher than that of the Cologne Cathedral, and with the exception of Ulm Minster and the Eiffel Tower, it will be the highest structure in the world when measured from the street-level. Years will elapse before its completion, but when finished the Cathedral of St. John the Divine will be the noblest ecclesiastical building in America, rivalling the grand cathedrals of England and the Continent.

The First Presbyterian Church is the oldest local society of that denomination. It was formed in 1717, and the early meetings were held in the City Hall. In 1719 the famous Wall-Street Church was opened, and here George Whitefield preached in 1740. The church now occupied by the parish, on Fifth Avenue, between West 11th and 12th Streets, was erected in 1845. It is a rich Gothic structure, of graceful and stately proportions, and with a dignified and spacious interior. The first pastor was James Anderson, a Scotch clergyman, installed in 1717. Dr. John Rodgers, "the Father of Presbyterianism" in New York, was another early minister. Dr. Howard Duffield is now in charge.

The Presbyterians began their services in 1706, with private meetings at the houses of a few families of Presbyterian sympathies. In 1707 the Rev. Francis McKemie preached to a small congregation in a private house, and baptized a child. He was arrested by order of Lord Cornbury and thrown into prison, but was soon released. From 1719 to 1809 there was but one Presbyterian church, the Wall-Street, with the church in Beekman Street, erected in 1768, and that in Rutgers Street, built in 1797, as Collegiate charges. The Collegiate relation was dissolved in 1809. The Presbyterian churches of the city are divided among the Presbyterians proper, the Reformed Presbyterians and the United Presbyterians. The first is much the strongest, having 53 churches, while the others have

FIRST PRESBYTERIAN CHURCH, FIFTH AVENUE, BETWEEN 11TH AND 12TH STREETS.

but five each. The Presbyterian Church is to New York what Congregationalism is to New England, a strong and aggressive religious force. It has 30,000 members.

The Scotch Presbyterian Church, recently on 14th Street, was organized in 1756 by a party of seceders from the old Wall-Street Church, under the name of the First Associate Reformed Church. The chief cause of the formation of the new society was difference of opinion regarding the use of musical instruments in the church. The first pastor was the Rev. John Mason, a Scottish clergyman, and the first church stood on Cedar Street. In 1837 the congregation removed to a church on Grand Street ; and in 1853 the church on West 14th Street was opened. Rev. Dr. David G. Wylie is the pastor. The church in 1893 occupied a new edifice, at 96th Street and Central Park West.

The Brick Presbyterian Church, at Fifth Avenue and 37th Street, one of the most important Presbyterian churches in the city, was erected in 1858, supplanting the old Brick Church, which had stood since 1767 on the corner of Beekman and

Nassau Streets. The new church is a partial reproduction in brick and brownstone of the older edifice, on a much larger scale ; and its interior, recently redecorated by La-Farge, is very attractive. The parish was formed by members of the First Presbyterian Church, and for forty-two years

BRICK MEETING-HOUSE, PARK ROW, NASSAU AND BEEKMAN STREETS. IN 1800.

the two branches continued their organic connection, with one session and the same trustees. The first pastor was the famous Dr. John Rodgers. He was succeeded in 1810 by the Rev. Dr. Gardiner Spring, who remained in office for sixty-two years. The Rev. Dr. Wm. G. T. Shedd, late of Union Theological Seminary, was one of

his colleagues. The present pastor, the Rev. Dr. Henry Van Dyke, was installed in 1883, and his ability as a pulpit orator has attracted a large and representative congregation. Its Christianity is simple, practical, and non-sectarian.

The Fifth-Avenue Presbyterian Church was organized in 1808, and its first church was erected on Cedar Street in that year. The Rev. John Brodhead Romeyn became the first pastor, retaining his connection with the parish until his death, in 1825. In common with all the earlier churches, the Cedar-Street parish made several removals farther up-town ; in 1834, to Duane Street ; in 1852, to its first Fifth-Avenue church, at the corner of 19th Street, when the corporate name was changed to the present title ; and again, in 1875, to its present location, at the corner of 55th Street. It is an ornate Gothic structure of imposing proportions, and the interior differs widely from the traditional simplicity

BRICK PRESBYTERIAN CHURCH, NORTHWEST CORNER OF
FIFTH AVENUE AND 37TH STREET.

and plainness of the older Presbyterian churches. There is an abundance of rich coloring and elaborate carving; light woods are effectively used in the panelling of the walls; and the floor slopes gradually down from the entrance to the pulpit, giving something of the effect of a public hall. The pastor, Rev. John Hall, D. D., LL. D., was installed November 3, 1867. The church is foremost, probably, in its gifts to missionary and benevolent work in the Presbyterian denomination, if not in the United States; and occupies a position of noble prominence among the Christian societies of the world.

The University-Place Presbyterian Church was organized in 1845, by a colony from the older Duane-Street Church. The present substantial stone church, on University Place, at the corner of East 10th Street, was erected in 1844 by private subscription. In 1870 the congregation received a large and important addition to its numbers from the Mercer-Street Church, which, after a prosperous existence since 1835, had been so greatly weakened by the building of up-town churches that it was compelled to sell its place of worship to the Church of the Strangers, and unite with the University-Place congregation. Thus strengthened and invigorated, the parish has enjoyed continued prosperity. The Rev. Dr. George Alexander is pastor.

The West Presbyterian Church was organized in 1829, with eighteen members, and its first house of worship was erected on Carmine Street, in 1832. There, for many years, the congregation grew and prospered. The present ecclesiastical structure, on West 42d Street, near Sixth Avenue, was erected in 1862. It is a noble example of the decorative Gothic style, with lofty roof and gabled entrance and tapering spire. The auditorium, seating 1,200, is striking and attractive. Four broad

FIFTH-AVENUE PRESBYTERIAN CHURCH, FIFTH AVENUE AND 55TH STREET.

and sweeping arches span the interior, one at either side and end, crossing near their spring from the gallery floor. The large round arch at the pulpit end is supported by massive pillars of polished stone, and roomy galleries sweep in a circle around three sides of the auditorium. A large chapel and spacious parish-rooms are connected with the church. Under the care of the Rev. Dr. John R. Paxton, one of the best-known preachers in the city, the West Church has gathered a large and fashionable congregation, with a goodly record of practical charities.

The **Fourth-Avenue Presbyterian Church**, at 286 Fourth Avenue, corner of 22d Street, was long in charge of the Rev. Dr. Howard Crosby, so well known as a reformer and earnest worker in the temperance cause. The church was built in 1856, and Dr. Crosby, in virtue of his prominence in public affairs, as well as his solid merits as a pulpit orator, attracted a large and influential congregation. The Fourth-Avenue Church became one of the most noted in the city, active in reform movements and greatly given to practical Christian work among the poor and wretched. The church is substantially built, after the Gothic manner, and has an attractive interior, but its chief claim to public notice is its goodly record in the past. It adjoins the 23d-Street Branch of the Young Men's Christian Association, and a view of the church is shown elsewhere with the Association Building.

The **Madison-Square Presbyterian Church**, at Madison Avenue and 24th Street, was organized in 1853, in response to the growing demand for churches in

MADISON-SQUARE PRESBYTERIAN CHURCH, MADISON AVENUE AND 24TH STREET.

what was then the up-town portion of the city. Its original membership was drawn mainly from the Central Presbyterian Church, in Broome Street, and the Rev. Dr. William Adams left the pastorate of the Central Church to assume that of the new organization. Public worship was begun in the chapel of the Union Theological Seminary; and subsequently the services were held in Hope Chapel, on Broadway, until the present building was ready for occupancy, in December, 1854. The church is built of brownstone, in a simple style of Gothic architecture; and contains, besides the auditorium, which has a seating capacity of 1,200, a large Sunday-school room and lecture-room. In November, 1873, after a long and fruitful pastorate of more than twenty years, Dr. Adams tendered his resignation, in order to assume the duties of the Presidency of the Union Theological Seminary. In 1875 the Rev. Dr. William Tucker was installed as pastor. He resigned in 1879, to assume the chair of sacred rhetoric in Andover Theological Seminary. The present pastor, the Rev. Dr. Charles H. Parkhurst, was installed in 1880. The history of the church has been a record of continuous progress, and its present membership is nearly 800. A mission Sunday-school, started in 1858, has gradually grown into the Adams Memorial Church, at 211 East 30th Street, which is now ecclesiastically independent, and dependent financially only in a slight degree. The resources of the parent church, no longer required in this direction, are now devoted to the maintenance of the Mission and Church House at 30th Street and Third Avenue, where there is being carried on a variety of religious and humane work.

The Church of the Covenant was founded in 1860 by the Rev. Dr. George L. Prentiss, in the interest of the New School of Liberal Presbyterians. For some time the services were held in the chapel of the Home for the Friendless, in East 23d Street. The church was formally organized in 1862, and the graceful stone building at Park Avenue and 35th Street was dedicated in 1865. Few of the more modern structures surpass it in beauty of design, spaciousness and attractiveness. Dr. J. H. McIlvaine is the pastor.

ADAMS MEMORIAL CHURCH, PRESBYTERIAN, 211 EAST 30TH STREET.

The Westminster Presbyterian Church, at 210 West 23d Street, has 500 members. Its commodious stone edifice, near Seventh Avenue, has recently been extensively improved ; and it is hoped that the church will long maintain this valuable down-town position. The pastor is Dr. Robert F. Sample, well known as a preacher and author.

The Madison-Avenue Presbyterian Church was organized in 1844, and in 1871 took possession of the Gothic building which had been erected at Madison Avenue and 53d Street, to meet the need of a Presbyterian church in that vicinity. It is a lofty brownstone structure, in the simple Gothic style so much affected in the ecclesiastical architecture of the middle of the present century, which was largely imitative in character. The large auditorium, seating nearly 1,600, is decorated in neutral tints. The church has enjoyed the services

CHURCH OF THE COVENANT, PRESBYTERIAN, PARK AVENUE AND 35TH STREET.

24

WESTMINSTER PRESBYTERIAN CHURCH,
210 WEST 23D STREET.

of a succession of powerful preachers. Under the pastorate of the Rev. Dr. Charles L. Thompson it has become one of the most influential of the Presbyterian churches in the city. In 1892 it was converted into a People's Church, with free pews, and a variety of educational, philanthropic and religious enterprises.

The Central Presbyterian Church, at 220 West 57th Street, was built in 1878. It is a large and sightly stone structure, with tower and pinnacles, and a spacious auditorium, decorated with light colors. The society was formed by the Rev. William Patton, who in 1820 began preaching to a handful of people in a school-room on Mulberry Street. A church was built on Broome Street in 1821. Dr. Patton continued with the parish until 1834, building up a strong and zealous congregation of nearly 1,000 members. During all its changes of location and ministers the church has prospered, becoming one of the prominent Presbyterian societies. Its pastor is Rev. Dr. W. Merle Smith.

The Phillips Presbyterian Church, at Madison Avenue and East 73d Street, built in 1858, is a lofty brick edifice in the Gothic style of architecture. The auditorium is nearly square, with arched ceiling and pleasing decorative work on the walls. The organ occupies an elevated position at the east end of the church and is flanked on either side by two small galleries. The parish was formed in 1844, and its church, erected by the generous gifts of James Lenox, stood in East 15th Street. Rev. Dr. George L. Spining is the pastor.

The Park Presbyterian Church, at 86th Street and Amsterdam Avenue, was founded in 1853, and called the 84th-Street Presbyterian Church. Francis L. Patton, President of Princeton University, was pastor for awhile. In 1879 the present pastor, Rev. Anson P. Atterbury, took charge. In 1882 a new location was purchased; and two years later the society moved into the new building. The church is prospering greatly.

The West-End Presbyterian Church, at Amsterdam Avenue and 105th Street, is an example of the rapid multiplication of new and beautiful church edifices in the upper part of the city. The church was organized in 1888, and for two years worshipped in its attractive chapel in the

CENTRAL PRESBYTERIAN CHURCH,
220 WEST 57TH STREET.

CHURCH OF THE PURITANS, PRESBYTERIAN, 15 WEST 130TH STREET.

rear of the church, pending the completion of the latter. The corner-stone was laid June 22, 1891. The church is constructed of yellow pressed brick, with ornamental line work, in the Romanesque style, and presents an extremely picturesque external appearance, with its stately corner tower and highly decorated round-arch entrances on the avenue. The auditorium is spacious and tastefully decorated, and a large gallery extends around three sides. The Rev. Dr. John Balcom Shaw is the pastor.

The Church of the Puritans, at 15 West 130th Street, near Fifth Avenue, is one of the leading churches of Harlem, and has grown with great prosperity and vigor. It was organized in 1872, as the Church of Harlem. The present name arose the Rev. Dr. George B. Cheever, who gave to funds resulting from the sale of the lease Puritans in Union Square, which had for reputation from the character of its people and ability of Dr. Cheever. This noble was coupled with the condition that the Harlem church should adopt the name of the older society. One of the finest church buildings in New York was then erected and fully paid for, by the aid of the Church Extension Committee of the New-York Presbytery and the self-sacrificing offerings of its members. The church is Gothic in architecture, and beautifully decorated, in simple and elegant taste, much of the carved

Second Presbyterian from the generosity of the new church the of the Church of the long years a national and the public spirit gift of about $87,000

PARK PRESBYTERIAN CHURCH, AMSTERDAM AVENUE AND WEST 86TH STREET.

woodwork and plaster-work having been designed and executed by Rev. Dr. Edward L. Clark, the pastor for more than twenty years, until 1893. The church has steadily advanced in a noble and liberal spirit of Christian love and charity. It has partaken of the wide influence of the church after which it was named, and has been a power for righteousness in the great community of Harlem.

The Washington-Heights Presbyterian Church, at 155th Street and Amsterdam Avenue, was built in 1860. The Rev. Dr. Charles A. Stoddard was its pastor for 25 years, during which time the church was built and paid for. He resigned to become editor of the *New-York Observer.* The Rev. Dr. John C. Bliss is the present pastor. Isaac L. Peet, LL. D., of the Deaf and Dumb Institution, the officers of the Juvenile Asylum and the Colored

WASHINGTON-HEIGHTS PRESBYTERIAN CHURCH, AMSTERDAM AVENUE AND WEST 155TH STREET.

Orphan Asylum, Shepherd Knapp, William A. Wheelock, F. N. DuBois and many others, have been, or are, members of this congregation. The building occupies ground which once formed part of the estate of Audubon, the naturalist, and over which the battle of Harlem Heights was fought ; and some mementoes of this battle were found in digging for foundations. The church is free from debt, and is in a prosperous and healthy condition. It is a landmark in this locality.

The Rutgers Riverside Presbyterian Church dates back to 1798, when this and the Brick and Wall-Street societies formed the three collegiate Presbyterian churches of New York. Milledoler, McClellan, McCauley and Krebs were its early pastors. The handsome church on Madison Avenue pertained to the Madison-Avenue society, which united with the Rutgers. In 1888 the

RUTGERS RIVERSIDE PRESBYTERIAN CHURCH, BOULEVARD AND 73D STREET.

church was sold to the Freemasons. This famous old society is now flourishing amain, in its beautiful new home at the Boulevard and 73d Street. The Rev. Dr. R. R. Booth is the pastor.

The Riverdale Presbyterian Church was organized in 1863, and the present church-building, a very pretty Gothic structure, designed by Renwick, was completed the same year. The first pastor was Rev. Dr. George M. Boynton. He was followed in 1867 by Rev. Dr. H. H. Stebbins, in 1874 by Rev. Charles H. Burr, and in 1879 by Rev. William R. Lord. Rev. Ira S. Dodd was installed in 1883, and is the present pastor. For many years the Riverdale Church has maintained a mission at Spuyten Duyvil. In 1889 a beautiful new chapel, called, after the old one, the Edgehill Chapel, was completed at Spuyten Duyvil, where it is the only

FIRST METHODIST PLACE OF WORSHIP IN NEW YORK, 120 WILLIAM STREET.

house of worship. The evening service of the church is now held there. There is also a flourishing Sunday-school and Society of Christian Endeavor at Spuyten Duyvil. The morning service is held at the church at Riverdale. The Riverdale Church is the most northerly in the New-York Presbytery. The gray stone church and parsonage are among the most picturesque and beautiful in suburban New York.

The First Reformed Presbyterian Church, at 123 West Twelfth Street, was opened in 1849. The society, organized in 1797, was the first Reformed Presbyterian organization in America. The early meetings were held in school-rooms, shops and other humble places, until the building of a small church in Chambers Street, in 1801. In 1845 the Union Presbyterian Church on Prince Street was purchased. For nearly three-quarters of a century the church had but two pastors, Dr. Alexander McLeod and his son, Rev. John Niel McLeod, who labored faithfully for this devoted

flock. Later pastors have been Wm. Wylie, 1874; J. M. Stephens, 1887; and James D. Steele, Ph. D., the present incumbent, installed in 1891.

The John-Street Methodist-Episcopal Church, the first organized society of that denomination in America, was formed by Philip Embury in 1766, with four or five members. The meetings were held in Embury's house, and later in a rigging loft on William Street, until 1768, when a stone church, 60 feet long and 42 in width, was built in John Street, and called Wesley Chapel. The exterior walls of the church were covered with blue plaster, and for some years the interior was left unfinished, the only means of ascent to the galleries being by means of ladders. At that period in the colonial history no public services could be performed in churches except such as were established by law, and a fire-place and chimney were among

JOHN-STREET METHODIST-EPISCOPAL CHURCH,
44 JOHN STREET.

the internal fittings of the building, in order that it might legally be regarded as a private dwelling. A second church was erected on the same site in 1817; and in 1841 the third and present structure was built, somewhat smaller than the earlier building, with two brick houses, one on each side, as a source of income. The external appearance of the church, which is Doric in its style, is simple and plain, and the interior is devoid of any striking features. The only relics of the old John-Street Church which have been preserved are its venerable clock, the gift of John Wesley, and its library. The site of the church, 44 John Street, has been called "the cradle of American Methodism." The John-Street Church has been the mother of many churches. It has long been the Mecca of American Methodists.

Its pastor is the Rev. F. G. Howell. The Methodist-Episcopal Church was formally organized in America in 1773. In 1817 there were five churches of that denomination in New York: the John-Street; the Forsyth-Street, consecrated in 1789; the Duane-Street, in 1797; the Two-Mile-Stone (now Seventh-Street); and the Allen-Street. The denomination now ranks among the foremost in the city, with 57 churches and 14,000 members.

The Seventh-Street Methodist-Episcopal Church was formed in 1786 by the Rev. William Veloe, a zealous local preacher from the John-Street Church. The earlier meetings were held in a private residence,

ASBURY METHODIST-EPISCOPAL CHURCH, WASHINGTON SQUARE
AND WASHINGTON PLACE.

and were known as the "Two - Mile - Stone Meetings." Later the Village Academy on the Bowery was used for the meetings, and here Bishop Asbury preached. The first church edifice was erected in 1818, near the Academy, and became known as the Bowery Village Church. The building was soon removed to 7th Street, near Second Avenue, and here the tumult of a long revival so troubled the wealthy families who had colonized St. Mark's Place, that they gladly offered to give two lots near Third Avenue and other considerations to have the church removed. The offer was accepted, and the church was moved to the present site. The more modern edifice was erected in 1836, and is a plain brick structure of

MADISON-AVENUE CHURCH, METHODIST-EPISCOPAL, MADISON AVENUE AND EAST 60TH STREET.

the Grecian temple style, with large columns at the front. The chief interest of the church is its age. The pastor is the Rev. J. V. Saunders.

The **Asbury Methodist-Episcopal Church**, at the corner of Washington Square East and Washington Place, is a rich old society, with an average Sunday congregation of fewer than a hundred, owing to the general occupation of the vicinity

ST. ANDREW'S METHODIST-EPISCOPAL CHURCH, WEST 11TH STREET, NEAR COLUMBUS AVENUE.

by foreigners. Its two towers are familiar features in the picturesque environment of Washington Square. In 1893 its members joined the Washington-Place M. E. Church.

The **Madison-Avenue Methodist-Episcopal Church**, an impressive brownstone building in the Romanesque style, at Madison

SWEDISH METHODIST-EPISCOPAL CHURCH, LEXINGTON AVENUE AND EAST 52D STREET.

Avenue and East 60th Street, was built in 1882. Its most striking external features are the graceful tower and the pleasing variation of its lines. The auditorium is large and tastefully decorated. This was General Grant's spiritual home during his last years; and the large and fashionable congregation sustains many practical and beneficent charities.

St. Andrew's Methodist-Episcopal Church, on 76th Street, near Columbus Avenue, has grown out of a prayer-meeting held 25 years ago, on West 69th Street, by Townsend H. Harrington. Under the auspices of the New-York City Sunday-School and Missionary Society it began, in 1882, to occupy a neat stone chapel at West 71st Street, near Columbus Avenue. The present church was com- the early Romanesque and is one of the hand- sides the church, there is novel and charming as a stained-glass windows; lated.

Church is a plain and

pleted and dedicated June 8, 1890. It is in style, the front being of Indiana limestone; somest Methodist churches in the city. Be- a chapel and parsonage. The interior is place of worship, and has several exquisite and the whole is admirably lighted and venti-

The Swedish Methodist-Episcopal spacious structure at the corner of Lexington Avenue and East 52d Street, and has a large and devout constituency among the Scandina- vians of the city.

Calvary Metho- dist-Episcopal Church is said to have the largest congrega- tion of any church of that denomination in the city, although it is of recent formation, the organization having been effected in 1883. In 1887 a commodious brick edifice was built at the corner of Seventh Avenue and 129th

CALVARY METHODIST-EPISCOPAL CHURCH, SEVENTH AVENUE AND WEST 129TH STREET.

Street, under the pastorate of Rev. F. M. North, D. D., and largely through the generosity of the late J. B. Cornell. In 1890, in the pastorate of Rev. James R. Day, D. D., this edifice was more than doubled in its seating capacity, and is now the largest Protestant church auditorium in the city. The church is Romanesque in style, with a massive tower, impressive from its size but not strikingly picturesque in treatment. It is attractively furnished and decorated, and abundantly lighted from three large Catharine-wheel windows and numerous smaller ones, and from a beautiful stained-glass opening in the flat panelled ceiling. A spacious gallery, with graceful horseshoe curve, accommodating 800 people, sweeps around three sides of the auditorium, and there is a feeling of roominess and light which adds to the general attractiveness. A large lecture-room and several Sunday-school rooms are connected with the church. The pastor is the Rev. Dr. James R. Day.

The Park-Avenue Methodist-Episcopal Church is at the corner of Park Avenue and 86th Street, near Central Park. It is an ancient society, dating its origin from about the year 1836, when its little congregation of five members began to meet in a chamber over a grocery store. Then for a time it held meetings at the house of Gilbert Bates, at Third Avenue and 84th Street; and afterwards it bought the church of the Bowery Village, and re- erected it at Third Avenue and 86th Street. This little band of wor- shippers retained its connection with the Harlem Mission until after the great revival of 1842, when it became inde- pendent. Its new church on the old site was dedicated by Bishop Janes, in 1859; and in 1884 its pres- ent handsome brownstone church was dedicated by Bish- op Warren. Under the place where the preacher stands are several of the great tim- bers shaped by Philip Em- bury, and used in the origi- nal John-Street Church, and afterwards in the Bowery Church. The society has now 600 members, and is flourishing nobly, under the ministration of the Rev. Fer- dinand C. Iglehart.

PARK-AVENUE METHODIST-EPISCOPAL CHURCH, PARK AVENUE AND 86TH STREET.

St. James' Methodist-Episcopal Church, at Madison Avenue and 126th Street, is a noble outgrowth of the historic Harlem Mission. Its early meetings were held at John James's house, on 125th Street, between Third Avenue and Lexington Avenue; in a store on Third Avenue; in 1831 in the Academy on 120th Street, between Second and Third Avenues; and in its church built in 1834 on 125th Street between Third and Fourth Avenues. In 1869 the society bought land at its present site; and in 1870 Bishop Janes laid the corner-stone of the present fine brownstone church, which was dedicated in 1871, at which time the society received the name of St. James's. This handsome and attractive edifice is adjoined by a chapel and a parsonage. The society has over 700 members. Its pastor is the Rev. Jacob E. Price, D. D.

The First
Baptist Church
was formed in
1762, by the re-
organization of the
Gold-Street con-
gregation, and un-
der the zealous
ministry of the
Rev. John Gano,
which lasted
through the Revo-
lutionary era, when
the people were
scattered, and the
church became a
stable. A larger
stone church was
opened in 1802;
followed by a still

JUDSON MEMORIAL BAPTIST CHURCH, WASHINGTON SQUARE AND THOMPSON STREET.

more spacious temple, at Broome and Elizabeth Streets, in 1842. In 1871 the great
Gothic church at Park Avenue and 39th Street was dedicated; and when the
encroachments of trade made this locality undesirable, the property was sold, in
1890, and the society occupied the brick chapel on West 81st Street. The First
Church has had but nine pastors, in 131 years; and among
them were the Rev. John Gano, the patriotic Revolutionary
chaplain, who offered the prayer of thanksgiving at Newburgh;
the Rev. Dr. Spencer H. Cone, long-time President of the American and Foreign Bible Society and the American Bible
Union, and one of the leaders in the re-translation of the
Scriptures; and Rev. Dr. Thomas B. Anderson, pastor from 1862
to 1878, a genial, scholarly and eloquent divine. The Rev.
Isaac M. Haldeman became pastor in 1884. The new edifice
of the First Baptist Church on 81st Street,
between West-End Avenue and the Boulevard, is an architectural gem, and has
but few superiors in the
metropolis.

ST. JAMES METHODIST-EPISCOPAL CHURCH, MADISON AVENUE.

The Baptists began work
in New York before 1669;
and their first preacher, William Wickenden of Rhode
Island, was imprisoned for
several months. The first
church, founded in 1712,
died in 1720; and its successor, founded in 1745, advanced but slowly, holding
worship for some years in a
rigging-loft in Horse and

Cart Lane (now William Street). In 1760 the society built a small stone church on Gold Street. The city now has 44 Baptist churches, with 14,000 members, who support many commendable institutions.

The Judson Memorial Baptist Church, on Washington Square, succeeds the old Berean Baptist Church, organized in 1838, and formerly worshipping in Downing Street. The imposing group of buildings in Washington Square was completed in 1892, at a cost of $450,000, as a memorial to the Rev. Dr. Adoniram Judson, the first American foreign missionary. The main building, Greco-Romanesque in style, is a handsome structure of ornate buff brick, with a conspicuous tall square tower, surmounted by a cross which at night is illuminated by electricity. It contains a beautiful auditorium, with massive columns and marble wainscoting, and

stained windows ; a spacious Sunday-school room ; a day-school, where children under ten years of age receive religious and secular instruction ; and the young men's apartments, including a social room, reading-room and library, and gymnasium. A house for children and other apartments occupy the square tower ; and adjoining is the Judson, a large apartment-house belonging to the church, its revenue being devoted to the support of the Children's House

FIRST BAPTIST CHURCH, BOULEVARD AND WEST 79TH STREET.

and other philanthropic activities. The excellent music is rendered by a chorus choir of 100 young persons. The work of the church is mainly among the crowded population of the neighborhood, which is rapidly increasing, owing to the replacement of small old-fashioned dwellings by tall apartment-houses, holding from twelve to sixteen families each. The Rev. Dr. Edward Judson is pastor. The architects were McKim, Mead & White.

Baptist Church of the Epiphany, Madison Avenue and 64th Street, is the home of a strong religious organization. It is one of the oldest Baptist societies in the city, with a history running back in unbroken succession to the year 1791, when a few members of the Second Baptist Church organized the Fayette-Street Baptist society, and in 1795 erected a small wooden meeting-house, on the corner of Oliver and Henry Streets. There the congregation remained until 1860, when a new church was built in 33d Street. Still later, a larger and finer church was occupied, on 53d Street, but a troublesome lawsuit led to the dispossession of the congregation, and the erection of the present brownstone Gothic edifice in 1882. The Madison-Avenue front is quite imposing, with its lofty gable and double

towers. The attractively decorated auditorium has a high open roof, and seats about 1,000.

Calvary Church is one of the strongest Baptist congregations, as its ecclesiastical home is one of the finest. The parish was organized in 1846; its first pastor and many of its members coming from the old Stanton-Street Baptist Church. Its first place of worship was Hope Chapel, on Broadway; but so great was the success of the work, under the Rev. Dr. John Dowling, that in 1854 a large brownstone edifice was erected on 23d Street. One of

BAPTIST CHURCH OF THE EPIPHANY, MADISON AVENUE AND EAST 64TH STREET.

the noted pastors of the church was the Rev. Dr. Gillette, who acted as the spiritual adviser to the conspirators who murdered President Lincoln. The present pastor is the Rev. Dr. Robert S. MacArthur, one of the most eloquent preachers in the city. The church was erected in 1883. It occupies a commanding position on West 57th Street, near Seventh Avenue, and close by the new Music Hall. It is Gothic in style, substantially built of Albion red sandstone and Lockport stone; and with its tall steeple, smaller tower, and long extended front it makes an imposing show. Above the central doors is a magnificent Catharine-wheel window, twenty feet in diameter, filled with richly stained and jewelled glass. The interior appointments are beautiful and complete. The main auditorium, sloping down from the entrance toward the pulpit, has a seating capacity of nearly 1,500, and is abundantly lighted by many windows of richly colored glass, some of them being memorials. In the centre of the lofty ceiling is a large lantern, whose central part is carried up into a dome, with sides and top filled with painted glass, producing a very rich effect. Galleries, in a horseshoe curve, are carried around three sides of the auditorium, and behind the imposing bronze pulpit and over the baptistery, a triplet of richly carved panels with central medallions form an effective background. The organ is one of the largest and finest in the city, containing 41 speaking registers, divided among three manuals. On the east of the auditorium is a beautiful chapel for special services. The membership is over 1,900, and the parish is the centre of much religious and humane work, one of its adjuncts being a mission on 68th Street, near the Boulevard, which is doing a valuable work in that vicinity.

The North Baptist Church, at 234 West 11th Street, was erected in 1882, to replace the church on Christopher Street, which had been built in 1828. It is an attractive Gothic building, with a large and pleasant auditorium. The society was organized in 1827, with twelve members, and the early meetings were held in the school-house on Amos (now West 10th) Street. The congregation afterwards removed to the old Green-wich-Village Watch-house, where the Rev. Jacob H. Brouner began a long and successful pastorate. Rev. John J. Brouner, the present pastor, was installed in 1869.

Trinity Baptist Church was founded in 1866 by Dr. J. Stanford Holme, who began preaching in a small hall on West 52d Street. A large congregation was soon gathered, and in 1870 the church of the Eleventh Presbyterian society, at 141 East 55th Street, was purchased, and here the congregation has remained and prospered.

The Baptist Tabernacle, at 166 Second Avenue, adjoining the Historical Society, was formed in 1839 by members of the older Mulberry-Street Church. In 1850 the church left Mulberry Street, and erected the present Gothic edifice during

CALVARY BAPTIST CHURCH, 57TH STREET, BETWEEN SIXTH AND SEVENTH AVENUES.

Dr. Edward Lathrop's pastorate. In 1886 the present pastor, Dr. D. C. Potter, remodelled the interior, making it an amphitheatre. He also added the large parish-house adjoining. The church has important missions and country houses, and one of the largest and finest organs in the city. The late Dr. A. C. Kendrick and Dr. Wayland Hoyt were among its pastors.

The Madison-Avenue Baptist Church is another of the leading societies of this denomination. It was organized in 1839, as the Rose-Hill Baptist Church. Its first meeting-house, on Lexington Avenue, is now occupied by the Moravian Brethren. The substantial stone edifice at Madison Avenue and East 31st Street was erected in 1858. The large auditorium, seating nearly 1,200, is tastefully decorated. Dr. Henry M. Saunders is the pastor.

MADISON-AVENUE BAPTIST CHURCH, MADISON AVENUE AND EAST 31ST STREET.

The Fifth-Avenue Baptist Church, at 6 West 46th Street, was erected in 1861. It is a plain brownstone building, with a large and tastefully decorated auditorium. Its pulpit was acceptably filled for forty years by Dr. Thomas Armitage, who resigned in 1888. The society was organized in 1841, and before the removal to 46th Street it worshipped in a church on Norfolk Street. Because of its prominent and wealthy members, it is regarded as one of the foremost Baptist congregations of New York.

St. Matthew's Church, at 354 Broome Street, is the oldest Lutheran society in the city. In 1841 the church in Walker Street was purchased from the English Lutherans, and in 1868 the church in Broome Street was bought from the Baptists, and has ever since remained the ecclesiastical house of the German Lutherans in its vicinity. The Lutherans were early comers to New York. They first attempted to hold services in 1653, about the time of the Indian massacres at Pavonia and Hoboken; but Governor Stuyvesant issued a proclamation, the first in New York against freedom of conscience, forbidding the people to assemble 'for any public service contrary to that of the Reformed Church.

He was rebuked by the Dutch West India Company for his intolerance, and the Rev. Ernestus Goetwater was sent out from Holland to organize a Lutheran church. But he was ignominiously sent back, and the members were heavily fined. According to the old Dutch records, still extant, and in the custody of this church, the congregation again sought recognition in 1656, but it was again refused. The Lutheran Church was formally recognized by the English Governor, Richard Nicolls. The document bears date 1664. Their first church-edifice stood near where now Bowling Green

FIFTH-AVENUE BAPTIST CHURCH, 6 WEST 46TH STREET.

is. According to an order of the Dutch, who had again taken possession of the island, it was razed to the ground, with many other buildings, because it was deemed an obstacle to a proper defence in case of an attack. But the government paid the congregation 45 guilders in cash, and gave it a new plot of ground to build on. The documents bearing on this transaction bear the signatures of A. Colve, Governor, and N. Bayard, Secretary. The property which the government gave in lieu of the former ground and church is designated as " No. 5, west of Broadway, between the property of George Cobbet and the City-wall"; date, "May 22, 1674." It was four rods square. Up to 1749 the services were held entirely in the Dutch language, although the Germans preponderated as eight to one. From that time the Germans demanded services in their own tongue. When this was refused, they separated, and organized as the Lutheran German Christ Church, and bought an old brewery on what is now Cliff Street. In 1767 they built the "Swamp Church," at the corner of Frankfort and William Streets. In the year 1789 the two congregations united again, under the name "United German Lutheran

TIFFANY MANSION
ST. JAMES' LUTHERAN CHURCH, MADISON AVENUE AND EAST 73D STREET.

Churches in the City of New York." In the year 1866 their name was changed by an act of the Legislature to "German Evangelical Lutheran Church of St. Matthew." The pastor of this venerable and historic church is the Rev. J. H. Sicker.

St. James' Lutheran Church, at Madison Avenue and East 73d Street, is the home of the first English Lutheran congregation organized in the city. The society was formed in 1827, and its first church, the gift of Pierre Lorillard, was in Orange Street. Following the constant up-town movement, it has made three removals ; in 1843 to Mulberry Street ; then to Stuyvesant Square ; and in 1890 to its present location. The church is an excellent example of the Gothic Romanesque. It is built of pink Milford stone, with brownstone trimmings. A portico, with a balcony and carved pillars, surmounted by a stone cross, forms the Madison-Avenue entrance. Stone pillars with embossed capitals separate the nave from the aisles, and lofty Gothic arches span the chancel and transepts. The richly decorated chancel, with a beautiful marble altar ; the great rose window on Madison Avenue, representing Christ in glory ; the baptismal font, modelled after Thorwaldsen's Angel of Baptism, in the Copenhagen Cathedral ; and other works of art, make the interior attractive. All the interior decorations and the memorial window are the work of the Tiffany Company. The Rev. Dr. J. B. Remensnyder is the pastor.

The Evangelical Lutheran Church of the Holy Trinity, at 47 West 21st Street, was organized in 1868 by a few members of St. James's Church, to provide an English service for the Lutheran residents of the West Side. The Rev. G. F. Krotel, then pastor of St. Mark's Lutheran Church, in Philadelphia, accepted a call to the pastorate ; and the Reformed Dutch Church, formerly the scene of the ministry of the celebrated Dr. Bethune, was leased, and named the Church of the Holy Trinity, in memory of the original Trinity Lutheran Church, built on Manhattan Island two hundred years before. During the 25 years of its history it has grown to be the largest English Lutheran congregation in the city, and has contributed liberally to general church work. The building has recently been re-decorated. Dr. Krotel still retains his position as pastor.

St. Peter's Lutheran Church, at Lexington Avenue and East 46th Street, is a sombre structure in appearance, with its high gable, fronting on the avenue, and its severe square tower rising from the centre of the front. The society was organized in the year 1862, and has been prospered. The Rev. Dr. E. F. Moldenke is the pastor.

The Gustavus Adolphus Church (or Svenska Lutherska Gustaf Adolf Kyrkan, as it is called in the Swedish tongue), is in East 22d Street, near Third Avenue. It is attended by a considerable number of Swedish people, and the affairs of the congregation are in a flourishing condition.

SVENSKA LUTHERSKA GUSTAF ADOLF KYRKAN, LUTHERAN, 22D STREET, NEAR THIRD AVENUE.

The Broadway Tabernacle Church (Congregational) was organized in 1840, and until 1857 worshipped in the Tabernacle built in 1836, by an earlier Congregational society, on Broadway, between Leonard and Worth Streets. During the long pastorate of Dr. Joseph P. Thompson, a great anti-slavery preacher and worker, many stirring scenes were enacted within its walls. The present church, a large Perpendicular Gothic building of stone, at Sixth Avenue and 34th Street, was completed in 1859, and remodelled in 1872. The Rev. Dr. William M. Taylor was pastor from 1872 to 1892. The Rev. Dr. Henry A. Stimson became pastor in 1893.

The first Congregational minister to hold services in the city was the Rev. John Townley, about 1804, and a Congregational church was formed in 1805. Its first building was erected in Elizabeth Street, in 1809, but after a few years of fruitless struggle, under a heavy debt, it was sold to the Asbury colored Methodists, and the congregation disbanded. An Independent Congregational church was organized in 1817, but in 1821 it was united with the Presbyterians. Other organizations were made later, but the strength of the closely related Presbyterian denomination has acted unfavorably upon the growth of New-England Congregationalism in New York, and there are only seven churches in the city.

All Souls' Church, at 245 Fourth Avenue, was the first Unitarian organization in New York. The society was incorporated in 1819, as the "First Congregational Church of New York," from the outcome of a few services held by William Ellery Channing. Edward Everett preached at the dedication of the church, in Chambers Street, in 1820. The Rev. Henry Ware, Jr., was the first pastor, and his successor was Dr. Henry W. Bellows, the President of the Sanitary Commission during the war. The present church was erected in 1855 by J. Wray Mould, the famous and eccentric architect. It is of brick, trimmed with Caen stone, in the form of a Greek cross, and was the first experiment made in this country toward a Byzantine

BROADWAY TABERNACLE, CONGREGATIONAL, SIXTH AVENUE AND WEST 34TH STREET.

style of architecture, though the remarkable tower drawn in the original design was never completed. The full-length bronze bas-relief of Dr. Henry W. Bellows, by Augustus St. Gaudens, is considered one of his best works. It can be seen by ringing the bell at the north door. The entrance-porch is effective in treatment, and the large auditorium is unobstructed by pillars. A central lantern rises above the roof, and

25   ALL SOULS' UNITARIAN CHURCH, FOURTH AVENUE AND EAST 20TH STREET.

the transepts are spanned by lofty round arches. A large parish-house adjoins the church. Rev. Theodore C. Williams is the pastor. All Souls' was the church of the poet Bryant and of Peter Cooper, and among its present attendants are Joseph H. Choate, Dorman B. Eaton and Daniel H. Chamberlain.

The Church of the Messiah is a well-proportioned brownstone building in the Gothic style, with a large and attractive interior. The parish was formed in 1825 by a few members of the older Chambers-Street society. The first church, in Prince Street, was destroyed by fire in 1837; and two years later another was built on Broadway, near Washington Square, and called the Church of the Messiah. In 1867 the present church was erected, at the corner of Park Avenue and East 34th Street. Orville Dewey was once pastor of the church, which is now in charge of the Rev. Dr. Robert Collyer.

The Lenox-Avenue Unitarian Church, the youngest Unitarian society in New York, has a handsome new building at Lenox Avenue and 121st Street. Rev. Merle St. Croix Wright is pastor.

The Church of the Divine Paternity is the strongest Universalist congregation. The building is a brownstone Gothic edifice at Fifth Avenue and 45th Street, and dates from 1865. The society was formed in 1839, and the first church stood in Elizabeth Street, running through to the Bowery, between Hester and Canal Streets. In 1845 the society moved to more commodious quarters, in Murray Street, just west of Broadway. In 1848 a third building was erected, on Broadway, between Prince

CHURCH OF THE MESSIAH, UNITARIAN, PARK AVENUE AND EAST 34TH STREET.

and Spring Streets; and here, under the Rev. Dr. Edward H. Chapin, the parish increased rapidly in strength and influence. The Rev. Charles H. Eaton is the present pastor.

The society was the fourth Universalist organization in the city. Towards the close of the last century the Rev. John Murray and other preachers of Universalism held services, and induced several prominent members of the John-Street Methodist Church to unite in the "Society of United Christian Friends of New York," formed in 1796. The next year a small church was built, in Vandewater Street, and Edward Mitchell was installed as pastor. He was an eloquent preacher, and in 1818 a large brick church was erected in Duane Street. Mr. Mitchell died soon afterward; and the congregation disbanded. A second society was organized in 1824. There are now three Universalist churches in New York.

The Church of The Strangers, at 299 Mercer Street, was purchased by Commodore Vanderbilt in 1870, and presented to the Rev. Dr. Charles F. Deems, as a token of interest in his work. Dr. Deems, who had been a Methodist-Episcopal clergyman, in North Carolina, came to the city in 1866, and began to preach in the chapel of the University of New York. His practical and independent presentation of the truths of Christianity attracted large audiences, and in 1868 a church was organized and called The Church of The Strangers, on account of its special field of work among sojourners in the city. It has no organic connection with any of the denominations, and remains faithful to its original work, which is a source of great blessing to the strangers within our gates.

The Broome-Street Tabernacle, at 395 Broome Street, is a station of the New-York City Mission and Tract Society, and the centre of an important work among the 60,000 English-speaking people in its vicinity, for whom there is no other Protestant church. It is a substantial brick building, with a large auditorium, a reading-room and library, a gymnasium, and numerous smaller rooms. The Lodging-House Missionary Society carries on an aggressive missionary work in the lodging-houses in the vicinity of the Tabernacle, and numerous other societies are actively engaged in philanthropic work, resulting in great good in

CHURCH OF THE DIVINE PATERNITY, UNIVERSALIST, FIFTH AVENUE AND WEST 45TH STREET.

this populous district. The minister in charge is the Rev. C. H. Tyndall.

The Church of the New Jerusalem, at 114 East 35th Street, a substantial stone building in the Doric style, was erected in 1859. The founder of the New Church (often called Swedenborgian) in New York was Edward Riley, who came from England in 1805. The society was organized in 1816, with the name of The Association of the City of New York for the Dissemination of the Heavenly Doctrines of the New Jerusalem; and in 1821 a small church in Pearl Street was purchased, and the Rev. Charles I. Doughty installed as pastor. The Pearl-Street church was sold to the Zion Baptist society in 1838, and the services were held in various places until the erection of the 35th-Street building; and this, and a mission at 356 West 44th Street, and a German church on Chrystie Street, are the only New-Church places of worship in the city. Rev. Samuel S. Seward is pastor.

The Church of the Disciples of Christ, at 323 West 56th Street, a substantial brick building in the Gothic style, was erected in 1883, and is the spiritual home of the oldest local congregation of that denomination. Its pastor is the Rev. Dr. B. B. Tyler. At different periods in its history the society has worshipped in halls and churches on Hubert, Greene, 17th and West 28th Streets, and it has grown and increased with gratifying certainty.

The Disciples date from about the year 1827. Their purpose is to unite Christians in a visible fellowship on the basis of Primitive Christianity, as described in the New Testament — its creed — its ordinances — its life. They number nearly 1,000,-000. Their greatest strength is in the West and South, where they are known as "Christians," or "Christian

CHURCH OF THE STRANGERS, 299 MERCER STREET.

Church." They are sometimes called "Campbellites" (which name, however, they repudiate), from Alexander Campbell, one of their early preachers. There are three churches of Disciples in New York.

The Catholic Apostolic Church is a handsome structure, at 417 West 57th Street. The congregation was organized in 1850, and the early services were held in a small room in the University of the City of New York. About 1855 a church was purchased in West 16th Street. This was sold to the French Presbyterian society in 1886, when the present edifice was opened. The Catholic Apostolic people are better known as

CHURCH OF THE NEW JERUSALEM, SWEDENBORGIAN, 114 EAST 35TH STREET.

BROOME-STREET TABERNACLE, BROOME STREET AND
CENTER MARKET STREET.

Irvingites, from the Rev. Edward Irving, a Scottish clergyman, who is popularly regarded as the founder of the movement. (This name they themselves repudiate.) One of the distinctive features of the sect is a return to apostolic methods and principles; another is "the preparation of the church as a body for the coming and kingdom of the Lord." Daily services are held at 6 A. M. and 5 P. M., and the Holy Communion is celebrated every Sunday morning. There are about 400 members. The church building was planned by F. H. Kimball. There is also a small German congregation.

The Swedish Evangelical Bethesda Church, at 240 East 45th Street and on 127th Street, supports three missionaries in China and three in Kongo, Africa. The church was organized in 1878, by a few members of the Swedish Lutheran Church, who left that body by reason of differences of opinion on matters of doctrine and discipline. There are 300 members. The pastor is the Rev. Professor K. Erixon.

The Reading-Room and Church for Seamen is a picturesque structure at the corner of Houston and West Streets, in the midst of the busy North-River traffic district. It is maintained by the Society for Promoting the Gospel among Seamen.

The Friends' Meeting-House, on Stuyvesant Square, a plain but substantial brick building, with a large school-house connected, was erected in 1860, and is one of the two Quaker places of worship in the city, the other being an equally plain building with a brownstone front, on Gramercy Park. The first Quakers came to New Amsterdam in 1657, fugitives from New England, and received but scanty welcome from Peter Stuyvesant, who arrested two of the women for

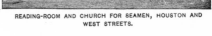

READING-ROOM AND CHURCH FOR SEAMEN, HOUSTON AND
WEST STREETS.

preaching in the streets. One of the men, Robert Hodgson, was arrested at Hempstead, Long Island, whither he had gone intending to preach, and haled before Gov. Stuyvesant, who used him harshly until Mrs. Bayard, the Governor's sister, prevailed upon him to allow the unwelcome visitor to depart in peace. The first meeting-house was built in Little Green Street in 1700, and in 1775 a second was erected in Pearl Street. After the great schism of 1827, the Orthodox Friends built a third meeting-house in Henry Street, leaving the Hicksite party in possession of the others. Later, these were sold, and the two now in use were erected.

The First Moravian Church, at Lexington Avenue and 30th Street, is the fourth edifice occupied by this congregation since the corner-stone of its first church

was laid, June 16, 1751, at the corner of Fulton and Dutch Streets, by Bishop Peter Boehler and the pastor, Rev. Owen Rice, a native of Wales. Its present pastor is Rev. Edward T. Kluge. The society was formed in 1741. The present pastor of the German Moravian Church, 636 Sixth Street, between Avenues B and C, is Rev. William H. Rice, a great-great-grandson of the pastor of 1751. This second Moravian congregation was organized in 1853.

The First Reformed Episcopal Church, at Madison Avenue and East 55th Street, is the only church of that denomination in the city. It is a handsome stone structure, with a large and simply decorated auditorium. It was built in 1876, soon after the formation of the Reformed Episcopal Church, which was organized by a number of Episcopal clergymen and laymen, under the leader-

CATHOLIC APOSTOLIC CHURCH, WEST 57TH STREET, BETWEEN NINTH AND TENTH AVENUES.

ship of Bishop G. D. Cummins, who objected to what they considered the Romanizing tendencies of the Prayer Book. Rev. Dr. William T. Sabine, a former Episcopal clergyman, is in charge of the parish.

The Hebrew-Christian Church, the first of its kind in America, began in 1882 with its present pastor, the Rev. Jacob Freshman, a converted Jew, who had resolved to devote himself to evangelizing the Hebrews of New York. For some time the meetings were held in a small room in the Cooper-Union building, and in the lecture-room of the Fourth-Avenue Presbyterian Church ; but in the year 1885 a private house, at 17 St. Mark's Place, was purchased and fitted up for the work. The audience-room, seating about 150, and lighted by stained-glass windows, is on the ground floor, while the remaining rooms are used by the missionary for various purposes connected with the work, which has met with a fair degree of success.

St. Patrick's Cathedral is the head of the great Archdiocese of New York. Roman Catholics visited Manhattan Island as early as

FRIENDS' CHURCH AND SEMINARY, STUYVESANT SQUARE, EAST 16TH STREET, CORNER OF RUTHERFORD PLACE.

1629, but when Father Isaac Jogues, the first priest to visit the island, came here in 1643, after his escape from the Mohawks, he found only two of his co-religionists. Jesuit fathers labored here at intervals between 1683 and 1785, when the first congregation was formed. Severe laws were enacted against the Catholics, but with no serious results, until the execution of John Ury for alleged participation in the Negro Riot of 1741, and on suspicion of being a Catholic priest. Governor Dongan was an ardent Catholic, as was his royal master, King James, and during his administration, in the closing years of the seventeenth century, a number of Catholic families of repute settled in the city, and a college was founded. In

FIRST REFORMED EPISCOPAL CHURCH, MADISON AVENUE AND EAST 55TH STREET.

1785 Sieur de St. Jean de Crevecœur, the French consul, and three others were incorporated as the Trustees of the Roman Catholic Church in the City of New York, and from that time the Church has steadily grown in numbers and power, largely through the immense foreign immigration. There are 83 Catholic churches and a long list of homes, asylums and schools. There are 400,000 Roman Catholics in the city, and besides the churches for English-speaking persons, there are others for Germans, Italians, Frenchmen, Canadians, Bohemians, Syrians, Afro-Americans, Poles and other nationalities.

St. Patrick's Cathedral, on 5th Avenue, between 50th and 51st Streets, is one of the grandest ecclesiastical buildings in the country, and has cost the greatest sum of money. It was projected by Archbishop Hughes, in 1850, and soon afterward the plans were drawn, by James Renwick, the architect of Grace Church. The corner-stone was laid in 1858, and the Cathedral was opened in 1879. The building is now nearly completed, according to the original plans, only the Lady Chapel remaining to be constructed. The style of the architecture is the Decorated Gothic of the thirteenth century, of which the cathedrals of Rheims and Cologne are examples ; and, with the mansion of the archbishop and the rector's residence, it occupies the entire block bounded by Fifth and Madison Avenues, and 50th and 51st Streets. It is built of white marble, and its leading dimensions are : Length, 322 feet; breadth, including chapels, 120 feet; breadth of nave and choir, 97 feet ; length of transepts, 172 feet ; height of nave, 100 feet ; height of aisles, 54 feet. The principal front, on

ARCHBISHOP'S AND RECTOR'S RESIDENCES.
ST. PATRICK'S CATHEDRAL, ROMAN CATHOLIC, MADISON-AVENUE AND 51ST-STREET SIDES.

Fifth Avenue, consists of a central gable, 156 feet in height, flanked by twin spires, 328 feet high. The grand portal is richly decorated, and buttresses, pinnacles and carved ornamentation abound in rich profusion.

The interior is particularly impressive. Massive clustered marble columns support the lofty groined roof ; the organ-gallery in the nave, between the towers, has a richly moulded front and ceiling ; and a magnificent rose window, 26 feet in diameter, filled with costly glass, dominates the western end, and forms a fitting pendant to the high altar in the sanctuary, in the eastern end. The altar was made in Italy of purest Carrara marble, and its front is inlaid with alabaster and precious stones. The lower front is divided into niches and panels ; the former containing statues of the four Evangelists, and the latter presenting in bas-reliefs the Last Supper, the Carrying of the Cross, the Agony, and the Betrayal. The tabernacle,

ST. PATRICK'S CATHEDRAL, ROMAN CATHOLIC.
FIFTH AVENUE, 50TH AND 51ST STREETS.

ARCHBISHOP'S RESIDENCE, ST. PATRICK'S CATHEDRAL,
MADISON AVENUE AND 50TH STREET.

above the altar, was carved in France, and its three niches contain statues of Our Lord, St. Peter, and St. Paul. The altar of the Blessed Virgin, at the eastern end of the north aisle, is made of French stone, delicately sculptured in panels, on which are carved scenes connected with the life of Christ. At the eastern end of the south aisle is the bronze altar of the Sacred Heart, with four statues, representing the sacrifices of the old dispensation and, in the central niche, Jesus holding a chalice. The columns on each side, surmounted by statues of St. Peter and St. Paul, were the gift of Pope Pius IX. West of the sacristy is the elaborate bronze altar of St. Joseph, and in a side chapel is the altar of the Holy Family, above which hangs a fine painting of the Holy Family, by Costazzini. The Cathedral is seated for 2,600 people, and nearly as many more can be accommodated in the aisles. The interior is lighted by 70 windows, the majority being memorial windows made in Chartres, France, at a cost of over $100,000. The total cost of the building has been not far from $3,000,000, and $500,000 will be necessary to complete it.

St. Peter's Church, at Barclay and Church Streets, is the oldest Roman Catholic organization in the city. The first church, a brick building, 48 feet wide and 81 feet long, was erected in 1786, and torn down in 1836, when the present stone church in the Ionic style was erected in its place. The interior is spacious, and contains a fine marble altar. The ceiling is frescoed, and there are 12 large stained-glass windows.

St. Patrick's Church is the oldest existing Catholic church-building in the city. It was built in 1815, at Mott and Prince Streets, and until the opening of St. Patrick's Cathedral, in 1879, it was the cathedral church of the See of

ST. PETER'S CHURCH, ROMAN CATHOLIC, BARCLAY AND CHURCH STREETS.

ST. PATRICK'S CATHEDRAL, ROMAN CATHOLIC.
THE HIGH ALTAR IN THE SANCTUARY, AT THE EASTERN END.

ST. PATRICK'S CHURCH, ROMAN CATHOLIC, MOTT AND
PRINCE STREETS.

New York. In earlier days the massive Gothic building, with its richly decorated auditorium, was one of the sights of the city; but with the departure of the Archbishop it lost much of its ancient fame, and is now merely the parish-church of the Catholics who live in the neighborhood.

The Church of St. Benedict the Moor is an impressive classic building, at 210 Bleecker Street, in one of the ancient and crowded quarters of the city. The congregation is mainly composed of colored people.

St. Stephen's Roman Catholic Church was organized in 1850, and a portion of the large Italian Renaissance building, on 28th Street, between Third and Lexington Avenues, was opened in 1855. This was enlarged and richly decorated in 1865. It extends through to 29th Street. It is cruciform in shape, and the interior is extremely beautiful. Above each of the transept galleries are large rose-windows, and the side windows of the nave are filled with richly stained glass. A fine painting of the Crucifixion surmounts a lofty marble altar in the sanctuary. The beautiful high altar and the two rich side altars cost $40,000. St. Stephen's has long been one of the fashionable Catholic churches, and for many years its choir has been acknowledged as one of the finest in the country. The Rev. Dr. J. W. Cummings founded this church, and Dr. Edward McGlynn held the pastorate from 1866 until 1887. During his term of office a large Orphans' House and an Industrial School for girls were built. Father Colton is now the rector.

The church property extends through the whole block from 28th Street to 29th Street.

CHURCH OF ST. BENEDICT THE MOOR, ROMAN CATHOLIC,
210 BLEECKER STREET.

St. Francis Xavier's Church, at 36 West 16th Street, near Sixth Avenue, was erected in 1882, and is in charge of the Jesuit Fathers. It is a massive stone structure in the Roman Basilica style, and is constructed in the substantial manner which characterizes the work of the Jesuits. A lofty porch, with massive stone pillars, and a vestibule, both with vaulted stone ceilings, give entrance to one of the grandest church interiors in the city. The church is cruciform in shape; and the lofty vaulted and richly decorated ceiling of the nave is supported by stone columns carrying a triforium gallery, pierced with round-arched openings. The prevailing tone of the decorations gives an effect of luminosity, and there is a profusion of ornamentation in relief. The high altar is a costly marble structure, and on either side of the sanctuary stand the altars of the Blessed Virgin and St. Joseph. In the transepts are the altars of St. Aloysius and the Sacred Heart, all in marble, with statues and carvings. The walls are filled with large paintings of Scriptural scenes. Twelve hundred electric lights have been placed in the church, which is illustrated on page 285. On this site stood the old church of the same name, founded in 1847. The Infanta Eulalia of Spain visited St. Francis Xavier's in 1893.

The Church of St. Paul the Apostle, at Ninth Avenue and 59th Street, is one of the greatest Catholic churches in the city, second only to the Cathedral in size and magnificence. It is in charge of the Paulist Fathers, a missionary order founded in 1858 by the late Very Rev. Isaac Hecker, who, with four other converts from Protestantism, began a remarkable series of missions throughout the United States. The community then established has since increased to twenty-five priests and sixteen theological students. The Paulist Fathers devote all the time they can spare from the missions to the preparation and spread of Catholic literature. In connection with the great Church of St. Paul they have a large convent and school-house, and lately built a printing-house, from which they issue their monthly publications, *The Catholic World, The Young Catholic,* calendars, sermons, tracts, etc. The cornerstone of the first church was laid in 1859, and of the present church in 1876, while the solemn opening took place in 1885. It is the second largest church edi-

CHURCH OF ST. PAUL THE APOSTLE, ROMAN CATHOLIC, NINTH AVENUE AND WEST 59TH STREET.

fice in the country, being 284 feet long and 132 feet wide. The walls are constructed of rough stone, and there is very little attempt at mere ornament, the architect aiming to obtain simplicity and dignity by the size and massiveness of the building, correctness of detail and harmonious grouping. The main façade, on Ninth Avenue, approached by a double flight of granite steps, is 134 feet wide, with a central compartment flanked by two towers 38 feet square, and with a total height of 300 feet when the spires are built. The style of architecture is the Thirteenth-Century Gothic, adapted to meet the special needs of the Fathers. The spacious and impressive interior, with its side aisles and passages, has a seating capacity of nearly 5,000. The lofty nave arches are carried by columns of polished Syracuse limestone, four feet in diameter, alternately round and octagonal, with carved caps and moulded bases over each arch ; the tracery windows of the clerestory give ample light from above, leaving a large expanse of wall space for effective decorative work. The windows, twenty-seven feet in length and twelve in

ACADEMY OF THE HOLY CROSS FOR YOUNG LADIES, AND CHURCH OF THE HOLY CROSS, ROMAN CATHOLIC, 335-343 WEST 42D STREET.

width, are of the finest workmanship. Those in the sanctuary represent the Queen of Angels surrounded by hundreds of angels in the centre, and flanked on either side by the four great archangels, all in adoration of the Blessed Sacrament on the altar. These were made in Munich. The fourteen tracery windows in the nave, the work of the American artist LaFarge, are unrivalled for richness of color. The sanctuary floor is well elevated above that of the nave, and contains the high altar, of variegated marble, with a lofty baldichino, whose canopied roof is supported by polished columns of Numidian marble. The great organ stands behind the high altar, and on each side are the stalls for the choir and the dignitaries of the Church. On the left of the sanctuary, at the head of the south aisle, is the altar of the Blessed Virgin, constructed of Siena marble and beautiful Mexican onyx, and surmounted by a lofty canopy, beneath which is a large marble statue of the Virgin. At the head of the north aisle is the altar of St. Joseph, similar in treatment, with a marble statue of the saint. At the end of the south aisle, and near the entrance, is a beautiful baptistery, with marble font, enclosed by a substantial marble rail. In the side chapels of the same aisle are altars of St. Agnes, The Annunciation and St. Justinus the Martyr. The side chapels of the north aisle contain the altars of the Sacred Heart, St. Catharine of Genoa and St. Patrick. The total cost of all the altars was not far from $50,000, and of the whole church $500,000. The magnitude of the interior is best shown by a few figures : The length of the nave and chancel is 257 feet, the width 60 feet, and the height 96 feet, while the aisles have

ST. CECILIA'S CHURCH, ROMAN CATHOLIC, EAST 106TH STREET, NEAR LEXINGTON AVENUE.

a combined width of 50 feet, giving an auditorium of immense size and striking and impressive perspective effect. The impression of immense space, height and solitude of the interior is increased by the treatment of the ceiling, which is painted a deep blue and studded with stars. It is concave in form, and the stars and constellations which thickly stud its surface are arranged from exact maps made by one of the Paulist Fathers, to represent their positions on January 25, 1885, the festival of the conversion of St. Paul, the patron-saint of the church. The decoration of the church is in the hands of the well-known artist LaFarge, and looks its best when lighted at night. The Annunciation altar has a fine copy of the Michael Angelo at Bruges ; and St. Justinus' altar has a bronze reredos, by James Kelly. Here, every Sunday evening, can be heard the best congregational singing of English hymns in New York. The singing at the other regular services is done by a surpliced choir of 100 men and boys. The group of buildings of which St. Paul's is the centre forms one of the strongest fortresses of Catholicism in New York.

CHURCH OF OUR LADY OF GOOD COUNSEL, ROMAN CATHOLIC, 236 EAST 90TH STREET.

The Church of Our Lady of Good Counsel, at 236 East 90th Street, is one of the youngest of the Catholic churches. The building, a handsome structure in the decorated Gothic style of architecture, with a front of Rutland marble, was completed in 1892, and dedicated on September 18th. There are two entrance-porches recessed into the front of the church, with steps which turn toward each other and unite in an outer lobby, which is screened from view by the front main wall. There are a number of handsome stained-glass windows, which were made in Munich. The high altar of marble came from Venice, and four smaller altars were made in the quarries of Carrara. Five paintings, over the high altar, are the work of Sig. Rossi, a prize-winner of the Paris Salon. The parish is a new one, established in 1886, and the corner-stone of the church was laid in May of that year. Rev. William J. O'Kelly is the rector, and he has four assistants.

Other Interesting Catholic Churches are St. Andrew's, away down-town, at City-Hall Place and Duane Street; St. Bernard's, a noble Gothic building on West 14th Street; the Holy Cross, on West 42d Street; and St. Cecilia's, on East 106th Street.

The B'Nai Jeshurun, "Children of Jeshurun," is the oldest Anglo-German Hebrew congregation in the city. It was founded in 1825 by a few German and Polish Jews, who left the Spanish synagogue on Mill Street, and adopted the Polish or German ritual, in place of the Portuguese, in use in the former congregation. The early meetings were held in a small hall in White Street, but in 1826 the former Presbyterian Church in Elm Street

ST. ANDREW'S CHURCH, ROMAN CATHOLIC, DUANE STREET AND CITY-HALL PLACE.

was purchased and remodelled. In 1850 a large synagogue was erected on Greene Street, followed in 1866 by a second in West 34th Street. In 1885 the large and impressive edifice on Madison Avenue, near East 65th Street, was erected, at a cost of $200,000. It is built of stone and pressed brick, in the Spanish-Moresque style, with twin towers, and an imposing façade. The audi-

ST. BERNARD'S CHURCH, ROMAN CATHOLIC, 332 WEST 14TH STREET.

torium is decorated in white and gold, and harmonizes with the Moorish exterior. Its seating capacity is 1,200, and the congregation is the leading orthodox Hebrew

TEMPLE EMANU-EL, HEBREW, FIFTH AVENUE AND 43D STREET.

body in the city, holding conservatively to the old Mosaic standards, and paying little regard to the changeful spirit of the nineteenth century. Dr. Henry S. Jacobs is the Rabbi; and Rev. Stephen S. Wise the junior minister.

The Jews were early settlers in Manhattan, and in 1695 there were twenty Hebrew families in the city; but their petition for permission to establish a place of worship was refused by the Provincial authorities. A Jewish congregation was formed early in the last century, and in 1729 the first synagogue was opened, in Mill Street, near Beaver. The Crosby-Street Synagogue was a spacious and elegant building. With the rapid increase in the Jewish population, others have been erected, and there are now 47 synagogues and temples, some of them magnificent edifices, and many charitable institutions, well-supported by the Jewish people.

The Temple Emanu-El, at Fifth Avenue and East 43d Street, is one of the finest and most costly synagogues in the world. The congregation was formed in 1845, as a reformed Hebrew society. It was "a day of small things" with the infant congregation for some years, and the earlier meetings were held in the Grand-Street court-room. In 1850 a church on Chrystie Street, which had been deserted by its Christian congregation, was purchased and remodelled. The first Rabbi was the Rev. Dr. Leon Merzbacher, one of the early Jewish reformers. In 1856 the Baptist church on East 12th Street was secured for the congregation, and here they remained until 1868, when their modern magnificent temple was completed, at a cost of nearly $600,000. Like all the finer Jewish synagogues of the city, it is Moorish in design and decoration, with twin towers and an impressive front on

TEMPLE BETH-EL, HEBREW, FIFTH AVENUE AND 76TH STREET, OPPOSITE CENTRAL PARK.

Fifth Avenue. The auditorium will seat nearly 2,000 people. The decorations are of the most elaborate character, conceived and carried out in the Moorish manner, with massive columns spanned by the peculiar Saracenic arch, a lofty clere-story, and a fine pulpit and ark. Leopold Eidlitz was the architect. The Rev. Dr. Samuel Adler, father of Felix Adler, was long the Rabbi of the congregation, which is one of the most liberal in the city, as it was the first established; and it is now the only one maintaining regular Sunday services, in addition to the usual Saturday service. Its music is celebrated for stateliness and brilliancy, and very effectively accompanies the impressive ritual of the ancient Hebrew Church. The present Rabbis are the Rev. Drs. Gustav Gottheil and Joseph Silverman.

The Temple Beth-El, at Fifth Avenue and 76th Street, is one of the costliest and most imposing religious buildings in the city. It is constructed of Indiana limestone, and its architectural features show a blending of the Byzantine and Moorish styles. Its front is 102 feet long on Fifth Avenue, and it extends back 150 feet on 76th Street. The land and building cost $750,000. The main entrance takes the form of a massive arch, with a screen of columns and small arches, and richly foliated bronze gates. The dome is enriched with lines of gilded ribbing. The main audience-hall has a lofty arched ceiling and galleries surmounted by large round arches. Beneath the great arch at the eastern end is an apsidal recess, containing the organ-loft, pulpit and shrine, the latter a magnificent structure of onyx

SHAARAI TEPHILA SYNAGOGUE, HEBREW, 127 WEST 44TH STREET.

columns and arches with capitals of gold, all richly decorated. The Congregation Beth-El was formed in 1874 by the union of the Congregations Anshi-Chesed and Adas-Jeshurun, the former being the first German Jewish congregation in the country, dating back to 1828. The Adas-Jeshurun Congregation, under the ministry of the Rev. Dr. D. Einhorn, became the leading Jewish reformed synagogue, and when the Beth-El Congregation was formed, it worshipped in the Lexington-Avenue synagogue until the Temple Beth-El was completed in 1891. Under Dr. Einhorn's successor, the Rev. Dr. K. Kohler, the reforming tendencies of the congregation have steadily strengthened, and it is now the leading exponent of modern liberal Judaism.

The Shaarai Tephila, "Gates of Prayer," at 127 West 44th Street, was erected in 1865. It is a magnificent building in a modified Moorish style of architecture, of Newark freestone, with trimmings of Dorchester stone. The spacious interior, seating 1,200, is richly decorated in contrasting colors. Four slender iron

AHAVATH CHESED SYNAGOGUE, HEBREW, LEXINGTON AVENUE AND EAST 64TH STREET.

TEMPLE SHEARITH ISRAEL, HEBREW, 5 WEST 19TH STREET,
NEAR FIFTH AVENUE.

columns support the roof on transverse and longitudinal arches, and all the interior fittings are of the most costly character. Above the richly inlaid and carved ark or shrine is a large rose window. The synagogue cost $200,000. The congregation was formed in 1845 by members of the Elm-Street Synagogue. The Rabbi is the Rev. Dr. F. de Sola Mendes.

The Rodoph Sholom, "Followers of Peace," organized in 1842, and formerly worshipping in Clinton Street, now owns the former Beth-El Synagogue, erected in 1873 at a cost of $250,000. It stands at Lexington Avenue and 63d Street, and is a lofty stone building in the Spanish-Moresque style. The interior is elaborately decorated in the Oriental manner prevailing among the Jewish synagogues. The congregation is large and influential. The Rabbi is the Rev. Aaron Wise.

The Ahavath Chesed, "Neighborly Love," was founded in 1850 by some of the moderate reform Hebrews. For some years it occupied a former Christian church on Avenue C. The stately synagogue, at 652 Lexington Avenue, was erected in 1872. It is built of stone, in the Moorish style, and the front has five elevations; a central one for the main entrance, with a tower and a stairway wing on each side. The towers are 122 feet high, square at the base, changing to octagons near the top, and crowned by gilded metal cupolas. The interior is very beautiful, with arabesque decorations and graceful Moorish arches and tall pillars. The Rabbi is the Rev. Alexander Kohut.

CONGREGATION SICHRON EPHRAIM, HEBREW, EAST
67TH STREET, NEAR THIRD AVENUE.

The Temple Shearith Israel, in West 19th Street, close to Fifth Avenue, is one of those structures of unfamiliar appearance which makes New York cosmopolitan in architecture. The front presents the appearance of two very high stories, each with its capital supported by double columns. The entrance is broad and high, and the windows are capped with semi-circular arches. The temple is surmounted by a Moorish dome, which is prominent for a considerable distance. The Temple Shearith Israel looms high over the houses of West 19th Street, with its classic front and ponderous dome.

The congregation, which is of the orthodox type, and is composed mainly of English-speaking Hebrews, is in a sense an offshoot from a very old Portuguese congregation of Newport, R. I., and as such it claims to be the oldest Jewish congregation now existing in New York. Rev. H. Pereira Mendes is the Rabbi, and Rev. Abraham H. Niets assistant.

The Sichron Ephraim synagogue, on East 67th Street, near Third Avenue, is a handsome piece of Saracenic architecture, with a North-African sentiment in its tall and unique tower and the arcades along its front.

The synagogue was built in 1890, by Jonas Weil, a wealthy Hebrew, and a new congregation was organized from the orthodox Hebrews residing in the vicinity. A portion of the work of the organization is the mainte-

BETH ISRAEL BIKUR CHOLIM, HEBREW, LEXINGTON AVENUE AND EAST 72D STREET.

nance of a religious school, which holds sessions on Tuesday and Thursday afternoons and Sunday forenoons. Rev. Dr. Bernard Drachman is the Rabbi.

The Beth Israel Bikur Cholim synagogue, in a fine neighborhood, at Lexington Avenue and 72d Street, is a spacious and commodious temple, with a rich and vivid interior. The society was formed in 1859, by the union of the Congregation Beth Israel and the Society Bikur Cholim; and worshipped in White Street and then in Chrystie Street until 1887, when it joined the great up-town movement of the churches. It is one of the foremost of the orthodox Jewish congregations. The Rabbi is Herman Lustig.

Other forms of worship abound in the great metropolis, in many sects, and with hundreds of societies, conclaves, missions and chapels. There are Christian

Israelites, Reformed Catholics, German Evangelicals, True Dutch Reformed, Christian Scientists, and many others.

The Greek Church holds its services at 340 West 53d Street, for the members of the large Greek colony.   The Rev. Paisius Ferendinos is archimandrite.

The First Society of Spiritualists, the only organized Spiritualistic society in the city, holds weekly meetings in Music Hall, on West 57th Street.   "Seances" and meetings of the Spiritualists are also held in private houses.

Mahommedanism is being preached to the New-Yorkers by Mohammed Webb, a native of this city, and longtime a consul in the East Indies.   He is supplied with large funds, by wealthy Moslems of Bombay and Allahabad, and lectures and distributes Mohammedan literature.

The Chinese Joss House occupies the upper floor of a building at 10 Mott Street.   It is a small room containing the shrine, before which lights are kept constantly burning.   The shrine is a magnificent specimen of Chinese carved work.

Religious Societies and Associations, devoted to the advancement of the cause of religion, in charities, preaching, literature, and many other ways, abound throughout this great city.

CHINESE JOSS HOUSE, 16 MOTT STREET.

The magnificent system of the Catholic hierarchy is exemplified here in a perfect manner, and all the vast interests connected with the Papal Church are governed with the precision and security of an ancient province of Rome.

The Church Missions' House, at Fourth Avenue and East 27th Street, is one of the noblest of the new buildings of the year 1893. The architects are R. W. Gibson and Edward J. N. Stent, and the style is a very rich and unusual variety of the Flemish, with clustered columns, pinnacles and statues.   The lower part is of rock-faced granite, and the rest of the building of Indiana limestone, with a steel frame.   The land and structure cost $420,000.   Its central gable is crowned by a statue of Faith.   This edifice is not a diocesan affair, but pertains to the whole American Church, by whose freewill offerings it was erected.   Here are to be the headquarters of the Domestic and Foreign Missionary Society and other great Episcopal associations.

The Domestic and Foreign Missionary Society of the Protestant Episcopal Church in the United States of America, at 22 Bible House, was founded in 1820 and incorporated in 1846.   It supports 21 bishops and gives stipends to 1,200 missionaries; and has missions, orphanages, hospitals, schools and colleges in Africa, China, Japan, Greece and Hayti; also among the negroes and Indians. It supports many lay-readers and women-workers. This society is the established agency of the entire American Episcopal Church, and is under the direction of the General Convention. It disburses $600,000 yearly.

The Diocesan House, 29 Lafayette Place, was opened in 1888, as a See House for the Episcopal Church in the Diocese of New York. The house originally belonged to Miss Catherine L. Wolfe, the munificent benefactor of the Metropolitan Museum of Art and of Grace Church; and was given by her for its present purpose. Extensive alterations were made in the original building, and the Diocesan House is now an ecclesiastical-looking edifice, conveniently arranged for the purpose for which it is intended, containing the offices of the Bishop of the Diocese, Arch-deacon of New York, Presiding Bishop of the Episcopal Church, Standing Committee of the Diocese, Secretary of the House of Bishops, a large reception-room, a reading-room, sleeping-rooms for the members of the Clergy Club, and a large hall, called Hobart Hall, in memory of the great bishop of that name, in which is kept the Diocesan library.

CHURCH MISSION HOUSE, PROTESTANT EPISCOPAL, FOURTH AVENUE AND 22D STREET.

The New-York Protestant Episcopal City Mission Society was founded in 1830, and chartered in 1833 "to preach the Gospel to the poor, and to relieve the unfortunate." Acting under its charter, the society led the way in the establishment of free churches for the middle and poorer classes of the city population. Later, when this need no longer existed, it inaugurated a mission work among the public institutions of the city and adjacent islands, and out of this work have grown many of the best benevolent institutions of the city, such as the House of Mercy; St. Barnabas' House; the Midnight Mission; the New-York Infant Asylum; the Sheltering Arms; the House of Rest for Consumptives; and many others. The society now employs eleven clergymen, two lay-readers, and women visitors in its work at its mission stations, the city jails, hospitals and courts. The missions of the society are St. Ambrose Chapel, on Thompson Street; the Rescue Mission, on Mott Street; St. Barnabas' Chapel, mission-house and schools, on Mulberry Street; and three chapels. The yearly expenditure is about $50,000. The Mission-House is at 38 Bleecker Street, where there is a free reading-room for males.

The Protestant Episcopal Church Missionary Society for Seamen in the City and Port of New York, at 77 Houston Street, was founded in 1841. It supports three chapels, as many reading-rooms, and a sailors' home. Every Episcopal Church in the city is required to make a yearly contribution for this society.

The **Presbyterian House**, at Fifth Avenue and 12th Street, was the former residence of the Lenox family, and the scene of many notable events in the social history of the city. This stately old mansion now contains the Home and Foreign Mission Board rooms, the Board of Church Erection, the Woman's Boards, and other great Presbyterian societies. It was virtually a gift from the Lenox family.

The **Board of Foreign Missions of the Presbyterian Church**, at the Presbyterian House, 53 Fifth Avenue, was established in 1834, and received its charter in 1862. The Foreign Board sustains missions in China, India, Siam, Japan, Korea, Africa, Central America, Brazil, Chile, Columbia, Mexico, Syria, Persia, and among the Chinese and Japanese in the United States, expending $1,000,000 yearly.

DIOCESAN HOUSE, EPISCOPAL CHURCH, 29 LAFAYETTE PLACE.

The **Board of Home Missions of the Presbyterian Church**, U. S. A., began its work in 1802, and received its present charter in 1872. It employs about 2,100 missionaries and teachers, in nearly every State and territory of the Union, including Alaska, maintaining missions among foreign populations, Indians, Mexicans, Mormons, Alaskans and mountain-whites. Its yearly appropriations are $950,000.

The **Methodist Mission House** is a noble stone and brick building, eight stories high, erected in 1889, at a cost of $1,000,000. It contains the offices and sales-room of the Publishing Agents, the press-rooms, composing-rooms and bindery, where thousands of books and pamphlets are manufactured yearly; the offices of the missionary society; a large chapel; the library; Board-room; Bishop's room; and a number of private offices. A picture will be found in another chapter.

The **Methodist Book Concern**, at Fifth Avenue and 20th Street, is the eldest auxiliary of American Methodism. It was established in 1779, when the Rev. John Dickins was appointed book steward, and began publishing books for the Methodist Church, with a borrowed capital of $600. The first New-York office of the Concern was in Church Street. Later the business was transferred to Mulberry Street; still later to Broadway and 11th Street; and then to Fifth Avenue and 20th Street. The profits of the Concern are used for the support of old and disabled ministers, widows and orphans, and during the century of its existence it has paid the Methodist Church for these purposes more than $1,500,000.

The **New-York City Church Extension and Missionary Society of the Methodist Episcopal Church** was chartered in 1866 to plant and support Sunday-schools, churches and missions in the city of New York. It extends financial aid to 23 churches and missions, at an annual expense of $40,000.

The Reformed Church Building, at 25 East 22d Street, contains the Boards of Domestic Missions, of Foreign Missions, of Publication, of Education, and the Women's Committees of Foreign and Domestic Missions. Here also is a large assembly-room for the special use of the clergy.

The Board of Domestic Missions of the Reformed Church in America, at 25 East 22d Street, was formed in 1832 to promote the extension of the Reformed Dutch Church in America. At present the Board aids 115 missionary pastors, and supplies ministers to 170 churches and missions, at a yearly expense of $65,000.

The Board of Foreign Missions of the Reformed Church in America, at 25 East 22d Street, was organized in 1837. It has missions in China, India and Japan, where it maintains 66 missionaries and 325 native assistants. About $110,000 are disbursed yearly.

The New-York City Baptist Mission Society, in the United Charities Building, at Fourth Avenue and 22d Street, was founded in 1870, and re-organized

PRESBYTERIAN HOUSE, FIFTH AVENUE AND EAST 12TH STREET.

in 1891, to sustain missions in the lower part of the city ; to establish new churches in the upper part ; to preach the gospel to the foreign populations ; to circulate religious and denominational literature ; to promote Baptist educational work ; to provide for the training of Sunday-school teachers, and other Christian workers; and to conduct various charities in connection with churches and missions.

The Bible House, owned by the American Bible Society, is a great brick edifice covering the whole block bounded by Third and Fourth Avenues and Astor Place and Ninth Street. It is six stories high and has an open court in the centre. The original cost of the property was about $300,000, provided for by special contributions, so that not a dollar of the ordinary benevolent contributions to the society was used in the purchase of the lot or the erection of the building. It contains the offices, library, and publishing departments of the society, and is the local headquarters of the following societies : American Sunday-School Union ; American

Home-Missionary Society; Congregational Church Building Society; American Missionary Association; American Board of Commissioners for Foreign Missions; Domestic and Foreign Missionary Society of the Protestant Episcopal Church; American Church Building Fund Commission; New-York Sabbath Committee; New-York Bible Society; Christian Aid to Employment Society; National Women's Christian Temperance Union; Women's Union Missionary Society; Willard Tract Repository; the *Christian Herald*, and a number of other religious publications.

The **American Bible Society** was organized in the City of New York in May, 1816, by delegates from 35 local Bible societies which had been previously formed in various portions of the United States. Its constitution declares that its sole object is to encourage a wider circulation of the Holy Scriptures without note or comment. Its field is the world. Its founders expressed the purpose to extend its operations to other countries, whether Christian, Mohammedan or Pagan. It is an unsectarian institution. Its 36 elected managers are identified with various branches of the Christian Church, while its affairs are conducted without denominational bias or control. It is also a benevolent institution. Its founders and their successors have always aimed by all wise methods to place the Holy Scriptures within the reach of all. Its publications are in no case sold at a profit. Those who can may buy them at the mere cost of manufacture, while those who cannot are supplied without price. The total receipts of the Society to March 31, 1893, were $26,546,248, but over eleven millions of this amount were received in payment of books sold at cost or less than cost. This aggregate also includes over $4,500,000 received from legacies. The Society has aided in the translation, printing or distribution of the Scriptures in 95 languages and dialects. The total number of volumes issued to April, 1893, was 56,926,771. The issues of the past five years are equal to those of the first forty years of the Society's operations. The Society has four times conducted a general Bible supply of the United States. The entire distribution of the Scriptures in the fourth re-supply was 8,146,808 volumes, in 27 different languages. Besides these special efforts the Society has constantly supplied the Scriptures to seamen, the immigrants, the freedmen, the soldiers, the inmates of humane and criminal institutions, and to mission churches and Sabbath-schools. The foreign work is conducted directly by its own agents and colporteurs, and indirectly through the foreign missionary societies of the various Christian denominations in the United States, or through the Bible societies established in other lands. There are six special agencies on the Western Continent — LaPlata, Peru, Venezuela, Brazil, Mexico and Cuba. During the ten years ending March 31, 1893, 538,237 volumes were sent from the Bible House to Latin America, including Cuba. There are five special agencies on the Eastern Continents, — the Levant, Persia, China, Siam, and Japan and Korea. The Scriptures are circulated in the Levant Agency in about thirty languages, and the total issues for 35 years to December 31, 1892, amount to 1,306,814 copies. Over 2,500,000 copies have been circulated in China since 1876. The Society's work is helped by buying and circulating its publications; by commending the Scriptures to others; by coöperating with the auxiliary Bible societies; by donations to the Society for its benevolent work. During the 77 years of the Society's history eleven persons have held the office of president — the first being the Hon. Elias Boudinot, LL.D., and the present being the Hon. Enoch L. Fancher, LL.D. The Rev. Edward W. Gilman, D.D.; Alexander McLean, D.D.; and Albert S. Hunt, D. D., are the corresponding secretaries. William Foulke is treasurer, and Caleb T. Rowe is general agent. The noble work of the American Bible Society has helped to shed God's light on all lands, heathen or Christian.

THE BIBLE HOUSE OF THE AMERICAN BIBLE SOCIETY.
THIRD AND FOURTH AVENUES, FROM 8TH TO 9TH STREETS, OPPOSITE ASTOR PLACE.

The **New-York Bible Society** was organized in 1823, and incorporated in 1866, as an auxiliary of the American Bible Society, to distribute copies of the Bible in the city and harbor of New York, and to raise funds in aid of the former society.   Its office is in the Bible House.   During 1891 it distributed nearly 100,000 copies of the Bible.

The **New-York Sabbath Committee,** 31 Bible House, was formed in 1857, by prominent laymen of different denominations, to protect and promote the observance of Sunday, by securing and enforcing just and wise Sunday laws, and by cultivating a sound public sentiment by documents, addresses and the press.   The committee was incorporated in 1884.   It has exerted a wide influence over our land, and a number of its documents have been reprinted in Europe.

The **New-York City Mission and Tract Society,** in the United Charities Building, was established in 1827 and incorporated in 1866.   It is the leading

FOURTH-AVENUE PRESBYTERIAN CHURCH.   ASSOCIATION HALL.   23D STREET.
YOUNG MEN'S CHRISTIAN ASSOCIATION, 23D STREET AND FOURTH AVENUE.

city missionary society, and its field of work is New York below 14th Street.   It sustains six mission stations, five Sunday-schools and sixty missionaries, at a yearly expense of $70,000.   It is entirely undenominational.

The **American Home Missionary Society,** at 34 Bible House, was organized in 1826 and incorporated in 1871, "to assist congregations unable to support the Gospel ministry, and to send the Gospel and the means of Christian education to the destitute within the United States."   It is the home missionary society of Congregationalism, and now employs 2,000 missionaries, expending yearly not far from $700,000 in its religious and educational work.

The **American Tract Society,** at 150 Nassau Street, was organized in 1825 for the publication and circulation of religious literature.   It is undenominational,

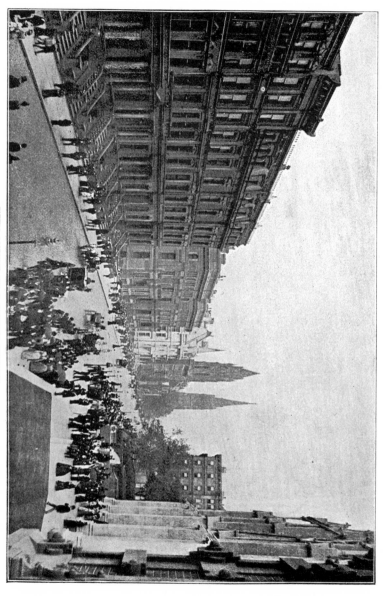

FIFTH AVENUE ON A SUNDAY MORNING.
LOOKING NORTH FROM THE CATHEDRAL.

and has issued more than 8,000 distinct publications, books, tracts, wall-rolls, etc., including
supplies for immigrants in many languages. The
work is carried on largely through colporteurs,
of whom there are now 174 working in different
States. It has published thousands of books
and tracts at foreign mission-stations. The
society expends over $300,000 yearly.

**The American Seamen's Friend So-
ciety** was established in 1828 to promote the
spiritual and temporal welfare of seamen. It
supports missionaries and homes in numerous
home and foreign ports, and provides loan
libraries for ships, besides rendering aid to suffering and needy seamen. Its annual expenditures are about $40,000 ; and it has an office at
76 Wall Street.

**The Society for Promoting the Gospel
Among Seamen in the Port of New York**
is better known as the New-York Port Society.
It was founded in 1818, and its headquarters

HARLEM BRANCH, YOUNG MEN'S CHRISTIAN
ASSOCIATION, 5 WEST 125TH STREET.

are at 46 Catharine Street, where it maintains the Mariner's Church, a library and a
reading-room at a yearly cost of $16,000.

The Salvation Army has been working here for nearly ten years, and now has
500 officers and soldiers in the city.
The National headquarters of the
Army are at 111 Reade Street.
There are large " barracks " where
nightly and Sunday meetings are
held, at 122 West 14th Street, 14
Fourth Avenue, 39th Street and
Sixth Avenue, 232 East 125th
Street, West 11th and Bleecker
Streets, 153 East 72d Street, and
340 East 8th Street. There is a
large Food and Shelter Depot, and
three Slum Posts, a Slum Crèche,
and a Rescue Home for fallen
women. The Army is doing energetic and blessed work in its hearty
fashion among classes of people
who most need help.

**The Young Men's Christian
Association** was organized in
1852, for the mental, social, physical, and spiritual improvement of
young men. The main Association
Building, at Fourth Avenue and
East 23d Street, is a large stone
edifice built in 1869, at a cost of

YOUNG MEN'S INSTITUTE, Y. M. C. A., 222 BOWERY.

GERMAN BRANCH, Y. M. C. A., 140 AND 142 SECOND AVENUE, NEAR 9TH STREET.

$500,000. It contains reception-room, parlors, reading-room, a lecture and concert hall, seating 1,300 people, a smaller lecture-room, numerous class-rooms, a library of 42,000 volumes, a gymnasium, bowling-alleys and baths. To aid in its work among the young men of the city, the Association has established fourteen branches in different sections, and employs the endeavors of 81 young men in superintending its work. Seven fully equipped gymnasiums, in charge of competent men, afford facilities for physical culture. The well-stocked libraries, containing over 60,000 volumes ; the various reading-rooms, where more than 1,000 newspapers, magazines and reviews are kept on file ; and the class-room instruction in 23 different lines of practical study, provide mental food for the studious-minded. Frequent religious meetings, Bible-classes, and public addresses minister to the spiritual needs of the members and their friends ; while the social element is fostered by frequent entertainments, lectures and receptions. The total membership of the various branches is 7,200, and the average daily attendance for 1892 was nearly 4,000. A prominent feature of the Association work is aiding deserving young men to obtain situations ; and recently a Students' Movement has been organized, to maintain religious meetings and Bible-classes in the colleges in the city. The general offices of the Association are at 40 East 23d Street, just west of the main Association Building, which is now designated as the 23d-Street branch. It was made a branch in 1887, and is the centre of local Association work, and of many kindly and civilizing influences.

The Bowery Branch, 153 Bowery, was organized in 1872, to aid young men out of employment and in temporary destitution, with free meals and beds.

The Harlem Branch, formed in 1868, has an attractive building, at 5 West 125th Street, containing a reading-room, parlor, library, gymnasium, entertainment hall and class-rooms.

RAILROAD BRANCH, Y. M. C. A., MADISON AVENUE AND 45TH STREET.

The East 86th-Street Branch was organized in 1884, and occupies two buildings at 153 and 155 East 86th Street, with a well-equipped gymnasium, bowling alleys, lecture-hall and bath-rooms. The buildings also contain a reading-room, library, parlor, reception-room, bicycle room and junior department rooms.

The Young Men's Institute, at 222 Bowery, is a branch of the Young Men's Christian Association, and was built in 1885, at a cost of $150,000. The building is in the style of the English Renaissance, with a frontage of 50 feet on the Bowery, and a depth of 96 feet. The first story is trimmed with Nova-Scotia sandstone, and special prominence is given to the entrance vestibule. An impression of height is conveyed by the gables and the mansard roof, on which has been constructed a flooring for summer-evening meetings and entertainments. There are six stories in the front and two in the rear, and the interior is conveniently divided. On the ground floor, at the right of the spacious vestibule of tiled brick and oak, is the large reception-room, attractively finished and furnished, with a wide-mouthed fire-place and cushioned-seats. A well-equipped gymnasium is in the rear of the

reception-room; and beneath are the bowling-alleys, locker-rooms, and baths. The second story contains a large reading-room and the library, finished in mahogany, a lecture-hall, and other rooms. On the third story are several large class and committee rooms, finished in cherry, and connected with each other by sliding doors. Several large class-rooms and the secretary's private room occupy the fourth story, and on the fifth floor there are private bath-rooms, a large class-room and the janitor's apartments. The object of the Institute is to provide for the physical, intellectual and spiritual welfare of the young men living in its vicinity. Its member-

YOUNG WOMEN'S CHRISTIAN ASSOCIATION, 7 EAST 15TH STREET, NEAR FIFTH AVENUE.

ship is over 600, with an average daily attendance of 200. There are classes in technical studies; and summer outings.

The German Branch, on Second Avenue, was organized in 1881 for work among the East-Side Germans, by whom it is greatly appreciated.

The French Branch, at 114 West 21st, was formed in 1889; and it offers the attractions of a reading-room, library, gymnasium, restaurant, employment bureau and parlor to the great numbers of French-speaking young men in its vicinity.

The Washington-Heights Branch, on 155th Street, near the Boulevard, furnishes a reading-room, library, parlors, gymnasium and bowling-alley.

The Railroad Branch was organized in 1875, and occupies the beautiful and elegantly equipped Railroad Men's Building, erected for it in 1887 by Cornelius Vanderbilt, at a cost of $75,000. The building is on Madison Avenue and 45th Street. It is unique in many respects, and is the outgrowth of Mr. Vanderbilt's desire to provide the employees of the railroads which enter the Grand Central station with a modern club-house, suited to their needs. It contains a reading-room, a library of 7,000 volumes, social rooms, a gymnasium, bowling-alleys, sleeping-rooms, and a lunch-room.

The West-72d-Street Branch was organized in 1889, and provides a reading-room, library, sleeping-rooms and lunch-room at the round-house of the New-York Central & Hudson-River Railroad.

The Association Boat-House is on the Harlem River ; and the athletic grounds are at Mott Haven.

The Young Women's Christian Association was founded in 1870, and incorporated in 1873, to aid self-supporting young women by providing special training in such industries as are adapted to them ; to assist them to obtain employment; and to provide opportunities for self-culture. The building of the Association is at 7 East 15th Street, and contains a library of 20,000 volumes, a reading-room, and numerous class-rooms. A Bible-class and social meetings are features of the work ; and there is an employment bureau, a board directory, and free classes in type-writing, stenography, physical culture, needle-work and art, and a salesroom for

APPRENTICES' LIBRARY.

MARGARET LOUISA HOME OF THE Y. W. C. A., 14 EAST 16TH STREET.

the work of consignors. The Association conducts a seaside cottage. There is a branch at 1509 Broadway, with classes in cooking, millinery and physical culture.

The Margaret Louisa Home of the Young Women's Christian Association is at 14 and 16 East 16th Street, communicating with the main building of the Association. It is a beautiful six-story structure, designed by R. H. Robertson, in the Romanesque style, fire-proof, and everywhere abounding in light and air. The main floor has the parlors, offices and restaurant ; and four floors above are occupied by 78 chambers, with 104 beds. This institution is for Protestant self-supporting women, with references, as a safe and very comfortable temporary home, at moderate rates of board. The building was erected (at a cost exceeding $200,000)

27

and presented to the Association by Mrs. Elliott F. Shepard, the oldest daughter of Cornelius Vanderbilt.   At the laying of the corner-stone in December, 1889, the services were conducted by the Rev. Drs. John Hall and W. R. Huntington, and Hon. Chauncey M. Depew.   The home was opened to the public January 19, 1891.

The Hebrew Institute, dedicated in 1891, at East Broadway and Jefferson Street, is a noble fire-proof building, 87 by 92 feet, and five stories high.   The lower part is occupied by an entertainment and lecture hall, seating 710 persons ; the first floor, by kindergarten and industrial-school rooms ; the second and third floors, by ten class-rooms, and the Aguilar Free Library and Y. M. H. A. reading-room ; the top floor, by a gymnasium, lockers and baths, a cooking-room and the manual training workshop ; and the paved roof by a summer-garden.

The Young Men's Hebrew Association was founded in 1873 to advance

the moral, social, intellectual and religious welfare of Hebrew young men.   It adopts the general methods of the Young Men's Christian Association, and occupies the building at 721 Lexington Avenue, with a branch at East Broadway and Jefferson Street.

The Young Women's Hebrew Association, at 721 Lexington Avenue, and at the Hebrew Institute, corner of Jefferson Street and East Broadway, was founded in 1888.   The rooms are open for conversation, games and dancing for members, as well as for instruction.   Entertainments of a musical and literary character are frequently given for members

HEBREW INSTITUTE, EAST BROADWAY AND JEFFERSON STREET.

and their friends.   During the summer of 1891 the association opened a summer-home for working girls at Sea Cliff, Long Island, at nominal rates.

It is difficult to estimate the enormous continual outlay of money, talent and toil in the behalf of religious work on Manhattan Island, and especially among the poor and degraded classes, who stand most in need of elevation and up-building.   Certainly the religious people of the city do not withhold from giving most liberally, not only of their funds, but also (and of greater importance) of their own individual and personal efforts.   The splendid churches from the Battery to Harlem River have all been erected by voluntary contributions, and the immense cost of their maintenance is similarly borne.   In like manner, continuous streams of money are flowing through the treasuries of the great missionary and philanthropic societies, to do good all over the wide world.   However sordid some aspects of New York may appear, it has much of the heroic, the beautiful and the noble.   This, however, is not much in evidence, in obedience to the injunction of the Divine Teacher, and its benevolent activities are conducted quietly, in the secret shadow of humility.

Charity and Benevolence.

**Institutions and Associations for the Poor and Unfortunate—
Homes, Asylums, and Temporary Relief.**

THE many public and private organized charities of the city are bewildering in
their variety and all-comprehensive in their work. The useful *New-York
Charities Directory*, published yearly by the Charity Organization Society, summa-
rizes the benevolent resources of the city as follows : Public charities, 28 ; for temporary relief, 83 ; for special relief, 51 ; for foreigners' relief, 26 ; for permanent
relief, 67 ; for medical relief, 101 ; for defectives, 16 ; reformatory, 16 ; miscellaneous, 232 ; making a grand total of nearly 700 charitable and benevolent institutions.

The Commissioners of Public Charities and Correction, three Commissioners appointed by the Mayor, have charge of the charitable and correctional
institutions, and receive all applications for relief, or admission to the hospitals, etc.
The office is at 66 Third Avenue. The yearly appropriations exceed $2,000,000.

The United Charities Building, at the corner of Fourth Avenue and 22d
Street, was erected and presented jointly to the Charity Organization Society, the
Children's Aid Society, the Association for Improving the Condition of the Poor,
and the New-York City Mission and Tract Society, by the munificence of John S.
Kennedy, and with the expectation that many other charities of the city will be
gathered under its roof, and that their efficiency and economy will be promoted
thereby. It is a magnificent seven-story fire-proof edifice, erected in 1891-93, at a
cost exceeding $700,000. The lower stories are of granite, and those above are
of stone and brick, leading up to a noble tiled roof. The architects were R. H.
Robertson and Rowe & Baker. Besides the offices of the four great unsectarian societies, the building contains a beautiful little hall, commodious bath-rooms for the Children's Aid Society, safe-deposit vaults for archives, a library of books about charities, the New-York Cooking School's restaurant, four studios, and many fine offices.

The Charity Organization Society of the City of New York, in the United
Charities Building, was inaugurated in 1882, to secure the concurrent action of the
various public and private charities of the city, and to act as a source of information
on all matters relating to benevolent work. It aims to raise the needy above want,
to prevent begging and imposition, to diminish pauperism, to encourage thrift, self-
dependence and industry, and to aid the poor by teaching and enabling them to
help themselves. At the main office a central registry is kept of all applicants for,
and recipients of, charitable relief, with a record of all that is known of their past history. To this registry more than 500 churches and societies and upwards of 1,000
private families contribute information concerning their beneficiaries. To systema-
tize the work, the city is divided into districts, in charge of local committees for
investigation and relief. The society bestows no alms from its own funds, but obtains

the needed relief from the proper existing sources. Its affairs are controlled by a Central Council, and in addition to its regular work it maintains a Penny Provident Fund, a Laundry and a Wood-yard. The society publishes monthly *The Charities Review*, discussing social and economic questions.

The New-York Association for Improving the Condition of the Poor, in the United Charities Building, organized in 1843 and incorporated in 1848, aims by systematic and scientific management to improve the condition of the working

UNITED CHARITIES BUILDING, FOURTH AVENUE, NORTHEAST CORNER OF 22D STREET.

classes, and to elevate their physical state. Its plan is to promote whatever tends to the permanent improvement of the condition of the working people ; to uplift their home-life and habits ; to improve the sanitary condition of their dwellings ; to supply baths in convenient localities, and at small cost ; to provide fresh-air benefits for those who cannot supply such for themselves ; and whenever the necessity arises, to get relief for the destitute and deserving, making employment its basis. It further endeavors to prevent indiscriminate and duplicate almsgiving ; to secure the community from imposture ; and to reduce pauperism by ascertaining and rectifying its accidental causes. It is controlled by a board of managers and executive committee, and supported by voluntary contributions. It is non-sectarian in character, and recognizes no distinction of race or nationality. It supports the People's Baths, at 9 Centre Market Place, where baths at any temperature can be had the year round for five cents. It maintains a Harlem Branch ; and covers the entire city. It conducts six branches of work, registration, relief, sewing, sanitary, fresh-air and public baths. It has the co-operation of the responsible charitable agencies of the city.

In 1891 there were 37,626 beneficiaries; 17,518 aided by the Fresh-Air department; 19,000 bathers at the People's Baths; and 906 aided by work. There were 16,051 visits to and for the poor; and the sum of $44,333 was disbursed.

Trinity Church Association, at 209 Fulton Street, was organized in 1879, and incorporated in 1887, to carry on general charitable work in the lower part of the city. It maintains the Trinity Mission House, at 209 and 211 Fulton Street, as headquarters for work among the poor, where they may apply for relief; a kindergarten for young children; a kitchen-garden, where 25 little girls receive instruction in general housework; a Down-Town Relief Bureau; a Provident Dispensary; a Sea-side Home for Children, near Islip, L. I., and a Training-School for young girls in household work. The yearly expenditures are about $10,000.

DEPARTMENT OF PUBLIC CHARITIES AND CORRECTION, THIRD AVENUE AND EAST 11TH STREET.

The Down-Town Relief Bureau, at 209 Fulton Street, was founded in 1882 for general out-door relief work among the poor in the lower wards of the city. It is supported by Trinity-Church Association and by voluntary contributions. Five thousand applicants were aided in 1892, at an expense of $35,000.

The Society of St. Vincent De Paul in the City of New York was organized in 1835, and chartered in 1872. Its leading objects are the cultivation of the Christian life; the visitation of the poor and sick; educational work among children; and general charitable work. Nearly all the local Catholic churches have separate conferences of the society, each confining its work to the limits of its own parish. There are upwards of fifty local conferences, all under the jurisdiction of the Particular Council of New York, which holds monthly meetings at the Cathedral School-house, 111 East 50th Street.

The University Settlement Society was formed for the purpose of bringing men of education and refinement into closer relations with the laboring classes of the city, for mutual instruction and benefit. It aims to establish "Settlements" in the tenement-house districts, where college men interested in the work may live, and mingle with their poor neighbors, on terms of perfect equality, somewhat after the plan of the famous Toynbee Hall, in London. It maintains the Neighborhood Guild, at 26 Delancey Street, which includes kindergartens, a gymnasium, boys' and girls' clubs, a reading-room and circulating library, penny-provident bank, concerts, and lectures, besides dancing, cooking, sewing, singing and other classes. It has organized the Tenth-Ward Social Reform Club, to establish public baths, laundries, kitchens, lavatories, parks, co-operative stores, sick benefit societies, etc.

The College Settlement, at 95 Rivington Street, was established by women college-graduates, in 1889. The residents, with outside helpers, conduct clubs for women, boys and girls ; classes in cooking, millinery, dressmaking, embroidery, kitchen-garden, wood-carving, drawing, singing, literature and municipal govern- ment ; a library and reading-room ; a penny-provident fund ; and a kindergarten.

The **League of Theosophical Workers,** organized in 1891, with head- quarters at 144 Madison Avenue, is a central exchange, through which individual members of the Theosophical Society and branches work so that better results may be accomplished.　The objects of the League are to relieve the sufferings of man- kind, physical, mental and moral.　The means employed are general, mainly through the propaganda of the science of Theosophy and of the doctrine of the universal brotherhood of man.　Cases of charity are given such attention as the funds of the League permit, but the means employed tend more especially to the eradica- tion of the cause of evil and sorrow than to the alleviation of physical effects.

The **Five-Points House of Industry** is one of the best-known charitable institutions of the country.　It has had a long and glorious history.　For many years the Five Points of New York, the meeting-place of Baxter, Worth and Park Streets,

FIVE-POINTS HOUSE OF INDUSTRY, 155 WORTH STREET, OPPOSITE PARADISE PARK.

bore an evil name and fame throughout the world.　Dickens wandered into its dens of iniquity in 1841, and described its horrors.　With a few dilapidated wooden build- ings, thickly peopled with human beings of every age, color and condition, it was an abode of atrocious crime and vice, avoided by peaceful citizens, and regarded with anxiety by the police.　As early as 1830 earnest Christian efforts were made to regenerate this degraded neighborhood.　A mission was started on Baxter Street, and a day-school opened, mainly under the auspices of the Central and Spring-Street Presbyterian Churches.　No very promising results followed.　In the spring of 1850 the Rev. Lewis Morris Pease, a Methodist clergyman, was commissioned by the Conference to open a mission at the Five Points, under the guidance of the Ladies' Home Missionary Society of the Methodist Episcopal Church.　Differences of opinion regarding the best methods of work soon caused a separation between the society and Mr. Pease, who immediately, on his own responsibility, leased a number of houses, and opened the Five-Points Home.　His success was so great that generous gifts were made for the extension and support of the work, and in 1854 a board of trustees was formed, and the Home incorporated as the Five-Points House of Industry. In its early years the work of the Home was largely among the abandoned women of the neighborhood, but of late it has labored mainly among the children. A commodious brick building was erected in 1856; and here, with additions, the work has been successfully carried on. Over 40,000 inmates have been received in school, and provided with homes, sent to their friends, or placed in other institutions. The leading features of the work are the preservation of children from crime and destitution; and the providing for them of homes, support, and religious and secular education. The institution also boards children of poor parents at merely nominal rates; shelters women while they are seeking work as servants; and affords temporary relief to destitute families in its neighborhood. Over 700 were sheltered in the Home during 1892, while 1,023 pupils received instruction in the day-schools. The infirmary and free dispensary gives free treatment to 1,600 cases yearly, and a lay missionary is constantly employed among the poor and destitute classes in the vicinity. The yearly expenses average $40,000, and are met by voluntary contributions and grants from the public funds. Morris K. Jesup is president of the Board of Trustees; and William F. Barnard is the superintendent of the Home.

The Five-Points Mission, at 63 Park Street, was organized in 1850, by the Ladies' Home-Missionary Society of the Methodist-Episcopal Church. The work at the Five Points was begun in a former dram-shop at the corner of Cross and Little Water Streets. The need of larger accommodations led to the purchase, in 1852, of that lazar-house of crime, the Old Brewery, in Park Street, which, built long before the city extended to the vicinity, had been for many years the resort of thieves and murderers, and the scene of many

FIVE-POINTS MISSION, 63 PARK STREET, OPPOSITE PARADISE PARK.

horrible crimes. This nest of iniquity was speedily demolished, and its place was filled by a group of buildings, comprising a chapel, parsonage, school-house, bathing-rooms, dining-rooms, etc., and tenements for poor families. This Mission has been a potent factor in the regeneration of the entire neighborhood, its chief object being so to educate children as to make them capable of self-support. The work is both religious and philanthropic. There is much missionary work done among the poor of this part of the city; and the Mission also provides for the physical welfare of many children and adults. It has in successful operation the Boys' and Girls' Shoe-Club; the Cooking-School for Girls; the Day-School, in which 600 pupils are enrolled; the Free Library and Reading Room for men and boys; the Fresh-Air Fund; and the Girls' Sewing-School. Over 6,000 individuals and 600 families were assisted during 1892; and nearly 100,000 dinners were served to hungry mouths. Church and Sunday-school services are held regularly. A much larger evangelistic and school building, with modern appliances, is about to be erected here.

The Bowery Mission and Young Men's Home, at 105 Bowery, was founded in 1880, for aggressive Christian work among the young men living in that locality, in which there are only two Protestant churches for an English-speaking population of 30,000. The work has been uniformly successful, over 300,000 young men having attended the evening meetings, many of whom have been reclaimed from evil lives. There are evening and Sunday religious meetings; a reading-room and library; and a lodging-house, where 125 persons can be boarded at a low rate. A distinctive feature of the work is the visitation of the lodging-houses in the neighborhood, of which there are sixty, crowded nightly with young men.

The Old Jerry McAuley Water-Street Mission, at 316 Water Street, was established in 1872 by Jerry McAuley, at one time a convict in the State Prison at Sing Sing, and afterwards a notorious river-thief about New York. He was converted in prison by Orville Gardner, the converted pugilist, and reclaimed in 1868, at a little prayer-meeting at Franklin Smith's house. This change of heart was of profound benefit to thousands of outcasts,

OLD BREWERY, SITE OF THE FIVE-POINTS MISSION.

and in 1872 McAuley opened the Water-Street Mission, which has become famous for the good it has accomplished among the fallen men and women of the Fourth Ward, thousands of whom have been transformed into useful members of society by its work. The original mission, which occupied a former dance-house, was replaced in 1876 by the present well-arranged building. Services are held nightly, and substantial aid is extended to those who desire to lead better lives. The work is entirely among the degraded ones of a district teeming with crime, and presents many interesting features. The yearly expenses of the Mission, which are met by voluntary contributions, are $6,000. S. H. Hadley is superintendent.

The Cremorne Mission, at 104 West 32d Street, was opened in 1882 by Jerry McAuley, for rescue work among the fallen and inebriate men and women of the West Side. It occupies a part of the building once known as the Cremorne Garden, a notorious resort in its day. There is no home in connection with the Mission, its work consisting mainly of nightly religious services of a revival character. Many converts have been made and much good accomplished in the last ten years.

Scores of societies have been organized for the protection and endearment of children, and they have done a mighty work in alleviating the sufferings of the little ones, born to misery in the dives of the great metropolis.

The New-York Society for the Prevention of Cruelty to Children,
the first of its kind in the world, was organized in 1875, under the provisions of the general law of that year, providing for the institution of such societies in the different counties of the State. Its objects are the prevention of cruelty to children, and the enforcement by all lawful means of the laws relating to, or in anywise affecting, children, and the care of children pending investigations. All magistrates, constables, sheriffs and police officers are required by law to aid the society in its work, which has been a source of incalculable benefit to the poor waifs of the city, too often at the mercy of hard

THE NEW-YORK SOCIETY FOR THE PREVENTION OF CRUELTY TO CHILDREN, FOURTH AVENUE AND 23D STREET.

and cruel taskmasters or depraved parents. The society is governed by a board of directors, who elect the members; these are of three classes — regular, honorary and life members. A life membership costs $100; regular members pay $5 yearly; and honorary members are those who have been active in aiding the work of the society. The offices and reception-rooms for children are at 297 Fourth Avenue, corner of East 23d Street. Elbridge T. Gerry is the President; Dallas B. Pratt, Treasurer; and E. Fellows Jenkins, Superintendent.

NEW-YORK INFANT ASYLUM, AMSTERDAM AVENUE AND WEST 61ST STREET.

The New-York Infant Asylum was founded in 1865, and chartered in 1871, for the protection, care and medical treatment of young unmarried women during their confinement, needy mothers and their infants, and foundlings. The asylum, at Amsterdam Avenue and 61st Street, is a large and well-appointed building; and there is an efficient staff of attendants and nurses. During 1892, 1,400 inmates were cared for, at an expense of $100,000. The institution has a country home and nursery at Mount Vernon, N. Y., to which poor mothers and children are sent during the summer months.

The New-York Foundling Hospital was incorporated in 1869, and until 1891 it was known as the Foundling Asylum of the Sisters of Charity. The Asylum comprises a group of buildings at 175 East 68th Street, with accommodations for 700 children and 300 adults; and is fitted up in a most complete and thorough manner. Its objects are the reception, care and education of foundlings and abandoned children, who are brought up in the Christian faith; the influencing of the mothers to lead useful and honest lives; and obtaining homes in the West for indentured children. Mothers who are willing to act as nurses are admitted with their infants. Nearly 1,400 infants are cared for yearly at their homes by the Outdoor Department. In connection with the Asylum, and under the same management, there is a Chil-

NEW-YORK FOUNDLING ASYLUM, 175 EAST 68TH STREET, NEAR THIRD AVENUE.

dren's Hospital, for the inmates of the institution; a Maternity Hospital; and a Day Nursery and Kindergarten School. There is also an annex at Spuyten Duyvil, accommodating 150 children. The yearly expenses reach $300,000.

St. Joseph's Day Nursery of the City of New York, at 473 West 57th Street, was incorporated in 1890. It receives and cares for during the day the children of working-women, irrespective of color or creed. The children receive kindergarten instruction, and have two meals daily. The average daily attendance is 50. Here also is a free employment bureau for domestic help.

The Bartholdi Creche, at 105 East 22d Street, was founded in 1886, and incorporated in 1890. During the summer months it maintains a seaside cottage at Randall's Island for poor mothers with sick infants and children under 12, who are unable to leave the city for a prolonged stay at any of the more distant seaside homes. A trained nurse and assistant are constantly in attendance, and cots and hammocks, pure milk, tea and coffee are provided. A ferry is maintained at the foot of East 120th Street for all who hold tickets, which are issued free of charge by the Charity Organization Society, the dispensaries, and other similar institutions. About 3,000 women and children are received each year.

The "Little Mothers'" Aid Society, at 305 East 17th Street, was founded in 1890 to furnish summer-day excursions for little girls compelled to take charge of younger children while their parents are at work, and who, therefore, cannot receive the benefit of other fresh-air charities. During the winter it provides entertainments, and classes in cooking and sewing, and supplies clothing and other necessities to the deserving.

The Tribune Fresh-Air Fund was established in 1877 by the Rev. Willard Parsons, sixty children having been sent out into the country for a brief stay during the

CHILDREN'S AID SOCIETY, CENTRAL OFFICE, 24 ST. MARK'S PLACE.

year. In 1878 the cause was championed by the *Evening Post*, and in 1882 the Fund was transferred to the *New-York Tribune*, which has had charge of the work since that time. The children are selected by Christian workers among the poor in New York, Brooklyn and Jersey City, and are given a fortnight's stay in the sweet peacefulness and healthfulness of farm-houses, far away in the green and sunlit

open country, where they are received, not as boarders, but as guests, generous readers of the *Tribune* paying all transportation expenses. There are no office expenses, and all the receipts are used for the benefit of poor children. During 1892 nearly 15,000 children were aided by this charity, at an expense of $28,000. Since 1877, 110,000 children have been sent into the country, and over $280,000 has been contributed for the work. Besides the children sent for long sojourns among the fields and woods, 85,000 have been given shorter outings in the country, usually of a day or so.

St. John's Guild was organized in 1866 by twelve gentlemen, who had been touched by the sight of the sufferings and privations of the thousands of New-York's tenement-house children, of whom a recent census of the Board

CHILDREN'S AID SOCIETY : NEWSBOYS' LODGING-HOUSE. 9 DUANE STREET, CORNER OF WILLIAM STREET.

CHILDREN'S AID SOCIETY : BOYS' LODGING-HOUSE,
SEVENTH AVENUE AND 32D STREET.

of Health shows more than 160,000 under the age of five, with as many more between five and fifteen. The city had made no adequate provision for healthful out-door exercise for these little dwellers in the crowded tenement-houses, and the death-rate among them was appalling. St. John's Guild is organized for the express purpose of assisting sick children and their mothers, by trips down the harbor in the Floating Hospital Barge, and by food and nursing at the Seaside Hospital on Staten Island. As many as five trips a week are made during the summer, and over 30,000 mothers and children receive the benefits of invigorating sea breezes. At the Seaside Hospital, 1,000 children and more than 500 weary mothers yearly are admitted and tenderly cared for. Since the organization of the Guild over half a million sick children and mothers have had the benefit of excursions down the bay. The Guild has a membership of 700 representative citizens, and is a favorite channel of beneficences. It embodies and exemplifies the true spirit and method of charitable effort, and is conspicuous for its application of the most careful business system and practice to every department of its work. The trustees have recently inaugurated a new feature in the work of ministering to the vast multitude of poor children, by opening the first of a series of small hospitals for children, which they hope to establish in the centres of densely populated districts. The new hospital, opened in 1892, is on West 61st Street, near Amsterdam Avenue. Others will follow as soon as the necessary funds are forthcoming, and will alleviate much of the harshness of life for the unfortunate children of the poor.

CHILDREN'S AID SOCIETY : EAST-SIDE BOYS' LODGING-HOUSE AND
INDUSTRIAL SCHOOL, 287 EAST BROADWAY.

The **Children's Aid Society,** one of the most helpful charities, was organized in 1853 by the late Charles Loring Brace and a few other gentlemen, who had been engaged in teaching some of the little arabs of the streets. The society was incorporated in 1856, "for the education of the poor, by gathering children who attend no schools into its industrial schools, caring and providing for children in lodging-houses, and procuring homes for them in the rural districts and in the West." In 1892 35,659 children were cared for, of whom nearly 3,000 were provided with homes. The offices of the society are at 24 St. Mark's Place. As supplementary to its work it maintains : The East-Side Mission, a fragrant charity, whose work is to distribute flowers daily during the summer months among the sick and poor ;

Free Reading-Rooms for Young Men, in Sullivan and 44th Streets; the Health Home at West Coney Island, comprising cottages and dormitories where mothers with sick children are given a grateful outing; the Sick Children's Mission, at 287 East Broadway, with a staff of ten physicians and four nurses, who visit the sick poor at their homes and supply free medical attendance, medicine and food for sick children, of whom 1,500 are treated yearly; a Summer Home at Bath Beach, Long Island, where over 4,000 tenement-house children are given a week's outing by the seaside each year; six lodging-houses, five for boys and one for girls, in which, during 1892, over 6,000 boys and girls were fed and sheltered; and twenty-two industrial and ten night schools, in which 12,000 children

CHILDREN'S AID SOCIETY : LODGING-HOUSE AND INDUSTRIAL SCHOOL FOR CRIPPLED BOYS, SECOND AVENUE AND 44TH STREET.

were taught and partly fed and partly clothed during 1892. One of the industrial schools is located in each of the lodging-houses for boys, and the two branches of the work are very closely interwoven. The lodging-house for girls is at 307 East 12th Street. Those for boys are at 9 Duane Street, 295 East 8th Street, 287 East Broadway, Second Avenue and East 44th Street, and Seventh Avenue and West 32d Street. A special feature of the Second-Avenue establishment is the industrial instruction for crippled boys. An adjunct is a brush-shop, in which a dozen crippled boys are employed, and 150 are at work pending permanent employment. The Children's Aid Society has found homes for 80,000 children, many of whom are educated and influential men and women. They become adopted children of the farmers, in field-work and house-work, and are loved and cared for and educated.

The Leake and Watts Orphan House, one of the most benevolent in design and meritorious in mission of all the city charities, was incorporated in 1831 as a free home for full orphans between the ages of three and twelve years, in destitute circumstances. This graceful charity owes its origin to the benevolence of John G. Leake, a wealthy New-York lawyer, who died in the early part of the century, leaving his large fortune to Robert Watts, the son of an old friend, on condition that he should assume the name of Leake. In case of a failure to comply with this provision, or of the death without heirs of the testator, the estate was to be applied to the founding of an orphan asylum. After a long lawsuit, it was decided that Mr. Leake had left no direct heirs, and that Robert Watts could inherit the property. He, however, died before he could comply with the condition mentioned in the will, and the estate passed into the hands of a board of trustees, who obtained a charter for an asylum under the name of the Leake and Watts Orphan Home. In 1843 they erected buildings in 113th Street. Here the institution cared for homeless and friendless orphans, educating them and, at the age of fourteen, obtaining Christian homes for them. In 1886 the estate was sold to the trustees of the Cathedral of St. John the Divine, for a building site, and the pleasant and spacious home now occupied was built at Ludlow, near the northern boundary of the city.

The Roman Catholic Orphan Asylum was founded in 1825, and incorporated in 1852, superseding an older society called the Roman Catholic Benevolent Society, which received its charter in 1817. The original location of the asylum was

ROMAN CATHOLIC ORPHAN ASYLUM (BOYS), FIFTH AVENUE AND 51ST STREET.

on Prince Street, but in 1851 the present asylum for boys at Fifth Avenue and 51st Street was completed. It is one of the largest and best-equipped orphan asylums in the country, and has accommodations for 500 lads. An additional wing is being built as a trade-school, and will accommodate 200 more boys. The girls' asylum was completed in 1890, and is of the same substantial character as that of the boys, but somewhat larger, accommodating 800 girls. In both the boys' and girls' departments provision is made for the religious, moral and technical instruction of the inmates. The work is carried on with a thoroughness which is characteristic of the Catholic Church. The new and admirable building on Madison Avenue was completed in 1893.

St. Joseph's Orphan Asylum in the City of New York, at 89th Street and Avenue A, was founded in 1858, and incorporated in 1859, for the support of orphans, half-orphans and homeless and neglected children of German parentage, who are cared for until they are sixteen years old, or until homes or occupations could be provided. The home is a large building, accommodating 750 inmates, and costing $65,000 a year. It is in charge of the Sisters of Notre Dame.

The Orphans' Home and Asylum of the Protestant Episcopal Church in the City of New York, one of the most important charities of its class, was founded in 1851, at the request of a few ladies connected with St. Paul's Chapel, to whom a child had been entrusted by a dying father, with the injunction that it should be brought up in the faith of the Protestant Episcopal Church. The asylum was incorporated in 1859, for the care, support and religious training of orphans and half-orphans, who are received between the ages of three and eight, and may be retained

ORPHANS' HOME AND ASYLUM OF THE PROTESTANT EPISCOPAL CHURCH, LEXINGTON AVENUE AND EAST 49TH STREET.

— the boys until they are twelve, and the girls until they are fourteen, when homes are provided for them. In common with other kindred institutions, religious, moral, intellectual and technical instruction is imparted to the inmates, the aim being to fit them to become useful and upright members of society. The smaller children are kept at the summer-home during the warm months, and the older ones enjoy vacations there. The home, at Lexington Avenue and East 49th Street, has accommodations for 150 inmates. A new home is greatly desired. The yearly expenses are $27,000, and there is an endowment fund of $212,000.

The Orphan Asylum Society in the City of New York is the oldest and one of the best-endowed institutions of its class in the country. It was founded in March, 1806, to minister to the wants of the parentless children of the community, and train them up in the paths of virtue. The work was begun in a small way by leasing a house in Greenwich Village. The act of incorporation came in 1807, and in the following year a suitable building was erected, not far from the first temporary quarters. A desirable location on Riverside Drive and West 73d Street was secured in 1835, and a large building was immediately erected, with accommodations for 250 children. The location is a charming one, overlooking the Hudson, and the grounds are attractively laid out. Orphans not above ten years of age are admitted

ORPHAN ASYLUM SOCIETY, RIVERSIDE DRIVE AND WEST 73D STREET.

to the home, and given thorough moral, mental and manual training, until they reach the age of fourteen, when Christian homes are obtained for them. The home is usually taxed to the utmost of its capacity. It is free and unsectarian. Its yearly expenses are $32,000, two-thirds of which are met by the income from invested funds.

The Eighth-Ward Mission was established in 1877, and maintains a home at Charlton Street, where orphan boys too old to be retained in other institutions, and unable to support themselves, are cared for and educated, and assisted in their efforts to obtain permanent employment. The Mission also supports an industrial school, where young girls are taught sewing and other household work ; and the Brown Memorial Home, at Sing-Sing-on-the-Hudson, a summer home for boys.

The Society for the Relief of Half-Orphan and Destitute Children in the City of New York was organized in 1835 and incorporated in 1837. Protestant children of both sexes, between the ages of four and ten, are received and properly cared for at a charge of $4 a month. Until 1890 the home was in West 10th Street. Then it was removed to a more desirable location on Manhattan Avenue, between 104th and 105th Streets, where a building had been erected for it. It has 200 inmates ; and the work is similar in character and scope to that of other orphan asylums, the object being the intellectual and moral training of the bereaved children of working people until homes can be provided for them.

The American Female Guardian Society and Home for the Friendless was founded in 1834, "to protect, befriend and train to virtue and usefulness those for

whom no one seemed to have a thought or pity." For a number of years the work was carried on entirely by w o m e n, with great energy, fearlessness and success. In 1846 a successful appeal was made to the public for funds sufficient to b u i l d a Home for the Friendless, and in 1848 a substantial and convenient house was erected at 32 East 30th S t r e e t. T h e r e is a H o m e C h a p e l, fronting on East 29th Street. Here homeless girls, and boys not over eleven years of age, are received and cared for until they can be placed in Christian h o m e s. Besides the Home, the society supports a Home - School

AMERICAN FEMALE GUARDIAN SOCIETY AND HOME FOR THE FRIENDLESS,
HOME CHAPEL, 29 EAST 29TH STREET AND 32 EAST 30TH STREET.

in East 29th Street, and twelve industrial schools, where the children of poor parents are clothed and taught. The work is supported by voluntary subscription and by a yearly grant from the public-school fund. In 1892 there were 450 inmates in the Home, and 5,832 pupils in the schools. The yearly expenses are $130,000.

The Sheltering Arms, one of the graceful charities for "The children in the midst," in which New York so generously abounds, was founded in 1864 by the Rev. Dr. T. M. Peters, then and now rector of St. Michael's Church, for the reception and care of homeless and destitute children, between five and twelve years of age, for whom no other institution in the city made provision. Here the blind, the deaf and dumb, the crippled and the incurables, are received and tenderly cared for until they are old enough to enter other suitable institutions. For six years this charity occupied a house given to it, rent free, by the founder, but in 1870 it removed to more roomy quarters at Amsterdam Avenue and 129th Street, where

SHELTERING ARMS, AMSTERDAM AVENUE AND WEST 129TH STREET.

ample accommodations for 200 waifs are provided. Whole orphans and infants are not received, and the children are not surrendered to the institution, but are held subject to the order of the parents or other relatives, being sent to the public schools and trained to household and other work. The yearly expenses are $17,000, and there is an endowment fund of $100,000.

The Children's Fold is a charity organized in 1867 to provide homes for homeless children between the ages of four and ten. They receive religious training, and education in the public schools. There are three families; two for boys, in Westchester County, and the other for girls, on 155th Street. The three homes have nearly 200 inmates, and each is in charge of its own "house-mother," with a general superintendent in charge of all. The yearly expenses are $17,000.

The Howard Mission and Home for Little Wanderers, known far and wide for the extent and value of its work, received its charter in 1864. Its purpose is to aid poor, neglected and helpless children, and worthy families among the very poor, by providing food, clothing, shelter and Christian love and sympathy, expressed in all practical ways. The homes of poor widows or disabled fathers are kept together by relief; the sick are relieved; and children are educated and kept, and at last placed in selected Christian families. The Mission has relieved more than 150,000 persons. It is purely unsectarian. The Mission-House and Home is at 225 East 11th Street, quite accessible to a region of squalor, wretchedness, vice and poverty, which provides many clients for the care of the officers of the mission.

St. Christopher's Home, formerly at Riverside Drive and West 112th Street, and now at Ingleside, near Dobbs Ferry, is under the patronage of the Methodist Episcopal Church. It was founded in 1882 as a home for destitute and orphan Protestant children between the ages of two and ten years. About 100 inmates are received yearly, who are taught some useful occupation to enable them to obtain self-supporting employment. Admission is free to those whose parents or friends are unable to contribute to their support.

28

The United Relief Works of the Society for Ethical Culture is an organization chartered by the Legislature for charitable and educational purposes, and entirely unsectarian in character. It was founded in 1879 ; for the last eleven years its quarters have been at 109 West 54th Street. It maintains the Working-man's School, comprising a Kindergarten ; a fully graded school (for children from six to fourteen years of age) based on the kindergarten principle, and a Normal Class for the training of kindergartners'; a Fresh-Air Fund, and a District Nursing Department. The annual expenses are $28,000.

The Children's Charitable Union was organized in 1877 to establish and maintain kindergartens for destitute young children, and to educate young women as kindergarten teachers. The school of the Union is at 70 Avenue D, where 75 poor children are taught daily and are fed at noon. The expenses are met by private charity.

The Asylum of St. Vincent de Paul is a large and well-arranged house at 215 West 39th Street. The institution was incorporated in 1868 for the reception,

care and religious and secular education of destitute and unprotected orphans of both sexes, preferably of French birth or parentage, over four years old. It is in charge of the Roman Catholic Sisters "Marianites of the Holy Cross," and is connected with the Church of St. Vincent de Paul. There are about 250 inmates, for whom a fresh-air fund provides seaside trips in summer. It is supported by voluntary contributions, and grants from the public funds. The architect was W. H. Hume.

The Dominican Convent of Our Lady of the Rosary, also known as the House of Our Lady of the Rosary, is at 329 East 63d Street. It was established in

ST. VINCENT DE PAUL'S ASYLUM, 215 WEST 39TH STREET.

1880 by the Sisters of St. Dominic, for religious, charitable, educational and reformatory work among young girls. Homeless and destitute girls between the ages of 2½ and 14 are admitted free, educated, and trained in the Catholic faith ; and when 16 years of age, provided with good homes. The convent educates nearly 500 girls yearly, at an expense of $60,000, which is partly met by a grant from the public funds.

The New-York Catholic Protectory was incorporated in 1863, to care for destitute Catholic children of the following classes ; 1st, children under fourteen years old, entrusted to it for care or protection ; 2d, those between the ages of seven and fourteen, who may be committed to its charge by magistrates as idle, truant, vicious or homeless ; 3d, those of the same age transferred from other institutions by the Commissioners of Public Charities and Correction. The protectories proper are at Westchester, N. Y., and the office and House of Reception are at 415 Broome Street. The Boys' Protectory is in charge of the Brothers of the Christian Schools, and the inmates are educated and taught useful trades. The Girls' Protectory is in charge of the Sisters of Charity, who educate the girls, and teach them housework and other industrial employment. This is one of the largest institutions of its class in the country, and cares for over 3,000 children yearly. The annual expenses, of $425,000, are met by grants from the public funds, voluntary contributions, and the sale of articles made by the inmates.

The Mission of the Immaculate Virgin, which occupies a large brick building at Lafayette Place and Great Jones Street, was incorporated in 1870 as a home for destitute boys under 16 years of age, who receive secular and religious education, and are taught habits of industry and self-reliance. Newsboys, bootblacks, and

other youthful workers who are able to pay, are allowed meals and lodgings at $2 a week, and in every case of destitution meals and lodgings are given free. The institution is in charge of St. Joseph's Union, a Catholic benevolent society. There is a country branch, at Mount Loretto, Staten Island, to which invalid inmates of the home are sent for an outing in the summer months. The Mission usually has in its care 2,000 boys, many of whom obtain situations through its employment bureau. The institution receives a large yearly grant from the public funds.

St. Joseph's Industrial Home for Destitute Children was established in 1868 by the Sisters of Mercy,

MISSION OF THE IMMACULATE VIRGIN AND ST. JOSEPH'S UNION,
LAFAYETTE PLACE AND GREAT JONES STREET.

as a branch of the Institute of Mercy. The home is at the corner of Madison Avenue and 81st Street, and has accommodations for 750 children. It affords a home and an industrial education to destitute young girls of good character, and also receives children over three years of age, who may be committed to its charge by a magistrate. In connection with the parent-house there is the Institution of Mercy, at Tarrytown, delightfully situated amid charming rural scenery.

St. Ann's Home for Destitute Children, at Avenue A and East 90th Street, is a Catholic charity, founded in 1879, for the care and education of destitute children over two years of age, who may be entrusted to it by parents or guardians, or committed by a magistrate. The Home is a large and cheerful edifice, with accommodations for nearly 300 inmates. It is in charge of the Sisters of the Good Shepherd, who receive the suffering regardless of creed, and give them a happy and comfortable home, in the mournful absence of their parents.

The House of the Holy Family, at 136 Second Avenue, was founded by the Rt. Rev. Mgr. Preston, formerly Vicar-General of the Archdiocese and Domestic Prelate to His Holiness Leo XIII., and was incorporated in 1870. The interior

administration was entrusted to the Sisters of the Divine Compassion. The work is the rescue, care and education of vagrant and tempted children and young girls, who are there trained and educated morally, intellectually and industrially. The House receives 500 inmates annually, and provides homes and occupation for deserving members when they wish to leave. The Sisters also conduct the House of Nazareth, at White Plains, for the care of young children still innocent, but who have been rescued from impending evil.

Many associations have been formed for the education, defence and relief of women, from the young girls just looking out upon life, up to the venerable grand-dames almost ready to pass away.

HOUSE OF THE HOLY FAMILY, 136 SECOND AVENUE.

The Ladies' Christian Union of the City of New York was organized in 1859 to promote the moral, temporal and religious welfare of women, particularly self-supporting young women, by providing them with home-like boarding-houses. The society maintains two homes : The Young Women's Home, at 27 Washington Square North, where nearly 100 respectable working-girls, other than house-servants, are lodged and boarded, at from $3 to $6 a week ; and The Branch Home, at 308 Second Avenue, where the same privilege is given to 40 self-supporting girls and women.

The Working Women's Protective Union was formed in 1863, to protect working women against the exactions and oppressions of unscrupulous employers. In every possible way the Union seeks to stand between the female wage-earner and the employer who would defraud her of her scanty wage. It also aids the same class in their efforts to obtain employment, and maintains a library at its office, 19 Clinton Place. Household servants are not included in its clients.

The Working Girls' Vacation Society, at 222 West 38th Street, was founded in 1883 to provide a two weeks' vacation for respectable unmarried working-girls who have satisfactory recommendations and a physician's statement that a vacation is needed. Railroad fares and board are provided, at the nominal rate of $1.50 a week. The society also pays the fares of working-girls to their friends in the country, and gives frequent day excursions in New-York harbor. Applications are made through clergymen, city missionaries or the Charity Organization Society. In 1892 776 girls were sent into the country for two weeks, 73 fares paid, and over 5,000 Glen-Island excursion-tickets furnished.

The Female Assistance Society was organized in 1813 for the relief of poor women in sickness. It has no house or home for its beneficiaries, and does its work by house-to-house visitation of those who apply for aid.

The Society for the Employment and Relief of Poor Women was founded, in 1844, to supply work at remunerative prices to poor women able and willing to work, who, having young children, or from sickness, are unable to leave their homes to obtain employment. About 100 applicants are aided yearly by the society, which has a repository at 146 East 16th Street, and an office at 104 East 20th Street.

The House and School of Industry, at 120 West 16th Street, was founded in 1851, to relieve poor women by furnishing them with plain and fine sewing, at living prices. Instruction in needle-work is also given to large classes of young girls. The yearly number of beneficiaries is about 125. The Home has a very attractive and comfortable brick building.

St. Mary's Lodging-House for Sheltering Respectable Girls, at 143 West 14th Street, was founded in 1877 by the "Friends of the Homeless," for the comfort and protection of respectable young women in search · of work, who are given the comforts of a pleasant home free of cost, until they are able to support themselves. The object of the Home is to protect its inmates from the numerous temptations that beset unemployed girls in all large cities. Nearly 2,000 young women were received in 1892.

HOUSE AND SCHOOL OF INDUSTRY, 120 WEST 16TH STREET.

The Institution of Mercy, on 81st Street, between Madison and Fourth Avenues, was opened in 1848, for the care and protection of destitute young women of good character, whom it trains in some useful pursuit, and assists in securing employment. About 400 young women are aided yearly by this charity, which is in charge of the Sisters of Mercy.

The New-York Female Asylum for Lying-In Women, at 139 Second Avenue, was incorporated in 1827, to provide free accommodation and medical attendance during confinement, to respectable indigent married women. It also gives the same aid to similar cases at their homes, and trains wet nurses for their profession.

St. Barnabas' House, at 304 Mulberry Street, is one of the numerous noble charities of the Episcopal City Missionary Society. It was established in 1865, as a temporary refuge for destitute and homeless women and those recently discharged from hospitals, cured, but needing rest; and a temporary home for destitute and homeless children. In connection with the House, and as auxiliary to its work of relief, there is a dispensary; a free day-nursery; an employment society for women; a fresh-air fund; a free library; an industrial school, where needle-work is taught; and a chapel where frequent religious services are held. During 1892 nearly 1,300 women and children were aided, 82,000 meals supplied to hungry applicants, and 18,630 lodgings given to the homeless.

The Isaac T. Hopper Home, at 110 Second Avenue, was opened in 1845 by the Women's Prison Association to assist liberated female prisoners with advice and encouragement; to provide them with a home and work; and to watch over them during the transition from prison-life to freedom. The aims of the management of the Home, which was named in memory of Isaac T. Hopper, the founder of the Women's Prison Association, are to prevent the recently liberated prisoners from falling back to their former evil courses, and to make an upright life easier for them. The privileges of the institution are free to the inmates, of whom there are about fifty.

The Riverside Rest Association, at 310 East 26th Street, provides a temporary home for friendless women who have been discharged from the public institutions on Blackwell's Island, and, so far as possible, procures work for them. It also cares for women who are addicted to drink, or victims of the opium habit, or immoral, and transfers them to the suitable institution for each case. The association was founded in 1887, and the Home has accommodations for 30 inmates.

The unfortunate women of the town, who are numbered here by legions, also have pitying hands outstretched to help them.

The New-York Magdalen Asylum was established in 1833 by the New-York Magdalen Society as a home for fallen women. It was the first American charity of its class. For twenty years it occupied a building on West 25th Street, but in 1850 the large brick building on 88th Street, between Madison and Fifth Avenues, was erected. In 1893 it occupied a new building, at the foot of 139th Street and North River. The asylum accommodates 125 inmates, and every effort is made to reclaim them by kindly treatment and also by teaching them different kinds of work, so that they may support themselves honestly.

The House of Mercy is a Protestant Episcopal home for fallen women, pleasantly located at Inwood-on-the-Hudson (at 206th Street). It originated in 1850, in the Christian labors of Mrs. Wm. Richmond, the wife of the then rector of St. Michael's, in aid of the abandoned women who found no hand outstretched to help them. Her labors resulted in the purchase of a suitable building at the foot of 86th Street, in 1856. The work was there carried on until 1891, when the present quarters were secured. The south wing, known as St. Agnes Hall, is devoted exclusively to the moral and industrial training of young girls between twelve and eighteen years of age. The rest of the edifice is devoted to the work among the older inmates. The House of Mercy is in charge of the Sisters of St. Mary, and a regular chaplain is provided. Legacies, donations and grants from the public funds are relied on to meet the expenses.

The House of the Good Shepherd, at the foot of East 90th Street, was founded in 1857 by five nuns of the Order of Our Lady of the Good Shepherd of Angers, a Catholic sisterhood founded in France as long ago as 1661, by Père Eudes. It is a house of refuge for fallen women and girls who desire to reform. Although founded and maintained by members of the Catholic communion, the privileges of the institution are free to all, regardless of creed, and there is kindly treatment of all who apply for help and shelter. The inmates are allowed to remain until a thorough reformation is effected, when permanent homes are secured, or employment is found for them. The House of the Good Shepherd is the largest of its kind in the city, having accommodation for 500 inmates, and it has been the means of restoring hundreds of Magdalens to industrious, useful and respectable lives.

St. Joseph's Night Refuge was founded in 1891 by the Friends of the Homeless. The Refuge is in the rear of 143 West 14th Street, and is open to all homeless women, no questions being asked or references required. There are 100 beds. Yearly, over 3,500 wandering women received shelter; and 7,000 meals are given to poor people in the neighborhood. In connection with the Refuge there is a laundry and sewing-room, where employment is given to inmates willing to work.

The Midnight Mission, at 208 West 46th Street, was opened in 1866, for the reclamation of fallen women, who are here given homes, and, if found worthy, aided in obtaining permanent homes or employment. It is in the charge of the Sisterhood of St. John Baptist, an order of the Protestant Episcopal Church.

The Florence Crittenton Mission for Fallen Women was established, in 1883, by Charles M. Crittenton, in memory of his little daughter Florence, and has

since been maintained by him, mainly at his own expense. The Mission is at 21 and 23 Bleecker Street, in the immediate vicinity of Mott Street and the Bowery, and finds its work ready to its hand. Its purpose is to reclaim the fallen women of the neighborhood, by providing them with lodging and food until they are strong enough to go out to work for themselves, and by Gospel meetings, which are held nightly until midnight. Many fallen women and dissolute men have been reclaimed here. The nightly services are quite interesting, and often bring out some heart-breaking experiences.

The Margaret Strachan Home and Mission, at 103 and 105 West 27th Street, is the outcome of a venture of faith begun in 1883 by Margaret Strachan, a poor seamstress. Her daily walks to and from her work brought her in contact with the licentiousness then rife in the vicinity of

FLORENCE CRITTENTON MISSION, 21 BLEECKER STREET.

27th Street, and she resolved to devote her life to the work of rescuing the fallen women in that part of the city. She rented a house; hung out a rude sign, bearing the legend, "Faith Home," and began the work, which she continued until her death, in 1887. She succeeded in interesting some of her patrons. The work increased to such an extent that the adjoining house was rented, and in 1887 both houses were purchased by the Mission, which was incorporated in that year. After the death of the founder the name was changed to the Margaret Strachan Home, and the work has been continued with remarkable success. The lower story of one of the houses is fitted up as a chapel, and Gospel-meetings are held there every night for the inmates, of whom there are about thirty. In the other house there are two pleasant parlors, and the sleeping-rooms are above, in both houses. The Home and Mission engages the attention and care of a number of wealthy ladies.

The Wetmore Home and several other institutions of similar character are actively engaged in the work of relieving the bitter distress of the social outcasts.

Invalids' Homes and the distress of incurables have aroused the pity of thousands, who have banded themselves together into societies to alleviate the woes thus seen.   One of the best of these is the Montefiore Home, described farther on.

The Home for Incurables, at Third Avenue and 182d Street, near Fordham, is one of those useful but mournful charities made necessary by the incurable nature of many diseases.   Its pleasant and well-ventilated buildings stand in a park of twelve acres, surrounded by shade-trees.   It was incorporated in 1866, and receives incurables of the better class at a charge of $7 a week.   There are 180 beds, one-third of them free.   The yearly expenses of $55,000 are met by voluntary contributions and the income of an endowment fund.

The House of the Holy Comforter Free Church Home for Incurables is well named, for if any are in sorest need of comfort it is the unfortunate for whom this home stands open.   The house is one of the numerous beneficent charities of the Protestant Episcopal Church, and was founded in 1880 to provide a free home for the care of destitute Protestant women and children of the better class suffering

HOME FOR THE RELIEF OF THE DESTITUTE BLIND, AMSTERDAM AVENUE AND WEST 104TH STREET.

from incurable diseases.   All patients are received on a three-months' trial and tenderly cared for by the Sisters of the Annunciation of the Blessed Virgin Mary, who are in charge of the work.   The house is at 149 Second Avenue, and the work involves the yearly expenditure of $7,000.

The New-York Home for Convalescents, at 433 West 118th Street, was opened in 1878 to afford gratuitous temporary care, employment and other assistance to worthy Protestant poor people, discharged as cured from the hospitals, but not yet able to resume their usual occupations.   This very necessary charity receives 300 inmates yearly, and is supported by private munificence.

The Lazarus Guild of the New-York Skin and Cancer Hospital was formed in 1891, to provide clothing, old linen and sick-room delicacies for the patients, as well as to raise funds for the endowment of free beds in the hospital.

The Society for the Relief of the Destitute Blind of the City of New York and vicinity, founded in 1869, maintains a house for the indigent and friendless blind of both sexes, at 104th Street and Amsterdam Avenue, with privileges free to those unable to pay ; and at $10 a month to others. Employment at fair wages is given to those able to work at mattress-making, re-seating chairs and all kinds of knitting-work. During 1892 the expenditures were $9,000, and 150 inmates were received.

The Sisters of Bon Secours, whose convent is at 1195 Lexington Avenue, devote their lives to the nursing of sick persons at their own homes. A number of these saintly nuns are consecrated to work for the sick poor, amid their surroundings of deprivation and destitution. Sister Eulalie de Barcelona is the Superior.

SISTERS OF BON SECOURS, LEXINGTON AVENUE AND 81ST STREET.

Homes for the Aged. — There are half-a-dozen comfortable and well-maintained homes for aged women, as well as for aged couples, and for men and women suffering from friendlessness and penury.

The Association for the Relief of Respectable, Aged, Indigent Females is one of the oldest of the city's charitable institutions. It charter runs back to 1814, a time when there was no other refuge than the poor-house for those gentlewomen who, having in their youth known better things, had in their old age fallen upon evil days. The society had no suitable home for its pensioners until 1833, when

a subscription list was opened, which John Jacob Astor headed with $5,000. Petrus Stuyvesant gave three lots of land in East 20th Street, and here the Asylum was erected, in 1838, followed in 1845 by a second building for the Infirmary. The asylum is now located on Amsterdam Avenue, at 104th

ASSOCIATION FOR THE RELIEF OF RESPECTABLE, AGED, INDIGENT FEMALES, AMSTERDAM AVENUE AND WEST 104TH STREET.

PRESBYTERIAN HOME FOR AGED WOMEN, 47 EAST 73D STREET.

Street, and here aged indigent gentlewomen find a pleasant and congenial home, as their faces turn toward the setting sun. Gentlewomen over sixty years of age are admitted on payment of $200 and the surrender of any property they may possess at their death. In addition to the regular inmates of the Home, the society supports a number of outside pensioners, at a total yearly expense of $56,000.

The Presbyterian Home for Aged Women, at 47 East 73d Street, was established in 1866, at the instance of a few ladies, to provide a refuge for aged and indigent female members of the local Presbyterian and Reformed Churches. Applicants for admission must be over 65 years old, and must pay a small weekly sum for board, in return for which they are given a pleasant home and tender care. Fifty inmates can be accommodated. The yearly expenses are met by contribution.

St. Luke's Home for Indigent Christian Females originated in an application made to the Rev. Dr. Tuttle, Rector of St. Luke's Church, by an aged woman for a place in which to spend her declining years. The good rector was compelled to refuse, as there was then no such home in the city. "But," said he, "please God, there soon will be"; and he immediately set about providing one, with such success that a house was soon leased and fitted up. In 1852 a house was opened, and in 1854, after an appeal to the leading city parishes, a building adjoining St. Luke's Church, in Hudson Street, was purchased. The present cheerful and commo-

ST. JOSEPH'S HOME FOR THE AGED, 207-215 WEST 15TH STREET.

dious house, at Madison Avenue and 89th Street, was built in 1870, and here the declining years of 65 good women are made pleasant and happy. The Home is open for the communicants of any of the Protestant Episcopal churches in the city which contribute to its support. The applicant must be 50 years of age, and must surrender any property she may possess, and pay an entrance-fee of $300.

The Peabody Home for Aged and Indigent Women was founded in 1874 by the Peabody Home and Reform Association, as a free and unsectarian home for poor but worthy women, who must be over 65 years, and in destitute circumstances. The home is pleasantly located on Boston Road, West Farms, and cares for 25 inmates, at a yearly expense of $5,000.

St. Joseph's Home for the Aged is an enormous building at 207-215 West 15th Street. This great charity was founded in 1868, and is under the charge of the Sisters of Charity of St. Vincent de Paul. It is entirely for the comfort of aged women; and has 350 inmates, of whom 100 pay according to ability.

The Home for Old Men and Aged Couples, a charity of the Protestant Episcopal Church, was incorporated in 1872, for members of the classes indicated, who are communicants of the Episcopal Church. The Home is at 487 Hudson Street, and here aged married couples are allowed to dwell comfortably together during their closing years.

The Home for the Aged of the Little Sisters of the Poor of the City of New York was incorporated in 1871, to provide a home for old persons

HOME FOR THE AGED, LITTLE SISTERS OF THE POOR, 207 EAST 70TH STREET.

of both sexes, irrespective of religion and belief. They must be over 60 years old, and destitute. There are two homes in the city; one at 207 East 70th Street, for applicants from the East Side; and another at 135 West 106th Street, for those from the West Side. The two homes give gratuitous care to nearly 500 inmates. They are in charge of the Little Sisters of the Poor, a Catholic charitable order instituted a quarter of a century ago, in France, by a poor priest and two working-girls.

The Methodist Episcopal Church Home of New-York City, a large brick edifice at the corner of Amsterdam Avenue and 93d Street, was incorporated in

1850 to provide a refuge for the aged and infirm destitute members of the Methodist Church. Applicants must have been members of that denomination for at least ten years, the last five in connection with one of the local churches. They must be of sound mind. No entrance fee is charged, but all property must

HOME FOR THE AGED, LITTLE SISTERS OF THE POOR, COLUMBUS AVENUE AND WEST 106TH STREET.

be surrendered to the Home, which supplies clothing, employment and medical and other necessary care. One hundred and twenty-five aged and infirm pensioners are cared for in the institution.

The Baptist Home for Aged and Infirm Persons was established in 1869 by the Ladies' Home Society of the Baptist churches of the city of New York, as an abiding-place for aged, destitute or infirm members of the Baptist churches. Applicants for admission must have been members of one of the Baptist city churches for at least five years, must be recommended by the pastor and deacons of the church to which they belong, and must pay an admission-fee of $100 each ; in return for which they receive a home, clothing, medical attendance and religious privileges. The home has about 100 inmates, who are cared for at a yearly expense of $15,000. It is in charge of a board of managers. The building stands on 68th Street, between Park and Lexington Avenues.

The Samaritan Home for the Aged of the City of New York was incorporated in 1867, in order to relieve the crowded condition of other similar institutions.

METHODIST EPISCOPAL CHURCH HOME, AMSTERDAM AVENUE AND WEST 93D STREET.

The first building stood on West 37th Street. The cheerful and commodious home at 414 West 22d Street was opened in 1870. The object of the institution is to provide a haven of rest for aged Protestants of either sex, over 65 years of age, on payment of an admission-fee of $250. Forty-five inmates are provided for, and there is an endowment fund of $40,000. The affairs of the Home are in charge of a board of managers.

The **Chapin Home for the Aged and Infirm,** at 151 East 66th Street, was opened in 1869 as a home for aged and infirm persons of both sexes, in reduced circumstances, who must be recommended by the board of managers. An applicant must be over 65 years old, and must pay an admission fee of $300, a physician's examination fee of $5, and a burial fee of $50, and surrender all property in possession at the time of admission. There are 70 inmates; and an invested fund of $60,000.

The **Isabella Heimath,** corner of Amsterdam Avenue and 190th Street, was established in 1875, by the late Mrs. Anna Ottendorfer, at Astoria, as a home for indigent old women. The institution on its completion in 1889 was presented by

ISABELLA HEIMATH, AMSTERDAM AVENUE AND 190TH STREET.

Oswald Ottendorfer to a society incorporated under the title Isabella Heimath. It is for the maintenance and care of the aged and the sick, without regard to creed, sex or nationality, comprising a home for the care of indigent persons — of at least sixty years of age — unable to support themselves, and without relatives to support them; and a hospital for chronic invalids without means. Consumptives, or patients suffering from infectious diseases, epileptics, idiots, and those requiring constant personal attendance, cannot be admitted. There is a convalescent ward, in which convalescents who need rest after an acute disease or a surgical operation are admitted for a limited time. The admission to all departments is gratuitous. There are 176 beds. The hospital is equipped with Worthington pumps, electric lights, and other conveniences and safe-guards.

Many avocations and trades, as confederated in modern times, have established extensive charitable agencies for their own people, when fallen on unhappy days, and have also made provision for helping their young people.

The Actors' Fund of America, at 12 West 28th Street, was incorporated in 1882 for the relief of needy actors and other persons connected with the stage. Its active founder was A. M. Palmer, who has constantly been its president. Its funds are derived from membership dues, and the proceeds of the annual benefit performance held in many theatres throughout the country. During 1892 over 400 persons were relieved, at an expense of $28,000. In 1892 a grand fair held in Madison-Square Garden netted nearly $200,000 for the fund.

The General Society of Mechanics and Tradesmen, at 18 East 16th Street, is one of the oldest local organizations. It was founded in 1785 for the general improvement of mechanics and tradesmen. It has a large membership; is in a flourishing condition; and has become a valued friend to the young men and women who avail themselves of its many privileges. Its leading features are the Free Library, at 18 East 16th Street, a public circulating library, founded in 1820; the mechanics' schools, furnishing free instruction in stenography, type-writing, and mechanical and free-hand drawing to worthy young men and women; courses of free lectures every winter; and free scholarships in the New-York Trade Schools. It supports its indigent members, and pensions the widows and orphans of deceased members.

The New-York Society for the Relief of Widows and Orphans of Medical Men was formed in 1842 to render aid to the needy widows and orphans of deceased members. In special cases, other near relatives, who had been dependent upon the deceased, are aided. Twelve widows and four orphans received assistance in 1892, at an outlay of $4,000.

The Exempt Firemen's Benevolent Fund, at 174 Canal Street, was founded in 1791, under the name of the Fire Department Fund, by a few members of the old volunteer force, at a convivial meeting. A charter was obtained in 1798, providing for the maintenance and increase of the fund. For many years the beneficiaries were few in number, and a large surplus accumulated. This was lost in the great fire of 1835, which ruined the fire-insurance companies in which it had been invested. The citizens, however, contributed $24,000; and when the volunteer system was superseded by the paid Fire Department, in 1865, the fund was placed in charge of the Association of Exempt Firemen, which had been formed in 1841. At that time the fund amounted to $90,000. Now it is nearly $200,000, and the income is expended for the benefit of indigent and disabled firemen, or their widows or children. The Fire Department has a fund amounting to nearly $500,000, the income of which is used in the same manner.

The maritime class, the sailors who go down to the sea in ships, are admirably protected by charitable funds, mainly of their own institution.

The Sailors' Snug Harbor, at New Brighton, Staten Island, was established in 1801, by Captain Robert Richard Randall, who bequeathed to it considerable tracts of city real estate, now of enormous value. The asylum buildings are very extensive, and the grounds contain 180 acres, attractively laid out. The Snug Harbor is a home for aged, infirm and superannuated sailors, who must be native-born, or, in case of those of foreign birth, must produce documentary evidence that they have served at least five years in vessels flying the American flag. The home is in charge of a board of trustees, and there is ample accommodation for 1,000 inmates. The institution has a yearly income of over $300,000, and is self-supporting.

Webb's Home for shipbuilders, now approaching completion, on Fordham Heights, palatial, endowed with millions, is intended partly for a home for aged and destitute master-shipbuilders and their wives.

The Marine Society of the City of New York, in the State of New York, at 19 Whitehall Street, was incorporated as early as 1770, for the improvement of maritime knowledge, and the relief of indigent members who are or have been masters of ships, or their widows or orphans. It is supported by voluntary contributions and membership dues. It aids nearly 50 widows yearly.

The Home for Seamen's Children was founded in 1846 by the Society for the Relief of the Destitute Children of Seamen. It is pleasantly located at West New Brighton, Staten Island, and about 130 children are cared for and educated yearly. No one is received for a shorter period than a year ; and a small weekly payment is required from parents who are able to contribute to the support of their children. The inmates, unless claimed by friends or guardians, are retained in the home until fourteen years of age, when suitable homes are obtained for them.

The Mariners' Family Asylum of the Port of New York, the only institution of its kind in the United States, was incorporated in 1854, as a home for the destitute sick or infirm mothers, wives, widows, sisters or daughters of seamen of the port of New York. Applicants must be over 60 years of age, and pay an admission fee of $100. The asylum is located at Stapleton, Staten Island, and about $5,000 is spent yearly in caring for the fifty pensioners.

The Seamen's Christian Association, at 665 Washington Street, was founded in 1888, and maintains a chapel, reading and writing room for seamen and boatmen, where religious and moral entertainment is provided for them. The "Rest" is open daily from 2 P. M. until 10 P. M., and here "Jack" may always find a hearty welcome. Religious services are held every evening.

Foreign Relief Societies.— An interesting manifestation of charity is in its application to various races from abroad. The great network of Jewish philanthropies is entirely built up and maintained from the abounding wealth and liberality of the Hebrew-American population. On the other hand, the African asylums, and the beneficent works done among the Chinese, the Italians and certain other immigrant colonies are maintained at the cost of the older population of the city. Among these fraternal groups are : The Italian Benevolent Society, founded in 1857 ; the German Mission-House Association, 1867 ; the Spanish Benevolent Society, in 1882 ; the Norwegian Relief Society, in 1883 ; the Hungarian Association, in 1884 ; the Jewish Immigrants' Protective Society, in 1885 ; the Polish Benevolent Society ; and the Greek Benevolent Society, in 1891.

St. George's Society, at 7 Battery Place, was established in 1786, succeeding an older society with similar aims, which had existed before the Revolution. It was incorporated in 1838. Its object is to afford relief and advice to indigent natives of England and the British Colonies, or to their wives, widows or children, in the cities of New York and Brooklyn. Its income can be expended only in charity. The persons eligible to membership are : natives of England or any of its dependencies, and their sons and grandsons, and British officers and their sons, wherever born.

St. Andrew's Society of the State of New York was founded in 1756 and incorporated in 1826. It is one of the oldest existing benevolent societies in the country. Its objects are the promotion of social and friendly intercourse among the natives of Scotland and their connections and descendants in the city and vicinity, and the relief of such as may be indigent. If employment cannot be found for the industrious poor in the city, the society pays their passage to any other place where work may be offered.   In 1892 2,300 persons received assistance.   The society has a permanent fund of about $75,000 ; and 450 members.   Its main office is in the United Charities Building, with a branch at 287 East Broadway.

St. David's Society, at 21 University Place, was founded in 1835, and incorporated in 1846, for the relief of needy Welsh people.   Welshmen and their descendants, and persons married to Welsh women, are eligible to membership.

The Irish Emigrant Society, at 51 Chambers Street and 29 Reade Street, was founded in 1841, and incorporated in 1844, to afford advice, protection and relief to needy Irish immigrants.   It is an outgrowth of the Social Benevolent Society of the Friendly Sons of St. Patrick, the successor of the Friendly Brothers of St. Patrick, which existed previous to the Revolution.   The Society of the Friendly

Sons of St. Patrick was organized in 1784, and became very active in extending aid to indigent natives of Ireland in the city, especially in aiding newly arrived immigrants in obtaining employment.   Since the founding of the Emigrant Society it has turned its activity in other directions.

La Societe Francaise de Bienfaisance (French Benevolent Society) was organized in 1809, and incorporated in 1819, to assist needy Frenchmen by providing medical advice, medicines, food, clothing, money, and temporary shelter for those in need or sickness.   It depends entirely on the generosity of the public for its yearly expenses,

SWISS BENEVOLENT SOCIETY, 108 SECOND AVENUE.

which average $20,000.   The society maintains a relief bureau, bureau of immigration, night refuge, dispensary, hospital and home, at 320 West 34th Street.

The Young Women's Home Society of the French Evangelical Church in the City of New York, at 341 West 30th Street, was organized in 1888 and incorporated in 1890, to provide unemployed governesses, teachers and domestics of French birth with homes and board.   It also supplies needy applicants with clothing, money and medical attendance, and procures employment for them.   The Home furnishes rooms and board for 24 inmates, at a cost of $4 a week each. Nearly 1,000 worthy cases are assisted yearly, at a cost of $7,000.

The Belgian Society of Benevolence, at 135 Duane Street, was incorporated in 1871, for the relief of indigent Belgians and their descendants.   Its funds are derived from private subscriptions largely from the natives of the Low Countries.

The Swiss Benevolent Society, the title of which indicates the scope of its work, maintains a home at 108 Second Avenue, where needy natives of Switzerland are cared for.

The Leo House for German Catholic Immigrants is for the protection and care of recently-landed German Catholic immigrants, who are aided by advice, financial assistance in extreme cases, and in all other possible ways.   The society in charge was incorporated in 1889. The House itself, at 6 State Street, is one of the few old-time mansions that have survived all the changes of the modern city. It was for many years the home of James Watson, the first president of the New-England Society of New York, and in its parlors that society was founded.

The Mission of Our Lady of the Rosary, at Castle Garden (7 State Street), receives yearly over 4,000 young immigrant girls, and cares for them until they meet their friends, procure work, or proceed on their journeys. It has neither State nor municipal aid, and is supported through the generosity of the charitable. The Rev. M. Callaghan is director.

The Lutheran Pilgrim House, at 8 State Street, was opened in 1885, for benevolent and humane work among the poorer classes of German Lutheran

LUTHERAN PILGRIM HOUSE.   MISSION OF OUR LADY OF THE ROSARY.   LEO IMMIGRANT HOUSE.
MISSION AND EMIGRANT HOUSES, ON STATE STREET.

immigrants, for whom a lodging-house, temporary employment, advice, and all other needful assistance is provided. The House is supported by the Lutheran churches.

The Evangelical Aid Society for the Spanish Work of New York and Brooklyn, at 1345 Lexington Avenue, was founded in 1886 to carry the Gospel to the Spanish-speaking people in their own language, to provide missionaries to visit them in their houses, to relieve the sick and help the poor, and to establish Sunday and industrial schools.

St. Bartholomew's Chinese Guild, at 23 St. Mark's Place, was founded in 1889 for the improvement, spiritual elevation and religious training of the Chinese. It renders legal aid to its beneficiaries, and cares for the sick and dying in the city and vicinity. There are nearly 700 members, who have the privileges of a reading-room, library and gymnasium, and receive instruction in the manual arts. The guild is supported by St. Bartholomew's Episcopal Church and by its membership dues.

29

The Colored Orphan Asylum and Association for the benefit of colored children, in the city of New York, is due to the earnest labors of two ladies, Miss Anna H. Shotwell and Miss Murray, who in 1836 began to work in behalf of the neglected colored children of the city. As the result of their labors, at a time when the negro was generally regarded as nothing more than the white man's chattel, the Association for the Benefit of the Colored Orphans was formed, the

first of its kind in the country, and a small house on 12th Street was purchased. The association was incorporated in 1838, and in 1842, after repeated appeals to the Common Council, a grant was obtained of twenty-two lots of land on Fifth Avenue, and a suitable building was erected. This was destroyed in the

COLORED ORPHAN ASYLUM, WEST 143D STREET, NEAR TENTH AVENUE.

Draft Riot of 1863, in spite of heroic efforts to save it. Instead of rebuilding on the old site, the managers secured a location on West 143d Street, between Tenth Avenue and the Boulevard, and the present home was erected. With the passing away of the old prejudice against the negro the institution has steadily gained in the confidence and good will of the community. Colored orphans of both sexes, between the ages of two and ten years, are received and gratuitously provided for, except in cases where the children are intrusted to the society by parents or guardians, when a nominal fee of seventy-five cents a week is charged. All the inmates are instructed in home industries, and at the age of twelve indentured into families or at trades. The leading design of the home is not merely to rescue from poverty, and minister to the physical comforts and necessities of those committed to its care, but to elevate the character, develop the faculties and impart a knowledge of religious and moral obligations and duties. About 350 children are cared for. The expenses are met by private subscriptions and grants from the public school fund.

The Colored Home and Hospital of the city of New York originated in 1839, in the labors of a few women, who sought to alleviate the condition of the indigent colored population. In 1845 the society was incorporated and $10,000 was secured from the State, for a suitable structure. The group of buildings, at 65th Street and First Avenue, was erected in 1849, and comprises the home, a chapel, a hospital for general diseases, and a lying-in hospital. The privileges of the home are free to all indigent colored residents of the city, and are open to non-residents upon the payment of a fixed sum quarterly. The Commissioners of Public Charities have the right to place in the institution adult destitute, infirm, sick and incurable colored persons of either sex, for whose support partial provision is made from the public funds.

The New-York Colored Mission, at 135 West 30th Street, was founded in 1871 for the religious, moral and social elevation of the colored people in the city. It seeks to attain its purpose by means of frequent religious services, by Sunday-school instruction, by its free employment office, reading-room and library, and by the zealous labors of a missionary, who visits the sick and poor, and gives relief in food and clothing and other necessaries. It also has a lodging-room, where colored women can obtain lodgings at nominal rates. Nearly 6,000 lodgings are furnished yearly. A sewing-school for women and young girls is also in successful operation. The yearly expenses are $5,000, and are met by private contributions.

The United Hebrew Charities of the City of New York, at 128 Second Avenue, was formed in 1874 by the union of the Hebrew Benevolent and Orphan Asylum Society; the Hebrew Benevolent Fuel Society; the Hebrew Relief Society; the Congregation Darech Amuno Free Burial Fund Society, and the Ladies' Hebrew Lying-in Society. Its objects are to afford relief of all kinds to worthy Hebrews, and by co-operation to prevent fraud. The city is divided into districts, with visitors and physicians attached to each district; the sick are visited in their homes; immigrants from Europe and other places are aided; and the worthy Hebrew poor are assisted in many ways. In 1892 nearly 40,000 persons were aided; situations were obtained for 5,000 applicants; and 20,600 lodgings and 64,000 meals were furnished.

The Hebrew Benevolent and Orphan Society of New York was incorporated in 1822, and reincorporated in 1860. It maintains a large asylum, one of the best appointed in the country, at Amsterdam Avenue and 136th Street, where

Hebrew orphans and indigent boys and girls are sheltered and educated. The building has a capacity of 1,000. The origin of the society is touching. Many years ago a Hebrew soldier of the Revolution lay dying in the City Hospital, and expressed a desire to see some of his co-

HEBREW BENEVOLENT ORPHAN ASYLUM, AMSTERDAM AVENUE AND WEST 136TH STREET.

religionists, a number of whom visited him. Becoming interested in the suffering soldier, they collected a small fund, and after his death, they found themselves in possession of $300, which was made a nucleus of the larger sum with which the asylum was founded. Wm. H. Hume designed the present building.

The Home for Aged and Infirm Hebrews of the City of New York, at West 105th Street, near Columbus Avenue, was opened in 1848, and incorporated in 1872. Aged and infirm Hebrew New-Yorkers, of either sex, over sixty years of age, are received here and given a home in their declining years. About 160 are cared for yearly, at an expense of $30,000.

The Hebrew Sheltering Guardian Society of New York was formed in 1879, to found and maintain an asylum where Jewish infants, orphans, half-orphans and deserted children, not admitted into other institutions, might be received, cared

for and educated until they could be provided with homes or permanent employment.   The asylum buildings are at Eleventh Avenue and 151st Street, for infants
and grown-up boys, and at the Boulevard and 150th Street, for girls.   In addition to its regular work, the institution gives temporary employment, food and
shelter to former inmates out of employment, and furnishes meals to poor persons
and children not connected with the asylum.   The yearly expenses are $60,000.

The **Montefiore Home for Chronic Invalids**, at the Boulevard and West
138th Street, a useful Hebrew charity, was established in 1884, to afford shelter in

MONTEFIORE HOME FOR CHRONIC INVALIDS, BOULEVARD AND WEST 138TH STREET.

sickness to such invalid residents as, by reason of incurable disease, are unable to
obtain treatment at other institutions.   Incurables of both sexes, discharged from
the city hospitals, are received and cared for, irrespective of their religious belief.
The families of the patients are also relieved, when deprived of the labor of the
breadwinner, from the income of the Julius Hallgarten Fund.   There is also a Discharged Patients' and Climatic Cure Fund, the income of which is used to send
improved patients to Vineland, N. J., or to Colorado, for a few months' change of
air and scene.   In 1892 this charity cared for 300 inmates and over 200 out-door
patients, at a cost of $73,000.

The **Ladies' Deborah Nursery and Child's Protectory** was founded in
1878, for the reception, care and education of destitute Hebrew children from four
to fourteen years old, who may be committed to its keeping by magistrates.   The
buildings are at 95 East Broadway, for boys, and East 162d Street, near Eagle
Avenue, for girls.   The inmates are cared for and instructed in some trade or household work until they are able to support themselves.   The average number received
yearly is 375.

The **Aguilar Aid Society** was founded in 1890 to assist the up-town Jewish
poor on the East Side with fuel, clothing, groceries, and in special cases money, and
also to provide Passover supplies to those unable to purchase them.

The **Hebrew Sheltering Home**, 210 Madison Avenue, was opened in 1889,
to aid Hebrew immigrants by furnishing free temporary lodgings and food, and
assistance in obtaining employment.   During 1892 4,000 immigrants were assisted.

The **Young Women's Hebrew Association**, 721 Lexington Avenue and
206 East Broadway, was founded in 1888 to advance the cause of Judaism, to promote culture among women, and to improve the moral and intellectual welfare of

girls of over fourteen years, and of women of the laboring and immigrant classes. Lessons are given in the domestic arts, cooking, physical culture, dressmaking, etc., mainly to Russian immigrants, who are also taught the rudiments of English.

Miscellaneous Charitable Societies abound on every side, and quite defy classification. A few of them may be mentioned, almost at random, in order to exhibit the wide sweep of metropolitan kindliness.

The New-York Fruit and Flower Mission, at 104 East 20th Street, was founded in 1870. It distributes flowers, fruits and delicacies among the sick in hospitals, asylums and tenement-houses, and sends Christmas greetings to sick children in houses and hospitals.

The New-York Bible and Fruit Mission to the Public Hospitals is an important local charity, organized in 1876 for work among the sick in public hospitals. Weekly visits are made to all the hospitals in charge of the Department of Public Charities and Correction, and flowers, food, fruit and reading-matter are distributed to the patients. The institution is also en-gaged in useful philanthropic work among the poor, and labors to reform criminals and inebriates. The Mission Building at 416 to 422 East 26th Street contains a chapel, where services are held every evening; a coffee-house and restaurant, where meals and tickets for food are sold at moderate prices; a lodging-house for men, which furnishes lodgings and baths at low rates; a broom factory, which gives employ-ment to men out of work, convalescents from the hos-pitals, and discharged con-

HOME FOR AGED AND INFIRM HEBREWS, 125 WEST 105TH STREET, NEAR COLUMBUS AVENUE.

victs; a reading-room and circulating library; and a sewing-school for young girls. Other branches of the mission work are the Penny Provident Fund, the Fresh-Air Fund, and the Loan-Relief Bureau. During 1892 85,000 meals were furnished at the coffee-house; 33,000 men were registered at the lodging-house; and the sum of $2,200 was paid out in wages at the broom factory.

The Christmas Letter Mission, was organized in Europe in 1871, and in the United States in 1881. It is a charming charity, formed to distribute Christmas messages of consolation and encouragement among the inmates of hospitals, prisons and other similar institutions. These messages are written by friends of the move-ment. In 1892 nearly 2,500 letters of Christmas greeting were distributed among the inmates of the local institutions, and over 35,000 in the United States.

The Island Mission for Cheering the Lives of the Poor and Sick, at 102 Waverly Place, is an unsectarian charity, formed in 1887, to brighten and cheer the lives of the inmates of the public charitable institutions by means of pictures, books and entertainments, and by providing the ordinary comforts of life for the aged, infirm and insane. It is supported entirely by private charity.

The Hospital Book and Newspaper Society, at 21 University Place, is a department of the State Charities Aid Association. It was formed in 1874, and its mission is to receive and distribute gratuitously among the inmates of the local hospitals and asylums, books, newspapers and other reading matter. Nearly 60,000 books and papers are distributed yearly.

The Needlework Guild of America, New-York Branch, was founded in 1891 to provide new and suitable garments for the inmates of the local hospitals, homes and other charities, and to unite all who are interested in that special field of charitable work. The guild has no office, but does its work privately, by house-to-house meetings among the members.

The Ladies' Fuel and Aid Society, at 199 Henry Street, was incorporated in 1888. It distributes coal, provisions, clothing and other necessaries of life to the worthy and suffering of any class or creed, assists in obtaining employment, and renders any other assistance thought to be wise and good. In 1893, 2,325 families were aided. Other fuel and aid societies are : The Hebrew Benevolent Fuel Society (1869), the Earle Guild (1876), and the East-Side Ladies' Aid Society (1889).

The New-England Society in the City of New York, at 76 Wall Street, was organized in 1805, as a charitable and literary association. It had but a feeble growth for many years, but after the opening of the Erie Canal, in 1825, many New-Englanders settled in the city, and infused new life into the society, which has for many years been a flourishing and popular institution. There is a committee on charity, which distributes the money voted by the board of officers to the beneficiaries, who are the widows and orphans of deceased members. The society has 1,500 members. Daniel G. Rollins is its President ; and L. P. Hubbard, Secretary.

The Penny-Provident Fund of the Charity Organization Society was established in 1889, to inculcate habits of providence and thrift among the poor, by supplying them with facilities for small savings, such as the savings-banks do not afford. The plan is similar to that of the English Postal Savings System. Deposits of one cent and upwards are received and receipted for by stamps attached by a Stamp-Card, given to each depositor. As soon as a sufficient amount has been deposited in this small way, the depositors are encouraged to open accounts in some savings-bank. Over 210 local stamp-stations have been established in various parts of the city, and more than 60,000 persons have made deposits, varying from one cent to larger sums. The central office is at Fourth Avenue and 22d Street.

The Christian Aid to Employment Society, at 50 Bible House, was incorporated in 1888, to assist worthy men and women to suitable employment. No worthy applicant is refused aid because of inability to pay a fee. A small charge is made to employers for services rendered.

The German Legal Aid Society, at 35 Nassau Street, was incorporated in 1876, to render free legal advice and aid to persons too poor to employ a lawyer. It has aided over 50,000 persons, and has collected for claimants over $350,000. Formerly the work was confined to Germans, but it is now international in character, and distributes its benefits to all applicants.

The Ladies' Union Relief Association was formed in 1865 for the care and relief of sick and disabled soldiers and their families, and of the widows and orphans of those who fell in the War of the Rebellion. Its work at present consists mainly in obtaining pensions for those entitled to them, and in granting out-door relief, not exceeding $10 a month, to those who have claims upon the National Soldiers' Home at Washington. It is managed by a board of women trustees.

The International Telegraph Christian Association, American Branch, was founded in 1890, to promote religion and Christian fellowship in telegraph-offices. The parent organization is of English origin. The American Branch has already established six Junior branches in different parts of the city, where messenger and telegraph boys under sixteen years of age receive moral, social and physical benefits ; and a Senior Branch for letter-carriers. The address of the General Local Secretary is 70 West 36th Street.

The Tenement-House Chapter of the King's Daughters and Sons, Madison Street, was organized in 1892 to bring the members of the Order into personal relation with the dwellers in tene-ment-houses, whose moral and physi-cal elevation is the principal aim of the organization. In cases of special need, such aid as seems best suited to each case is given ; and nursing, sick-room comforts and food are supplied to the sick. A valuable fresh-air work is done among the children dur-ing the summer months. The head-quarters of the King's Daughters are at 158 West 23d Street, in the former home of David M. Morrison.

KING'S DAUGHTERS, 158 WEST 23D STREET.

The Ladies' Mission of the Protestant Episcopal Church of the Public Institutions of the City of New York was incorporated in 1862. The membership is composed of charitably inclined women of the Episcopal Church, who are willing to devote a portion of their time to visit-ing the inmates of the numerous local public institutions, including special prison-work on Blackwell's Island. During 1892 over 25,000 visits were made by the members of the mission.

The Guild of St. Elizabeth, at 440 West 23d Street, was organized in 1876 to minister to the sick and poor in the public institutions at Bellevue Hospital, and on Blackwell's, Ward's, Hart's and Randall's Islands.

The Istituto Italiano (Italian Home) is a charitable organization, founded in 1889 by Gian Paolo Riva, the Italian Consul-General, and other prominent Italian residents, to maintain a hospital and to give advice to Italian immigrants, dissemi-nate information among them, and promote their welfare in various ways. It has occupied its present quarters, at 179 Second Avenue, near East 11th Street, since February, 1891. Its work has been comparatively limited because of lack of funds. Giovanni Starace is president.

The New-York Society for Parks and Playgrounds for Children, at Room 7, 36 Union Square, was founded in 1891 to supply fresh air, sunshine and healthful recreation to as many as possible of the 400,000 children crowded into the stuffy tenement-houses of the city. The first playground started by the society, at Second Avenue and 92d Street, accommodates 500 children, at an expense of only

ITALIAN INSTITUTE AND ITALIAN HOME, 179 SECOND
AVENUE, BETWEEN EAST 11TH AND EAST 12TH STS.

$5 a day. It is proposed to open other similar grounds, provided with swings, see-saws, wagons, wheelbarrows, shovels, heaps of sand and jumping-ropes as rapidly as funds are forthcoming. The economy of the work is such that all this can be provided at an outlay of one cent a day for each child in attendance, and the value of the work is out of all proportion to its cost. The expenses are met by voluntary contributions.

Many Old-time Charities of New-York City have in recent years wisely removed their establishments into the neighboring country, where, amid verdurous forests, lapsing waves and pure sweet breezes, their unhappy patrons may find some better chance of recovery and sanity. Thus on the shores of the Hudson, and overlooking the blue sea from Long Island and Staten Island, now stand many asylums formerly poisoned by the stenches and oaths of the down-town slums. The latest to move out of the city was the Babies' Shelter of the Church of the Holy Communion, which has been removed to St. Johnland, the Church Industrial community on Long Island.

The heroic attacks of Grace, St. Bartholomew's, Trinity, Judson Memorial, and other churches and secular bodies are continuously delivered against the powers of the slums, and with marked effect. The University and College Settlements, encamped in the heart of the "Suicide Ward," or the "Typhus Ward," where over 60,000 people are packed into 110 acres, are to erect a grand building, to be a centre of regenerative influences. Thousands of active philanthropists are daily saving New York from the poison of its depraved and degraded humanity and the venom of pauperized peasant immigration, by a self-imposed round of brave and self-denying and fragrant charities. Although this city is a sink into which pour the crime and poverty of all countries, the efforts of its philanthropic societies have resulted in a perceptible diminution of crime, especially among boys and girls, and therefore in an incalculable saving to the community — and to Humanity.

LEAGUE OF THEOSOPHICAL WORKERS, 144 MADISON AVENUE,
BETWEEN 31ST AND 32D STREET.

The Sanitary Organizations.

Board of Health and Health Statistics—Hospitals and Dispensaries—The Morgue—Curative Institutions—Insane, Inebriate and other Asylums.

THE general sanitary condition of New York is fairly good, in view of the many unfavorable conditions necessarily prevailing in all large cities. The average annual death-rate of about 25 in 1,000, while somewhat higher than that of most American and many foreign cities, is not abnormally high, when the large yearly influx of immigrants, the crowded condition of the tenement-houses, and the number of patients from other cities, who come here for treatment in the hospitals, are taken into consideration. The average yearly number of deaths is not far from 40,000, fully 8,000 of which occur in the numerous public and private institutions, and about 25,000 in houses containing three or more families. One drawback to a satisfactory sanitary status is the difficulty of keeping the many miles of streets in a cleanly condition, a trouble which is not so strongly felt in smaller cities. Strenuous efforts are made by the Street Department to improve the condition of the streets, and to remove all these menaces to the public health.

The Board of Health controls the sanitary affairs of the city. In its present form it was established in 1873. It consists of the President of the Board of Police, the Health Officer of the Port, and two Commissioners, one of whom must have been a practising physician for five years previous to his appointment. The Commissioners hold office for six years, and are appointed by the Mayor, independent of the Board of Aldermen. A large corps of medical inspectors is constantly employed in the cure and prevention of disease, in the inspection of houses, and for the enforcement of the health-laws and the sanitary code. There is also a night service of such physicians and surgeons as are willing to undertake the work, who answer all night-calls that may be sent to them from the different police-stations; a vaccinating corps; a disinfecting corps; and an organization of meat and milk inspectors; all of which are potent factors in promoting the general healthfulness of the city. The Board also has charge of the Reception Hospital, at the foot of East 16th Street, built in 1885 for the temporary care of contagious cases while awaiting transportation to the Riverside Hospital, on North Brother Island, which was erected in 1884 for the treatment of such contagious diseases as cannot well be isolated at home, as well as similar cases from Quarantine; and the Willard Parker Hospital, at the foot of East 16th Street, opened in 1884 for cases of scarlet fever and diphtheria.

The Quarantine Service is administered by three Commissioners of Quarantine appointed by the Governor for three years, and a Health Officer, for two years. The Commissioners are authorized by law to make all needful regulations for the examination and (when necessary) the detention of all incoming vessels. The State of New York furnishes residences for the Health Officer and his three assistants, at the boarding station at Fort Wadsworth, Staten Island. These officials are obliged to board every vessel subject to quarantine or visitation, immediately after her arrival at the boarding station ; to ascertain the sanitary condition of the vessel and all its passengers by strict examination ; to send all sick passengers to the Quarantine Hospital; and to determine what persons and vessels are to be detained in Quarantine.   The property of the Department comprises the Hospital Ship, used as a residence for the deputy health officer and a boarding station for all vessels arriving from infected ports; Swinburne Island, on which is the hospital for contagious diseases; Hoffman Island, used for the detention and purification of well persons arriving in infected vessels ; the Crematory, on Swinburne Island ; the upper boarding station at Fort Wadsworth, Staten Island ; and a steamer for daily communication between all points of the Quarantine establishment.

Hospitals are more numerous in New York than in any other city on the continent.   There are nearly eighty of these ''inns on the highway of life where suffering humanity finds alleviation and sympathy,'' and many of them are among the largest and most magnificent buildings in the city.   The newer ones are built of warm red brick, and fitted with the latest and most efficient heating and ventilating apparatus.   There is no kind of bodily suffering that may not find skillful treatment and kindly nursing in one or the other of these healing homes, where the most eminent physicians and surgeons give freely of their time and skill to the inmates.   The wealthy patient may command all the luxuries a fine private home could give, and the poor man unable to pay may enjoy comforts impossible to him in his

BELLEVUE HOSPITAL, FIRST AVENUE, EAST 26TH STREET, AND EAST RIVER.

own narrow dwelling.   Fully 100,000 patients are treated yearly in these curative institutions, more than three-quarters of them without any payment for the care and skill which restore them to health or smooth the pathway to the grave ; and the death-rate is less than eight per cent.   Nearly all the larger hospitals have an ambulance service in constant readiness to answer calls for help, and some have training-schools, where nurses are taught the duties of their calling, and trained in those kindly ministrations which often are more potent factors in the patient's restoration to health than all the skill of the physician.

Bellevue Hospital is a great charity institution. It receives gratuitously the sick poor of the city. The first stone of the original building was laid in 1811, and in 1816 it was opened as a hospital, almshouse and penitentiary, under the direction of the Common Council. At that time the medical staff consisted of one visiting and two young resident physicians. In 1826 the Hospital and Almshouse were separated; and in 1848 the Bellevue grounds were divided, a large part sold to private purchasers, and the convicts and paupers sent to Blackwell's Island. In 1849 the Common Council was superseded by a board of ten governors, who in 1860 gave place to the Commissioners of Public Charities and Correction, who now have charge of the Hospital. Until 1849 the members of the hospital staff were appointed by the Common Council, but in that year the present system of appointment after a rigid competitive examination was inaugurated. At that time the Junior, Senior and House Services were each of six months' duration; the service was divided into four medical and two surgical divisions; and the physicians rotated, serving three months on

STURGIS SURGICAL PAVILION, BELLEVUE HOSPITAL, FOOT OF EAST 26TH STREET.

the male, and three months on the female side. In 1866 this service was rearranged into four medical and four surgical divisions, each having male and female sections, while the physicians no longer rotated. This method is still in force, but the number of wards has increased to forty, with 768 beds, making Bellevue one of the largest institutions of its kind in the world.

The entrance to the hospital grounds, comprising 4½ acres, lying between East River and First Avenue, is on 26th Street, through an arched gateway built in 1885. Immediately to the left of the entrance gate is the Marquand Pavilion, a one-story brick building erected in 1877 by Frederick and Henry Gurdon Marquand in memory of their brother, Josiah P. Marquand, who died from the effects of an operation. It is a medical ward for women and children, and contains 18 beds for adults and 16 for children. Nearly opposite, on the right, is the Insane Pavilion, a low brick building erected in 1879 by the city for people who become insane. It accommodates 25 patients, who are kept five days to allow of communication with their friends, and arrangements for their transfer to suitable institutions. The one-story brick pavilion to the north is the Sturgis Surgical Pavilion, built in 1879 by Mrs.

William H. Osborne in memory of her father. Immediately opposite is the long stone building of the old almshouse, four stories in height, which forms the centre of the hospital. The long prison-like structure comprises a central division, with side wings, giving a total length of 350 feet. The buildings, including the north-east wing, built in 1855, have external balconies and staircases for each story, affording ample means of escape in case of fire, and also space for exercise. The central portion of the building contains the reception-room, store-room, Warden's office, the library, the consulting-room, and a notable operating-room, the largest in the country, with a seating capacity of 1,000. In the rear, on First Avenue, is the Townsend Cottage, where cases of uterine tumors are received. This building, and the adjoining chapel and library, were erected in 1888 by Mrs. R. H. L. Townsend as a thank-offering for recovery from sickness. An Alcoholic Pavilion was built in 1892, for the reception of male and female patients suffering from the improper use of stimulants. Since 1873 a superior grade of nurses has been obtained from the Training-School for Nurses. The immediate care of the hospital is entrusted to a medical board, appointed by the Commissioners of Public Charities and Correction, and comprising three consulting and twelve visiting surgeons, three consulting and sixteen visiting physicians. The House Staff includes four physicians and four surgeons, and three assistants to each, none of whom receives any other compensation for his services than suitable accommodations and a small yearly allowance for board.

The exceptionally large number of patients, averaging 14,000 yearly, has made the hospital one of the most valuable in the country for the study of diseases of every kind. This exceptional condition led in 1861 to the founding of the Bellevue-Hospital Medical College, one of the leading schools of medicine and surgery in the country, occupying a building in the hospital grounds, on East 26th Street.

The free dispensary service of the hospital, one of its most valuable features, was established in 1866, and treats 100,000 patients yearly, besides the large number of

GOUVERNEUR HOSPITAL, GOUVERNEUR SLIP AND FRONT STREET.

cases which are sent to different hospitals. The Ambulance Service is an important feature in the work of the hospital, as may be seen from the fact that nearly 5,000 calls are answered yearly.

Under the same management as Bellevue are the Adult, Children's and Infants' Hospitals and the Idiot and Epileptic Asylum on Randall's Island; the Emergency Hospital, at 223 East 26th Street; the Gouv-erneur Hospital; the Harlem Hospital, at 533 East 120th Street; the Hart's Island Hospital for the reception of convalescents; the Fordham Reception Hospital, at Fordham, N. Y.; the Insane Asylum for Males and the Ward's Island Hospital; and on Blackwell's Island the Charity and Convalescent Hospitals, Female Insane Asylum, the Hospital for Incurables, and the Paralytic and Alms-House Hospitals, mostly large stone buildings, with a combined capacity of fully 5,000 beds, forming the largest group of associated charities under one management in the world, a proof of the liberality of New-York City in caring for its sick and afflicted poor. In fact, the public and the private medical institutions indicate New York's intelligence as well as its generosity.

The Morgue, on the Bellevue-Hospital grounds, is a one-story building of 62 by 83 feet, containing an office, autopsy-room, room for refrigerator, and two special rooms where the remains of the deceased are laid out, that friends may view the bodies, or hold religious services previous to their burial. It was opened in 1866, and contained at that time four marble tables. A corpse remains in the Morgue for 72 hours, more or less, according to condition and weather, and if not identified it is removed to the City Cemetery, on Hart's Island, for interment. The clothing is preserved for six months, and if not then identified it is destroyed. All bodies are photographed, and the photographs are carefully preserved as a possible means of future identification. There are usually from three to five bodies awaiting identification, and the sight is anything but a pleasant one. The number of bodies received here exceeds 4,000, the average being from 175 to 235 yearly. The number of bodies received here annually, from all sources, averages about 8,000, including Morgue cases proper (the unknown dead).

The Gouverneur Hospital, at Gouverneur Slip and East River, is an emergency hospital, in charge of the Department of Public Charities and Correction. It occupies the old Gouverneur-Market building, and was established in 1885.

The Charity Hospital, on Blackwell's Island, was opened in 1852 for the city's indigent sick. The original wooden building was destroyed by fire in 1865, and a large granite edifice was opened in 1870. It is four stories high, and extends across the southern end of the island. With the outlying pavilions of the maternity, epileptic and nervous wards it contains 1,000 beds. There are thirteen male and twelve female wards. The number of patients received yearly is 6,800. The medical and surgical staff comprises twenty-four physicians and a large number of attendants. In 1886 a training-school for female nurses was opened in the castellated stone building erected in 1872 for a small-pox hospital. A training-school for male nurses was established in 1887, and these schools have done much to improve the quality of the nursing in the hospital.

The Ward's-Island Hospital, on Ward's Island, was opened in 1876, for the treatment of all classes of diseases, both male and female. It is under the Commissioners of Public Charities and Correction.

The New-York City Asylums for the Insane on Blackwell's, Ward's and Hart's Islands, and at the City Farm at Central Islip, are in charge of the Commissioners of Public Charities and Correction. The buildings are of enormous extent ; and upwards of 6,000 patients are cared for at one time, at a cost of $800,000 annually. The accommodations are inadequate, and many plans for relieving the crowded condition of the asylums have been proposed. Those now in progress are the use of the large building on Ward's Island, formerly occupied for the uses of the State Commissioners of Immigration (but long since abandoned), the removal of all the insane to Ward's Island and Central Islip, Long Island, and the expenditure of $1,500,000 in new buildings. Several unsuccessful attempts have been made to transfer the city insane to the care of the State, which has a uniform system of hospitals, where it is claimed the patients would receive better care. Passes to visit the asylums may be obtained from their heads, or from William Blake, 66 Third Avenue. The general medical superintendent is Dr. A. E. MacDonald.

The New-York City Asylum for the Insane, on Blackwell's Island, was opened in 1848, and is now used for women only. The buildings occupy extensive grounds on the northern end of the island, and have accommodations for about 1,300 patients. The main building is a four-story granite structure, and contains the office, rooms for the house staff, and eight wards for patients. In each ward there is a large sitting-room for the inmates, and all the wards open into a spacious central rotunda. In 1881 a stone building, accommodating 500 patients, was erected at the southern end of the grounds, for acute cases ; and in 1892 a brick building was opened for chronic cases.   There are also ten wooden pavilions, one brick pavilion, a laundry, bath-house, superintendent's residence, and a Roman Catholic chapel on the grounds. The amusement building contains a large hall with a stage and piano, where dances and entertainments are given frequently for the amusement of the patients, and a work-room where mats, brushes, rugs, carpets, and fancy articles are made by the inmates.   The patients are kept without restraint, and every possible effort is made to ameliorate their condition, by allotting them some occupation to employ their minds.   Twice a day they are given an hour's exercise in the grounds, in charge of the attendants ; and once a week they are given baths, under the supervision of the resident woman-physician.   About 2,500 patients are received yearly ; and the daily census averages nearly 1,900.   Dr. E. C. Dent is medical superintendent.

The New-York City Asylum for the Insane, on Ward's Island, has been used for male patients only.   It is a large brick building, with towers and turrets, and has trimmings of Ohio freestone, presenting a fine architectural appearance.   It was opened in 1871, and accommodates, with out-lying buildings, over 2,200 patients.   The number of admissions during the past year was 750, and the total

NEW-YORK CITY ASYLUM FOR THE INSANE (WOMEN), BLACKWELL'S ISLAND.

number under treatment for the year was 2,498.   The asylum has a resident medical staff of sixteen physicians.   The general treatment is that in vogue in advanced and progressive asylums ; and all patients capable of appreciating them are provided with occupation and amusements.   Dr. W. A. Macy is medical superintendent.

The New-York City Asylum for the Insane, on Hart's Island, was opened in 1878, for the reception and care of chronic cases of female insane.   The buildings comprise a number of pavilions.   In 1886 the former Hart's-Island Hospital was discontinued, and the pavilions utilized for insane of both sexes.   There are accommodations for about 1,000 patients.   Dr. G. A. Smith is medical superintendent.

The New-York Hospital is the oldest local institution of its class. As early as 1770 a number of public-spirited citizens contributed for the erection of a hospital in the city, and a charter was obtained from the Provincial authorities in the following year. Considerable sums of money were contributed in England, and the Provincial Legislature made a grant of $2,000 a year for twenty years towards its support. The corner-stone of the first building was laid in 1775, and when nearly completed the structure was destroyed by fire, entailing a loss of $35,000. The Legislature made a grant of $20,000 for its rebuilding, and the work was

NEW-YORK CITY ASYLUM FOR THE INSANE (MEN), WARD'S ISLAND.

begun. The building was nearly completed again, when the outbreak of the Revolution turned men's thoughts into other directions. The unfinished building was occupied by the British and Hessian soldiers as a barrack and hospital, and it was not until January, 1791, that it was in a proper condition to receive patients. Eighteen sick persons were then admitted. The original buildings were near Broadway, between Worth and Duane Streets. In 1869 they were torn down, and a new structure was erected on West 15th Street, between Fifth and Sixth Avenues. This was opened for the reception of patients in March, 1877. The hospital has been liberally aided by the State. In addition to the grants already mentioned, a grant of $10,000 a year was made in 1792, which was increased to $20,000 in 1795, and still further increased to $25,000 in the following year. The Bloomingdale Asylum for the Insane, opened in 1821, is a branch of the New-York Hospital. In 1799 an arrangement was entered into with the United-States Treasury Department whereby the hospital was to receive a stipulated sum for the care of sick and disabled seamen. Under its present administration it is a general hospital for the reception and care of both pay and free patients, the latter constituting nearly 80 per cent. of the 5,200 patients taken yearly. Private patients are received and treated at varying rates, the price in the general wards being $7 a week, and for private rooms from $15 to $35 a week. The New-York Hospital's many advantages have made it one of the best schools of medicine and surgery in the country, and no pains are spared to render it valuable to students by furnishing every possible facility for the study and treatment of disease. Clinics are regularly given in cases arising in the practice of the house, to which students from all the local medical colleges are admitted. As early as 1796 a library was founded for the use of physicians and students, and it now numbers upward of 19,000 volumes. In 1840 a pathological cabinet, now one of the most important in the city, was begun, and has grown into a large collection of specimens of morbid anatomy, casts, drawings, etc., embracing nearly 3,000 specimens. A training-school for nurses was opened in 1877, which has graduated over

200 nurses.   The new building, opened in 1877, is said to be one of the most luxu-
riously appointed hospitals in the world.   It is seven stories high, with a mansard
roof, and has accommodations for 200 patients, with their attendants.   Stone, iron
and red brick form the constructive materials, and the building is as nearly fire-
proof as is possible to the builder's art.   In the rear, on West 16th Street, is the
venerable Thorn mansion, an old-time structure, used as an administration building
for the executive offices of the hospital ; and a handsome brick building, completed
in 1891, and occupied by the library, the pathological museum and the training-
school for nurses.   The hospital is heated by steam, and artificial ventilation is

secured by means
of a large fan, which
forces a current of
fresh air through
the wards and cor-
ridors.   The kit-
chens and laundries
are in the upper
stories, above the
wards.   An unusual
and pleasing feature
of the hospital is
the solarium, a
large room on the
upper story of the
administration
building, covered
with a canopy of
translucent glass,
filled with plants
and flowers, fount-
ains and aquaria, a
sunny and healthful
resting-place for
convalescents.   On
other stories are the
large operating and
autopsy rooms, the
general wards, pri-
vate apartments for

NEW-YORK HOSPITAL, WEST 15TH STREET, NEAR FIFTH AVENUE.

pay patients, and the offices.   The corporation is controlled by a board of twenty-six
Governors.   Besides the hospital proper it supports the Bloomingdale Insane Asylum ;
the House of Relief, or Emergency Hospital, at 160 Chambers Street, where 2,000
cases of accidents are received yearly ; and a dispensary, where upwards of 20,000
patients are annually given free treatment and advice.   The ambulance services respond to more than 4,000 calls yearly, and are of great service in many emergencies.
During 1892 the total number of patients in all departments of the hospital was
38,118, and the grand total since its foundation is 577,630.   The former site of the
hospital is covered by substantial iron-front buildings, occupied by a number of the
strongest houses in the dry-goods trade.   Merritt Trimble (president of the Bank
for Savings) is president of the hospital ; and George P. Ludlam is superintendent.

BLOOMINGDALE ASYLUM FOR THE INSANE.

30   VARIOUS BUILDINGS IN THE ASYLUM GROUNDS AT BOULEVARD, WEST 117TH AND WEST 120TH STREETS.

The Bloomingdale Asylum was occupied by the insane patients of the New-York Hospital in 1821, when what is now known as the "main building" was opened. The asylum is substantially built of brick and stone, and has long occupied a commanding site on Harlem Heights, at the Boulevard and 117th Street, over-looking the Hudson and surrounding country. For many years no better location could have been found. The rapid growth of the city in that vicinity has made a change of location desirable, and the land and buildings have been sold to Columbia College. Bloomingdale will remove in 1894 to new and imposing structures at White Plains, N. Y. About 450 patients are received yearly, who are divided into classes, according to the nature of their mental aberration; and suitable methods of treatment are adopted for each class, the so-called moral method being largely employed, supplemented by the best-known scientific and medical treatment; harsh measures and all unnecessary confinement being strictly prohibited. The asylum has some free beds, but most of the patients are required to pay, in proportion to their ability; and thus a quiet hospital has been provided, for those of moderate means, as well as the rich, who are suffering from mental disease, where they can be assured of kind and skilful treatment. During 1892, 442 patients were treated, of whom 144 were new cases. During the year 43 patients were discharged as cured; 36 as improved; 18 as unimproved; and 38 died. The accommodations for the insane having become inadequate at the New-York Hospital, the Governors applied to the Legislature in 1815 for aid to construct new buildings elsewhere, and a grant was given them for that purpose of $10,000 yearly, to date from 1816 to 1857. Accordingly, in 1816 a plot of ground was purchased at Bloomingdale Heights, then seven miles from the city, and buildings were erected thereon and completed in 1821.

The Roosevelt Hospital, at 59th Street and Ninth Avenue, was referred to in 1874 by an eminent English surgeon as "Without exception the most complete medical charity in every respect" that he had ever seen. It owes its existence to the princely bequest of James H. Roosevelt, who, dying in 1863, left his whole estate "for the establishment, in the City of New York, of a hospital for the reception and relief of sick and diseased persons, and for its permanent endowment." The amount received from the bequest was a little more than $1,000,000; and, after long and careful consideration, the nine trustees under the will decided to adopt the pavilion plan. The corner-stone was laid October 29, 1869; and the hospital was formally opened November 2, 1871. The cost of the grounds, which embrace the entire block lying between Ninth and Tenth Avenues and 58th and 59th Streets, and the build-ings constructed thereon up to 1893, together with their equipment, amounted to about $1,200,000. The original design was for a central administration building, with two pavilions on each side for patients and their attendants, to be connected with the administration building by covered corridors, and yet so far apart from each other as to secure light and ventilation for all. The money at the disposal of the trustees did not admit of the execution of the entire plan. The buildings con-structed comprise the following: 1st. The administration building, in the centre of the block facing on 59th Street, a four-story brick edifice containing the offices, examining room, apothecary's department, staff dining-room, etc., on the first floor; on the second floor, the private apartments of the superintendent, a reception-room for the trustees, a medical-board room, and an amphitheatre for clinical instruction, etc.; on the third floor, a few rooms for private patients; and on the fourth floor, two surgical wards — one for women, and the other for children. 2d. In the rear of this, facing on 58th Street, is a building used for kitchen, laundry, store-rooms, sewing-room, linen-room, and dining and sleeping-rooms for out-ward help; while in the basement, and running east, are the boiler-room, engine-rooms, fan-room, and various agencies for heating and ventilating all the buildings. 3d. East of the administration building, and fronting on 59th Street, is the Medical Pavilion, a four-story structure, with wards on each floor for patients, as well as living quarters for members of the house staff and nurses. 4th. East of the Medical Pavilion is the Surgical Pavilion, containing a ward for 36 male patients, with rooms for members of the house staff and male nurses. 5th. East of the Surgical Pavilion is the new Syms Operating Theatre, built through the liberality of William J. Syms, who left $350,000 for the purpose of construction, equipment and maintenance. Of that amount $150,000 is reserved for maintenance. It is believed to be the best-appointed operating building in this or any other country. The exterior is of brick, with granite trimmings, and built in the most substantial manner. The main amphitheatre occupies the centre, and is semi-circular in shape, with abruptly rising seats, to allow an unobstructed view of the operating table from all parts of the room. In the basement are the janitor's apartments, the engine-room, and

ROOSEVELT HOSPITAL AND SYMS OPERATING THÉATRE, NINTH AVENUE AND WEST 59TH STREET.

the fan-room for ventilating. The first story contains, besides the amphitheatre, a special operating room, an operating room for septic cases, a private reception-room, a reception-room for patients, an examining room, two etherizing rooms, a photographic room, a microscopic room, a bandage-preparation room, a bandage-storage room, an instrument-washing room, and the instrument room. The floors are of mosaic tile, and in many cases the walls are wainscoted in marble. On the second floor, south front, are four rooms for the reception of patients after operation, and on the floor above that six other rooms for nurses, etc. 6th. There is also the small and perfectly appointed McLane Operating Room, opened in 1890, the gift of Dr. James W. McLane, the President of the College of Physicians and Surgeons, in memory of his son, James W. McLane, Jr., and designed solely for the use of the gynæcological service. 7th. Adjoining the administration building on the west is the Out-Patient Department, which received over 83,000 visits during 1892, of patients who were cared for there without taxing the ward accommodations of the hospital.   There are 180 beds for patients in the hospital. 8th.   The dead-house and ambulance stable are in a separate building.   Fourteen beds have been endowed in the Roosevelt Hospital, in the sum of $5,000 each.   In 1892 2,788 patients were treated, of whom 1,159 were discharged as cured, 948 improved, 210 not improved, and 307 died, leaving 164 under treatment.   During the same period 3,768 patients were treated in the accident room who were not detained for ward treatment, and the calls of the ambulance during the year numbered 1,905. From the opening of the hospital to the beginning of 1893, 39,104 patients had been treated, 34,741 of them gratuitously, so that the institution well deserves its name of a great free hospital, whose charity is bounded only by its ability to care for those who seek its aid.

The Presbyterian Hospital in the City of New-York comprises an imposing group of brick buildings, occupying the entire block between Madison and Park Avenues, and extending from 70th Street to 71st Street.   The group comprises the operating pavilion, erected in 1892 ; the administration building, completed in 1872 ; the dispensary, opened in 1888 ; the chapel, pathological department, and an isolating pavilion, erected in 1889 ; two surgical pavilions and a surgical administration building, opened in 1890 ; and the laundry ; all constructed of pressed brick, and connected by corridors, as at the Roosevelt Hospital.   The Presbyterian Hospital was founded in 1868, and the first buildings were opened in 1872, on land given by James Lenox, who took a deep interest in the work.   In 1889 most of the original buildings were destroyed by fire, and as a result the entire scheme was re-arranged, with a view to secure greater efficiency, convenience and economy.   The new edifices embody the latest and best methods of hospital construction, and are admirably adapted to their purpose.   The operating pavilion, administration building and dispensary are on 70th Street.   In the rear of the latter, on Madison Avenue, is the chapel, and near it the isolating pavilion.   On 71st Street are the large medical and surgical pavilions and a surgical administration building, with a second surgical pavilion on Park Avenue.   These pavilions provide 22 wards, having 330 beds, with a possible increase to 450, and numerous other rooms for a great variety of purposes, such as reception-rooms, parlors, dining-rooms, doctors' parlors, and consultation rooms ; 22 private rooms, for paying patients ; press-rooms, drying-rooms, pantries, dormitories, solaria, etc.   The buildings are entirely fire-proof, being constructed of masonry and iron throughout ; and the system of ventilation is as perfect as could be devised ; the great factor in the system being the lofty dispensary tower on Madison Avenue, which has at its base a large battery of steam-driven fans.   The tower and the fans open into an immense underground duct, connecting by smaller branches with all the hospital buildings, except the Isolating Pavilion and the Pathological Department, which have independent systems of ventilation. · While the foul air is drawn from the buildings by these great fans, fresh air, taken from a considerable height above the ground, is forced into them by other fans, thus ensuring a constant current of pure air in all the wards.   The heating and plumbing arrangements are of the most approved pattern, and the comfort of the patients is still farther secured by the ample lighting facilities of the wards, which are 16 feet in height, and painted in delicate tones of color.   The Children's Ward, with its long rows of dainty cribs, is especially attractive.   One noteworthy feature of the interior arrangement is the provision of rooms for cases where death must speedily ensue, thus freeing the wards from the depressing effects of death-bed scenes.   The new operating pavilion has three halls for surgical operations, each with a series of adjoining rooms, that add much to the comfort, completeness and success of the best surgical work. The amphitheatre seats 100 persons, and is abundantly lighted by a ceiling light and three great side-lights. The wainscoting and floors are of marble. The smaller operating rooms afford facilities for operations where retirement is essential to success and spectators are undesirable. The pathological department is fully equipped with the best modern appliances; and the new dispensary building, a lofty hall 100 feet in length, lighted by three-story windows, and surrounded by doctors' rooms, provided with every convenience for the treatment of patients, is a model of its class. The buildings represent an outlay closely approaching $1,200,000. Everything that the best medical and surgical skill can suggest, and the lavish expenditure of money can secure, is done for the relief of the patients. While the hospital is largely supported by members of the Presbyterian and Reformed Churches, it is entirely undenominational in its work, less than ten per cent. of the patients being Presbyterians, and over fifty per cent. being Roman Catholics. Of the 3,300 patients cared for yearly over 3,200 are treated gratuitously; and scarcely more

PRESBYTERIAN HOSPITAL, MADISON AVENUE AND EAST 70TH STREET.

than $3,000 is received from pay patients. The dispensary treats upwards of 70,000 patients yearly, and dispenses about 22,000 prescriptions, while the ambulance service answers 1,500 calls. The entire plant is lighted by both gas and electricity, the latter light permitting surgical operations under ether to be performed with safety night or day. The hospital is also equipped with powerful Worthington pumps.

The Mount-Sinai Hospital was originally known as "The Jews' Hospital in the City of New York." It was founded in 1852 by a number of benevolent Hebrews, headed by Sampson Simson, who gave a lot of land on 28th Street. It was opened in 1855, and remained in the first location until 1872, when it took possession of its group of buildings on Lexington Avenue, extending from 66th Street to 67th Street. The land is leased from the city for ninety-nine years, at a nominal rental of $1 a year.   Brick and stone form the constructive materials.   The group comprises three five-story buildings, connected by closed corridors.   Like most other so-called private hospitals, Mount Sinai has two grand divisions — the medical and

the surgical — each having four wards; a gynæcological department, classed as surgical; and a children's ward. It has also an eye and ear department, to which six rooms, each containing two beds, are allotted. These are on the first floor of the administration building, on Lexington Avenue.   On the same floor are the

MOUNT-SINAI HOSPITAL, LEXINGTON AVENUE, EAST 66TH AND 67TH STREETS.

directors' room, the offices of the superintendent and the admitting physician, a sitting-room and a library containing 2,000 volumes.   The remaining floors are given up to private rooms, those of the house staff and the superintendent, the synagogue and operating rooms.   The wards for women and children occupy the northern wing, on 67th Street ; and the men's wards are in the southern wing.   The arrangement is alike for all the wards, each containing from 20 to 25 beds, ranged along the sides of the room.   All the wards are kept scrupulously clean, and abundantly lighted and ventilated.   In the rear of the administration building is the isolation-house for contagious cases, the laundry building, and the morgue.   In summer the intervening court-yard forms a pleasant lounging-place for convalescent patients.   The kitchen and dining-rooms are in the basement of the main building.

Just across the way, in 67th Street, is the Dispensary Building, erected in 1890, at a cost exceeding $125,000.   It is connected with the hospital by a warm and well-lighted tunnel under the street, and is thoroughly fire-proof.   The first story of the front is of Belleville stone, and the remaining five stories are of salmon pressed brick and terra cotta.   On the right is the entrance to the free dispensary, which, with its reception-rooms and smaller operating and examination rooms, occupies the first two stories of the building.   There are eye, ear, throat, venereal and general departments. The last annual report shows that over 70,000 patients were treated, and upwards of 58,000 prescriptions dispensed, in most cases free of cost.   On the left side of the building is an entrance to the rooms of the Ladies' Auxiliary Society and the Training School for Nurses, which occupy the upper stories.   The Ladies' Auxiliary Society is an important factor in the work of the hospital.   It was established in 1872, and finds an ample field of work in providing clothes and bedding for the unfortunate sick and needy.   The Training-School for Nurses was opened in 1881, and has graduated many well-trained nurses.

Although Mount-Sinai was founded and is sustained by benevolent Hebrews, it does not limit its ministrations to members of that faith, but admits patients of all nationalities and creeds. About eight per cent. of the patients are Russian Jews; and of the 3,000 cases yearly admitted, ninety per cent. are free patients. Mount-Sinai receives a larger proportion of the annual Hospital-Sunday collection than any other of the local institutions, as its percentage of free patients is the largest. Unlike most of the other local hospitals, Mount-Sinai makes only provision for clinical instruction for a limited number of students, but devotes all its energies to the care of its inmates, seeking to make its work educational only to the limits of the house staff, and medical students and practicing physicians and surgeons who are invited to be present at operations. This was the first hospital in the city to admit women to membership on its house staff, and although none are now serving, their absence is not due to any change in the rules, but because the young men have stood the highest in the rigid competitive examinations required of all applicants for positions. Women are still on the general staff, but they have charge of a division in the children's department, in the dispensary. The administration of the hospital is under the control of a board of directors, elected by the members. Besides directing all expenditures of money, and regulating the general policy of

the institution, they have the appointment of the medical and surgical staff, all the members of which serve without pay, for the term of two years. The hospital accommodates 220 patients, including those in private rooms, who pay from $12 to $40 a week, and have whatever advantages come from isolation and an abundance of room. The report for 1892 shows the number of applications for admission to have been 5,669; number of patients treated, 3,159; number of consultations in the dispensary, 91,449; number of prescriptions in the dispensary, 74,883; total amount of receipts, $127,230; amount of expenditures, $109,689; permanent fund, $179,500; number of members and patrons, 4,016. Of the 3,159 patients admitted during 1892 1,679 were discharged as cured, 851 as improved, 156 as unimproved, 20 were sent to other institutions, and 247 died in the hospital.

MOUNT-SINAI HOSPITAL DISPENSARY AND NURSES' HOME, 151 EAST 67TH STREET, NEAR LEXINGTON AVENUE.

St. Luke's Hospital, at Fifth Avenue and 54th Street, holds a unique place among the local hospitals, as it is not merely a hospital, but also a religious house. The superintendent is a clergyman of the Protestant Episcopal Church; the central feature of the building is a large chapel; and the services of the Church are recited daily in the wards. While maintaining the highest standard of scientific work, it is the most home-like of the local hospitals, and the relations between patients, physicians and nurses are as nearly as possible the same as would obtain in private families under like conditions. The beginnings were made in 1846, when Rev. Dr. William A. Muhlenberg, then rector of the Church of the Holy Communion, took up a collection of $30 for the work. In 1850 an appeal to the public

ST. LUKE'S HOSPITAL, FIFTH AVENUE AND WEST 54TH STREET.

resulted in the formation of a corporation and in subscriptions amounting to $100,000. In 1854 the Sisters of the Holy Communion opened an infirmary, in a house on Sixth Avenue, where upwards of 200 patients had been treated when the work was transferred to the newly erected St. Luke's, in 1858. The building fronts on West 54th Street, and faces south, with a length of nearly 300 feet. Its general plan is that of an oblong parallelogram, with wings at each end, and a central chapel flanked by two towers. The building stands well back from the street, with a large lawn intervening, and is constructed of brick, painted a modest drab. The chapel is well lighted and ventilated. There are nine wards for medical and surgical cases, including three wards for consumptives. All acute, curable and non-contagious cases are received, and treated free, if necessary. There are 224 beds. To the extent of accommodation, no patient whose disease is suitable for treatment is turned away because unable to pay for board. Over 2,000 patients are treated yearly, at an expense of about $100,000. In connection with the hospital there is a training-school for nurses, established in 1888. The popularity of St. Luke's has been such as to make larger accommodations necessary, and the trustees have recently purchased a spacious tract of land on 113th Street, near the proposed Cathedral of St. John the Divine, where they will erect magnificent new buildings.

The corner-stone of the new St. Luke's Hospital was laid May 6, 1893, in the presence of the trustees of St. Luke's, of Columbia College, of the Teachers College and of the Cathedral, the medical staff of the hospital, the bishops of New York and of Long Island, and a large body of vested clergy. The site to be occupied by the new hospital extends from 113th Street to 114th Street, and from Morningside Avenue to Amsterdam Avenue, with the principal front on 113th Street, adjacent to the grounds of the Cathedral. The new hospital is to be com-

ST. LUKE'S HOSPITAL, NOW BUILDING ON WEST 113TH STREET, NEAR MORNINGSIDE PARK.

posed of nine semi-detached buildings, four facing on each street, and with the lofty administration building in the centre. The architect is Ernest Flagg. The amount of money invested, when the entire establishment is completed, will be in excess of $2,000,000. The buildings will be five stories high, and thoroughly fire-proof and fitted with every modern appliance. The administration or central building is named in honor of Dr. Muhlenberg, and the pavilions to be built at first bear the names of Minturn, Norrie, and Vanderbilt, benefactors of the hospital. Other pavilions will be built as the money is furnished and the necessities of the work require. Although St. Luke's was founded by the Episcopal Church, and is practically a religious house of that denomination, it is entirely unsectarian in the range of its benefactions. Up to October 18, 1892, 36,050 patients had been treated in its wards, and of these 38½ per cent. were Episcopalians, 33 per cent. were Protestants of other sects, and 27½ per cent. were Roman Catholics.

Lebanon Hospital was organized in 1889 and incorporated in 1891. It purchased the building formerly occupied by the Ursuline Convent, at 150th Street and Westchester Avenue, and very thoroughly remodelled and reconstructed it so that it might be suited for the purpose in mind. It is not only a hospital, but a convalescent home, and is intended for the worthy poor who need fresh air, rest and medical care. There are beds for 500 patients, besides ample and commodious offices for the general departments of the institution. It was founded by benevolent Hebrews, but there is

NEW-YORK OPHTHALMIC HOSPITAL, THIRD AVENUE AND EAST 23D STREET.

nothing of a sectarian character about the Lebanon Hospital, which is open to all sufferers, without distinction as to their race or creed. The president is Jonas Weil.

National Hospitals have been established in several localities, by the foreign colonies residing in New York, for the benefit of their sick and unfortunate members and compatriots. These institutions serve a most kindly and worthy purpose in taking care of the weary immigrants, often thrown upon our shores almost in destitution, exhausted by the long sea-voyage, devastated by home-sickness, and almost ready to succumb. The Chinese Hospital, for the moon-eyed Celestials of New York, is in the neighboring city of Brooklyn, and draws its support from philanthropic Americans. It is for the reception, care and maintenance of, and the giving of medical and surgical advice exclusively to, Chinese afflicted with maladies or physical injuries or weaknesses, deformities or infirmities, excepting contagious diseases. The French Hospital, at 320 and 322 West 34th Street, receives about 500 sick poor French people yearly, giving the indigent free treatment. This fine charity is conducted by the French Benevolent Society. The Norwegian Relief Society maintains the Norwegian Deaconess Home and Hospital, with 30 beds. It has

lately been removed from East 57th Street to Brooklyn. The Swiss Home, at 108 Second Avenue, gives medical attention to Swiss who are without means. The strong local societies of Scots, Irishmen, Englishmen, Welshmen, Hollanders, Spaniards, Russians, Belgians, Poles, Hungarians and other foreigners have provision

LEBANON HOSPITAL, WESTCHESTER AVENUE AND 150TH STREET.

for looking out for their sick and injured fellow-countrymen, mainly by the aid of the great city hospitals. The Germans, however, have two or three finely equipped establishments (as described elsewhere); and the tide of Italian immigration of late years pouring through this port has caused the erection of two hospitals entirely for people of this nationality, taking care of above 2,000 patients yearly. The best facilities, care and attention, however, are provided at the great public hospitals, and as there are no restrictions as to race or creed, these noble institutions are wide open to our impecunious European and Asiatic guests.

St. Vincent's Hospital of the City of New York, at 195 West 11th Street, was founded in 1849, and for some years occupied a house in West 13th Street. In 1857 the building of the Catholic Half-Orphan Asylum in West 11th Street was secured. The work of the hospital increased to such an extent that a large four-story brick building was erected in 1882, at the corner of West 12th Street and Seventh Avenue, giving the hospital accommodations for nearly 200 patients. The Sisters of Charity of St. Vincent de Paul, a Roman Catholic order instituted in

France in 1633, have charge of the hospital, which, since its foundation, has received and treated upwards of 50,000 cases, the average number now admitted being nearly 2,500. No charge is made to persons unable to pay for treatment, and these form a majority. The hospital has an ambulance service which answers upwards of 2,000 calls yearly. Although a Catholic institution, patients are admitted without regard to their religious belief, and St. Vincent's occupies a prominent position among the local hospitals.

The Hahnemann Hospital of the City of New York is a general hospital for the reception of such free and pay patients, not suffering from incurable or chronic diseases, as may desire to be treated by homœopathic methods. It was chartered in 1875, two older institutions, the New-York Homœopathic Surgical Hospital, incorporated in 1872, and the New-York Homœopathic Hospital for women and children, incorporated in 1848, uniting under the name of the Hahnemann Hospital. The substantial four-story brick and stone building on Park Avenue, between 67th and 68th Streets, was erected in 1878, and has accommodations for about seventy patients. There are four well-lighted and pleasant wards, one each for men and children, and two for women, besides an endowed room for firemen, containing three beds; one for saleswomen, containing two beds; one for policemen, containing one bed; and the Anthony Dey room, with one bed. In 1887 the Ovariotomy Cottage was erected on the grounds, and in 1891 the Dispensary was opened. In addition to its free beds, the hospital provides a quiet and comfortable home for the sick and suffering of all classes under homœopathic treatment; and persons requiring surgical operations, or taken ill with any disease not contagious, can be received and obtain the best medical and surgical treatment and skilled nursing, their comfort and sensibilities being always considered and secured. Private patients pay at rates varying from $18 to $40 a week. A gift of $5,000 endows a bed in perpetuity; one of $3,000 during the donor's lifetime; and the same amount endows a bed in perpetuity in the Children's Ward, a cheery apartment containing beds and cribs for the little ones. About 2,000 patients are treated yearly. The managers contemplate the erection of a maternity hospital and the establishment of a training-school for nurses.

HAHNEMANN HOSPITAL, PARK AVENUE, BETWEEN EAST 67TH AND 68TH STREETS.

St. Francis Hospital, at 605 to 617 5th Street is a general hospital for the gratuitous treatment of the poorer classes. It was opened in 1865, and is in charge of the Roman Catholic order of the Sisters of the Poor of St. Francis. No contagious or incurable cases are admitted, but all others are received and treated without charge, when unable to pay. There are 240 beds; and about 2,700 patients are admitted yearly.

GERMAN HOSPITAL, PARK AVENUE AND EAST 77TH STREET.

The German Hospital and Dispensary of the City of New York, at Park Avenue and 77th Street, was incorporated in 1861. Patients of every nationality, color and creed are received, and treated gratuitously, when they are unable to pay. Private patients are charged from $15 to $35 a week. There are 165 beds. Upwards of 2,500 patients are treated yearly, a large proportion of them being free patients. The dispensary department was opened in 1884, and gives free treatment and advice to nearly 30,000 cases yearly. A nominal fee of ten cents is charged to those who are able to pay. The annual expenses of the hospital and dispensary are met by voluntary subscriptions, and the interest of an endowment fund of $170,000.

The Manhattan Dispensary and Hospital is a brick building at Amsterdam Avenue and 131st Street. The dispensary was opened in 1862, and treats about 8,000 patients yearly. The hospital was opened in 1884, and contains seventy beds. Medical and surgical treatment is given free to patients who are unable to pay for relief, and pay patients are charged from $7 to $35 a week. Upwards of 600 cases are cared for yearly.

MANHATTAN HOSPITAL, AMSTERDAM AVENUE AND WEST 131ST STREET.

St. Elizabeth's Hospital, at 225 West 31st Street, is in charge of the Sisters of the Third Order of St. Francis of Assisium. It was founded in 1870; and all persons in need of surgical or medical aid, except contagious, insane and violent cases, are admitted, and treated by their own physicians when desired. The charges vary from $8 to $35 a week, and there are 90 beds.

The New-York Post-Graduate Medical School and Hospital, at Second Avenue and East 20th Street, a school for clinical instruction to practitioners of medicine, was opened in 1882 for the treatment of general diseases. Patients who are able to pay are charged from $7 to $20 a week ; and no contagious or chronic cases are admitted. There are women's wards, men's wards, orthopædic wards for children, and an entire building for babies' wards. The hospital has 114 beds, and upwards of 800 new patients are admitted yearly. The directors are building a fine six-story fire-proof structure for the school and hospital, at Second Avenue and 20th Street. During the year 502 physicians attended the school.

The Christopher Columbus Hospital is at 41 East 12th Street. It was opened in 1890, for the free medical and surgical treatment of both sexes ; and receives all classes of patients, except those suffering from contagious diseases. It is in charge of the Catholic Salesian Sisters of the Sacred Heart of Jesus.

St. Mark's Hospital of New-York City is at 177 Second Avenue. It was incorporated in 1890, and receives general charity and pay patients. Private cases pay from $15 to $50 a week, and have the privilege of selecting their own physicians. The hospital is small, treating 600 patients yearly. It numbers among its staff physicians of national repute.

St. Joseph's Hospital was opened in 1882, by the Sisters of the Poor of St. Francis, for the reception and care of consumptives, and a limited number of other chronic and in-curable diseases which cannot be properly treated in other hospitals. But no acute diseases, affections of the mind and nervous system (such as insanity, idiocy and epilepsy), chronic surgical diseases, cases of deform-

ST. JOSEPH'S HOSPITAL, BROOK AND ST. ANN'S AVENUES, EAST 143D AND 144TH STREETS.

ity or aged persons are admitted. The building occupies the entire block between East 143d and 144th Streets and Brook and St. Ann's Avenues, and is well adapted for its purpose, everything possible in the way of improved sanitary conditions, pleasant surroundings and skilled medical treatment, being provided to alleviate the sufferings of the patients. St. Joseph's is one of the handsomest of the New-York hospital buildings, and is favorably placed in the open country, not far from St. Mary's Park, beyond the Harlem River. There are 300 beds ; and admission is free to the poor, without regard to nationality, creed or color.

The Seton Hospital for Consumptives, on the Spuyten-Duyvil heights, is a magnificent Italian Renaissance structure of brick, built in 1892-93, at a cost of $300,000, for 250 patients. Its minutest details have been arranged by the most eminent specialists, and this is the best hospital for consumptives in the world. It is conducted by the Sisters of Charity.

The Beth-Israel Hospital Association was incorporated in 1890. It maintains a free hospital and dispensary at 206 East Broadway and 195 Division Street. The hospital contains 50 beds ; and the dispensary treats yearly 12,000 patients.

The **Flower Surgical Hospital** was opened in 1890, by the authorities of the New-York Homœopathic College, on Avenue A, between East 63d and East 64th Streets.   Surgical cases only are taken here, and 200 cases are received annually.   The dispensary averages 25,000 free prescriptions yearly.

The **Sloane Maternity Hospital**, at the corner of Tenth Avenue and 59th Street, has been pronounced by many home and foreign physicians to be a model lying-in hospital.   It was erected in 1886 and 1887 by William D. Sloane, whose wife, a daughter of the late William H. Vanderbilt, endowed the institution by making all its beds free in perpetuity.   It is built of brick, with mouldings of granite and terra cotta, and its construction is fire-proof throughout.   The flooring of the halls and the wainscoting of the stairways are of white marble ; the wards and operating rooms are floored with white vitrified tiles.   In the basement are the laundry, kitchen, servants' dining-room, coil chamber, and fan for warming and ventilation ; a bath-room, where newly admitted patients are thoroughly cleansed before going to the wards ; and a locker-room for the safe-keeping of the clothing worn by patients on admission to the hospital.   On the first floor are the rooms of the house-physician, the assistant house-physician, and the matron ; a reception-room, a din-

THE WOMAN'S HOSPITAL IN THE STATE OF NEW YORK, PARK AVENUE AND EAST 50TH STREET.

ing-room for the house staff, the manager's room, and a large examination room. The second floor contains three wards with 20 beds, a delivery-room, sleeping-rooms for the nurses, the drug-room, and a dining-room.   On the third floor there are five wards, containing 25 beds, a delivery-room, the apartment of the principal of the training-school for nurses, two isolating rooms, and sleeping-rooms for the ward-nurses.   The total number of beds is 45.   In the attic are the rooms of the house-servants.   The lying-in wards are used in rotation.   Each one, having been occupied by five patients, is thoroughly cleansed and the furniture washed with a solution of carbolic acid.   Each of the delivery-rooms contains a table of special design, and the high character of the service is shown by the fact that in 2,500 cases, many of them emergency cases brought to the hospital in ambulances, only 13 deaths are recorded. The hospital is in charge of the College of Physicians and Surgeons, which is the Medical Department of Columbia College.

The Woman's Hospital in the State of New York, the first of its class established in the world, was founded in 1854 by Dr. J. Marion Sims, at that time the leading expert in female diseases in the world, and the discoverer of a new method of treatment, which has revolutionized the prac-

SLOANE MATERNITY HOSPITAL, TENTH AVENUE AND WEST 59TH STREET.

tice of medical surgery as applied to female complaints. The institution began its work in 1855, in a house built for a private residence, on Madison Avenue. The hospital was incorporated in 1857, and in 1866 it was removed to 50th Street, between Lexington and Park Avenues, where two commodious brick buildings have been erected, with accommodations for 150 patients, and completely equipped with all necessary conveniences for the treatment of this class of complaints. Each county in the State is entitled to one free bed, and the medical and surgical attendance is gratuitous. At the Dispensary 1,500 outdoor patients receive treatment yearly. The yearly expenses, met by voluntary subscriptions and the income of an endowment fund of $152,000, are about $70,000.

The New-York Infirmary for Women and Children, on Stuyvesant Square (East), near 16th Street, was founded in 1854 by Drs. Elizabeth and Emily Blackwell, who were the pioneers among women physicians. It is the only hospital in the city (except the Homœopathic Hospital) where women and children can be treated by women physicians. Its doors are open to all classes for medical or surgical treatment. The present hospital accommodates 65 patients, and additions soon to be made will double its capacity.

During 1892 341 patients were treated, and of this number more than half were free. The dispensary, where over 28,000 patients received free treatment during the

NEW-YORK INFIRMARY FOR WOMEN AND CHILDREN, 5 LIVINGSTON PLACE, OPP. STUYVESANT SQUARE.

NEW-YORK DISPENSARY FOR WOMEN AND CHILDREN, 15TH STREET AND LIVINGSTON PLACE.

year, occupies the first floor of the college building, 321 East 15th Street. The Woman's Medical College of the New-York Infirmary moved into its present commodious building, corner of Stuyvesant Square and 15th Street, in 1890. Twenty-one students graduated in 1892. The Training School for Nurses was united in 1891 with the New-Haven Training School, the nurses from the latter school coming to the Infirmary for obstetrical and gynæcological training. The Nurses' Home is at 327 East 15th Street.

The Nursery and Child's Hospital in the City of New York was opened as a day-nursery in 1854, largely through the instrumentality of Mrs. Cornelius DuBois. The original location was in St. Mark's Place; and in 1857 a hospital was added as a necessary adjunct of the work, and the institution became incorporated under its present name. In 1855 a substantial brick building, 119 feet by 60 feet, with two wings, was erected on the present site, at Lexington Avenue and 51st Street. In 1863 a foundling asylum was built, but for four years it was used as a soldiers' home, for the reception and care of sick and wounded soldiers. In 1867 the building reverted to the institution, and has since been used as a lying-in hospital. A new three-story brick building, erected in 1888 in memory of Miss Mary A. DuBois, for many years a directress of the institution, contains the wards and offices of the corporation. Upwards of 600 mothers and 1,000 children are received yearly and cared for, at an expense of $100,000, which is met by voluntary subscriptions.

The New-York Medical College and Hospital for Women, at 213 West 54th Street, was founded

NURSERY AND CHILD'S HOSPITAL, LEXINGTON AVENUE AND EAST 51ST STREET.

in 1863. The treatment is homœopathic, and the aim is to provide a
hospital for self-supporting young
women, whose only home is the
boarding-house, where, when over-
taken by sickness, they may receive
skilful treatment from physicians of
their own sex at a moderate cost,
or free of expense when necessary.
The larger part of the service, both
in the hospital and dispensary, is
gratuitous, and a steadily increasing demand for the services of
women physicians in the treatment
of women and children has made
the present leased building inadequate, and a larger structure is

NEW-YORK MEDICAL COLLEGE AND HOSPITAL FOR WOMEN,
213 WEST 54TH STREET.

contemplated to meet the needs of the work. The building now occupied has
accommodations for thirty patients. During 1891 174 cases were treated, with only
six deaths. During the same period, at the dispensary, upwards of 1,500 patients
were treated and 5,000 prescriptions dispensed. This is the only local homœopathic
hospital where women physicians are exclusively employed, and the maternity ward
shows the remarkable record of but one mother lost in thirty years.

St. Mary's Free Hospital for Children, at 407 West 34th Street, was organized in 1870 and incorporated in 1887, for the medical and surgical treatment of
children between the ages of two and fourteen years. It is in charge of the Sisterhood of St. Mary, a Protest-
ant Episcopal order, and
accommodates 70 patients.
The yearly expenses are
about $14,000, and upwards
of 400 cases are treated
yearly. In connection with
the hospital, there is a free dispensary for children, where
5,000 suffering children are
treated yearly; the Noyes
Memorial House, at Peeks-
kill, N. Y., for patients who
have been treated in the
Hospital, and whose diseases
assume an incurable form;
and a Summer Branch House,
at Rockaway Beach, Long
Island, for convalescent children.

ST. MARY'S FREE HOSPITAL FOR CHILDREN, 407 WEST 34TH STREET.

31

**The Laura Franklin
Free Hospital** in the City of
New York, at 19 East 111th
Street, a three-story brick

LAURA FRANKLIN FREE HOSPITAL FOR CHILDREN,
19 EAST 111TH STREET.

building, was opened in 1886 for the free medical and surgical homœopathic treatment of children between two and twelve years of age. It is in charge of the Sisters of St. Mary, a Protestant Episcopal order. It accommodates fifty patients, and is supported by voluntary subscriptions.

St. Andrew's Convalescent Hospital, at 213 East 17th Street, was opened in 1886 for the reception and care of women and girls over 15 years of age, of good character, and in need of rest, nursing and medical treatment. All cases, except those suffering from nervous or contagious diseases, are admitted free. There are twelve beds. The hospital is in charge of the Sisterhood of St. John the Baptist, a Protestant Episcopal order founded at Clewer, England, in 1851.

The Yorkville Dispensary and Hospital in the City of New York, at 1307 Lexington Avenue, was incorporated in 1886, to maintain an out-door service for the treatment of women and children. It is also a maternity charity, furnishing medical and nursing attendance to poor women during confinement. As yet it has no accommodations for in-patients, but confines its work to out-door relief. It is supported by voluntary subscriptions.

The New-York Mothers' Home of the Sisters of Misericorde, at 523 to 537 East 86th Street, was incorporated in 1888, to provide and maintain maternity hospitals and children's asylums in the State of New York. At present the society maintains a maternity hospital, for destitute women and young unmarried girls, hitherto respectable, about to become mothers. There are accommodations for 125 free and 30 pay patients, with private rooms. During 1892 206 women and 167 children were cared for, at an expense of $12,000.

The Babies' Hospital of the City of New York, at 657 Lexington Avenue, was incorporated in 1887, for the care of poor sick children under two years of age. It has accommodations for 30 babies ; and in 1891 expended upwards of $13,000 in its work. In connection with the hospital there is a dispensary for children ; a country branch, at Oceanic, N. J. ; and a training-school for children's nurses, where young girls of good character, over 18 years of age, are taught the management and training of sick and well children.

The Lying-in Hospital of the City of New York was founded in 1798. A suitable building was procured on Cedar Street ; and Robert Lenox, Dr. David Hosack, and other leading citizens were appointed managers. It soon became evident that the funds of the society were insufficient to meet the expenses, and an arrangement was made with the New-York Hospital by which that institution should receive the income of the funds, on condition that the governors should provide a lying-in ward. This arrangement continued until 1827, when the lying-in asylum was reorganized, and began an independent work. The society has no home or hospital for its beneficiaries, but renders assistance to them in their houses.

The Ladies' Hebrew Lying-In Society, at 58 St. Mark's Place, is a branch of the United Hebrew Charities. It was incorporated in 1877, and cares for poor Hebrew mothers during confinement, and supplies medical aid, food, nurses and clothing to all deserving cases. The yearly disbursements are about $2,000.

The New-York Eye and Ear Infirmary, at 218 Second Avenue, was the first institution opened in the city for the treatment of diseases of the eye and ear. The work was begun in 1820, by two young physicians, Edward Delafield and J. Kearney

BABIES' HOSPITAL, 657 LEXINGTON AVENUE, CORNER EAST 55TH STREET.

Rogers, who leased two small rooms in a house on Chatham Street, and announced their readiness to treat all eye and ear diseases. Within seven months over 400 patients were treated, and many cases of partial blindness were cured. As a result of the first year's work, a society known as the New-York Eye Infirmary was organized, in 1821 ; and in 1824 the old Marine Hospital of the New-York Hospital was leased. This was occupied until 1845, when a house in Mercer Street was purchased and fitted up for the use of the society. In 1854 an appeal to the Legislature

NEW-YORK EYE AND EAR INFIRMARY, SECOND AVE. AND EAST 13TH ST.

and the public resulted in a grant and subscription amounting to $30,000, which was used in the erection of a commodious building on Second Avenue. In 1890 the corner-stone of a new and larger building was laid, and in the following year a hospital wing containing 70 beds was opened for the free treatment of patients. An average of 700 patients are received yearly. The dispensary department gives advice and treatment to 60,000 cases annually.

The New-York Ophthalmic Hospital, at Third Avenue and East 23d Street, is a hospital for the treatment of diseases of the eye, ear and throat, and a college affording clinical instruction in the diverse forms of these diseases. It was incorporated in 1852, and after many years of useful work, in cramped and insufficient quarters, the present four-story brick building was erected, in 1871, at a cost of $100,000, the gift of Mrs. Emma A. Keep. It is conveniently arranged for its purpose, and contains reception and operating rooms for out-door patients, numerous wards and private rooms for those whose cases require a prolonged stay at the hospital, and two large contagious wards, entirely isolated from the other patients. The hospital is free to those unable to pay for the service of a physician, the directors and surgeons serving without compensation, and it is one of the great charities deserving of confidence and support. It is the only institution in the country authorized by law to confer the degree of Surgeon of the Eye and Ear upon properly qualified students, and the steady growth of its work is shown by the fact that while only 830 patients were treated during the first year of its existence, in 1890 it treated over 13,000 cases, received 400 resident patients, and issued more than 53,000 prescriptions. The large visiting and consulting staff comprises many eminent specialists, and the institution enjoys an enviable reputation for its skilful treatment of the difficult diseases of which it makes a specialty.

The Manhattan Eye and Ear Hospital was chartered in 1869, and occupies a substantial brick building at 103 Park Avenue, corner of 41st Street. It is supported

by voluntary contributions, and is intended solely for the treatment of those who cannot pay for medical aid. Besides the ophthalmic and aural departments there is one for nervous diseases, and one for throat diseases; and an isolated ward for the treatment of contagious diseases of the eye. Upwards of 13,000 cases are treated yearly. The administration is in the hands of a board of directors; and the

MANHATTAN EYE AND EAR HOSPITAL, PARK AVENUE AND EAST 41ST STREET.

medical staff is composed of many of the best-known physicians and surgeons of the city, who give freely of their time and skill for the relief of the unfortunate. The work has already outgrown the accommodations, and to relieve the pressure upon the day clinics, as well as to meet the wants of those unable to leave their work during the day, night clinics have been established in some of the departments; and the directors are contemplating the enlargement of the building so as to increase the usefulness of the institution, which has long been recognized as one of the best of its class. The hospital has an endowment fund of $80,000; the C. R. Agnew Memorial Fund of $12,000; and seven endowed beds.

The New York Ophthalmic and Aural Institute, at 46 East 12th Street, was opened in 1869 as a dispensary and hospital for the treatment of diseases of the eye and ear, and a school of ophthalmology and otology. Patients unable to pay are, so far as the resources of the institute will permit, received, provided for, and treated in the hospital without charge. Dispensary patients (about 8,000 a year) are treated gratuitously. The Institute leases the building it now occupies, and in 1891 treated nearly 400 in the hospital, where 160 cataracts were successfully extracted. About one-third of the patients receive free treatment.

The New-Amsterdam Eye and Ear Hospital, at 212 West 38th Street, a substantial brick building, was opened in 1888 for the treatment of eye and ear diseases. There are also nose and throat departments. It is supported by voluntary subscriptions. Seventy patients are treated yearly; and 175 operations are made; while the dispensary department gives free treatment to upwards of 2,000 needy applicants.

The New-York Cancer Hospital, at Central Park West and 106th Street, was founded in 1884, for the treatment of all sufferers from cancer, whose condition

NEW-YORK CANCER HOSPITAL, CENTRAL PARK WEST AND 106TH STREET.

promises any hope of cure or relief. The building is of recent construction; replete with all the modern improvements and appliances; and has 130 beds. About 600 new patients are admitted yearly, two-thirds being free. The charges for pay patients vary from $7 to $30 a week; and the yearly expenses are nearly $40,000.

The New-York Skin and Cancer Hospital, at 243 East 34th Street, was incorporated in 1883, for the free treatment and care of the poor afflicted with cancer and skin diseases. It has accommodations for 100 patients, and maintains a country branch hospital for chronic cases at Fordham Heights, a dispensary for the free examination and treatment of the poor, and the Guild of St. Lazarus, which assists in providing necessary clothing, sick-room comforts and delicacies for the inmates of the hospital.

The Metropolitan Throat Hospital, at 351 West 34th Street, was incorporated in 1874. It affords free treatment to those who are unable to pay special fees for all affections of the nose and throat. The institution is unsectarian, is supported entirely by voluntary contributions, and treats 1,000 cases yearly, aside from the much larger number of those who simply make visits for treatment.

The New-York Society for the Relief of the Ruptured and Crippled began its work in a small way in 1863, in a building on Second Avenue. Its founding was due to Dr. James Knight, whose long medical experience among the poor had convinced him of the need of some provision for the gratuitous treatment of cases of hernia and deformity. The rapid increase of the work soon made large accom-

modations necessary ; and in 1867 a hospital was opened at the corner of 42d Street and Lexington Avenue. It is an ornamental structure of brick and stone, five stories in height, with accommodations for 200 inmates, most of whom receive gratuitous treatment, the annual expenses of $50,000 being met by an appropriation from the city, private subscriptions, and a grant from the Hospital Sunday-Fund. Upwards of 9,000 cases are yearly treated in the hospital and out-door department, the large majority receiving advice, apparatus and treatment free of charge.

The New-York Orthopedic Dispensary and Hospital, at 126 East 59th Street, was established in 1866. It receives and treats destitute persons suffering from diseases and deformi-

NEW-YORK SOCIETY FOR THE RELIEF OF THE RUPTURED AND CRIPPLED, LEXINGTON AVENUE AND EAST 42d STREET.

ties of the spine and joints, infantile paralysis, bow-legs, club-foot and similar ailments, besides such cases as can not get proper treatment at home.

St. Bartholomew's Hospital and Dispensary, at 300 West 36th Street, was organized in 1888, for the gratuitous treatment of the poor suffering from skin and certain other diseases. Over 600 patients are treated yearly at the Dispensary. Although managed by Episcopalians, the hospital is unsectarian in character.

The New-York Pasteur Institute, at 1 West 97th Street, the first one of its class in America, was opened in 1890 for the anti-hydrophobic treatment of rabies according to the method of M. Pasteur. Its founder was Dr. Paul Gibier, a pupil of Prof. Pasteur. Since the opening of the Institute, 2,000 patients have been received, of whom 1,200 have been sent back, after having their injuries properly dressed, it having been demonstrated that the animals attacking them were not mad. In the remaining 300 cases the anti-hydrophobic treatment was resorted to, with a loss of only three patients. In all cases patients unable to pay for treatment have been inoculated and cared for free of charge. In 1893 the Institute occupied the Central-Park Sanatorium, at Central Park West and 97th Street, a six-story fireproof building, admirably equipped.

The New-York Christian Home for Intemperate Men was established in 1877 to rescue victims of intemperance and the opium habit by bodily rest, mental repose, religious influence, and freedom from annoyance, irritation or temptation. No drugs or nostrums are used, but every possible means is employed to divert the minds of the patients and to keep them happily occupied. The Home, at 1175 Madison Avenue, has accommodations for 75 inmates. None is received for a stay of less than five weeks. During 1892, of the 247 inmates received, 188 professed conversion, and of these 143 remained steadfast. The refuge of the Home is free to residents of the city who are unable to pay ; and otherwise the rates vary from $8 to $20 a week, according to the room selected. The yearly expenses are about $22,000, and there is an endowment fund of $50,000.

The Vanderbilt Clinic was opened in 1888 as a free dispensary for the poor. It is in charge of a board of five managers, but allied with the College of Physicians and Surgeons ; and stands on land belonging to the college, at the corner of 60th Street and Amsterdam Avenue. It is a large three-story brick building, similar in design to the Sloane Maternity Hospital ; and was erected and endowed by the four sons of the late William H. Vanderbilt, who gave the money for the purchase of the half block on which the College of Physicians and Surgeons, the Sloane Maternity Hospital and the Vanderbilt Clinic now stand, and with which the college buildings

INFIRMARY OF FIVE-POINTS HOUSE OF INDUSTRY, 155 WORTH STREET.

were erected. Besides its dispensary department, where nearly 125,000 patients received free treatment and advice during 1892, the building contains numerous small rooms for the direct practical teaching of diagnosis and treatment to the students of the college, and a theatre for clinical lectures which accommodates an audience of 400. Although of recent foundation, the Vanderbilt Clinic has already become an important medical institution.

The New-York City Dispensary, at White and Centre Streets, was established in 1791 on Tryon Street, afterward Tryon Row, which extended along the north-eastern side of the City-Hall Park, between Chambers and Chatham Streets. In 1796 the Dispensary was incorporated by the Legislature, and in 1805 it was united with the "Kinepox Institution," which had been established in 1803 for vaccinating the poor with cow-pox instead of small-pox. In 1828 the three-story brick building now in use was opened. During the cholera season of 1832 it is said that the Dispensary physicians "were found in every part of the widely extended city, stopping, as far as they were able, the ravages of the plague." The institution treats 50,000 patients yearly, at a cost of $25,000. Since its foundation, dispensaries of many kinds have been established throughout the city, and are doing a noble work in relieving suffering humanity.

The **Infirmary of the Five-Points House of Industry,** at 155 Worth Street, is maintained by the charitable organization from which it takes its name. It treats 2,000 patients yearly.   Two stories were added to the building in 1892.

The **Church Hospital and Dispensary** of the Protestant Episcopal Church was organized and incorporated in 1892 to concentrate and centralize Church medical work upon the most modern scientific medical principles, to provide a visiting staff, and to give special care to the worthy poor who are averse to receiving medical aid from a public clinic.

The **German Dispensary** was opened in 1857, and has been of vast benefit to the population of the crowded German quarter and to the poor of New York in general.

OTTENDORFER FREE LIBRARY.   GERMAN DISPENSARY.   LYING-IN-HOSPITAL.

THE GERMAN DISPENSARY, 137 SECOND AVENUE, BETWEEN 8TH AND 9TH STREETS.

The present handsome and commodious building at 137 Second Avenue was erected in 1883 by Mrs. Anna Ottendorfer.   It contains a medical library of about 5,000 volumes.

The **Northern Dispensary** was founded in 1827.   It is at Christopher Street and Waverly Place, and furnished medical and surgical aid to over 1,000,000 indigent persons.   It is supported by voluntary gifts.

The **Good-Samaritan Dispensary** (formerly the Eastern Dispensary, opened in 1832), at 75 Essex Street, was opened in 1891.   Upwards of 1,250,000 patients have been aided, and 160,000 cases receive treatment yearly, the number of prescriptions dispensed being about 110,000.

The **DeMilt Dispensary** occupies a building at 23d Street and Second Avenue.   It was opened in 1851, and its service includes the district lying between 14th and 40th Streets and Sixth Avenue and the East River.   It treats upwards of 30,000 cases yearly and dispenses nearly 70,000 prescriptions.   It has cared for nearly 1,000,000 patients and given out 2,000,000 prescriptions.

The **Northeastern Dispensary,** at 222 East 59th Street, was founded in 1862. It is a large medical and surgical relief institution, treating 22,000 cases yearly, and dispensing upwards of 60,000 prescriptions.

The Harlem Dispensary, at Fourth Avenue and 125th Street, was opened in 1868. The district comprises that part of the city north of 100th Street and east of Eighth Avenue. Upwards of 7,000 cases are treated yearly.

The German Poliklinik, 78 Seventh Street, is managed mostly by German physicians, for the poor in the vicinity. It was opened in 1883, and affords medical relief to 15,000 patients yearly.

Other Local Dispensaries, aside from those mentioned above and those connected with the hospitals, include the West-Side German, opened in 1872 ; the Dispensary of the Trinity-Church Association, 1880 ; the Dispensary of St. Chrysostom's Chapel, 1880 ; the New-York Dispensary for Diseases of the Skin, 1869 ; the Homœopathic Dispensary, 1870 ; the Northwestern Dispensary, 1852 ; the Yorkville Dispensary, 1887 ; and the Eclectic Dispensary, at 239 East 14th Street. Each of these is of notable service in the locality which it covers.

The New-York Training-School for Nurses was founded in 1873, for the instruction of intelligent women in hospital and private nursing. It was the first school for nurses opened in this country, and was the outgrowth of a desire on the part of a few charitable and public-spirited women to elevate the standard of nursing in the Bellevue and other public hospitals. Previous to the opening of the school the male and female nurses in Bellevue Hospital had been the product of chance, physical misfortune, and practical politics, and the service left very much to be desired. The first class was graduated in 1875, and consisted of six well-trained nurses, most of whom entered upon their duties in Bellevue. The work of the school has been such as to elevate the nursing service in all the local hospitals, and the graduates have in many instances been called upon to establish similar schools in other cities, and even in Italy, China and Japan. When the school was opened, in 1873, only five applicants presented themselves, but such has been the growth of the work that 1,500 applications for admission are now received yearly, and the school always has its full quota of 68 students. The requirements are exacting. The candidates must be from 25 to 35 years of age, and physically and mentally fitted for their calling. At the expiration of a short probationary period, those who have proved satisfactory are engaged for a two-years' course of theoretical and practical training, which includes lectures by eminent physicians and surgeons and actual service in the wards of Bellevue. The school building is at 426 East 26th Street, opposite the entrance to Bellevue. It is a four-story brick

ITALIAN CLUB.　　　　　ECLECTIC DISPENSARY.
ECLECTIC DISPENSARY AND ITALIAN INDEPENDENT CLUB,
237 AND 239 EAST 14TH STREET.

structure, and was built in 1887 by Mrs. William H. Osborne. It contains a kitchen, parlor, dining-room, library, lecture rooms and sleeping apartments for the nurses. The distinctive garb of the nurses is blue and white seersucker, with a white apron and cap and linen collar. Over 400 nurses have been graduated.

The D. O. Mills Training-School for Male Nurses occupies a substantial brick building, erected in 1888 in the Bellevue-Hospital grounds, at the foot of East 26th Street. It is arranged and fitted up as a home for the nurses during their two-years' course of study, which is on the same lines as that of the training-school for female nurses, nearly opposite. Several classes have been graduated from the school, and there are now fifty-seven inmates, all of whom serve in the male wards of the hospital. It is a generous charity, founded by Darius O. Mills.

The New-York Post-Graduate Medical School Training-School for Nurses, at 163 East 36th Street, was founded in 1885 for the instruction and training of hospital and private nurses. It has graduated upwards of 250 nurses.

The New-York County Medical Society, at 19 West 43d Street, is the oldest local organization of doctors. It was established in 1806 "to aid in regulating the practice of physic and surgery, and to contribute to the diffusion of true science, and particularly the knowledge of the healing art." It is authorized to examine students in medicine, and to grant diplomas to such as are duly qualified.

The New-York Medical and Surgical Society was founded in 1834 for the discussion of professional topics. The membership is limited to thirty-two, and the meetings are held at the residences of the members.

The New-York Academy of Medicine, at 119 West 43d Street, was established in 1847, and incorporated in 1851, for the cultivation of the science of medicine; the advancement of the profession; the elevation of the standard of medical

NEW-YORK ACADEMY OF MEDICINE, 19 WEST 43D STREET.

education and the promotion of the public health. It is a large and important organization, and has sections in pediatrics, obstetrics and gynæcology, the theory and practice of medicine; neurology, orthopedic surgery, materia medica and therapeutics; laryngology and rhinology, surgery, ophthalmology and otology, and public health and hygiene. The fine Academy building was opened in 1890. It is Romanesque in style and ornate in treatment, and contains numerous meeting and reception-rooms and a large medical library, which is open to the public. The Academy is one of the leading institutions of its kind in America, and its membership includes many eminent physicians and surgeons. It has a library of 50,000 volumes.

The Scientific Meeting of German Physicians was established in 1857, for the exhibition and study of interesting pathological specimens, and the report and discussion of notable medical and surgical cases. It has a membership of about 90; and the monthly meetings are held at 110 West 34th Street.

The Medico-Chirurgical Society of German Physicians meets bi-monthly at 411 Sixth Avenue. It was organized in 1860, for "the cultivation of medical science and the promotion of the honor and interest of the profession."

The Medico-Historical Society was founded in 1864, for the preservation and publication of interesting and valuable facts regarding the medical history of the city. Among its other valuable publications mention may be made of its yearly Medical Directory, which contains valuable information and statistics relating to the many local benevolent and medical institutions.

The New-York Ophthalmological Society was organized in 1864, for the improvement of its members in ophthalmic and aural studies. There are thirty members ; and the meetings are held bi-monthly at the members' houses.

The Medico-Legal Society was founded in 1866, and incorporated in 1868, for the study and advancement of the science of medical jurisprudence. The membership comprises regular practitioners of the medical and legal professions in good standing, leading scientists, and eminent literary men, 1,000 in number.

The New-York Dermatological Society was formed in 1869, for the study and investigation of the causes of skin diseases, the best curative methods, and all subjects connected with dermatology.

The New-York Neurological Society meets monthly at 17 West 43d Street, for the advancement of the science of medicine in all its relations to the nervous system. It was established in 1872, and has 75 members.

The American Laryngological Association was

VANDERBILT CLINIC, CORNER 60TH STREET AND AMSTERDAM AVENUE.

founded in 1878, for the study of diseases of the throat. Its headquarters are at 20 West 31st Street.

The New-York Clinical Society is devoted to the consideration of medical and surgical topics in their clinical and therapeutical aspects. The membership is limited to twenty, and monthly meetings are held at the houses of the members.

The New-York Surgical Society holds bi-monthly meetings at the New-York Hospital, for the discussion of interesting surgical cases occurring in the hospital practice. It was founded in 1879.

Other Medical Societies are the American Microscopical Society of the City of New York, founded in 1865 ; the New-York Medical Union, 1865 ; the Harlem Medical Association, 1869 ; the Yorkville Medical Association, 1870 ; the Association for the Advancement of the Medical Education of Women, 1874 ; the New-York Therapeutical Society, 1877 ; the Materia Medica Society, 1881 ; the Practitioners' Society of New-York, 1882 ; the Society of Medical Jurisprudence, 1883 ; the Manhattan Medical and Surgical Society, 1883 ; the Lenox Medical and Surgical Society, 1885 ; and the Hospital Graduates' Club, 1886. Most of these societies hold meetings at stated times, and discuss important topics.

Convalescent Homes have been established in many of the pleasant places near New York, for invalids to recover in. Among these are All Saints' Convalescent Homes for men and boys, at Oak Summit, Ruhberg and Farmingdale; the Fresh-Air and Convalescent Home, at Summit, N. J.; the New-York Home for Convalescents, at 433 East 118th Street; and others of like nature.

The Sanitary Aid Society, at 94 Division Street, was incorporated in 1885. It investigates evasions and violations of existing sanitary laws, prosecutes the offenders, and endeavors to educate public opinion on this important subject. It maintains the Model Lodging-House and Dormitories, at 94 Division Street, where a bed and bath, with access to a reading-room and library, are supplied to sober single men at a nominal cost. The house has 140 beds, and lodgings are furnished to 50,000 applicants yearly.

The Ladies' Health Protective Association, of New York, at 27 Beekman Place, was organized in 1884, to protect the health of the people of the City of New York by taking such action as may be necessary to secure the enforcement of existing sanitary laws and regulations, also calling the attention of the authorities to any violations thereof, and procuring the amendment of such laws and regulations when necessary.

DEMILT DISPENSARY, SECOND AVENUE AND 23D STREET.

The Hospital Saturday and Sunday Association at 79 Fourth Avenue, was founded in 1879, to get funds for the local hospitals, by collections in the churches, etc. In 1892 $60,000 were distributed among the hospitals.

The New-York Diet-Kitchen Association was incorporated in 1873, to provide the destitute sick with nourishing food, free of cost, upon a written requisition of any of the house and visiting physicians of the local dispensaries. It supports five diet-kitchens, in various parts of the city, and assists 15,000 persons yearly.

The American Veterinary College Hospital, at 139 West 54th Street, was opened in 1886 for the reception and care of animals needing treatment. Upwards of 3,000 domestic animals are treated yearly. In the dispensary horses and other animals belonging to the poor are treated free of charge. Since its opening over 7,000 animals have been received, and upwards of 2,500 operations performed.

The New-York College of Veterinary Surgeons has a large and efficient hospital for domestic animals, at 332 East 27th Street.

Reformatories and Corrections.

The Police Courts, Prisons, House of Refuge, Penitentiary, Work-House, House of Correction, Etc.

THE prevention, detection and punishment of crime and, when possible, the reformation of the criminal, form important features in the municipal activity of New York. All arrested persons are taken to the nearest station-house, and thence at the earliest possible moment they are brought before one of the six police-courts, where they are charged with specified offences and committed, bailed or discharged, according to the nature of the evidence against them.

The Police-Courts have original jurisdiction over minor offences. They are held at the Tombs, Jefferson-Market Court-House, Essex-Market Court-House, Yorkville, Harlem and Morrisania. Drunkenness, assault and battery, and thieving make the bulk of the work. Nearly all the convictions are disposed of by fines, or by short terms of imprisonment in the city institutions on Blackwell's Island. The courts have power to examine prisoners accused of serious crimes, and to hold them for trial in the higher courts. In fact, they have an extended jurisdiction and a wide latitude in the exercise of their powers. They stand next to the common people, and their province is not only to punish offences, but it is even more important to correct abuses and to adjust family and neighborhood differences. For these reasons, the justices, who are appointed by the Mayor, are not often members of the legal fraternity. They are men of practical sense and experience in the every-day affairs of life, and that they have knowledge of the character, the foibles and the needs of the people with whom they come most in contact is regarded as more important than that they have legal lore. They hold office for ten years, and have salaries of $8,000 a year.

The Tombs, at Franklin and Centre Streets, is a large granite building, occupying an entire block. It is the city prison; and covers the site of the pre-Revolutionary gibbet, which was planted on a small island in the Collect Pond. The most notable execution on the island was that of seven negro slaves, in 1741, for alleged complicity in the negro riot of that year. The Collect Pond was a small sheet of water, separated from the river by a strip of marsh-land. The early experiments of John Fitch in steamboat navigation were made in 1796, on the pond. It was filled in 1817. The Tombs was built in 1840, and some of its granite stones came from the old Bridewell, erected in City-Hall Park about 1735, and torn down in 1838. The building is a pure specimen of Egyptian architecture; and it is deplorable that its really noble proportions are dwarfed by its location in a low hollow. The name arose from its gloomy and funereal appearance and associations. It appears as a single lofty story, with windows extending to the cornice. The main entrance is on Centre Street, through a lofty porch, supported by massive stone columns. Projecting entrances and columns vary the somewhat monotonous appearance of the sides of the building. The Tombs Police-court is on the right of the entrance, and the Court of Special Sessions is on the left.   The latter is connected with the prison in the rear by a bridge, known as the "Bridge of Sighs," from the fact that condemned prisoners are led across it, after conviction.   The entrance to the prison proper is on Franklin Street, through a locked and barred grating.   The warden's office is on the left of the entrance ; and a short hallway leads the visitor to the cells, 300 in number.   These are arranged in tiers, one above the other, with a corridor for each tier.   In addition to the old granite building, two smaller prisons of yellow brick were erected in 1885, to relieve the crowded condition of the Tombs.   Criminals awaiting trial in the Special Sessions or Tombs Police courts are detained here, as well as those accused or convicted of more serious crimes.   Executions formerly took place in the central courtyard, but since the introduction of electrocution, all executions occur at the State prisons at Sing Sing and Auburn.   The Tombs prison is in charge of the Department of Public Charities and Correction.   The yearly number of committals is about 25,000.

The **Jefferson-Market Prison** is a minor city prison, virtually a branch of the Tombs, and an adjunct of the Jefferson-Market Police-Court.   There is such a prison attached to each of the police-courts, for the temporary detention of persons accused of or convicted of crime.   The Jefferson-Market Police-Court and prison, and the market from which they take their name, occupy different portions of a unique and handsome brick structure of irregular shape and considerable architectural beauty, at Sixth Avenue, Greenwich Avenue and West 10th Street.   It was built in 1868.   One of its features is a tall tower, on the northeast corner, in which is a clock with an illuminated dial.

The **Ludlow-Street Jail** is a large brick building in the rear of the Essex Market, extending from Ludlow Street to Essex Street.   It was built in 1868, and is used for the safe-keeping of persons arrested under writs issued to the Sheriff of the

LUDLOW-STREET JAIL, LUDLOW AND ESSEX STREETS.

County of New York, who has charge of the jail.   Those who have violated the United-States laws are also confined there, the Government paying a stipulated daily sum for each prisoner.   Sheriff's prisoners who are willing and able to pay for the privilege are allowed superior accommodations, and the system has led to many abuses, which the Legislature has often attempted to correct.   Persons arrested for debt were formerly confined here, but the practice is now done away with, as contrary to the Federal laws.   A debtors' prison was built in 1735, on the City Commons, near the present City Hall.   During the Revolution it was used as a prison by the British, and in 1840 it was converted into the present Hall of Records, which is thus the oldest public building in the city, and the only Revolutionary prison remaining in the country. It is a low brownstone building, in the Doric style ; and stands near the entrance to the East-River Bridge.

THE TOMBS. THE PLACE OF DETENTION FOR CRIMINALS AWAITING TRIAL.
FRANKLIN, CENTRE, LEONARD AND ELM STREETS.

Blackwell's Island, purchased by the city in 1828, for $50,000, is a long, narrow island in the East River, extending northward 1½ miles, from opposite East 50th Street to East 84th Street, and containing about 120 acres. It is the principal one of the group of islands upon which are most of the public reformatory and correctional and many of the charitable institutions for which New York is famous. Upon it stand the Charity Hospital, the Penitentiary, Alms-House, Hospital for Incurables, Work-House, Asylum for the Insane, and other institutions. Most of the buildings are of granite, of imposing size, and built after the turretted and battlemented designs of feudal times. They have all been erected by convict labor, as was also the sea-wall surrounding the island. The name of the island commemorates Robert Blackwell. He married the daughter of Captain John Manning, who in 1673 surrendered New York to the Dutch. After his disgrace, Manning retired to his farm on Blackwell's Island, then known as Hog Island; and after his death it became the property of his daughter. It remained in the Blackwell family for many years. The old Blackwell homestead, a low rambling wooden house, built nearly 125 years

THE PENITENTIARY, BLACKWELL'S ISLAND.

ago, still stands, and is used as the residence of the warden of the Alms-House. The warden of the Penitentiary occupies a picturesque stone cottage, standing on an elevated plateau, just north of the Penitentiary. The island contains much fertile land, and gardening and farming are carried on by the convicts. The population is about 7,000 persons, all in care of the Commissioners of Public Charities and Correction, from whom permits to visit the island must be obtained. The island-ferry leaves the foot of East 26th Street twice daily.

The Penitentiary on Blackwell's Island is a stone building, 600 feet long, with a long projecting wing on the north. The main building was erected in 1832, and the northern wing in 1858. The material used in its construction was the grey stone from the island quarries. It is four stories in height, castellated in design, and contains 800 cells, arranged back to back, in tiers, in the center of the building. A broad area runs entirely around each block of cells; and each tier is reached by a corridor. Persons convicted of misdemeanors are confined here, and the number of prisoners averages nearly 1,000 a day. Over 3,000 offenders are received yearly, of whom 400 are women. Each of the cells bears a card, giving the inmate's name, age, crime, date of conviction, term of sentence, and religion. All inmates are compelled to follow some trade or occupation. Stone-cutting in the quarries on the island, and mason-work on the buildings which the city is constantly erecting, furnish employment to a large number; others are employed in the rough work of the

SCENES ON BLACKWELL'S ISLAND.

THE ALMS-HOUSE CHAPEL, OLD BLACKWELL RESIDENCE, AND OTHER BUILDINGS.

Department of Public Charities and Correction; and still others work at the various trades which they followed before their incarceration. Most of the women prisoners are employed in sewing, or as cleaners in the female department. Each cell contains two canvas bunks, and all are kept freshly whitewashed and scrupulously clean. Solitary confinement is not practised, except as a punishment for insubordination; and in spite of the fact that the inmates of the Penitentiary are to be seen at work all day in various parts of the island, and with a seemingly insufficient guard, escapes are almost unknown, only one prisoner having got away in ten years. This immunity from escapes is due to the exceptionally strong natural safeguards afforded by the insular position of the institution, and the tremendously swift flow of the tide in the river, which makes it possible to guard nearly 1,000 criminals with fewer than 20 guards and about 35 keepers. To this same fact, as well as to the open-air life of the prisoners, is due the exceptionally healthy condition of the inmates.

As early as 1796 the Legislature provided for two State prisons, one at Albany, and one in New-York City. The first Newgate Prison, in Greenwich Village, was

WORK-HOUSE, BLACKWELL'S ISLAND.

opened in 1797, but it soon became crowded, and in 1816 the Penitentiary was built, on the East-River shore at Bellevue. In 1848 the Bellevue grounds were divided, and the convicts were removed to Blackwell's Island.

The Work-House, on Blackwell's Island, was built in 1852, to take the place of an older building which had been erected early in the century in the Bellevue grounds, on East 23d Street, where portions of the massive stone walls are still to be seen. The Bellevue grounds once extended from East 23d Street to East 27th Street, and from the river to Third Avenue, but in 1848 they were divided, and the larger portion sold for business purposes and dwellings. The Work-House is of granite, three stories in height, and comprises a long wing running north and south, and two cross wings, running east and west. The main building is about 600 feet long, and contains 221 cells, arranged in tiers against the side walls, and separated by a broad hallway. The cells are large, airy and well-lighted, and the entire building is kept immaculately neat. The offices are in the west wing; and the kitchen in the east wing. The Work-House is intended to be an institution for the punishment of the large class of petty criminals, always abounding in large cities. Most of the

BLACKWELL'S ISLAND INSTITUTIONS.

THE CHARITY HOSPITAL, PENITENTIARY WORKSHOPS, AND CHURCHES.

22,000 inmates yearly committed to the institution belong to the class known as "drunks." Many of them are old offenders, who have become almost permanent residents. Some of the inmates are daily drafted to perform household and other duties in the other public institutions controlled by the Commissioners of Public Charities and Correction. Those who remain at the Work-House are kept busily engaged in some useful occupation — much of the clothing, bedding, etc., used in the other institutions being made here. The average daily number of inmates is about 1,000, and about the same number are furnished to other institutions. The terms of commitment range from five days to one year, the majority of committals being for short periods, for drunkenness or disorderly conduct. Chief among the reformatory methods adopted at the institution are the Protestant and Roman Catholic religious services. The large percentage of short-term sentences makes the Work-House a house of detention, rather than a house of correction, or reformation. Destitute persons not criminals are committed to this cheerless abode upon their own application to the Commissioners.

The Branch Work-House, at Hart's Island, occupies a number of buildings formerly belonging to the Hart's-Island Hospital, which was given up in 1887. It is intended to relieve the overcrowding of the main Work-House, and it receives yearly about 2,500 prisoners.

The Alms-House, on Blackwell's Island, was built, in 1846, by convict labor, from the granite of the island quarries. The original buildings were two in number — one on the south for women, and one on the north for men. They are similar in design and treatment, and, with the later additions, they afford accommodations for 2,000 of the city's paupers. The grounds of the Alms-House occupy the central portion of the island, and contain about a dozen buildings, including the five now occupied by the Alms-House proper, the two older stone buildings, and three brick structures erected in 1889–91; the Alms-House hospital for women, a number of wooden buildings, opened in 1881; the hospital for incurables, opened in 1866; the pretty little Episcopal Chapel of the Good Shepherd, erected in 1888 by George Bliss as a memorial; the old Blackwell mansion; the Alms-House Hospital, for men; and other buildings used for various purposes connected with the management of the institution. There is a large reading-room in the basement of the chapel; and much active religious work is done among the inmates by the Episcopal City Mission Society, the Roman Catholics, and numerous charitable guilds. Over 3,000 paupers are annually received and cared for, and in their pleasant island-home they are more comfortably situated than are thousands of the dwellers in the crowded tenement-houses of the city. The first alms-house was built in 1734, on the Commons, now City-Hall Park, alongside the Bridewell. It was of stone, two stories high, and served also as a house of correction and a calaboose for unruly slaves. A new building, on the same site, was opened in 1795, just after the breaking out of an epidemic of yellow fever in the city, and for some time it was used as a hospital for the victims of the fever. In 1816 a large building was opened on the Bellevue grounds, which was occupied by the hospital and the almshouse until 1828, when they were separated, and in 1846 the paupers were removed to Blackwell's Island.

Randall's Island, near the union of the East River and Harlem River, comprises about 100 acres. Located upon it are the House of Refuge, the Idiot Asylum, Nursery, Children's and Infant's Hospitals, schools, and other charities provided for destitute children. Passes to visit the city institutions may be obtained from the Commissioners of Public Charities and Correction, but are not needed at the House of Refuge, which is open daily until 4 P. M.

The House of Refuge, on Randall's Island, was erected in 1854, and is a reform school for juvenile delinquents of both sexes. It is in charge of the Society
for the Reformation of Juvenile Delinquents, the oldest organization of its class in
the country. It was founded in 1817, as the " Society for the Prevention of Pauperism ;" and one of its first important works was the investigation of the prison
systems of England and the United States. In 1823 it was merged into the Society
for the Reformation of Juvenile Delinquents. The first House of Refuge was opened
in 1825, in the old barracks on Madison Square. In 1839 the Refuge was removed
to the Bellevue grounds, at East 23d Street and East River, where it remained
until the Randall's Island location was occupied, in 1854. The grounds of the institution are on the southern end of the island, and comprise a tract of 37½ acres, upon
which numerous buildings have been erected from time to time, to meet the needs
of the work. They are of brick, in the Italian style of architecture. The two

FEMALE ALMS-HOUSE, BLACKWELL'S ISLAND.

main buildings are nearly 1,000 feet in length, and will accommodate 1,000 inmates.
Children brought before police magistrates for misdemeanors are committed to the
institution. The yearly number of committals approaches 400. The boys and
girls are kept apart. They are taught useful trades, and are instructed in the common English branches. The secretary is Evert J. Wendell.

The Prison Association of New York, at 135 East 15th Street, was founded
in 1846 to improve the penal system, to better the condition of prisoners, and to aid
reformed convicts after their discharge. Daily visits are made to the Tombs and
the police-courts, and all needful aid is given to those prisoners who are deemed
worthy. The association has been instrumental in introducing many reforms in
prison management. In 1888 it founded the United-States Press Bureau, to give
employment to deserving ex-convicts in the collection and sale of newspaper clip-
pings.

The New-York Juvenile Asylum, at 176th Street and Amsterdam Avenue,
was incorporated in 1851 as a reformatory home for truant and disobedient children,
committed by magistrates or surrendered by parents or friends. The asylum is a
large stone building, with accommodations for 1,000 inmates, who receive moral,
mental, and industrial training, and are provided with homes when they reach a

suitable age.   Truant and disobedient children between the ages of 7 and 14 years, belonging in the city, are received; and the institution draws $110 from the city treasury for each child supported during the year.   This amount is supplemented by a grant from the public school funds and by private gifts.   The thoroughness of the work is shown by the fact that of the many children who have been placed in western homes, not more than five per cent. have proved to be incorrigible or guilty of serious misconduct.   There is also a House of Reception at 106 West 27th Street, where the children are kept for a few weeks before being sent to the asylum.

The Wetmore Home for Fallen and Friendless Girls, at 49 Washington Square, was founded in 1865, with the late Apollos R. Wetmore as president, to protect young girls against temptation, and to rescue them when they have been led astray.   Mr. Wetmore took a warm interest in the work, and upon his death, in 1881, the present building was purchased, and named the Wetmore Home, in his

NEW-YORK JUVENILE ASYLUM, AMSTERDAM AVENUE AND 176TH STREET.

memory.   Since the opening of the institution over 3,000 young women and girls have been admitted to its shelter.   Instruction is given in housework and sewing, and the inmates are aided in procuring employment.

The American Society for the Prevention of Cruelty to Animals, at 10 East 22d Street, is one of the most widely known of the many civilizing influences of the city.   It was founded in 1866, by the late Henry Bergh, who remained its President until his death in 1888.   The first laws for the prevention of cruelty to animals were enacted in 1866, and have been amended by successive legislatures until they are the best of their kind in existence.   Nearly every State and Territory has adopted similar laws, with societies to enforce them, and which are in communication with the parent institution.   The headquarters are open perpetually. Thousands of complaints are received yearly of cruelty to animals, all of which are thoroughly investigated, and the evils remedied.   No animal is too insignificant for attention.   The society has ambulances for the removal of disabled animals; a patrol service for rendering first aid to injured and sick animals; and a force of uniformed officers, who have authority to arrest and prosecute offenders found violating any of the humane statutes of the State. By numerous publications and the work of sixty affiliated societies, it has developed a strong public sentiment; and the good work it has accomplished to mitigate and prevent suffering to animals is incalculable. Its monthly official journal is called *Our Animal Friends.* The Society has prosecuted 17,000 cruelists; suspended over 50,000 animals from labor by reason of disabilities; humanely destroyed 34,000 horses and other animals, injured or diseased past recovery; and removed 6,000 disabled horses in ambulances. The President, John P. Haines, has been connected with the organization for many years, and under his guidance the humane work has been greatly extended.

The New-York Society for the Suppression of Vice, at 41 Park Row, was incorporated by the Legislature of the State of New York in 1873, through the efforts of Anthony Comstock, its secretary, aided by a few public-spirited citizens. Its object is the enforcement of all laws for the suppression of obscene literature, pictures, and articles for indecent and immoral use, including gambling in its various forms, lotteries, and pool-selling. It seeks the defence of public morals by preventing the dissemination and seed-sowing of criminal influences. Through the efforts of this society five acts were passed in 1873 by Congress prohibiting the importation into this country, or the dissemination by mail, or in provinces under the exclusive jurisdiction of the United States, of obscene books, pictures or articles. Through its efforts stringent laws were enacted the same year in New-York State, and since then in various other States. Branch organizations have been established in New England and the Southern and Western States. Nearly 2,000 arrests have been made, and 45 tons of obscene matter and 17 tons of gambling material and paraphernalia have been seized and destroyed. Upon persons convicted, 324

SOCIETY FOR THE PREVENTION OF CRUELTY TO ANIMALS, FOURTH AVENUE AND EAST 22D STREET. *

years' imprisonment and more than $120,000 of fines have been imposed. The annual expenses are about $10,000, which are met by voluntary contributions. Through the efforts of this society stringent laws were enacted by Congress in 1889 prohibiting "green-goods" swindlers and other fraudulent devices from using the mails.

The Society for the Prevention of Crime, with spacious and commodious offices at 923 Broadway, was organized in 1877 and incorporated in 1878. Its special and peculiar mission is the attempt to remove the sources and causes of crime, by the enforcement of existing laws and the enactment of new ones, and by arousing public opinion, more particularly regarding the excise laws, gambling, and public nuisances in general. Under the direction of its former President, the late Rev. Dr. Howard Crosby, the society accomplished a vast amount of work, and incurred a corresponding degree of hostility from those upon whom the laws have no other restraining

* Taken down in 1892, to make room for new Episcopal Church Missions House.

power than that due to the fear of detection and punishment.   The society employs a number of agents to detect violations of the law.   The present President, the Rev. Dr. Charles H. Parkhurst, is well known as the author of the crusade against the brothels and gambling-houses of the city, as a result of which the Grand Jury in 1892 found a sweeping indictment against the Police Department.

The Home of Industry and Refuge for Discharged Convicts was founded in 1879, and incorporated in 1882.   Its object as stated in the articles of

incorporation is "To do good to the souls and bodies of men," but its labors are confined to the criminal class.   A small house at 305 Water Street was secured for the initial stages of the work, and after several removals they located in 1891 in a large and commodious building of their own at 224 West 63d Street.   Since its start, 3,000 ex-convicts have been received into the "Home," 1,400 of whom have obtained employment. The yearly expenses are $8,000, of which fully one-fourth is earned by the inmates, chiefly at broom-making.   The yearly average of inmates is 40.   Gifts are greatly needed to pay indebtedness existing.

HOME OF INDUSTRY AND REFUGE FOR DISCHARGED CONVICTS, 224 WEST 63D STREET.

The National Christian League for the Promotion of Social Purity, at 33 East 22d Street, was organized in 1886, and secured by special act of Congress in 1889 a National charter.   Its aims are to elevate public opinion regarding the nature and claims of social purity, with its equal obligation upon men and women ; to enlist and organize the efforts of Christians in protective, reformatory, educational and legislative work ; and to supply employment and furnish advice and various forms of aid to girls and women in need.   The League holds two meetings a month.   At these meetings papers are read, taking up any department of the subject, after which discussion follows.   The work is done specially through ten committees.

The Society for the Purification of the Italian Quarters may be classed as among the reformatory organizations of the city, since its work is the important one of driving disorderly houses and disreputable people from the Italian quarters of the city.   It was organized in 1890, and, in addition to the work outlined above, it endeavors to do away with the crowded condition of the Italian tenement-houses.

The Lunacy Law Reform and Anti-Kidnapping League, at 10 East 14th Street, was founded in 1890 to protect sane persons against unjust and unlawful imprisonment in insane asylums and hospitals, and to secure humane treatment and the protection of their legal and constitutional rights to those suffering from insanity. Legal and medical advice is freely given to all deserving applicants.